European Family Therapy Association Series

Founding Editors

Maria Borcsa
University of Applied Sciences, Nordhausen, Thüringen, Germany

Peter Stratton
University of Leeds, Leeds, West Yorkshire, UK

More information about this series at http://www.springer.com/series/13797

Angela Abela • Sue Vella • Suzanne Piscopo
Editors

Couple Relationships in a Global Context

Understanding Love and Intimacy Across Cultures

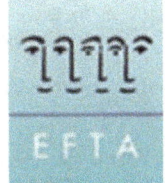

Editors
Angela Abela
Department of Family Studies
Faculty for Social Wellbeing
University of Malta
Msida, Malta

Sue Vella
Department of Social Policy and Social Work
Faculty for Social Wellbeing
University of Malta
Msida, Malta

Suzanne Piscopo
Department of Health
Physical Education and Consumer Studies
Faculty of Education
University of Malta
Msida, Malta

ISSN 2569-877X   ISSN 2569-8796 (electronic)
European Family Therapy Association Series
ISBN 978-3-030-37711-3   ISBN 978-3-030-37712-0 (eBook)
https://doi.org/10.1007/978-3-030-37712-0

© Springer Nature Switzerland AG 2020
This work is subject to copyright. All rights are reserved by the Publisher, whether the whole or part of the material is concerned, specifically the rights of translation, reprinting, reuse of illustrations, recitation, broadcasting, reproduction on microfilms or in any other physical way, and transmission or information storage and retrieval, electronic adaptation, computer software, or by similar or dissimilar methodology now known or hereafter developed.
The use of general descriptive names, registered names, trademarks, service marks, etc. in this publication does not imply, even in the absence of a specific statement, that such names are exempt from the relevant protective laws and regulations and therefore free for general use.
The publisher, the authors, and the editors are safe to assume that the advice and information in this book are believed to be true and accurate at the date of publication. Neither the publisher nor the authors or the editors give a warranty, expressed or implied, with respect to the material contained herein or for any errors or omissions that may have been made. The publisher remains neutral with regard to jurisdictional claims in published maps and institutional affiliations.

This Springer imprint is published by the registered company Springer Nature Switzerland AG
The registered company address is: Gewerbestrasse 11, 6330 Cham, Switzerland

Foreword

Mario Benedetti, perhaps the most famous Uruguayan poet of love, writes that to be totally, completely, absolutely in love, one must be certain of being loved back, certain of being capable of inspiring love. Whether or not this feeling of mutual and reciprocated absorption of love is universal, it lies at the center of what contemporary love ideals are in many cultures. Even in those contexts where marriage is arranged, the hope is that reciprocal love will evolve in time. Nevertheless, there is a lot more to coupling than love. South Americans like Benedetti have always known that couple relationships are like tangos, complex and passionate dances of closeness and distance, emotion and skill, support and companionship. Far from being islands of love, couples are and have always been part of historical and ecological contexts that make deep incursions into their private lives, incursions largely unacknowledged or unspoken by most. Each couple's responses are also deeply shaped by internal processes generated by personal temperaments and individual life histories.

Marriage, or more precisely couplehood, is not a "doomed" institution as many have prophesied but is, as Stephanie Coontz prophetically affirmed, a "transformed" institution. All societies are becoming more diverse and multicultural and, in spite of persisting differences, globalization also exposes couples to common themes worldwide. The message of this book for theoreticians, researchers, and practitioners is clear: a couple's issues are not inherent simply or only to the couple. Many of the issues, such as power dynamics, the raising of children, and decisions around lifestyle, love, and intimacy are manifestations of the social constructions of the larger cultural groups to which the members of the couple belong. These issues assume different centrality at earlier or at later points in the life cycle of couples, or also appear with poignancy among intercultural couples as they seek shared meaning.

To understand these complexities and work with increasingly diverse forms of contemporary couple relationships, we need comprehensive, multilevel ecosystemic models that encompass micro-, meso-, and macro-processes. Each one of the chapters in this timely and ambitious volume aptly titled *Couple Relationships in a Global Context* makes major contributions to a multidimensional, multilevel understanding of couples in many cultural contexts by embracing both complexity and empathic resonance with love concerns today. Increasingly, diverse social constructions and power inequities based on gender, race, class, sexual orientation, and cultures across the globe are featured in ways that not only enlighten broader sociocultural and sociopolitical influences on a couple's wellbeing but also invites self-reflection on the part of practitioners. Reading the pages of this book reminds us about how much our values and beliefs about couples are deeply embedded in our own culture and ecological niche and how unwittingly and yet erroneously we may consider those as normative.

In the development of family systems theory, couples were often seen as a subset of family therapy for which no additional constructs or training were necessary. Once the family was engaged, therapists would slowly and carefully uncover couple's problems that needed attention. Today, in many places in the world, couples seek help on their own and most therapists (including individually trained ones) regardless of orientation have a large portion of their practices dedicated to the treatment of couples, perhaps to an even larger extent than to the treatment of families. For many years in the literature of couple and family therapy, advanced interventions assumed a one-size-fits-all universal applicability. In time, cultural perspectives were introduced with pointers about adaptation or modification of those interventions to fit cultural values or beliefs that required knowledge of various ethnic groups. This initial approach could, in spite of its best intentions, border on formulas or stereotypes. Over time, the complexity of variabilities of cultural beliefs, rituals, customs, or identities and the power differentials afforded by gender, race, and socioeconomic class are finally being grappled with.

It is laudable and gratifying that this book invites the reader to find out about these differences and inequities with curiosity and respect and a fresh sense of discovery rather than *a priori* knowledge, or a colonizing attitude of cultural competence on the part of the clinician. Instead, the pages of this book open doors to cultural humility. Examples are questioning the usual polarities between individualistic and collectivist cultures; the need to examine dichotomies between arranged and romantic marriages; or the conviction that the legalization of same-sex marriages is sufficient to reduce persistent stigma or the need for alertness to the interaction between social pressures on personal life cycle decisions like a woman's age of marriage and newly evolving societal aspirations of a woman's more autonomous life course. Instead of simplistic answers, many chapters underscore fundamental changes in the institution of marriage worldwide, but changes that are best described with a both/and approach that may reflect more accurately the coexistence of disparate, and sometimes contradictory values in many couples' lives today. Views of marriage in India, France, Ireland, Scandinavia, Arab countries, or others do not remain static; all evolve—though they may differ in the depiction of transitional smoothness versus tense conflict or competing forces between conservative and modern couplehood in areas such as premarital sex, women's roles, informal or formalized love relationships, or acceptance of divorce. In spite of the global spread of women's rights, patriarchy is still alive causing marital power imbalance, an imbalance that presents serious challenges to clinicians trained in modern Euro American values.

Another admirable aspect of this volume is the freedom the editors bestowed on the authors. Couples' issues are approached from many angles. The chapter materials are based on demographic quantitative data, legal information, sociological inquiry, discourse analysis, fiction such as novels, or films, political backdrops, or the impact of physical landscapes or climate on intimate relationships or focusing on the depth of attachment histories or personal trauma. These multiple contexts contribute to a richness of perspectives and resources, including substantial information and robust reviews of relevant scholarly literature that can be used for textbook purposes. This variety is sprinkled with vividly expressive anecdotal evidence, with illustrative vignettes that breathe life into abstract concepts and also with fuller case studies. As an experienced couple and family therapist, I was pleasantly surprised by learning new things I did not know about today's couples.

As a young trainee in the 1970s in Chicago, Illinois, USA, I had an outstanding supervisor. He was a reserved, parsimonious Norwegian from the North. I learned from him that in his country when couples quarreled intensely, they seldom voiced their disagreements openly. Their strategy was to seek individual isolation until their storm passed. Typically, he told me, the man would go into the woods, perhaps sleep in a cottage, be nourished by nature and silence and return home 1 or 2 days later when the conflict had abated. Almost never would he or his wife refer back to the topic of quarrel. It puzzled me at the time to think how our "talk therapy" culture would deal with this type of coping, and the likelihood that we would see it as a deficit. The book that Abela, Vella, and Piscopo have assembled would encourage therapists to view this pattern with curiosity, respect, and the possibility of underlying strengths over deficits. Furthermore, the chapters on providing therapeutic support would wisely explore the cultural preferences and the impact of intergenerational styles of relating as well as the influence of communities of support on couple's conflict patterns.

Each contributor reflects on contemporary changes and variations in couple formation, the result for the reader is a fascinating immersion in other cultures as well as an expansion of perspectives about coupling today in their own countries. Timely attention is given to the social, ethical, and moral dilemmas precipitated by the proliferation of information communication technologies such as cell phones or the modern options of meeting partners online, or of forming relationships at long distance and also the emergence of couple's therapy online. All current developments require therapists to be very much on board today.

This comprehensive book is a living example of the systemic contextual thinking that family therapy has always stood for in its understanding of how larger social systems play a significant role in shaping emotional states and relational bonding. It can contribute to theory building about the connections between the microlevel of sex, money, work, or parenting in individual couples and the larger social and cultural constructions of gender, race, class, religion, and family roles. It can also inspire practitioners to develop psychoeducational modules that could help couples externalize or resist oppressive cultural and sociopolitical injunctions. The authors may have different ways of knowing and may come from different discourses and traditions, but they all chart various parts of the complex territory of couples' relationships in today's world.

The editors do a masterful job of outlining the book's mission and vision in the preface and introductory chapter and in the closing chapter, which they title simply as policy implications; they bravely take on the task of providing the most useful cogent analysis of five fundamental organizing principles with which to view couples as portrayed in various chapters.

The magnifying lens focused intensely on couples that this book provides is appropriately psychosocial while also remaining deeply committed to the uniqueness and emotional health of each couple. All the chapters represent the complexity, breadth, and depth we need to do effective couples work. Our call as couple and family therapists is to affirm the systemic postmodern basis of our field of study and practice as a discipline, as a profession, and as a service in the public interest. This book is a major contribution to this endeavor.

Celia Jaes Falicov
Department of Family Medicine and Public Health
University of California,
San Diego, USA

Preface

Living in a couple relationship is the most popular choice for adult persons worldwide. This remains true in spite of widespread changes, such as evolving family forms and lifestyles and corresponding changes in family law; a rise in self-chosen or circumstantial singledom; and the broader realities of globalization, migration, and the pervasiveness of technology. True to our systemic understanding, through this volume we seek to provide a global perspective on couple relationships which takes into account both culture and context. In spite of the apparent dichotomy between collectivist and individualistic cultures, we contend that there are common themes and a shared humanity that unite us across continents. This search for what unites us is what urged us to deepen our understanding of couple relationships beyond the western perspective within which much contemporary literature is set.

This volume is written by authors who are mostly couples and/or family therapists, as well as other family practitioners, researchers, and policy specialists from all over the world. The volume takes into account the contextual forces which are influencing the couple relationship today. It explores how these relationships are shaped by different belief systems surrounding love, intimacy, and sexuality and the ways in which these are shaping couple relationships. Light is shed on the challenges couples face in different parts of the world, particularly around the impact of rising expectations of equality between men and women, and between same-sex and opposite-sex couples. The influence of the family on couple relationships and the impact of children are also brought to the fore. Therapeutic implications are discussed, and almost each chapter has a few vignettes illustrating a particular aspect of the couple relationship. These vignettes are either taken from existing literature or are closely parallel to authentic stories of clients (whose identity has been carefully concealed).

The volume comprises 25 chapters and is divided into five parts. In Part I, the introductory chapter provides an overview of the volume by highlighting why we consider it important to look at couple relationships, and the meaning of love and intimacy across cultures and in an increasingly interconnected world. We then present an overview of the different sections of the book and various ways of intervening with couples from a systemic perspective. The second chapter highlights the significance of the couple relationship across the globe and outlines salient findings defining this relationship. Two vignettes illustrate some of the challenges encountered by couples, including income inadequacy and infidelity.

Part II is about couple relationships in different countries and regions of the world. In this section, we have chapters about Scandinavia, France, India, the Arab region, China, and Malta. All of these chapters present couple relationships in the sociocultural context in which they are embedded. They take into account not only traditional couple relationships, but also current trends such as evolving expectations of the couple relationship and the challenges that couples face. Contextual influences such as globalization, the use of technology, economic constraints, and work-life balance are discussed. The descriptions of the romantic ideal and the meaning of love, intimacy, and sexuality across cultures are of particular interest, as are insights on power and closeness in relation to gender. The influence of the family, including the family of origin, and the impact of children are often also addressed.

Part III is about couples in diversity. A broad array of couples are portrayed, reflecting the many ways in which love is expressed among couples in the twenty-first century. These couple relationships are breaking traditional boundaries and include intercultural couples, same-sex couples, those falling in love in later life, polygynous marriages from an Arab-Islamic perspective and couple relationships where one of the partners has a disability. Other couples living in diverse relationships are also referred to in other parts of the volume: polyamorous relationships feature in the chapter about infidelity, while couples living apart together are included in the chapter on online couple therapy.

Part IV deals with global trends and includes chapters on how couple relationships are framed in the media, the impact of smartphones on relationships, and the search for a partner through online dating and its impact on psychotherapy. Other authors help us understand long-term relationships, fidelity, and non-monogamy and why and how couples leave relationships. Last but not least, we thought it would be apt to have a chapter on singledom.

Part V is specifically about therapy, support, and policy implications. This is not to say that therapeutic approaches only feature in the last part of the volume. Most of the contributors in this volume are couple therapists, and it was only natural for them to present their topic from a clinical perspective. However, we also wished to look at how couples may be supported outside a clinical setting. Thus, one chapter looks at ways of supporting the couple through a parenting program, while another looks at the support of couples at a community level. A chapter discusses online couple therapy, describing an innovative approach by therapists to reach out to couples who live apart together and who may find it difficult to go to a clinic. The last chapter of the volume is about policy perspectives on couple relationships, bringing together those principles and instruments that emerged through foregoing chapters as common to diverse regions around the world.

Msida, Malta

Angela Abela
Sue Vella
Suzanne Piscopo

Acknowledgements

We wish to express our sincere gratitude to numerous organizations and individuals who have made possible this international volume on couple relationships in the twenty-first century. Our first thanks go to the Malta Foundation for the Wellbeing of Society and to the President Emeritus of Malta, Her Excellency Marie-Louise Coleiro Preca. While all resident academics at the University of Malta, we also make up the National Centre for Family Research (NCFR) within this Foundation. As NCFR, we conducted a national survey on life and relationship satisfaction among couples and single persons between 2015 and 2017, which work was supported and encouraged by Her Excellency and the administrative staff of the Foundation.

Eager to extend our work beyond Malta, and supported by the Foundation and the International Commission on Couple and Family Relations, an international conference on *The Couple Relationship in the Twenty-first Century* was held in February 2018 at the Grandmaster's Palace in Valletta, Malta. This conference brought together scholars from various regions and disciplines to reflect on emergent trends, with particular focus on the romantic ideal, power and closeness, and diversity across the globe. Many of the participants in this conference, together with other renowned scholars, have contributed to this volume and we also extend our heartfelt thanks to them. It has been a pleasure and privilege to work with all the authors from different continents and to learn so much about developments in their fields and countries.

We are especially grateful to the European Family Therapy Association, which kindly accepted to publish this volume in the European Family Therapy Series. Special thanks go to the series editors, Maria Borcsa and Peter Stratton, for their enthusiasm, guidance, and support throughout the preparation of this book and to the publishing staff of Springer.

We hope that a wide range of readers may find this volume useful, and that this compilation of chapters is a worthy contribution to the literature on couple relationships which are so central to our happiness and flourishing. We also hope that you will enjoy reading this volume as much as we have enjoyed working on it.

Contents

Part I The Significance of the Couple Relationship

1. Understanding Love Relationships in a Global Context: Supporting Couples Across Cultures 3
   Angela Abela, Suzanne Piscopo, and Sue Vella

2. The Significance of the Couple Relationship in the Twenty-First Century................................. 19
   Angela Abela

Part II How Couple Relationships Are Changing in Different Parts of the World

3. The Existential and Relational Meaning of Intimacy and Love for Couples in Scandinavia: Through a Lens of Scandinavian Fiction and Drama 41
   Anne Kyoung Sook Øfsti

4. The Evolution of the Couple in France over the Past 30 Years...... 55
   Michel Maestre

5. Changing Couple Relationships in India 71
   Lina Kashyap

6. Couple Relationships in the Arab Region: Changes and Renegotiations 85
   Hoda Rashad, Zeinab Khadr, and Eman Mostafa

7. Couple Relationships in China 107
   Dan Wang and Yan Xia

8. Couple Relationships in Mediterranean Malta 125
   Suzanne Piscopo, Sue Vella, and Angela Abela

Part III Couples in Diversity

9 **Home Is Where the Heart Is: Aporias of Love and Belonging in Intercultural Couples** 145
Reenee Singh

10 **Stigma, Social Change and the Well-Being of Same-Sex Couples** 159
David M. Frost

11 **Falling in Love in Later Life** 177
Margaret Hellie Huyck

12 **Polygamous Marriages: An Arab-Islamic Perspective** 193
Alean Al-Krenawi

13 **The Couple Relationship When One of the Partners Has an Acquired Physical Disability** 207
Elaine Schembri Lia

Part IV Global Trends in Couple Relationships

14 **Framing Couples in the Media: Coupledom, Well-Being and Comedy** 227
Brenda Murphy

15 **Keeping Couples Together when Apart, and Driving Them Apart when Together: Exploring the Impact of Smartphones on Relationships in the UK** 245
Mark McCormack and M. F. Ogilvie

16 **Online Dating: Modern Options of Searching for a Partner and Its Implications for Psychotherapy** 261
Christiane Eichenberg, Jessica Huss, and Cornelia Küsel

17 **Fidelity, Infidelity, and Non-monogamy** 279
Tina Timm and Adrian Blow

18 **Understanding Long-Term Couple Relationships** 295
Carrie Cole and Donald Cole

19 **Why and How Couples Leave Relationships: A Twenty-First Century Landscape** 311
Jim Sheehan

20 **Between the Couple and Living Alone** 329
Lynn Jamieson

Part V Supporting Couple Relationships

21 Systemic Therapy and Narratives of Attachment 347
Arlene Vetere

**22 Supporting Parents as Partners: The Couple Context
of Parenting, a Personal and Academic Journey** 359
Carolyn Pape Cowan and Philip A. Cowan

**23 Supporting Links Between Living Apart Together (LAT)
Couples Through Online Couple Therapy** 375
Pierre Cachia

**24 No Couple Is an Island: Communities of Support
in Couple Relationships** 391
Kevin Schembri

25 Policy Perspectives on Couple Relationships 403
Sue Vella, Angela Abela, and Suzanne Piscopo

Index 425

About the Editors

Angela Abela, PhD, is a Professor and founding Head of the Department of Family Studies at the University of Malta, where she teaches clinical psychology and family therapy trainees. She also teaches Master's students in Family Studies, and supervises research. She chairs the National Centre for Family Research of the Malta Foundation for the Wellbeing of Society. As a clinical psychologist, family therapist, and systemic supervisor, she works with couples, children, and their families and supervises practitioners working in this area. She is a consultant for Parliament and the Maltese government. She is lead author of the Strategic Policy on Positive Parenting for Malta launched in 2016. Angela has served as an expert for the Council of Europe in the area of children and families for many years. Her research projects include studies on marital satisfaction, couple conflict and family violence, families living in poverty, lone parent families, parenting, and children in out-of-home care. In 2014, she co-edited *Contemporary Issues in Family Studies: Global Perspectives on Partnerships, Parenting and Support in a Changing World* with Wiley-Blackwell and co-authored *Intervening after violence, Therapy for couples and families* with Springer (2017). She is an associate editor of *Clinical Child Psychology and Psychiatry,* an international advisory editor of *Contemporary Family Therapy* and is on the editorial board of *Children Australia*.

Sue Vella, PhD, is a senior lecturer in the Department of Social Policy and Social Work at the University of Malta, where she lectures in social policy. Prior to joining University, Sue had almost 20 years of experience in the public sector. After graduating, she was a founder member of the Domestic Violence Unit which today is known as the Foundation for Social Welfare Services. She has since held top management positions at the Employment and Training Corporation and Malta Enterprise and has served on various organizational boards and policy committees. She was a member of the EU's Employment Committee for 7 years, including 2 years as Vice-President and Chair of the Committee's technical group. Sue is currently a member of the National Centre for Family Research, Chairperson of the Church's Institute for Research in Malta, and a member of the Board of Trustees of Richmond Malta. Her research interests include families, the mixed economy of care, housing, employment, and migration, and she has recently published on long-term care; poverty in the media; and wellbeing.

Suzanne Piscopo, PhD, is the founding head of the Department of Health, Physical Education and Consumer Studies, Faculty of Education, University of Malta. She is an Associate Professor in Nutrition, Family and Consumer Studies, mainly training prospective home economists, teachers, and early childhood educators. Professor Piscopo is a Registered Nutritionist and Registered European Health Promotion Practitioner and is frequently invited as a guest speaker in school and community events and on the media, tackling subjects related to food, health, consumption, and finance within the family and societal context. She is currently involved in various international and national projects addressing social determinants of health, the Mediterranean diet, elderly health, prison health, and sustainability education. Over the years, Professor Piscopo has been appointed to multiple national Councils and Advisory Committees. She is a member of the National Centre for Family Research within the Malta Foundation for the Wellbeing of Society and is co-researcher in studies on couple relationships and on access to quality food.

About the Contributors

Alean Al-Krenawi, PhD, is Professor and Chair of the Bachelor of Social Work program, Spitzer Department of Social Work, Ben-Gurion University of the Negev. His work focuses on challenges facing indigenous and minority populations in the Middle East, North America, and the West. He has conducted extensive research on the effects of cultural phenomena that were previously unexamined in scholarly and professional literature. This work is utilized in academia, policy-making, and professional practice throughout the world. His work has also brought to the fore the "unheard voices" of weakened and disadvantaged groups that are often sidelined in various cultural contexts as a result of ethnicity or other social determinants.

Adrian Blow works as a couple and family therapy intervention researcher and educator at Michigan State University (MSU). Adrian is a Professor in the Human Development and Family Studies department where he directs the Couple and Family Therapy program. He obtained his PhD from Purdue University in 1999. After Purdue, he joined the faculty at Saint Louis University where he worked for 6 years. He subsequently joined MSU in 2005. His research is focused on families and trauma, military families, infidelity in committed relationships, and on change processes in interventions pertaining to Systemic Family Therapy. He has acquired over two million dollars in research grants as Principal Investigator, published numerous peer-reviewed publications (60) and book chapters (12). He has mentored many students and in 2017 was awarded the American Association for Marriage and Family Therapy (AAMFT) Training Award, which recognizes excellence in family therapy education. He has served the field of Systemic Family Therapy in a number of capacities and was the AAMFT Board Secretary from 2012 to 2014, and Board Treasurer from 2016 to 2019.

Pierre Cachia, DCplPsych, is a senior couple psychoanalytic psychotherapist and a counseling psychologist with a background in systemic practice and Gestalt therapy. His doctoral research focused on the conceptualization of relational normality in the practice of couple psychotherapy. Over the past 3 years, he led the setting up of the Online Couple Psychotherapy Service at Tavistock Relationships in London which he currently heads. He is a full member of the British Psychoanalytic Council, the United Kingdom Council for Psychotherapy and is a chartered member of the British Psychological Society. He maintains a private practice offering services to individuals, couples, and professionals seeking clinical supervision in London and online.

Carrie Cole is the Director of Research for The Gottman Institute and runs The Gottman Institute Love Lab. She has co-authored journal articles with Drs. John and Julie Gottman. Carrie is an honor graduate of The University of Texas with a Master's degree in Counseling Psychology. She is a licensed professional counselor and an approved LPC supervisor. Her work with couples includes couple's therapy, workshops, seminars, and intensive marathon sessions. Carrie's passion for working with couples led her to found the Center for Relationship Wellness together with her husband, Dr. Don Cole. She has always had a profound interest in using a scientific approach to psychotherapy. Having discovered the scientific research of Dr. John Gottman in graduate school, Carrie realized her dream and became a Certified Gottman Method Couples' Therapist and Certified Gottman Method Workshop Leader in 2007.

Carrie is a Master Trainer for The Gottman Institute and trains other therapists in the Gottman Method of Couples Therapy by conducting Level 1, Level 2, and Level 3 trainings yearly. She is also a consultant for the certification program. She has led The Art and Science of Love weekend workshop for couples since 2008. Carrie was a presenter at the 2008 Gottman Annual Conference, the American Congress of Obstetrics and Gynecology in 2012, and appeared as a guest on the Deborah Duncan Show in Houston, TX. Carrie has co-authored a number of workshops and has been interviewed and quoted in several newspapers and magazines including The Chicago Tribune, Time, Cosmopolitan, Redbook, Real Simple, Women's Health, and Woman's World.

Donald Cole, D.Min. LPC-S, LMFT-S, LMHC, is the Clinical Director at The Gottman Institute. He is a licensed Professional Counselor, a licensed Marriage and Family Therapist, and an approved supervisor in both disciplines. Dr. Cole received the Doctor of Ministry degree in Pastoral Counseling and Psychotherapy from Garrett-Evangelical Seminary at Northwestern University in 1993. Dr. Cole, along with his wife, Carrie Cole, co-founded the Center for Relationship Wellness, a private practice for therapy, consultation, and training in Houston, Texas and Seattle, Washington. Dr. Cole is also a Master Trainer in the Gottman Method Couples' Therapy. He offers all levels of training in Gottman Method for therapists throughout the United States and several other countries. He also serves as a consultant for therapists completing their final training in Gottman Method. Along with his wife Carrie, he presents The Art and Science of Love Workshop to couples. Dr. Cole has authored a number of workshops including: The Unique Challenges of Second Marriages, Ethics in Couples Therapy, Domestic Violence and Law Enforcement and Living as God's Family: Relationship Enhancement for Congregations and has presented to a wide range of audiences including, the American Association of

Pastoral Counselors and the American Congress of Obstetrics and Gynecology. As an ordained Lutheran Pastor and Native American, Dr. Cole has served on the Board of Directors of the Oaks Indian Center where he helped design programs for staff training and family restoration.

Carolyn Pape Cowan, PhD, Adjunct Professor of Psychology, Emerita at the University of California, Berkeley has co-directed three longitudinal studies of how family relationships affect children's adaptation. With Philip Cowan and Marsha and Kyle Pruett, she developed a group intervention for parents of young children, in which health professionals work to strengthen parents' relationships as partners and parents. Seven US, Canadian, and UK trials show positive benefits for parents' and children's development in middle-class, working-class, and low-income parents from varied ethnic backgrounds. Co-author with Philip Cowan of *When Partners Become Parents: The Big Life Change for Couples* (1992, Basic Books, 2000, Erlbaum), co-editor of *Fatherhood Today: Men's Changing Role in the Family* (Wiley, 1988), and *The Family Context of Parenting in Children's Adaptation to Elementary School* (2005, Erlbaum), and author of numerous scientific journal articles, Cowan consults internationally about the development and evaluation of interventions for partners who are parents.

Philip A. Cowan, Professor of Psychology, Emeritus at the University of California, Berkeley, served as Director of the Clinical Psychology Program and the Institute of Human Development at UC, Berkeley. He has authored numerous scientific articles and *Piaget: With Feeling* (Holt, Rinehart, & Winston, 1978), co-authored *When Partners Become Parents: The Big Life Change for Couples* (Basic Books, 1992; Erlbaum, 2000), and co-edited four books and monographs, including *Family Transitions* (Erlbaum, 1991), and *The Family Context of Parenting in the Child's Adaptation to School* (Erlbaum, 2005). Along with Marsha Kline Pruett and Kyle Pruett, Philip and Carolyn Cowan have been evaluating and consulting on interventions with fathers and their partners in the United States, Canada, and most recently, the United Kingdom, and Malta. Their most recent work focuses on the family policy implications of their 40+ years of preventive intervention work with families from a range of backgrounds and economic circumstances.

Christiane Eichenberg completed her PhD at the University of Cologne in 2006 and finished her habilitation at the Ilmenau University of Technology in 2010. She is a Professor and Head of the Institute of Psychosomatics, Medical Faculty at the Sigmund Freud Private University, Vienna. She is also a psychotherapist (psychoanalysis). She published more than 60 peer-reviewed papers in journals and also published books about e-mental health, self-treatment and self-medication, psychotraumatology and online-counseling. She gives oral presentations at international conferences.

David M. Frost is an Associate Professor in Social Psychology in the Department of Social Science at University College London. His research interests sit at the intersections of stress, stigma, health, sexuality, and close relationships. His primary line of research focuses on how stigma, prejudice, and discrimination constitute minority stress and, as a result, affect the health and wellbeing of marginalized individuals. He also studies how couples psychologically experience intimacy within long-term romantic relationships and how their experience of intimacy affects their health. His research has been recognized by grants and awards from the National Institutes of Health (USA), the Society for the Psychological Study of Social Issues, and the New York Academy of Sciences.

Jessica Huss is a psychologist and a consultant with a current focus on personnel and executive development. She is doing her PhD at the University of Kassel, Germany. Her main research focus is e-therapy, online interventions, and serious games.

Margaret Hellie Huyck has been a gerontologist for over 50 years. She received her PhD from the University of Chicago Committee on Human Development in 1970, specializing in Adult Development and Aging. She taught in the psychology department at Illinois Institute of Technology for 42 years. A Fellow of the Gerontological Society of America, Margaret has published many articles and books on aging. Her focus on how gender shaped the life course is reflected in many of her publications. In addition to her academic work, she has been involved with OWL—the Voice of Women 40+—for several decades and served as the President of the National Board until it closed recently. She was widowed in 2015 after 54 years of marriage; she has two adult daughters and one granddaughter. She is now in a new loving relationship.

Lynn Jamieson is a Professor of Sociology at the University of Edinburgh. She was President of the British Sociological Association between 2014 and 2017 and is Co-Director of the Centre for Research on Families and Relationships (www.crfr.ac.uk). Her main research focus is on families, relationships, living arrangements, life course, and social change. Prof. Jamieson's recent publications include: Jamieson, L. (2016) *Families, Relationships and 'Environment': Unsustainability, Climate Change and Biodiversity Loss*; *Families Relationships and Societies*, 5, 3, 335–355; Jamieson and Simpson, (2013) *Living Alone: Globalization, Identity and Belonging*. At present, she is collaborating on projects which include *Family Futures in Italy, Spain and the UK* (CRFR and ESRC Centre for Population Change) and *Working across qualitative longitudinal studies:—A feasibility study looking at care and intimacy* (ESRC National Centre for Research Methods). Prof. Jamieson is Co-editor of the Palgrave Macmillan series, *Studies in Family and Intimate Life*, and of the Policy Press journal, *Families Relationships and Societies*.

Lina Kashyap, PhD, a social work educator, retired in 2013 from the Tata Institute of Social Sciences (TISS), a renowned Deemed University in Mumbai, India, after a career in social work spanning almost five decades. At TISS, Professor Kashyap headed the Department of Family and Child Welfare for 12 years, initiated and headed the Centre for Disability Studies for 2 years, and served as the Deputy Director (Pro Vice-Chancellor) of the Institute for 5 years. Post retirement, Professor Kashyap was associated with the Institute as an Emeritus Professor for 3 years. During her tenure at TISS, she worked with a team of international Family Educators to establish the Global Consortium for International Family Studies (GCIFS) which now offers a comprehensive and unique online MA program in International Family Studies. Professor Kashyap has served as the Founder Chairperson of GCIFS for 6 years.

Zeinab Khadr is a Senior Research Scientist at the Social Research Center (SRC) of the American University in Cairo, where she was appointed in 1998. She has a PhD in Demography from the University of Michigan and is currently also an Associate Professor at the Department of Statistics, Faculty of Economics and Political Science, Cairo University. Khadr has extensive teaching and research experience. Her research interests include measuring health disparities, family arrangement in older ages, development of urban areas, as well as marriage and family stability. At the SRC, Khadr has been the Principal Investigator of several research projects including "Marriage Market," "Marriage and Family Formation among the Youth in Egypt," "Urban Inequity," "Social Determinants of Health and Health Equity in the Arab region" and "Health Equity and Integrated Health and Poverty Alleviation Policies." She has also been the local Principal Investigator on the project "Validation of Gender Differences in Disability and Care."

Cornelia Küsel got a diploma (Mag.Phil.) in Educational Sciences, with main focus on Psychotherapy Research and Counseling from the University of Innsbruck, Austria. She currently works at the Computer Science Department, Bundeswehr University in Munich, Germany, as research associate and PhD candidate. Research topics are e-mental health, online interventions, PTSD, and eating disorders.

Elaine Schembri Lia is a Clinical Psychologist, a Family Therapist, and a Systemic Practitioner. One of Elaine's special interests as a professional is resilience, specifically understanding how individuals and families going through difficulties can be supported to thrive in their lives and to move on from their adversities. Among other practices, Elaine also works with children, adolescents, and adults diagnosed with disability and their families, both within the public sector and within the private domain. Given that to date there is a dearth of services in the area locally, Elaine is committed to contribute to the development of services and to the training of professionals to psychotherapeutically support individuals and families challenged with disabilities. Elaine has delivered training seminars, workshops, lectures, and presentations about the topics of disability, resilience, and the family in Malta and abroad. She has also published research in the area.

Michel Maestre is a clinical psychologist and has been working as a couple and family therapist since 1985. He is the Founding President of the Association of Family Therapists in North France and a past Board Member of the French Society of Family Therapy. He has sat on the European Family Therapy Association Board since 2004 and is also a member of its Training Institutes Committee. In 1989, he founded the PSYCOM Training Institute in Couple and Family Therapy in the city of Villeneuve d'Ascq in France where he still holds the position of Director and Trainer. He also chairs *La Clinique du Couple*, a Couple Therapy Center, which offers its services in six different cities in France. Michel is a Lecturer at the Catholic University of Lille and at Paris VIII University and has authored various articles and a book on Family Therapy. As the first family and couple systemic therapist to be working in private practice in Northern France, over the past 30 years, Michel has accumulated considerable experience in his professional work with couples and, through his research, has observed a significant evolution of the couple and conjugality in France.

Mark McCormack is a Professor of Sociology in the Department of Social Sciences at the University of Roehampton, London. Prior to Roehampton he was an Associate Professor at Durham University, where he was also Co-Director of its Centre for Sex, Gender and Sexuality. His research examines how social trends related to gender and sexuality map onto everyday experiences of individuals in society. A core focus has been documenting how the decrease in homophobia in Britain and the United States influences the experiences of young people, including an expansion of socially acceptable gendered behaviors for male youth and improvement in life experiences of gay and bisexual youth. He is lead author of *Discovering Sociology*, an introductory sociology textbook, published with Red Globe Press, and author of *The Declining Significance of Homophobia*, published by Oxford University Press.

Eman Mostafa has a Master's degree in Demography from the Cairo Demographic Center and has been working as a demographic researcher and grant technical associate for several years. He has extensive experience in preparing, reviewing, and analyzing literature and statistical tables for different papers and reports, as well as designing, developing, implementing, analyzing, and reporting of field research. His work has spanned a vast range of areas including Health Equity, Social Determinants of Health, Marriage Dynamics, Gender and Fertility, and Sexual and Reproductive Health.

Brenda Murphy is an Associate Professor at the University of Malta and teaches in the Department of Gender Studies. Prior to that she was Director of the Edward de Bono Institute for the Design and Development of Thinking, and Senior Lecturer with the Department of Communication Studies. She has served as Head of Department, is a Research Associate with the Mediterranean Institute, chaired the Gender Advisory Committee at the Malta Broadcasting Authority, held the posts of President and General Secretary for UMASA, and worked with H.E the President of Malta in the President's Foundation to spearhead gender training for media practitioners. She is also an Expert for the European Commission and European Parliament on issues around media and gender. She is a collaborative researcher with several institutions —the European Institute for Gender Equality (EIGE) and COST and has been the National Coordinator for the Gender Monitoring Media Project (GMMP) since 2000.

Anne Kyoung Sook Øfsti is an Associate Professor at VID Specialized University, Oslo, Norway, where she is responsible for the professional training of couple and family therapists.

Her doctoral thesis is entitled *Some Call it Love. Exploring Norwegian therapists' discourses about Love and Intimacy*. She has presented about her work in Norway and in other countries and has also published in peer-reviewed journals. Currently, she is the Editor for the Scandinavian Journal: *Fokus på familien* (Systemic Practice and Family therapy). She has extensive professional experience as a couple and family therapist and supervisor. In 2014, she debuted as a novelist, with the title *If only we had all day* which is a story about shame, guilt, forgiveness, and hope and of course family relations.

M. F. Ogilvie is a PhD candidate in the Department of Sociology at Durham University. An elite volleyball player, his research examines the development of homosocial and homoerotic cultures among athletes from the United Kingdom and the United States, further adding to studies of masculinities in team sports. His research also explores the dynamics of these intercultural contexts and examines the gender dynamics between men and women on these elite teams. He has also conducted research on the experiences of transgender athletes, published in the edited book, *Playing Against Gender: Transgender Athletes in Sport*, and on bisexuality in sport in the edited book, *LGBT Athletes in the Media*.

Hoda Rashad is the Director of the Social Research Center of the American University in Cairo and holds a doctorate in population studies from the University of London. Dr. Rashad has been sought as a resource person and expert for a number of national and international organizations, including: Member of the WHO Commission on Ending Childhood Obesity (2014–2016) and WHO Commission on Social Determinants of Health (2005–2008), member of a committee to establish the Arab Council of Social Sciences (2006–2008), Vice Chairman of the Dutch Development Assistance Research Council (RAWOO) (2002–2007), and member of the governing body of the Global Development Network (GDN) (2001–2004). On the national front, Dr. Rashad has served as a member of the Senate (2004–2011), the National Council for Women (2000–2011) and the Social, Humanity and Population Science Council of the Egyptian Academy of Scientific Research and Technology (2009–2012).

Kevin Schembri lectures in canon law at the Faculty of Theology and the Faculty of Laws at the University of Malta. He coordinates two Master's programs and forms part of the Department of Pastoral Theology, Liturgy and Canon Law. Schembri earned his undergraduate degrees and a licentiate in theology and pastoral ministry from the University of Malta. He then graduated with a licentiate and a doctorate in canon law from the Pontifical Gregorian University in Rome. He is a Catholic priest and also serves as defender of the bond and promoter of justice at the Metropolitan Tribunal of the Archdiocese of Malta. His book-length monograph *Oikonomia, Divorce and Remarriage in the Eastern Orthodox Tradition* appeared as volume 23 in the *Kanonika* book series.

Jim Sheehan is Professor of Family Therapy and Systemic Practice at VID Specialized University, Oslo, and faculty member in the School of Psychotherapy at University College Dublin. Jim is a social worker, registered family therapist, and systemic supervisor in Ireland where he lives and practices. Jim has published extensively on the topics of hope and despair in psychotherapy, narrative and forgiveness, and the supervision of family therapists and systemic practitioners. His most recent publication is Sheehan, J. (2018) *Family Conflict After Separation and Divorce: Mental Health Professional Interventions In Changing Societies.* London: Palgrave.

Reenee Singh is the Director of the London Intercultural Couples Centre and editor of the Journal of Family Therapy. She is also co-director of the Tavistock Family Therapy and Systemic Research Centre and visiting Professor in the School of Psychology at the University of Bergamo, Italy. Currently, she is the editor of the *Journal of Family Therapy*. Renee is a UKCP accredited systemic psychotherapist with 25 years of clinical experience and the author of two text books and many academic papers. She presents her research at international conferences and teaches cross-cultural therapy and research at Universities and training institutions all over the world.

Tina Timm, PhD, is an Associate Professor in the School of Social Work at Michigan State University (USA) where she teaches graduate students specializing in clinical social work. Dr. Timm is a Clinical Fellow of the American Association for Marriage and Family Therapy and licensed as both a marriage and family therapist and a clinical social worker. Her research focuses on couples and families with an emphasis on issues related to sexuality. She completed post-graduate training at Masters and Johnson Institute in sex therapy and sexual trauma. She has been doing clinical work for over 26 years in a wide range of settings and is a frequent presenter on topics related to the integration of sex therapy into clinical practice, affair recovery, trauma informed treatment, and attachment.

Arlene Vetere is Professor of Family Therapy and Systemic Practice at VID Specialized University, Oslo, Norway; Affiliate Professor of Family Studies at Malta University; Visiting Professor of Clinical Psychology at Università degli Studi di Bergamo, Italy; and Visiting Professor of Psychology at Northampton University, UK. Arlene is a clinical psychologist and systemic psychotherapist, registered in the United Kingdom, where she lives. Arlene specializes in working therapeutically with couples and families where violence is of concern. Arlene was president of the European Family Therapy Association for two terms, from 2004 to

2010. She has co-authored and co-edited 11 books that reflect her longstanding interest in family relationships, violence in the family, and healing and repair in close relationships using an integrative systemic attachment narrative approach.

Dan Wang is a doctoral student in the Department of Child, Youth and Family Studies in the College of Education and Human Sciences at the University of Nebraska-Lincoln, USA. Her research focuses on global family health and wellbeing, specifically studying family dynamics within different contexts including migration, community, and poverty. Dan has a strong background in identifying and interpreting contextual influences on family relationships, with her intercultural experience in China and the United States, and as a result of her professional experience in quantitative and qualitative research design, implementation, analysis, and dissemination. She has been working on several grants and projects in the fields of cross-cultural studies, as well as on the evaluation of programs for co-parenting interventions for couples in dissolution and for poverty simulation to assist the public to change their attitudes toward people in poverty.

Yan Xia is a Professor in the Department of Child, Youth and Family Studies in the College of Education and Human Sciences at the University of Nebraska-Lincoln, USA. She holds a PhD in Family Science and an MS with specialization in Marriage and Family Therapy. Her research focuses on strengths and challenges in stress coping among Asian-American and Chinese families, and she has recently studied youth and family resilience during China's socioeconomic transition and family migration process. Professor Xia collaborated to form the Global Consortium for International Family Studies and has worked extensively with local, national, and international communities on youth and family service program development and evaluation. She has served as Chair of the International Section, National Council on Family Relations (USA) and presided at the UN 20th International Year of the Family Research Forum. Professor Xia has been a Certified Family Life Educator since 2001.

Part I
The Significance of the Couple Relationship

Chapter 1
Understanding Love Relationships in a Global Context: Supporting Couples Across Cultures

Angela Abela, Suzanne Piscopo, and Sue Vella

1.1 Introduction

The couple relationship is typically associated with the hope of fulfillment of our need to be loved and cherished in the course of our adult life. Such hope is rooted in our human need for safety, love and connection to a significant other. This might explain why choosing to be in a couple relationship has endured over time in different cultures across the globe and is a predominant choice for the majority of adult persons.

As is amply explained in the next chapter on the significance of the couple relationship, a fast-growing body of knowledge is now pointing towards the vital importance of meaningful relationships for our well-being. The quality of the couple relationship features prominently in this regard. Therapists, researchers and policy makers all point towards the psychological, psychosomatic and physical ill effects, which can ensue when the couple relationship stumbles or fails. Moreover and in spite of the fact that children are no longer necessarily born and brought up in the

---

A. Abela (✉)
Department of Family Studies, Faculty for Social Wellbeing, University of Malta, Msida, Malta
e-mail: angela.abela@um.edu.mt

S. Piscopo
Department of Health, Physical Education and Consumer Studies,
Faculty of Education, University of Malta, Msida, Malta
e-mail: suzanne.piscopo@um.edu.mt

S. Vella
Department of Social Policy and Social Work, Faculty for Social Wellbeing,
University of Malta, Msida, Malta
e-mail: sue.vella@um.edu.mt

© Springer Nature Switzerland AG 2020
A. Abela et al. (eds.), *Couple Relationships in a Global Context*,
European Family Therapy Association Series,
https://doi.org/10.1007/978-3-030-37712-0_1

context of a couple relationship, the majority of them still are, and the influence of the parents on the children's quality of life is enormous.

Given the importance of this relationship, this volume is written by couple therapists, and other family practitioners and policy specialists from different parts of the world with the aim of highlighting how the couple relationship is evolving across the globe. Contextual influences such as globalization, economic influences, the technological advances in communication and the way cultural belief systems shape behaviour will be highlighted. The romantic ideal and the meaning of love, intimacy and sexuality are of particular interest as is the sharing of power in the couple relationship and its relationship with gender. The influence of the family on couple relationships and the impact of children will also be taken into account. The book highlights the challenges that today's couples are facing and explores innovative ways of supporting them and their families in therapy and in the community, and concludes with a chapter on the couple relationship through policy. It is being hoped that this understanding will help clinicians and policy makers gain new insights about this important relationship, how it can be sustained and how we can best promote the well-being of couples and families across the globe.

This chapter provides an overview of the key aspects that are highlighted in this book, namely the importance of the cultural contexts in which the couple relationship is embedded. The effect of globalization and the impact of technological advances in communication on the couple relationship will be taken into account. The way love and intimacy in couple relationships are expressed in different parts of the world and how the emergence of diversity has broken barriers in love relationships will be highlighted. Power and gender in couple relationships will also be discussed. To conclude, reference will be made to ways of supporting couples and their families from a therapeutic perspective, at a community level as well as through policy.

1.2 The Influence of Culture on Couple Relationships

In spite of the increasing globalization, the cultural context in which we live shapes our beliefs as to what makes a good quality relationship. And yet "the influence that culture has on us is likely to be at least in part implicit (Watts-Jones, 2010) beyond our awareness and beyond our mastery" (Rober & De Haene, 2014, p. 16). It is precisely for this reason that understanding how couple relationships are constructed in the different cultural contexts has become increasingly important for family practitioners. Hence, our need to give the book a global perspective. This volume gives importance to couple relationships in different parts of the world from East and West, North and South and includes accounts by couple therapists and other family practitioners from China, India, the Arab world, France, Scandinavia and Malta.

As editors coming from a small city state, we are very aware that we cannot simply rely on what is going on in the West to make sense of vital relationships. Understanding cultural diversity has become even more relevant, considering that we live in an increasingly globalized world characterized by a rise in interconnectedness precipitated by the communication and technology revolution; large migration flows and ongoing demographic shifts, which have increased multiculturalism across the globe, especially in big cities.

1.3 Love and Intimacy Across Cultures

In their cross-cultural research, Shaver, Wu, and Schwartz (1992) noted that love in the context of a couple relationship is considered to be a universal emotion. Human beings identified love, joy, anger, sadness and fear as five universal emotions pertaining to our basic repertoire of emotions. Fehr and Russell (1991) added hate in their analyses of basic emotions. Karandashev (2017), like Hazan and Shaver (1987), speaks of love as a biologically based emotion. When a couple is in love, "they are aware of this from their gut feelings, without needing to express it in words" (Karandashev, 2017, p. 3). As an anthropologist, he makes reference to the fact that love is understood by all races, religions and cultures, although its interpretation may vary according to the cultural context in which it is embedded. It is therefore not surprising that couple relationships are highly prevalent across the globe.

Individualism and collectivism may be considered as key cultural dimensions that influence interpersonal behaviour. Cross-national scholars like Triandis et al. (1986) and Hofstede (2001) report that individualism is prevalent in European countries and Western societies in general; whereas, collectivism is more predominant in Asia, Africa and Latin America.

Hiew, Halford, and Liu (2014) explain these two dimensions. They argue that in individualistic cultures, the attributes of the individual persons come to the forefront including their feelings and preferences. Their sense of independence and their ability to fulfill their individual dreams are highly valued by themselves and by society at large. On the other hand, in collectivist cultures, one tends to see oneself as part of an interdependent network, and value is placed upon living harmoniously and fulfilling one's obligation towards the other members of the network.

In terms of love relationships, Hiew et al. (2014) argue that individualistic cultures give more importance to romantic love, psychological intimacy and sexual pleasure in their relationship with their partner. Intimacy characterized by reciprocal self-disclosure regarding very personal issues is strongly related to couple satisfaction. Collectivist cultures value respect, mutual understanding and support. Gratitude and admiration are also given priority.

In spite of this apparent dichotomy, we would like to argue that there are running threads across the East and West with regards to the construction of a romantic ideal. In spite of the fact that in Western countries independence and the fulfilling of personal dreams are considered important, an interdependent network does exist in these societies characterized by intergenerational solidarity (Izuhara, 2010) and reciprocity and support (Smart, 2007). This is also the case in Malta, where the characteristics of a loving couple relationship include reciprocity and respect but also communication, intimacy and love (PFSW, 2017). Admiration for one's partner is also very common.

At the same time, women's fight for gender equality in the East has brought about a shift in the set of values embraced by young women. Chinese women value independence (Jankowiak, Shen, Yao, Wang, & Volsche, 2015) and there is a reluctance among women in Japan, Taiwan and Korea to co-reside with the husband's in-laws (Raymo, 2014). As is explained by Lina Kashyap in Chap. 5 of this volume, highly educated Indian women too aspire to move out and discontinue living under the same roof with their husband's family at some point. In these cultures, more emphasis is now put on one's identity as a couple rather than the patrilocal family.

The rise in individualization and the weakening of the traditional family form had its roots in the cultural revolution of the 1960s, which took place in the West. In the mid-1980s, Lesthaeghe (1995) introduced the theory of the second demographic transition to make sense of the changes in family life in the West. The couple relationship was at the centre stage of these changes, as fertility levels declined, parenthood was postponed and some choose to have children outside marriage. Formalizing the couple relationship through marriage became a choice rather than a social expectation. A rise in divorce and an increase in living alone and in bringing up children on one's own were also prevalent, whereas an increasing number started to cohabit. Amato, Booth, Johnson, Johnson, and Rogers (2007) have coined the term *alone together couples* for an emerging group of couples in America who showed more individualistic characteristics. These couples share less activities together, have less friends in common and are less likely to belong to the same club or organization. Unlike companionate couples who enjoy shared activities, they interact much less with each other but equally enjoy a high level of happiness. Some of these behaviours are now emerging in non-Western countries. Births outside marriage, though small in number and considered as a social taboo, are slowly increasing in Eastern countries such as India (Katke, Saraogi, & Pagare, 2014), China and Japan. Parents who bear children outside marriage face a criminal penalty for adultery in the MENA region (Fisher, 2015). On the other hand, China and South Korea have divorce rates above the European and OECD averages (Budd, 2017) and there is an increasing number of women in Taiwan, Japan and Singapore who prefer to remain single. Similar to women in the Arab countries, most of the women who remain single in these countries are highly educated as they are finding it difficult to reconcile their work with the caring responsibilities on the home front (The Economist, 2011). When commenting on the status of marriage across the globe in the twenty-first century, Budd (2017, p. 4) points out that "what looks like fundamental cultural differences between West and East are often differences of timing and degree. Marriage is being transformed almost everywhere, and in many of the same ways. But different countries are at different stages of the journey."

Another interesting shift in collectivist cultures is that marriage is increasingly in the hands of the young people themselves. In Japan, for example, it is now a thing of the past for the parents to choose their children's future wife or husband. In China, where flirting is looked down upon, dating apps facilitate the connection of millions of couples (The Economist, 2018) The use of smartphones has also made it easier for young people in countries like India to court secretly. Parents are still involved in the marriage arrangements and do not mind as long as they feel that the choice of partner is a sensible one, usually meaning that it is within religious and caste boundaries. Many parents in India now make use of dating websites to choose an eligible spouse for their children, and they discuss this with them as they increasingly wish their children to have a say in the choice of their future spouse (Budd, 2017). In Arab countries, a number of marriages happen after the first contact, and subsequent meetings would have taken place over the internet or through the mobile phone. Shopping malls are considered as an ideal location for dating. As Anser (2014) reports:

> New technologies, readily accessible to people regardless of sex, age, language, religious belief, class or residence, contribute to breaking of barriers and shift the boundaries between private and public domains. It has become relatively easy to communicate, to meet and to converse not only in virtual communities but in person also. (p. 64)

In many Western countries, dating sites have become very popular as is suggested by Eichenberg, Huss and Kusel in Chap. 16. In the United States, one-sixth of first encounters facilitated through dating apps lead to marriage. Another one-sixth meet on other online venues (The Economist, 2018). Interestingly, studies in the United States have reported that the likelihood of marriage breakdown for those who met online was significantly less than for those who met in the real world (Rosenfeld, Reuben, & Falcon, 2016).

1.4 Couple Diversity as a Hallmark of the Twenty-First Century

Love is increasingly becoming a force to be reckoned with and is breaking cultural, religious and racial barriers to the extent that diversity in couple relationships has increased in an unprecedented way in the twenty-first century. Part III of this volume is about couples in diversity. Same-sex couple relationships are now legally recognized in almost two of every three countries in the world. Couples in exclusive long-term happy relationships flourish, next door to others, which break down or are shaken by infidelity. A small percentage of couples enjoy polyamorous relationships in the West. Polygamy on the other hand is on the decline in Arab countries, but is still highly prevalent among the Bedouin population in Israel and in West Africa. Falling in love in later life is no longer the prerogative of male film stars. Similarly, persons with a disability can now express their sexuality and enter into a romantic relationship. Many men are moving away from the macho culture and it is not uncommon for them to also ask for affection rather than simply wish to have sex (Abela, 2016).

According to a European study, around 9% of couples are in a living apart together (LAT) relationship in Western European countries (Mortelmans, Pasteels,

Régnier-Loilier, Vignoli, & Mazzuco, 2015). The reasons behind these choices are not always individualistic, contrary to what is suggested by Amato and Hayes (2014). Many of these couples are still in the traditional dating phase and may eventually decide to move in together. Some divorced couples on the other hand may wish to give priority to the care of their children by choosing not to disrupt their living space when entering a new couple relationship. Such motivations have also emerged in our qualitative research on couple relationships in Malta (PFSW, 2017) particularly among couples who can afford it. In Chap. 23 of this volume, Pierre Cachia discusses some of the themes that these couples present and how they can be supported through online therapy.

Increased opportunities resulting from globalization and the rising connectedness afforded by technology have also led couples, even married ones, to live apart together. For instance, one partner may make a career move to another country, which would necessitate communicating via technological devices from a distance as well as meeting every so often. By way of example, I will cite the current situation in the Gulf countries with the majority of the population being single and male, mostly from Europe or the United States. These men work away from their families aiming to reap a rewarding and generous pay packet (Anser, 2014). Work in Brussels with the European Union has also created opportunities for bureaucrats and diplomats who travel back home to spend the weekend with their loved ones. They return to their office on Monday morning often carrying their hand luggage behind them as they arrive straight from the airport. Wang and Xia in Chap. 7 also make reference to Chinese men who leave the rural regions to go and work in the city leaving their wife and children behind them.

The situation may be very similar to that of migrants from low- to middle-income countries. At the moment, many Eastern Europeans take advantage of better salaries and the increasingly accessible cheap air flights to work in other EU countries. Many leave their family behind and go abroad. They live in one room or share an apartment and spend their time working for very long hours, whilst visiting their loved ones as often as they can afford to. Trask (2010) makes a special reference to poor immigrant women who are sought out to perform caring jobs. These women leave their loved ones including their children to earn money and be able to send remittances back home. Trask (2010, p. 141) points out that they are "particularly vulnerable and easily oppressed. Much domestic service is paid under the table without regard for labor laws, and involves elements of exploitation." However, many of these poor and working-class women are resilient and succeed in "refashion(ing) their identities, and roles within their families, their communities and host societies" (Trask, 2010, p. 144).

These migration flows (reaching 258 million persons not living in their birth country in 2017 United Nations, 2017) include those couples leaving their country of origin together, as well as singles. Situations whereby couples and families have had to adjust to a new culture or those who meet a partner in the country of destination have alerted us to the importance of making sense of culture in our relationships more than ever before. Intercultural couple relationships are on the increase and have further accelerated with the technological advances in communication and the introduction of online dating websites. In spite of the fact that intercultural couples tend to face bigger challenges (see Chap. 9 in this volume by Renee Singh), their prevalence is now reaching 1 in 10 in different parts of the world including the United Kingdom, France, South Korea and in some areas of Japan. According to the Australian Bureau of Statistics, marriages between partners of different countries have risen by 12 percentage points in a decade. In Australia, almost one in three registered marriages were intercultural in 2016 and are even higher in Hawaii and Singapore.

How do we position ourselves as family and couple therapists in the midst of this unprecedented change? Since its inception, family therapy and systemic psychotherapy have given considerable importance to culture (Bateson, 1972). Cecchin's emphases on curiosity in 1987 also promoted a stance that shuns a colonizing attitude towards families, and situates the therapist in the position of a learner. This stance is always considered to be helpful, given that dealing with difference is a constant in couple relationships irrespective of whether the individual partners come from a different country. Each partner in a couple relationship (even if from the same country and socio-economic background) inevitably brings a different baggage. Burnham (2012) and his colleague Roper-Hall have created an acronym called Social GGRAAACCEEESSS aiming to help practitioners be reflexive and mindful about such difference. The letters in the acronym stand for gender, geography, race, religion, age, ability, appearance, class, culture, ethnicity, education, employment, sexuality, sexual orientation and spirituality.

Very often couples come to us to discuss their dilemmas. They want us to help them to reflect as they find themselves letting go of the values their family of origin had instilled in them, to take the role of pioneers in the way they construct meaningful relations with significant others. They may be struggling to connect with their partner's family of origin or may have difficulty having their partner accepted by their own family. Some may face difficult decisions on whether to stay in a relationship or to leave it. These realities call for family practitioners who are able to have conversations with them, which can generate new meaning (Anderson & Goolishian, 1988). Falicov (2005) notes that many immigrants try to become increasingly bi-cultural and thus more able and resilient as they negotiate the two different worlds that they inhabit. Others struggle and expect therapists who are able to work with difference and are sensitive and respectful towards them (Yon, Malik, Mandin, & Midgley, 2018). Krause (2012) gives a lot of importance to the reflexivity of the therapist when addressing issues of culture, a

> "reflexivity which encompasses recursiveness between the different aspects of meaning, interpretation, and experience held or expressed by persons (either clients or therapists) *as well as* the self reflexivity of both the therapist and clients *vis-à-vis* their own history, development, and background and the contexts in which they participate." (p. 9)

Krause hopes that this kind of positioning of the therapist helps to broaden meaning for clients. In this respect, this knowledge about oneself and others moves slightly away from the postmodernist notion of not knowing (Rober & De Haene, 2014).

Whilst reflexivity and cultural sensitivity are important when working with difference, we agree with Rober and De Haene (2014, pp. 16, 18) that we need to be conscious of the fact that "there is a shared humanity that can be an important resource in intercultural therapy" and that in our therapeutic encounter we must first and foremost "remain present and responsive as human beings to the family members' utterances."

1.5 Power and Gender in Couple Relationships Across Cultures

Power matters in couple relationships. Various authors from diverse schools of thought have noted how power dynamics are informed by the socio-cultural context surrounding the couple relationship. The various authors of this volume have in turn argued how the changing socio-economic, political, religious and cultural beliefs in their respective countries have a direct impact on the shaping of couple behaviour.

This comes across very strongly in the different contexts. Gender plays a very important role with women having to fight for an equal status with men in different parts of the globe. Whereas, in most countries, power originally rested with men, greater consciousness of the need for equality came about as different political, economic and cultural forces came into play. It is also significant to note that as women accessed higher education, they became more vocal in claiming their rights. In many countries, including non-OECD ones, women are in fact superseding men in terms of obtaining a tertiary level of education. This shift is spreading across the globe (OECD, 2018).

Anser (2014) makes reference to how what has been termed as a "spinsterhood" crisis is affecting women with a high level of education in all Arab countries today. Others are making their wishes very explicit:

> It would seem that well-educated women with high aspirations are disillusioned and frustrated by the dominant patriarchal order. Consequently, they decide to concentrate on their career and pursue their dreams of freedom and achievement. … brides also insist on including specific conditions in the marriage contract, such as the right to education, the right to work, and the right to have their own separate residence … divorce is granted in return for a financial payment, and has been invoked to prevent situations of polygamy (Anser, 2014, p. 65).

The younger generation of Arab women are now intent on reconciling their wish for marriage and having children with getting a good education and participating in the labour market. Young men are also in agreement with this trend (Khadr, 2016).

In spite of the increasing number of women continuing their education in China, the gender pay gap between male and female employment and the lack of available jobs for women devalues the work women do outside the home and this has an effect on the sharing of family responsibilities inside the home. Women are less happy when they have to do everything themselves at home over and above their job. Gender inequality and intimate partner violence are typical reasons for divorce.

Intimate partner violence in particular is becoming increasingly unacceptable with women who divorce more likely to have experienced domestic violence in their marriage. In rural areas, traditional roles between husband and wife are still very much ingrained with women taking responsibility and care on the home front, including the care of the elderly, whereas men are the ones who bring the income home (Basu, Zuo, Lou, Acharya, & Lundgren, 2017). Wang and Xia, the authors of Chap. 7 on couple relationships in China, note that rural migration of male farmers has at times given more autonomy to the women who stay behind. However, they point to research reporting that when it comes to important decisions including those related to handling family finances, men ultimately tend to take those decisions single-handedly.

In India, men also have more power than women. Traditionally authority rested with the eldest male in the family who even had the right to choose a husband for his daughter. Nevertheless, almost all female university students now expect equal relationships. Tilak (2015) reports that according to the last national census, which was carried out in 2011, 12, 43% of University students were female. According to Lina Kashyap, who wrote our chapter about couple relationships in India, female university students still accept to live with their husband's family at least for the first few years of marriage. However, they expect that their individual needs are met and would like to steer away from the submissive role their respective mothers had taken.

In Malta, women now outnumber men when it comes to higher education. In spite of this trend and legal reforms on equal pay for women and men, Maltese females still experience a gender pay gap. It is estimated that in the next 4–5 years Malta will reach the European Union average for female labour market participation (Carabott, 2019), a shift that was considered important to sustain the viability of the pension system and the country's economic growth. These changes have had an impact on the couple relationship and on every other aspect of family life. In the last decade, the first author has witnessed young couples who used to come for couple therapy because of the unequal division of household chores. Husbands felt entitled to make use of a demand-withdraw style of conflict in the 1990s and this did not impact on the marital satisfaction of the wife or husband even when this was the predominant style adopted. On the other hand, when a woman-demand/man-withdraw style was predominant, both husband and wife were dissatisfied (Abela, Frosh, & Dowling, 2005). This was no longer the case a decade later when demand-withdraw styles of conflict triggered dissatisfaction irrespective of gender (Abela, 2014). Abela notices that women are increasingly reluctant to stay silent in the face of abuse from their husbands. Victims are now protected by law, which entered into force in 2006. As is happening in other Mediterranean countries, the social construction of masculinity and femininity is changing.

In the West, this change started to take place a few decades earlier. The cultural revolution of the 1960s brought about a paradigm shift. Gender, patriarchy and inequality were hotly debated issues. Women progressively sought work outside the home and dual earner families increased steadily in the following decades. Equality became apparent especially in the case of couples that had a higher level of education. Women in employment also felt that they had more weight in decisions taken by the couple and in the division of household chores. An INSEE study (2015) showed that in France many men were participating more on the home front although they tended to opt for softer options such as games and social activities with children as opposed to supervising homework or chauffeuring children around to take part in extra-curricular activities. Nevertheless, as Michel Maestre reports in Chap. 4, in France, division of household chores is increasingly considered as the politically correct thing to do and is no longer brought to therapy as an issue that couples disagree about.

Iceland, Finland, Norway and Sweden rank highest at closing the gender gap according to the 2018 Gender Global Gap report published by the World Economic Forum. And yet on a structural level, men have more power than women even in these countries (Sanandaji & Förlag, 2016).

These accounts from different parts of the world reflect how gender equality forms part of a global cultural change that is also reflected in the interactions between couples. This does not imply that we should assume that gender equity is in place. Even in Western countries, couples especially heterosexual ones may experience power imbalance and even abuse. A survey that was carried out across the 28 EU member states in 2012 reported that just over one in five women experienced physical and/sexual violence either with their current or previous partner (European Union Agency for Fundamental Rights, 2014). The effects of patriarchy are still very widespread in spite of the fact that gender equality is what these countries aspire to.

A number of family therapists have long been drawing attention to how structural power imbalance between the sexes penetrates the couple relationship. McDowell et al. (2017) argue however that therapists often fail to address societal context, culture and power in the couple relationship. The authors highlight the importance of socio-culturally attuned practice, which promotes equity. They advocate for a third-order lens by applying trans-theoretical guidelines that may be used whatever the conceptual clinical model. This is because power imbalance hinders intimacy in the couple relationship and triggers depression. The worth and identity of each partner are important for intimacy and affiliation to thrive in couple relationships (Knudson-Martin, 2013). Even dominant partners lose out as they may feel that they cannot make themselves vulnerable lest they lose their ground, whereas those taking a submissive position are afraid to express their wishes for more equality.

Clinicians may consider that intervening with couples from traditional cultures is particularly delicate to take on. However, research with couples from Iran by Moghadam, Knudson-Martin, and Mahoney (2009) suggests that women who were not treated equally wished to be more equal in their relationship with their husband. In spite of a gendered division of labour, when husbands were attentive to their wives and asked for their views even about finances, couples were happier and more intimate. As is evidenced in the chapters by Wang and Xia and Kashyap, there is also evidence of a shift towards gender equality in collectivist cultures as has also been researched by Quek (2009) in Singapore and in Chinese American dual earners (Quek, Knudson-Martin, Rue, & Alabiso, 2010).

Couple therapists note that power imbalances may also be present in gay couple relationships. However, Jonathan (2009) reports that these couples were more intent on the notion of equality and made an effort to address such issues in one way or another in their relationship. In this respect, gay couples tend to be quite equal between them (Gottman, 2011).

1.6 The Impact of Technology and the Media on the Couple Relationship

Several authors in this volume have made reference to how couples relate to each other in the context of a technological revolution. McCormack and Ogilvie in Chap. 15 alert us to the pros and cons of the smartphone in couple relationships. This digital device has permeated unimaginable geographic markets and revolutionized how people date and communicate. The smartphone has facilitated a sense of togetherness not only for couples who may be living apart but also for those who are not together during the day because of work. Messaging and romantic chatting among couples are now possible through several apps including Whatsapp, Messenger and Facetime.

Nevertheless, the smartphone can have the opposite effect when the couple are together. Some of the apps on this device can be addictive and may hinder partners from spending quality time together. Other distractions include easy access to one's email, which facilitates the intrusion of work commitments during time with one's partner and other family members.

Technology has also made infidelity easier. Partners can easily access sexually explicit internet material from their devices, Ipad or desktop. Muusses, Kerkhof, and Finkenauer (2015) report that in most studies, relationship quality including sexual satisfaction is found to be suffering when one of the partners resorts to such behaviour. Men are more likely to resort to problematic pornography use and Szymanski and Stewart-Richardson (2014) report that men with more avoidant and anxious attachment style are more prone to do so. In this respect, negotiation skills and good communication are important for couples to remain satisfied with their quality time as a couple. Women's self-esteem is affected when they discover that their partner is resorting to pornography. Women often feel that they have to be the aesthetic sex and conclude that they are not good enough for their husband.

Moira Weigel (2016) in her book on digital dating also highlights how we are living in an economy, which drives women, mostly through advertising, to sell themselves on the dating market. In this respect, dating becomes a profitable market for the cosmetics and fashion industries inciting women (and men) to improve the way they look in order to get the perfect match. Older women and men fall prey to this as well. By way of example, according to the American Society for Aesthetic Plastic Surgery, one million Americans a year, mostly coming from privileged backgrounds, opt for Botox in a society that is becoming increasingly visual and where women who opt for these interventions want to look younger. Many of the men want to look good in spite of their age in an increasingly ageist professional setting, whilst others may also be interested to find a younger woman as their partner (Maisel et al., 2018).

Other potential sources of alienation for today's couples include the commercialization of love. Illouz (1997) calls this the commodification of romance whereby romance is associated with leisure consumption such as having a candle-lit dinner at a restaurant, taking a romantic weekend break and giving and receiving gifts. The media and advertising in particular send the message that the more one is extravagant, the more romantic is the experience. Hochschild (2012) also makes reference to how commodification is now entering our private life and is giving a new twist to important family celebrations such as birthdays, which are now being organized by a birthday planner. As Murphy points out in Chap. 14, the media portray an idealized version of commodified romance, glossing over the more mundane lived experiences of a romantic relationship. In our qualitative study on the expectations and lived experiences of couples in Malta, our participants complained that the media provides an idealized image of romantic relationships that did not necessarily correspond with their daily experiences. They also complained about the fact that they had to work very long hours to be able to meet their high expectations. Those on a minimum wage experienced financial stress and struggled to earn sufficient income (PFSW, 2017). This phenomenon is very present in the West, but also in other parts of the world due to the influence of American capitalism across the globe (Illouz, 1997). Recent studies (e.g. Jankowiak et al., 2015) accentuate the importance of material factors for sustaining a romantic relationship in China.

1.7 Supporting Couple Relationships

Sustaining good quality couple relationships over time is proving to be quite a challenge in the twenty-first century. People across the globe have increasingly high expectations of their intimate relationship. Lack of satisfaction on a psychological and a sexual level leads many people to stray (Perel, 2017, Timm and Blow in this volume) and eventually drift apart even if still connected through their children. We also know that so many other couples stay happily together for a lifetime (see Cole & Cole Chap. 18).

What support do couples need? The last part of this volume turns its focus on this important question. Various authors address this issue from a different perspective and highlight the importance of attachment theory in couple therapy, the value of online therapy especially for couples who are living apart together, the importance of supporting parents without losing sight of the couple relationship and support in the community. The last chapter is an overarching one that seeks common themes in couple relationships across the chapters and sets them in a context of global trends in couple relationships.

1.8 Conclusion

The observation that was made by Moira Weigel in one of her interviews seems to be very apt as a conclusion to this introductory chapter. Love does not die and desire does not die, because if they did, then we would be living in a world where hope is killed and dreams cease to exist. We hope that this volume will provide readers with insight into what it means to be in a couple relationship in the twenty-first century, and enhance our understanding of the vital importance of this relationship and how we can best support couples in today's world.

References

Abela, A. (2014). *Changing dynamics in Maltese marriages.* Paper presented at the First European Conference on Systemic Research in Therapy, Education and Organizational Development.

Abela, A. (2016). Family life. In M. Briguglio & M. Brown (Eds.), *Sociology of the Maltese islands* (pp. 18–46). Luqa: Miller Publishing.

Abela, A., Frosh, S., & Dowling, E. (2005). Uncovering beliefs embedded in the culture and its implication for practice: The case of Maltese married couples. *Journal of Family Therapy, 27*(3), 3–23.

Amato, P. R., Booth, A., Johnson, D. R., Johnson, D. R., & Rogers, S. J. (2007). *Alone together: How marriage in America is changing.* New York, NY: Harvard University Press.

Amato, P. R., & Hayes, L. N. (2014). 'Alone together' marriages and 'living apart together' relationships. In A. Abela & J. Walter (Eds.), *Contemporary perspectives on partnerships, parenting and support in a changing world* (pp. 31–45). Malden: Wiley.

Anderson, H., & Goolishian, H. A. (1988). Human systems as linguistic systems: Preliminary and evolving ideas about the implications for clinical theory. *Family Process, 27*(4), 371–393.

Anser, L. (2014). Divorce in the Arab Gulf countries. In A. Abela & J. Walker (Eds.), *Contemporary issues in family studies: Global perspectives on partnerships, parenting and support in a changing world* (pp. 59–73). London: Wiley Blackwell.

Basu, S., Zuo, X., Lou, C., Acharya, R., & Lundgren, R. (2017). Learning to be gendered: Gender socialization in early adolescence among urban poor in Delhi, India, and Shanghai, China. *Journal of Adolescent Health, 61*(4), S24–S29.

Bateson, G. (1972). *Steps to an ecology of mind: Collected essays in anthropology, psychiatry, evolution, and epistemology* (p. 381). Scranton: Chandler Publishing Company.

Budd, J. (2017, November 23). Special report: Marriage. A looser knot: The state of marriage as an institution. *The Economist.* Retrieved from https://www.economist.com/special-report/2017/11/23/the-state-of-marriage-as-an-institution

Burnham, J. (2012). *Culture and reflexivity in systemic psychotherapy: Mutual perspectives* (p. 139). London: Karnac Books.

Carabott, S. (2019, February 6). Gender pay gap caught up with Malta. Times of Malta. Retrieved from https://timesofmalta.com/articles/view/gender-pay-gap-caught-up-with-malta-president.701269

Cecchin, G. (1987). Hypothesizing, circularity, and neutrality revisited: An invitation to curiosity. *Family Process, 26*(4), 405–413.

European Union Agency for Fundamental Rights. (2014). *Violence against women: An EU wide survey. Main results.* Luxembourg: Publications Office of the European Union.

Falicov, C. J. (2005). Emotional transnationalism and family identities. *Family Process, 44*(4), 399–406.

Fehr, B., & Russell, J. A. (1991). The concept of love viewed from a prototype perspective. *Journal of Personality and Social Psychology, 60*(3), 425.

Fisher, B. (2015). Why non–marital children in the MENA region face a risk of statelessness. *Harvard Human Rights Journal Online, 32*, 1–8.

Gottman, J. M. (2011). *The science of trust: Emotional attunement for couples.* New York, NY: WW Norton & Company.

Hazan, C., & Shaver, P. (1987). Romantic love conceptualized as an attachment process. *Journal of Personality and Social Psychology, 52*(3), 511. https://doi.org/10.1037/0022-3514.52.3.511

Hiew, D. N., Halford, W. K., & Liu, S. (2014). Loving diversity: Living in intercultural couple relationships. In A. Abela & J. Walker (Eds.), *Contemporary issues in family studies: Global perspectives on partnerships, parenting and support in a changing world* (pp. 87–99). London: Wiley Blackwell.

Hochschild, A. R. (2012). *The outsourced self: Intimate life in market times.* New York, NY: Metropolitan Books.

Hofstede, G. (2001). *Culture's consequences: Comparing values, behaviors, institutions and organizations across nations.* Thousand Oaks, CA: Sage Publications.

Illouz, E. (1997). *Consuming the romantic utopia: Love and the cultural contradictions of capitalism.* Berkeley: University of California Press.

Institut National de la Statistique et des Études Économiques (INSEE). (2015). *2015 annual report.* Retrieved from https://www.insee.fr/en/information/2404445

Izuhara, M. (2010). New patterns of family reciprocity: Policy challenges and ageing societies. In M. Izuhara (Ed.), *Ageing and international relations: Family reciprocity from a global perspective* (pp. 149–159). Bristol: The Policy Press.

Jankowiak, W., Shen, Y., Yao, S., Wang, C., & Volsche, S. (2015). Investigating love's universal attributes: A research report from China. *Cross-Cultural Research, 49*(4), 422–436.

Jonathan, N. (2009). Carrying equal weight: Relational responsibility and attunement among same–sex couples. In C. Knudson-Martin & A. R. Mahoney (Eds.), *Couples, gender, and power: Creating change in intimate relationships.* New York, NY: Springer.

Karandashev, V. (2017). *Romantic love in cultural contexts.* Basel: Springer.

Katke, R. D., Saraogi, M. R., & Pagare, P. (2014). Rising incidence of unwed mothers in India; associated social parameters & institutional guidelines for managing them. *International Journal of Reproduction, Contraception, Obstetrics and Gynecology, 3*(4), 942–946.

Khadr, Z. (2016). *Marriage market in urban settings in Egypt: A socio-ecological framework.* Retrieved from: http://schools.aucegypt.edu/research/src/Documents/Marriage%20Market%20Report/Marriage%20market%20in%20urban%20settings%20in%20Egypt.pdf

Knudson-Martin, C. (2013). Why power matters: Creating a foundation of mutual support in couple relationships. *Family Process, 52*(1), 5–18.

Krause, I. B. (2012). *Culture and the reflexive subject in systemic psychotherapy.* London: Karnac Books.

Lesthaeghe, R. (1995). The second demographic transition in Western countries: An interpretation. In K. O. Mason & A.-M. Jensen (Eds.), *Gender and family change in industrialized countries* (pp. 17–62). Oxford: Clarendon Press.

Maisel, A., Waldman, A., Furlan, K., Weil, A., Sacotte, K., Lazaroff, J. M., … Cartee, T. V. (2018). Self-reported patient motivations for seeking cosmetic procedures. *JAMA Dermatology, 154*(10), 1167–1174.

Moghadam, S., Knudson-Martin, C., & Mahoney, A. R. (2009). Gendered power in cultural contexts: Part III. Couple relationships in Iran. *Family Process, 48*(1), 41–54.

Mortelmans, D., Pasteels, I., Régnier-Loilier, A., Vignoli, D., & Mazzuco, S. (2015). *Analysis of determinants and prevalence of LAT.* Families and Societies Working Paper Series 25. Retrieved from http://www.familiesandsocieties.eu/wp-content/uploads/2015/01/WP25MortelmansEtAl.pdf

Muusses, L. D., Kerkhof, P., & Finkenauer, C. (2015). Internet pornography and relationship quality: A longitudinal study of within and between partner effects of adjustment, sexual satisfaction and sexually explicit internet material among newly–weds. *Computers in Human Behavior, 45*, 77–84.

McDowell, T. Knudson-Martin, C. Bermudez, J. M. (2017). *Socioculturally attuned family therapy: Guidelines for equitable theory and practice*. Routledge, Abigdon, United Kingdom

OECD. (2018). *Education at a glance 2018: OECD indicators*. Retrieved from https://read.oecd-ilibrary.org/education/education-at-a-glance-2018_eag-2018-en#page1

Perel, E. (2017). *The state of affairs: Rethinking infidelity*. London: Hachette Book Group.

PFSW (2017) Sustaining Relationships, The Expectations and lived experiences of Maltese couples. San Anton Palace Attard Malta

Quek, K. M. (2009). WE consciousness: Creating equality in collectivist culture. In C. Knudson-Martin & A. R. Mahoney (Eds.), *Couples, gender and power: Creating change in intimate relationships* (pp. 193–214). New York, NY: Springer.

Quek, K. M. T., Knudson-Martin, C., Rue, D., & Alabiso, C. (2010). Relational harmony: A new model of collectivism and gender equality among Chinese American couples. *Journal of Family Issues, 31*(3), 358–380.

Raymo, J. M. (2014). Demographic change and its impact on relationships in Japan and East Asia. In A. Abela & J. Walker (Eds.), *Contemporary issues in family studies. Global perspectives on partnerships, parenting and support in a changing world* (pp. 328–340). London: Wiley Blackwell.

Rober, P., & De Haene, L. (2014). Intercultural therapy and the limitations of a cultural competency framework: About cultural differences, universalities and the unresolvable tensions between them. *Journal of Family Therapy, 36*, 3–20.

Rosenfeld, M. J., Reuben, T. J., & Falcon, M. (2016). *How couples meet and stay together, waves 1, 2, and 3: Public version 3.04*. Stanford, CA: Stanford University Libraries.

Sanandaji, N., & Förlag, T. (2016). *The Nordic gender equality paradox*. Retrieved from http://nordicparadox.se/wp-content/uploads/2016/02/The-Nordic-gender-equality-paradox.pdf

Shaver, P. R., Wu, S., & Schwartz, J. C. (1992). Cross-cultural similarities and differences in emotion and its representation. In M. S. Clark (Ed.), *Review of personality and social psychology* (pp. 175–212). Newbury Park, CA: Sage.

Smart, C. (2007). *Personal life: New directions in sociological thinking*. Cambridge: Polity Press.

Szymanski, D. M., & Stewart-Richardson, D. N. (2014). Psychological, relational, and sexual correlates of pornography use on young adult heterosexual men in romantic relationships. *The Journal of Men's Studies, 22*(1), 64–82.

The Economist. (2011, August 20). *The decline of Asian marriage: Asia's lonely hearts*. Retrieved from https://www.economist.com/leaders/2011/08/20/asias-lonely-hearts

The Economist. (2018, August 18). *Briefing. Sexual selection: Putting the data into dating*. Retrieved from https://www.economist.com/briefing/2018/08/18/how-the-internet-has-changed-dating

Tilak, J. B. (2015). How inclusive is higher education in India? *Social Change, 45*(2), 185–223.

Trask, B. S. (2010). *Globalization and families: Accelerated systemic social change*. New York, NY: Springer.

Triandis, H. C., Bontempo, R., Betancourt, H., Bond, M., Leung, K., Brenes, A., et al. (1986). The measurement of etic aspects of individualism and collectivism across cultures. *Australian Journal of Psychology, 38*, 257–267.

Watts-Jones, T. D. (2010). Location of self: Opening the door to dialogue on intersectionality in the therapy process. *Family Process, 49*(3), 405–420.

Weigel, M. (2016). Flirting with humanity: The search for an artificial intelligence smart enough to love. *New Republic, 247*(6), 18–27.

Yon, K., Malik, R., Mandin, P., & Midgley, N. (2018). Challenging core cultural beliefs and maintaining the therapeutic alliance: A qualitative study. *Journal of Family Therapy, 40*(2), 180–200.

Chapter 2
The Significance of the Couple Relationship in the Twenty-First Century

Angela Abela

2.1 Introduction

According to The Guardian (Beaumont-Thomas, 2017), Ed Sheeran was the most frequently streamed artist on Spotify in 2017 and his song *Thinking out Loud* became the first song to hit 500 million streams in October 2015. The lyrics promise long-lasting love:

> When your legs don't work like they used to before
> And I can't sweep you off your feet
> Will your mouth still remember the taste of love
> Will your eyes still smile from your cheeks
>
> And darling I will be loving you 'til we are 70
> And baby my heart could still fall as hard at 23
> And I'm thinking 'bout how people fall in love in mysterious ways
> Maybe just the touch of a hand
> Oh me I fall in love with you every single day
> And I just wanna tell you I am…

This song's popularity suggests that we can only be truly sustained by everlasting romantic love, in spite of the fact that it is unrealistic to expect to be in such a perpetual state with a partner. Beall and Sternberg (1995) argue that the yearning for everlasting romantic love is simply a social construction. Others attest that besides the social layer, there is a biological basis to this yearning in that "romantic love is an attachment process—a *biosocial* (emphasis added) process by which affectional

A. Abela (✉)
Department of Family Studies, Faculty for Social Wellbeing,
University of Malta, Msida, Malta
e-mail: angela.abela@um.edu.mt

bonds are formed between adult lovers, just as affectional bonds are formed earlier in life between human infants and their parents" (Hazan & Shaver, 1987, p. 511). In my clinical work with couples and also in the course of my conversations with those I encounter in my daily life, many people have often told me that they feel actualized when experiencing a meaningful connection with their significant others. On a global level, cross-cultural anthropologists have attested that romantic love is a powerful emotion that we feel in our body and which forms part of the six basic emotions that all human beings experience no matter where they are living (Karandashev, 2017) the others being joy, anger, sadness, fear and hate.

2.1.1 The Rise in Singledom

On the other side of the continuum, psychologist De Paulo claims that "There's never been a better time to be single" (De Paulo, 2018).

In the United States, the number of people living without a spouse or partner rose to 42% from 39% a decade ago (Fry, 2017). In Germany, 41.4% lived alone in 2015. According to Mitchell (2006), the rise in singledom can be attributed to greater individualism and changing gender roles. Today, many who are living alone are better off financially compared to years gone by and can afford a comfortable life. They can also stay connected with friends and family through social media (Beaujot, 2012).

The rise in singledom has permeated the East–West divide. Well-educated women in Arab countries are opting to remain single if the conditions for marriage are based on a dominant patriarchal order. Divorce is also increasing at a very fast rate in the Arab countries (Anser, 2014). In Japan, Korea and Taiwan, women with a higher educational level are also rejecting marriage. They would rather focus on their career first and have children later. Many of these women end up not marrying at all because they are not particularly keen on taking family responsibilities, including the care of the husband's elderly parents in a society where men expect to take a backseat when it comes to sharing household responsibilities. These countries have also experienced a rapid increase in divorce (Raymo, Park, Xie, & Yeung, 2015). In terms of life satisfaction, the key difference between happy and unhappy single persons has to do with whether the independence is a choice (Mitchell, 2006). Loneliness may contribute towards poorer mental health in single persons.

In a study that we carried out at the Maltese National Centre For Family Research within the President's Foundation for the Wellbeing of Society (PFWS, 2016) on couples and singles in Malta with a nationally representative sample of just under 2500 individuals, it transpired that almost 68% of those who were single were not interested in having a relationship and this disinterest remained very high across age cohorts. The predictors of "happy singledom" were income adequacy (as has already been mentioned in the international literature by Mitchell), the type of lifestyle they were leading and the fact that they and their families experienced well-being (PFWS, 2016).

2.1.2 The Predominance of the Couple Relationship

In spite of the rise in singledom, those in a couple relationship still constitute the majority of adult persons.

The European Social Survey (2016) takes into account those aged between 18 and 55 to examine marriage rates across different groups of countries. In the "traditional" group of countries, around 53% are married, whereas almost 19% of those who are unmarried are living with a partner. The traditional group of countries includes Poland, Russia, Slovenia and Israel. In the "middle" group of countries, approximately the same proportion of persons are in a couple relationship, but there is a clear difference in status as 49% are married and around 29% of those who are unmarried are living with a partner. This middle group of countries included Germany, the Netherlands, United Kingdom, Belgium, Czech Republic and Ireland. In the third group comprising Sweden, Norway, Finland, Denmark and France around 44% are married, whereas almost 40% of those who are unmarried are living with a partner. Comparisons with statistics issued in 2008 show that the incidence of couple relationships has either increased or remained the same. Cohabitation has however gone up in traditional and middle group countries over the past 8 years, whereas marriage has decreased. Nevertheless, marriage continues to be more popular than cohabitation. This enduring preference for marriage also holds true for the Scandinavian countries and France even though the rate of married couples exceeds that of cohabiting couples by only 5%. As Abela and Walker argue "the symbolic importance of marriage remains high" (2014a, p. 1) even in the case of minority groups.

Types of couple relationships that were once banned, such as intermarriage amongst different racial groups or same-sex relationships, today form part of the changing social landscape of many societies across the globe. The meaning of this change in societal norms and in how we make sense of romantic relationships is best captured in the popular meme "Love is Love." Although in some societies, intercultural and gay relationships are still not fully accepted, they have become increasingly common especially in big cities such as London where it is predicted that by 2030 half of the population will be foreign born. By 2017, same-sex relationships were legal in 124 countries around the world, whereas 72 countries were found to criminalize sexual activity between persons of the same sex (Carroll & Mendos, 2017). Twenty-six countries in the West have legalized same-sex marriages, whereas 15 countries recognize civil unions. In the United States, just 1 in 10 lesbian, gay, bisexual and transgender adults are married to somebody of the same sex (Jones, 2017). In Britain, Sweden and the Netherlands, marriages between women outnumber those between men maybe suggesting that women have a greater preference for sealing their romantic relationship through marriage (The Economist, 2017a).

2.2 Good Quality Couple Relationships Enhance Well-being

Good quality couple relationships are central to health and well-being, and enhance well-being in all societies (Benjamin, Marshall, & Ferenczi, 2014; Tasfiliz et al., 2018).

Being in a good relationship is associated with lower levels of depression amongst both men and women (Leach, Butterworth, Olesen, & Mackinnon, 2013). On the other hand, when the couple relationship is bad, this is associated with poor mental health and higher anxiety in partnered women compared to those who are single (Leach et al., 2013). The latter authors postulate that high expressed emotion may be considered as one explanation linking poor mental health to poor quality relationships. There are clear links between relationship distress and depression, anxiety, increased blood pressure and increased risk of heart attacks (Kiecolt-Glaser & Newton, 2001; Proulx, Helms, & Buehler, 2007). Alcohol misuse may also be influenced by relationship distress (Leonard & Eiden, 2007). There is also a link between chronic stress such as couple distress and addictions including smoking and substance misuse (Al'Absi, 2007).

Sixty percent of those with depression cite relationship problems as the main cause and therapy for relationship distress may alleviate up to 30% of major depression (Sserwanja & Marjoribanks, 2016).

2.2.1 What Makes a Good Quality Couple Relationship

We all enter couple relationships with our own set of expectations regarding the role we wish our partner would play and how he or she would relate towards us. In our qualitative study amongst 23 adult participants in Malta who were all in a heterosexual couple relationship at the time of the study (PFWS, 2016), a satisfying relationship was characterized by respect, communication, trust and love. Fidelity, reciprocity and shared companionship were also highlighted. The importance of these relational qualities became particularly crucial when facing life challenges, which are common to all couples. They were also evident in the way conflict and disagreement were managed and how decisions were taken. The extent to which one felt understood during these moments, and the generosity, affection, intimacy and humour, which were shared with one another contributed to or detracted from the partners' sense of well-being. Support and encouragement received from and performed for one's spouse were also found to be beneficial by Minnotte, Pedersen, and Mannon (2010) who studied 96 heterosexual couples. Many studies that delve into what makes good quality relationships are North American. However, few cross-cultural studies that exist show that there are common threads across different cultures. For example, responsiveness between partners is important in North America and in Japan, although it is given less importance in Japan (Tasfiliz et al., 2018). Another study in peri-urban Ethiopia reports that commitment and trust were equally important in this culture (John, Seme, Roro, & Tsui, 2017).

Another correlate of marital satisfaction underlined in research includes sexual satisfaction, with good quality communication found to strengthen this correlation (Millman, 2012). Married couples who reported high levels of relationship satisfaction were found to disclose more positive affect and sexual preferences (Coffelt & Hess, 2014). This coincides with Rehman et al.'s (2011) findings with newlywed couples, where positive behaviours in both sexual and nonsexual conflict were slightly associated with higher relationship satisfaction. According to Twenge, Sherman, and Wells (2017), there exists a decline in sex in the United States. The authors wonder whether this is a reflection of a higher incidence of depression and an increasing use of antidepressants, and/or the increasing access to entertainment.

In the case of dual-earner couples, who are in the majority in most Western countries, findings illustrate that perceived unfairness in the division of domestic chores was associated with poorer relationship quality amongst women but not men (Britt-Lutter & Nazarinia, 2014). Carlson, Miller, and Sassler (2018) have shown that couples (whether cohabiting or married) who shared childcare and housework reported greater satisfaction and better sex lives.

Greater flexibility of gender roles is on the rise in couple relationships. Men are increasingly doing more on the homefront. In the United Kingdom, academics at Oxford have shown that the gap in hours of housework between men and women has narrowed from 174 h in 1974 to 74 h in 2005. In the United States, the gap fell by 38 min a day between 2003 and 2006 and by 28 min between 2011 and 2015 (Altintas & Sullivan, 2016).

Individuals who reported a high use of planning and management skills, which they adopted as a couple, and who had a positive attitude towards multiple roles reported higher levels of relationship satisfaction in a study conducted with 402 dual earners in Portugal, as did those who adjusted by also cutting back on work (Matias & Fontaine, 2012). A more recent study underlines the association between collaboration between the couple and perceived fairness of household and childcare division of tasks (Knutson, 2014), which in turn was associated with better marital quality in husbands and wives alike.

2.2.2 *Is There Such a Thing as a "Good Fit" in the Couple Relationship?*

All the above qualities and skills contribute towards a good quality relationship. But how do couples find a good comfortable fit between them once the mysterious falling in love process takes place? There is now ample evidence that shows that those attachment patterns that are developed with significant others at a very young age form the basis for adult relationships (Fonagy et al., 1996; Hazan & Shaver, 1987; Main, Kaplan, & Cassidy, 1985).

Bowlby (1973) considered the nurturing experience in an infant's first years to provide a necessary core on which children can build a capacity for trusting others and for believing that there are persons out there who resemble the primary caregiver and who are responsive and can support them in moments of need. The experience also gives these persons the confidence to believe that others will be empathic towards them and will respond to their needs in a loving way.

When one feels secure and confident in a relationship, there is a greater disposition to be generous and flexible and relaxed. The availability, responsiveness and supportiveness of a romantic partner are considered crucial for romantic relationships to flourish (Mikulincer et al., 2006). Being in a satisfactory relationship may reinforce partners' engagement in more relationship maintenance behaviours, hence enhancing a predisposition to behave in ways that further benefit the relationship (Schoebi, Karney, & Bradbury, 2012). In my opinion, it is this sense of confidence and this learnt ability to regulate one's emotions in the face of frustration as well as the ability to contain hate in a framework of love that creates the capacity for a good fit in the couple relationship.

It is not always the case that infants have a positive relational experience with their primary caregiver/s. Some infants are neglected, coerced, rejected or abused and these children find it much more difficult to trust that others will ever have the capacity to empathize with them, comfort them or have their best interests at heart. Their attachment style is anxious ambivalent, avoidant or fearful. These insecure attachment styles are actually open to change through subsequent experiences that bolster the resilience of individuals who have gone through difficult and at times traumatic experiences. But when this does not happen, they develop a sense of anxiety when relating to their loved ones, the main reason being that they do not see themselves as lovable and therefore fear an attack or abandonment. Goldner, Penn, Sheinberg, and Walker (1990) and Bartholomew (1997) further argue that such individuals seek to connect with those who are vulnerable like them and that such a combination may not augur well for a durable fit between the two.

Knoke, Burau, and Röhrle's (2010) study amongst married couples highlighted that emotional loneliness and attachment style are central to partners' self-reported relationship quality. Individuals who reported experiencing insufficient emotional closeness and intimacy tended to evaluate their relationship poorly in terms of adequate communication, affection, mutuality and happiness between the couple. Anxious attachment was also related to reduced couple satisfaction. This may be explained by the negative perception of persons with an anxious attachment style, which usually gears them towards cues that might reinforce their fear of being abandoned or attacked.

Of course a comfortable fit in the couple relationship is not only based on the biological human need to connect and on the psychological sequel of a particular attachment pattern, yet I believe that emotional security augurs well for a good accommodation between a couple. Usually it would take 2 years for such a fit to develop and this duration is similar to the time taken for an attachment pattern to develop between a primary caregiver and baby.

A cross-cultural study on adult romantic attachment across 62 regions suggests that there exist cultural variations in terms of attachment style. Secure attachment was only rated as the highest type of attachment in 79% of the countries, suggesting that the ecology of the country had a big impact on attachment style. Stress was mentioned as a plausible explanation for the seven African countries. In the case of East Asian countries, it was hypothesized that the collectivist traditions give more importance to how much one is of value to others than to oneself. This was perhaps why preoccupied attachment was higher in these regions. The authors also wondered whether the translations of the instruments in the different cultures could have led to misunderstandings and therefore make the point that further research is needed to ascertain the universality of adult romantic attachment across cultures (Schmitt et al., 2004).

2.3 How Do Couple Relationships Unfold?

Increasing diversity has become considerably more noticeable across the past 50 years, as the "more traditional pathways to getting married are being eroded and are giving way to a range of options for making, breaking and remaking couple relationships" (Abela & Walker, 2014a, p. 1). Although living together as an unwed couple was historically prohibited by cultural norms, marriage is no longer an expected requirement for couples (Abela & Walker, 2014b). Children born of cohabiting couples are now more commonplace in the United States, United Kingdom and Northern Europe (Abela & Walker, 2014b). Recent evidence challenges the idea that cohabiting relationships are less stable, and research is increasingly illustrating that both marriage and cohabitation may enhance well-being (Musick & Bumpass, 2012).

Entering a couple relationship following divorce has also become increasingly common, often leading to remarriages and stepfamilies (Falke & Larson, 2007). Several studies indicate no differences in relationship satisfaction when comparing first marriage to remarriage (Amato, 2007; Skinner, Bahr, Crane, & Call, 2002) though divorce becomes progressively more likely as one remarries a second and a subsequent time (Pryor, 2014). Similarly, individuals in consensually non-monogamous relationships have been found to have comparable rates of relationship quality and life satisfaction to those in an exclusive romantic relationship, further suggesting that relationship structure is not a guarantee of psychological and relational well-being (Rubel & Bogaert, 2015). Such findings aptly shift the focus onto the quality of relationships (as has already been pointed out further up) rather than the structure or legal status of relationships.

Through a longitudinal study following 464 newlyweds over their first 4 years of marriage, Lavner and Bradbury (2010) identified that distinct trajectories of change in marital satisfaction corresponded to divorce rates 10 years later. Spouses who reported relatively high levels of satisfaction, which remained stable, or had minimal decline, over 4 years had a later divorce rate that ranged between 9% and 26%, in contrast to a range of 40–60% divorce rate amongst spouses who reported low initial satisfaction scores and immediate declines after marriage.

Such findings were replicated in a later study by Lavner, Bradbury, and Karney (2012), with spouses in the low-satisfaction group displaying marital dissolution rates three to four times higher than spouses in the moderate- and high-satisfaction groups. Nevertheless, in both studies, some spouses who were unhappy in the first 4 years of marriage remained married. This may be explained by literature suggesting that commitment may—in spite of difficulties—serve to stabilize couple relationships when the couple's inclination to maintain the relationship is high (Schoebi et al., 2012).

On the other hand, some couples who fared well in the first 4 years of marriage were still found to dissolve their marriage in the subsequent 6 years (Lavner et al., 2012; Lavner & Bradbury, 2010). This coincides with earlier findings by Amato and Hohmann-Marriott (2007), which illustrate that half of those individuals who eventually divorced had reported relatively high initial levels of marital happiness and low projected probability of divorce. Such findings raise the question of what causes couple relationships with high levels of marital satisfaction to eventually deteriorate. A study by Lavner, Bradbury, and Karney (2012) revealed that couples who divorced, despite reporting high levels of relationship satisfaction during their first 4 years of marriage, were not low on initial commitment, yet scored higher on negative communication (for instance, destructive disagreement, invalidation, blame) and on their display of anger and contempt as newlyweds.

Common features that emerged in low-distress marriages that ended in divorce in Lavner et al.'s (2012) study similarly included lack of support, anger, contempt, invalidation, disagreement and blame, in comparison with couples who remained married. These processes had already been studied by Gottman in 1977 in his love lab as he videotaped couples interacting and negotiating differences between them, which led him to identify the four "horsemen of the apocalypse" predicting divorce, namely criticism, defensiveness, contempt and stonewalling (Gottman, 1993).

However, in a recent longitudinal study with newlyweds, Lavner, Karney, and Bradbury (2016) concluded that communication behaviours rarely predict relationship satisfaction. Instead, satisfaction was found to predict communication. I am more inclined to believe that there exists a recursive virtuous process between couple satisfaction and a mutually constructive communication style as suggested by Schoebi et al. (2012) further above. Recent findings highlight the negative impact of emotion dysregulation on relationship quality and couple intimacy (Tani, Pascuzzi, & Raffagnino, 2015). This once again leads me to reflect on the importance of emotion regulation for good relationships and how important it is for parents to be supported in the regulation of their infants' emotions.

2.4 Children and the Couple Relationship

2.4.1 The Desire for Children

In the United States, 55% of the young adult population aged between 18 and 34 said that having a child was not an important milestone of adulthood (Vespa, 2017). This would appear to be equally true amongst higher educated women in richer countries, as they are having fewer children at a later age (with some resorting to fertility treatment). The total fertility rate has gone down in different parts of the world, and the decline is more pronounced in the Western World where it stands at 1.76 in the United States (World Bank, 2017) and 1.59 in the European Union (Eurostat, 2019). Financial concerns (including rising childcare costs and the impact motherhood has on the pay packet) as well as the increasing difficulty with sustaining a good work life balance keep men and women back from having the number of children they would ideally like to have in the United States (Cain Millar, 2018). Similarly, Tanturri (2014) highlights how the high costs of children and the new demographic transition with its new value system based on individualistic needs contribute to low fertility.

In a study that was carried out on a national representative sample, Riskind and Patterson (2010) found that only 37% of lesbian women wished to have children compared to 68% of heterosexual women. In the case of gay men, 54% expressed such a wish when compared to 67% of heterosexual men. In the long run, however, gay men were less likely to have a child when compared to lesbian women.

In spite of demographic developments, the desire for children continues to be an essential feature of the great majority of couple relationships with only a small percentage choosing not to have children, ranging from 4% to 9% of couples in industrialized nations (Avison & Furnham, 2015). The stability of the couple relationship and positive feelings towards the partner influence women to have children (Fischer, Stanford, Jameson, & DeWitt, 1999). In another study amongst 1613 White British married couples without children, the reason why respondents wanted children revolved around values about giving love, making a family and having a child that is biologically related to both members of the dyad (Langdridge, Sheeran, & Connolly, 2005). In a qualitative study amongst Australian heterosexual couples, the desire to have a child was considered to be a natural progression of being a couple, as well as an internal drive and a desire to see oneself reflected in another human being (Riggs & Bartholomaeus, 2016).

2.4.2 *The Impact of the Couple Relationship on Children*

Family stability and the quality of the relationship between the parents have a significant impact on the life chances of the children. Children who come from a family where the parents are happy together enjoy better physical and mental health (Meltzer, Gatward, Goodman, & Ford, 2000), better emotional well-being (Harold et al., 2011) and do better at school. Conflict between parents can result in increased anxiety, withdrawal and depression, and behavioural problems including hostility and aggression.

By the age of 16, 42% of children in the United Kingdom do not live with both parents (DWP, 2015). In the study by RELATE, which was carried out in England and Wales in 2016 on couple relationships, parents of children under 16 were more likely than couples with younger children to be in a distressed relationship. In Malta, lower levels of satisfaction were associated with parenting adolescents than younger children (PFWS, 2016).

In the study by Gabb, Klett-Davies, Fink, and Thomae (2013), homosexual parents scored higher on relationship maintenance behaviours than heterosexual parents. The latter were found to be the group least likely to invest in "couple time," to seek shared interests, to be there for one another and talk openly with each other, and to say "I love you."

Piscopo in 2014 found that happily married Maltese couples experienced attunement, generosity and fulfilment through parenthood. Interestingly, husbands' marital satisfaction increased when involved in performing emotion work for children, yet was found to decrease when their level of emotion work reached or exceeded that of their wives.

In spite of the fact that fertility rates have generally decreased, parents have increased the time they spend with their children. An analysis conducted in 11 rich countries estimates that the average mother spent 54 min per day caring for children in 1965 but 104 min in 2012. Men have increased child caring from 16 min to 59 min. A gap has opened between working-class and middle-class parents. By 2012, the more educated ones were spending half an hour more a day with their children, stimulating them through play and other educational activities such as reading (Dotti Sani & Treas, 2016).

2.5 Couple Satisfaction over Time

Knoke et al.'s (2010) study amongst married couples reports that marital quality also declined as couples grew older. This contrasts with previous literature (Gagnon, Hersen, Kabacoff, & Van Hasselt, 1999), wherein a decrease in relationship quality is expected in middle age, followed by a renewed increase in marital quality for older couples. Knoke et al. attribute this finding to the age range of their participants, given that the median age was 39 years. A decrease in relationship quality is expected for individuals in middle age. Indeed, research indicates that levels of marital satisfaction tend to decrease over the first 15 years of marriage, at which point many marriages may end in divorce (Kahr, 2012). In a recent study by Amato and James (2018) who made use of six waves of data from the Marital Instability over the Life Course Study with 1617 participants, happiness declined during the first 20 years of marriage and then remained stable for the entire cohort. They found however that overall happiness did not decline in marriages that did not eventually experience a divorce. On the contrary, happiness increased slightly in marriages that remained stable especially for husbands. Sheeran must be aspiring to form part of the latter couples in his song.

2.5.1 Older Couples

In a qualitative study exploring the marital experiences of five couples married for over 40 years, partners identified togetherness and having children/grandchildren as important aspects when describing relationship satisfaction (Nimtz, 2011). Furthermore, attitudes of commitment, respect and humour emerged as themes relevant to marriage longevity, in addition to acts of communication, compromise and support (Nimtz, 2011).

Research amongst older couples also highlights the association between marital quality and illness, including dementia. De Jong-Gierveld, Broese van Groenou, Hoogendoorn, and Smit (2009) researched emotional loneliness amongst 755 married participants in Holland aged between 64 and 92 taking into account the quality of the marriage. Between 20% and 25% were found to be suffering from emotional loneliness. Health problems, lack of emotional support from the spouse, infrequent conversations between the couple and a poor or nonexistent sex life were the factors impinging on the sense of loneliness. For some reason, women in second marriages felt more emotionally lonely, as did men whose wives had a disability. Poor connections with the children and with friends increased their sense of loneliness. Ultimately, the loss of a loved one is often experienced as a time of intense grief for the surviving partner.

2.6 The Fragility of the Couple Relationship

Couple relationships have become increasingly fragile. This is even more so in the West. In a study that was carried out in the United Kingdom, almost one in five people who were in a couple relationship could be described as distressed at a point in time (Sserwanja & Marjoribanks, 2016). In Malta, which is a country forming part of the traditional group of countries in Europe, 20% of married couples were estimated to be distressed in 2005 (Abela, Frosh, & Dowling, 2005) and this went up to 24.6% in 2015 (Abela, 2016). According to the Office for National Statistics (2018), in the United Kingdom, 42% of marriages end in divorce. In the United States, between 40% and 50% of married couples also divorce (American Psychological Association (APA), 2018).

Rates of distress and even divorce are higher for inter-cultural couples than for couples of the same culture (Bratter & Eschbach, 2006; Kalmijn, de Graaf, & Jansen, 2005). Lesbians too seem to be at higher risk for marriage breakdown than gay men in spite of their tendency to marry more frequently than the latter. In the Netherlands, which legalized same-sex marriage in 2001, 82.1% of opposite-sex marriages which took place in 2001 were still intact in 2016 compared to 69.6% of marriages between women and 84.5% between men (The Economist 2017a). This finding merits further exploration in view of findings from the large-scale research project carried out in the United Kingdom by Gabb et al. (2013) who sought to investigate quality and stability in long-term adult couple relationships. They reported that homosexual participants were more positive and happy in relation to the quality of their relationship and relationship maintenance in comparison with heterosexual participants. The authors do not distinguish between gay and lesbian couples.

There are a number of process variables that contribute towards relationship breakdown, which have already been mentioned above, including emotional dysregulation and negative communication styles. However, an important structural variable that also merits discussion is income inadequacy. Countless studies have reported that poverty triggers depression and distress in relationships between couples (Kalmijn, Loeve, & Manting, 2007) and in parents (Abela & Renoux, 2014). As Jamieson (1999) puts it in her critique of Gidden's notion of pure relationships "much of personal life remains structured by inequalities" (p. 477).

Together with relationship quality, income adequacy was the other predictor for life satisfaction in the NCFR study in Malta. Problems at work, mental health and other health problems as well as facing big problems in general were the other predictors of unhappiness in this study. I will illustrate this through a personal anecdote.

Not long ago, a taxi driver started a conversation with me on my way to the airport. I asked for a receipt. We started talking about the cost of living and he told me that he was on the minimum wage. "Il-paga pjaga" he uttered. (The two Maltese words rhyme and there is an alliteration; it means that the salary is a grievance) He told me that he earned Eur800 a month. That is 26 euros a day I calculated. What could I buy for our daily living with 26 euros? How much would I need to pay the other bills? Would the in-work benefits and the Children's Allowance suffice to bridge the gap? I would need a carton of milk, cereal, some eggs, a packet of pasta, a few groceries to prepare the school lunch for the kids and some vegetables and meat for a meal in the evening.

"Do you have children?" I asked.

"Yes, three", he replied and then he added "I am separated."

There was disappointment in his voice. After a few moments of silence he added "She went with someone else. He knew how to caress her better than I did."

Again I could feel the sadness and the inadequacy.

"Is she still with him?" I asked

"No" he replied.

When I arrived at my destination I kept thinking about the story which this man narrated to me, and of the Maltese proverb which says that without money you can neither hug nor kiss.

Economic factors are an important predictor of conflict amongst married and cohabiting couples and financial hardship is associated with more conflict (Hardie & Lucas, 2010; Kalmijn et al., 2007).

In the United States, those in the working class are less likely to marry and when they do, their relationship is more likely to break down (Carbone & Cahn, 2014). In the United Kingdom, 65% of top professionals got married in 2017 according to the Labour Force Survey (as cited in the Economist, 2017b). For those with routine jobs, this went down to 44% and it was 40% for the unemployed.

2.7 The Meaning of Love and Intimacy

Marrying by choice today seems to put more emphasis on the romantic ideal. Many increasingly appear to be marrying later in life, possibly cohabiting prior to marriage, or not marrying at all (Abela & Walker, 2014b; McGoldrick, 2011).

Although such developments may contribute towards a more fulfilling couple relationship for both partners, this also enhances the concept of choice, hence underscoring the fact that long-lasting couple and marital relationships are no longer taken for granted. Whilst all the participants in the NCFR 2016 study agreed that trust and fidelity were fundamental for the couple relationship, they attributed the fragility of couple relationships to media influences, including social media, a weakened sense of commitment, weakening of social norms around fidelity and exclusivity, the long hours spent in the company of others at work, which even led to more socializing with them outside of work. Esther Perel (2017), in her recent book *The State of Affairs,* argued that fidelity may be the last taboo that couples want to break and explored the tension between the need that human beings have for security and for freedom.

Many scholars have written about the motives, contextual forces and cultural ideas that propel individuals into affairs (Blow & Hartnett, 2005). Dissatisfaction with the relationship is the predominant predictor of infidelity. Human beings yearn for a meaningful connection with their partner and when this is lacking, and there is emotional loneliness, the meaning of an affair may be mostly about yearning for this emotional connection and an assurance that one is still loveable. The difficulty in connecting is often left unexpressed and it is only after the infidelity that some couples seek help to talk about intimacy and try to get closer to each other. Perel (2017) points out that even loving couples may struggle with desire and may seek to express it outside the relationship. She is inspired by Mitchell (2002), who argues that romance thrives on novelty, mystery and danger and that reconciling the erotic and the domestic is difficult and fragile. According to Mitchell, anxiety, repression and constraint by one of the partners further increases the urge from the other to find freedom elsewhere. However, Sue Johnson (as cited in Bobrow, 2017) argues that where there is a secure attachment between a couple, active deception is warded off. I too believe that those who enjoy a secure attachment with their loved one have the capacity to be reflective, are empathic and would keep the other partner in mind as they go about their daily lives.

Similarly, Gottman (as cited in Bobrow, 2017) thinks that it is not true that those in a happy couple relationship seek affairs. In this respect, fidelity is still important for good solid relationships and although a few may both be satisfied and happy with an open relationship, many are distraught as the following vignette portrays:

This is a story of a humble man who came to me because he discovered that his wife was having a romantic relationship with another woman. He would weep as he would tell me the story and then take out his cotton handkerchief and wipe his eyes. He would put so much pressure that I almost used to fear that his eyelids would be torn.

"What shall I do?" he would ask me desperately. I would try as best as I could to help him make sense of what had been going on in his relationship with his wife.

In the meantime, his wife would leave and spend the weekend away from home presumably with her partner. He would stay behind with their son.

The man was waiting for his wife to come back to him. He was ready to continue living with his wife even if she continued with her relationship with her partner. I love her he would tell me. I felt like telling him No! His broken heart was taxing me.

As the months rolled by, he increasingly tried to understand his wife and slowly attempted to hold her hand once again.

Months later, he told me how they lay on the bed one summer afternoon and listened to an old Italian song which they loved in their youth when they were still courting. They held hands … Then they both had a shower and went out for a drink by the seaside.

2.8 Conclusion

In different parts of the world, couple relationships and marriage in particular are being gradually stripped of the many roles that were traditionally expected of men and women. What has really come to matter is the personal relationship and the quality of such a relationship.

Where is the couple relationship going? Are we aware that our close relationships are crucial for our well-being? Is our increasing intolerance of couple relationships that are not of good quality matching up to our investment in the relationship? And how is the State helping those who need support as they struggle to create a better version of their existence?

In the next sections of this book, we hope to provide some of the answers to these questions by understanding in more detail how couple relationships are evolving in the different cultural contexts, what are the global trends in couple relationships and some innovative ways of supporting couples and their families.

References

Abela, A. (2016). Family life. In M. Briguglio & M. Brown (Eds.), *Sociology of the Maltese islands*. Malta: Millers Publications.

Abela, A., Frosh, S., & Dowling, E. (2005). Uncovering beliefs embedded in the culture and its implications for practice: The case of Maltese married couples. *Journal of Family Therapy, 27*(1), 3–23.

Abela, A., & Renoux, M. C. (2014). Families living on the margin in affluent societies. In A. Abela & J. Walker (Eds.), *Contemporary issues in family studies: Global perspectives on partnerships, parenting and support in a changing world* (pp. 302–316). West Sussex: Wiley Blackwell.

Abela, A., & Walker, J. (2014a). Changing couple and family relationships. In A. Abela & J. Walker (Eds.), *Contemporary issues in family studies: Global perspectives on partnerships, parenting and support in a changing world* (pp. 1–4). West Sussex: Wiley Blackwell.

Abela, A., & Walker, J. (2014b). Global changes in marriage, parenting and family life: An overview. In A. Abela & J. Walker (Eds.), *Contemporary issues in family studies: Global perspectives on partnerships, parenting and support in a changing world* (pp. 5–15). West Sussex: Wiley Blackwell.

Al'Absi, M. (2007). *Stress and addiction: biological and psychological mechanisms*. Cambridge, MA: Academic Press.

Altintas, E., & Sullivan, O. (2016). 50 years of change updated: Cross-national gender convergence in housework. *Demographic Research, 35*(16), 455.

Amato, P. R. (2007). Transformative processes in marriage: Some thoughts from a sociologist. *Journal of Marriage and Family, 69*(2), 305.

Amato, P. R., & Hohmann-Marriott, B. (2007). A comparison of high-and low-distress marriages that end in divorce. *Journal of Marriage and Family, 69*(3), 621–638.

Amato, P. R., & James, S. L. (2018). Changes in spousal relationships over the marital life course. In D. F. Alwin, D. H. Felmlee, & D. A. Kreeger (Eds.), *Social networks and the life course* (pp. 139–158). New York, NY: Springer.

American Psychological Association. (2018). *Marriage and divorce*. Retrieved from https://www.apa.org/topics/divorce/

Anser, L. (2014). Divorce in the Arab Gulf countries. In A. Abela & J. Walker (Eds.), *Contemporary issues in family studies: Global perspectives on partnerships, parenting and support in a changing world* (pp. 59–73). West Sussex: Wiley Blackwell.

Avison, M., & Furnham, A. (2015). Personality and voluntary childlessness. *Journal of Population Research, 32*(1), 45–67.

Bartholomew, K. (1997). Adult attachment processes: Individual and couple perspectives. *British Journal of Medical Psychology, 70*(3), 249–263.

Beall, A. E., & Sternberg, R. J. (1995). The social construction of love. *Journal of Social and Personal Relationships, 12*(3), 417–438.

Beaujot, R. (2012). Changes in patterns and trends. *Aging, 5*, 24.

Beaumont-Thomas, B. (2017, December 5). Ed Sheeran named most-streamed artist on spotify in 2017. *The Guardian*. Retrieved from https://www.theguardian.com/music/2017/dec/05/ed-sheeran-named-most-streamed-artist-on-spotify-in-2017

Benjamin, K., Marshall, T., & Ferenczi, N. (2014). Romantic ideals, mate preferences and anticipation of future difficulties in marital life: a comparative study of young adults in India and America. *Frontiers in Psychology, 5*, 1355. https://doi.org/10.3389/fpsyg.2014.01355

Blow, A. J., & Hartnett, K. (2005). Infidelity in committed relationships I: A methodological review. *Journal of Marital and Family Therapy, 31*(2), 183–216.

Bobrow, E. (2017, December/January). What's wrong with infidelity? *The Economist*. Retrieved from https://www.1843magazine.com/features/whats-wrong-with-infidelity

Bowlby, J. (1973). *Attachment and loss: Volume II: Separation, anxiety and anger*. London: The Hogarth Press and the Institute of Psycho-Analysis.

Bratter, J. L., & Eschbach, K. (2006). 'What about the couple?' Interracial marriage and psychological distress. *Social Science Research, 35*(4), 1025–1047.

Britt-Lutter, S., & Nazarinia, R. R. (2014). Relationship quality among young couples from an economic and gender perspective. *Journal of Family and Economic Issues, 35*, 241–250. https://doi.org/10.1007/s10834-013-9368-x

Cain Millar, C. (2018, July 5). Americans are having fewer babies. They told us why. *The New York Times*. Retrieved from https://www.nytimes.com/2018/07/05/upshot/americans-are-having-fewer-babies-they-told-us-why.html

Carbone, J., & Cahn, N. (2014). *Marriage markets: How inequality is remaking the American family*. New York, NY: Oxford University Press.

Carlson, D. L., Miller, A. J., & Sassler, S. (2018). Stalled for whom? Change in the division of particular housework tasks and their consequences for middle-to low-income couples. *Socius, 4*, 1–7. https://doi.org/10.1177/2378023118765867

Carroll, A., & Mendos, L. R. (2017). State-sponsored homophobia. In *A world survey of laws, criminalisation, protection and recognition of same-sex love* (12th ed.). Geneva: International Lesbian, Gay, Bisexual, Trans and Intersex Association (ILGA).

Coffelt, T. A., & Hess, J. A. (2014). Sexual disclosures: Connections to relational satisfaction and closeness. *Journal of Sex & Marital Therapy, 40*(6), 577–591.

de Jong-Gierveld, J., Broese van Groenou, M., Hoogendoorn, A. W., & Smit, J. H. (2009). Quality of marriages in later life and emotional and social loneliness. *Journals of Gerontology Series B: Psychological Sciences and Social Sciences, 64*(4), 497–506.

De Paulo, B. (2018, March 9). There's never been a better time to be single. *CNN*. Retrieved from https://edition.cnn.com/2018/01/05/health/single-people-partner/index.html

Department for Work and Pensions. (2015). *Social justice outcomes framework: Family stability indicator—Update*. Retrieved from https://assets.publishing.service.gov.uk/government/uploads/system/uploads/attachment_data/file/509320/social-justice-family-stability-indicator-2013-2014.pdf

Dotti Sani, G. M., & Treas, J. (2016). Educational gradients in parents' child-care time across countries, 1965–2012. *Journal of Marriage and Family, 78*(4), 1083–1096.

ESS Round 8: European Social Survey Round 8 Data (2016). *Data file edition 2.1. NSD—Norwegian Centre for Research Data, Norway—Data Archive and distributor of ESS data for ESS ERIC.* https://doi.org/10.21338/NSD-ESS8-2016.

Falke, S. I., & Larson, J. H. (2007). Premarital predictors of remarital quality: Implications for clinicians. *Contemporary Family Therapy, 29*(1–2), 9–23.

Fischer, R. C., Stanford, J. B., Jameson, P., & DeWitt, M. J. (1999). Exploring the concepts of intended, planned, and wanted pregnancy. *Journal of Family Practice, 48*(2), 117–118.

Fonagy, P., Leigh, T., Steele, M., Steele, H., Kennedy, R., Mattoon, G., … Gerber, A. (1996). The relation of attachment status, psychiatric classification, and response to psychotherapy. *Journal of Consulting and Clinical Psychology, 64*(1), 22.

Fry, R. (2017, October 11). *The share of Americans living without a partner has increased, especially among young adults*. Pew Research Center. Retrieved from https://www.pewresearch.org/fact-tank/2017/10/11/the-share-of-americans-living-without-a-partner-has-increased-especially-among-young-adults/

Gabb, J., Klett-Davies, M., Fink, J., & Thomae, M. (2013). Enduring love? Couple relationships in the 21st century. In *Survey findings: An interim report*. Berkshire: Open University.

Gagnon, M. D., Hersen, M., Kabacoff, R. I., & Van Hasselt, V. B. (1999). Interpersonal and psychological correlates of marital dissatisfaction in late life: A review. *Clinical Psychology Review, 19*(3), 359–378. https://doi.org/10.1016/S0272-7358(97)00048-2

Goldner, V., Penn, P., Sheinberg, M., & Walker, G. (1990). Love and violence: Gender paradoxes in volatile attachments. *Family Process, 29*(4), 343–364.

Gottman, J. M. (1993). The roles of conflict engagement, escalation, and avoidance in marital interaction: A longitudinal view of five types of couples. *Journal of Consulting and Clinical Psychology, 61*(1), 6.

Hardie, J. H., & Lucas, A. (2010). Economic factors and relationship quality among young couples: Comparing cohabitation and marriage. *Journal of Marriage and Family, 72*(5), 1141–1154.

Harold, G. T., Rice, F., Hay, D. F., Boivin, J., Van Den Bree, M., & Thapar, A. (2011). Familial transmission of depression and antisocial behavior symptoms: Disentangling the contribution of inherited and environmental factors and testing the mediating role of parenting. *Psychological Medicine, 41*(6), 1175–1185.

Hazan, C., & Shaver, P. (1987). Romantic love conceptualized as an attachment process. *Journal of Personality and Social Psychology, 52*(3), 511. https://doi.org/10.1037/0022-3514.52.3.511

Jamieson, L. (1999). Intimacy transformed? A critical look at the 'pure relationship'. *Sociology, 33*(3), 477–494.

John, N., Seme, A., Roro, M. A., & Tsui, A. O. (2017). Understanding the meaning of marital relationship quality among couples in peri-urban Ethiopia. *Cultural Health Sex, 19*(2), 267–278. https://doi.org/10.1080/1361058.2016.1215526

Jones, J. M. (2017, June 22). *In U.S., 10.2% of LGBT adults now married to same-sex spouse.* Retrieved from https://news.gallup.com/poll/212702/lgbt-adults-married-sex-spouse.aspx

Kahr, B. (2012). Foreword. In A. Balfour, M. Morgan, & C. Vincent (Eds.), *How couple relationships shape our world: Clinical practice, research, and policy perspectives* (pp. xvii–xxxi). London: Karnac Books.

Kalmijn, M., de Graaf, P. M., & Jansen, J. P. G. (2005). Intermarriage and the risk of divorce in the Netherlands: The effects of differences in religion and in nationality, 1974-94. *Population Studies, 59*, 71–85.

Kalmijn, M., Loeve, A., & Manting, D. (2007). Income dynamics in couples and the dissolution of marriage and cohabitation. *Demography, 44*(1), 159–179.

Karandashev, V. (2017). *Romantic love in cultural contexts.* Basel: Springer.

Kiecolt-Glaser, J. K., & Newton, T. L. (2001). Marriage and health: His and hers. *Psychological Bulletin, 127*(4), 472.

Knoke, J., Burau, J., & Röhrle, B. (2010). Attachment styles, loneliness, quality, and stability of marital relationships. *Journal of Divorce & Remarriage, 51*, 310–325. https://doi.org/10.1080/10502551003652017

Knutson, K. M. (2014). *The effects of collaborative and non-aggressive communication on the relationship between the division of labor(s) and marital quality for dual-earner couples* (Unpublished doctoral dissertation). University of Kansas.

Langdridge, D., Sheeran, P., & Connolly, K. (2005). Understanding the reasons for parenthood. *Journal of Reproductive and Infant Psychology, 23*(2), 121–133.

Lavner, J. A., & Bradbury, T. N. (2010). Patterns of change in marital satisfaction over the newlywed years. *Journal of Marriage and Family, 72*(5), 1171–1187.

Lavner, J. A., Bradbury, T. N., & Karney, B. R. (2012). Incremental change or initial differences? Testing two models of marital deterioration. *Journal of Family Psychology, 26*(4), 606.

Lavner, J. A., Karney, B. R., & Bradbury, T. N. (2016). Does couples' communication predict marital satisfaction, or does marital satisfaction predict communication? *Journal of Marriage and Family, 78*(3), 680–694.

Leach, L. S., Butterworth, P., Olesen, S. C., & Mackinnon, A. (2013). Relationship quality and levels of depression and anxiety in a large population-based survey. *Social Psychiatry and Psychiatric Epidemiology, 48*(3), 417–425.

Leonard, K. E., & Eiden, D. R. (2007). Marital and family processes in the context of alcohol use and alcohol disorders. *Annual Review of Clinical Psychology, 3*, 285–310. https://doi.org/10.1146/annurev.clinpsy.3.022806.091424

Main, M., Kaplan, N., & Cassidy, J. (1985). Security in infancy, childhood, and adulthood: A move to the level of representation. *Monographs of the society for research in child development.*

Matias, M., & Fontaine, A. M. (2012). Can we have it all? The work–family coping profiles of dual-earners. *Family Science, 3*(3–4), 255–265.

McGoldrick, M. (2011). Becoming a couple. In M. McGoldrick, B. Carter, & N. Garcia-Preto (Eds.), *The expanded family life cycle: Individual, family, and social perspectives* (4th ed., pp. 193–210). Boston, MA: Pearson Education.

Meltzer, H., Gatward, R., Goodman, R., & Ford, T. (2000). *The mental health of children and adolescents in Great Britain.* London: HM Stationery Office.

Mikulincer, M. (2006). Attachment, caregiving, and sex within romantic relationships: A behavioral systems perspective. In M. Mikulincer & G. S. Goodman (Eds.), *Dynamics of romantic love: Attachment, caregiving, and sex* (pp. 23–44). New York, NY: The Guilford Press.

Mikulincer, M., Shaver, P. R., & Slav, K. (2006). Attachment, mental representations of others, and gratitude and forgiveness in romantic relationships. In M. Mikulincer & G. S. Goodman (Eds.), *Dynamics of romantic love: Attachment, caregiving, and sex* (pp. 190–215). New York: The Guilford Press.

Millman, R. D. (2012). *Communication as a moderator of the interplay between newlyweds' sexual and relationship satisfaction* (Unpublished master's dissertation). Simon Fraser University, British Columbia.

Minnotte, K. L., Pedersen, D., & Mannon, S. E. (2010). The emotional terrain of parenting and marriage: Emotion work and marital satisfaction. *The Social Science Journal, 47*(4), 747–761.

Mitchell, S. A. (2002). *Can love last?: The fate of romance over time*. New York, NY: W.W. Norton & Company.

Mitchell, B. A. (2006). Changing courses: The pendulum of family transitions in comparative perspective. *Journal of Comparative Family Studies, 37*(3), 325–343.

Musick, K., & Bumpass, L. (2012). Re-examining the case for marriage: Union formation and changes in well-being. *Journal of Marriage and Family, 74*(1), 1–18.

Nimtz, M. A. (2011). *Satisfaction and contributing factors in satisfying long-term marriage: A phenomenological study* (Unpublished doctoral dissertation). Liberty University, Virginia.

Office for National Statistics. (2018). *Divorces in England and Wales: 2017. (Statistical bulletin)*. Retrieved from https://www.ons.gov.uk/peoplepopulationandcommunity/birthsdeathsandmarriages/divorce/bulletins/divorcesinenglandandwales/2017/pdf

Perel, E. (2017). *The state of affairs: Rethinking infidelity-A book for anyone who has ever loved*. New York, NY: Harper Collins Publishers.

Piscopo, M. (2014). *No fairy-tale… but it works: A quantitative study of the process of forming and maintaining a happy marital relationship in Malta* (Unpublished master's dissertation). University of Malta.

President's Foundation for the Wellbeing of Society. (2016). *Sustaining relationships: Couples and singles in a changing society*. Retrieved from The President's Foundation for the Wellbeing of Society website http://pfws.org.mt/wp-content/themes/pfws/loadfile/Sustaining_Relationships_Final[1].pdf

Proulx, C. M., Helms, H. M., & Buehler, C. (2007). Marital quality and personal well-being: A meta-analysis. *Journal of Marriage and Family, 69*(3), 576–593.

Pryor, J. (2014). Marriage and divorce in the Western world. In A. Abela & J. Walker (Eds.), *Contemporary issues in family studies: Global perspectives on partnerships, parenting and support in a changing world* (pp. 46–58). New York: Wiley.

Raymo, J. M., Park, H., Xie, Y., & Yeung, W. J. J. (2015). Marriage and family in East Asia: Continuity and change. *Annual Review of Sociology, 41*, 471–492.

Rehman, U. S., Janssen, E., Newhouse, S., Heiman, J., Holtzworth-Munroe, A., Fallis, E., & Rafaeli, E. (2011). Marital satisfaction and communication behaviors during sexual and non-sexual conflict discussions in newlywed couples: A pilot study. *Journal of Sex & Marital Therapy, 37*(2), 94–103.

Relate. (2016). *Happy families? Family relationships in the UK today*. Retrieved from https://www.relate.org.uk/sites/default/files/the_way_we_are_now_-_happy_families.pdf

Riggs, D. W., & Bartholomaeus, C. (2016). The desire for a child among a sample of heterosexual Australian couples. *Journal of Reproductive and Infant Psychology, 34*(5), 442–450.

Riskind, R. G., & Patterson, C. J. (2010). Parenting intentions and desires among childless lesbian, gay, and heterosexual individuals. *Journal of Family Psychology, 24*(1), 78.

Rubel, A. N., & Bogaert, A. F. (2015). Consensual nonmonogamy: Psychological well-being and relationship quality correlates. *The Journal of Sex Research, 52*(9), 961–982.

Schmitt, D. P., Alcalay, L., Allensworth, M., Allik, J., Ault, L., Austers, I., … Zupan ÈiÈ, A. (2004). Patterns and universals of adult romantic attachment across 62 cultural regions: Are models of self and of other pancultural constructs? *Journal of Cross-Cultural Psychology, 35*(4), 367–402. https://doi.org/10.1177/0022022104266105

Schoebi, D., Karney, B. R., & Bradbury, T. N. (2012). Stability and change in the first 10 years of marriage: Does commitment confer benefits beyond the effects of satisfaction? *Journal of Personality and Social Psychology, 102*(4), 729.

Skinner, K. B., Bahr, S. J., Crane, D. R., & Call, V. R. (2002). Cohabitation, marriage, and remarriage: A comparison of relationship quality over time. *Journal of Family Issues, 23*(1), 74–90.

Sserwanja, I. & Marjoribanks, D. (2016). *Relationship distress monitor: Estimating levels of adult couple relationship distress across the UK*. (Relate Research Report). Retrieved from https://www.relate.org.uk/sites/default/files/relationship_distress_monitor_0.pdf

Tani, F., Pascuzzi, D., & Raffagnino, R. (2015). Emotion regulation and quality of close relationship: The effects of emotion dysregulation processes on couple intimacy. *BPA-Applied Psychology Bulletin (Bollettino di Psicologia Applicata), 63*(272).

Tanturri, M. L. (2014). Why fewer babies? Understanding and responding to low fertility in Europe. In A. Abela & J. Walker (Eds.), *Contemporary issues in family studies: Global perspectives on partnerships, parenting and support in a changing world* (pp. 136–150). West Sussex: Wiley Blackwell.

Tasfiliz, D., Selcuk, E., Ginyaylin, G., Slatcher, R. B., Corriero, E., & Ong, A. D. (2018). Patterns of perceived partner responsiveness and wellbeing in Japan and the United States. *Journal of Family Psychology, 32*(3), 355–365. https://doi.org/10.1037/fam0000378

The Economist. (2017a, November 23). *Adam and Steve: Getting used to gay unions.* Retrieved from https://www.economist.com/special-report/2017/11/23/getting-used-to-gay-unions

The Economist. (2017b, November 23). *Marriage in the West.* Retrieved from https://www.economist.com/special-report/2017/11/23/marriage-in-the-west

Twenge, J. M., Sherman, R. A., & Wells, B. E. (2017). Declines in sexual frequency among American adults, 1989–2014. *Archives of Sexual Behavior, 46*(8), 2389–2401.

Vespa, J. (2017). *The changing economics and demographics of young adulthood: 1975–2016* (Report No. P20-579). Retrieved from https://www.census.gov/content/dam/Census/library/publications/2017/demo/p20-579.pdf

World Bank. (2017). *Fertility rate, total (births per woman).* Retrieved from https://data.worldbank.org/indicator/sp.dyn.tfrt.in

Part II
How Couple Relationships Are Changing in Different Parts of the World

Chapter 3
The Existential and Relational Meaning of Intimacy and Love for Couples in Scandinavia: Through a Lens of Scandinavian Fiction and Drama

Anne Kyoung Sook Øfsti

3.1 Introduction

My intention in this chapter is to explore couples and coupledom with Scandinavia as a background and frame.

It might be sound to claim that when it comes to adult intimate life, the longing for belonging and attachment is universal and central to desire. However, that which decides the content of our dreams of love is also socioculturally inspired and informed by the different discourses available for people to take up. As an example, 50 years ago in Scandinavia, marriage between homosexuals was impossible, and "homophilia" was a diagnosis and a taboo. Now, same-sex marriage is allowed and in Norway, it is also possible for couples to be married in the Church.

3.1.1 Scandinavia as Context

Geographically, "Scandinavia" refers to Denmark, Norway, and Sweden. These countries are similar linguistically, and there are two main coexistent language groups, Scandinavian and Sami. The geography of Scandinavia is extremely varied. In Norway, there are the fjords and the Peak Mountains. In Denmark, the landscape is open, flat, with long sand dunes along the coast, and in Sweden, there are lakes and moraines. The climate is cold, wet, and rainy in the North and West, and in the mountains, one finds an alpine tundra climate. Despite this ruggedness, in the south of Scandinavia, it can quite be mild, thanks to the Gulf Stream (https://en.wikipedia.org/wiki/Scandinavia).

A. K. S. Øfsti (✉)
Oslo, Norway
e-mail: anne.ofsti@vid.no

© Springer Nature Switzerland AG 2020
A. Abela et al. (eds.), *Couple Relationships in a Global Context*,
European Family Therapy Association Series,
https://doi.org/10.1007/978-3-030-37712-0_3

Do different cultural landscapes, climates, and nature form the dreams, the expectations, the relationships, and attitudes of different populations? Is love a different experience in a Norwegian fjord far from next-door neighbors and a long way to hospitals, banks, schools, and workplaces than in a city?

I think the answer is yes. Once, many years ago, I lived and worked in the North of Norway, a small place with borders to Russia and Finland. The population consists of Norwegians, Sami, Russian, and Finnish people. When I later became a leader of Family Therapy Guidance Center in a small city close to Oslo, the capital of Norway, I found myself wondering about differences in attitudes, values, and practices concerning coupledom.

As a simple observation, in the North, there was more quarreling around gender issues, housework, and child-raising, whereas in the South, it was more common for existential questions to arise around the themes of quality of life and living a successful life as a couple: do we want to be in this relationship, if we don't understand each other?

However, in this chapter, I am not aiming to be an anthropologist or ethnographer, claiming universal truths about or pointing out traits of the Scandinavian population. As a family therapist, novelist, and researcher, I am preoccupied with narrative and how narratives form people's lives and are in turn formed by them. I have selected readings of famous Scandinavian novels and film; fictional sources, as fiction and narratives do not present the information of manuals or textbooks on how to live love, but rather it is possible to think, believe, act, and feel when the various expectations of love become difficult. Fiction is a fruitful resource through which to gain insight into the lives of ordinary people.

3.1.2 A Scandinavian Discourse About Scandinavians?

The famous Danish author Hans Christian Anderson wrote the poem, "I am a Scandinavian" in 1839 after a visit to Sweden. Andersen became a supporter of early political *Scandinavism*. He declared after his visit that he understood how related the Swedes, Danes and Norwegians were: "I sensed the beauty of the Nordic spirit, the way the three sister nations have gradually grown together. We are one people, we are called Scandinavians!" (Andersen, 1846/2000).

What kinds of qualities and peculiarities represent the community Andersen held up as an inspiring entity? It is said that the author was walking in the Swedish woods when he became enlightened by the notion of the *Scandinavian*. Clearly, nature played a role, and the familiarity of language. But was there more? A mentality? A profound understanding of brave, solitary people who can survive cold climates, harsh storms, and modest harvests?

When asking colleagues and friends informally about myths and prejudices concerning Scandinavians and Scandinavia, they all respond the same way: Scandinavians are "blonde," and in keeping with the familiar metaphor, also naive.

Scandinavians are also reserved and "cold," distant (quite like the Nordic landscape) so they need time before they warm up and become inclusive and warmhearted.

I have read articles about Scandinavia claiming that the weather is terrible, and it is very expensive. Scandinavians are also spoken of in terms such as sexually liberated, feminist, hardworking, and attached to nature and traditions. The soul of the people is one of frugality, and well known for its humanism, charity, and adventurous spirit, as witnessed by such famous representatives as Fridtjof Nansen, Alfred Nobel, Henrik Ibsen, and Tor Heyerdahl.

3.1.3 Sociopolitical Structures

A contemporary sociological gaze on Scandinavia focuses on political processes and progressive movements such as state feminism, secularization, and globalization. These political discourses are important influences in understanding changes in romantic love and coupledom in Scandinavia. For instance, in Norway, the Church is no longer the official religion as in 2012 laws were passed dividing the State and the Church. The ideal of romantic love has been traditionally rooted in Protestantism and a common understanding of marriage as instituted by God.

In a Nordic context, structural egalitarianism has deep historical roots from after the Second World War to the present. The Nordic countries are characterized by a strong welfare state and highly structured working life. In 1987, a politician and researcher described the concept of State feminism (Hernes, 1987). State feminism underlies political and normative assumptions about gender equality and social justice, producing woman-friendly policies that focus on parental leave, childcare, and minimum age restrictions for marriages involving foreigners from cultures in which child marriage is common. State feminism is explored in relation to women's political participation and representation and women's ability to influence policies of gender equality. Also, feminist processes are not only structurally organized to support equal rights to work and economic equality, but also mental models that promotes equal access for women to forms of intimacy and emotional dynamics.

3.2 Courtly Love in Conflict with a Passionate–Romantic Discourse

The Danish–Norwegian author, Sigrid Undset received the Nobel Prize for the trilogy *Kristin Lavransdatter* in 1928. The novel follows Kristin Lavransdatter, a woman living in Scandinavia in the Middle Ages, from her birth to her death. It is a love story and it is a story about obligation, pride, honor, and shame.

When I was 11 years old, I read the book for the first time. The reading experience was marvelous, and I could not stop; it was a page-turner—and it demonstrated for me the meaning of love in life. This was strange in many ways as the trilogy portrayed a family life in Norway in the middle ages with descriptions of customs, beliefs, the environment, and nature, which were quite unlike the existences of adults in a nuclear family in the 1970s.

Sigrid Undset wrote primarily historical novels, and although she portrayed her characters in a medieval context, she wrote about existential, moral, religious, and psychological phenomena that are equally valid and recognizable throughout all eras. Once Sigrid Undset commented that *times change, so do customs and beliefs, but the hearts of men do not change*. My reading of that quotation is that people will always long for closeness and love.

In *Kristin Lavransdatter*, Christianity provides the backdrop and the arrangement of marriage was in the form of alliances between significant men and their families to increase status and property. For the couple, the marriage was founded on expectations for and combinations of economic convenience and courtly love. By definition, courtly love is "a highly-conventionalized code of conduct for lovers" (http://americanheritage.yourdictionary.com/courtly-love).

The hero in the novel is Kristin's father, Lavrans Bjorgulfson, the master of Jorundgaard. He belongs to a highly regarded lineage in Norway known as the Sons of Lagmand. His greatest joy is his daughter Kristin. About his marriage to his wife Ragnfrid, Undset writes that "Lavrans was married at a young age; he was only 28…but after his marriage he lived quietly on his own estate…rather moody and melancholy and did not thrive among the people in the south" (Undset, 2014).

3.2.1 Historical Courtly Love and a more Contemporary Discourse of Love as Virtue

In my study, *Some call it love* (Øfsti, 2008), I identified the discourse *love as virtue*, which talks about love as a way to mature together. This discourse is inspired by Evans (2003) who engaged with philosophers from the Enlightenment as well as classic novelists such as Jane Austen in describing the path of our culture away from unstable sensitivity toward trustworthy sense and rationality. The love ideal of Austen is recognizable as a discourse framed in terms of love as a virtue one must refine; love means to mature together in a sense of shelter, and as a stance in opposition to erotic passion and the dangers of falling in love (Øfsti, 2008). The notion of virtue was and is relevant for three important reasons. First, it is a spiritual value and thereby permits a connection between ideological perspectives and life crises. Second, virtue is a well-known and inherited concept in traditional marriage counseling as the first therapists were often priests. Third, virtue also reflects the use of a practice or a method; being virtuous is doing virtuous acts. Virtuous love, then, fits well as a discourse when narrative friction is experienced, because it reconciles the discursive needs of the romantic pull, as for instance in monogamy, and the pain and doubt that can be encountered and that can challenge faith in, and motivation for, continuing love. A discourse constructing love as a virtue, then, arises in a context in which the act of love demands an active effort and sacrifice by the partner/s.

As the reader will see, love as a virtue differs from courtly love, as courtly love emphasizes emotions and a contract based on romantic love more than the arrangement of alliances and a conduct of behavior in the more aristocratic sense. It is a more literary script from the Middle Ages portraying knights and kings and lawful men as courtly.

Lavransdatter takes his responsibility seriously in getting his daughter properly married, and she is expected to marry Simen Darre, heir to the neighboring estate:

And after Kristin had grown accustomed to his round face and his way of speaking, she was entirely satisfied with her betrothed and pleased that her father had arranged the marriage for her. Fru Aashild was invited to the banquet. Ever since the people of Jørundgaard had taken up with her, the gentry of the nearest villages had once again begun to remember her high birth, and they paid less attention to her strange reputation; so now Fru Aashild was often in the company of others. After she had seen Simon, she said, "He's a good match, Kristin. This Simon will do well in the world-you'll be spared many types of sorrow, and he'll be a kind man to live with. But he seems to me rather too fat and cheerful. If things were the same in Norway today as they were in the past and as they are in other countries, where people are no sterner toward sinners than God is Himself, then I would suggest you find yourself a friend who is thin and melancholy-someone you could sit and talk to. Then I would say that you could fare no better than with Simon."

3.2.2 *The Intrigue: Courtly Love in Conflict with Passionate Being-in-Love*

Despite her Christian upbringing and her love for her father, Kristin is drawn away from her father's beliefs and values. She falls in love with the handsome, playful, and irresponsible knight, Erlend Nikolausson. Through an unfortunate sequence of events, the sweet and innocent child is emboldened and takes on a semi-reckless approach to her relationship with Erlend. While away from home at a nunnery and while she is betrothed to Simon Darre, Kristin and Erlend become lovers and Kristin forces her will to marry Erlend despite her father's wishes. Without ruining the end of the story for those who have not yet read it, their relationship becomes dangerous and devolves into catastrophe. I read this novel primarily as a sad love story. The loving couple get into violent conflict and become destructive toward one another. This becomes a tale of a love story destroyed. However, in this text, Undset ultimately paints a picture of the ideal of a love inspired by humility, duty, and virtue blessed by God.

As a couple therapist, I have seen this struggle played out as a conflict between the ideals of virtuous love (self-sacrifice, obligation to promises, and shared care of children) and a more romantic discourse, emphasizing the notion of not being able to withstand falling in love, love at first sight, and the dream of the "only one," or the one true love.

3.2.3 The Romantic Dream—Encountering Modern Times, Liberation, and Progress Toward the "Pure Relationship"

The Swedish moviemaker and author Ingmar Bergman has been one of the most influential Nordic artists, narrating and displaying the Scandinavian temperament, attitudes, and inner struggles on the big screen. He captures, presents, and represents family life, dysfunctional relationships, and individual struggles in the cultural environment and atmosphere of living in Scandinavia.

In 1974, the drama *Scenes from a Marriage* was broadcast on television in Scandinavia. The film is a portrait of a failing marriage consisting of 5 h of searching dialogue between the two protagonists, Johan and Marianne. The drama takes place over a 10-year period, each episode of the TV series providing a snapshot of their relationship during that time. When we first see Marianne and Johan they have been married for 10 years. The married couple seem happy, at first. Their union looks both extraordinary and comfortable. We see Marianne and Johan go about their domestic routines, affectionate and tender with one another. In the first episode, Marianne and Johan have another couple round for dinner. The guests descend into bitter arguments and a hurtful slanging match. But Marianne and Johan, although shocked by the terrible state of their friends' marriage, can calmly say, "That will never happen to us." It is a middle-class dream: Johan is a professor, and Marianne is a lawyer, they have two daughters and their relational dynamic is built on respect and independence.

M*arianne* 1: Do you think it's possible two people can spend their entire lives together?
J*ohan* 1: That's just an insane convention we inherited from God knows where. There should be 5-year contracts. Or an agreement that remains valid for 1 year that you can also terminate.
M*arianne* 1: For us, too?
J*ohan* 1: No, not for us.
M*arianne* 1: Why not for us?
J*ohan* 1: Because you and I are the exception to the rule. You and I won the Fools' Lottery.
M*arianne* 1: So you think we'll stay together our entire lives?
J*ohan* 1: What a strange question. (Mann, 2017)

Then the story takes a different turn. Johan confesses that he must leave her as he has fallen in love with another woman. After he leaves, the tone of the dialogue changes, becoming more bitter, more accusing, and mutually hurtful. This struggle between liberation from bonds and holding onto the union begins to be a private fight about intimacy.

When *Scenes from a marriage* was shown on Swedish television, the streets of Stockholm and Oslo were empty of people as an overwhelming majority prioritized viewing it. Ingmar Bergman's popular television series was said to have doubled divorce rates in Sweden. How can we understand the influence of this drama on Scandinavian culture? Bergman hit a nerve among Scandinavians; he had insight into how a well-functioning marriage and family life should be constructed and lead. However, the popularity of the drama lies nevertheless in the curious ways such a marriage can fail. Its popularity lies in both a recognition of and a desire to understand the modern move toward divorce as a choice. More than encouraging divorce, the series most likely touched on crucial changes appearing in society in the 1970s in the wake of the sexual revolution and developing conceptions of love and marriage. Divorce and the choice of several potential constellations in the love relationship occurred in the late-modernist or postmodern era. In Scandinavia, gender issues, equality, and movements toward postfeminist stances were on the agenda. On the one hand, couples were expected to form families and "nest"; on the other hand, expectations of self-realization of the individual had become more acceptable, as well as something of an imperative.

Below, I have presented excerpts from the dialogue. Reading them closely, one can see the emergence of a kind of reflexivity. Johan says that they are emotional illiterates, and this signals a sub-discourse of romantic love and expectations of intimate, emotional discussions. Marianne speaks about loneliness in an existential manner when she says that people are not strong all on their own. Marianne argues around expectations related to gender issues and sex. Arriving with the wave of feminist thought and liberation processes, it has now become possible to argue and negotiate about equality, role-play, and how sex and desire can be constructed. In Scandinavia, there has been a distinct feminist move characterizing reflections around gender issues and the varied positioning available to women. This is reflected in the discussions about sex between the partners and Marianne's immediate defensiveness, as if she is being blamed for her occasional lack of desire:

Johan: We're emotional illiterates. We've been taught about anatomy and farming methods in Africa. We've learned mathematical formulas by heart. But we haven't been taught a thing about our souls. We're tremendously ignorant about what makes people tick.

Marianne: I think about you… and I think about myself and about the future. I can't see how you're going to cope without me. Sometimes I think in desperation, "I must look after Johan. He's my responsibility. It's up to me to make sure he's all right. That's the only way our lives will be worthwhile."

Johan: I don't believe people are strong all on their own. You have to have someone's hand to hold.

Marianne: I felt inadequate at work and at home, and I was a washout in bed too. I was hedged in by all the griping and endless demands! Goddamn you! Was it so strange that I used sex for leverage? I was outnumbered, having to fight you, both sets of parents and society! When I think about what I endured, I could scream! I tell you this: never again! You sit there whining about conspiracies. Well, it serves you right! I hope you'll have it rammed down your throat that you're a useless parasite.

Johan: You're being utterly grotesque!

Marianne: So what? That's what I've become! (Mann, 2017) Bergman, (1973).

Another of the central themes of this drama is the issue of guilt. Bergman admits in his autobiography that he felt a tremendous weight of guilt for leaving successive wives and families and this guilt is transferred to Johan's character. Remember also that Bergman was the son of a Lutheran Priest. When Marianne tries to help Johan pack for his trip to Paris, saying that he was never any good at it, he lashes out and is abusive toward her. He cannot face the guilt of having her help him while injuring her. Then, after a calm and business-like breakfast, as he puts on his raincoat and prepares to leave the house, she begs him to reconsider, asks him how he can be so cruel, and he pushes her away, literally prying her arms from around his neck, and rushes out.

3.2.4 The Romantic Discourse Squeezed Between the Demands of Nostalgia and Desire for Liberty and Choice

A romantic discourse encompasses marriage, monogamy, and love and invoking one invokes them all (Willig, 2001). Romantic love is expressed in the following terms: "if you love me, you will want to marry me and remain faithful forever." Johan and Marianne approve and confirm one another this way in the initial scene. Here, marriage and monogamy are necessary conditions in a romantic discourse, which takes much of its force from expectations of harmony and stability, as seen in a happy and unthreatened couple/family structure. In *Scenes from a marriage*, Johan falls in love with another woman, and thereby breaches the contract of monogamy, and this leads to divorce.

"Oh, how romantic!" is an exclamation that immediately invites us into a framework of love in which roses, champagne, and candlelight are natural symbols of an appealing, old-fashioned style of courtship. In the sequence below taken from my thesis, one of the informants is contrasting contemporary couples' social behavior with how things were "back then" when T was young, a kind of nostalgia:

> T: I think nowadays young people…. they go out separately. They have different needs. So, she goes with her friends and he gets jealous and then he goes to a pub with his friends […] Unlike in my time, when they either went together or stayed at home [together]. [Going out] separately to the pub… It's become very common. I don't think it's healthy (Øfsti, 2008).

The reason I address this excerpt from my analysis with the screenplay from *Scenes from a marriage* is that I think it demonstrates the deep-seated nostalgia of romance as we know it, the "good old days," and the process toward "pure relationship." In Scandinavia, I think these two processes go hand in hand: sentimentality, the desire for stability and safety along with acknowledgment of the forces of individualization and the desire for freedom.

As a couple therapist, I find these dilemmas highly relevant for the various dialogues that occur among couples, especially the questions about the experience of how difficult it can be to develop long-term relationships. Here there is conflict between the traditional romantic promise, forever yours, with the individual's doubt about what the "glue" of the relationship consists in when the choice of leaving is always present. Øfsti, (2010).

3.3 The Pure Relationship, the Plot, and Longing Depicted in the Swedish Novel, *Willful Disregard*

This novel by the Swedish author Lena Andersson published in 2013 has been broadly discussed among booklovers in Scandinavia. The protagonist is a 31-year-old essayist Ester Nilsson. Ester is described as a successful modern woman living with an unexciting but reliable boyfriend, Per, and is contentedly devoted to intellectual pursuits. She is bright, thoughtful, and rational.

One day she receives an invitation to give a lecture about the renowned artist Hugo Rask, with whom she immediately develops a fascination. Immediately after her lecture, Rask declares, "no outsider has ever understood me so profoundly and precisely" and suggests they should go for a drink. Ester falls in love. She knows in an intuitive way that the two of them will relate. As an early strategy of self-defense (so as not to let this fascination threaten her relationship) she tells herself that she thinks she would like her partner, Per, to socialize with Rask.

How can we understand this first moment of attraction? The encounter between Hugo and Ester cannot be explained by physical desire for him, as in traditional romantic narratives where the male hero is usually tall, dark, and handsome. Rather, Ester is determined to dazzle him with her lecture, believing that men like him were "receptive to the power of intellectual formulations and their erotic potential" (Andersson, 2016). Rask delivers a perfect flirtatious statement when he says, "no outsider has ever understood me so profoundly and precisely," and emphasizes that Ester is particularly competent in her special view of him.

Rask's statement correlates with Anthony Giddens' description of the "pure relationship." While romantic love as an ideal has had a huge impact on how intimacy is organized in late modernity, it has at the same time been challenged by what Giddens has called the "pure relationship" (Øfsti, 2008), The "'pure relationship' […] refers to a situation where a social relation is entered into for its own sake, for what can be derived by each person from a sustained association with another; and which is continued only in so far as it is thought by both parties to deliver enough satisfaction for each individual to stay within it" (Giddens, 1992, p. 58). The ideal of the pure relationship tends away from the traditional model of marriage toward a post-traditional form in which the relationship is seen as a means to self-development; the expectation is rather that, when the relationship no longer serves the purpose of self-realization, it will be terminated.

For Ester, hearing that she has seen and grasped Hugo Rask as no one else has done, is a relational invitation that makes Ester and Hugo special for one another. This ideal of seeing the personality of the other and the striving for a unique identity is interwoven into an understanding of the importance of being perceived as an individual, in-depth, in the struggle to be someone special and in intimacy as a self-development project.

Another concept of Giddens describes emotional ties, "confluent love":

Opening oneself to the other, the condition of what I shall call confluent love, is in some ways the opposite of projective identification, even if such identifications sometimes set up a pathway to it. Confluent love is active, contingent love, and therefore jars with the "for-ever", and "one and only" qualities of the romantic love complex. […] Confluent love presumes equality in emotional give and take, the more so the more any particular love tie approximates closely to the prototype of the pure relationship (Giddens, 1992, pp. 61–62).

The pure relationship and the confluent aspect of love as representations of intimate relationships correlate with a contemporary development I refer to as "a call for emotional peak experiences." This development focuses on the individual's need to be entertained and to maximize fulfilment. Philosophically speaking, we could say that the individual orients herself relationally toward pleasure and satisfaction more than duty and virtue. In such a trend, the couple's compass points toward frequent and rapid emotional events rather than lasting and cyclical experiences. In this light, being in love is the "jewel in the crown" of emotional peak experiences (Øfsti, 2008).

In the novel, Ester leaves her boyfriend and throws herself into an imaginary relationship with Hugo. She believes they are a couple, because the intensity of their chain of meetings and shared events is compelling and increasing. From an outsider, it seems that Rask consumes her thoughts. Ester is struggling between rationalizing and analyzing the relationship, and at the same time, helpless in the face of her overpowering feelings for Hugo. She throws herself into a love that starts to direct all her waking movements. With classic, torturous uncertainty, she puzzles over the meaning of every encounter and the crushing blank of Hugo's frequent absences.

In terms of the pure relationship, reflexivity is necessary, producing questions such as, "Is everything all right in our relationship?" and "How is this relationship contributing to my self-development?" Ester submits to a reflexive loop throughout the story. She notices the power imbalance early on: "Hugo never followed up anything Ester said. Ester always followed up what Hugo said. Neither of them was really interested in her but they were both interested in him."

"Let's be in touch later," he said cautiously.

"Only if you feel like it."

"Or if you feel like it."

"No, I'm afraid that's not how it works. It's if you feel like it that we'll be in touch."

He dashed out after a quick, harassed kiss (Andersson, 2016).

Although romantic love has its foundation in housekeeping, economic concerns, gender differences, children and, for some, moral and religious commitment, the pure relationship is instead a relationship based on sexual and emotional equality, embarked upon solely for its own sake and for the mutual satisfaction of the partners.

Beck and Beck-Gernsheim (1995) explore the dilemmas and challenges concerning love that arose in late modernity through individualization and secularization. They explore the gap between the Old Era and the New Era, where New Era refers to "a collision of interests between love, family and personal freedom." Characteristic of the Old Era was that definitions of roles and functions were clearer; men and women of middle-class upbringing anywhere in the Western world desired to marry, and to bear and rear children. The New Era refers to a condition in which almost everything is a matter of choice: relationships, jobs, and marriage, with the possible consequence of a conflict of interests between couple relationships, family/children, and personal freedom. However, common to both the old and new eras is the importance of displaying a good "self-biography" and this involves showing off one's relational status.

Ester's expectations after she and Rask have finally had sex once or twice are that they are now in a steady, defined relationship. The problem is that Hugo seems to be more interested in her thoughts and their communication, while Ester is longing for security and emotional and erotic exchange. Traditionally in a romantic, heterosexual discourse, the male erotic lust is taken for granted. Nevertheless, in the novel, Hugo is uninterested. In the shed of the new discourse, how do people attract one another? In romantic role-play one falls in love. What must the contract become for getting into a relationship? The question this novel is asking is: can a woman win a man solely with intellectual firepower?

3.3.1 Dialogical Love and the Emphasis on Being Seen as a Psychological–Relational Being

Psychological language and knowledge have become incorporated into folk knowledge, and I find it interesting that the emphasis on emotions, the value of good dialogues, the needs for self-government and reflection, and to a certain degree confession, permeates the discourse of coupledom (Madsen, 2009). Madsen proposes that there are problematic aspects with this development that are seldom recognized due to a widely held assumption that "the more psychology, the better for everyone" (Rose, 1989/1999).

In the relationship between Ester and Rask, the uncertainty and vague dynamics between them upsets Ester, and she becomes emotionally trapped, as in a kind of addiction, such as that of gambling: win a little 1 day, lose dramatically the next. However, what I find interesting when discourses about coupledom get entangled in this struggle is that the solutions become therapeutic. A recurring concern with psychological solutions however, is that they often provide individual solutions to structural problems such as unemployment, poverty, inequality, and social mobility As a result, psychologists may be inadvertently increasing the burden on the shoulders of the people they are meant to help and, at the same time, our capacity to understand individual suffering in the light of major historical and political changes in society is becoming increasingly clouded (Madsen, 2009).

The novel can also be read in a moralistic framework, as asking whether human beings are responsible for vulnerabilities in others. When you involve yourself emotionally and intimately with another toward whom you do not intend to commit yourself, are you morally responsible for the impact this might have on the other person? This is what Ester claims of Hugo in the novel, since he has offered attention to her, as if they were going to have a steady and intimate relationship.

This novel is also written in the context of a postmodern, individualistic discourse, in which the persons involved are free to choose; at the same time, they are also very alone in deciding what it is that should qualify as a compass for being a couple.

3.4 Scandinavia Today: A Crucible of Discourses and Experiences and the Movement Between Nostalgia and New Ways of Being Intimate

In this chapter, I have presented different discourses of coupledom in Scandinavia. There may be some experiences representative of Scandinavia that differ slightly from those common to other countries and continents. I am not sure. Looking again at the history of Scandinavia, one can see a certain geographical isolation from the European continent. However, with globalization and processes of migration, and economic growth, Scandinavia resonates closely with impulses that are common worldwide. It is not my intention to argue for a unique Scandinavian discourse. Rather, I want to remind the reader how important it is to understand the interchange between different aspects such as geography (the topographic landscape), historical traditions, religion and values, the structural and economic conditions and the cultural landscape, and the contributions these make to discourses.

The crucible or in the words of Beck and Beck-Gernsheim, *the normal chaos of love,* is an apt description. In Scandinavia, as in the Western World, it is difficult to dictate the ways how family, marriage, parenthood, sexuality, or love should have significance, what they should or could be. As seen in this chapter, these vary in substance, exceptions, norms, and morality from individual to individual and from relationship to relationship.

In a collision of ideals, the meaning of love and of the way of being a couple, are being squeezed between old and new ideals and practices. For the Scandinavians, the new era represents diversity, and possibility and at the same time, anxiety, and risks. Being aware of the cultural and historical context, we might get a better understanding of the personal dilemmas, which can occur, since in the end, love and forms of intimacy are essential for human beings—and the complexity of intimate relationships needs to be understood and further explored by politicians, writers, therapists, and the individual people themselves.

References

Andersson, L. (2016). *Willful disregard*. New York: Other Press. LLC.
Beck, U., & Beck-Gernsheim, E. (1995). *The normal Chaos of love*. Cambridge: Polity Press.
Bergman, I. (1973). Scener ur ett äktenskap. Cinematograph AB.
Evans, M. (2003). *Love: An unromantic discussion*. Cambridge: Polity Press.
Giddens, A. (1992). *The transformation of intimacy: sexuality, love and eroticism in modern societies*. Cambridge: Polity Press.
Hernes, H. (1987). *Welfare state and women power: Essays in state feminism*. Norwegian University Press.
Madsen, O. J. (2009). Psykologi, samfunn og etikk. *Tidsskrift for Norsk Psykologforening, 46*(2), 144–152.
Mann, E. (2017). Scenes from a marriage. Screenplay.
Øfsti, A. K. S. (2008). *Some call it love: Exploring Norwegian systemic couple therapists' discourses of love, intimacy and sexuality*. London: University of East Londo.
Øfsti, A. K. S. (2010). *Parterapi: kjærlighet, intimitet og samliv i en brytningstid*. Oslo: Universitetsforlaget.
Rose, N. (1989/1999). *Governing the soul the shaping of the private self*. London: Free Association Books.
Undset, S. (2014). *Kristin Lavransdatter*. New York: Penguin Random House.
Willig, C. (2001). *Introducing qualitative research in psychology adventures in theory and method*. Philadelphia: Open University Press.

Chapter 4
The Evolution of the Couple in France over the Past 30 Years

Michel Maestre

4.1 Introduction

Over the past three decades, clinical psychologists and couple therapists have witnessed an intense evolution of the couple in France, particularly when one considers the origins of the concept of the couple. In the 1960s, people did not speak of couples but of a *ménage* (household). In French, the word *ménage* indicates performing household tasks. Therefore, *se mettre en ménage* translates to setting up house together and could, by analogy, indicate taking care of the house and domestic tasks. The setting up of house together continued to evolve in its permutations so that in the 1970s and 1980s, the relationship status of French individuals was one of the following:

- Single: A very poorly perceived status after the age of 25, especially for women who were often mocked and called 'old girls';
- Engaged: An emotional association between two young people, with marriage as its sole prospect and where the young woman and the young man were called 'intendeds';
- Married: A status adopted for better or for worse, and where the marriage could only be thought of as being for life;
- Widowed: A circumstance where widowers and widows could remarry and were even encouraged to do so;
- Divorced: A status that was quite rare and very poorly perceived, to the extent that hardly any pupils in elementary school had divorced parents.

M. Maestre (✉)
Université Catholique de Lille, Lille, France

Université de PARIS 8, Saint-Denis, France

PSYCOM Institute in Villeneuve d'Ascq, Lille, France

In addition, almost without exception, in the poorest families both parents worked. This in contrast to the post-second World War era where it was expected that the mother, and, by extension, the wife, would stay at home to take care of the home and raise the children while the husband, and head of the family, left for work to provide for the family's financial needs.

Clearly, over a span of 50 years, society has changed considerably in France, just as it has for couples within this society. In this chapter, these changes will be considered from the following points of view: Legislation, trends in couple relationship status, how household tasks are organised by couples and how the problems described in couple therapy have changed over the course of the last 30 years.

4.2 A Historical Perspective on the Couple and the Law in France

Up until the French Revolution, the only type of marriage that was recognised was religious marriage. The parish records at the time were therefore considered to be civil records. With the French Revolution, marriage was republicanised and on 20 September 1792, a new law introduced civil marriage to France. This took away the authority held by the Church and instead meant that marriages were recorded at the Town Hall. This form of marriage therefore became the only valid form in the eyes of the law and this still holds today. French people are still free to have a religious ceremony, as a part of whatever religion they practice, but only once they have had a civil service. Not respecting this rule is considered an offence.

In 1804, the Napoleonic Code defined the conditions and initiation of marriage. Marriages were now contracted before a municipal officer, meaning the mayor or his or her representative, and this individual was responsible for keeping the civil records. Based on this law, marriage could be revoked by divorce. If the two spouses wished, the marriage could be dissolved on the simple claim of incompatible characters or personalities. It is interesting to note that Napoleonic law gave French people marriage and divorce at the same time, whereas Catholicism did not accept divorce. Indeed, with the law of 8 May 1816, under the Restoration and with the return of Catholicism as the state religion in France, divorce was abolished. It would be reintroduced many decades later by the law of 27 July 1884; but only one type of divorce was allowed—divorce for a just cause.

With respect to partner status, there was inequality between the husband and the wife up until 1938. Only after this date could a married woman enter into a contract or take legal action without the authorisation of her husband. It took another few decades, specifically with the law of 13 July 1965 regarding the reform of marital law, for French wives to obtain even more independence from their husbands. This new law gave women the right to open a bank account, write cheques and have a job without needing their husband's permission.

Starting in the 1970s, alongside changing social habits, the pace of legislation accelerated and a number of couple and family laws were put into force:

- 4 June 1970: Law on joint parental authority, which modified the civil code and replaced paternal power with joint parental authority;
- 3 January 1972: Law stating that all children have the same rights and the same responsibilities with regards to their parents, whether they were born inside or outside of wedlock;
- 11 July 1975: Law that modernised the right to divorce and henceforth recognised three types of divorce, including that of two spouses divorcing based on mutual consent;
- 27 July 1987: Law extending the exercise of parental authority by two parents to unmarried couples and divorced couples; meaning that all parents are, by law, equally recognised in the exercise of their authority, whether or not they are married. This latter law saw the start of a disassociation between parental responsibility and marriage. In a certain sense, this law implied that couples who formed families could now be unmarried.

Another milestone came about on 15 November 1999 when a new law established the civil solidarity pact, commonly known in French as PACS (*pacte civil de solidarité,*). PACS is a contract between two people, regardless of their sex. The two partners commit to a life together and to jointly contributing to the couple's expenses. They also have a duty to help and support each other. PACS is different from marriage. Within the framework of PACS, there is no joint ownership of goods, there is no divorce (meaning that either of the partners can leave the other without any formalities), and there is no automatic adoption by one partner of a child adopted by the other partner. Therefore, PACS means, in part, that unmarried couples are recognised as couples, whether they are heterosexual or homosexual (Martin & Théry, 2001). This law was taken one step further when as of 17 May 2013 marriage became legally available to same-sex couples (Erlanger, 2013). This law is called the 'Law of Marriage for All' (Government of France, 2013).

In summary, looking at the evolution of the couple in France, it can be said that up until the French Revolution of 1789, the Catholic Church presided over marriages. Divorce, which was forbidden by the Church, was not possible because it was considered that God joined the partners together, tying them to each other until one of them died. With the enactment of the Civil Code in 1804, which is still applied today throughout most of Europe, the right to marriage and divorce was conferred at the same time. It was not until the twentieth century that the law regulating couples began to change more rapidly, with the equality of married partners, the recognition of children conceived outside of wedlock, and the recognition of unmarried and homosexual couples with PACS. The beginning of the twenty-first century saw the extension of marriage to all couples, whether homosexual or heterosexual. With this law, France became the 9th European country and the 14th country worldwide to legalise gay marriage. In 2014, same-sex couples represented 4% of all unions (INSEE, 2015a).

4.3 How Do People Enter Into Life as Couples in France Today?

In a study by Rault and Régnier-Loilier published in 2015, the authors offer extensive detail on how people's lives together as couples began and developed in France. The authors explain that after the cultural revolution of 1968, cohabitation before marriage and being part of a consensual union became possible. Previously, the institution of marriage was the only context recognised as allowing couples to have a sexual relationship and conceive children. Up until then, living together outside of marriage or being separated conferred stigma, as did sexuality outside of the marital framework, especially for women. With this backdrop in mind, this section will highlight key elements from the Rault and Régnier-Loilier landmark publication.

4.3.1 Age at Time of Marriage or Entering Couplehood

Rault and Régnier-Loilier (2015) describe how marriage started to take place later and became less common over the years in France. After the Second World War, in the 1950s, most people were already married by the age of 30 (74% of women and 66% of men) and even 25 (64% of women and 49% of men); whereas a quarter of a century later, only 16% of women and 7% of men were already married by the age of 25. Marriage started to become less 'automatic'. Religious ceremonies too became less common: while almost 9 out of 10 first marriages that took place in the early 1970s were accompanied by a religious ceremony, this was only the case for 6 out of 10 marriages 35 years later. The authors explain that the age at which people first live together as a couple has changed twice. First, the first relationships occur later. While half of men and women born in the early 1950s had already been part of a couple at the age of 21.6 and 23.2 years, respectively, this median age increased to 22.8 and 25.8 years for the generations born in the mid-1970s. Longer educational careers and the increase in unemployment are the primary reasons for this shift of entering couplehood at an older age. However, more than a rejection of life as a couple, this trend rather portrays a delay in the first relationship. In other words, it was less common for the generations born around 1970 than for those in the post-war period to have already been part of a cohabitating couple at the age of 25. One must point out here that, irrespective of when they were born—post-war or around 1970, at 30 years of age rates of cohabitation were similar for the two groups, and by 40–45 years of age they were more or less the same.

For more recent generations (those born between 1978 and 1987), while the duration of educational careers is no longer increasing, the trend in cohabitation is stabilising and even reversing for men. Men born in the 1980s are more likely to have lived as part of a couple at 25 years of age than men who were born in the late 1970s. This could be explained in part by the abolition of military service (passed in 1997) which affected all generations born after 1979 as they no longer had to leave the home to fulfil this duty. Also, despite slightly longer educational careers, women continue to form their first cohabitating couple relationship earlier than men, and the age difference between partners persists, even though it is tending to decrease.

In fact, the median age at the first experience of living as a couple is 21.5 years for women and 24 years for men from the 1978 to 1987 generations whose studies stopped before the baccalaureate, compared to 23.6 and 26.3 years, respectively, for those with a higher degree up to a baccalaureate plus 2 years.

4.3.2 Moving in Together

Moving into a new home together is less common than it was previously. In the post-war generations, the two partners were often both employed at the beginning of their relationship (66% of women and 54% of men for those born around 1950); a stable situation that facilitated cohabitation. In later generations, it was less common for both partners to be employed (34% of women and 31% of men born between 1978 and 1982) and more common for them to still be students at the onset of their relationship. The persistence of an age gap between partners, combined with a longer educational career for women, often lead to a situation in which the man was employed and the woman was a student (27% of situations described by men and 24% of those mentioned by women), whereas the reverse situation—the man studying and the woman working—remained rare (3%). This economic, career, and lifestyle difference impacted on cohabitation decisions.

Focusing on the generation born in 1978–1982, it is still fairly rare for these individuals to move in with their sexual partner. This is particularly striking in women whose sex life now begin at an age closer to that at which it does for men. For those born between 1948 and 1952, the male and female were first partners in that particular couple in more than three quarters of cases. This was not so for a third of women (38%) born 30 years later. Notably, it is more common for couples to move into the man's home (approximately one in four of women and men) than it is to move into the woman's home (approximately one in six).

4.3.3 Previous Experience as a Couple

Nowadays, it is more likely to have a first partner who has already lived with a partner. Whilst only 9% of women and 5% of men born in 1948–1952 formed their first couple with someone who had already lived as part of a couple, this scenario is prevalent among more than a quarter of women and men born in 1978–1982. It is not so common, however, to have a first relationship with someone who already has children. Moreover, first relationships are not necessarily those that lead to children. The trend is for individuals to have multiple significant romantic relationships during their adulthood, some of which may involve cohabitation. The percentages have been increasing over the years as evident from Table 4.1.

Considering the frequencies in Table 4.1, one might surmise that younger generations tend to describe relationships of their youth as significant or 'serious', when they would not have been described as such by older generations (Rault & Régnier-Loilier, 2015). Whilst this over-valuation is possible, the Epic study (2019) suggests otherwise. This study reported that in 1950, 10% of men had had two or

Table 4.1 Percentage of males and females having had at least two significant romantic relationships by 25 or 30 years of age

	Born 1948–1952		Born 1978–1982	
	At least two relationships		At least two relationships	
Max. Age	Men %	Women %	Men %	Women %
25 years	9	6	29	36
30 years	3	5	16	19

Source: Adapted from Rault and Régnier-Loilier (2015); INED-Épic (2019)

more significant relationships in their life by age 25, whereas this figure increased to 35% by 1985. Similarly, in 1950, 14% of 25-year-old women had already had two or more significant relationships in their life, and this figure increased to 44% in 1985. In other words, there were more women than men who reported having experienced more than two significant relationships by the time they were 25. This difference can be explained by the difference in ages between members of a couple, even though this is tending to decrease. Essentially, 25-year-old women are more often in relationships with older men.

There have been multiple changes in the concept of the couple, beginning in the 1960s. These include diversification of types of partnerships, with the decrease in marriage and, more recently, the rise of civil partnerships (PACS), and the availability of marriage to same-sex couples. There has also been an increase in the number of romantic relationships that occur in individual trajectories. These days, one's first couple relationship often takes place while the participants are still completing their studies. The relationship very often takes the form of experimentation with a lifestyle, and is less often undertaken with the potential prospect of marriage and establishing a family.

4.4 The Evolution of Couple Formation and Dissolution in More Recent Years

An INSEE (*Institut National de la Statistique et des Etudes Economiques*—National institute of Statistics and Economic studies) (2015b) study indicates that 123,500 divorces were announced in 2014, compared to 134,000 in 2010. After having reached a peak in 2005, the number of divorces remained relatively stable until 2010. Since then, there has been a downward trend. This recent decrease in divorces is largely due to a slight decrease in requests for divorce, and not so much to a decrease in the number of marriages. If the 2014 divorce rate continues, 44% of marriages that took place that year will end in divorce. In addition, these days, as it has been since the 1970s, the risk of divorce is highest at 5 years of marriage (Bellamy, 2016; Mazuy, Barbieri, & D'Albis, 2014). In 2014, one out of four marriages was a remarriage for at least one of the two partners, and 1 out of 10 was a remarriage for both partners. The age at the time of remarriage has been increasing since 1980. Previously, divorced men who married in 2014 were on average 50 years old, and women 46 years old.

The INSEE (2015b) study corroborates what is often seen in couple therapy consultations; namely that couples form primarily to be a couple and later, potentially, have a family. In fact, the number of non-cohabitating couples in France is increasing (Régnier-Loilier, 2017). Buisson and Lapinte (2013) provide the following figures:

> As at 2011, in mainland France, out of 32 million adults who state that they are in a couple, 72% are married and share the same residence as their partner of a different sex. Seven million are in a consensual union, and 1.4 million are civil partners (PACS). Among adults who state that they are in a couple, 4% also indicate that their partner does not live in the same home. More than half of these are under 30 years old. Of those between 30 and 59 years of age, one person out of ten who are in a couple does not live with his or her partner in the absence of having a child together. Non-cohabitation is mainly relevant to consensual unions. (p. 1, translation from French)

One can easily propose, therefore, that a new form of married life is developing in France. According to sociologist Arnaud Régnier-Loilier (2016), more than a new way of being a couple, it is perhaps more a new step, either toward separation or toward moving in together. This does not necessarily mean that non-cohabitating couples are less stable. As Régnier-Loilier (2016) indicates in his article 'Partnership trajectories of people in stable non-cohabiting relationships in France', between 2005 and 2008, 46% of non-cohabitating couples went on to separate. In comparison, 94% of cohabitating couples who were followed as part of his study were still living together after 3 years. The rate of break-ups is thus higher for non-cohabitating than it is for cohabitating couples. However, it is important to note that 22% of individuals who were 'living apart together' were still leading the same lifestyle 3 years later, while 72% of these couples had ended up moving in together.

Couples in France actively choose their form of coupledom more now than they did in the past. They experience the relationship before sharing a home. Many forms of life together are available to them, mainly as a non-cohabitating couple, as a consensual union, as civil partners (PACS) and as a married couple. Having a family is no longer the aim of being a couple, as more and more couples and women choose not to have children. But even though non-cohabitating couples are more numerous, this is still a way of testing out life together. Divorce is not an inevitability anymore. Couples consider separation even if they have young children. There are more and more so-called 'blended' or 'single parent' families. An INSEE study (2015b, 2015c) showed that the number of single parent families has continued to increase for the past 50 years. It was 2.5 times higher in 2005 than in 1968. In 2005, 17.7% of children under the age of 25 were part of a single-parent family, compared to 7.7% in 1968. More frequent couple break-ups are the basis of this increase. Up till 1968, or around the mid- to late-twentieth century, single-parent families occurred mainly due to the early death of one parent, most often the father.

4.5 The Couple and Division of Responsibilities

In France, as in all Western countries, the 1970s introduced citizens to birth control. This scientific advance was accompanied by a change in customs that promoted the equality of the sexes. But till this day, this equality is distributed unevenly among different levels of education in France: It is more apparent in university environments, somewhat less so in working-class environments, and has been slow to be applied in everyday life.

> I still smile today when, at the end of the couples' therapy session, I see a wife take the cheque book out of her bag and give it to her husband so that he can write the cheque. This must have to do with a behavioural memory of a time when the wife was not allowed to pay directly. (Author)

A study by the INSEE (2015b, 2015c) addressing the division of household tasks among members of a couple between 1985 and 2010 revealed that this division of tasks between men and women had changed little in 25 years. In 2010, women still performed 71% of domestic tasks and 65% of parenting activities. In particular, women dominated in the care of the essential domestic tasks within a couple, but they did less of them in 2010 than they did in 1985. The main reason was that more women had joined the workforce and, therefore, had less time to dedicate to household tasks. The INSEE study further showed how the increase in women's employment had affected social norms and the way in which women perceived their role within the household. Essentially, the fact of working gave them more weight in decisions made within the couple, as well as in the division of domestic tasks.

It follows from the above, that the amount of time that men spend on household tasks has also changed little in 25 years. Yet the study showed that men were dedicating more time to their children, with the rate doubling in 25 years. This change was particularly apparent in young fathers aged 18–30; being the male age group that spent the most time with their children. Laws on parental leave for fathers as well as for mothers after the birth of their child (2001) and the law affirming the equality of joint parental responsibility (2002) have been suggested as having facilitated this change (INED, n.d.). Nonetheless, the study authors also noted that parental activities with children, similar to domestic tasks, remain strongly gendered: Almost three quarters of child care, supervision of schoolwork or taking children to different activities were carried out by mothers. Only playing games and other social activities were shared equally between men and women. In effect, the increase in parenting time for men during the 25-year period was primarily linked to their greater involvement in caregiving and games. As for women, they dedicated most of their parenting time to taking children to activities and caring for the children.

The other striking observation from the INSEE study is that egalitarian couples were more common. In 2010, 27% of men performed more domestic tasks than their female partner, compared to 17% in 1985. This increase may seem somewhat low, but it points to a larger social and cultural change, with less distinct roles for men and women. The concept of a traditional couple with a stark division of labour between the partners, one performing in the professional sphere and the other in the domestic sphere, is no longer strongly prevalent (INSEE, 2015b, 2015c). Interestingly, the study also revealed that couples had a tendency to resemble each other in terms of participation, so that women who were very involved in parenting and domestic tasks had partners who were also very involved.

This INSEE study corroborates my observation of couples in therapy. Wives complain less and less often about disparities in who performs domestic tasks or how the partners' involvement in child-raising is divided. We should note that, today, sharing tasks and work is politically correct, with the reference model being equality. Forty years ago and more, men who took care of young children or performed domestic tasks were not well perceived by their peers.

4.6 Changes in the Needs of Couples in Therapy over the Past 30 Years

This section will be presented as an anecdotal narrative by the author who, as a clinical psychologist and couples therapist working for more than 30 years in the field, has witnessed first-hand the evolution of the couple in France. The vignettes described are based on real-life scenarios from clinical practice.

4.6.1 Consulting a Couple Therapist

When I began to counsel couples in the mid-1980s, few therapeutic options were available and requests for consultation were rare. Consulting a psychologist or psychotherapist could be considered a sign of a mental or psychological problem, or even insanity. Today, when I encounter couples in a therapeutic setting, it is not rare for them to both be in individual therapy and for their children to be in therapy or seeing a speech therapist or learning specialist. These days in France, and in particular in large metropolitan areas, it is fairly 'well-regarded' to consult a psychologist. In a little more than 30 years, lifestyles and the relationship between the public and psychotherapy service have changed dramatically in France.

4.6.2 Needs Expressed During Couple Therapy

The needs expressed during couples therapy have also changed substantially. Thirty years ago, they primarily had to do with marital disputes, most commonly about the following themes; boredom with the relationship, conflicts between parents with regards to how their children should be raised, and the relationship between spouses once the children had left home. Back then and even now, for some parents it is almost as if the couple has been put in parentheses for several years whilst childrearing is taking place. Similarly, some couples also sought and still seek therapy later in life, at the end of their career or at retirement, or during a period of unemployment. These contexts plunge them into a new, shared life that is not interrupted by a day's worth of activities outside of the house. Thus a semi-permanent and sometimes difficult cohabitation ensues.

One can delve more deeply into how the needs of couples in therapy have changed in 30 years. In the 1970s and 1980s, they mostly had to do with expectations and repairing the marital relationship which life events had disturbed. The couples that sought therapy were motivated by the myth of marital longevity. A couple that had been together for a long time was considered to be a 'good couple'. Quantity was prized without questioning the quality of the relationship. Separation and divorce were perceived, above all, as a failure. Seeking out a couple therapist was deemed by the couple as the last means of avoiding divorce. How many times have I heard, 'You are our last hope!'

Couples' needs were also circumscribed by the specific context of an established couple. The most common problems were associated with erosion of the couple, as they did not know how to reinvent themselves adequately, and thus progressively succumbed to boredom. At the same time, the two circumstances of children leaving home and/or the couple entering retirement, put the couple back into each other's company on a continual basis after years of separate activities. This frequently had a negative impact on the relationship.

Nowadays, the fear of divorce is less significant and separation is considered a possibility. Fewer younger or older people wish to force themselves to remain in an unhappy marriage. At the same time, it seems as though there is an aspiration within French society to succeed in one's personal life, meaning one's marital, sexual, parental and professional life. It is not uncommon for members of a couple to allow themselves to be tempted by a temporary extramarital affair in order to make up for a lack of affection or sex life, or even, paradoxically, to indirectly attract the attention of a partner who they feel has neglected them. Extramarital affairs come up more and more easily in consultation. The number of extramarital affairs seems to be equal in terms of frequency for men and women. They are mostly perceived as a sign of dysfunction and, less often, as the trigger for an inevitable separation.

4.6.3 Divorce as a Symptom of Dysfunction

Based on the experience of consultations with couples in therapy today, it seems that a request for divorce by married couples, or separation for unmarried couples, acts as a symptom. This is evident when considering that the systemic family approach, and in particular the work from the school of Palo Alto (Watzlawick, Weakland, & Fisch, 2014), have used the term 'symptom' to mean a sign of dysfunction. The role that the symptom plays in the system to which it belongs is interrogated systematically. As explained by Dominique (2010), the main value that the symptom has for the subject who seeks therapy is that it is a sign; a sign that something is not right. Medically, a symptom is defined as a sign taking the place of a link and a representation between two elements; the first, the symptom, which is known and visible, is the effect of the other, unknown, invisible element. 'Symptoms are signs of traumatic events', said Freud in 1909 (cited in Freud & Breuer, 1955).

For couples seeking therapy, a request for divorce or separation expressed by one of the members of the couple can be understood as his or her last attempt to get the other partner to act and prompt the couple to help itself. This request thus appears to be paradoxical as it can mean both 'I want to leave you' and at the same time 'Let's take steps to stay together'. This type of request is also reminiscent of the form taken by some suicide attempts, which are in fact a cry for help! At the first meeting, the partner who could be left most often appears to be suddenly discovering the dramatic state of the marital situation. During the first sessions, he or she will begin to understand that his or her partner has sent them many signals of distress in the past which they did not see, before the actual request for a divorce or separation was enunciated. This request would be understood here as a symptom whose role would be to lead the couple to seek psychotherapeutic counselling.

4.6.4 Perspectives on Extra-Marital Relationships

It is interesting to draw a parallel between the request for divorce or separation by one of the partners and the extra-marital relationship. First, the psychotherapist must check how the couple started out; the implicit contract that took place between the two members of the couple. For example, one understanding could be: 'If you cheat on me I will leave you'. Or another could perhaps be: 'If it happens and if it's not important, I prefer not to know'. The extra-marital relationship must be situated in the specific context of the couple and not compared to what is commonly accepted (or not accepted) in French society. The extra-marital relationship, when it is experienced by a couple, must be understood as a betrayal of one by the other, and is not exclusively limited to whether or not sexual relations took place outside of the couple. Before the 1950s, in France, when marriage was standard and divorce prohibited, some sexual relationships outside of the couple could be accepted, as long as they were not known of or seen, and above all as long as the other partner was not humiliated. These days, as members of a couple choose each other in order to have a happy married life, it is the question of betrayal that is the most poignant, whether or not there is a sexual relationship with another person.

Case 1

I worked with one couple, where the male partner was called Pierre and was 43 years old. He was a high school chemistry teacher, did not talk much and claimed to be, above all, scientific. He felt that 'talking is useful for exchanging information, that's all!' He could spend several minutes side-by-side with his son without speaking, whilst doing a DIY project for example. He would appreciate the relationship in silence. The female partner was named Jacqueline and was 41 years old. She worked in management. She was a friendly woman and could spend hours on the telephone with her sister or one of her friends talking about everything and nothing. The important thing for her was to communicate, to interact with other people, to do things together. She often reproached Pierre for not talking to her enough, whilst he complained of feeling obligated by his wife to talk when he had nothing to say.

The event that led to the consultation was that Pierre was spending more and more time playing on his computer or smartphone. He was visiting an internet site where people met up to discuss various topics. While he said little in real life, it was apparent that he became more talkative in a virtual context. Pierre would visit this site without hiding his behaviour and, from time to time, when his wife was present, Jacqueline would come up behind him to ask what he was doing, discreetly glancing at the conversations. One day when she did so, he had asked a woman he was 'chatting' with to take off her t-shirt and show him her breasts. This request made Pierre laugh a lot and made Jacqueline shout a lot as she perceived this conversation as an extra-marital relationship, as a betrayal.

Case 2

I was also witness to another clinical example of the virtual world intruding on a couple's reality. Julie was 35 years old, and Lucien was 37. The consultation took place on Réunion, which is a French island in the Indian Ocean 10,000 km from mainland France. The request for a consultation came after Julie fell in love with a gentleman who lived in Lyon in mainland France. Their conversations took place via a dating site and continued by video Skype. The two 'lovers' had never touched each other, had never met in person, had never kissed, had never had sexual relations, yet nevertheless, for the couple who asked for a consultation, it was as if everything had happened in real life. For Lucien it was a true betrayal, and for Julie it was a wonderful encounter. She clearly planned to leave her husband and head to mainland France to be with her lover, who she had never seen in person! The husband was devastated and felt betrayed, even though his wife had never cheated on him in real life.

Case 3

I met a couple in their 30s, with two children, and who did a lot of things together. But after 10 years of life together and the birth of the children, boredom set in and the wife's libido dissipated to the great displeasure of her husband. She stopped working when their second child was born in order to have more time to take care of the children. The couple was seeking consultation because of their distant relationship and the loss of sexual desire. They attended more than 10 sessions in two series of consultations. The therapy helped, and the couple relearnt how to take pleasure in doing things together. Their sexual encounters remained rare however. The wife eventually found a new job, their communication improved, she lost weight and became more attractive to her husband. During a therapy session, they told me that the wife had just gotten back in touch with a friend, a man who was about 15 years older than them. He lived on Réunion, and they live in mainland France. The wife wished to see this old friend who she had started speaking with again online. He primarily represented a father figure for her. She explained that he understood her better than her husband, and at the same time she asserted that she loved her husband and appreciated the positive changes that had occurred in their relationship. The husband was hesitant. He found himself in what we call in systemic family therapy 'a double bind': Either he let her go to Réunion but run the risk of her not returning, or refuse to let her go and make her unhappy. He risked losing her in both cases. He did not have a 'plan C' and could not extract himself from this double bind. The wife tried to reassure him that she would come back. And this is indeed what happened. She went on her trip and came back to her family as planned. But the stay on Réunion further increased the interest that she had in this man. A few months later the couple informed me that the gentleman from Réunion was moving to France to be closer to his friend. The husband was devastated and still did not know what to do. In the end he accepted that his wife spent the weekend with this older man who had become her lover. At the end of the therapy, the couple separated. The wife went to live with her new companion, and the husband, who did not know how to get his wife back, was very unhappy and was left with the prospect of mourning the loss of their relationship.

Luckily, there are also many situations in which, after an extra-marital relationship, the couple reconnect with each other through communication and sexuality, almost as though the lived risk of losing each other had reminded them both of the true value of the couple and the importance of restoring the quality of the relationship. One can thus infer that, in 2018, in France, an extra-marital relationship often acts as a sign of dysfunction addressed to the other partner, and also as an apparently effective means of bringing two partners together again and signalling the start of a new life together as a couple.

4.6.5 Recently Formed Couples Who Request Consultation

There is another type of request for consultation these days that did not exist 30 years ago, namely the request from couples who, at the beginning of their relationship, are afraid of failing and wish to undergo couple psychotherapy to prevent any potential difficulties that they could encounter later on. I am always amazed by these couples who come to a consultation after having been together for only 2 or 3 months, who are confusing the natural difficulties associated with becoming a couple with the problems that couples encounter after many years of life together. Suffice it to say that couple psychotherapy does not work as a preventative measure. It is essential that a couple has been together for some time (more than 1 year, at a minimum) before psychotherapy can be considered.

4.6.6 Homosexuals Seeking Therapy

Ever since the law on marriage for all was passed, and therefore homosexual couples were allowed to marry, there has been a change in mentality facilitating a greater acceptance of homosexual couples. To the best of my memory, I did not provide counselling for any homosexual couples before 2000. When the first couples began to request consultations, the person who made the appointment never failed to mention their homosexuality and to ask if it was possible to attend couple therapy with a same-sex partner. In contrast, ever since the 2013 law was passed, people only rarely mention their homosexuality when they make an appointment, and prior to the session it is only apparent from two first names of the same gender. I should add that, after the first minute or two, the therapist does not pay any more attention to this, except of course if homosexuality and its recognition are part of the problem that the clients wish to discuss.

4.6.7 Contemporary Views on Couplehood and Parenthood

The way that French people represent themselves these days has changed. Previously, people wanted primarily to establish a family, and forming a couple was essentially the first step on the path to forming such family. The objective of life seemed to be exclusively to give life and continue the process of giving rise to new generations, as has been going on since humanity began. These days, people want to be happy as a couple and build a life together. We have moved from parenthood to couplehood; from the couple as a means to the couple as an end. It is almost as if these two roles, couplehood and parenthood, are no longer two floors in the same house, but two different houses. Indeed, these days you can be a parent without being part of a couple. Single people adopt children and raise them, and couples live full lives together without wishing to establish a family.

Another important change is that the couple is a group of belonging. It has become disconnected from the concept of physical location; meaning that nowadays couples also exist outside of the concept of sharing daily life together. Living near Lille, which is approximately 240 km north of Paris and is connected to the capital via a high-speed train (1 h by train), I know couples where one member works in Paris but lives in northern France, commuting daily. In contrast, in some couples each member has his or her own home, one in Paris and the other in Lille, or even in Brussels (30 min by Eurostar). Thus, for a still small yet growing number of couples, a dissociation within the couple's relationship, specifically the couple as a group of belonging and where the couple lives, is developing progressively. In the past, when speaking of a couple and/or a family, one spoke of the *foyer* (household), implying that the community, the group of belonging, was such that all of its members gathered around the *foyer* (fire) that fed them and kept them warm. These days, you can consider yourselves to be a committed couple and live in separate places. Of course, long-distance lovers seek to meet up as often as possible; but strangely, with the development of social networks, dating sites and digital tools, people can also get to know each other and, in some cases, fall in love at a distance. Nowadays, more and more French couples meet and begin their relationships through social media or dating sites.

4.7 Conclusion

The concept of the couple takes many forms in contemporary France. Marriage is still the most common form of relationship, especially with the arrival of children. Before marriage or married life, many couples live apart, whether because they live far from each other or because they wish to try out the relationship before committing to it further. Today, there are forms of shared life other than marriage, such as consensual unions and PACS. Married life is no longer restricted to heterosexual couples, and both marriage and PACS are available to heterosexual couples. What is certainly significant is the value accorded to couple relationships. The number of significant romantic or couple relationships experienced by the age of 25 has increased regularly in recent years. It is as if the need for companionship and a more intimate relationship is felt more strongly; and given that the union can take different formats and that there is a shift to a greater acknowledgement of the partner's education or career needs and more shared household related tasks, couple are more willing to cohabitate. Yet, social norms around gender roles and around expectations from marriage or unions still carry components of traditional expectations. In some couple therapy sessions, this is fairly evident and reconciling the traditional and modern perspectives and behaviours of a couple requires sensitivity to each partner's stage along the trajectory of acceptance of the other and effort to make a relationship work.

References

Bellamy, V. (2016). 123 500 divorces en 2014: Des divorces en légère baisse depuis 2010, *INSEE Première No. 1599 (French Version)*

Buisson, G., & Lapinte, A. (2013). Le couple dans tous ses états: Non-cohabitation, conjoints de même sexe, Pacs…, *INSEE Première No. 1435 (French Version)*, p. 1

Dominique, N. (2010). Le symptôme dans tous ses états. *Figures de la Psychanalyse, 1*(19), 131–140.

Erlanger, S. (2013, May 18). Hollande signs French gay marriage law. *The New York Times*. Retrieved April 19, 2019, from https://www.nytimes.com/2013/05/19/world/europe/hollande-signs-french-gay-marriage-law.html

Freud, S., & Breuer J. (1955). Studies on hysteria. In J. Strachey & A. Strachey (Eds. & Trans.), *The standard edition of the complete psychological works of Sigmund Freud* (Vol. 2). London: Hogarth Press

Government of France. (2013). *Mariage pour tous: Le projet de loi est définitivement Adopté*. Government of France. Retrieved April 19, 2019, from https://www.gouvernement.fr/action/le-mariage-pour-tous

INED (Institut National D'Études Démographiques). (2019). *EPIC (Étude des parcours individuels et conjugaux). Study on individual and conjugal trajectories*. Retrieved April 19, 2019, from https://epic.site.ined.fr/en

INED (Institut National D'Études Démographiques). (n.d.) *Paternity leave in France*. Retrieved April 19, 2019, from https://www.ined.fr/en/everything_about_population/demographic-facts-sheets/focus-on/paternity-leave-in-france/

INSEE (Institut National de la Statistique et des Études Économiques). (2015a). *2014 demographic balance: Fewer deaths*. INSEE Première No. 1532. Retrieved April 19, 2019, from https://www.insee.fr/fr/statistiques/1283853

INSEE (Institut National de la Statistique et des Études Économiques). (2015b). *The many varieties of unions: Non-cohabiting partnerships, same-sex couples, civil unions… and more*. INSEE Première No, 1435. Retrieved April 19, 2019, from https://www.insee.fr/en/statistiques/1281437

INSEE (Institut National de la Statistique et des Études Économiques). (2015c). *Couples et Familles: Press kit*. Retrieved April 19, 2019, from https://www.insee.fr/en/statistiques/fichier/2127926/PK_Couples_et_familles.pdf

Martin, C., & Théry, I. (2001). The PACS and marriage and cohabitation in France. *International Journal of Law, Policy and the Family, 14*(3), 135–158.

Mazuy, M., Barbieri, M., & D'Albis, H. (2014). Recent demographic trends in France: The number of marriages continues to decrease. *Population (English Edition), 69*(3), 273–322.

Rault, W., & Régnier-Loilier, A. (2015). First cohabiting relationships: Recent trends in France. *Population & Societies, 521*. Retrieved April 19, 2019, from https://www.ined.fr/fichier/s_rubrique/23603/population.societies.2015.521.first.cohabiting.relationships.en.pdf

Régnier-Loilier, A. (2016). Partnership trajectories of people in stable non-cohabiting relationships in France. *Demographic Research, 35*(40), 1169–1212. https://doi.org/10.4054/DemRes.2016.35.40

Régnier-Loilier, A. (Ed.). (2017). *A longitudinal approach to family trajectories in France: The generations and gender survey*, INED Population Studies (Vol. 7). Basel: Springer.

Watzlawick, P., Weakland, J. H., & Fisch, F. (2014). *Changement paradoxe et psychothérapie*. Paris: Seuil.

Chapter 5
Changing Couple Relationships in India

Lina Kashyap

5.1 Introduction

Couple relationships in India and in many parts of South East Asia are generally seen as spousal relationships within the institution of marriage. Although in large urban areas today there is a minority group of young people who have opted for live-in relationships, the latter is still quite rare in India. For better or worse, Indians still believe in the institution of marriage.

In the spousal relationship, the partners' behaviour towards each other is continually influenced by three dynamics, namely: issues related to power and control; issues related to how each spouse conveys his/her feelings (likes and dislikes) about the other person; and issues related to the respect or disrespect for each other person's ideas, values and differences (Farrell, Simpson, & Rothman, 2015). The spousal relationship is also continually influenced by the prevailing and changing socio-economic, political, religious and cultural ethos of a society. As society changes over time, it brings about diversity in the attitudes and values of people, specifically about marriage as an institution and spousal relationships within it. This, in turn, influences each spouse's perception of the romantic ideal in their marital relationship, the level of individuality the spouses accord to each other and any dominance by one partner.

This chapter will offer a brief overview of the romantic ideal and power dynamics in the major forms of marriages in India from the ancient to the present times. It will highlight the changing perceptions of Indian youth and their families about marriage as an institution and the influence on dynamics of the marital relationship. Vignettes from discussions with 21 to 27 year old students in the author's class on 'Marriage Counselling' at the Indian university where she was teaching will provide insights to the couple scenario in India as lived by this group of young people.

L. Kashyap (✉)
Retired Professor and Former Deputy Director, The Tata Institute of Social Sciences, Mumbai, Maharashtra, India

5.2 *'Gandharva Vivah'* or Self-Chosen Marriages in Ancient India

Traditionally, there were many classical forms of marriages in ancient India. One of the earliest and most common forms of marriage in Rig Vedic times (from 300 BC to 600 BC) was self-chosen marriages—*Gandharva Vivah*—based on mutual attraction between a man and a woman, with no rituals, witnesses or family participation and which did not require the consent of parents or anyone else (Pandey, 1969). In classical literature, this ancient marriage tradition has been described as one where the woman selects her own husband. They meet each other of their own accord in their ordinary village life, or in various other places such as regional festivals and fairs, begin to enjoy one another's company, and eventually consensually agree to live together. This free choice and mutual attraction were generally approved by their kinsmen (Pandey, 1969).

Thus, women in the Rig Vedic era in India enjoyed an honourable place in the social life of the community. They had the freedom to select their male partner, they could educate themselves, and widows were allowed to remarry. In family matters, though custom and tradition invested the husband with greater powers in the management of the household, in many respects wives were regarded as equal to their husbands and were treated as *'Ardhanginis'* or the better half. Both husband and wife were regarded as the joint heads of the household. The wife was, however, expected to be obedient to the husband, helping him in the performance of his duties, including the religious ones.

As the Vedic religion evolved into classical orthodox Hinduism (ca. 500 BC), large sections of Indian society moved towards patriarchy and caste-based rules which prevented intermixing of ethnic groups and castes. During this period, kinship groups gained prominence as the primary social unit to which all individuals were expected to owe their allegiance. Marriage started being perceived as an event which not only impacted the two individuals concerned, but actually deeply impacted the entire family for both Indian Hindus and Muslims alike and became perceived as a way to form and maintain family alliances (Pandey, 1969).

After the Mogul invasion of India in the sixteenth and seventeenth centuries, Hindu ideology brought about a social shift from diversity of marriage types to a situation where social pressures compelled the girl's family to seek arranged early marriages. Consequently, over time, *Gandharva* marriages based on love and free will became controversial and were discouraged on religious and moral grounds as they were considered unrighteous, lustful, disrespectful of parents and dangerous to society (Pandey, 1969). Parental control of marriage may have emerged during this period as a way to prevent the intermixing of ethnic groups and castes (Hoiberg & Ramchandani, 2000). Early marriages, in which girls were married before they reached puberty, also became prevalent, though not universal. Under this system of early arranged marriages, women were stripped of their traditional independence and honourable status in a variety of ways and placed permanently in male custodianship: first of their fathers in childhood, then of their husbands through married life, and finally of their sons in old age (Kant, 2003). This emergence of early arranged marriages in the Indian subcontinent was consistent with similar developments elsewhere, such as Indonesia and in the Malay–Muslim societies of South East Asia (Jones, 2010).

5.3 Arranged Marriages in Traditional Indian Society

In traditional Indian society, the extended multi-generational or joint family system was more common than the nuclear family system. The traditional family structure was patriarchal, patrilineal and patrilocal, where roles, responsibilities and the control and distribution of resources were strictly determined by age and gender. Total authority rested with the eldest male member of the family. Women were considered inferior to men, although their status increased with age, having sons, and ascending to the head of the domestic household in old age. There was segregation and seclusion of women and the family rarely invested in their education. The young daughter's socialisation was designed to equip her for the demands of her adult roles as wife, daughter-in-law and mother.

Marriage in traditional Indian society was an important event and everyone had to marry. The traditional concept of Hindu marriage was that it was a sacrament, a social obligation and required for the perpetuation of the lineage. It was more economically and socially oriented and took place between two families rather than two individuals. Marriages were mostly endogamous and were generally arranged by parents and members of the kinship group, with class and caste positions and religion as important considerations. Research in this area has demonstrated that arranging marriages has prevailed as an important focus of family attention from the fourth century up till the twenty-first century (Medora, Larson, Hortacsu, & Dave, 2002; Mukhopadhyay & Seymour, 1994). Although non-Hindu Indian groups conceptualise marriage somewhat differently (for instance, Muslims see it as a contract rather than a sacrament), their traditions are equally insistent on premarital virginity, religious endogamy and a father's right to bestow his daughter on the man of his choice.

Arranged marriages can appear as an alien and somewhat 'backward' tradition of marriage practice to Euro-American Western eyes, as they explicitly involve, from a very early stage, the importance of family, kin and community. They are often assumed to be devoid of romantic love (at least at the outset) and more focused on socio-cultural and pragmatic choice (Smart & Shipman, 2004). However, while it is true that in the traditional concept of arranged marriages, practical concerns such as caste, socio-economic class and religion were the primary selection criteria for a marital partner and relationship maintenance, actual idealistic views on love and romance were strongly supported within the cultural milieu. In many classical Indian folklore and mythical love stories, romantic love is usually held in high esteem. There are many songs and folk tales which talk about brides scheming to win their men's primary love away from mothers (Netting, 2010). What needs to be understood here is that although family and kinship ties were indeed the central organising aspect of arranged marriages, this does not mean that the idea of romantic love was absent (Chantler, 2013). The conceptualisation of love in the Indian context included both romantic love, as well as the notion of commitment—not just to each other, but also as part of a wider family and kinship system. In the traditional arranged marriage system, while the marital pair were not 'in love' with each other at the start of their marriage, they had a firm belief that once they committed themselves to the marital relationship romantic love would develop between them over time.

When one looks at the power dynamics in the traditional form of arranged marriages, one finds that the system of marriage, the manner of negotiation between the two families, the rites of marriage (the father of the bride performing the ritual of *kanyadan*—'gift of a maiden'), and the payment of dowry, actually set the seal of inequality on the marital relationship. Indeed, the dowry, made up of durable goods, cash and real or movable property, that the bride's family was expected to give to the bridegroom, his parents and his relatives as a condition of the marriage (Jethmalani & Dey, 1995), actually put great financial burden on the bride's family (Siwan, 2007). In many cases, the dowry system has led to crimes against women, ranging from emotional abuse, to injury and even death (Rao & Correya, 2011). The payment of dowry has now long been prohibited under specific Indian laws, including the Dowry Prohibition Act of 1961 and, subsequently, by Sections 304B and 498A of the Indian Penal Code (Agrahari, 2011).

One must also note that, traditionally, the marital partners were also influenced by gender-based traditional values and norms in their perception and practice of marital roles. In fact, boys and girls were socialised into these roles right from childhood. The wife's status was clearly viewed as inferior and subordinate to that of her husband, not only by men but also by women themselves. The woman commanded respect and honour only to the extent that she excelled in her role as a mother and wife. As wife and mother she was expected to keep the interests of her husband and children above her own. Typically, her own perception was that she needed her husband and children for her own identity and self-esteem and believed that her children and husband needed her. Ramu (1988) who studied roles and power in traditional conjugal relationships reported that the majority of husbands wanted to be seen as decision makers and their wives helped them to maintain such an image.

Present day grandparents are of the generation that had conventional arranged marriages, in which the young couple were allowed to see each other only once or twice before the wedding. In rural areas, matches were arranged between strangers without the couple meeting each other. The boy's family generally had an upper hand and received inquiries and photographs from representatives of several girls' families. The boy's family sometimes sent their relatives to meet the most promising candidates and then went on tour themselves to meet the young women and make a final choice. In other words, parents and other relatives came to an agreement on behalf of the couple. In cities, however, there was more pre-marriage interaction, especially among the educated classes. Photographs were exchanged and sometimes the couple was allowed to see each other and ask each other a few questions with relatives present. Whereas their ancestors had heard mythical love stories, this generation of couples encountered romance in novels, Indian films and short stories which showed the happiest outcomes for partners with similar social backgrounds and for couples in arranged marriages who grew to love each other over time (Uberoi, 2006).

In sum, whereas on the one hand youth from rural India can see and benefit from a general increase in awareness of legislation, fairness and dignity when it comes to issues like child marriages and dowry (Sandhya, 2013), on the other hand, the caste system and parental influence still play a dominant role in choosing marriage partners in these regions. Even in the present times, one still hears about incidents such as so-called 'honour killings' where either the female or male has married 'inappropriately' out of their caste (Deol, 2014). In such instances, relatives, usually male, commit acts of violence against daughters, sisters or mothers to reclaim their family honour from real or suspected actions that are perceived as having brought shame on the family or even the community. These acts of violence can result in mutilation or even death (Kaur, 2014). Most of the honour killings are decided and ordered by the 'custodians of honour', also known as 'caste *Panchayats*', '*Khap Panchayats*' or '*Katta Panchayats*' and which comprise members of a particular caste who can dispense judgement (Rana & Mishra, 2013). Between 2014 and 2017, approximately 500 people—mostly females—died due to honour killings in India (Chandran, 2017). The intermingling of different castes or religions, particularly in marriage, remains taboo in many rural populations; but well-off urban families also resort to drastic action, especially when it involves a higher-caste woman marrying a lower-caste man. As young people become better educated they are emboldened to hold fast to their partner and relationship wishes, opposing both their families and other socio-cultural traditions. This may have detrimental and serious outcomes on their well-being.

It is useful to point out that the terms 'arranged marriage' and 'love marriage' are still used as opposites in India. Traditionally, parents used to associate 'love marriages' with premarital sex, pollution of high castes by lower ones, an attempt by their children to evade their obligations towards their family, and a threat to their very identity. Many parents, especially from the higher socio-economic and caste strata, fought tenaciously to maintain control of a daughter or son. Simultaneously, the young person would curb their desires and own self-interest and, even if they loved somebody, they would hesitate to consider marriage if their parents persisted in their disapproval of the person.

Vignette 1

Reena fell in love with a man of her age who was working in the same company as her. He was from a lower caste than her and was from a small town in South India. When her parents came to know about the affair, they were both angry and tearful, and attempted to convince Reena that this man was actually trying to take advantage of her because of their better financial position and status in society. Reena agreed not to meet the man again and to resign from her job. Within the next three months a marriage was arranged for her with a man who lived in the UK and had a well-paid job.

5.4 Arranged Marriages in Contemporary Times

The last two decades of the twentieth century and the first two decades of the twenty-first century have witnessed far-reaching socio-economic-political changes in Indian society as a result of neoliberalism and globalisation. These changes have, in turn, brought about significant shifts in the attitudes and values of the people, specifically about how marriage as an institution and spousal relationships within it are viewed in Indian society.

With expanding social reform and female emancipation that accompanied economic and literacy growth after India's independence in 1947, many predicted the gradual demise of arranged marriages in India and the inexorable rise of so-called 'love marriages' (Hoiberg & Ramchandani, 2000). However, despite the far reaching social changes of the past 60 years, in twenty-first-century India, the arranged marriage tradition has proved to be surprisingly robust and arranging marriages has remained an important focus of family attention (Hoiberg & Ramchandani, 2000). The role of finding a spouse for their child is still taken very seriously by parents who see it as their main obligation to their children, along with providing them a good education. This is evidenced in a comment by one mother to her friend when she was in the process of arranging a marriage for her son: *'We are not just looking for a wife for our son but also a daughter-in-law for our family. Of course we are not going to force him to marry someone he is incompatible with. However, his marriage will affect everyone in the family, so we have to select very carefully and then hope for the best'.*

But how do contemporary young Indians and their families view the institution of marriage and what are their views about the couple relationship? Research on the family has not been accorded the importance it should have been given and is one of the less developed areas of social research in India. Given the dearth of research on this topic, the chapter will refer to discussions among young university students 21–27 years of age which were held during a course on 'Marriage Counselling'. (For the sake of confidentiality, pseudonyms will be used throughout.) These students were very articulate as many of them were currently going through the process of their families finding a 'good' life partner for them. The comments and observations made by the different student groups during these classes over the span of about 10 years since the early 2000s can offer a broad understanding of the changing perception towards marriage as an institution and marital roles in contemporary Indian society. At the same time, one acknowledges that these views pertain to a particular group of young people and may not be representative of prevailing attitudes and practices in other groups in both urban and rural regions.

5.4.1 Students' Perception of Marriage

In a discussion of their perception of marriage in contemporary times, most of the university students involved were looking forward to getting married and entering a new phase in their lives. Having said that, all the students were unanimous in their opinion that, unlike in the past, they no longer considered marriage as an inevitable state, but a matter of choice—whether to marry at all, whom to marry and when. Shobha, a very bright student had her own ideas about her future: *'I have told my parents that I would prefer not to marry at all as I want to concentrate on my career. I have no time to date and have not yet come across any man who has interested me'*. Another bright student, Sita, had rejected a man from her own caste who held a prestigious high paid job. His parents used to proudly boast that they had received proposals from more than 100 girls and she had been one of the few girls shortlisted by them for a meeting. Her candid explanation for rejecting this much sought after man was as follows:

> During the first meeting itself, when I asked him what he thought of working women, he very arrogantly stated that in his frame of reference his future wife's career would always be secondary. In fact, in that half hour's meeting, he spoke most of the time and hardly allowed me to say much. Though my parents were very sad and disappointed, after they heard my reasons they accepted my decision and have been very supportive and sweet.... My grandmother ... is still hoping that I will get back to him.... According to her, he was such a good catch... and I must learn to compromise and adjust. I have no regrets at all. I definitely want to be the one to decide and not anybody else whom to marry and whether I want to work after marriage or not.

5.4.2 Students' Views on Arranged and Love Marriages

In a particular discussion about the issue of choice, the debate about the merits and demerits of 'arranged' and 'love' or 'self-chosen' marriages was lively and insightful. For more than half the students in the class, their families had started receiving marriage proposals which generally contained a resumé, horoscope and photograph of the prospective young boys or girls. Shortlisting and discussions on the promising proposals were already underway within the family. The students were also included in the discussions, yet significantly, at least half of them preferred that their parents chose a marriage partner for them. When asked to elaborate on their reasons for this preference, Asha explained, *'I feel that my parents are wiser and have my best interests at heart. Also, if I marry with my parents' approval and blessings, I can always count on them to help me if I am ever in any difficulty'*. Rohit, who was the first member of his village to have managed to go to college, had a similar perspective:

> My parents have sacrificed a lot to send me to college in Mumbai. I will have to marry a girl whom my parents and other relatives choose for me and she will have to be from my caste. It is my social obligation to my parents and my family. I will be patient with her and I know that we will learn to love each other.

However, other young people wanted to maintain some say in the choice of their partner and negotiated this with their parents. Manisha was quite demanding:

> I have told my parents that I agree that they look for a marital partner for me, but have also informed them that I want to be allowed to have more meetings alone with the prospective man and be given enough time to make a decision. I have also negotiated with them that I will only agree to marry if I find that the man selected by them is compatible with me at an individual level.

Nilesh who was from Delhi, very succinctly outlined a pragmatic stance to the matter looking at both the short term and long term:

> To my mind, falling in love is risky business because backgrounds of the couple may be diverse and their expectations from each other unrealistic. I also think that the physical attraction could be a passing phase and so cannot be the basis for a marriage. On the other hand, I think that arranged marriages are more stable because they guarantee similarity of religion, food and social class. I have told my parents that I am willing to marry a girl who is physically presentable, well-educated and she must have a good nature and disposition so that we can become good companions and friends. I am sure love will grow. I am not too concerned about her family background.

A few of the students in the classes who were currently dating argued in favour of love or self-chosen marriages. The female students among them felt that a love relationship would be an equaliser; that the woman would be able to negotiate for greater understanding and equality with her partner and try to neutralise male dominance whilst working towards a more egalitarian couple relationship. Neela who was in a serious relationship with a fellow student had a set plan:

> We have decided to get married to each other. After both of us complete our post graduate degrees, we will both first look for a job. Each one of us will then approach our parents, not to announce our engagement, but to ask their permission to marry. We will try to convince them that we are compatible in every way, our horoscopes match and we love each other. We know our parents. Initially, they may resist the idea, but we think they will finally give their consent once they realise we are not trying to break the family and want their approval and support.

There is a trend now in India for couples like Neela and her friend who came to know each other on their own and become involved romantically, to go through the process of an arranged marriage with that specific partner in mind. Since arranged marriages result in a deep meshing and unification of extended families and are believed to contribute to marital stability, many young couples today try to orchestrate their marriages with each other through the processes of an arranged marriage. These marriages are often referred to as 'self-arranged marriages' or 'love-cum-arranged marriages'.

As indicated earlier, one of the most prominent changes that have occurred in partner selection is increased freedom of choice. Young Indians are negotiating with their parents to have more opportunities to meet partners themselves, more time to make a decision and more latitude for rejecting an offer. What is also significant is that during the discussions with the university students, irrespective of whether they were in favour of arranged or love marriage, all of them expressed a strong support for romantic love, which they believed should be an integral part of married life. Even in arranged marriages they trusted that love would develop between partners over time.

5.4.3 Students' Expectations from Marriage

Another revealing discussion among the students evolved around the most important characteristics young people would look for in the person they would like to marry, and in the kind of marital relationship they aspired for. A number of significant changes from the traditional attitudes and values emerged. For instance, attributes in men included being well educated, kind, honest and understanding, as well as having a stable job and decent salary and coming from a family who was highly regarded in the community. A number of students felt that physical appearance was also important, but not necessarily top of the list.

Almost all the female students in the various discussion felt that equality should underline the husband–wife relationship. Asha made it a point to show her precise thinking: *'For me, equality does not mean that my husband and I should share exactly the same roles around the house. For me, equality means that both of us should work together to divide our responsibilities fairly'*. The issue of developing a mutually respectful relationship with the partner and with in-laws was also highlighted, especially considering that some initial years of marriage might involve cohabiting with parents. As Lata explained:

> Most of us are aware and have accepted that at least for the first few years of marriage we will be living in a joint family with our husband's parents and relatives. That being the case, I feel that I should not be the only one to make all the adjustments as my mother had to. I am very clear that my marital family must respect my individuality. I would like a partner who has the maturity and confidence to offer me a more equitable relationship and to support me to develop a more equitable relationship with my in-laws for myself and for us as a couple.

The importance of each partner facilitating an environment where their partner was conferred love and respect by the marital parents was a common assertion.

5.4.4 *Summary Overview of Evolving Attitudes and Practices with Respect to Marriage*

The perceptions shared by the university students is in consonance with studies that have pointed out that, even in the twenty-first century, arranged marriages have continued to be accepted without any difficulty as a legitimate way of finding a mate even among all classes of Indian society (Hoiberg & Ramchandani, 2000). Young Indians have moved away from the traditional perception of marriage as a social obligation for the perpetuation of lineage. They now consider that people should get married for love, companionship and individual happiness which is a radical shift in perspective. Moreover, young Indians are not only seeking someone who is socially suitable, but they are also seeking a partner who is compatible with them on an individual level and who can meet their personal needs for connection and intimacy.

Given the above shifts in expectations, many aspects of arranged marriages have evolved for the better in twenty-first-century India. The caste system in urban regions is somewhat less rigid and the preferences of the couple are taken into account. It is possible to marry outside of the sub-caste, or one's own language, or province as long as the partner is still within the same caste. With the legal banning of child marriages and the legal age of marriage now 18 years for females and 21 years for males, families are delaying the marriage of their sons and daughters until they have acquired university degrees, and of the sons until they have a stable job. In India, getting a good marriage proposal depends heavily on the educational qualifications of the male and female. Therefore, parents even from the lower middle class of society make many sacrifices in order to pay for their children's higher education, which is highly subsidised by the government and therefore not as expensive as in many Western countries. Another related change that has come about pertains to the criteria for selection of the life partner. In urban areas in particular, greater emphasis is now placed on women's education and employment status, rather than just efficiency in the domestic arena.

Parental attitudes have also changed. Parents are now showing an increased willingness to adjust to their children's romantic aspirations as they have realised that their adult children have their own beliefs and attitudes about love and romance, about marital life, and what qualities they are seeking in a lifetime partner. Consequently, with changing times, as Shukla and Kapadia (2007) have pointed out, the definition of arranged marriage has been suitably expanded to place 'the individual will' at the heart of the process, thus gradually shifting its focus from serving social and religious obligations to meeting the needs of individuals. Moreover, parents now allow the prospective partners to interact more freely, over the phone or even face-to-face. The concept of courtship has also gained favour, with the couple getting the opportunity to know each other, sometimes for as long as a year between the engagement and the actual marriage dates. Young men and women are now rarely forced to marry someone against their wishes and both men and women (men more than women) are allowed a right of refusal of the partners. On their part, the young people are reluctant to marry someone whom their parents disapprove of as they still believe that, in India, children and parents need each other throughout the entire course of life (Netting, 2010). The role of the parents in contemporary times seems to have moved from being the main decision makers in the marriage of their children, to allowing their children more choice in the selection of their life partners, while continuing to look after the material aspects of arranging marriages.

The whole procedure of arranging marriages has also seen some major modernisation as Indian youth and their families, from practically all strata of society, have found ways to adapt this mode of marriage to accommodate to the changing socio-economic realities and the aspirations of the Indian youth. With the loosening of kinship bonds, many urban parents no longer have the social reach that they had before the rise of nuclear families, especially in cities in India. Therefore, though families may still use their personal networks, caste directories and newspaper advertisements, now marriage proposals are increasingly being solicited through the internet with the rise of matchmaking websites such as *shaadi.com* (*shaadi* is the Indian word for wedding), which claims to be the largest matrimonial service in the world. Notably, whether through conventional means or more modern channels, young people are being brought together by their parents and allowed to get to know each other. Decisions to get engaged often happen after a few meetings. In some cases, the relationship forms quite strongly from the outset, whereas in other instances it might take some time to solidify.

Vignette 2

Neha is a university student who had recently got engaged. Her parents initially put an advertisement in the national Newspapers soliciting proposals from interested males but were not happy with the proposals they had received. One day, her father's friend told her parents about a young man from their own caste who had a similar socio-economic background. The parents showed interest so the friend gave them the young man's biodata, horoscope and some photographs. Neha read his bio and saw his photos. She decided he looked quite nice and agreed to meet him. Their horoscopes also matched. Soon after the families met in the boy's house and Neha and the young man were invited to go to another room and talk to each other alone. Neha was feeling very jittery and had no clue what to say to him. But he immediately put her at ease in the way he asked her about herself. She liked him the moment she saw him. They agreed to meet a second time. He picked her up from home and they went to a restaurant. They could not stop talking to each other and only when they noticed that the waiter was hovering around them did they realise that 3 h had passed They met twice more and Neha realised that although they had similar opinions about some things, they also had very different opinions about a lot of other things. However, she felt he respected her views and did not try to impose his views on her. She also realised that she was comfortable with him. After their last meeting, she had decided to marry the man but did not tell him anything because she first needed to consult her parents. The parents were happy, as well as relieved, as they too had liked the boy and so they conveyed Neha's approval to the boy's family and in a week's time they were engaged.

Vignette 3

Rita had been engaged for over a year. She was shortlisted by her fiancé's family through the online portal *shaadi.com*. They thought she would fit in suitably with their family. Rita met her fiancé alone only twice before he conveyed to his and her parents that he would like to marry Rita. At the time of her engagement Rita felt she was getting engaged to a stranger and it was quite a frightening feeling. But somehow everything changed after the engagement. She is now used to his being part of her life and of at least speaking to him on the phone every day, if not meeting. When they do not meet or speak to each other for 2 days at a stretch she feels that something is wrong in her life. She is not sure whether this would translate to what is called 'romantic love', or having 'fallen in love', but she is certain that she will be living her whole life with her fiancé and do so very willingly and very happily.

In a recent study, Gala and Kapadia (2014) found that while commitment to a relationship was very important to emerging adults in India, they expressed strong support for romantic love as well, which they believed should be an integral part of married life. Even in arranged marriages they trusted that love would develop between partners over time. According to Netting (2010), whereas their ancestors heard mythical love stories and their parents encountered romance in novels and films, young Indians today can imagine love marriage as a real possibility for themselves.

5.5 Conclusion

Young Indian people are redefining their beliefs about love and romance, their attitudes towards marital life, and what qualities they are seeking in a lifetime partner. They seem to be willingly stepping out of their traditionally demarcated roles and moving towards a more egalitarian concept of marriage. It is apparent from the narratives of the young university students, as they spoke about love and family-arranged marriages, that they did not see themselves caught between mutually exclusive systems. In fact, the distinction between arranged and love marriages is becoming increasingly blurred. Young people today are actually bypassing the conventional dichotomy of love-versus-arranged marriage and using the best of both approaches, either simultaneously or by actually constructing new combinations. They are combining hegemonic Indian traditional values and individualistic romantic values as they commit themselves to support their parents' and their family's cherished customs by matching horoscopes and bringing the bride into her husband's family, while seeking a conjugal partnership that is intimate, egalitarian and loving (Netting, 2010). In return, it appears that parents are increasingly allowing their adult children to choose their own partners, provided these are presented to parents for approval.

It is clear that contemporary shifts in marriage planning and practices are allowing for a dynamic relationship between love and material conditions in India. Therefore, to focus initially on the material, which arranged marriages seem to do, is not necessarily to debar romantic love, as even in self-arranged or love marriages once a couple makes a decision to marry, the couple has to sort out the material aspects related to getting married. Hence, such a conceptualisation actually blurs the boundaries between love and arranged marriage practices. Although differences still exist in the socio-cultural expectations and practices of urban and rural regions with respect to relationships and marriage, young Indian people seem to be willing to look beyond the material and beyond tradition to seek a partner for a mutually fulfilling relationship and, as far as possible, still respects parental desires.

References

Agrahari, G. (2011). *Law relating to dowry prohibition, cruelty, and harassment: An up-to-date, lucid, and exhaustive commentary with case law on the Dowry Prohibition Act, 1961*. Delhi: India Law House.

Chandran, R. (2017). *In south India, a 20-year-old survivor of honor killing turns crusader.* Thomson Reuters Foundation. Retrieved April 19, 2019, from https://www.reuters.com/article/us-india-women-crime/in-south-india-a-20-year-old-survivor-of-honor-killing-turns-crusader-idUSKBN1EN0O4

Chantler, K. (2013). What's love got to do with marriage? *Families, Relationships and Societies, 3*(1), 19–33.

Deol, S. S. (2014). Honour killing in India: A study of the Punjab state. *International Research Journal of Social Sciences, 3*(6), 7–16.

Farrell, A. K., Simpson, J. A., & Rothman, A. J. (2015). The relationship power inventory: Development and validation. *Personal Relationships, 22*(3), 387–413.

Gala, J., & Kapadia, S. (2014). Romantic love, commitment and marriage in emerging adulthood in an Indian context: Views of emerging adults and middle adults. *Psychology and Developing Societies, 26*(1), 115–141. https://doi.org/10.1177/0971333613516233

Hoiberg, D., & Ramchandani, I. (2000). *Students' Britannica India: Select essays*. India: Popular Prakashan.

Jethmalani, R., & Dey, P. K. (1995). Dowry deaths and access to justice. In R. Jethmalani (Ed.), *Kali's Yug: Empowerment, law and dowry deaths* (pp. 36–38). Delhi: Har Anand Publications.

Jones, G. W. (2010). *Changing marriage patterns in Asia*. Asia Research Institute: Working paper no. 131. Retrieved April 19, 2019, from http://www.ari.nus.edu.sg/wps/wps10_131.pdf

Kant, A. (2003). *Women and the law*. India: APH Publishing.

Kaur, R. (2014). Honour killing: A global scenario. *International Research Journal of Management Sociology & Humanity, 5*(11), 206–214.

Medora, N. P., Larson, J. H., Hortacsu, N., & Dave, P. (2002). Perceived attitudes towards romanticism; a cross-cultural study of American, Asian-Indian, and Turkish young adults. *Journal of Comparative Family Studies, 33*(2), 155–178.

Mukhopadhyay, C. P., & Seymour, S. (1994). *Women, education, and family structure in India*. Boulder, CO: Westview Press.

Netting, S. N. (2010). Marital ideoscapes in 21st-century India: Creative combinations of love and responsibility. *Journal of Family Issues, 31*(6), 707–726.

Pandey, R. (1969). *Hindu saṁskāras: Socio-religious study of the Hindu sacraments*. New Delhi: Motilal Banarasidass Publications.

Ramu, G. N. (1988). Marital roles and power: Perceptions and reality in an urban setting. *Journal of Comparative Family Studies, 19*(2), 207–228.

Rana, P. K., & Mishra, B. P. (2013). Honor killings: A gross violation of human rights and its challenges. *International Journal of Humanities and Social Science Invention, 2*(6), 24–29.

Rao, A., & Correya, S. S. (Eds.). (2011). *Leading cases on dowry*. New Delhi: Human Rights Law Network. Retrieved April 19, 2019, from https://hrln.org/wp-content/uploads/2017/09/Leading-Cases-on-Dowry.pdf

Sandhya, S. J. (2013). Mate selection preferences among college students in Bagalkot, Karnataka. *Journal of Humanities and Social Science, 15*(1), 55–59.

Shukla, S., & Kapadia, S. (2007). Transition in marriage partner selection process: Are matrimonial advertisements an indication? *Psychology and Developing Societies, 19*(1), 37–54.

Siwan, A. (2007). The economics of dowry and bride price. *Journal of Economic Perspectives, 21*(4), 151–174.

Smart, C., & Shipman, B. (2004). Visions in monochrome: Families, marriage and the individualization thesis. *The British Journal of Sociology, 55*(4), 491–509.

Uberoi, P. (2006). *Freedom and destiny: Gender, family, and popular culture in India*. Delhi: Oxford University Press.

Chapter 6
Couple Relationships in the Arab Region: Changes and Renegotiations

Hoda Rashad, Zeinab Khadr, and Eman Mostafa

6.1 Introduction

Couple relationships in the Arab region are being shaped within two types of opposing forces. Such forces produce conflicting influences on the positioning of marriage among different potential forms of couple relationships, as well as on the dynamics of the relationship between partners within a couple.

The first type of forces impacting couple relationships includes a wide array of forces supporting individual control and freedom of choices. Key among these forces are the changing values regarding gender dynamics, equity, and reproductive rights. These are augmented by the increased opportunities for social interactions between sexes, as well as significant changes in the acquisition of individual attributes, allowing more autonomy of youth and supporting their ability to defy societal and parental expectations. This first group of forces fosters a move away from marriage unions and toward less formal types of relationships. It also fosters more equitable dynamics within such relationships. The expectations are that these relationships are based on individual choices and feature more closeness and romantic emotions.

The second type of forces includes the centrality of marriage in people's livelihoods, together with the traditional division of gender roles. The centrality of marriage derives from perceiving marriage as a signal of lifetime achievement and as

---

H. Rashad (✉) · E. Mostafa
The Social Research Center, The American University in Cairo, Cairo, Egypt
e-mail: hrashad@aucegypt.edu; emanmost@aucegypt.edu

Z. Khadr
The Social Research Center, The American University in Cairo, Cairo, Egypt

Faculty of Economics and Political Science, Cairo University, Cairo, Egypt
e-mail: zeinabk@aucegypt.edu

granting the only legitimate and religiously and socially approved license for sexual relations and reproduction. Indeed, the Arab societies have not bestowed their moral acceptance upon nonformal couple relationships. Such relationships are seen as defying religious codes. The term "Harram," implying not abiding by religious doctrines, is invoked to reflect the epitome of disapproval. Religious and cultural oppositions to nonformal sexual unions are quite strong. Thus, nonformal sexual unions are shrouded with secrecy and shunned by society. Children who are born out of wedlock are discriminated against and marginalized, and so-called "honor killing" continues to be resorted to in more conservative social groups. Indeed, a recent study soliciting views on whether women should be virgins when they marry received a high percentage of agreement ranging from 61% to 82% in Morocco and Lebanon, respectively (El Feki, Heilman, & Barker, 2017). Notably, these two countries are generally known to be more liberal than most other Arab countries.

It is worth highlighting that nonformal relationships do not entail any legal and institutional rights. A clear example is evidenced in how common law *Urfi* marriage is perceived and addressed in legal and institutional settings. *Urfi* marriage is defined as a non-registered marriage that meets the religious criteria of marriage (acceptance, witnesses, and announcement). However, in many Arab countries, such marriages (particularly those which are not publicly announced) do not enjoy societal approval and legislative protection. They are perceived as illicit affairs and do not carry with them any legal rights for partners of the unions. Only recently has the ability of women to obtain divorce from *Urfi* marriage (but not other legal stipulation applicable to married partners), and recognition of the legal rights of offspring, come about in some Arab countries.

The traditional expectations of gender roles within formal marriage unions are another widespread force within the second group of forces. Such a force derives from a societal endorsement of assigning the breadwinning responsibility to the husband; an endorsement that is perceived by many as not contradictory to gender equality, but as existing alongside an assertion of equality between sexes. This perception is mainly anchored in widely accepted religious interpretations and supported by legislative stipulations. The religious interpretation argues that such division of roles is not indicative of gender inequality and is more in tune with widely practiced asymmetries in responsibilities. In other words, since the husband is the breadwinner, he has more rights and is the guardian of the household. The legislative stipulation enforces breadwinning and financial support roles as pertaining to the household males (e.g., husbands, brothers, uncles).

This second type of forces, therefore, sustains the institution of marriage as framed by a patriarchal division of roles and responsibilities. The expectations are that the relationships governed by the second group of forces lend themselves to pressured or even forced marriage arrangements and are characterized by uneven power relationships and less closeness and romantic ideals.

The objective of this chapter is to investigate the potential impact of these competing forces on two aspects of couple relationships, mainly the positioning of marriage and the dynamics within it. This chapter also investigates two important dimensions of couple relationships that interact closely with positioning and dynamics of marriage. These dimensions are the level of satisfaction within marital unions and the possible emergence of a new framework of conscious choice exercised by youth in marriage formation.

6.2 Positioning of Marriage Among Other Forms of Couple Relationships

Given the ongoing societal shifts, it is worth investigating some of the changes surrounding the institution of marriage—whether marriage continues to be the dominant form in couple relationships and which are the other new forms of relationships.

6.2.1 Dominance of Marriage Unions

A number of earlier studies have described the many changes that Arab countries have experienced in terms of the timing, intensity, and stability of marriage, as well as in the characteristics of marriage and marriage partners (Hopkins, 2001; Osman & Shahd, 2001; Rashad & Osman, 2001; Rashad, Osman, & Roudi-Fahimi, 2005). The analysis in the following section draws heavily on two more recent studies (Rashad, 2015; Rashad & Khadr, 2017) after adjusting some of the measures used by introducing more up-to-date and more relevant statistics.

As a general overview, marriage patterns in the Arab region have moved from a uniform base of early and universal marriage toward delayed and nonuniversal marriage. Arab countries, however, have progressed differently along this path. Table 6.1 summarizes the current status of Arab countries within the groupings of relatively moderate changes, more significant changes and in transition.

One group of Arab countries (nine countries) has continued to have large proportions of youth marrying at an early age, and has experienced moderate delays in average age at marriage with spinsterhood remaining at a low or medium level. Another group (seven countries) has experienced more significant changes. The proportion of adults marrying young is low, and there are significant delays in average age at marriage and a marked increase in spinsterhood. A few remaining countries are in a transitional phase, but are mainly moving toward the second group.

The picture is less well documented for marriage dissolution. At one level the perception is that marriage dissolution is quite high, that divorce is increasing at an alarming rate, that it occurs mainly within short marriage duration and that the Gulf countries face a particularly serious challenge. This perception is supported by articles in social media raising the alarm, and by studies using non-precise measures of the phenomenon in question. Many of these refer to the number of divorce cases per day or per hour and sometimes even per second (Abd Allah, 2016; Abdul Ghafour,

Table 6.1 Groupings of Arab countries by the nature of changes in the tempo and density of marriage

Country	Early marriage %	Age at marriage Average years	Never married %
Significant changes			
Libya	2.0	31.2	31.6
Kuwait	n/av	27.5	24.5
Lebanon	6.0	28.3	23.7
Algeria	3.0	29.1	23.1
Tunisia	2.0	28.5	17.1
Bahrain	n/av	26.9	32.0
Djibouti	5.0	26.9	12.7
Moderate changes			
Somalia	45.0	20.4	1.3
Mauritania	34.0	21.6	5.8
Sudan	33.0	21.9	7.4
Comoros	32.0	24.2	4.3
Yemen	32.0	23.0	6.0
Iraq	24.0	22.0	11.1
Syria	18.0	25.4	11.4
Egypt	17.0	22.1	3.1
Palestine	15.0	23.5	10.6
In transition			
Morocco	13.0	26.3	22.9
Jordan	8.0	25.0	13.7
Qatar	4.0	25.8	12.3
UAE	n/av	25.3	7.6
Oman	n/av	25.6	7.2
Saudi Arabia	n/av	24.9	6.0

n/av.: Data not available

Changes: Significant change: Low proportion of early marriage before age 18 (2–6%), delayed marriage (age 27–31 years), high spinsterhood (13–22%); Moderate change: Fairly high proportion of early marriage before age 18 (15–45%), low (age 20–24 years) to moderate (age 25–26 years) delay in getting married, low spinsterhood (<12%); In transition: Low to moderate proportion of early marriage (4–13%), moderate (age 25–26 years) delay in getting married, low to moderate spinsterhood (6–23%)

Measures: Early marriage: % women aged 20–24 who married before their 18th birthday; Age at marriage: Average number of years spent in single status; Spinsterhood: % never married (women 35–39 years of age)

Sources: (1) United Nations, Department of Economic and Social Affairs, Population Division (2015) World Marriage Data 2015; (2) United Nations, Department of Economic and Social Affairs, Population Division (2013) World Marriage Data 2012; (3) UNICEF (n.d.) UNICEF Data: Monitoring the Situation of Children and Women; (4) Roudi-Fahimi and Ibrahim (2013) Ending Child Marriage in the Arab Region

2015; Olarte, 2010; Pathak, 2013; Younes, 2016). Others use the number of divorce cases relative to number of marriage cases (Al Munajjed, 2010; El Haddad, 2003). Clearly, as stated in Rashad and Khadr (2017), these statistics cannot capture the prevalence and incidence of divorce as they need to be related to those exposed to the risk of divorce (number in marital unions) and to a time frame.

The crude divorce rate (divorces per 1000 inhabitants) of eight Arab countries ranges between 0.7 and 2.6 which, when compared to the global range of 0.4–4.6 (Divorce Sciences, 2016), suggests that only two of the eight Arab countries (Bahrain, Jordan) can be considered to experience mid-level divorce rates. Kuwait is an exception, and is among the highest on the global scene, with a crude divorce rate of 4.5 per 1000 inhabitants (GCC Statistical Center, 2016).

A more sensitive indicator of the prevalence of divorce is provided by relating the number of currently divorced women to those ever married. Table 6.2 documents that the prevalence of divorce is quite high in Gulf countries and that Kuwait, in particular, is exceptionally high. It also shows that in Egypt the prevalence is the lowest among the seven countries considered. In addition, the data on the percentages of divorced women in younger age groups lend support to the perception of a trend for marriages of shorter durations, particularly among Gulf countries and Jordan.

Indeed, this increasing incidence of divorce among younger age groups (reflecting shorter marriage durations) is confirmed by 2015 data by age groups in Egypt. The divorce incidence rate for those aged 25–29 is 1.3, and increases at young ages to reach 2.7 for those aged 18–19. In contrast, the divorce rate is only 0.9 for those aged 35–39 and decreases to 0.4 for those aged 55–59 (CAPMAS, 2016, 2017).

Table 6.2 Percent divorced women among ever-married women aged 15–49 in select Arab countries

Age groups	Kuwaiti women 2011	Bahraini women 2010	Saudi women 2010	Egyptian women 2017	Jordan DHS 2012	Algeria census 2008	Tunisia MICS 2011–2012
15–19	4.4	4.6	2.5	0.3	4.8	1.9	7.7[a]
20–24	5.8	5.4	4.8	0.7	3.0	2.0	1.4
25–29	7.8	5.1	2.1	1.4	3.4	2.6	1.1
30–34	8.8	5.0	3.8	2.1	4.0	3.3	2.4
35–39	9.4	5.4	6.0	2.4	3.0	3.9	3.6
40–44	9.4	5.8	5.4	2.6	2.7	4.2	3.5
45–49	9.4	6.3	10.0	2.6	4.0	4.2	2.3
Total	8.5	5.5	5.0	1.7	n/av	n/av	n/av

Note: National women in GCC countries; n/av.: data not available
Sources: Bahrain Central Informatics Organization (2015), Population, Housing, Buildings, Establishments and Agriculture Census 2010; Kuwait Central Statistics Bureau (n.d.) Population, Housing, Buildings and Establishments 2011; Saudi Department of Statistics and Information (n.d.). Detailed Results of Population and Housing Census 1431H; CAPMAS (2017) Population Census 2017. For Jordan, Algeria and Tunisia: United Nations, Department of Economic and Social Affairs, Population Division (2015); World Marriage Data 2015
[a]Based on a few number of cases

Also data from Egypt indicate that 43% of recent divorce cases occur within the first 5 years of marriage (CAPMAS, 2016).

Clearly, while the analysis of marriage dissolution is an area calling for much more in-depth study, and while the level of divorce is not exceptionally high in general, the perceptions of an increasing trend and a concentration of divorce within marriages of short duration, as well as a higher divorce rate in Gulf countries, appear valid.

The previous changes are bound to have an impact on the dominance of the marriage institution among the many other potential forms of couple relationships. Also a higher proportion of the population living in nonmarital unions is expected to result in an increase in other new forms of couple relationships. Acknowledging these hypotheses, the dominance of marriage was investigated in various Arab countries. Figure 6.1 shows that, with very few exceptions, the population ever married in the age group 30–49 dominates all Arab countries and there is a higher percentage of females than males in this category. The notable exception is in the two Gulf countries of Bahrain and Kuwait, where the percentages are very likely affected by a large proportion of foreign workers (particularly males) in their population. The change in marriage patterns in these countries has started to touch on the dominance of marital unions within this older group.

Figure 6.2 pertains to the younger age group (20–29) and tells a completely different story. In all the nine Arab countries considered, a higher percentage of males have never been in a marital union (between 52.71% and as high as 91.61%). For

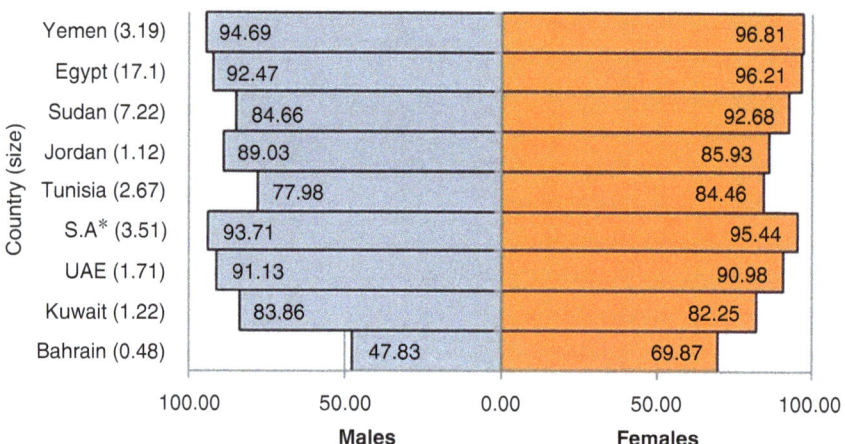

Fig. 6.1 Percentages of population aged 30–49 ever married and the size of the total population in this age group in millions by sex and country (Source: Rashad, 2015). ∗S.A. data refers to nationals only

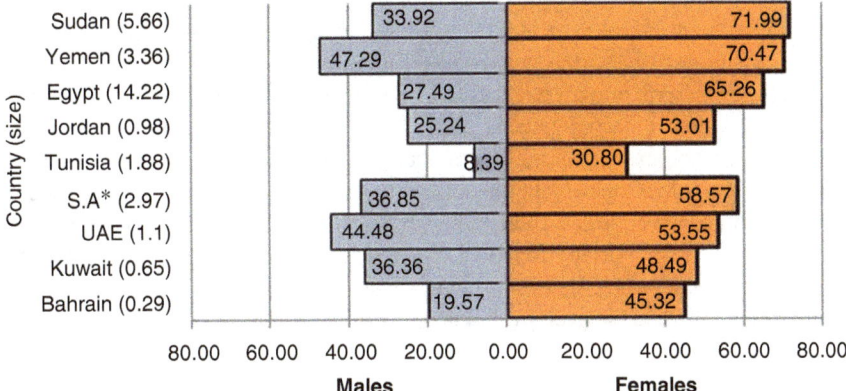

Fig. 6.2 Percentages of population aged 20–29 ever married and the size of the total population in this age group in millions by sex and country. (Source: Rashad, 2015). *S.A. data refers to nationals only

females, the percentages that have never been married is less than half the population in six out of the nine countries (ranging from 28.01% to 46.99%). Nonetheless, there is still a sizeable percentage of females who have never been married in this age group.

In brief, marriage continues to dominate, but its dominance is significantly receding among the younger generation. The implications of a sizeable, predominantly young social group, living outside marriage unions, but within a conservative context are bound to be quite significant. A number of dimensions related to these implications have been touched upon (Khadr & El-Zeini, 2001; Rashad, 2000), particularly demographic macro-level dimensions that lend themselves to aggregate data analysis (e.g., fertility levels, household structures, living arrangements). Other implications of a more sociological nature have been sparsely studied, forced to be limited to small areas and more anthropological types of analysis or to conceptual theorizations.

6.2.2 New Forms of Couple Relationships

Nonconventional marital unions and sexual relations outside marriages are traditionally taboo behaviors, but which are currently more openly acknowledged in public discourse. Nowadays, many articles and debate forums address these unconventional forms of couple relationships. In Egypt, for example, the perception of significant increase in *Urfi* marriages, particularly among high school and university students, is widely shared. Additionally, the changes in legislation to allow children born out of wedlock to acquire birth certificates is an implicit acknowledgment of the practice.

In the Gulf countries, the increase in studies investigating *Messyar* and *Muta'a* marriages is another open acknowledgment. These marriages involve a type of temporary marriage contract where the husband and wife are able to renounce some marital rights, such as living together. The practice is often used in some Islamic countries to give legal recognition to nonconventional unions and transient cohabitation arrangements. However, the acknowledgment of these forms of relationships does not imply societal endorsement. Accurate measurement of prevalence is also lacking.

A pioneering study (El Tawila & Khadr, 2004) conducted in Egypt revealed that around 70% of unmarried male youth and 59% of unmarried female youth in the age group 18–30 believe that relationships between couples (not necessarily sexual) are very common. When these youth were probed about their actual experience, around a third of males and a quarter of females stated that they are experiencing a relationship with the other sex, though underreporting is likely given the reluctance to admit these relationships. Both males and females stated that these relationships are detrimental to the female's reputation and would affect her future marriage prospects. The question on actual engagement in sexual relations was an indirect one. Only 13% of males and around 4% of females stated that they knew a close acquaintance who was actually engaged in a sexual relationship. An earlier study conducted in Egypt on a sample of university students reported that 26% of males and 3% of females stated that they had engaged in at least one sexual encounter (El Zanaty & El-Daw, 1996). It is acknowledged that this latter data may not reflect the current realities.

In the El Tawila and Khadr (2004) study, the spread of *Urfi* marriages was difficult to measure. Around 8.5% of males and 4% of females stated that they knew someone in such a marriage. What is interesting is that despite the negative attitudes toward these marriages, the majority expressed that it provides a better framing than engaging in open sexual relationships. So while the general attitude is that most cases for *Urfi* marriages are a pretext and cover for premarital sex, such a pretext was quite valued: Males felt that such a pretext is a shield against any potential accusation of adultery; females considered it a reassurance that they were not violating religious doctrines and offered some degree of legitimacy.

As suggested earlier, other forms of nonconventional marriages that are perceived as increasing using anecdotal evidence are *Muta'a* and *Messyar*. *Muta'a* is an arrangement bound by a time frame and is practiced by a sect of Moslems (e.g., Shi'ites in southern Lebanon). *Messyar* is an arrangement in which a man marries without any of the financial responsibilities (whether before or during relationship) that a standard Arab marriage requires. This form of marriage mainly features in the Gulf countries where non-married females tend to enjoy high levels of education and financial autonomy. Notably, due to the evolution of *Messyar* marriage "Islamic society may be far happier with consensual sexual relations as long as those actions are legitimized by marriage" (Al-Nasr, 2011 p. 50). These newer forms of marriages are short-term marriages that enjoy some forms of religious and legal legitimacy in Islamic countries. They provide a frame for Arab youth that allows satisfaction of sexual desires outside formal unions.

Vignette
Basem, a 32-year-old man, got married for the first time 7 years ago. He had sought a wife with a good upbringing—who could raise children and keep the family together and someone he could trust and talk to. In the first few weeks of his marriage to Zeinab he could see that she would do anything to make him happy and was very thankful, but he still felt there was something missing in their relationship. After a few months of marriage he was continually dissatisfied and they often ended up quarreling. At one point he struck up an affair with a female workmate who he was attracted to physically. They would get together whenever his wife went to visit relatives. Basem eventually decided to change things and get secretly married through the *Urfi* marriage (a legal contract where the State is not involved) because he wanted it to be *halal* and thus meet with cultural approval. He did not inform his wife, although he was legally obligated to, and she never found out. He continued living with his first wife who was immersed in raising their young daughter and simultaneously enjoying his *Urfi* partner.

One day Zeinab learnt that Basem had another wife. At first there was disbelief. Then there was anger. She felt offended, insulted, cheated, unappreciated, and distraught. In time, and with much difficulty, she settled down to a life where she shared her husband, the father of her child, with another woman. But the mental stress and emotional hurt remained. She never really recovered from the experience and, gradually, any passion she had ever had for Basem died. Zeinab eventually decided to file for divorce.

(Adapted from Primo, 2015)

6.3 Marriage Dynamics: Power and Closeness Within Marital Unions

Couple relationships are investigated in this section under two dimensions dealing with gender equity attitudes and practices in the private sphere.

6.3.1 Attitudes Around Gender Equity

Tables 6.3 and 6.4 provide some attitudinal statistics related to gender equality in private and public life in Egypt, Lebanon, Morocco, and Palestine. The assumption is that the more equitable the values are, the less likely the relationship between

Table 6.3 Percentage of adult male (M) and female (W) respondents who agreed with selected statements on gender attitudes in private life, based on IMAGES MENA 2016

Indicators	Egypt M (%)	Egypt W (%)	Palestine M (%)	Palestine W (%)	Morocco M (%)	Morocco W (%)	Lebanon M (%)	Lebanon W (%)
Household division of responsibilities								
A woman's most important role is to take care of the home and cook for the family	87	77	80	59	71	49	n/av	n/av
A man should have the final word about decisions in the home	90	58	80	48	71	47	n/av	n/av
Changing diapers, giving baths to children, and feeding children should all be the mother's responsibility	98	85	77	68	72	54	n/av	n/av
I think it is shameful when men engage in caring for children or other domestic work	10	17	19	14	37	24	19	12
Spousal control								
Husband wants to know where his wife is at all times	93	86	88	85	91	80	n/av	n/av
Husband does not allow his wife to wear certain clothes	98	65	91	77	88	66	n/av	n/av
Husband controls when his wife can leave the house	91	69	85	63	69	45	n/av	n/av
Husband expects wife to agree to have sex when he wants to	96	84	87	80	62	79	n/av	n/av
If a husband provides financially, his wife is obliged to have sex whenever he wants	16	33	43	25	n/av	n/av	n/av	n/av
A woman should be able to refuse to have sex with her husband when she does not want to	80	73	67	82	n/av	n/av	n/av	n/av
Perceptions of masculinity and femininity								
To be a man, you need to be tough	27	23	40	20	62	57	35	32
It is a man's duty to exercise guardianship over his female relatives	78	79	82	64	77	56	35	45
Boys are responsible for the behavior of their sisters, even if they are younger than their sisters	80	61	76	26	64	50	37	20

n/av.: Data not available
Source: El Feki, S., Heilman, B. and Barker, G., Eds. (2017) Understanding Masculinities: Results from the International Men and Gender Equality Survey (IMAGES) – Middle East and North Africa. Cairo and Washington, D.C.: UN Women and Promundo-US

couples is governed by power dynamics. Three general features emerge: First, a non-negligible percentage of respondents hold non-equitable and patriarchal views. Second, a much higher percentage of men than women express such non-equitable attitudes, indicating that women are only slowly experiencing an important move among men away from patriarchal values. Third, of the four countries considered, respondents from Egypt hold much more traditional views. Egypt is then followed by Palestine; whereas Morocco and Lebanon express less patriarchal attitudes.

Table 6.4 Percentage of adult male (M) and female (W) respondents who agreed or strongly agreed with selected statements on gender attitudes in public life, based on IMAGES MENA 2016

Indicators	Egypt M (%)	Egypt W (%)	Palestine M (%)	Palestine W (%)	Morocco M %)	Morocco W (%)	Lebanon M (%)	Lebanon W (%)
Female education and employment								
More rights for women mean that men lose out	35	17	35	18	41	19	24	10
If resources are scarce, it is more important to educate sons than daughters	35	16	40	18	22	8	32	12
A married woman should have the same right to work outside the home as her husband	31	75	52	73	55	89	79	86
When work opportunities are scarce, men should have access to jobs before women	98	88	83	70	73	71	57	31
Women at work								
Support equal salaries for men and women in the same position	74	93	n/av	n/av	80	93	n/av	n/av
Willing to work with female colleagues at the same level	86	96	n/av	n/av	78	94	n/av	n/av
Willing to work with female boss	55	88	n/av	n/av	70	87	n/av	n/av
Women in leadership								
There should be more women in positions of political authority	29	68	42	59	67	91	75	88
Women are too emotional to be leaders	74	53	67	52	42	32	45	23
Women who participate in politics or leadership positions cannot also be good wives or mothers	53	35	40	21	35	31	41	22
Women should leave politics to men	57	40	59	41	29	22	31	16
A woman with the same qualifications can do as good a job as a man	77	89	63	81	82	94	77	92
Gender equality								
The idea that men and women are equal is not part of our traditions and culture	52	60	59	54	50	48	32	65
We have already achieved equality between women and men in society	70	52	36	32	58	49	30	17
We need to do more to promote the equality of men and women	58	73	75	87	56	87	68	87

n/av.: Data not available
Source: El Feki, S., Heilman, B. and Barker, G., Eds. (2017) Understanding Masculinities: Results from the International Men and Gender Equality Survey (IMAGES) – Middle East and North Africa. Cairo and Washington, D.C.: UN Women and Promundo-US

It should be noted that there are clear deviations of attitudes within the private and public spheres. In the private sphere, the majority of men (and a non-negligible percentage of women) express attitudes supporting traditional division of responsibilities, as well as husbands' control over their wives. In contrast, the attitudes toward women's rights, abilities and participation in public spheres becomes more positive in general. Of particular relevance is that, among males, between 56 and 75% accept that more needs to be done to promote the equality of men and women. Among women, the corresponding percentages are much higher—between 73 and 87%.

It appears that men in Arab societies have grown more accustomed and less resistant to gender equity in the public sphere, yet they are less accepting in the private sphere when it comes to their wives enjoying the full benefit of their improved resources and public status. Congruently, women appear to be more forceful regarding their public roles, but less so in the private sphere. Many of them, though, are expressing real frustrations. A typical example of such frustration is well expressed in an open exchange on Facebook cited below:

> In the Middle East, almost 100% of the housework is done by women. Even if she has a job she still has to do everything related to housework, because "it's the way women things have always been". As a female who is born and lives in the Middle East, I just thought that one day I will HAVE to do all the things I see women do around me. This has put me off the whole marriage thing.
>
> Islam never indicated that a woman should not work and keep her time for the house and the housework, and it never indicated that the husband should not help with housework. If anything, Prophet Muhammad-Peace upon him-used to help with housework that's my point.

How progressive or conservative the values are may not necessarily be an accurate indication of the closeness in couple's relationships, though it would be fair to infer that such closeness may derive from similarity in values. The expectation would be that the less divergent the attitudes between couples, the less tense the interactions between them. Figure 6.3 is an attempt to investigate the convergence and divergence of values between males and females in different countries using the data from Tables 6.3 and 6.4.

It must be pointed out that the data available did not allow husband–wife comparisons and also the scale used to measure convergence is quite arbitrary. Hence, Figs. 6.3 and 6.4 should be seen as providing a general indication of the similarity in gender attitudes. Nevertheless, the dominance of two particular shades indicates that the noted difference between males and females in gender attitudes do not reach a level that make them significantly divergent. The few cases where the attitudes of both men and women are diametrically opposed are those mainly related to husband's control in household decisions, wives' freedom of movement, as well as the equal right of women to work outside the home.

Very few studies have attempted to probe the actual dynamics between husbands and wives within the home. The limited data is confined to division of household chores and the occurrence of domestic violence. In terms of household chores, the available data (El Feki et al., 2017) indicate that husbands rarely engage in traditional household or childcare activities. The contributions of husbands start to become significant only when the chores are related to the perceived male domain, such as house repairs and buying food. Furthermore, a large percentage of husbands

	Egypt	Palestine	Morocco	Lebanon
Household division of responsibilities				
A woman's most important role is to take care of the home and cook for the family				n/av
A man should have the final word about decisions in the home				n/av
Changing diapers, giving baths to children, and feeding children should all be the mother's responsibility				n/av
I think it is shameful when men engage in caring for children or other domestic work				
Spousal control				
Husband wants to know where his wife is at all times				n/av
Husband does not allow his wife to wear certain clothes				n/av
Husband controls when his wife can leave the house				n/av
Husband expects wife to agree to have sex when he wants to				n/av
If a husband provides financially, his wife is obliged to have sex whenever he wants			n/av	n/av
A woman should be able to refuse to have sex with her husband when she does not want to			n/av	n/av
Perceptions of masculinity and femininity				
To be a man, you need to be tough				
It is a man's duty to exercise guardianship over his female relatives				
Boys are responsible for the behavior of their sisters, even if they are younger than their sisters				

KEY
- Convergent: Both genders 65% or more; both genders 35% or less
- Minimally divergent: Difference of 20 % points or less
- Divergent: Difference more than 20-30 % points
- Highly Divergent: One gender 65% or more and the other gender 35% or less
- n/av Data not available

Fig. 6.3 Convergence and divergence of gender attitudes on practices in private life. Source: Based on El Feki, S., Heilman, B., and Barker, G., Eds. (2017). Understanding masculinities: Results from the international men and gender equality survey (IMAGES) – Middle East and North Africa. Cairo and Washington, D.C.: UN Women and Promundo-US

report that they control the weekly budget, pay bills, and individually make decisions on spending money.

In terms of domestic violence, Table 6.5 shows that as many as one in five males in Egypt reported that they resorted to physical violence during the 12 months preceding the survey (El Feki et al., 2017). Levels reported by males in Palestine, Morocco, and Lebanon were lower and ranged between 3.3 and 8.2%. The level of emotional violence was quite high, starting from 13.2% in Lebanon and reaching as

	Egypt	Palestine	Morocco	Lebanon
Female education and employment				
More rights for women mean that men lose out				
If resources are scarce, it is more important to educate sons than daughters				
A married woman should have the same right to work outside the home as her husband				
When work opportunities are scarce, men should have access to jobs before women				
Women at work				
Support equal salaries for men and women in the same position		n/av		n/av
Willing to work with female colleagues at the same level		n/av		n/av
Willing to work with female boss		n/av		n/av
Women in leadership				
There should be more women in positions of political authority				
Women are too emotional to be leaders				
Women who participate in politics or leadership positions cannot also be good wives or mothers				
Women should leave politics to men				
A woman with the same qualifications can do as good a job as a man				
Gender equality				
The idea that men and women are equal is not part of our traditions and culture				
We have already achieved equality between women and men in society				
We need to do more to promote the equality of men and women				

KEY
- Convergent: Both genders 65% or more; both genders 35% or less
- Minimally divergent: Difference of 20% points or less
- Divergent: Difference more than 20-30% points
- Highly Divergent: One gender 65% or more and the other gender 35% or less
- n/av Data not available

Fig. 6.4 Convergence and divergence of gender attitudes on practices in public life. Source: Based on El Feki, S., Heilman, B., and Barker, G., Eds. (2017). Understanding masculinities: Results from the international men and gender equality survey (IMAGES) – Middle East and North Africa. Cairo and Washington, D.C.: UN Women and Promundo-US

high as 53.8% in Egypt. Furthermore, more than a fifth and up to half of the males in the considered countries accepted the statement that "There are times when a woman deserves to be beaten"; and even higher proportions indicated that women should tolerate violence to keep the family together.

In summary, the patriarchal system expressed in division of household responsibilities and the domination of male power is noticeably prevalent in the studied countries.

Table 6.5 Percentage of ever-married male respondents having manifested violence against women during the previous 12 months and attitudes toward violence against women, based on IMAGES MENA 2016

Indicators	Egypt	Palestine	Morocco	Lebanon
Physical violence (during last 12 months)	21	8	5	3
Emotional violence (during last 12 months)	54	26	29	13
There are times when a woman deserves to be beaten	53	34	38	21
A woman should tolerate violence to keep the family together	90	63	62	26

Source: El Feki, S., Heilman, B. and Barker, G., Eds. (2017) Understanding Masculinities: Results from the International Men and Gender Equality Survey (IMAGES) – Middle East and North Africa. Cairo and Washington, D.C.: UN Women and Promundo-US

6.4 Marriage Satisfaction

Marriage satisfaction is a direct indication of the closeness of couples in marital union. Research on Arab countries dealing with marriage satisfaction and distress is minimal. The few articles that exist (Al-Darmaki et al., 2016, 2017; Onsy & Amer, 2014; Thabet, Abu Tawahina, Sarraj, & Panos, 2009) are based on very small sample studies and, consequently, do not offer a solid measure of the prevalence of satisfaction and its determinants. Some insights from these studies, however, can be obtained and these are relevant to the current analysis.

Many of these studies cited the relevance of the time spent together and of communication as determinants of satisfaction among couples. Religiosity was positively associated with satisfaction. The link between marriage satisfaction and mental/psychological health was demonstrated in a number of these studies. In particular, a positive correlation between marital satisfaction and life satisfaction and self-esteem was reported. An interesting finding (Al-Darmaki et al., 2016) was that men reported higher levels of marital satisfaction than women. The study noted that the gender roles and traditional family interrelationships favor men and contribute to their sense of marital satisfaction. On the other hand, the study noted that inconsistencies between expectations of women to adhere to their traditional roles and women's increased liberal attitudes toward their role in society may be an explanation why women had lower levels of satisfaction with the marital union than men. The study also posited that women themselves have a tendency to apply different or higher standards than men when assessing marital satisfaction. Indeed, drawing on the potential link between individual well-being and marital satisfaction, the findings of the IMAGE MENA study may be relevant in this regard: The study reported that from 40% to 51% of women exhibited depressive symptoms, as opposed to 20–28% of men (El Feki et al., 2017).

Another indication of marital dissatisfaction can be inferred from the level of divorce discussed earlier. Some would argue that the increase in divorce rates between young couples is indicative of different gender expectations, noting that younger females are much more assertive in seeking equity and participation in public life. Yet, the validity of using divorce and depression rates to infer findings on marital satisfaction can be debated on the grounds that the increase in divorce rates is not necessarily a sign of increasing tension within marriage, but simply reflects the increased ability to break away from unsatisfactory relationships. Similarly, the level of well-being is shaped by many societal and political factors and cannot be related to marriage satisfaction without the necessary research.

6.5 A Framework of Conscious Choice

This section is an attempt to conclude by reconciling the many findings presented earlier: significant changes in marriage formation and dissolution, alongside a patriarchal system continuing to play a dominant force in marital unions, as well as a suggestion of a non-negligible level of dissatisfaction. The reconciliation proposes that the delays in marriage formation and the increase in divorce rates are both a calculated choice to address the incompatibility of the prevailing patriarchal marriage dynamics with increased female aspirations for autonomy and self-realization. The question here is whether the delays in marriage formation are linked to the gender dynamics that are witnessed within marriage. Does the younger generation continue to value marriage and are they willing to pursue it at all cost, or can the delay in marriage be partly explained by a framework of conscious choice exercised by youth?

The value of marriage is reflected in a number of studies. For example, the most common view in a recent study that discussed attitudes toward marriage, family formation, and work of 27 non-married Qatari female university students aged 18–29 years, was that marriage is "natural, normal and desirable for women" (Hawkins, Qutteina, & Yount, 2017, p. 161). The IMAGES MENA study (El Feki et al., 2017) showed that the majority of women and men in Egypt, Morocco, and Palestine (between 53% and 73% of women, and between 54% and 75% of men) agreed with the statement that, "It is more important for a woman to marry than for her to have a career." Similarly, in a qualitative study by the Population Council in Egypt (Amin & Al-Bassusi, 2004), the majority of the 27 young working women stressed that delayed marriage was not an indication of devaluation of marriage, but rather a response to the need to accumulate sufficient funds to meet the establishment of a new household and marriage costs.

It is worth noting that a number of studies identified delayed marriage as a mechanism for women to balance their aspirations and societal pressure (Golkowska, 2014; James-Hawkins et al., 2017; Ayachi, 2014). These studies suggested that the ongoing societal transformation toward supporting women's education and participation in the labor market have raised young women's aspirations for higher education and self-realization through their work and career. They also argued that these aspirations are confronted with the societal pressure to conform to the rigid patriarchal values, norms, and traditions that maintain the clear gender division of labor within the family (Golkowska, 2014). The same observation was expressed by

Hawkins et al. (2017): "Young women are in a quandary, caught between social expectations to become wife and mother and pursuit of personal educational and workforce goals" (p. 156). Likewise, Ayachi (2014) have stated that the current generation of young people "can be regarded as a transitional group who combine the wishes and desires of parents with their own personal choices. It is a compromise between the old and the new order during a time of social change" (p. 321).

With specific reference to Gulf countries, El Haddad (2003) commented on the "spinsterhood crisis" among well-educated middle class women and those who occupy high ranking jobs. The study noted that these women tend to delay marriage to achieve their aspirations and are often busy in realizing such aspirations. Similarly, a recent study on the marriage market in Cairo (Khadr, 2016) showed that only 33.8% of young women and 29.2% of young men considered that marriage is more important than higher education, while 66.1% of young women and 70.5% of young men disagreed with a statement that "a young woman should marry once a suitable suitor is available even if she is still in school or University." Quite significantly, 87% of these young women and 82% of the young men asserted that marriage should be initiated after young women's completion of their higher education.

An interesting finding demonstrating the strong association between higher aspirations and celibacy (or delayed marriage) is available in Abdallah (2009). This study of the Palestinian women in Jordanian Camps reported that among the third generation of Palestinian women who came to age during the 1970s, celibacy was a choice due to higher aspirations and individualization of choice. This was the result of increased education availability, combined with overall welfare of the residents of these camps because of improvement in financial well-being as a result of a period of migration to Saudi Arabia and other Gulf States. Contrastingly, among the fourth generation of Palestinian women who came to age in the 1990s, celibacy is dreaded. The involuntary return of Palestinians from the Gulf States following the Gulf war was subject to the political environment that excluded these Jordanian camps from the Oslo agreements and thus diminished young women's personal ambitions beyond institution of marriage. Young women in this generation were marrying at an early age before reaching their twenties, some even at the age of 15.

This latter experience of Palestinian women was observed among young Syrian women living in Jordanian Camps, where early marriage of young women was considered a good strategy by the whole family to escape the camps. Al Akash and Boswall (2016) reported how young Nesreen (16 years) agreed to marry to save her whole family from living in a tent and starving. They also described how some parents agreed to marry their daughters as young as 11 years to protect them from being raped inside or outside the camp.

As the above demonstrates, attempts to achieve a balance between young women's aspirations and the societal pressure to maintain the patriarchal family tradition have substantially transformed young people's perception of marriage from being their divine and sole life goal into one of many lifecourse aspirations. This new perception has allowed not only a conscious renegotiation of the timing of marriage and its continuity, but also influenced the criteria for partner selection and the role of intimacy in the initiation of marriage. Furthermore, traditional practices characterizing marriage, such as consanguinity, also became subject to renegotiation.

An interesting observation in the Egypt marriage market study by Khadr (2016) was that the pursuit of love and intimacy were not the central drivers in forging marriage unions. The study observed that while love and conjugal emotion had not played a role in marriage formation among older generations due to societal pressure and family involvement in the marriage process, intimacy and love were also losing ground in the marriage process among the young generations due to their realistic perspective of life, cultural norms and traditions, and the ongoing social transformations and challenges. Indeed, young people in Egypt were more practical in their choice of their future mate. The study did show that three-fourths of young women and men preferred to enter marriage through love, but this preference did not rank highly when women were asked about the most preferred attributes for their future husbands.

Figure 6.5 presents results from the Egypt marriage market study (Khadr, 2016) and shows that having a reliable personality and trustworthy attributes (such as being responsible, coming from a good family, respecting one's mate, being religious) occupied the highest rankings, while being a lovable person ranked far down the same list. Furthermore, while nearly half (46.5%) of young women reported that they would not marry someone they did not know, about half (49.3%) reported that they would give them a chance. On the other hand, 63.8% of young men reported that they would not marry someone they did not know, whereas 30.8% would give them a chance. In this respect, in a somewhat earlier study, Amin and El Bassusi (2004) quoted a young woman as saying, "I do not believe in love … I want to marry a man who is rich, successful and able to take responsibility. He should be older than me by 20 years, one who has fixed monthly income. I would like the man to be prepared and ready for marriage not one who has a room or who is still looking for a flat or one who is going to live with his mother" (p. 22).

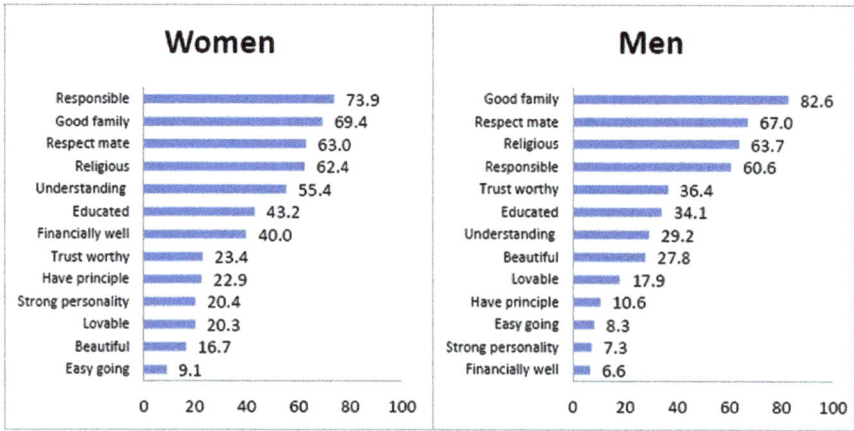

Fig. 6.5 Preferred attributes of future partner as expressed by males and females in Egypt. Source: Khadr (2016). Marriage Market in Urban Setting in Egypt: A Socio-ecological Framework

Similar results were observed among Kuwaiti women, where 66% of an index of mate selection preference was accorded to balanced personality (Hajeeh & Lairi, 2009). In Palestinian Camps of Jordan, Abdallah's (2009) four-generation comparison of married women revealed that current generations of young women were becoming more practical in their approach to marriage and "love marriage" was seen as utopian and not expected due to the political situation in these camps and the power of family groups within this context.

Another renegotiated dimension of marriage is the marriage contract itself. El Haddad (2003) reported a study by Bagadar (2003) indicating that in Jeddah, Saudi Arabia "most marriage contracts included conditions set by the bride including her right to study, to work and to have her own house (not to live with the man's parents)" (p. 8). He further added that some women reserve the right of divorce in their contract if their husband had another wife.

6.6 Conclusion

To conclude, couple relationships, particularly among the young generations in the Arab region, are caught between two opposing forces. Transformations are occurring, but the speed and degree of change vary widely among countries, and between males and females. The investigation of the role of love and intimacy in shaping couple relationships merits much more in-depth analysis and probing. The current evidence depicts a level of practicality in partner selection, as well as a degree of tension within marriage. It suggests that power relationships remain dominant. It also points to a transitional phase were women are more assertive in claiming their rights and exercising them in different formats.

References

Abd Allah, M. (2016, April 17). Rise in the number of divorce cases in the Arab world. Reasons and numbers. *Raseef* 22. Retrieved October 10, 2017, from http://raseef22.com/life/2016/04/17/%d8%a7%d8%b1%d8%aa%d9%81%d8%a7%d8%b9-%d8%a3%d8%b9%d8%af%d8%a7%d8%af-%d8%ad%d8%a7%d9%84%d8%a7%d8%aa-%d8%a7%d9%84%d8%b7%d9%84%d8%a7-%d9%82-%d9%81%d9%8a-%d8%a7%d9%84%d9%88%d8%b7%d9%86-%d8%a7%d9%84%d8%b9/

Abdallah, S. (2009). Fragile intimacies: Marriage and love in the Palestinian camps of Jordan (1948–2001). *Journal of Palestine Studies, 38*(4), 47–62.

Abdul Ghafour, J. (2015, May 9). Saudi divorce rate high: The 'message' is clear—Stop abusing social media. *Arab News*. Retrieved October 10, 2017, from http://www.arabnews.com/saudi-arabia/news/744426

Al Akash, R., & Boswall, K. (2016). Listening to the voices of Syrian women and girls living as urban refugees in Northern Jordan—A narrative ethnography of early marriage. In N. Ribas-Mateos (Ed.), *Migration, motilities and the Arab Spring. Spaces of refugee flight in the Eastern Mediterranean*. Cheltenham: Edward Elgar Publishing.

Al-Darmaki, F., Ahammed, S., Hassane, S., Abdullah, A., Yaaqeib, S., & Dodeen, H. (2017). Antecedents and consequences of marital satisfaction in an Emirati sample: A structural equation model analysis. *Marriage & Family Review, 53*(4), 365–387.

Al-Darmaki, F., Hassane, S., Ahammed, S., Abdullah, A., Yaaqeib, S., & Dodeen, H. (2016). Marital satisfaction in the United Arab Emirates: Development and validation of a culturally relevant scale. *Journal of Family Issues, 37*(12), 1703–1729.

Al-Munajjed, M. (2010). *Divorce in Gulf Cooperation Council countries: Risks and implications*. Dubai: Booz & Company.

Al-Nasr, T. (2011). Gulf Cooperation Council (GCC) women and misyar marriage: Evolution and progress in the Arabian Gulf. *Journal of International Women's Studies, 12*(3), 43–58.

Amin, S., & Al-Bassusi, N.-H. (2004). Education, wage work, and marriage: Perspectives of Egyptian working women. *Journal of Marriage and Family, 66*(5), 1287–1299.

Ayachi, S. (2014). Mate selection and marriage stability in the Maghreb. In A. Abela & J. Walker (Eds.), *Contemporary issues in family studies: Global perspectives on partnerships, parenting and support in a changing world*. Hoboken, NJ: John Wiley & Sons, Ltd.

Bagadar, A. (2003). Issues and problems of marriage in Gulf Council States. Executive Bureau of the Council of Labor and Social Affaires Ministries of the GCC and the Marriage Funds of the UAE.

Bahrain Central Informatics Organization. (2015). *Population, housing, buildings, establishments and agriculture census 2010*. Retrieved October 16, 2017, from http://www.cio.gov.bh/cio_eng/default.aspx

CAPMAS. (2016). *Annual bulletin of marriage and divorce statistics 2015*. Cairo, Egypt: Central Agency for Public Mobilization and Statistics.

CAPMAS. (2017). *Population census 2017*. Retrieved October 16, 2017, from http://www.capmas.gov.eg/

Divorce Science. (2016). *World divorce statistics: Comparisons among countries*. Retrieved October 10, 2017, from https://divorcescience.org/for-students/world-divorce-statistics-comparisons-among-countries/

El Feki, S., Heilman, B., & Barker, G. (Eds.). (2017). *Understanding masculinities: Results from the international men and gender equality survey (IMAGES)—Middle East and North Africa*. Cairo: UN Women and Promundo-US.

El Haddad, Y. (2003). Major trends affecting families in the Gulf countries, in United Nations: Department of Economic and Social Affairs (Family). *Major trends affecting families: A background document*. Retrieved October 10, 2017, from https://www.un.org/development/desa/family/publications/major-trends-affecting-families.html

El Tawila, S., & Khadr, Z. (2004). *Patterns of marriage and family formation among youth on Egypt*. National Population Council, Research Management Unit and Center for Information and Computer Systems, Faculty of Economics and Political Science, Cairo University, and Social Research Center, The American University in Cairo.

El Zanaty, F., & El-Daw, A. (1996). *Behavioral research among Egyptian university students* (Unpublished Report). International Medical Technology Egypt (MEDTRIC), Family Health International, Behavioral Research Unit.

GCC Statistical Center. (2016). *Marriage and divorce statistics in the GCC countries 2010-2015* (Annual Bulletin Issue No. 2). Retrieved October 15, 2017, from https://gccstat.org/en/

Golkowska, K. U. (2014). Arab women in the gulf and the narrative of change: The case of Qatar. *Interdisciplinary Political and Cultural Journal, 16*, 51–64.

Hajeeh, M., & Lairi, S. (2009). Marriage partner selection in Kuwait: An analytical hierarchy approach. *The Journal of Mathematical Sociology, 33*(3), 222–240.

Hawkins, L., Qutteina, Y., & Yount, K. (2017). The patriarchal bargain in a context of rapid changes to normative gender roles: Young Arab women's role conflict in Qatar. *Sex Roles, 77*(3–4), 155–168.

Hopkins, N. (2001). The new Arab family. *Cairo Papers in Social Science, 24*(1/2). Cairo: American University in Cairo Press.

Khadr, Z. (2016). *Marriage market in urban settings in Egypt: A socio-ecological framework.* Social Research Center, The American University in Cairo. Retrieved April 19, 2019, from http://schools.aucegypt.edu/research/src/Documents/Marriage%20Market%20Report/Marriage%20market%20in%20urban%20settings%20in%20Egypt.pdf

Khadr, Z. & El-Zeini, L. (2001). Families and households: Headship and co-residence. *Cairo Papers in Social Science, 24*(1/2), 140–164. Cairo: American University in Cairo Press.

Kuwaiti Central Statistics Bureau. (n.d.). *Population, housing, buildings and establishments 2011.* Retrieved October 16, 2017, from http://www.csb.gov.kw/

Ministry of Health and Population [Egypt], El-Zanaty and Associates [Egypt], and ICF International. (2015). *Egypt demographic and health survey 2014.* Cairo: Ministry of Health and Population and ICF International.

Olarte, O. (2010, January 11). Divorce on the rise in Arab states. *Khaleej Times.* Retrieved October 10, 2017, from http://www.khaleejtimes.com/article/20100111/ARTICLE/301119907/1002

Onsy, E., & Amer, M. (2014). Attitudes toward seeking couples counseling among Egyptian couples: Towards a deeper understanding of common marital conflicts and marital satisfaction. *Procedia: Social and Behavioral Science, 140,* 470–475.

Osman, M., & Shahd, L. (2001). Age-discrepant marriage in Egypt. *Cairo Papers in Social Science, 24*(1/2), 51–61. Cairo: American University in Cairo Press.

Pathak, S. (2013, September 4). 10 reasons why UAE marriages fail: Rising divorce rate among expats and Emiratis worries counsellors. *Gulf News.* Retrieved October 10, 2017, from http://gulfnews.com/xpress/10-reasons-why-uae-marriages-fail-1.1227513

Primo, V. (2015). Polygamy in Egypt: Why I decided to marry a second wife. *Cairo scene.* Retrieved April 21, 2019, from https://cairoscene.me/In-Depth/Polygamy-in-Egypt-Why-I-Decided-to-marry-a-Second-Wife?fb_comment_id=995923153763398_999873900034990#faba49c86231cc

Rashad, H. (2000). Demographic transition in Arab countries: A new perspective. *Journal of Population Research, 17*(1), 83–101.

Rashad, H. (2015). The Tempo and intensity of marriage in the Arab region: Key challenges and their implications. In *DIFI Family Research and Proceedings 2015,* 2. Retrieved October 10, 2017, from https://doi.org/10.5339/difi.2015.2

Rashad, H., & Osman M. (2001). Nuptiality in Arab countries: Changes and implications. *Cairo Papers in Social Science,* 24(1/2), 20–50. Cairo: American University in Cairo Press.

Rashad, H., Osman, M., & Roudi-Fahimi, F. (2005). Marriage in the Arab world. *MENA Policy Briefs.* Washington, DC: Population Reference Bureau.

Rashad, H., & Khadr, Z. (2017). Family support policies: Facing challenges and achieving quality of life. *Policy Brief Paper,* 4. Forum of Arab Parliamentarians for Population and Development FAPPD (in Arabic).

Roudi-Fahimi, F., & Ibrahim, S. (2013). Ending child marriage in the Arab region. *MENA Policy Briefs.* Washington, DC: Population Reference Bureau.

Saudi Department of Statistics and Information. (n.d.). *Detailed results of population and housing census 1431H.* Retrieved October 16, 2017, from https://www.stats.gov.sa/

Thabet, A., Abu Tawahina, A., El Sarraj, E., & Panos, V. (2009). Marital satisfaction and mental health of Palestinians in the Gaza strip (Cohort II). *ArabpsyNET E. Journal, 21–22,* 84–89.

UNICEF. (n.d.) *UNICEF data: Monitoring the situation of children and women.* Retrieved, July 15, 2017, from https://data.unicef.org/topic/child-protection/child-marriage/

United Nations, Department of Economic and Social Affairs, Population Division. (2013). *World marriage data 2012* (POP/DB/Marr/Rev2012).

United Nations, Department of Economic and Social Affairs, Population Division. (2015). *World marriage data 2015* (POP/DB/Marr/Rev2015). Retrieved April 19, 2019, from https://www.un.org/en/development/desa/population/theme/marriage-unions/WMD2015.asp

Younes, N. (2016, June 21). Tunisia struggles with 14,527 divorces over judicial year. *Tunisia Live.* Retrieved October 10, 2017, from http://www.tunisia-live.net/2016/06/21/tunisia-leads-arab-world-in-divorces/

Chapter 7
Couple Relationships in China

Dan Wang and Yan Xia

7.1 Introduction

China has had a steadily increasing population since the Chinese economic reform, from 0.96 billion in 1978 to 1.39 billion in 2017. In the last decade, around 10 million couples registered for marriage each year and up to 4 million couples registered for divorce (National Bureau of Statistics of China, 2018a). Being influenced by traditional culture, socioeconomic development, and globalization, couple relationships in China are evolving, but some unique features remain stable. The forms of Chinese couples are becoming increasingly diversified: intracultural heterosexual married couples remain the majority, but "modern" forms such as cohabitation, intercultural marriage, and same-sex partnerships are also becoming prevalent (Jankowiak, 2017). Through the theoretical perspectives of human ecology and family life course development (Klein & White, 1996), this chapter aims to understand how Chinese couple relationships are evolving and how cultural and contextual factors are influencing couple relationships. To address this aim, three sets of research questions are asked. First, what is the meaning of love to Chinese couples and what attributes are they looking for when selecting partners? Second, what are the social, economic, and cultural factors that strengthen or weaken Chinese couple relationships? Third, what are the challenges in Chinese couple relationships? A critical analysis approach will be adopted to examine the influence of social changes on current Chinese dating and marriage. Based on a review of selected academic literature published in both Chinese and English, the chapter will offer insights into the meaning of love, into the development, formation and maintenance of intimate relationships, as well as into the various related challenges as perceived and

D. Wang (✉) · Y. Xia
Department of Child Youth and Family Studies, University of Nebraska-Lincoln, Lincoln, NE, USA
e-mail: dan.wang@huskers.unl.edu; rxia2@unl.ed

experienced in China. This will increase understanding of the current state of Chinese couple relationships, as well as identify any understudied areas.

7.2 Meaning of Love, Intimacy, and Sexuality

The meaning of love in China is associated with altruism, affection, self-actualization, emotional fulfillment, and sexual attraction (Jankowiak, Shen, Yao, Wang, & Volsche, 2015). Urban Chinese youth report that they know it when they are in love. When talking about what love meant to them, young adults attending university mentioned terms such as happy, sweet/romantic, commitment, joy, wedding-related, and sacrifice among others. They agreed that love makes a person stronger and better, and it brings happiness to life. Notably, both genders also agreed that males are expected to assume more responsibilities than females for initiating and maintaining a relationship. Similar to other cultures, and aligned with Sternberg's theory, the conventions of love in China also emphasize three components: passion, intimacy, and commitment. These components are exhibited through an increasing acceptance of premarital sex and cohabitation (Yu & Xie, 2015), a shared sense of togetherness and frequent communication, and discussion of love, responsibility, marriage and sexuality (Cao, Zhou, Fine, Li, & Fang, 2018). Partners develop and maintain intimacy mainly by spending time together, while dating or at home, and communicating constantly through face-to-face and digital media conversations (Farrer, 2014).

Although not all couples are comfortable to openly discuss sexuality, they agree that sexual pleasure is essential to a harmonious relationship, which is consistent with the findings in other contexts (Cao et al., 2018; Farrer, 2014; Schoenfeld, Loving, Pope, Huston, & Štulhofer, 2017). The commitment also includes avoiding extramarital affairs (Ho, Jackson, Cao, & Kwok, 2018).

In China, various types of couples perceive and practice love and intimacy similarly, but also differently. For instance, each year more than 40,000 intercultural couples register for marriage (National Bureau of Statistics of China, 2018b). For these couples love is about mutual attractiveness, equality, and psychological pleasure (Wang, 2017). Similarly, same-sex couples report that love goes beyond sex, and love, intimacy and respect are the bases for long-term intimate relationships (Huang, 2018). Currently, a lacuna exists in the research regarding same-sex couples, one reason being that the public health framework has reclassified homosexual individuals as at-risk individuals for AIDS/HIV due to unprotected sex. Thus, the majority of published studies focus on gay couples (Kong, 2016) who are at a higher risk of being infected with sexually transmitted diseases (Li, Li, Wang, & Lau, 2015) and less is known on the more emotional aspects of the relationships. In other words, China has evolved to allow open discussion about same-sex relationships, but within the public health framework.

To summarize, in addition to embracing affection and sexual attraction, contemporary Chinese couples seek emotional fulfillment in love and view commitment as a sign of love and extramarital affairs as serious breach of commitment.

7.3 Romantic Ideal and Mate Selection

The mate preferences of Chinese men and women remain relatively stable, with women emphasizing economic status and men of any age highlighting physical attractiveness (Zheng, 2015). Buss and Schmitt (2019) reviewed general mate preferences and mate selection strategies among couples, concluding that the mating decision depended on individual and contextual factors including mate value, sex ratio, as well as social and cultural norms. Acknowledging the gaps between mating desires and actual mating behaviors, they discussed the diverse short-term and long-term mating strategies of men and women regarding mate value and ecological contingent environments. They also indicated that mating psychology is evolving in the modern world due to exposure to different population groups and technology. Similarly, Chinese mate selection criteria and romantic ideal are also evolving. Chinese marriage has been changing over time, from the family-arranged marriage to self-arranged marriage or romantic choice. Accordingly, the most valued mate selection criterion is shifting from matched social and economic standing, to an individual's traits and characteristics, followed by parental preference and social environment as the main considerations (Jankowiak, 2017).

7.3.1 Personal Traits and Characteristics

Personal traits and characteristics are often mentioned as crucial considerations in Chinese mate selection. In general, honesty, health, kindness, and understanding are the top valued traits and characteristics. Women tend to focus more on certain traits related to personality (e.g., humorous and intelligent), capability (e.g., earning high income) and social status (e.g., powerful and high social status), whereas men tend to emphasize more certain traits related to household labor (e.g., a good housekeeper), willingness to have children, and physical attractiveness (Chen, Austin, Miller, & Piercy, 2015). An ideal mate to a female is either—already or potentially—materially successful and has sound moral character. An ideal mate to a male is young, sexually attractive, well-educated, and independent in a career (Ho et al., 2018). In addition, being influenced by traditional Confucianism, Chinese value the altruistic traits in relationships. Guo, Feng, and Wang (2017) categorized an individual's altruism into kin altruism (with relatives), reciprocal altruism (with allies or acquaintances), and general altruism (with unrelated persons). The two genders emphasize kin altruism in both long-term and short-term mate selection, especially filial piety; but males prefer altruistic traits more than females and females advertise themselves more with these traits.

7.3.2 Parental Preferences

Although arranged marriage has been legally forbidden since the 1950 Marriage Law, parents still influence young people's relationship decisions. A recent study found that the educational attainment of parents is related to young adults' attitudes and expectations. Lower parental education is associated with an expectation of romantic love, whereas higher parental education fosters an attitude of "realistic" love (Hu & Wu, 2019). In general, children and parents have some compatible expectations for a future spouse because they all advocate the traditional values, such as filial piety. However, they also have contradictory interests due to a different understanding of a relationship: young people regard the relationship as a path to happiness, so they value romantic love, whereas parents regard marriage as an exchange and an integration of resources of two families, so they emphasize matching social status (Jankowiak, 2017). The expectations for son-in-law and daughter-in-law are also diversified: the former emphasizes earning capacity and the latter emphasizes genetic quality and reproductive fitness (Guo, Li, & Yu, 2017).

7.3.3 Biased Social Context

The social environment is a stressor, especially for unmarried women over 27 years old, who are often discriminately tagged by the public and officials as "leftover women," or "*Sheng nu*" in Chinese (Fincher, 2016). These unmarried women, even those having an educated background and a successful career, are judged negatively by the public for their late marriage. In addition to the social stress, unmarried women are subject to their parents' concerns that they are "leftover" (Budgeon, 2016) so increasing the stress. As a compromise to the pressure from society and from parents, some educated women lower their mate selection criterion of physical attractiveness, but they are unwilling to forfeit their expectation for men who have a higher social and economic status than themselves, as they still observe the rule of "marrying up" (Schmitt, 2005).

7.3.4 Intercultural Couples and Same-Sex Couples

Intercultural couples and same sex-couples' mate selection criteria are similar to those of the general population in China, including considerations of individual traits and characteristics, parental preferences, and social environment. The most common combinations of intercultural couples are Chinese–Western couples, consisting of a Chinese woman with a Western man, and intra-Asian couples, consisting of a Chinese man with an Asian woman from a less developed foreign country such as Vietnam, Myanmar, and Laos (Wang, 2017). Chinese–Western couples mainly reside in the Western country, and the intra-Asian couples mainly stay in China. Socioeconomic status is the main priority among intercultural couples, though some of them also give value to physical attractiveness of the partner, as well as equality in a relationship.

Compared to the Taiwan area, there are fewer studies on mate selection of same-sex couples in mainland China for social and political reasons, and the studies on this topic with regard to mainland China are mainly qualitative (Jeffreys & Wang, 2018; Kong, 2016). A comparative analysis of mate selection among same-sex and different-sex couples in Taiwan shows that the two types of couples have similar mate selection criteria. However, same-sex couples are more comparable in age and education level, but more divergent in family background. In addition, parental influence has a larger effect on children's mate selection and dissolution of relationships among same-sex couples than different-sex couples due to the traditional desire to keep the family continuity (Lin, Yu, & Su, 2019).

7.4 Marriage and Same-Sex Couple Relationships

Chinese couples generally formalize their relationships through official marriage registration and a ceremony. Heterosexual couples officially register for marriage at a local government office and, following tradition, host a wedding ceremony to inform their family and friends. In China, same-sex marriage is not legal, and public and parental attitudes toward this vary. Thus, some same-sex couples conceal their relationship with a "fake" marriage using one of two strategies: First, a homosexual partner legally marries a heterosexual individual but secretly maintains an extramarital homosexual life. Or second, two pairs of homosexual partners of the opposite sex marry each other on the surface but maintain same-sex relationship secretly (Kong, 2016). Other same-sex couples choose to have a ceremony to inform close relatives and friends (Wu, Mou, Wang, & Atkin, 2018).

7.4.1 Marriage Registration and Wedding

For heterosexual couples, the marriage registration and ceremony might not happen simultaneously because couples want the recorded date on the marriage certificate to be meaningful or special, and because the ceremony happens only when the wedding company, hotel banquet hall, and guests are all available (Xu, DeFrain, & Liu, 2016). The wedding ceremony is typically hosted by the groom's family in the groom's hometown. The cost of a wedding ceremony is usually high; for example, the average cost in large cities like Shanghai was 32,000 USD 5 years ago and it is even higher now (Zhuang & Everett, 2018). The widely perceived wedding "necessities" also include providing housing for the couple and a brand-new car. These used to be provided by the groom and his family, but due to the high expense, nowadays the bride and her family are also willing to assume partial payment (Xu & Xia, 2014). Parental investment before marriage is legally regarded as a gift to the child alone; after marriage as a gift to the couple (Davis, 2014). Regardless of the efforts and high costs, parents usually insist on hosting the ceremony because of perceived importance and initial investment. After the marriage registration and ceremony, the two partners legally and morally formalize their relationship with this voluntary contract, which allows them to jointly own properties and share rights and responsibilities. Some people sign a prenuptial agreement and some sign a loyalty agreement after the wedding. The loyalty agreement serves as a contract to hold both partners morally responsible for being faithful to each other. Loyalty is more regarded as a moral issue than a legal one in local court cases when the plaintiff cannot provide sufficient evidence to demonstrate the existence of extramarital affairs. A study shows most couples in Shanghai and Guangzhou agreed that a prenuptial agreement was helpful, but they argued that the legality of the loyalty agreement was useless (Davis, 2014).

7.4.2 Low Marriage Rate and Late Marriage

The declining marriage rate and prevailing late marriage are notable in China. Although the traditional desire for forming and maintaining a family is universal and stable (Yeung & Hu, 2016), the marriage registration rate dropped 13.7% within 5 years from 2012 to 2016. The minimum legal marriage age for males and females in China is 22 and 20, respectively, but from 1990 the age of first marriage has been delayed from 21.4 to 25.7. Among the 177 million unmarried population above the age of 15, there are 32 million more males than females (National Bureau of Statistics of China, 2018a). There are also group and regional differences: women with higher education levels and financial independence in developed Eastern and urban areas of China delay marriage longer than their counterparts in Western and rural areas (Budgeon, 2016). Researchers have suggested that the phenomenon is partially explainable by the socioeconomic change of China and the globalization of the world (Ji & Yeung, 2014).

Hukou has lost the status of institutional incentive for early marriage in many cities. *Hukou* is a household registration system in China, differentiating individual benefits by their birthplace. People with an urban *hukou* used to enjoy more benefits on employment, housing, and insurance than those with rural household status. A rural *hukou* holder would automatically receive an urban status if he/she was married to an urban *hukou* holder. Thus, it was common to see an early intermarriage between a more educated rural spouse and a less educated urban spouse. However, with socioeconomic development, increased mobility, and local policy changes in

China, the link between marriage and *hukou* has been politically and economically weakened (Lui, 2016). Tian, Qian, and Qian (2018) have found that the more stringent local *hukou* policy has resulted in individuals being less likely to benefit from intermarriage and tradeoffs.

The increased gaps in socioeconomic status are also related to the late marriage and so-called "marriage squeeze" referring to the phenomenon that an adult at marriage age cannot find a mate in the marriage market (Zang & Zhao, 2017).

Women in contemporary China's labor market have a higher education than those before, allowing them to be more economically and emotionally independent (Dasgupta, Matsumoto, & Xia, 2015). In addition to the marriage squeeze among women with high socioeconomic status (biasedly tagged as "leftover women"), the marriage squeeze among males with low socioeconomic status is also apparent. The high ratio of unmarried men and women due to the one-child policy and marry-up aspirations leave fewer choices for rural men than before (Mu & Xie, 2014). Moreover, the notion of gender equality and femininity has become increasingly valued in Asian societies, and the trend of postponing marriage and birth has been found noticeable in East Asian countries, including China, Japan, Korea, and Taiwan (Raymo, Park, Xie, & Yeung, 2015).

7.4.3 Same-Sex Relationships

As indicated earlier, same-sex couples have not been allowed to officially register for marriage in China, so some of them choose to host a ceremony to disclose their relationship to parents, relatives, and friends. There are some studies on the attitudes toward same-sex couples, showing that these vary. In 2013, the Pew Research Center reported that over half of Chinese adults surveyed disagreed with the statement that homosexuality should be accepted; only one-fifth agreed. Chi and Hawk (2016) also found a general negative attitude toward same-sex couples among students in nine universities randomly selected from over 100 Eastern and Southwestern universities in China. They noted, however, that higher achieving urban female students with higher levels of maternal education and frequency of internet usage tended to have more positive attitudes than the rest. Indeed, social media plays an important role in reducing the public stigma of same-sex marriage, and this has also been found in a different study with 980 social media users (Wu et al., 2018).

A recent study in Hong Kong shows that although Chinese parents would like primary schools to educate their children about homosexuality, they are conservative about their own children establishing same-sex relationships and marriage (Ling & Chen, 2017). Indeed, Choi and Luo (2016) indicated that a main challenge for same-sex relationships was from parents. As similarly highlighted earlier, influenced by the traditional Chinese culture filial piety, Chinese parents value the continuity of the family line, so they and their adult children have to negotiate on the disagreements regarding offspring. Couples will eventually try to reduce interactions with parents and their familial network if they cannot reach an agreement.

7.5 Couple Relationship Satisfaction

Chinese couple relationship satisfaction is associated with the division of power, couple communication, and the relationship with children and extended family.

7.5.1 Power and Decision-Making

Shared power and decision-making are important to a satisfying and stable intimate relationship (Knudson-Martin, 2013; Kulik, 2011). Chinese couples constantly negotiate their power and roles in family decision-making. The traditional Chinese gender ideology and division of labor, that a husband is expected to work outside as the breadwinner and a wife to stay at home, bestows women with more power in mundane and children-rearing decisions and men more power in economic decisions (Qian & Qian, 2015; Shu, Zhu, & Zhang, 2013). This could be seen as a concrete example of the feminist theory which states that gender inequality is embedded in society, limiting women's equal opportunities to education and work, as well as undervaluing women's contribution at home (MacKinnon, 1989). Such a society further disadvantages women in the negotiation of labor and power exchange.

It is worth noting that compared to urban areas in China, rural areas observe a stricter gendered division of labor. Since China's reform in 1979, rural farmers have been migrating to urban areas as laborers. Among the 0.29 billion migrant workers, nearly 78% are married and 65.6% are men (National Bureau of Statistics of China, 2018a). One study also reported that about half of married migrant workers were not living with their spouse and children (Fan, Sun, & Zheng, 2011). This living apart, possibly at great distance, strains the couple's relationship. Some of the migrants develop an extramarital relationship, or have sex with high-risk partners (Chen, Yu, Luo, & Huang, 2016; Yu et al., 2017). Meanwhile, approximately 50 million rural women remain at home to work on the farm and take care of children and the elderly. They are studied as "left-behind women" who enjoy some autonomy to manage the household's basic living budget within the family when their migrant husbands are temporarily absent from home (Luo, Yang, Li, & Feldman, 2017). However, whether migration has changed the power distribution among migrant couples remains an argument (Wu & Ye, 2016) as Chinese migrant men report more individual decision-making than joint (Liu, Bell, & Zhang, 2019).

7.5.2 Communication

Communication is directly and indirectly associated with relationship satisfaction. Researchers have identified three communication patterns that affect a couple's relationship satisfaction: mutual constructive, demand–withdraw, or mutual avoidance communication (Chi, Epstein, Fang, Lam, & Li, 2013). Couples in a healthy and satisfying relationship tend to discuss issues and concerns in an open and honest manner, whereas those in a troubled relationship may either have one or both partners completely shut down.

Research by Hiew, Halford, van de Vijver, and Liu (2015) found that positive communication (such as self-disclosure) generally contributed to a higher level of relationship satisfaction across intracultural and intercultural couples in China. This comparison study also found that Chinese female partners show fewer positive communications than their Western counterparts. As the researchers point out, however, the indicator of positive communication only includes direct communication. Thus, as a culture that values nonconfrontation, it is not surprising that Chinese couples prefer indirect communication. In relation to this, Halford, Lee, Hiew, and van de Vijver (2018) compared the rate of indirect communication among Chinese couples, Western couples, and Chinese–Western intercultural couples in Australia and found that all three groups showed a low rate of indirect communication. It was proposed that Chinese immigrant couples might have adapted their communication to the new cultural environment.

Constructive communication is essential in nurturing and maintaining positive couple relationships (Galvin, Braithwaite, & Bylund, 2015). Yet this is sometimes logistically challenging in China where couples may choose or have to live apart for the common interests of the family. For example, a married young couple may work in different cities, or migrant farmer working parents may have to make a difficult choice to have one parent working in cities for better income while the other parent stays with their children and aging parents in the villages. In both instances, the couple may only be together during holidays. Another common scenario is when grandparents take care of their grandchildren, and rural couples seek low-skilled job opportunities in urban areas. Here males often work in the manufacturing or construction industry and females work in the service industry. Though most of these couples typically work in the same city, they only meet on weekends because of long hours of work and different means of transportation. These so-called "weekend couples" maintain communication and relationship mainly by new digital media such as mobile phones and social networking software (e.g., QQ and Wechat, an app similar to WhatsApp) (Luo et al., 2017). As the divorce rate is growing among couples (National Bureau of Statistics of China, 2018b), researchers need to study whether lack of constructive communication has a role, and what are the possible effective, constructive communications that could strengthen couple relationship and satisfaction in China.

7.5.3 Parenting and the Relationship with the Extended Family

Another factor affecting marital satisfaction is the couple's views of parenting and their relationship with their own parents. Couple relationships in China are not only about two married person, but also about their children and extended family. As such, there are frequent physical, emotional, and financial interactions or exchanges between the couple and their extended families. Xu and Xia (2014) indicated that Chinese couples choose to live with their parents for two major reasons: care for both the young and the old. Childcare centers in China are not always available in an area and/or affordable, so parents and in-laws move in with their adult children to provide childcare for the grandchildren (Du, Dong, & Zhang, 2019). At the same time, adult children see it as their familial obligation to help when their aging parents need assistance. Nonetheless, couples do disagree on parenting and caring for aging parents, as well as on decisions over infertility and the number of children to have (see Tao, Coates, & Maycock, 2012 for more on discussions about infertility and marital stability).

7.6 Couple Relationship Challenges

The number of divorce registrations in China shows an overall increasing trend, with the crude divorce rate rising from 1% to 3% since 1990 (National Bureau of Statistics of China, 2018b). Urbanization and the increased unemployment rate have been linked to the increased divorce rate in China (Zhang, Wang, & Zhang, 2014). Typical reasons for divorce among Chinese couples are identified as gender inequality, intimate partner violence, and family dysfunction (Johnson, Nguyen, Anderson, Liu, & Vennum, 2015; Liu et al., 2019; Yang, Poon, & Breckenridge, 2018), as well as pursuing personal freedom and dispute over property rights (Yeung & Hu, 2016). Although mental health plays an important role in the couple relationship, studies of mental health among Chinese couples mainly focused on vulnerable groups such as infertile couples (Chow, Cheung, & Cheung, 2016; Ying, Wu, & Loke, 2016), pregnant women (Wang et al., 2017) and same-sex couples (Li et al., 2016). Thus, there is a gap in knowledge. In addition, individuals who find it difficult to form intimate bonding, such as those with a high level of attachment avoidance, hold unrealistic expectations and experience dissatisfaction with the intimate partner and with in-laws (Liu, Wang, & Jackson, 2017). Of note is that infidelity is a major trigger to the dissolution of same-sex female couple relationships (Shieh, 2016).

7.6.1 Gender Inequality

Gender inequality is a context influencing the dynamics of couple relationships in mate selection, marriage, and dissolution in China. Chinese women's higher education level has neither brought them more, nor better, job opportunities. On the contrary, the overall female employment rate and relative income have been decreasing since the 1990s (Sinha Mukherjee, 2015). In particular, the gender role division in rural areas, where men work in gainful employment outside the home and women mainly stay at home to run the household, limits the rural women from participating in paid work and, therefore, from gaining income (Luo et al., 2017). Additionally, although laws forbid companies from discriminating against women during recruitment, many employers are reluctant to hire women with the consequence that this reduces the opportunities in the job market for women (Qian & Qian, 2015). Thus, Chinese women with less social and economic capital are disadvantaged in negotiating power regarding sharing of housework and parenting.

7.6.2 Intimate Partner Violence

Reported lifetime experience of violence as a victim within Chinese married couples mainly includes psychological violence (20%), physical violence (4%), and sexual violence (1%) (Yang et al., 2018). The three types of violence often occur simultaneously, but this varies according to type of violence, individual characteristics, and groups. Psychological and minor physical intimate partner violence (IPV) perpetration and sufferance as a victim are bidirectional, but sexual and severe physical violence is usually unidirectional. Chinese males tend to perpetrate physical and sexual violence, whereas women tend to perpetrate psychological violence. Chinese males report less violence sufferance than females, but quantitative studies on males as victims of violence is limited (Breckenridge, Yang, & Poon, 2019; Chen & Chan, 2019). Divorced women were more likely than married women to report having experienced all types of violence and controlling behavior (Lin, Sun, Liu, & Chen, 2018). Individuals report more recent violence sufferance than lifetime sufferance, suggesting this is an emerging phenomenon. In addition, migrant workers and rural women with less education reported being victims of violence more frequently than other groups (Hou, Cerulli, Marsha, Caine, & Qiu, 2018).

The prevalence of IPV is closely related to sociopolitical and cultural factors. IPV had not been clearly defined as a legal issue until 2016, when China issued its first national law against domestic violence, prohibiting domestic violence between couples, either married or cohabitating (National Law against Domestic Violence of the People's Republic of China, 2015). However, this law included only physical and psychological violence, but not sexual abuse. Nor did the law mention former partners, divorced partners, and same-sex partners (Breckenridge et al., 2019). Meanwhile, group comparison shows that individuals' definitions of IPV still vary by cultural context and notion. Chinese young adults who live in mainland China tend to have a narrower definition of IPV than those in the USA, Hong Kong, and Taiwan area. At the same time, those who advocate male dominance and live in rural areas tend to have a narrower definition than those who live in urban areas and perceive IPV as a crime (Jiao, Sun, Farmer, & Lin, 2016; Lin, Sun, Wu, & Liu, 2016). A qualitative study revealed that definitions might be related to Chinese males' personal perception of the severity of violence and cultural conception of masculinity (Simon & Wallace, 2018). Individuals with higher awareness as a result of exposure to printed media (e.g., book, magazines, and newspapers) tend to have a more negative attitude toward IPV (Wang, 2018).

Risk factors for suffering from IPV in China include having more than two children, unplanned pregnancy, gambling, alcohol use, and drug use (Lin et al., 2018;

Wang et al., 2017). Gender, age, and employment are not associated with the three major types of violence, but they are related to controlling behaviors (Lin et al., 2018). The cultural, somewhat insensitive, definition of psychological violence, together with the obligation to satisfy a partner's sexual demands are also risk factors (Breckenridge et al., 2019). Indeed, a study in Hong Kong found that approximately one-third of IPV victims refused on-site counseling (Choi et al., 2018) possibly because of the cultural influence. Thus, public policy initiatives are needed to promote equal access to education and employment for women to manage partners' controlling behaviors, to increase public awareness of IPV, and to develop culturally responsive services.

Vignette

Chang's appeal for divorce from Yong, her husband, is denied again by the court. In 2016, the year Chang submitted her first divorce application, the couple had been married for 18 years and they had three girls. Chang's grounds for seeking divorce were that Yong was addicted to gambling and spent his day at *Majiang* parlors. When he was at home he was always picking fights. Chang stated that she paid for most of family living expenses and Yong rarely cared for her and their children. She was physically and psychologically exhausted because of the frequent fights and double shifts of both working outside the home and taking care of their children. Yong did not show up in court, nor provide written responses. The court acknowledged Yong was addicted to gambling, missing work and neglecting family but denied Chang's request. The court explained that the dispute over household chores was not sufficient grounds for incompatibility (one of the legal bases to grant couple divorce when one spouse wants to divorce, but the other does not); and it was possible that the couple could improve mutual understanding and communication to rebuild their relationship. Chang appealed for a review of her divorce case and added domestic violence as evidence. Their oldest daughter also provided a statement that her father loved gambling and was ill-tempered, and there was no peace at home when her father was around. The court dismissed Chang's appeal based on three considerations: First, the additional evidence was submitted after the appeal court decision was made and thus it was not admissible. Also, the daughter's statement could not be considered as appropriate evidence because of the mother–daughter relationship. Second, Chang did not provide sufficient evidence to demonstrate her husband's gambling and domestic violence. Third, an intact family is necessary for the welfare of children and positive child development (The Supreme People's Court of the People's Republic of China, 2016, 2018).

Comments: This case and the court ruling in favor of the husband are from an authentic court case (pseudonyms have been for the husband and wife). Chang sought divorce to live in peace and to protect herself from a gambler husband. However, due to lack of court-accepted evidence to back up her argument, she was not granted a divorce. Chinese family and marriage laws protecting women and children (i.e., Marriage Law of the People's Republic of China, National Law against Domestic Violence of the People's Republic of China and The Law of the

People's Republic of China on the Protection of Minors) are general and ambiguous (i.e., grant divorce when there are other incompatibilities), making their execution dependent on interpretations of the judges of local courts. In this case, it appears that the local judge's decision was influenced first by the lack of understanding of the impact of addiction on children, as well as the lack of awareness of intimate partner violence, including the characteristics and impacts of the abuse. Secondly, the court tried to protect the children by keeping the family intact, weighing heavily on moral, family obligations. The well-being of Chang as a wife, a mother of three daughters and a gainfully employed person contributing to the family upkeep were not mentioned.

7.7 Conclusion

This chapter has critically analyzed the existing literature on couple relationships in China through the lenses of human ecology and family life course development. It incorporates traditional and modern social roles and relationships to highlight the adherence and changes of Chinese couple relationships at each stage (Klein & White, 1996). The review describes how individuals, family, societal contexts and Chinese culture interact with Chinese couple relationships, with one or more working as the dominant factors. It also explains that cultural, social, and economic forces directly or indirectly influence Chinese intimate relationships.

Driven simultaneously by individual preference, family interests, and social norms, mate selection has shifted, to some extent, from family arrangement and practicality to mutual attractiveness and romance, whereas the core values of marriage remain the same. Social norms are particularly significant for modern couples in that society has become more accepting of different living choices, such as homosexual partnership, cohabitation, and singlehood. The rigid gender roles in traditional Chinese culture tend to decrease Chinese couple relationships and relationship satisfaction. In contrast, shared power and decision-making, constructive communication, as well as quality relationships with children and extended family strengthen couple relationship satisfaction. In general, women reported lower marital satisfaction when they had to do double shifts, taking on both paid work and work at home. Educated, unmarried women are facing social biases. Increased gender inequality in the job market is associated with the lowered status of women, and a risky predicament for rural women or those who mainly work inside the home, which is further linked to the quality of relationships and IPV.

More research is essential on multiple fronts. Studies are needed to further investigate the association between communication styles and relationship satisfaction in the Chinese culture. There is also a gap in knowledge on how individual characteristics, such as education, geographical location and understanding of healthy intimate relationships, interact with family and economic contexts to predict relationship quality. Further research is also needed to understand how mental health affects couple relationships, as current research mainly examines how dysfunction in the relationship leads to mental health issues.

These findings pose a number of challenges. Current laws should be reinforced to ensure and protect women's equal access to education and employment. A more widespread awareness should also be raised about related deficiencies. One cost-effective approach is to implement public campaigns and support programs of family life education in order to increase the knowledge of family development, the awareness of IPV and addiction, as well as their impacts on marital relationship, and to increase skills of effective communication, age-appropriate parenting and managing stress and crisis among the general population. Another strategy is to develop research-supported and culturally responsive educational programs for equal, healthy, respectful relationships. The government should also focus on capacity-building, growing a profession that is specialized in helping couples and families understand family life development, and gain skills of communication, as well as stress and crisis management.

References

Breckenridge, J., Yang, T., & Poon, A. W. C. (2019). Is gender important? Victimization and perpetration of intimate partner violence in mainland China. *Health and Social Care in the Community, 27*(1), 31–42.

Budgeon, S. (2016). The 'problem' with single women: Choice, accountability and social change. *Journal of Social and Personal Relationships, 33*, 401–418.

Buss, D. M., & Schmitt, D. P. (2019). Mate preferences and their behavioral manifestations. *Annual Review of Psychology, 70*, 77–110.

Cao, H., Zhou, N., Fine, M. A., Li, X., & Fang, X. (2018). Sexual satisfaction and marital satisfaction during the early years of Chinese marriage: A three-wave, cross-lagged, actor–partner interdependence model. *The Journal of Sex Research, 56*(3), 391–407.

Chen, L., Yu, Z., Luo, X., & Huang, Z. (2016). Intimate partner violence against married rural-to-urban migrant workers in eastern China: Prevalence, patterns, and associated factors. *BMC Public Health, 16*(1), 1232.

Chen, M., & Chan, K. L. (2019). Characteristics of intimate partner violence in China: Gender symmetry, mutuality, and associated factors. *Journal of Interpersonal Violence*. Advance online publication. doi:https://doi.org/10.1177/0886260518822340

Chen, R., Austin, J. P., Miller, J. K., & Piercy, F. P. (2015). Chinese and American individuals' mate selection criteria: Updates, modifications, and extensions. *Journal of Cross-Cultural Psychology, 46*(1), 101–118.

Chi, P., Epstein, N. B., Fang, X., Lam, D. O. B., & Li, X. (2013). Similarity of relationship standards, couple communication patterns, and marital satisfaction among Chinese couples. *Journal of Family Psychology, 27*(5), 806–816.

Chi, X., & Hawk, S. T. (2016). Attitudes toward same-sex attraction and behavior among Chinese university students: Tendencies, correlates, and gender differences. *Frontiers in Psychology, 7*, 1592–1601.

Choi, A. W. M., Wong, J. Y. H., Lo, R. T. F., Chan, P. Y., Wong, J. K. S., Lau, C. L., & Kam, C. W. (2018). Intimate partner violence victims' acceptance and refusal of on-site counseling in emergency departments: Predictors of help-seeking behavior explored through a 5-year medical chart review. *Preventive Medicine, 108*, 86–92.

Choi, S. Y., & Luo, M. (2016). Performative family: Homosexuality, marriage and intergenerational dynamics in China. *The British Journal of Sociology, 67*, 260–280.

Chow, K. M., Cheung, M. C., & Cheung, I. K. (2016). Psychosocial interventions for infertile couples: A critical review. *Journal of Clinical Nursing, 25*, 2101–2113.

Dasgupta, S., Matsumoto, M., & Xia, C. (2015). *Women in the labour market in China*. Bangkok: The International Labour Organization.

Davis, D. S. (2014). Privatization of marriage in post-socialist China. *Modern China, 40*(6), 551–577.

Du, F., Dong, X. Y., & Zhang, Y. (2019). Grandparent-provided childcare and labor force participation of mothers with preschool children in urban China. *China Population and Development Studies, 2*, 347–368.

Fan, C. C., Sun, M., & Zheng, S. (2011). Migration and split households: A comparison of sole, couple, and family migrants in Beijing, China. *Environment and Planning A, 43*, 2164–2185.

Farrer, J. (2014). Love, sex, and commitment: Delinking premarital intimacy from marriage in urban China. In D. S. Davis & S. L. Friedman (Eds.), *Wives, husbands, and lovers: Marriage and sexuality in Hong Kong, Taiwan, and urban China* (pp. 62–96). Palo Alto, CA: Stanford University Press.

Fincher, L. H. (2016). *Leftover women: The resurgence of gender inequality in China*. London, UK: Zed Books Ltd.

Galvin, K. M., Braithwaite, D. O., & Bylund, C. L. (2015). *Family communication: Cohesion and change*. London, UK: Routledge.

Guo, Q., Feng, L., & Wang, M. (2017). Chinese undergraduates' preferences for altruistic traits in mate selection and personal advertisement: Evidence from Q-sort technique. *International Journal of Psychology, 52*(2), 145–153.

Guo, Q., Li, Y., & Yu, S. (2017). In-law and mate preferences in Chinese society and the role of traditional cultural values. *Evolutionary Psychology, 15*(3), 1–11.

Halford, W. K., Lee, S., Hiew, D. N., & van de Vijver, F. J. (2018). Indirect couple communication and relationship satisfaction in Chinese, Western, and Chinese–western intercultural couples. *Couple and Family Psychology: Research and Practice, 7*, 183–200.

Hiew, D. N., Halford, W. K., van de Vijver, F. J., & Liu, S. (2015). Communication and relationship satisfaction in Chinese, Western, and intercultural Chinese–Western couples. *Journal of Family Psychology, 30*(2), 193–202.

Ho, P. S. Y., Jackson, S., Cao, S., & Kwok, C. (2018). Sex with Chinese characteristics: Sexuality research in/on 21st-century China. *The Journal of Sex Research, 55*, 486–521.

Hou, F., Cerulli, C., Marsha, N., Caine, E. D., & Qiu, P. (2018). Using confirmatory factor analysis to explore associated factors of intimate partner violence in a sample of Chinese rural women: A cross-sectional study. *BMJ Open, 8*(2), e019465.

Hu, A., & Wu, X. (2019). Parental education and college students' attitudes toward love: Survey evidence from China. *Journal of Marriage and Family, 81*, 584. https://doi.org/10.1111/jomf.12561

Huang, S. (2018). Beyond the sex–love–marriage alignment: Xinghun among queer people in mainland China. In M. W. Yarbrough, A. Jones, & J. N. DeFilippis (Eds.), *Queer families and relationships after marriage equality* (pp. 136–149). New York, NY: Routledge.

Jankowiak, W. (2017). Mate selection, intimacy, and marital love in Chinese society. In X. Zang & L. Zhao (Eds.), *Handbook on the family and marriage in China* (pp. 53–74). Cheltenham, UK: Edward Elgar Publishing.

Jankowiak, W., Shen, Y., Yao, S., Wang, C., & Volsche, S. (2015). Investigating love's universal attributes: A research report from China. *Cross-Cultural Research, 49*, 422–436.

Jeffreys, E., & Wang, P. (2018). Pathways to legalizing same-sex marriage in China and Taiwan: Globalization and "Chinese values". In B. Winter, M. Forest, & R. Sénac (Eds.), *Global perspectives on same-sex marriage: A neo-institutional approach* (pp. 197–219). Cham, Switzerland: Springer Nature.

Ji, Y., & Yeung, W. J. J. (2014). Heterogeneity in contemporary Chinese marriage. *Journal of Family Issues, 35*, 1662–1682.

Jiao, Y., Sun, I. Y., Farmer, A. K., & Lin, K. (2016). College students' definitions of intimate partner violence: A comparative study of three Chinese societies. *Journal of Interpersonal Violence, 31*, 1208–1229.

Johnson, M. D., Nguyen, L., Anderson, J. R., Liu, W., & Vennum, A. (2015). Pathways to romantic relationship success among Chinese young adult couples: Contributions of family dysfunction, mental health problems, and negative couple interaction. *Journal of Social and Personal Relationships, 32*(1), 5–23.

Klein, D. M., & White, J. M. (1996). *Family theories: An introduction* (pp. 149–177). Thousand Oaks, CA: Sage Publications.

Knudson-Martin, C. (2013). Why power matters: Creating a foundation of mutual support in couple relationships. *Family Process, 52*(1), 5–18.

Kong, T. S. (2016). The sexual in Chinese sociology: Homosexuality studies in contemporary China. *The Sociological Review, 64*, 495–514.

Kulik, L. (2011). Developments in spousal power relations: Are we moving toward equality? *Marriage and Family Review, 47*(7), 419–435.

Li, D., Li, C., Wang, Z., & Lau, J. T. (2015). Prevalence and associated factors of unprotected anal intercourse with regular male sex partners among HIV negative men who have sex with men in China: A cross-sectional survey. *PLoS One, 10*(3), e0119977.

Li, X., Zhang, B., Li, Y., Antonio, A. L. M., Chen, Y., & Williams, A. B. (2016). Mental health and suicidal ideation among Chinese women who have sex with men who have sex with men (MSM). *Women and Health, 56*(8), 940–956.

Lin, K., Sun, I. Y., Liu, J., & Chen, X. (2018). Chinese women's experience of intimate partner violence: Exploring factors affecting various types of IPV. *Violence Against Women, 24*(1), 66–84.

Lin, K., Sun, I. Y., Wu, Y., & Liu, J. (2016). College students' attitudes toward intimate partner violence: A comparative study of China and the US. *Journal of Family Violence, 31*(2), 179–189.

Lin, Z., Yu, W. H., & Su, K. H. (2019). Comparing same- and different-sex relationship dynamics: Experiences of young adults in Taiwan. *Demographic Research, 40*, 431–462.

Ling, M. T. L., & Chen, H. F. (2017). Hong Kong's parents' views on sex, marriage, and homosexuality. *Journal of Child and Family Studies, 26*, 1573–1582.

Liu, J., Bell, E., & Zhang, J. (2019). Conjugal intimacy, gender and modernity in contemporary China. *The British Journal of Sociology, 70*(1), 283–305.

Liu, J., Wang, Y., & Jackson, T. (2017). Towards explaining relationship dissatisfaction in Chinese dating couples: Relationship disillusionment, emergent distress, or insecure attachment style? *Personality and Individual Differences, 112*, 42–48.

Lui, L. (2016). Gender, rural-urban inequality, and intermarriage in China. *Social Forces, 95*(2), 639–662.

Luo, C., Yang, X., Li, S., & Feldman, M. W. (2017). Love or bread? What determines subjective wellbeing among left-behind women in rural China? *Gender Issues, 34*(1), 23–43.

MacKinnon, C. A. (1989). *Toward a feminist theory of the state*. Cambridge, MA: Harvard University Press.

Mu, Z., & Xie, Y. (2014). Marital age homogamy in China: A reversal of trend in the reform era? *Social Science Research, 44*, 141–157.

National Bureau of Statistics of China. (2018a). *China's forty year reform: Social and economic development report series 21*. Retrieved, February 15, 2019, from http://www.stats.gov.cn/ztjc/ztfx/ggkf40n/201809/t20180918_1623598.html

National Bureau of Statistics of China. (2018b). *Marriage registration and divorce*. Retrieved, February 15, 2019, from http://data.stats.gov.cn/easyquery.htm?cn=C01

National Law against Domestic Violence of the People's Republic of China. (2015). *The national people's congress of the People's Republic of China*. Retrieved, February 15, 2019, from http://www.npc.gov.cn/npc/xinwen/2015-12/28/content_1957457.htm

Pew Research Center. (2013). *The global divide on homosexuality*. Retrieved, February 15, 2019, from http://www.pewglobal.org/2013/06/04/the-global-divide-on-homosexuality/

Qian, Y., & Qian, Z. (2015). Work, family, and gendered happiness among married people in urban China. *Social Indicators Research, 121*(1), 61–74.

Raymo, J. M., Park, H., Xie, Y., & Yeung, W. J. J. (2015). Marriage and family in East Asia: Continuity and change. *Annual Review of Sociology, 41*, 471–492.

Schmitt, D. P. (2005). Fundamentals of human mating strategies. In D. Buss (Ed.), *The handbook of evolutionary psychology* (pp. 258–291). Hoboken, NJ: Wiley.

Schoenfeld, E. A., Loving, T. J., Pope, M. T., Huston, T. L., & Štulhofer, A. (2017). Does sex really matter? Examining the connections between spouses' nonsexual behaviors, sexual frequency, sexual satisfaction, and marital satisfaction. *Archives of Sexual Behavior, 46*, 489–501.

Shieh, W. Y. (2016). Why same-sex couples break up: A follow-up study in Taiwan. *Journal of GLBT Family Studies, 12*(3), 257–276.

Shu, X., Zhu, Y., & Zhang, Z. (2013). Patriarchy, resources, and specialization: Marital decision-making power in urban China. *Journal of Family Issues, 34*(7), 885–917.

Simon, C. T., & Wallace, T. W. (2018). Disclosure of victimization experiences of Chinese male survivors of intimate partner abuse. *Qualitative Social Work, 17*, 744–761.

Sinha Mukherjee, S. (2015). More educated and more equal? A comparative analysis of female education and employment in Japan, China and India. *Gender and Education, 27*, 846–870.

Tao, P., Coates, R., & Maycock, B. (2012). Investigating marital relationship in infertility: A systematic review of quantitative studies. *Journal of Reproduction and Infertility, 13*(2), 71–80.

The Supreme People's Court of the People's Republic of China. (2016). *Yan and Sun divorce case first instance civil adjustment* [闫某与孙某甲离婚纠纷一审民事判决书]. China Judgement Online. Retrieved, February 20, 2019, from, http://wenshu.court.gov.cn/content/content?DocID=67729981-c0a5-4720-82f8-a73c012cd9a9&KeyWord=%E9%97%AB%E6%9F%90%7C%E5%AD%99%E6%9F%90%7C%E7%A6%BB%E5%A9%9A%7C%E6%B9%96%E5%8C%97

The Supreme People's Court of the People's Republic of China. (2018). *Yan and Sun divorce case retrial inspection and civil adjustment* [闫某、孙某离婚纠纷再审审查与审判监督民事裁定书]. China Judgement Online. Retrieved, February 20, 2019, from http://wenshu.court.gov.cn/content/content?DocID=403a662b-25e0-42b5-948a-a8cf013110b8&KeyWord=%E5%AE%B6%E6%9A%B4

Tian, F. F., Qian, Y., & Qian, Z. (2018). Hukou locality and intermarriages in two Chinese cities: Shanghai and Shenzhen. *Research in Social Stratification and Mobility, 56*, 12–20.

Wang, L. (2018). Influences of media exposure on Chinese university students' attitudes and perceptions of intimate partner violence. *Deviant Behavior, 39*, 1202–1216.

Wang, P. (2017). Foreign-related marriages in contemporary China, 1979–2013. In X. Zang & L. Zhao (Eds.), *Handbook on the family and marriage in China* (pp. 89–107). Cheltenham, UK: Edward Elgar Publishing.

Wang, T., Liu, Y., Li, Z., Liu, K., Xu, Y., Shi, W., & Chen, L. (2017). Prevalence of intimate partner violence (IPV) during pregnancy in China: A systematic review and meta-analysis. *PLoS One, 12*(10), e0175108.

Wu, H., & Ye, H. (2016). Hollow lives: Women left-behind in rural China. *Journal of Agrarian Change, 16*(1), 50–69.

Wu, Y., Mou, Y., Wang, Y., & Atkin, D. (2018). Exploring the de-stigmatizing effect of social media on homosexuality in China: An interpersonal-mediated contact versus parasocial-mediated contact perspective. *Asian Journal of Communication, 28*(1), 20–37.

Xu, A., DeFrain, J., & Liu, W. (2016). *The Chinese family today*. London, UK: Routledge.

Xu, A., & Xia, Y. (2014). The changes in mainland Chinese families during the social transition: A critical analysis. *Journal of Comparative Family Studies, 45*(1), 31–53.

Yang, T., Poon, A. W. C., & Breckenridge, J. (2018). Estimating the prevalence of intimate partner violence in mainland China—Insights and challenges. *Journal of Family Violence, 34*, 93–105.

Yeung, W. J. J., & Hu, S. (2016). Paradox in marriage values and behavior in contemporary China. *Chinese Journal of Sociology, 2*(3), 447–476.

Ying, L., Wu, L. H., & Loke, A. Y. (2016). The effects of psychosocial interventions on the mental health, pregnancy rates, and marital function of infertile couples undergoing in vitro fertilization: A systematic review. *Journal of Assisted Reproduction and Genetics, 33*, 689–701.

Yu, B., Chen, X., Yan, Y., Gong, J., Li, F., & Roberson, E. K. (2017). Migration stress, poor mental health, and engagement in sex with high-risk partners: A mediation modeling analysis of data from rural-to-urban migrants in China. *Sexuality Research and Social Policy, 14*(4), 467–477.

Yu, J., & Xie, Y. (2015). Cohabitation in China: Trends and determinants. *Population and Development Review, 41*, 607–628.

Zang, X., & Zhao, L. (2017). *Handbook on the family and marriage in China*. Cheltenham, UK: Edward Elgar Publishing.

Zhang, C., Wang, X., & Zhang, D. (2014). Urbanization, unemployment rate and China's rising divorce rate. *Chinese Journal of Population Resources and Environment, 12*(2), 157–164.

Zheng, T. (2015). *Tongzhi living: Men attracted to men in postsocialist China*. Minneapolis, MN: University of Minnesota Press.

Zhuang, Y. J., & Everett, A. M. (2018). A brief history of Chinese wedding and bridal photography tourism: Through the lens of top Chinese wedding photographers. In E. C. L. Yang & C. Khoo-Lattimore (Eds.), *Asian cultures and contemporary tourism* (pp. 79–100). Singapore: Springer.

Chapter 8
Couple Relationships in Mediterranean Malta

Suzanne Piscopo, Sue Vella, and Angela Abela

8.1 Introduction

Malta is a small archipelago nation strategically situated in the center of the Mediterranean Sea. The islands' size renders Malta a face-to-face community where interaction with the extended family is common and anonymity is unusual. Its geographical position and history of colonization play a significant role in the way of life of its inhabitants. A tourism-based economy, a rising number of economic migrants, a growing consumeristic and pluralistic society, and a shift from a homogenous Catholic culture to a predominantly secular one are all linked to the values, attitudes, and practices of the Maltese as individuals and as partners in a couple dyad.

S. Piscopo (✉)
Department of Health, Physical Education and Consumer Studies, Faculty of Education, University of Malta, Msida, Malta
e-mail: suzanne.piscopo@um.edu.mt

S. Vella
Department of Social Policy and Social Work, Faculty for Social Wellbeing, University of Malta, Msida, Malta
e-mail: sue.vella@um.edu.mt

A. Abela
Department of Family Studies, Faculty for Social Wellbeing, University of Malta, Msida, Malta
e-mail: angela.abela@um.edu.mt

8.2 The Couple Relationship in Europe and Its Southern Countries

In a recent 27-country European study on life satisfaction among those 15 years of age and older, the countries of the South, namely Greece, Italy, Portugal and Spain emerged as having some of the lowest levels of satisfaction, with only 46%, 65%, 56%, and 77%, respectively, of the studied population being very or fairly satisfied with life (Rajani, Skianis, & Filippidis, 2019). These findings are in contrast to the results for Malta and Cyprus where 92% and 83% of the respondents rated themselves as very or fairly satisfied with life. In the Rajani et al. (2019) European study, when compared to those who were single, widowed, or divorced, being married was associated with higher life satisfaction.

The question which automatically arises therefore is whether married status is still being sought in Europe and, if yes, what is the motivation.

According to the European Social Survey (2016), marriage remains the predominant manner in which couple relationships are formalized in Europe, but other forms of pair-bonding, such as cohabitation and Living Alone Together (LAT—unmarried couples in a stable couple relationship) are also gaining ground. A study by Rossi (2014) showed how European countries differ in the "pathways" to couple formation. Southern European countries, such as Malta, Italy, and Greece, are among the most frequent to choose the marriage pathway and, together with Spain, among the most frequent to choose the LAT pathway.

Yet there has been a steady reduction in marriage rates in most countries of Southern Europe in the past two decades, alongside a concomitant increase in cohabitation, with the latter being more common in Portugal and Spain and to a lesser degree in Italy (Olah, 2015). Looking at crude marriage and divorce rates for select Southern European countries (Table 8.1) one sees that there are differences between countries and also as compared to the EU-28 average (Eurostat, 2017). In 2017, Cyprus had the highest marriage rate, but also the highest divorce rate. Malta had the second highest marriage rate, but the lowest divorce rate; the latter was

Table 8.1 Marriage and divorce crude rates (per 1000) in selected Southern European countries and the EU-28 in 2000–2017

Country	Marriage		Divorce	
	2000	2017	2000	2017
Cyprus	13.4	6.8	1.7	2.2
Greece	4.5	4.7	1.0	1.8
Italy	5.0	3.2	0.7	1.5
Malta	6.7	6.3	[a]	0.7
Portugal	6.2	3.3	1.9	2.1
Spain	5.4	3.7	0.9	2.1
EU-28	5.2	4.4[b]	1.8	1.9[b]

Source: Compiled from Eurostat (2017), Marriage and Divorce Statistics
[a]Divorce was only introduced in 2011
[b] 2016 data

perhaps partially influenced by the fact that divorce legislation was only introduced in Malta in 2011. All told, shifts in formation and re-formation of couples in Southern Europe are clearly evident.

What motivates people to get married is also changing. Around the world and throughout the ages, in most societies marriage has been a crucial institution for structuring adults' intimate relationships, and for providing a stable context for conceiving and rearing children and integrating their fathers into their lives (Social Trends Institute, 2015).

A study by Camarero (2014) refers to pluralism and changes in relationship priorities in Europe. Camarero explains that there is no unified view on marriage in Europe, with Southern European countries such as Malta (79%), Italy (57%), and Greece (52%) standing out as being staunch supporters of a traditional "alliance" type of marriage—where marriage is undertaken as a necessary means to happiness. Malta, Italy, and Poland, all predominantly Catholic countries, are top supporters of "marriage for life." It is posited that for these latter countries, the value of marriage is rooted in cultural and religious norms, whereas for some other countries material well-being, personal gratification, or practical partnership might be the motivation for marriage.

The presence of children in the couple's household is also a distinguishing variable in Southern European countries versus other European countries. Olah (2015) reports that "the difference in the presence of children by partnership type is especially striking in Southern Europe" (p. 8) and that extended households with more than two adults with children are common, possibly reflecting "the pattern of adult children leaving the parental home at more mature ages in these regions, especially in Mediterranean countries, and/or young couples starting their family by moving in with the parents of one of the partners" (p. 10). Recent statistics back this interpretation. On average, young people leave the parental household at the age of 26 years in the EU (Eurostat, 2019). In contrast, in a number of the Southern countries the pattern is different where on average, young people in Malta leave home at 30.7 years, in Italy at 30.1 years, in Spain at 29.5 years, in Greece at 29.3 years, and in Portugal at 28.9 years of age. It is not unusual for Maltese young adults to reside with parents right up till the day they get married (Abela, Frosh, & Dowling, 2005; Visanich, 2018).

8.3 A Focus on Malta

In 2006, sociologist Anthony Abela posited that traditional values anchored in an "attachment to the church and religion, party politics, local and social solidarity, traditionalism and materialism, were gradually giving way to the reshaping of a national identity in a new social context" (p. 10). Fast forward 13 years and one can say that Malta has witnessed an upsurge in cultural diversity, stable economic growth, and an increasingly consumeristic society, which may have resulted in material and cultural enrichment on the one hand, but also the development of socioeconomic disparities on the other (Abela, 2016; Darmanin, 2018; National Statistics Office, 2019).

8.3.1 What Are the Trends in Couple Relationships in Malta?

As indicated earlier and also highlighted in work by Angela Abela (2009, 2016) on sociocultural contexts of families and couples in Malta, the institution of marriage still represents an important stage in the family life cycle; a bridge between youth and adulthood (Visanich, 2018). Overall, Malta ranks among the top countries with respect to marriage rates in the EU (Eurostat, 2017). However, the numbers of civil marriages are now higher than those of church-celebrated marriages. In 2010 there were 1547 church weddings and 740 civil weddings, whereas in 2018 there were 1129 church weddings and 1423 civil weddings (Scicluna, 2019). One must caution that the increase in civil weddings may be explained by a booming wedding tourism industry in Malta (OurWEDDING.com.mt [online]). In 2016, there were 835 foreign couples who got married in Malta, with 749 of these opting for a civil ceremony. The increase in civil weddings may also be due to the growing number of mixed-nationality marriages where a church wedding may not always be possible. In 2017, there were 1014 marriages between a Maltese person and a foreigner, as compared to 689 in 2008 (Malta Independent, 2018).

Four significant legislative developments in the past decade in Malta have contributed to changing patterns in couple formation on our islands. These were the introduction of divorce in 2011, of civil unions for same-sex couples in 2014, of cohabitation law in 2017, and of marriage for same-sex couples also in 2017. Some early indications regarding trends are available. For example, despite an initial spike when divorce was legalized, the number of divorces obtained in Malta has remained steady over the years, in the low to higher 300s annually (see Table 8.2), although an additional number of divorces were also obtained abroad. Nonetheless, as noted earlier, in 2017, Malta still had the lowest crude rate for divorce in the EU, at 0.7 per 1000 (Eurostat, 2017).

The average number of marriage separation cases initiated every day in 2018 in Malta was 3.6 (Scicluna, 2019). Of all separation cases initiated in 2018, close to three quarters were contentious, requiring a mediation letter or requiring Court Application, while just less than one quarter were amicable separations. Separation rates were stable for a few years, but have increased quite steeply since 2015 (see Table 8.2), with 1358 cases registered in 2018 (Mallia, 2019).

Research on whether and why separated Maltese individuals obtain a divorce and legally join in a new partnership (marriage or otherwise) is still in its infancy. A study by Abela, Casha, Debono, and Lauri (2015), conducted with 2006 married

Table 8.2 Marriage dissolution in Malta through divorce and separation, 2011–2016

	2011	2012	2013	2014	2015	2016
Divorces obtained, total	115	510	399	399	468	500
Divorces obtained, from Malta	42[a]	441	338	323	372	371
Registered separations	518	554	666	662	656	701

Source: Compiled from National Statistics Office, Malta (2018a)
[a]Divorce was introduced at the end of 2011

and previously married adults just before divorce was legalized, uncovered various attitudes toward divorce and remarriage. A striking finding relevant at the time was that the majority (67.4%) of respondents did not consider remarriage. Top reasons put forward were religious or social beliefs and values (20.3%), not to relive past bad experiences (19.6%) and old age or health (8.9%). Women and previously married adults were statistically more likely to offer the second reason. A more positive attitude to considering remarriage was evident in adults who were younger, of a higher socioeconomic status, previously married, non-parents or who had children who were not all born within marriage.

More recent research by Farrugia (2014), conducted after divorce had been legalized for some years, studied the process and impacts of remarriage among seven couples and found that a number of them had tried to salvage their marriage before resorting to marriage dissolution, that separation rather than divorce was the toughest aspect marking the breakdown, that resilience was required in order to face social stigma, overcome fear of another failure, address challenges faced as one transitioned to and shaped a new couple relationship and manage biological and step children. A prevalent attitude was that remarriage was sought for personal satisfaction, perhaps reflecting an increasing emphasis locally on achieving self-fulfillment and personal emotional satisfaction from marriage (Abela & Walker, 2014).

Vella (2015) conducted a study with 14 same-sex couples, 6 couples who were in a civil union and 8 who were not, immediately after the legalization of same-sex civil unions in 2014. Participants explained that the choice to commit themselves in civil union was based on gaining legal protections, facilitating presentation to others, and acceptance as a committed couple. They felt that civil union had offered an effective piece of legislation to present same-sex relationships in a society where the normative relationship is a heterosexual one. Some were very comfortable in their extended family and in the public sphere, which was also becoming more accepting of the manifestations of such union like holding hands. However, they were also aware of the low acceptance of discussions around the possibilities for bringing children into the union. Interviewees described how they lived a regular family life, with its chores and challenges like in any other household. Yet, they experienced domesticity and division of labor with a lack of gender differentiation. In a way, this fostered a more equal setting where "traditionalism combines with cohesiveness, making living a cooperative effort in which partners depend on one another" (Vella, 2015, p. 174).

8.3.2 What Makes for Satisfying Couple Relationships in Malta?

In 2016 and in 2017, The President's Foundation for the Wellbeing of Society (PFWS) launched two related research reports on couple relationships in Malta. A number of studies had been conducted over the years looking at marriage, divorce, remarriage, same-sex marriage, and parenting locally (e.g., Abela, 2009; Abela & Lanfranco, 2016; Abela et al., 2005, 2015; Borg, 2012, 2016; Farrugia, 2014; Vella,

2015), but this was the first time that a large-scale quantitative study was carried out that was nationally representative and specifically focused on factors which sustained relationships. This section will give an overview of the two PFWS sequential studies which have been conducted to date and which were also tabled at the Parliament of Malta (Session 65, P.L.873, December 18, 2017).

The first quantitative study used a Computer-Assisted Telephone Interview and collected data from a representative sample of 2469 adults who were either in a relationship or single, and who either had or did not have children. It explored various aspects of life and relationship satisfaction. The second qualitative study used focus groups and interviews to delve deeper into factors influencing relationship satisfaction which emerged from the first study. The sample comprised adults who had scored high or low on a relationship satisfaction scale.

8.3.2.1 The Profile of Maltese Couples

The research sample of the first PFWS (2016) study was predominantly of Maltese nationality (99%) and adhered to the Roman Catholic faith (99%). The importance of being in a relationship was evident from results which showed that 66.6% of the participants reported to be in a relationship and these included not only those who were currently married (100%) but also 53.3% of the divorced, 36.5% of the separated, 35.6% of the single, and 9.6% of the widowed participants. Such results confirmed that seeking to be in some form of committed relationship was a priority for the majority of Maltese adults and that secularization of local society and legal opportunities had very likely facilitated this happening (Abela, 2009; Abela & Walker, 2014). Some years ago, an alliance through marriage was seen as the only route to happiness, but now other pair-bondings outside of the marriage institution were becoming acceptable. In the PFWS (2016) study, 11% reported to be cohabiting and in a committed and exclusive relationship. Additionally, 93% of respondents in a relationship had Maltese partners, but 1 in 3 (31.3%) of divorced respondents had a foreign partner. Notably, the presence of children influenced the status of the couple relationship. Participants with dependent children, particularly those who were single or widowed, were more likely to report being in a committed and exclusive relationship.

8.3.2.2 Life and Relationship Satisfaction

In keeping with the literature already cited in the beginning of this chapter, in the PFWS (2016) study there was a positive correlation between being married or in a couple relationship and life satisfaction. Congruently, satisfaction in one's relationship was associated with life satisfaction. On a scale of 1–5 (from 1 lowest, to 5 highest), those who were married reported highest levels of life satisfaction (mean 4.22), followed, in descending order, by the single (mean 4.06), the separated (mean 3.71), the widowed (mean 3.64), and the divorced (mean 3.63).

Nine out of ten (90.4%) participants who were in a relationship described their relationship as "positive" or "very positive." The only significant predictor of satisfaction in one's current relationship was civil status: Married respondents had the highest positive responses, with a mean score of 4.5 (on a scale of 1–5, 5 being highest). However, a number of other factors were correlated with relationship satisfaction, namely age, employment status, and income adequacy.

Older adults (61+) were more likely to describe their relationship as "very positive." This could be related to comfort with each other's personalities, idiosyncrasies and practices, emotional regulation, and stronger ability to weather negative experiences (Lee & McKinnish, 2018; Mazzuca, Kafetsios, Livi, & Presaghi, 2018). It could also be related to their life stage in that perhaps having now retired, they were no longer experiencing challenging work problems which could spill over to the home environment, or perhaps they were no longer experiencing child-rearing problems since their children were now adults and possibly no longer residing in the same home.

In relation to parental status, parents reporting highest levels of relationship satisfaction had children younger than 9 years of age, whereas parents reporting lower levels of relationship satisfaction had adolescents. Additionally, dual earning couples with children were twice as likely to describe their relationship as "negative," "very negative," or "average" (10.5%) than those without children (5.1%). Indeed, research has shown that having a preschool child was associated with greater parental happiness in Southern Europe (Social Trends Institute, 2015). Moreover, in research with Spanish couples, persons not having children showed greater rates of satisfaction with the couple relationship than those with children (Urbano-Contreras, Martínez-González & Iglesias-García, 2018).

Employment status was also correlated with relationship satisfaction among Maltese adults (PFWS, 2016). The most satisfied couples were in a situation where one partner worked full-time whereas the other worked part-time. In the least satisfied couples both partners were unemployed and on benefits. Two factors could be at play here. Given that another finding was that the lower the income adequacy, the lower the relationship satisfaction, then couples' financial insecurity possibly took its toll on the relationship. This could be due to conflicts about money management and purchases, or a sense of inadequacy compared to felt needs and wants for themselves or their loved ones. On the other hand, the dual-earner couple may have found a work–life balance which suited them, so that by having a full-time and part-time status, income was deemed sufficient and there was time for communication and other couple and family activities. Data collected confirm the above conjectures, as when asked what they liked least in their relationship, adults' responses included, in order of magnitude: working too much leaving no time for the relationship, one partner always at work or rarely at home, poor communication and lack of financial security.

When those in a relationship were asked what they valued most in their relationship, the five topmost responses were: respect (25%), communication (18%), trust (16%), love (15%), and fidelity (9%). Young and middle-aged adults valued communication and trust most. Older age groups valued forgiveness and understanding most. Respondents reporting the highest relationship satisfaction mentioned communication most.

Vignette

Elizabeth and Walter have been married for 10 years and have two daughters. The couple believes strongly in respect and says this can only happen when a couple is capable of good communication. Elizabeth explains that she has always appreciated how her husband accepts her as she is and not for a dream that could be. So she also accepts her husband the way he is. She sees her husband as someone to turn to when she has a problem, a partner who helps to raise their family together. She values his loyalty toward her and the children, saying that loyalty is not just about keeping out of extramarital affairs, but that he does not let her down on important things and that his number one priority is their family. At one point, when they had their first daughter, she felt that her husband had forgotten her and was besotted with his newborn child. She was crying constantly; it affected her so much. So she told her husband that she felt she had become an outsider and it was breaking her. They spoke about this at length and in time a balance was found.

Walter explains that for him and his wife they are number one to each other. They both listen actively to each other and make time to be together alone. Especially now that their daughters are no longer infants, a few times a week they manage to go on a 20-min walk which they both enjoy doing. Sometimes they go to a café while their daughters are at private lessons. Walter looks forward to these dates with his wife.

8.3.3 An Ecosystem Analysis

In the above overview of the status of couples in Malta and life and relationship satisfaction among the Maltese couples studied in the PFWS (2016) research, it is evident that various interrelated factors are having an impact. These occur at different levels of the environment based on Bronfenbrenner's (1994) ecosystem framework; from the micro system (e.g., valued aspects of a satisfying relationship), to the meso system (e.g., schedule and type of couple employment), to the macro system (e.g., cultural affinity to couple bonding via marriage), and set within the chronosystem (e.g., influence of age and lifestage on relationship satisfaction; shifts in couple bonding trends).

The interplay of the various contextual and personal factors influencing a couple's relationship and marriage satisfaction has also been described in research with Maltese married, heterosexual, dual-earner couples with children who had been married for over 7 years (Piscopo, 2014). Key factors involved were perspectives of relationship formation and maintenance beyond "living happily ever after" (p. 72), flexibility in gender roles, strategies for handling of conflicts, shared enjoyment,

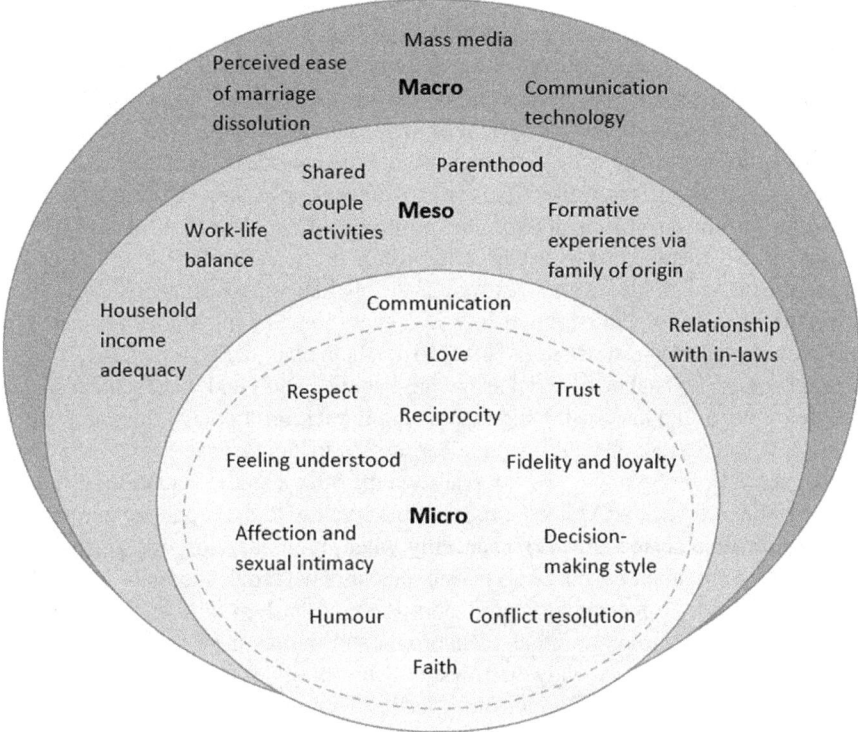

Fig. 8.1 Factors influencing couple relationships in Malta as emerging from the President's Foundation for the Wellbeing of Society sustainable relationships studies (PFWS, 2016, 2017)

attending to the needs of and appreciating one's partner, and being generous and loving. The below sections will show how the PFWS (2017) qualitative study corroborated and added to previous studies, referring to different factors in the macro, meso, and micro levels of a proposed socio-ecological model (Fig. 8.1).

8.3.3.1 Factors Influencing Couple Relationships: The Macro Level

The mass media were perceived by study participants as negatively impacting on the couple relationship primarily in two ways. Firstly, constant marketing was seen as fostering materialistic norms and thus leading to a reordering of people's priorities. This has added economic pressures among couples who feel they need to work more to augment their income and be able to maintain a "socially acceptable" lifestyle. In particular, parents seek to gratify their children's demands or give their children what they had perhaps lacked in their own childhood. One example mentioned was paying for extensive extracurricular activities, which sometimes led to conflicts among the parents on what was "essential." This consumeristic shift has a strong hold on contemporary society (Piscopo, 2012) with couples working longer hours to be able to participate in certain activities and buy certain goods.

The second observation by participants about the negative impact of the mass media was in relation to its portrayal of an idealized married life, based on romantic practices. The mass media were blamed for shaping unrealistic expectations of couple relationships and marriage. As a result, young people enter into a couple relationship with an immature attitude and ill-prepared for the practical realities of nurturing and maintaining a strong relationship in the face of routine household management and childcare tasks, as well as the challenges of unexpected periods of adversity. This trend and potential link with mass media depiction of married life has been highlighted elsewhere (Abela, 2016; Abela et al., 2005).

Technology was acknowledged as having its advantages and disadvantages with respect to nurturing and sustaining stable couple relationships. On the one hand it was appreciated as a practical communication tool to "touch base" with one's partner at intervals during a long working day. On the other hand, it was seen in a negative light on two counts: As intruding into time spent with one's partner (a resource which was often scarce already), especially when more attention was given to the mobile phone or tablet than to one's partner; and as a potential risk factor for infidelity as it facilitated opportunities for clandestine relationships with another individual, particularly through mobile technology and social media. These findings coincide with those of a study with Maltese university students in a committed relationship (Scicluna, 2017), indicating that technology is impacting both mature and younger partners in a relationship.

Perceived ease of marital dissolution is becoming increasingly evident in Malta even through casual conversations where people refer to recently married couples who are in the process of separation or divorce. As described earlier, Maltese couples traditionally married for life (Abela et al., 2005; Camarero, 2014) and marriage dissolution was far from one's mind as the knot was being tied. Trying to seek annulment when a church marriage was involved, or seeking divorce overseas when a civil marriage was involved were the only options available up till 2011 in order to be able to remarry. Neither of these were easy options from a time and expense perspective. Many people resorted to separation and eventually to informal cohabitation.

Several of the PFWS (2017) study participants expressed concern that marriage is now being entered into more lightly, as dissolution was perceived to be easier. All study participants stated that they had married intent on having a faithful, long-lasting commitment. They emphasized the need to work hard to sustain the relationship, especially where children were involved. Almost all, however, spoke about their perception of the fragility of marriage, partially substantiated by the broader societal perception that marital dissolution is "easy," both legally but also attitudinally with regards to weaker levels of commitment. As one male participant described it: "Today, [people] live with a suitcase behind the door, and as soon as the first problem crops up for the couple, it's goodbye" (cited in PFWS, 2017, p. 28). Participants also attributed this current perception of the ease of marriage dissolution to TV fiction series and to a weakening of social norms around fidelity and exclusivity.

8.3.3.2 Factors Influencing Couple Relationships: The Meso Level

Work–family balance and its association with couple well-being has been explored in a number of studies in Malta (Abela, 2009, 2016; Borg, 2012; Piscopo, 2014; Rizzo, 2009) wherein the need for less rigid gender roles in the home environment was underscored. In the PFWS (2017) study, this theme permeated the interview conversations for different reasons. All participants placed great value on spending quality time together as a couple. Yet, the struggle to balance work and family life was felt to negatively affect the couple relationship, especially when either one or both partners worked long hours or alternating shifts. Some explained that when they were still a childless couple, they arranged shift-work to be off work at the same time. Once they had children, however, they actually reversed this so one parent would always be off work to care for the children and do other household tasks while the other was at work. The possibility for telework generated conflicting feelings: while facilitating paid work from home, it often also impinged on couple time, such as when one of the partners started to catch up on the telework duties in the evening.

In the EU, a 40-h working week is still the norm for men, with the working week being longest during the parenting phase of life (European Foundation for the Improvement of Living and Working Conditions, 2018). For women, an average of 34 h per week is spent in paid employment, although the hours decrease during the parenting phase. Yet, women spend significantly more time than men in unpaid work, primarily taking care of children or dependent adults. Different studies have shown that the paid and domestic work-related gender activity gap is still pronounced for Southern Europe (Olah, 2015) and that problems combining work and life are most frequently reported by people with young children (Social Trends Institute, 2015). Locally, the Maltese National Commissioner for the Promotion of Equality (Laiviera, 2019) has noted that both women and men are increasingly seeking to reconcile employment and parenthood through taking advantage of available family-friendly measures and flexible working arrangements.

Another factor related to work–life balance which emerged from the PFWS (2017) study was that participants lamented how their partner's work colleagues often saw the partner more than they did during the day. Moreover, many of the women and men expressed concern that socializing with colleagues outside work hours increased the risk of infidelity. Such fear may negatively impact the relationship. As research with Portuguese adults has shown, even the imagination of infidelity is profoundly painful (Pazhoohi et al., 2019).

Household income adequacy was highlighted in both of the PFWS studies (2016, 2017) as related to couple well-being. In the PFWS (2016) study, inadequate income was one of the main factors associated with low relationship satisfaction and in the follow-up PFWS (2017) study participants stated unequivocally that often Maltese couples are working long hours to ensure an adequate income to meet their needs. Many participants considered it impossible to raise a family on one salary alone; multiple jobs were essential. In 2017, the at-risk-of-poverty rate (the number of persons living in households with a national equivalized income below the at-risk-of-poverty line) for all households with dependent children was 18.2%, and for single parent households it was an alarming 45.7% (National Statistics Office, 2018b). That income adequacy was highlighted by the PFWS studies participants as a potential source of strain on the couple relationship is understandable given the above figures.

Parenthood impacted the couple relationship in various ways as already partially described above with respect to life satisfaction, income, work–life balance, and the ages of the children. Traditionally, a main cultural expectation of a couple relationship was for there to be offspring who would be given priority over the couple itself (Abela et al., 2005). In the PFWS (2017) study this was still felt strongly; however, a slight shift was evident as the companionship of the partner was also given value and several participants with children maintained that the couple relationship should take priority over the parent–child relationship. One male expressed this quite bluntly, stating that "Children should know their place in the family. They are not number one, the number one is your partner..." (cited in PFWS, 2017, p. 48).

Participants who were parents consistently described children as influencing their relationship with their partner. Having children was described as a "blessing," but also as a stressor for the couple relationship. There were differing views on how to balance loyalties fairly toward one's partner and one's children. For some, the partner's closeness to their children led them to feel neglected, as if they were of secondary importance. At the same time, most participants with children made an effort to find time to be together and to talk to each other without the children present despite various constraints. As described by one parent, "We can't talk about certain things when our daughter is with us, for example when talking about discipline on children... So you go out together, for a coffee, even go out shopping together, because that is an important part of building the relationship" (cited in PFWS, 2017, p. 49).

Shared couple experiences were seen by participants in the PFWS study (2017) as enhancing the couple relationship and were deemed important to nurture from early on in the relationship. These experiences involved mindfully doing activities together and not just spending time together. Activities mentioned ranged from walking the dog, to jogging, to praying together every evening. In particular, engaging in joint leisure activities emerged as beneficial to promoting closeness among the couples, although even just showing interest in a partner's hobbies or compromising by joining in an activity a partner enjoyed, such as visiting certain museums when on holiday, were also seen as enhancing the couple bond. Research conducted with young Maltese heterosexual couples in a relationship of over 5 years (Borg, 2012) found that partner similarity in leisure pursuits reduced conflict. In another study with young Maltese adults (Borg, 2016), participants reported that they preferred being in a relationship "with someone with whom they share common ground" (p. 84).

The couple's *relationship with in-laws* was considered as potentially impacting the couple relationship both positively and negatively. As in previous research, in-laws were appreciated as a source of support and care for grandchildren, often taking responsibility for the younger children during after-school hours and holidays while parents are at work (Abela & Lanfranco, 2016). However, some couples in the PFWS study (2017) also referred to the unfortunate conflicts which occasionally arise between the partners as result of strong allegiances with one's parents, such as when there are frequent visits to parents or contrasting opinions of in-laws and partner. This sometimes strained the relationship between the couple. Results from a study by

Borg (2012) with young Maltese couples had similar results: these young adults were not keen on involving their parents in the couple's relationship, with some expressing belief that when parents are involved, more problems could arise between the couple.

Another generational factor which was raised by some participants in the PFWS (2017) study was the couple's *formative experiences as individuals within their family of origin*. These were perceived as having a significant role in molding perceptions around expectations from marriage and what facilitates or diminishes happy couple relationships. The influence of the family of origin was also mentioned in local research with couples by Borg (2016) where parents were considered as role models and thus one would typically seek a partner with similar qualities and values to their parents. Similarly, research by Piscopo (2014) indicated that processes observed in the family of origin which helped to build a happy couple relationship were emulated or built upon, and other less facilitative processes avoided, in the new couple.

8.3.3.3 Factors Influencing Couple Relationships: The Micro Level

In this section factors grounded in the data from the PFWS (2016, 2017) research will be presented in the form of a narrative. The main focus will be on communication—its manifestation and processes—since in both PFWS studies this emerged as highly significant.

In a stable and thriving couple relationship *communication* in different formats, based on different values and with varying goals is crucial. The ultimate goal is for each partner in the couple to be happy and for the couple as a dyad to be sustained. Partners in Malta want to *feel understood* and to be shown *respect*. They want to be "heard" by their partner, they want to have their needs considered as appropriate, they want to find a friend in their partner when needed, they want to have their apology accepted when they admit wrongdoing. Partners understand the *reciprocity* of all this and that it often requires effort. Partners also feel that respect is lacking if the other partner is unreliable and lets them down, or when one's dignity is not respected; especially if rights are ignored or, worse still, they feel exploited, ill-treated, or abused. Even if the relationship breaks down, partners can still maintain a respectful relationship, especially if they are parents.

Maltese partners want someone who is open, honest, and faithful, where "nothing is hidden." *Loyalty* and *fidelity* are paramount. A partner needs to be loyal through giving priority to the couple relationship over other roles and relationships. Fidelity should be maintained through considering the impact of any decisions and actions on the partner's feelings, even when the couple is not physically together. *Trust* is built with time and the beginning of a relationship is a period of uncertainty. As the relationship progresses, there is a sense of security that each partner is acting with mutual well-being in mind. Being afraid to discuss something for fear of being misunderstood by one's partner is destructive.

Partners seek to have someone who can *share in decision-making*. This involves discussion and mutual agreement, but also acknowledging that one partner may take the lead in decision-making in some areas, while the other partner takes the lead in others based on personal knowledge, skills, and experience. Just being aware of what is happening which can impact the couple or family is important. Conflicts are unavoidable and decisions on parenting and sharing of household chores are common sources of conflict. Irrespective of whether or not conventional gender prescriptions are followed, clarity and execution of work committed to is essential for both individual and couple well-being.

A lack of compromise and perceived selfishness in the partner are key hindrances to the resolution of intercouple disagreements. Any communication which is hurtful, criticizing, dismissive, or dishonest is particularly harmful. Constructive *conflict resolution* requires making time to talk through the differences or dilemma cooperatively, as a couple. It requires a sensitivity to the strong emotions often being experienced by either one or both partners and waiting to discuss when the situation is calmer. Being able to manage differences and resulting conflicts is more important than having commonalities among the two partners. When partners' different personalities complement each other, this is seen as contributing to a sense of harmony in the couple relationship and nurturing growth in each partner.

Faith can also help to sustain the relationship in different ways. Faith can work to strengthen commitment to the relationship and the ability to deal with more challenging periods. Some couples also include faith-related practices and rituals in their daily routines. *Humor* such as telling jokes and light banter can also add joy to the relationship.

Vignette

James is a self-employed mechanic and typically spends the whole day alone in his garage. He explains how he is often very tired when he gets home, but relishes the chats he has with his wife Pauline over a mug of tea. He knows she likes to be shown affection so makes the effort to give her a hug and say "I love you" as soon as he arrives. He admits that he is not an affectionate person, but believes that these small things count and it is easy to end up taking them for granted. He does not recall ever seeing his father kiss his mother as he was growing up.

Pauline believes that couples need to understand each other and to listen to each other. She knows her husband likes to talk a lot when they meet in the evening. He opens up about work matters, since he works alone and does not have friends. She confesses that sometimes she does not feel like hearing about his problems, but stays quiet and listens because she senses he needs to tell her. At the same time, this helps her know what is going on in his life. One thing that has started bothering her recently is that he has stopped joking with her. He used to make her laugh a lot and he laughed a lot too. She feels that maybe he is not happy with her anymore, because he is not joking the way he used to. Pauline believes that jokes and laughter broaden love and hopes that this change in her husband is just because he is very tired because of his work.

Communication among couples in Malta goes beyond the pure verbal interaction. *Affection* and emotional support can be shown through other endearing actions, such as hugs, meaningful gestures, and helpful behaviors. *Sexual intimacy* is valuable, but not the be-all and end-all of a relationship. *Love* is a choice one makes to stay with a particular person. It is manifested through showing patience, tolerance, and a willingness to do everything for the partner. It is about accepting one's partner as they are, yet also supporting them in their decisions and helping them to grow. Love progresses to a higher dimension when one is not simply loving for the purpose of personal gain.

This narrative of the various factors that Maltese respondents value in a relationship corroborates findings from other local studies (Borg, 2012; Compagno, 2018; Piscopo, 2014). Similar results included the value of building good communication practices which can lead to clarity of expectations from the marriage, deepening knowledge and understanding of the partner as the couple transitions from one stage to another (e.g., from childless to being parents), and nurturing a strong sense of connectedness.

8.4 Implications for Practice

The PFWS (2016) phase 1 study explored whether participants had ever sought relationship support and from where. Results showed that there were significant associations between help-seeking behavior and age and level of education, and strong associations with civil status and age of children. Those who had sought support were often between 26 and 65 years of age, of a higher level of education, divorced or separated, and/or parents of adolescents of 10–19 years of age. The topmost sources of support were members of the clergy (29.1%), or family therapists or marriage counselors (21.6%). The findings suggest that pastoral help is still popular, but therapy is picking up. Those facing serious difficulties, which include separation and divorce, but also those bringing up adolescents are more likely to seek help. Reasons why those with a lower level of education are not so forthcoming to seek help still need to be identified.

Results of both PFWS studies (2016, 2017) also made clear the need for relationship education. In 2016, Abela and Lanfranco had argued that marriage and relationship education can be one strategy to facilitate thriving couple relationships, yet this must be closely aligned to the realities which couples are facing in contemporary Malta at different stages of the life cycle. Similarly, Piscopo (2014) had recommended that relationship education should address the needs of couples in a more secular society and, as such, this education can no longer be offered solely by the Catholic Church in Malta at the premarriage stage. Other studies (Abela & Lanfranco, 2016; Abela, Farrugia, Casha, Galea, & Schembri, 2013; Attard Micallef, 2015) have concluded that in parenting skills training there should be a strong focus on the couple's needs as well.

The results from the Malta studies demonstrate that most individuals in a couple relationship seek to have a strong bond with their partners and are committed to avoid or overcome conflict and to prevail in times of adversity. This ties well with Schramm, Galovan, and Goddard's (2017) recommended shift in relationship education to focus on strengthening the couple's attachment, expanding on internal motivations. This can also help couples be better prepared for challenging periods in their life.

8.5 Conclusion

This chapter has provided insight into the structure, processes, and culture of couples in Malta within a Euro-Mediterranean context. It has addressed demographic, sociocultural, legal, structural, and biographical factors that synergistically mold couple relationships. In concert, the data and reflections may be used by practitioners, service providers, policymakers and others to identify opportunities to help couples: from facilitating responsible and informed entry into a couple relationship, to maintaining couple stability, to offering support when there is dysfunction, and to studying the diverse systems, dynamics and societal norms that help to shape, make or break couples. The ultimate goal should be to assist couples to experience vibrant, meaningful, and flourishing relationships.

References

Abela, A. (2009). The changing landscape of Maltese families. In J. Cutajar & G. Cassar (Eds.), *Social transitions in Maltese society* (pp. 23–50). Malta: Agenda Publications.

Abela, A. (2016). Family life. In M. Brigulio & M. Brown (Eds.), *Sociology of the Maltese Islands* (1st ed., pp. 17–46). Malta: Miller Publishing.

Abela, A., Casha, C., Debono, M., & Lauri, M. A. (2015). Attitudes about remarriage in Malta. *Journal of Divorce & Remarriage, 56*(5), 369–387. https://doi.org/10.1080/10502556.2015.1046799

Abela, A., Farrugia, R., Casha, C., Galea, M., & Schembri, D. (2013). *The relationship between Maltese adolescents and their parents* (Department of Family Studies Research Report, No. 1). Malta: Office of the President of Malta.

Abela, A., Frosh, S., & Dowling, E. (2005). Uncovering beliefs embedded in the culture and its implications for practice: The case of Maltese married couples. *Journal of Family Therapy, 27*, 3–23.

Abela, A., & Lanfranco, I. (2016). *Positive parenting national strategic policy: 2016 – 2024*. Malta: Ministry for the Family & Social Solidarity.

Abela, A., & Walker, J. (2014). *Perspectives on partnerships, parenting and support in a changing world*. Chichester: Wiley-Blackwell.

Abela, A. M. (2006). Shaping a national identity: Malta in the European Union. *International Journal of Sociology, 35*(4), 10–27.

Attard Micallef, H. (2015). *Stories of couples during their transition to parenthood* (Unpublished Professional Training in Systemic Family Psychotherapy dissertation). Institute of Family Therapy, Malta.

Borg, B. (2016). *Benefits or love? A micro-sociological inquiry on the formation of couple relationships played off in society* (Unpublished bachelor's dissertation). University of Malta, Malta.

Borg, P. (2012). *The lived experience of perceived similarities and differences of young adult couples in long-term relationships* (Unpublished bachelor's dissertation). University of Malta, Malta.

Bronfenbrenner, U. (1994). Ecological models of human development. In T. Husén & T. N. Postlethwaite (Eds.), *International encyclopaedia of education* (Vol. 3, 2nd ed., pp. 1643–1647). Oxford, UK: Elsevier.

Camarero, M. (2014). Marriage in Europe. *European Societies, 16*(3), 443–461. https://doi.org/10.1080/14616696.2013.878097

Compagno, R. (2018). *And they lived happily ever after: The story of being married for thirty years, a narrative study of heterosexual married men* (Unpublished bachelor's dissertation). University of Malta, Malta.

Darmanin, J. (2018). *Poverty, social exclusion and living conditions in Malta: An analysis using SILC*. Malta: Central Bank of Malta.

European Foundation for the Improvement of Living and Working Conditions. (2018). *Striking a balance: Reconciling work and life in the EU*. Luxembourg: Publications Office of the European Union.

European Social Survey. (2016). *European Social Survey Round 8 Data. Data file edition 2.1*. NSD, Norway: Norwegian Centre for Research Data. https://doi.org/10.21338/NSD-ESS8-2016

Eurostat. (2017). *Marriage and divorce statistics*. Retrieved June 30, 2019, from https://ec.europa.eu/eurostat/statistics-explained/index.php?title=Marriage_and_divorce_statistics#Fewer_marriages.2C_more_divorces

Eurostat. (2019). *When are they ready to leave the nest?* Retrieved June 30, 2019, from https://ec.europa.eu/eurostat/web/products-eurostat-news/-/EDN-20190514-1?inheritRedirect=true&redirect=%2Feurostat%2Fweb%2Fincome-and-living-conditions%2Fpublications

Farrugia, T. (2014). *The lived experience of couples in remarried relationships following divorce, in Malta* (Unpublished master's dissertation). University of Malta, Malta.

Laiviera, R. (2019, April 13). Gender equality: Improved work-life balance crucial. *Times of Malta*. Retrieved June 30, 2019, from https://www.timesofmalta.com/articles/view/20190413/life-features/gender-equality.707174

Lee, W. S., & McKinnish, T. (2018). The marital satisfaction of differently aged couples. *Journal of Population Economics, 31*(2), 337–362.

Mallia, M. (2019, January 30). Twice as many couples got married than separated in 2018. *Newsbook*. Retrieved June 30, 2019, from https://www.newsbook.com.mt/artikli/2019/01/30/4-separations-a-day-in-malta-4-a-month-in-gozo-in-2018/?lang=en

Malta Independent. (2018, June 6). More than a thousand Maltese married foreign partners in 2017. *Malta Independent*. Retrieved July 16, 2019, from http://www.independent.com.mt/articles/2018-06-06/local-news/More-than-a-thousand-Maltese-married-foreign-partners-in-2017-6736191212

Mazzuca, S., Kafetsios, K., Livi, S., & Presaghi, F. (2018). Emotion regulation and satisfaction in long-term marital relationships: The role of emotional contagion. *Journal of Social and Personal Relationships, 36*(9), 2880–2895. https://doi.org/10.1177/0265407518804452

National Statistics Office (Malta). (2018a). *International Day of Families: 2018, News Release 075/2018*. Valletta: National Statistics Office.

National Statistics Office (Malta). (2018b). *EU-SILC 2017: Salient indicators. News Release 120/2018*. Valletta: National Statistics Office.

National Statistics Office (Malta). (2019). *EU-SILC 2018: Estimates of Material Deprivation and Housing Problems. News Release 036/2019*. Valletta: National Statistics Office.

Olah, L.S. (2015). Changing families in the European Union: Trends and policy implications. *Families and Societies, Working Paper Series 44*. Retrieved April 22, 2019, from http://www.familiesandsocieties.eu/wp-content/uploads/2015/09/WP44Olah2015.pdf

OurWEDDING.com.mt. (2016). *Astonishing number of destination weddings in Malta since 2015*. Retrieved July 16, 2019, from https://www.ourwedding.com.mt/en/astonishing-number-of-destination-weddings-in-malta-since-2015

Parliament of Malta. (2017). *Session 65, P.L.873, December 18, 2017*. Retrieved April 22, 2019, from https://parlament.mt/13th-leg/plenary-session/ps-065-18122017-0900-am/

Pazhoohi, F., Silva, C., Pereira, L., Oliveira, M., Santana, P., Rodrigues, R., & Arantes, J. (2019). Is imagination of the infidelity more painful than actual infidelity? *Current Psychology, 38*(2), 572–578.

Piscopo, M. (2014). *No fairy-tale… but it works: A qualitative study of the process of forming and maintaining a happy marital relationship in Malta* (Unpublished master's dissertation). University of Malta, Malta.

Piscopo, S. (2012). Consumer culture. In C. Borg & R. Vella (Eds.), *Shooting Malta* (pp. 182–185). Malta: Midsea Books.

President's Foundation for the Wellbeing of Society. (2016). *Sustaining relationships: Couples and singles in a changing society*. Malta: PFWS.

President's Foundation for the Wellbeing of Society. (2017). *Sustaining relationships: The expectations and lived experiences of couples in Malta*. Malta: PFWS.

Rajani, N. B., Skianis, V., & Filippidis, F. T. (2019). Association of environmental and sociodemographic factors with life satisfaction in 27 European countries. *BMC Public Health, 19*(1), 534. https://doi.org/10.1186/s12889-019-6886-y

Rizzo, S. (2009). The dual-worker family: Combining working life with social life. *Bank of Valletta Review, 39*, 1–18.

Rossi, G. (2014). The complex relationship between values and couple patterns. *Journal of Comparative Family Studies, 45*(2), 173–199, 161, 165, 169. Retrieved June 30, 2019, from https://search-proquest-com.ejournals.um.edu.mt/docview/1586126286?accountid=27934

Schramm, D. G., Galovan, A. M., & Goddard, H. W. (2017). What relationship researchers and relationship practitioners wished the other knew: Integrating discovery and practice in couple relationships. *Family Relations, 66*(4), 696–711.

Scicluna, C. (2019, January 28). Number of marriage separations outnumber church weddings in 2018. *Times of Malta*. Retrieved June 30, 2019, from https://timesofmalta.com/articles/view/number-of-marriage-separations-outnumber-church-weddings-in-2018.700505

Scicluna, S. (2017). *Technology and the couple relationship: A qualitative study* (Unpublished bachelor's dissertation). University of Malta, Malta.

Social Trends Institute. (2015). *World family map 2015: Mapping family change and child well-being outcomes*. New York: Child Trends, Social Trends Institute.

Urbano-Contreras, A., Martínez-González, R. A., & Iglesias-García, M. T. (2018). Parenthood as a determining factor of satisfaction in couple relationships. *Journal of Child and Family Studies, 27*(5), 1492–1501.

Vella, M. (2015). *Same-sex civil unions in contemporary Malta: A sociological understanding* (Unpublished master's dissertation). University of Malta, Malta.

Visanich, V. (2018). Structure and agency: Changes in personal agency in the life domain of young women in Malta. *SAGE Open, 8*(1), 215824401875461. https://doi.org/10.1177/2158244018754613

Part III
Couples in Diversity

Chapter 9
Home Is Where the Heart Is: Aporias of Love and Belonging in Intercultural Couples

Reenee Singh

9.1 Introduction

Multiculturalism in couple relationships is a trend that is set to rise in Western countries. In the UK, 2.3 million people are living with or married to somebody from a different ethnic group, and 1 in 10 relationships is intercultural. The figures for London are even higher and it is predicted that by 2030, 50% of people living there will be foreign-born (2011 Census). Similarly, in Australia, as of March 2013, 26% of the national population of 23,263,969 was born overseas (Bhugun, 2016).

In the USA, almost 4 in 10, or 39% of Americans who have married since 2010 have married those from different religious groups (Murphy, 2015). In the UK, one might hypothesise that if one in ten relationships in England and Wales is between people of two different ethnic/cultural groups, it is likely that many of these will be interfaith relationships, or between people of two different religious groups.

This surmise gains more credence if one takes into account the 2011 Census, wherein 23,000 people in England and Wales were classified as having 'mixed religion' (Miller, 2012), pointing to the possibility of a number of interfaith unions between partners professing different religions.

Intercultural is a broad term that can refer to interracial, interfaith or interethnic differences. It is important to note that the term 'intercultural' can have different meanings in different cultures and contexts. For example, in India, intercultural refers to relationships where the partners come from different caste backgrounds and communities. In other countries, partners might identify as intercultural if they come from different class backgrounds or if they are from the same 'ethnic' background but grew up in different countries. I have worked with couples from the

---

R. Singh (✉)
Association of Family Therapy and Systemic Practice, Child and Family Practice,
London, UK

© Springer Nature Switzerland AG 2020
A. Abela et al. (eds.), *Couple Relationships in a Global Context*,
European Family Therapy Association Series,
https://doi.org/10.1007/978-3-030-37712-0_9

same religious background who identify as intercultural because of the difference in the strength of their religious beliefs.

At the moment, in the Western world, there seems to be a renewed interest in couple relationships across racial and cultural divides, evidenced in the media responses to Prince Harry and Megan Markle's wedding and in the recent number of films on this topic, for example, A United Kingdom, Loving, Victoria and Albert and The Big Sikh, to name a few.

It is almost difficult to imagine that until 1967, interracial relationships were illegal in the USA. Attitudes towards interracial marriages have changed considerably in the Western world and have led to a corresponding increase in interracial relationships. However, this increase could also be due to other factors such as globalisation, growing rates of migration and a changing demographic of ethnic groups. In the USA, Hispanics, Asians and people classified as being of 'Other' racial/ethnic backgrounds only made up 10% of the population in 1980, but today they make up 29% (Kopf, 2016). Thus, the opportunities for intermarriage are higher in contemporary times than they were 30 years ago. The data suggests gender, age and class differences, with younger people, men and those with higher education more likely to marry across racial and cultural divides.

9.1.1 Systemic Theoretical Frameworks

There is now a growing body of literature on interracial and intercultural couples (see, for example, Bhugun, 2016; Falicov, 1995, 2014; Hiew, Halford, & Liu 2014; Killian, 2001a, 2001b, 2003, 2008, 2012, 2013; Seshadri & Knudson-Martin, 2013; Singh & Dutta, 2010; Singh, Killian, Bhugun, & Tseng, in press). In this chapter, I would like to add to the burgeoning literature, focusing specifically on clinical practice.

An overarching systemic perspective that has particular relevance to intercultural couples is that of the family life cycle. Systemic theory posits that symptoms can arise in the transitions between one developmental stage and another, and signal the family's difficulties in making these transitions (McGoldrick, Carter, & Garcia Preto, 2015). With intercultural couples, an added level of conflict can emerge because of a lack of agreement about the meaning of the religious and cultural practices and the impact of such practices on parenting—for example, in the case of a family where one partner is Jewish and the other Catholic, whether the children should be christened or not, or have a Bar Mitzvah during the transition to adolescence. When working with intercultural couples, systemic practitioners can design innovative rituals that incorporate elements of both partners' cultural traditions, in order to facilitate transitions from one developmental stage to another (Singh 2017a, 2017b).

Another systemic framework which can be applied to intercultural couples is positioning theory. Based on social constructionist thinking, positioning theory has been adapted to working with families and organisations by Campbell and Huffington (2008). Within a discourse, for example, of romantic love, there are a number of available subject positions, and partners within a couple relationship can position each other and themselves within this discourse. Positioning can be interactive or reflexive, that is, we can position ourselves and each other. In intercultural couples, there is a danger that partners can position each other along racial and cultural lines, sometimes relying on cultural stereotypes in their exchanges—for example, in an intercultural couple where one partner is English and the other is Indian, the English partner may be positioned as 'cold' and 'inhospitable'.

How do we position ourselves as psychotherapists, working with intercultural couples? Falicov (2014) suggests that the clinical encounter with an intercultural couple requires the clinician to be self-reflexive about their own culture and cultural values. One of our most important tools is the use of ourselves and self-reflexivity. Whilst this is important in working with any couple, the system that is created when working with intercultural couples comprises the three cultures including that of each of the partners and the one of the therapist, thus increasing the possibilities for cultural alliances, splits and misunderstandings.

Burnham, Palma and Whitehouse (2008) devised the acronym the Social GRRAACCEESS to describe the interplay between aspects of difference, such as gender, race, and religion. Burnham (2012) expands this idea to discuss GRRAACCESS that are visible, invisible, voiced or unvoiced. The social GRRAACCESS are a useful way of thinking about how differences both between intercultural couples and between the couples and the therapist can be conceptualised. For example, the therapist could be visibly similar to one partner within an intercultural couple, but there could be a multitude of unvoiced differences between them. As a South Asian couples therapist, when working with an intercultural couple where the female partner is Bangladeshi, I could be seen as visibly similar to my client. However, the differences in age, class and religion between us may be difficult to bridge, and in fact, I may be able to relate more to the white British male partner. Hence, the complexities and nuances of difference can be unpacked using Burnham's (2012) framework.

Notions of whiteness and white privilege (Wallis & Singh, 2014) have been imported to working with intercultural couples, in order to help couples to understand the difference in the power dynamics within them. These ideas can provide safe ways of speaking openly about the vexed issues of 'race' and racism.

Killian (2001a, 2001b) discusses dominant and marginalised discourses used by interracial couples in the USA. Monocultural couples are still seen as the norm by wider society, with discourses of homogamy and colour blindness prevailing. Killian found that black partners' reactions to society's racism were thought of as being 'hypersensitive' by their white partners. He uses the wonderful expression 'crossing the borders' (Killian, 2001b) to describe interracial couples in the USA visiting all white or all black segregated neighbourhoods. During such times, the couples would physically separate so that they did not run the risk of being seen as a couple.

Killian uses the fascinating idea of 'universalising the particular' to demonstrate how an interaction between a couple can be linked to happenings in the wider socio-political context, for example, a row over one parent's overprotectiveness in a dual heritage family can be related to recent media coverage of racist attacks in the family's neighbourhood. However, generalising statements such as 'this is what white men are like' can be deconstructed and examined in the context of the couple's particular histories and beliefs.

Seshadari and Knudson Martin's (2013) grounded theory study of intercultural couples revealed that although couples experienced most issues as cultural issues, race only occurred during their interactions with 'others'. Based on their research, they advocate a strengths-based model for working with intercultural couples. Similarly, Bhugun's (2016) research focuses on the resiliencies and strengths of intercultural parents in Australia.

The study by Hiew et al. (2014) explores the belief systems of couples who come from European and Chinese ancestry, in Australia, with particular emphasis on the effect of culture in respect to communication and relationship standards. They argue that the individualism–collectivism continuum is a predominant cultural dimension that influences the way the different partners communicate and the relationship standards each partner holds.

An ongoing multisite research study (Ugazio, Fellin and Singh) explores the semantic cohesion between samples of monocultural and intercultural couples. The sample comprises 15 monocultural couples (both partners from the same country, that is British or Italian) and 15 intercultural couples where one partner is a migrant from the UK, Europe, USA or Australia, and the other is from Asia, Africa or Latin America. The migrant partner should not have moved to the Western country before the age of 12, and the couple should be cohabiting for at least a year. The data will comprise extracts from recorded sessions and will be analysed using the Family Semantics Grid (Ugazio & Castelli, 2017). Our research questions explore whether there are greater differences in the semantics between intercultural couples, as compared to monocultural couples, and if so, how intercultural couples negotiate and manage these semantics. For example, could it involve the migrant partner accommodating to the Western partner's semantic?

Falicov (2016) points to the complexity of practice with intercultural couples. She posits that for intercultural couples there is a difference in cultural content (values and beliefs), there are sociopolitical and economic inequalities and that these two levels impact on interactional processes. As systemic practitioners, we are trained to intervene at the level of process, but when working with intercultural couples, we have to be mindful of the level of content (differences in values and beliefs for example as related to parenting, religion, language and food) and the socioeconomic and power differences. Further, Falicov (2016) highlights that we must not assume that every intercultural couple will have difficulties nor that all their struggles are because of their intercultural differences.

In this chapter, through the use of clinical vignettes,[1] I will illustrate the complexities and dilemmas for intercultural couples and the clinicians who work with them, whilst acknowledging the strengths and resiliencies in such relationships. I will begin by discussing current sociopolitical contexts and discourses and how these are mirrored in our consulting rooms. I will then take up two interrelated themes that, to my mind, recur poignantly in the lives of every intercultural couple I have worked with—namely, the meaning of home and the meaning of love. I will end the chapter with a section on clinical implications—an overview of a few systemic techniques and interventions that I find particularly useful.

---

[1] One of the vignettes is a composite case example and the remaining two are of intercultural couples who have given their permission for their stories to be used for research/teaching purposes.

9.2 Sociopolitical Contexts

Clinical Vignette 1: When the Political becomes the Personal
'The day that Trump was elected, we had a bitter row', recounted an American client Marjorie, who is in a relationship with Carlo, an Italian settled in London. Marjorie was appalled that Trump had been elected and although Carlo was also unhappy with the outcome of the elections, he could not quite see Marjorie's perspective. A row about gendered differences erupted, with Marjorie invoking their cultural differences. How could Carlo, as an Italian man, understand and sympathise with women's plights and positions? How could he empathise with Marjorie, an American woman, living in this day and age?

Within the consulting room, when things had calmed down between them, Carlo and Marjorie could recognise that their positions had become polarised along gendered and cultural lines. It was easy for Marjorie to see Carlo as 'a typical, chauvinistic Italian male' and Trump's election victory led to her feeling unsafe and unprotected as a woman, hence relying even more on her political convictions and feminist position. For Carlo, however, Trump's migration politics were equally prescient. Carlo reminds us that Trump being in power concerned different people in different ways—women and men, citizens and migrants, and that localised concerns had impact beyond personal and state boundaries, indeed spread all over the world. In the clinical session, what this generated was a discussion about their own positions, highlighting the culturally located gendered roles and responsibilities of both within the relationship.

Hare-Mustin (1994), in her classic text on gendered discourses in family therapy, highlights that our consulting rooms often mirror societal discourses and prejudices. Thus, 'much of what couples and families bring to therapy nowadays has to do with Internet related problems, addictions and affairs, fears of racism and invidious xenophobia: gendered inversions to the household as the financial crisis results in women becoming primary breadwinners; and the impact of forced migration on family and couple relationships' (Singh, 2017b). p. v.

As psychotherapists, we often encounter the challenges our clients are confronted with as a reflection of the broader sociopolitical contexts of their lived realities (Singh & Dada, 2017). For example, at the moment in the UK, families are increasingly being divided along lines of Brexit Leavers and Remainers. If we think of our consulting rooms—and our therapeutic encounters with intercultural couples—as microcosms of wider society, we can intervene at the levels of 'universalising the particular' and 'particularising the universal' (Killian, 2001a, 2001b).

9.3 The Meaning of Home

Home can be thought of as a 'secure base' (Byng-Hall, 1995); a crucible in which family members learn about family rules, family scripts, hierarchies and roles. Homes are, of course, not always secure or safe places for all the family members, some of whom may wish to leave home. In other cases, family members may have to leave their homes and homelands.

Papadopoulos (2002) aptly describes the sense of 'nostalgic disorientation' faced by refugees and forced migrants when they have to leave their homes and move to another country. They miss the sights, sounds and smells of home, without being consciously aware of what they are missing. Similarly, Falicov (2014) uses the idea of ambiguous loss to depict this feeling of disorientation and confusion. Political events like Brexit can have a profound impact on intercultural couples' sense of safety and belonging in the home country.

Papadopoulous (2017) posits that home is not a unitary concept, and when migrants and refugees think of home, they are thinking at once about three different meanings of home—the home now, the old home then (that is, the home that they left which may have changed now as a result of social, political and economic changes) and the ideal home. The construct of the ideal home may be vastly different to the home that is currently inhabited. Confusions and misunderstandings may arise between partners of a couple if they are referring to one level of home, but their partner may be responding to a different meaning.

For intercultural couples, the process of creating a home together is often beset with difficulties and challenges. They may be confronted with difficulties in obtaining a visa to Western countries, not being able to work in the host country, experiencing racism and in many ways, not being able to feel 'at home' in their partner's country (Singh, 2014). Arguments can ensue between couples about whose territory they are living in. These arguments can often escalate during particular periods of the family life cycle, for example, when children are born, or when the parents of the migrant partner(s) are ageing or unwell.

Clinical Vignette 2: 'That area' is my home and my identity

Yasmin [and Ben] sought premarital couple's therapy, before making a decision about whether to get married or not. Yasmin is a Palestinian Arab woman and Ben is Jewish European. Yasmin's ancestors had to flee Palestine and settle in Jordan as a result of the conflict between Israel and the Palestine. In the first therapy session, they described a recent incident when they were at a party together, with Ben's friends and relatives. One of Ben's friends talked about how the Israelis had wanted the British to leave Israel. Yasmin was upset by this comment and Ben could not understand why.

When they talked about the incident, Yasmin explained that she was upset, not only because it was uncomfortable to be the only outsider at a Jewish gathering, but also because Ben's friend had designated Palestine as 'that area' and described it as a 'social construct'. Yasmin talked about how her ancestors had lost everything when they had been 'kicked out of Palestine'. Ben's friend's denying the existence of Palestine felt to Yasmin like a denial of a home and an identity. Yasmin spoke poignantly about how she valued the importance of Ben's homeland Israel, and was merely asking for a similar recognition of her own history. The incident at the party could be thought of as a microcosm of the couple's relationship.

Ben and Yasmin represent an intercultural couple where the clashes between them mirrored conflict in the wider sociopolitical contexts. In the case of other intercultural couples, where there may be no acceptance, or even knowledge about their union from one partner's family, the home can function as an encapsulated world and safe haven.

To conclude this section, the home that intercultural couples create can often feel like a safe container. This home, where cultural and religious traditions from both countries/cultures/religions are practiced, can have a hybrid character, and may not be recognisable to families from either culture. However, the outside world can sometimes intrude, and intercultural couples sometimes have to 'cross borders' (Killian, 2001b) and inhabit a world that marginalises the racial and cultural partner. In order for intercultural couples to be able to resolve this painful and deeply felt struggle, therapy can offer a way of helping interracial/intercultural couples to find 'separate cultural spaces' (Falicov, 2014) as well as safe ways of being together, in the outside world.

9.4 The Meaning of Love

The second theme that I will address in this chapter has to do with cultural constructions of love and intimacy and how these are inscribed in gender and power relationships.

Rosenblatt (2009) highlights that intercultural couples may struggle with different ideas about what marriage and coupleness involve. The two partners may be positioned very differently on an individualistic–collectivistic dimension and while one may value spending every weekend, festival and celebration with their family of origin, the other may wish for more distance from one or both families of origin.

In many cultures and religions, arranged marriages are the norm, and premarital sex is prohibited. Marrying outside one's own community, religion and culture could be associated with a sense of loss, dishonour and betrayal, and may impact the couple's sexual and intimate relationship. Further, the partners may come to their relationship with completely different templates of love, intimacy and togetherness, originating from their different cultural backgrounds. Partners from migrant or minority ethnic backgrounds, where the couple is often embedded within extended family relationships (Gabb & Singh, 2015b) may not be able to understand the construction of the couple as the primary dyad within the family. In non-Western cultures, the primary 'dyad' could comprise the father–son, mother–daughter, or other dyads based on social rather than biological ties. Relying solely on the couple relationship for emotional needs and support could result in feelings of loneliness and isolation. Having a community of other intercultural or mixed couples can help in overcoming the feelings of being alienated by providing a sense of connectedness (Singh, 2014).

Romance, love and intimacy can be expressed differently in different languages, cultural and class contexts and the nuances of this expression can get lost in translation. This may feel particularly poignant when the partners grew up speaking in different languages. The shared language that they agree to speak at home may not have the emotional overtones or scope for romantic expression that their own 'mother tongues' may have, and this may diminish the possibility of finding connection.

Rosenblatt (2009) describes the differences in power that 'may have been established decades or even centuries before the couple ever met' (p. 7). For example, a relationship between a white British man and Pakistani woman may be impacted by the postcolonial power relationships between the two countries, so that the white male partner does not bother to learn Urdu, his partner's language.

Sometimes, the younger generations want to break away from their parents' traditions and are not given permission to do so by their parents. Many feel torn between the loyalty towards their family of origin and the love towards their partner. Other families are more flexible and adapt to the changes. However, there could still be nuances of racism that one partner experiences from the other's family.

Gender and gendered roles are perhaps the most challenging areas for intercultural couples (Rosenblatt, 2009). Couples may struggle with the differences in gendered expectations between themselves and their partner, and this may be further complicated by parental expectations and societal cultural stereotypes, for instance, 'What can you expect from a chauvinistic Middle Eastern man?'

Clinical Vignette 3: Gender and Power
Tanvir and Isabella, a professional couple in their early 40s, came to see me as they had reached an impasse in their couple relationship, which was affecting their children, Hassan (9) and Rania (6). Tanvir was from a Pakistani Muslim background and Isabella was from a Spanish Catholic background. Both were born and brought up in the UK. They had been together for 15 years.

The couple had struggled at many points in their relationship. They had married against considerable parental opposition. Tanvir had wanted Isabella to convert to Islam, but her parents, who were staunch Catholics, had refused. Tanvir had agreed to get married in a registry office, but on the day of the wedding, had not been able to rebel against his parents' wishes and had left Isabella waiting at the registry office, furious. The couple broke up at this point, but got together again, 6 months later, with Isabella reluctantly agreeing to convert and to bring up the children they planned to have within the Muslim faith.

A few years later, their relationship had almost broken down over Tanvir and his family insisting on having Hassan circumcised. Isabella, once again, finally gave in. However, in the last 6 months, things had reached a crisis over Tanvir's conviction that Isabella was infatuated with his 27-year-old cousin, who was visiting from Pakistan. Isabella denied this vociferously, while admitting that she was going through a 'midlife crisis' and needed reassurance about her attractiveness to men. Tanvir secretly installed a CCTV camera in the house and recorded 'evidence' of the flirtation between Isabella and Husain (his cousin).

Tanvir and Isabella met before the terrible happenings of 9/11 in the USA and the bombings in London (July 2005). Particularly after Brexit, the couple and their two children experienced racism and Islamophobia, within the school, and even from Isabella's relatives, who viewed Tanvir's family with hostility and suspicion. In my work, I tried to open up a space where having these difficult conversations was possible. I drew on Killian's (2013) ideas about particularising the universal and universalising the particular.

In Tanvir and Isabella's family, how did the wider—universal—discourses of Islamophobia impact on their couple and parenting relationship? Isabella poignantly recounted how, as a family, they had stopped watching television during difficult times, as the news reminded them of the religious differences between them, which could become politicised. Similarly, they struggled to understand how they might cope with the (particular) racist bullying that Hassan encountered as located not only within their school contexts but as a symptom of a wider universal social malaise? How could they find ways to protect Hassan and intervene in the school system?

Honour, guilt, and shame have different meanings and are privileged differently in different religions and cultures. Tanvir and Isabella had endured a lot in their couple relationship but the one thing that their love could not conquer was related to a radical difference in gendered beliefs and values. Although Tanvir did not believe that Isabella had been unfaithful to him, he had lost trust and honour through her actions of shaming him by flirting with a younger member of his extended clan. Isabella could not understand how her actions, which she saw as an expression of her 'freedom' as a Western woman, could have such disastrous consequences. The impasse that opened up between them led her to then see Tanvir as the Muslim 'other' and her family and friends reinforced her positioning of him as an oppressor. Tanvir fought hard against this description, angry at being stereotyped, and pointing out that he had been liberal throughout their relationship.

I used Ugazio's (2013) theory of semantic polarities to posit that the couple had grown up with vastly different conversational realities within their extended families and societies. While Tanvir came from a semantic of belonging, which privileged honour and exclusion, Isabella came from a semantic of freedom, which valued freedom, exploration, and independence and risk-taking. How could they co-position themselves and each other within these semantics?

Isabella had hoped that by accepting Tanvir's version of events as she had by agreeing with the conversion and circumcision, he would eventually capitulate and that they could reconcile their differences. This time, however, Tanvir was impervious to Isabella's pleas and decided that he wanted to separate. Through our work, the couple began to realise that although they really loved each other, they were not able to continue to compromise on deeply engrained values that left them estranged from their family and friends, but mostly from themselves. They decided to separate amicably and continue to coparent.

9.5 Clinical Implications

The three clinical vignettes above demonstrate a range of systemic ideas, interventions, techniques and practices that I frequently use in my work with intercultural couples. I have argued in this chapter that as systemic clinicians, we should be prepared to think about the impact of wider sociopolitical contexts on our clients' lives. Further, we should be prepared to grapple with the complexities of how our clients understand the meaning of home and the meaning. In doing so, we must be careful not to impose our own assumptions and values on our clients. For example, many Western and Western-trained clinicians struggle to understand the meaning of arranged marriages, and assume that they are pathological or confuse them with forced marriages. Furthermore, although arranged marriages may work well in some cases, sometimes it may be difficult for one partner, especially if they do not feel physically attracted to their partner, and feel coerced to stay in the marriage, because of financial pressures or the stigma and shame that a divorce would bring to their extended families.

Similarly, home inevitably has different meanings for different couples. We may assume that our clients miss home, but some may experience living in the host country as a refuge or haven from their own contexts. They may be able to refashion their identities and adopt the practices of their host countries, with a great deal of facility. Bringing up children in a country that they did not grow up in may present both challenges and opportunities. Others may embrace the idea of dual or multiple homes and intercultural couples may learn how to live happily, if not seamlessly, between their different homes and countries.

Working with intercultural couples has prompted me to explore what culture, religion and faith meant in my own family. My parents' marriage was an interfaith one, my father being Sikh—albeit disowned and disinherited by his own father for cutting his hair—and my mother Hindu. Through creating my own spiritual ecogram (Hodge, 2005), I realised the identifying principle (Hardy & Laszloffy, 1995) in my family was that marrying across religious divides is the norm, and that it is possible and even desirable to accept and tolerate your partner's religious practices.

I sometimes share aspects of my own story with my clients where appropriate. In other cases, I will discuss my dilemmas in positioning myself because of culture, gender, religious, and linguistic similarities and differences.

As I have indicated elsewhere (Singh, 2017a), nonverbal and representational methods work well with intercultural couples, possibly because they eschew the difficulty of language differences. I use drawings, cultural genograms (Hardy & Laszloffy, 1995), culturegrams, ecograms and ecomaps, and emotional maps (Gabb & Singh, 2015a) in my work. Emotion maps could be seen as a graphic illustration of intercultural couples' homes, and given the significance of homes for intercultural couples, can be used to great advantage. As mentioned earlier, it is sometimes helpful to give partners permission to engage in their own cultural practices separately, whether this involves going to the mosque, synagogue, visiting friends and relatives without the other partner, as well as developing a shared cultural couple identity.

To conclude, many of the 'classic' systemic techniques that I use with intercultural couples such as internalised other interviewing (Tomm, 1987) and cultural genograms (Hardy & Laszloffy, 1995) could, of course, be used with any clinical couple but they seem especially useful in creating the ability for intercultural couples to empathise with and understand each other's cultural, racialised and religious experiences and meanings.

References

Bhugun, D. (2016). Parenting advice for intercultural couples/parents: A systemic perspective. *Journal of Family Therapy, 39*(3), 454–477.
Burnham, J. (2012). Developments in the social GRRRAAACCEEESSS: Visible-invisible and voiced-unvoiced. In I.-B. Krause (Ed.), *Culture and reflexivity in systemic psychotherapy. Mutual perspectives* (pp. 139–160). London: Karnac.
Burnham, J., Palma, D. A., & Whitehouse, L. (2008). Learning as a context for differences and differences as a context for learning. *Journal of Family Therapy, 30*, 529–542.
Byng-Hall, J. (1995). Creating a secure family base: Some implications of attachment theory for family therapy. *Family Process, 34*(1), 45–58.
Campbell, D., & Huffington, C. (2008). *Organizations connected. A handbook of systemic consultation*. London: Karnac.
Falicov, C. J. (1995). Cross-cultural marriages. In N. Jacobson & A. Gurman (Eds.), *Clinical handbook of couple therapy* (2nd ed., pp. 231–246). New York: Guilford Press.
Falicov, C. J. (2014). *Latino families in therapy* (2nd ed.). New York: The Guilford Press.
Falicov, C. J. (2016). Intercultural couples. In Plenary Presentation. European Family Therapy Association Conference, Athens.
Gabb, J., & Singh, R. (2015a). The uses of emotion maps in research and clinical practice with families and couples: Methodological innovation and critical inquiry. *Family Process, 54*, 185–197.

Gabb, J., & Singh, R. (2015b). Reflections on the challenges of understanding racial, cultural and sexual differences in couple relationship research. *Journal of Family Therapy 37*(2), 210–227.

Hare-Mustin, R. T. (1994). Discourses in the mirrored room: a postmodern analysis of therapy. *Family Process 33*(1), 19–35.

Hardy, K., & Laszloffy, T. (1995). The cultural genogram: Key to training culturally competent family therapists. *Journal of Marital and Family Therapy, 21*(3), 227–237.

Hiew, D. N., Halford, W. K., & Liu, S. (2014). Loving diversity. Living in intercultural couple relationships. In A. Abela & J. Walker (Eds.), *Contemporary issues in family studies: Global perspectives on partnerships, parenting and support in a changing world*. London: Wiley.

Hodge, D. (2005). Spiritual ecograms: A new assessment for identifying clients' strengths in space and across time. *Families in Society, 86*(2), 287–298.

Killian, K. D. (2001a). Reconstituting racial histories and identities: The narratives of interracial couples. *Journal of Marital and Family Therapy, 27*, 23–37.

Killian, K. D. (2001b). Crossing borders: Race, gender and their intersections in interracial couples. *Journal of Feminist Family Therapy, 13*, 1–31.

Killian, K. D. (2003). Homogamy outlaws: Interracial couples' strategic responses to racism and partner differences. *Journal of Couple and Relationship Therapy, 2*, 3–21.

Killian, K. D. (2008). Introduction. In T. Karis & K. Killian (Eds.), *Intercultural couples: Exploring diversity in intimate relationships* (pp. 1–11). New York: Routledge.

Killian, K. D. (2012). Resisting and complying with homogamy: Interracial couples' narratives. *Counselling Psychology Quarterly, 25*, 125–135.

Killian, K. D. (2013). *Interracial couples, intimacy and therapy. Crossing racial borders*. New York: Columbia University Press.

Kopf, D. (2016). Why is interracial marriage on the rise? *Priceonomics, 1*, 2016.

McGoldrick, M., Carter, B. A., & Garcia Preto, N. A. (2015). *The expanding family life cycle: Individual, family and social perspectives*. New York: Prentice Hall.

Miller, S. K. (2012, December 13). Mixed religion as identity: Who are these people?' Blog post. *The Huffington Post*.

Murphy, C. (2015, June 2). Interfaith marriage is common in the US, particularly among the recently wed. *Blog post*. Pew Research Centre Survey.

Papadopoulos, R. (2002). *Therapeutic care for refugees. No place like home*. London: Karnac.

Papadopoulos, R. (2017). Refugee aid: Can systemic research help? In Plenary Presentation at the 2nd International Systemic Research Conference, Heidelberg, Germany.

Rosenblatt, P. C. (2009). A systems theory analysis of intercultural couple relationships. In T. A. Karis & K. D. Killian (Eds.), *Intercultural couples. Exploring diversity in intimate relationships*. London: Routledge.

Seshadri, G., & Knudson-Martin, C. (2013). How couples manage interracial and intercultural differences: Implications for clinical practice. *Journal of Marital and Family Therapy, 39*(1), 43–58.

Singh, R. (2014). *Love across border control*. Media diversified. Retrieved from https://mediadiversified.org/2014/02/05/loving-across-border-control/

Singh, R. (2017a). Intimate strangers? Working with interfaith couples and families. *Australian and New Zealand Journal of Family Therapy, 38*(1), 7–14.

Singh, R. (2017b). Foreword. In J. Gabb & J. Fink (Eds.), *Couple relationships in the 21st century. Research, policy and practice* (2nd ed.). New York: Springer.

Singh, R., & Dada, M. (2017). *Intercultural couples in a divided world*. Discover Society. Retrieved from www.discoversociety.org

Singh, R., & Dutta, S. (2010). Working with intercultural couples. In R. Singh & S. Dutta (Eds.), *'Race' and culture. Tools, techniques and trainings. A manual for professionals* (pp. 95–100). London: Karnac.

Singh, R., Killian, K. D., Bhugun, D., & Tseng, C. (in press). Clinical work with intercultural couples. In: K. Wampler & A. Blow (Eds.), *Handbook of systemic family therapy* (Vol. 3). London: Wiley.

Tomm, K. (1987). *Internalized other interviewing*. Family therapy resources. AAMFT. 2011 census data. Retrieved from https://www.ons.gov.uk/census/2011census

Ugazio, V. (2013). *Semantic polarities and psychopathologies in the family. Permitted and forbidden stories*. London: Routledge.

Ugazio, V., & Castelli, D. (2017). The semantics grid of the therapeutic relationship. *TPM—Testing, Psychometrics, Methodology in Applied Psychology, 22*, 135–159.

Wallis, J., & Singh, R. (2014). Constructions and enactments of whiteness: A discursive analysis. *Journal of Family Therapy, 36*(Suppl 1), 39–64.

Chapter 10
Stigma, Social Change and the Well-Being of Same-Sex Couples

David M. Frost

10.1 Introduction

The last two decades have witnessed a tremendous amount of social and policy changes pertaining to same-sex relationships. At the time of this writing (early 2018), same-sex marriage was either performed or recognised in 32 countries throughout the world, and attitudes towards homosexuality and same-sex marriage are improving according to opinion polls in most 'Western' countries (Ayoub & Garretson, 2017; Fetner, 2016). However, it is important to recognise that the vast majority of countries across the globe do not legally recognise same-sex couples, and in some countries homosexuality continues to be criminalised. Even in countries with positive social and policy climates, many same-sex couples experience stigma and discrimination from co-workers, peers and family, which can be damaging for their relationships and for their health and well-being. This chapter provides a review and integration of recent theoretical and empirical contributions from the author and his colleagues (Frost & Fingerhut, 2016; Frost & LeBlanc, 2018; Hammack, Frost, & Hughes, 2019; LeBlanc, Frost, & Bowen, 2018; LeBlanc, Frost, & Wight, 2015) with the aim of highlighting the psychological and social factors that contribute to the well-being of same-sex couples in rapidly changing social and policy contexts.

D. M. Frost (✉)
Department of Social Science, University College London, London, UK
e-mail: d.frost@ucl.ac.uk

10.2 Similarities and Differences Between Same-Sex and Mixed-Sex Relationships

As recently reviewed by the author and his colleagues (Hammack et al., 2019), studies comparing same- and mixed-sex relationships have found very few differences between the two when using a multitude of indicators of relationship quality, including satisfaction, love, commitment, conflict and communication (Balsam, Beauchaine, Rothblum, & Solomon, 2008; Diamond, 2006; Kurdek, 2005; Peplau & Fingerhut, 2006). Early research pointed to a higher likelihood of dissolution among same-sex couples relative to mixed-sex couples (Blumstein & Schwartz, 1983). However, such comparisons were made in relation to mixed-sex married couples, which scholars have argued is not an appropriate comparison group due to lack of legal recognition available to same-sex couples (Hammack et al., 2019) at the time of this early comparative work on same- and mixed-sex relationships. Furthermore, research has indicated that the processes that predict commitment in relationships—such as investment, satisfaction and quality of alternatives—do not appear to differ between same-sex and mixed-sex relationships (Beals, Impett, & Peplau, 2002; Kurdek, 2008).

Although the majority of comparative research fails to detect differences between mixed- and same-sex relationships, there are several meaningful ways in which the lived experiences of same-sex couples are unique and which therefore deserve specific consideration (Hammack et al., 2019). Firstly, same-sex couples tend to report more equitable distributions of financial, housework and childrearing responsibilities than mixed-sex couples (Diamond, 2006; Goldberg, 2014; Kurdek, 2005; Peplau & Fingerhut, 2006). Additionally, some studies have shown that same-sex couples use more effective conflict resolution strategies than mixed-sex couples (Gottman et al., 2003; Kurdek, 2004; Rostosky & Riggle, 2017a). Due to their experience of social stigma and the exclusion from equal legal relationship recognition, same-sex relationships are often structured in ways that are designed to meet practical needs through sexual agreements that defy traditional expectations of monogamy and of heteronormative ideals (Adam, 2006; Degges-White & Marszalek, 2007; Hammack et al., 2019; Green & Mitchell, 2008; Lannutti, 2008; Weston, 1991). Illustrative research points to findings that sexual minority individuals and same-sex couples have been shown to have more open views regarding sexual exclusivity, and may be more likely to have 'open' relationships than mixed-sex couples (van Eeden-Moorefield, Malloy, & Benson, 2016; Rubin, Moors, Matsick, Ziegler, & Conley, 2014).

10.2.1 Unique Experiences of Same-Sex Couples

Although the research reviewed above predominantly shows that same-sex relationships have a lot in common with mixed-sex relationships across key indicators of relational health and functioning, there are two important underlying differences between same- and mixed-sex couples: gender and stigma (Diamond, 2006). Same- and mixed-sex relationships are inherently different because partners in same-sex couples share the same cisgender identity, while those in mixed-sex couples do not. Early work by Blumstein and Schwartz (1983) in their American Couples Study revealed that gender differences in sexual desires and activity frequency might explain results that female couples reported diminished frequency of sex relative to mixed-sex couples and male couples, with the latter couples reporting the greatest frequency of sex. Later attempts to explain this pattern of differences gave rise to speculation of what was termed 'lesbian bed death', where sexual frequency and desire were hypothesised to diminish rapidly over time in female couples due to 'pathologica' l levels of merger. There has been a tremendous amount of clinical discussion about this hypothesised phenomenon, but little empirical evidence to support it as a unique concern for female couples (Frost & Eliason, 2014). Scholars have also cited gender dynamics as an explanation for the previously discussed findings of more equitable levels of distribution of housework and greater role equality in same-sex relationships relative to mixed-sex couples (for a review, see Diamond, 2006).

The second fundamentally unique aspect of same-sex couples' lived experiences stems from the continued stigmatised status of same-sex relationships in most areas of the world (Diamond, 2006; Hammack et al., 2019). Much of the body of research on same-sex relationships has focused on how stigma as a contextual factor shapes their experiences and well-being. Stigma has been theorised to exist on several levels, starting with the most macro form of structural stigma (Hatzenbuehler, 2016). Structural stigma manifests in legal policies that discriminate against same-sex couples and sexual minority individuals, which often include marriage policies that directly or indirectly exclude same-sex couples from the rights, privileges and symbolic value of marriage. Although many countries in Europe and North America provide equal access to legal relationship recognition, most countries in the world do not provide equal legal recognition to same-sex and mixed-sex couples, including some developed 'Western' countries (e.g., the UK, Italy).

Notably, like mixed-sex couples, not all people in same-sex couples want to get married (Rothblum, 2005). Scholars have debated whether access to legal marriage will have beneficial effects for same-sex couples, or whether the availability of marriage will lead to pressure on same-sex couples to conform to heteronormative standards (Diamond, 2017). However, research has shown that many sexual minority individuals report wanting to be in long-term romantic relationships and to get married to a same-sex partner if they were allowed to be legally married (Baiocco, Argalia, & Laghi, 2014; D'Augelli, Rendina, Sinclair, & Grossman, 2007; Herek, 2006; Rostosky, Riggle, Rothblum, & Balsam, 2016).

Moving from a structural level to the level of attitudes, the lack of full public support for equal relationship recognition, which remains the case even in countries with legal equality, illustrates that many people in most societies view same-sex couples as lesser than mixed-sex couples. This difference is not likely limited to the political or legal level, but persists on a moral level as well (Frost & Gola, 2015). Exposure to these forms of prejudice and negative attitudes creates a social discourse of devaluation which likely has an effect on members of same-sex relationships. This devaluing discourse, which exists in addition to the denial of equal legal recognition, persists in many countries across the globe (Frost & Fingerhut, 2016; Herdt & Kertzner, 2006; Herek, 2006). Members of same-sex couples are often reminded of this separate and non-equal status in day-to-day interactions with their family, friends and co-workers, as well as by the news and public debate on social media (Frost & Fingerhut, 2016). As a result, many scholars have highlighted how such experience of legal and social devaluation constitutes minority stress (Brooks, 1981; Frost et al., 2017; LeBlanc, Frost, & Wight, 2015; Riggle, Thomas, & Rostosky, 2005; Russell & Richards, 2003) that likely has additional negative effects on members of same-sex couples' mental health and psychological well-being (Frost & Fingerhut, 2016; Hatzenbuehler, McLaughlin, Keyes, & Hasin, 2010; Herdt & Kertzner, 2006; King & Bartlett, 2006). Because these devaluing discourses call into question the general value of intimacy and relationships in sexual minority individuals' lives, their negative impact is likely to be felt by many people pursuing same-sex relationships, regardless of their desires to be legally married or publicly committed to one another. Indeed, barriers to the achievement of intimacy-related goals (e.g., getting married, finding a partner, buying a home) stemming from interpersonal (e.g., friends, family) and structural (e.g., laws, religious institutions) sources have been shown to partially explain inequalities in depression, psychological well-being, and social well-being (Frost & LeBlanc, 2014) that have often been observed between sexual minorities and heterosexuals (see King, Semlyen, Tai, Killaspy, Osborn, Popelyuk, et al., 2008 for a meta-analysis).

Members of same-sex couples experience stigma, prejudice and discrimination stemming from the devalued social status of their relationships on an interpersonal level, as well as the structural and broader social forms noted previously (Diamond, 2006; Frost & Meyer, 2009; Green and Mitchell, 2008; Peplau & Fingerhut, 2006). For example, research has shown that members of same-sex couples experience greater stress related to not being accepted and being misunderstood by other significant people, especially by their families, compared to single sexual minority men and women (Lewis, Derlega, Griffin, & Krowinski, 2003). Recent meta-analyses and systematic reviews highlight the growing evidence that these forms of interpersonal stress are associated with decreased relational health and functioning (see Doyle & Molix, 2015; Rostosky & Riggle, 2017b).

Despite continuing experiences of stigma, prejudice and discrimination at the structural and interpersonal levels, many members of same-sex couples are in happy, healthy and rewarding relationships (for a review, see Rostosky & Riggle, 2017a). However, in the context of constantly shifting social and policy climates across the globe, stigma maintains an unfortunate and important role in the lives of same-sex couples. This issue and its impacts will be discussed in more depth in the remainder of this chapter.

10.3 The Damaging Discourse Surrounding the Social Value of Same-Sex Couples in Shifting Policy Climates

Research has begun to examine how discourses surrounding changing laws and policies impact the members of same-sex couples' well-being and relationship quality. This section highlights one study by Frost and Fingerhut (2016) which examined how members of same-sex couples were impacted by the social discourse that emerged surrounding the last round of state-level voter referenda regarding same-sex marriage in the USA.

There are many historical examples wherein the rights of minority groups with disadvantaged social status have been subject to popular vote and judicial decision-making by members of dominant majority groups (such as women's right to vote in the USA; court decisions about laws prohibiting marriage between men and women of different races). Such public decisions are accompanied by social debates which centre on the social value of minority groups whose rights are being decided (women and interracial couples in the examples cited above). Voter referenda on same-sex marriage are perhaps the most prominent contemporary example of such policy decisions and their resulting social debates. Many countries (for instance, Australia, Romania, Germany, Italy and Northern Ireland in the UK) have since recently been debating the legal status of same-sex marriage. Members of same-sex couples living in these countries experience others in their families, communities, workplaces, and social networks debating the value of their relationships, either directly or indirectly, through their expression of support or disapproval for such coupling decision. What emerges from these debates, particularly from dissenting opinions, is a devaluing social discourse which has been hypothesised to have a negative effect on the lives and relationships of members of same-sex couples.

In this regard, research by the author and his colleagues (Frost & Fingerhut, 2016) directly examined the psychological and relational consequences of exposure to negative campaign messages surrounding marriage equality campaigns in the USA. Within the study, 62 same-sex couples (124 individuals) were surveyed every day for ten consecutive days leading up to the last wave of voter referenda on same-sex marriage in four USA states. The couples' daily encounters with messages about the same-sex marriage campaigns in their states (including billboards, social media postings and news discussions) were measured, along with their daily experiences of general stressors (such as finances, childcare and household chores), relationship quality and positive and negative affect. The study found that daily exposure to negative same-sex marriage campaign messages was associated with decreased relationship satisfaction, decreased positive affect and increased negative affect, controlling for daily fluctuations in general stress and baseline levels of depression and relationship satisfaction (Frost & Fingerhut, 2016). It is important to note that same-sex marriage campaigns succeeded in achieving marriage equality in these states, but these findings indicate that the campaign itself created a negative and damaging social discourse surrounding the social value of same-sex couples.

This study was the first prospective examination to document the ways in which the devaluing social discourse that precedes policy decisions regarding same-sex marriage can be damaging for same-sex couples' psychological and relational well-being. Additional findings on the effects of negative media messages on sexual minorities in contexts of voter referenda have since emerged from studies in Australia (Verrelli, White, Harvey, & Pulciani, 2019) and the Republic of Ireland (Dane, Short, & Healy, 2016), indicating that increased exposure to negative messages was associated with poorer well-being outcomes. These findings have been further bolstered by a combined analysis of television advertisements and national survey data on distress among sexual minorities in the USA during the last voter referenda, which further showed that heightened exposure to negative television advertisements was associated with higher levels of distress among sexual minorities (Flores, Hatzenbuehler, & Gates, 2018).

The US Supreme Court's (2015) ruling in Obergefell v. Hodges granted members of same-sex couples equal access to legal marriage; however, social debates surrounding same-sex marriage continue, and members of same-sex couples are still forced to engage with a potentially damaging social discourse. Similar debates have continued cross the globe, where the majority of societies do not allow members of same-sex couples to access equal legal marriage, and communities in many of these countries have been, or continue to be, in debates about access to equal legal recognition for same-sex couples. Thus, access to equal legal rights and protections for same-sex couples is constantly shifting and increasingly subject to pending popular vote, legislative action and judicial decisions. As more and more countries and communities take on the decision of legal access to marriage for members of same-sex couples, it is important for policymakers, social scientists and clinical and counselling psychologists to monitor the ways in which emerging devaluing social discourses surrounding such decisions may negatively affect the lives of same-sex couples living in such areas.

10.4 Minority Stress in the Lives of Same-Sex Couples

Another recent theoretical advancement which aims to understand the influence of the shifting social context on the health and well-being of members of same-sex couples is couple-level minority stress theory (LeBlanc et al., 2015). Frost and LeBlanc (2018), Frost and colleagues (2017), and LeBlanc and colleagues (2015) have proposed an extension of Meyer's (2003) original minority stress model, as summarised below.

Members of same-sex couples experience stress in ways that are similar to members of mixed-sex couples (such as managing finances, negotiating with families of origin, taking care of children and conflict with a partner), which are known to negatively affect well-being and relational health and stability (Bodenmann et al., 2007; Booth & Amato, 1991; Kiecolt-Glaser, Bane, Glaser, & Malarkey, 2003). Yet, in addition to experiencing these commonly recognised forms of stress, same-sex couples experience additional unique stressors that are not experienced by mixed-sex couples.

These stressors are referred to as minority stressors given they are related to the stigmatised and disadvantaged social status afforded to same-sex relationships by society (Frost, 2011b; Meyer, 2003). This next section details the unique nature of the couple-level experience of minority stress in same-sex relationships and potential ways in which understanding the experience of couple-level minority stress (LeBlanc, Frost, & Wight, 2015) can lead to enriched understandings of how social stigma can impact the health and well-being of members of same-sex couples.

10.4.1 Minority Stress Experienced by Individual Members of Same-Sex Couples

The original minority stress framework (Meyer, 2003) articulates five minority stressors that individual members of same-sex couples are potentially exposed to as a result of their stigmatised social status as sexual minority individuals. These include event-based forms of discrimination (e.g., prejudice events), chronic and everyday forms of discrimination, expectations of rejection, stigma concealment and internalised stigma. An increasing amount of research has shown that individual members of same-sex couples can be negatively impacted by these minority stressors in terms of their experiences of the quality of their relationships, as well as their mental health and well-being (see Rostosky & Riggle, 2017b for a review, and Doyle & Molix, 2015 for a meta-analysis). For example, members of same-sex couples may be more likely to experience discrimination in the form of threats and harassment, and/or more minor forms of social distancing and slights (Peplau & Fingerhut, 2006). Additionally, as noted previously, members of same-sex couples experience greater stress related to not being accepted and being misunderstood by other people in their lives compared to single sexual minority individuals (Lewis, Derlega, Berndt, Morris, & Rose, 2002), and this can be acutely distressful when it involves their families. Members of same-sex couples may also feel compelled to hide the fact that they have a same-sex partner in order to reduce potential exposure to discrimination and devaluation. However, concealing one's membership in a same-sex relationship can also be a cognitive burden and is, therefore, in and of itself stressful (Meyer, 2003). The stigmatised status of same-sex couples and same-sex desire may additionally become applied to individual members of same-sex couples' identities, which represents minority stress in the form of internalised stigma (Frost & Meyer, 2009).

10.4.2 Couple-Level Minority Stressors

The theory of couple-level minority stress (LeBlanc et al., 2015) represents an extension of the original minority stress framework through its central concept: When individual sexual minority persons become members of a same-sex couple, they may face increased vulnerability to couple-level minority stressors that are unique to same-sex couples and not attributable solely to members' experiences as sexual minority individuals. Couple-level minority stressors occur as a result of the continual stigmatisation of same-sex relationships. 'It is the source of this stress (i.e. society's marginalization of the relationship) that defines such stressors as couple-level minority stressors' (Frost et al., 2017, p. 456).

Couple-level minority stressors can manifest in the lived experiences of same-sex couples in multiple ways. For instance, the distinction between individual and couple-level minority stressors becomes clear when we consider the case of a woman who conceals her sexual orientation from her co-workers because they have said homophobic things in the workplace. This illustrates individual-level minority stress in the form of identity concealment and everyday discrimination. Consider what happens if this woman were to be married to a female partner with whom she co-parents two children. Her membership in a same-sex couple may result in experiences of additional stressors, above and beyond what she may experience as an individual sexual minority person. More specifically, beyond her hiding of her own sexual identity, she is now challenged with the potential need to conceal her relationship status as well, which is more difficult given the need to register beneficiaries of life insurance, designate an emergency contact, and request time off from work for care-related responsibilities. This exemplifies the shift to a couple-level minority stressor, which involves concealment efforts around management of the visibility of her relational and parental statuses. In this example, as is the case for all couple-level forms of minority stress, the fundamental source of minority stress lies in the stigmatised social status afforded to same-sex couples, rather than each member's sexual minority identity as an individual.

Although researchers have examined the dyadic nature of more generally experienced social stressors (Bolger, DeLongis, Kessler, & Wethington, 1989), research has yet to directly investigate the existence or substance of couple-level minority stressors. Frost and colleagues (2018), Frost and colleagues (2017), and LeBlanc and colleagues (2015) have hypothesised that couple-level minority stressors may negatively impact couples' relationship quality, as well as the health and well-being of each partner. The negative influence of couple-level minority stress may come about because of unexamined stress processes involving stressors that emerge in relational and social contexts (Milkie, 2010; Pearlin, 1999; Pearlin, Aneshensel, & LeBlanc, 1997; Pearlin & Bierman, 2013), and cannot be accounted for at the level of individual experience.

10.4.3 Dyadic Minority Stress Processes

Classic sociological research has established that various types of stressors may 'proliferate' and move from one life domain to another (Pearlin, 1999; Pearlin et al., 1997; Pearlin & Bierman, 2013). In this regard, minority stressors may also proliferate to the couple level from the individual level of experience. In other words, couple-level minority stressors can be conceptualised as a 'primary' source of minority stress that can move into other 'secondary' forms of relational stressors (LeBlanc et al., 2015).

For individual members of same-sex couples, the proliferation of individual-level minority stress in the context of the dyad of a same-sex couple may happen in the form of minority stress 'discrepancies' (LeBlanc, Frost, Alston-Stepnitz, et al., 2015), which have been defined as the degree to which individuals' levels of stress experience vary in relation to those of a significant other (Lyons, Zarit, Sayer, & Whitlatch, 2002; Wight, Beals, Miller-Martinez, Murphy, & Aneshensel, 2007). LeBlanc and colleagues (2015) note how when one partner has low levels of internalised homophobia relative to the other, stress may emerge from this discrepancy in multiple ways: it may become a source of relational conflict, or a barrier to desired intimacy. These same authors also note another form of minority stress proliferation which concerns instances of minority stress 'contagion'. This can occur when individual-level minority stressors faced by one partner negatively affect the relational health and well-being of the other partner. However, the mechanisms through which minority stressors may become contagious have not yet been subject to empirical investigation in the dyadic context of same-sex couples.

The core tenants of couple-level minority stress theory (Frost et al., 2017; Frost & LeBlanc, 2018; LeBlanc, Frost, Alston-Stepnitz, et al., 2015) have been summarised here in order to highlight their potential utility in improving the field's understanding of how stigma impacts the health and well-being of same-sex couples in a changing social climate. Thus far, the only systematic investigation of couple-level minority stress theory has been a large-scale qualitative study (Frost et al., 2017) which provided evidence for the existence of 17 unique couple-level minority stressors, which are now subject to quantitative and longitudinal research. This follow-up research was deemed crucial to formally investigate the degree to which these minority stressors represent an additional risk to same-sex couples' health and well-being, above and beyond minority stress experienced at the individual level.

10.5 Beyond Access to Equal Marriage

Preliminary evidence for the utility of couple-level minority stress theory in explaining mental health among same-sex couples can be seen in a recent study from LeBlanc and colleagues (2018). This research provides the first test of an association between couple-level stress stemming from perceived unequal social recognition of same-sex couple relationships and several indicators of mental health. This research will be summarised and discussed as it connects couple-level minority stress to overarching concerns regarding stigma and its associations with same-sex couples' well-being in a changing social and policy context.

As previously mentioned, many countries are undergoing rapid changes in the laws that determine the legal recognition of same-sex couples, which are intertwined with changing social attitudes about same-sex couples. For example, debates concerning the legal recognition of same-sex relationships in the USA have continued, despite the fact that marriage is now legal for same-sex couples across the country. As a result of this continued debate, members of same-sex couples may continue to perceive a lack of equal treatment and value for their relationship from society at large and the political and legal system that governs rights and benefits afforded to legal marriage. Previous qualitative research into same-sex couples' experiences of couple-level minority stress identified perceived unequal legal status as one such couple-level minority stressor, stemming from the stigmatised status afforded to membership in a same-sex couple (Frost et al., 2017).

Several studies have now established a link between legal recognition for same-sex couples and positive outcomes for sexual minority individuals' mental health (Riggle, Rostosky, & Horne, 2010; Wight, LeBlanc, & Lee Badgett, 2013; Wight, LeBlanc, De Vries, & Detels, 2012). This research bolsters longstanding evidence of the positive health benefits of legal marriage of mixed-sex couples (Hughes & Waite, 2009; Umberson, Thomeer, & Williams, 2013). Conversely, research on structural stigma has shown that the passage of laws banning same-sex couples from access to legal marriage can have negative impacts on sexual minority mental health (Hatzenbuehler, McLaughlin, Keyes, & Hasin, 2010). Together, this research can be taken to show that equal access to marriage can be beneficial to the health and well-being of same-sex couples. However, recent changes in the laws governing equal access to marriage may not be sufficient to offset the negative aspects of the social stigma that persists and continues to create a perception of unequal relationship recognition for members of same-sex couples.

LeBlanc et al. (2018) examined the degree to which the perception of unequal recognition—as a couple-level minority stressor—explained variation in mental health above and beyond legal relationship recognition. The authors predicted that members of same-sex couples with legal marital status would report more positive mental health outcomes compared to members of same-sex couples who were not legally married (following Wight et al., 2012; Wight et al., 2013). They further hypothesised that a perception of the social climate as not affording equal recognition to same-sex couples would be related to worse mental health for members of same-sex couples, regardless of legal marital status. Dyadic data from both members of 106 same-sex couples—diverse in terms of couple gender, how long they had known one another, region of the USA and race/ethnicity—were collected and analysed. The survey contained measures of legal marital status, perceived unequal social recognition and mental health outcomes (i.e., depressive symptoms, non-specific psychological distress and problematic drinking behaviour). Dyadic analyses were used to examine relationships among legal marital status, perceived unequal recognition of same-sex relationships and the previously mentioned mental health outcome measures.

The study's findings (LeBlanc et al., 2018) demonstrated that perceived unequal relationship recognition was predictive of poorer mental health, above and beyond whether or not members of same-sex couples were in a legally recognised relationship. Focusing on potential differences in mental health by levels of legal relationship recognition, the study found that members of same-sex couples recognised as registered domestic partners or civil unions (RDP/CUs), but not as legal marriages, demonstrated significantly lower levels of mental health compared to those with legal marriages and those with no legal relationship status. Those who were legally married reported the most positive mental outcomes, but were not statistically distinguishable from those with no legal recognition for their relationship.

Notably, the inclusion of the couple-level minority stress construct of perceived unequal recognition demonstrates the importance of looking beyond indicators of structural stigma (that is, legal marital status) in examining social determinants of sexual minority mental health and well-being (which social determinants have previously been established as correlates of distress and mental health [Hatzenbuehler et al., 2010; Riggle et al., 2010; Wight et al., 2012; Wight et al., 2013]). The study findings, although preliminary, illustrated a consistent and robust pattern of associations with multiple indicators of mental health, suggesting that the degree to which members of same-sex couples perceive their relationship to have unequal recognition is a meaningful factor underlying mental health outcomes. Indeed, LeBlanc et al. (2018) observed such associations net the effects of legal relationship status and other relevant factors (that is, couple gender, race/ethnicity, relationship length, income and education). In summary, although institutionalised forms of discrimination, such as unequal access to legal marriage, have documented associations with mental health in sexual minority populations (Hatzenbuehler et al., 2010), the lived experience of perceived inequality likely represents a more proximal form of minority stress (Meyer, 2003), one that potentially exists as shared lived experience at the couple-level (LeBlanc, Frost, Alston-Stepnitz, et al., 2015) 'and may even persist in contexts where structural stigma has been reduced or eliminated' (LeBlanc et al., 2018, p. 405).

These findings are relevant to the main arguments of the current chapter in many ways; most notably in that they demonstrate that expansion of minority stress constructs beyond the individual to the couple-level can potentially help to illustrate how social change manifests at the relational level and has implications for individual mental health. Findings also importantly highlight how equal access to legal marriage is an important social change, but not sufficient to eliminate longstanding social risk for mental health problems faced by sexual minority individuals and members of same-sex couples. The constantly shifting social and policy climate facing sexual minorities and same-sex couples continues to warrant attention from social scientists, public health scholars and policymakers in light of its potential impact on mental health.

10.6 Resilience Resources Relevant to the Experience of Couple-Level Minority Stress

This chapter has focused on how same-sex couples' experiences of the rapidly changing social climate—emphasising stigma and minority stress—can be damaging for the couples' mental health and well-being. Yet, as alluded to earlier, it is also important to recognise that many same-sex couples experience happy, healthy, rewarding and lasting relationships. Thus, an understanding of variability in the experience of couple-level minority stress and its potential association with same-sex couples' mental health and well-being is needed to improve knowledge of when and how members of same-sex couples are able to cope with, overcome and resist the negative effects of minority stress. The final section of this chapter will, therefore, focus on the resources that members of same-sex couples may rely on in their efforts to be resilient in the face of experiences of social stigma and the resulting minority stress.

There are several resilience resources that same-sex couples may utilise to cope with minority stress, as highlighted by Frost and colleagues (2018). Members of same-sex couples may utilise individual and dyadic coping strategies that are common among all couples, regardless of sexual orientation (Bodenmann, Meuwly, & Kayser, 2011; Bodenmann, Pihet, & Kayser, 2006; Rostosky & Riggle, 2017a). However, sexual orientation-specific resilience resources (Meyer, 2014) are of particular interest in the present discussion, given that they may be most useful in dealing with the unique aspects of minority stress that same-sex couples face. Some examples will be presented as a means to illustrate this in action.

Couples are faced with the challenge of establishing and maintaining intimacy within their relationships while contending with negative stereotypes about their relationships and resulting minority stressors. Some research has indicated that individuals in same-sex relationships utilise meaning-making strategies whereby they (a) emphasise the fact that minority stress is a social challenge that they can overcome, thereby becoming stronger as a couple, and (b) exercise 'positive marginality' by defining important relationship milestones for themselves rather than relying on heteronormative definitions of success in relationships (Frost, 2011a, 2011b; Rostosky & Riggle, 2017a). Indeed, the use of such 'redemptive' meaning-making strategies when contending with minority stress in same-sex relationships is associated with heightened closeness in relationships (Frost, 2014) and may then be protective against negative relationship outcomes, such as diminished relationship quality and functioning, and the potential for relationship dissolution.

There are also resilience resources that exist within sexual minority communities that may be instrumental in mitigating the negative effects of minority stress (Meyer, 2003). Such minority group-specific resilience resources centre around establishing psychological and affiliative bonds with other sexual minority group members and developing a sense of connectedness to sexual minority communities (Frost & Meyer, 2012; Meyer, 2014; Russell & Richards, 2003). Extending the concept of minority group-specific resilience resources to the experiences of same-sex couples, it can be argued that having a supportive social network that includes other same-sex couples will likely be helpful in dealing with couple-level minority stress (LeBlanc, Frost, Alston-Stepnitz, et al., 2015). This parallels classic research that shows the presence of 'similar others' to be beneficial for mental health and psychological well-being among stigmatised minority group members (Frable, Platt, & Hoey, 1998) and useful for making positive social comparisons (Crocker & Major, 1989). Additionally, members of same-sex couples might be best equipped to offer support when facing couple-level minority stress, given they likely have been through similar experiences and can thus offer tried-and-tested advice and support to manage and overcome the negative effects of couple-level minority stress (Frost, Meyer, & Schwartz, 2016).

10.7 Implications and Conclusions

In concluding this chapter, it is important to reiterate that many same-sex couples are in happy, healthy and rewarding relationships despite continuing stigma at the societal level (Rostosky & Riggle, 2017a). Yet as more and more countries continue to pass laws providing legal recognition, rights and benefits to same-sex couples, it is crucial to remember that most countries do not offer such protections and stigma in various forms continues to negatively affect the health and well-being of same-sex couples even in contexts of marriage equality. As a result, efforts are continually needed to combat stigma and minority stress at the social and policy level (such as anti-discrimination laws, and inclusive and affirming educational curricula) even in countries that are 'post-marriage' in their recognition of same-sex couples' rights.

Even though minority stress stems from societal stigma, which can only be eliminated through social and structural interventions (Meyer & Frost, 2013; Ouellette, 1998), many same-sex couples are in need of help from clinicians and counsellors to navigate minority stress in their lives (Moradi, Mohr, Worthington, & Fassinger, 2009). Helping sexual minority individuals and same-sex couples make sense of minority stress in their pursuit and maintenance of intimate relationships is an important challenge and opportunity for clinicians (Kertzner, 2004). Simultaneously, addressing the negative effects of minority stress is necessary to build resilience resources and reduce the potential detrimental impact of minority stress leading to negative outcomes in the domains of relational health and functioning, as well as individual well-being and mental health.

Clinical and counselling interventions focused on helping members of same-sex couples manage minority stress need to be expanded beyond the level of individual patient treatment modalities in order to include couple-level counselling and dyadic psychotherapies (e.g., Green & Mitchell, 2008). Within such couple-level interventions, clinicians and counsellors can likely enhance their efforts to assist members of same-sex couples in dealing with the additional unique couple-level minority stressors and dyadic minority stress processes which persist in the present times of rapid social change as a threat to the well-being of same-sex couples.

Additionally, as laws change and structural stigma may decline (Hatzenbuehler, 2014), social and interpersonal sources of minority stress will likely endure. For example, familial devaluation of one's same-sex partner and/or prohibitions against getting married and parenting (Frost & LeBlanc, 2018; Frost et al., 2017) may be more likely to contribute to relationship dissolution and divorce than structural inequality now that equal legal marriage is increasingly available for members of same-sex couples. Within this rapidly changing social context, utilising the couple-level minority stress framework in future research and interventions may be helpful in better understanding these social factors that lead to negative outcomes in the lives of same-sex couples.

References

Adam, B. (2006). Relationship innovation in male couples. *Sexualities, 9*(1), 5–26.
Ayoub, P. M., & Garretson, J. (2017). Getting the message out: Media context and global changes in attitudes toward homosexuality. *Comparative Political Studies, 50*(8), 1055–1085.
Baiocco, R., Argalia, M., & Laghi, F. (2014). The desire to marry and attitudes toward same-sex family legalization in a sample of Italian lesbians and gay men. *Journal of Family Issues, 35*(2), 181–200.
Balsam, K. F., Beauchaine, T. P., Rothblum, E. D., & Solomon, S. E. (2008). Three-year follow-up of same-sex couples who had civil unions in Vermont, same-sex couples not in civil unions, and heterosexual married couples. *Developmental Psychology, 44*(1), 102–116.
Beals, K. P., Impett, E. A., & Peplau, L. A. (2002). Lesbians in love: Why some relationships endure and others end. *Journal of Lesbian Studies, 6*(1), 53–63.
Blumstein, P., & Schwartz, P. (1983). *American couples*. New York: Morrow.
Bodenmann, G., Charvoz, L., Bradbury, T. N., Bertoni, A., Iafrate, R., Giuliani, C., ... Behling, J. (2007). The role of stress in divorce: A three-nation retrospective study. *Journal of Social and Personal Relationships, 24*(5), 707–728.
Bodenmann, G., Meuwly, N., & Kayser, K. (2011). Two conceptualizations of dyadic coping and their potential for predicting relationship quality and individual well-being: A comparison. *European Psychologist, 16*, 255–266.
Bodenmann, G., Pihet, S., & Kayser, K. (2006). The relationship between dyadic coping and marital quality: A 2-year longitudinal study. *Journal of Family Psychology, 20*, 485–493.
Bolger, N., DeLongis, A., Kessler, R. C., & Wethington, E. (1989). The contagion of stress across multiple roles. *Journal of Marriage and the Family, 51*, 175–183.
Booth, A., & Amato, P. (1991). Divorce and psychological stress. *Journal of Health and Social Behavior, 32*(4), 396–407.
Brooks, V. R. (1981). *Minority stress and lesbian women*. Lexington, MA: Lexington Books.
Crocker, J., & Major, B. (1989). Social stigma and self-esteem: The self-protective properties of stigma. *Psychological Review, 96*(4), 608.
D'Augelli, A. R., Rendina, H. J., Sinclair, K. O., & Grossman, A. H. (2007). Lesbian and gay youth's aspirations for marriage and raising children. *Journal of LGBT Issues in Counseling, 1*(4), 77–98.
Dane, S., Short, L., & Healy, G. (2016). *Swimming with sharks: The negative social and psychological impacts of Ireland's marriage equality 'NO' campaign*. Retrieved April 8, 2019, from https://espace.library.uq.edu.au/view/UQ:408120
Degges-White, S., & Marszalek, J. (2007). An exploration of long-term, same-sex relationships: Benchmarks, perceptions, and challenges. *Journal of LGBT Issues in Counseling, 1*(4), 99–119.
Diamond, L. (2006). The intimate same-sex relationships of sexual minorities. In D. Perlman & A. Vangelisti (Eds.), *The Cambridge handbook of personal relationships* (pp. 293–312). New York: Cambridge University Press.
Diamond, L. M. (2017). Three critical questions for future research on lesbian relationships. *Journal of Lesbian Studies, 21*(1), 106–119.
Doyle, D. M., & Molix, L. (2015). Social stigma and sexual minorities' romantic relationship functioning: A meta-analytic review. *Personality and Social Psychology Bulletin, 41*(10), 1363–1381.

Fetner, T. (2016). US attitudes toward lesbian and gay people are better than ever. *Contexts, 15*(2), 20–27.

Flores, A. R., Hatzenbuehler, M. L., & Gates, G. J. (2018). Identifying psychological responses of stigmatized groups to referendums. *Proceedings of the National Academy of Sciences, 115*(15), 3816–3821.

Frable, D. E., Platt, L., & Hoey, S. (1998). Concealable stigmas and positive self-perceptions: Feeling better around similar others. *Journal of Personality and Social Psychology, 74*(4), 909.

Frost, D. M. (2011a). Social stigma and its consequences for the socially stigmatized. *Social and Personality Psychology Compass, 5*(11), 824–839.

Frost, D. M. (2011b). Stigma and intimacy in same-sex relationships: A narrative approach. *Journal of Family Psychology, 25*(1), 1–10.

Frost, D. M. (2014). Redemptive framings of minority stress: Implications for closeness in same-sex relationships. *Journal of Couple & Relationship Therapy, 13*, 219–239.

Frost, D. M., & Eliason, M. J. (2014). Challenging the assumption of fusion in female same-sex relationships. *Psychology of Women Quarterly, 38*(1), 65–74.

Frost, D. M., & Fingerhut, A. W. (2016). Daily exposure to negative campaign messages decreases same-sex couples' psychological and relational well-being. *Group Processes & Intergroup Relations, 19*, 477–492.

Frost, D. M., & Gola, K. A. (2015). Meanings of intimacy: A comparison of members of heterosexual and same-sex couples. *Analyses of Social Issues and Public Policy, 15*(1), 382–400.

Frost, D. M., & LeBlanc, A. J. (2014). Non-event stress contributes to mental health disparities based on sexual orientation: Evidence from a personal projects analysis. *American Journal of Orthopsychiatry, 84*, 557–566.

Frost, D. M., & LeBlanc, A. J. (2018). Stress in the lives of same-sex couples. In A. E. Goldberg & A. P. Romero (Eds.), *LGBTQ divorce and relationship dissolution: Psychological and legal perspectives and implications for practice* (pp. 70–86). Oxford: Oxford University Press.

Frost, D. M., LeBlanc, A. J., de Vries, B., Alston-Stepnitz, E., Stephenson, R., & Woodyatt, C. (2017). Couple-level minority stress: An examination of same-sex couples' unique experiences. *Journal of Health and Social Behavior, 58*, 455–472.

Frost, D. M., & Meyer, I. H. (2009). Internalized homophobia and relationship quality among lesbians, gay men, and bisexuals. *Journal of Counseling Psychology, 56*, 97–109.

Frost, D. M., & Meyer, I. H. (2012). Measuring community connectedness among diverse sexual minority populations. *Journal of Sex Research, 48*(1), 36–49.

Frost, D. M., Meyer, I. H., & Schwartz, S. (2016). Social support networks among diverse sexual minority populations. *American Journal of Orthopsychiatry, 86*(1), 91.

Goldberg, A. E. (2014). Will I marry if my parents can't? Young adults with LGB parents consider marriage for themselves. *Journal of Family Issues, 35*(2), 151–180.

Gottman, J. M., Levenson, R. W., Swanson, C., Swanson, K., Tyson, R., & Yoshimoto, D. (2003). Observing gay, lesbian and heterosexual couples' relationships: Mathematical modeling of conflict interaction. *Journal of Homosexuality, 45*, 65–91.

Green, R. J., & Mitchell, V. (2008). Gay and lesbian couples in therapy: Minority stress, relational ambiguity, and families of choice. In *Clinical handbook of couple therapy* (Vol. 4, pp. 662–680).

Hammack, P. L., Frost, D. M., & Hughes, S. D. (2019). Queer intimacies: A new paradigm for the study of relationship diversity. *Journal of Sex Research, 56*(4-5), 556–592. https://doi.org/10.1080/00224499.2018.1531281

Hatzenbuehler, M. L. (2014). Structural stigma and the health of lesbian, gay, and bisexual populations. *Current Directions in Psychological Science, 23*(2), 127–132.

Hatzenbuehler, M. (2016). Structural stigma: Research evidence and implications for psychological science. *American Psychologist, 71*(8), 742–751.

Hatzenbuehler, M. L., McLaughlin, K. A., Keyes, K. M., & Hasin, D. S. (2010). The impact of institutional discrimination on psychiatric disorders in lesbian, gay, and bisexual populations: A prospective study. *American Journal of Public Health, 100*(3), 452–459.

Herdt, G., & Kertzner, R. (2006). I do, but I can't: The impact of marriage denial on the mental health and sexual citizenship of lesbians and gay men in the United States. *Sexuality Research and Social Policy, 3*(1), 33–49.

Herek, G. M. (2006). Legal recognition of same-sex relationships in the United States: A social science perspective. *American Psychologist, 61*(6), 607–621.

Hughes, M. E., & Waite, L. J. (2009). Marital biography and health at mid-life. *Journal of Health and Social Behavior, 50*(3), 344–358.

Kertzner, R. M. (2004). Psychotherapy with lesbian and gay clients from an adult life course perspective. *Journal of Gay & Lesbian Social Services, 16*(2), 105–111.

Kiecolt-Glaser, J. K., Bane, C., Glaser, R., & Malarkey, W. B. (2003). Love, marriage, and divorce: Newlyweds' stress hormones foreshadow relationship changes. *Journal of Consulting and Clinical Psychology, 71*(1), 176.

King, M., & Bartlett, A. (2006). What same sex civil partnerships may mean for health. *Journal of Epidemiology & Community Health, 60*(3), 188–191.

King, M., Semlyen, J., Tai, S. S., Killaspy, H., Osborn, D., Popelyuk, D., & Nazareth, I. (2008). A systematic review of mental disorder, suicide, and deliberate self harm in lesbian, gay and bisexual people. *BMC Psychiatry, 8*(1), 1–17.

Kurdek, L. A. (2004). Are gay and lesbian cohabiting couples really different from heterosexual married couples? *Journal of Marriage and Family, 66*(4), 880–900.

Kurdek, L. A. (2005). What do we know about gay and lesbian couples?. *Current Directions in Psychological Science, 14*(5), 251–254.

Kurdek, L. A. (2008). Change in relationship quality for partners from lesbian, gay male, and heterosexual couples. *Journal of Family Psychology, 22*(5), 701–711.

Lannutti, P. J. (2008). Attractions and obstacles while considering legally recognized same-sex marriage. *Journal of GLBT Family Studies, 4*(2), 245–264.

LeBlanc, A. J., Frost, D. M., Alston-Stepnitz, E., Bauermeister, J., Stephenson, R., Woodyatt, C. R., & de Vries, B. (2015). Similar others in same-sex couples' social networks. *Journal of Homosexuality, 62*(11), 1599–1610.

LeBlanc, A. J., Frost, D. M., & Bowen, K. (2018). Legal marriage, unequal recognition, and mental health among same-sex couples. *Journal of Marriage and Family, 80*(2), 397–408.

LeBlanc, A. J., Frost, D. M., & Wight, R. G. (2015). Minority stress and stress proliferation among same-sex and other marginalized couples. *Journal of Marriage and Family, 77*(1), 40–59.

Lewis, R. J., Derlega, V. J., Berndt, A., Morris, L. M., & Rose, S. (2002). An empirical analysis of stressors for gay men and lesbians. *Journal of Homosexuality, 42*(1), 63–88.

Lewis, R. J., Derlega, V. J., Griffin, J. L., & Krowinski, A. C. (2003). Stressors for gay men and lesbians: Life stress, gay-related stress, stigma consciousness, and depressive symptoms. *Journal of Social and Clinical Psychology, 22*(6), 716–729.

Lyons, K. S., Zarit, S. H., Sayer, A. G., & Whitlatch, C. J. (2002). Caregiving as a dyadic process: Perspectives from caregiver and receiver. *The Journals of Gerontology Series B: Psychological Sciences and Social Sciences, 57*(3), 195–204.

Meyer, I. H. (2003). Prejudice, social stress, and mental health in lesbian, gay, and bisexual populations: Conceptual issues and research evidence. *Psychological Bulletin, 129*, 674–697.

Meyer, I. H. (2014). Minority stress and positive psychology: Convergences and divergences to understanding LGBT health. *Psychology of Sexual Orientation and Gender Diversity, 1*(4), 348.

Meyer, I. H., & Frost, D. M. (2013). Minority stress and the health of sexual minorities. In C. J. Patterson & A. R. D'Augelli (Eds.), *Handbook of psychology and sexual orientation* (pp. 252–266). New York: Oxford University Press.

Milkie, M. A. (2010). The stress process model: Some family-level considerations. In W. R. Avison, C. S. Aneshensel, S. Schieman, & B. Wheaton (Eds.), *Advances in the conceptualization of the stress process: Essays in honor of Leonard I. Pearlin* (pp. 93–108). New York: Springer Science + Business Media.

Moradi, B., Mohr, J. J., Worthington, R. L., & Fassinger, R. E. (2009). Counseling psychology research on sexual (orientation) minority issues: Conceptual and methodological challenges and opportunities. *Journal of Counseling Psychology, 56*(1), 5.

Obergefell v. Hodges, 576 U.S. ____(slip. op.) (2015).

Ouellette, S. (1998). The value and limitations of stress models in HIV/AIDS. In: B. P. Dohrenwend (Ed.), *Adversity, stress, and psychopathology* (pp. 142–160). New York: Oxford University Press.

Pearlin, L. I. (1999). The stress process revisited: Reflections on concepts and their interrelationships. In C. S. Aneshensel & J. C. Phelan (Eds.), *Handbook on the sociology of mental health* (pp. 395–415). New York: Kluwer Academic/Plenum Press.

Pearlin, L. I., Aneshensel, C. S., & LeBlanc, A. J. (1997). The forms and mechanisms of stress proliferation: The case of AIDS caregivers. *Journal of Health and Social Behavior, 38*, 223–236.

Pearlin, L. I., & Bierman, A. (2013). Current issues and future directions in research into the stress process. In C. S. Aneshensel, J. C. Phelan, & A. Bierman (Eds.), *Handbook of the sociology of mental health* (2nd ed., pp. 325–340). New York: Springer Science + Business Media.

Peplau, L. A., & Fingerhut, A. W. (2006). The close relationships of lesbians and gay men. *Annual Review of Psychology, 58*, 405–424.

Riggle, E. D., Thomas, J. D., & Rostosky, S. S. (2005). The marriage debate and minority stress. *PS: Political Science & Politics, 38*(2), 221–224.

Riggle, E. D., Rostosky, S. S., & Horne, S. G. (2010). Psychological distress, well-being, and legal recognition in same-sex couple relationships. *Journal of Family Psychology, 24*(1), 82–86.

Rostosky, S. S., & Riggle, E. D. (2017a). Same-sex couple relationship strengths: A review and synthesis of the empirical literature (2000–2016). *Psychology of Sexual Orientation and Gender Diversity, 4*(1), 1–13.

Rostosky, S. S., & Riggle, E. D. (2017b). Same-sex relationships and minority stress. *Current Opinion in Psychology, 13*, 29–38.

Rostosky, S. S., Riggle, E. D., Rothblum, E. D., & Balsam, K. F. (2016). Same-sex couples' decisions and experiences of marriage in the context of minority stress: Interviews from a population-based longitudinal study. *Journal of Homosexuality, 63*(8), 1019–1040.

Rothblum, E. D. (2005). Same-sex marriage and legalized relationships: I do, or do I? *Journal of GLBT Family Studies, 1*(1), 21–31.

Rubin, J. D., Moors, A. C., Matsick, J. L., Ziegler, A., & Conley, T. D. (2014). On the margins: Considering diversity among consensually non-monogamous relationships. *Journal für Psychologie, 22*(1).

Russell, G. M., & Richards, J. A. (2003). Stressor and resilience factors for lesbians, gay men, and bisexuals confronting antigay politics. *American Journal of Community Psychology, 31*(3-4), 313–328.

Umberson, D., Thomeer, M. B., & Williams, K. (2013). Family status and mental health: Recent advances and future directions. In *Handbook of the sociology of mental health* (pp. 405–431). Springer: Dordrecht.

van Eeden-Moorefield, B., Malloy, K., & Benson, K. (2016). Gay men's (non) monogamy ideals and lived experience. *Sex Roles, 75*(1–2), 43–55.

Verrelli, S., White, F. A., Harvey, L. J., & Pulciani, M. R. (2019). Minority stress, social support, and the mental health of lesbian, gay, and bisexual Australians during the Australian Marriage Law Postal Survey. *Australian Psychologist, 54*(4), 336–346. https://doi.org/10.1111/ap.12380

Weston, K. (1991). *Families we choose: Lesbians, gays, kinship*. New York: Columbia University Press.

Wight, R. G., Beals, K. P., Miller-Martinez, D., Murphy, D. A., & Aneshensel, C. S. (2007). HIV-related traumatic stress symptoms in AIDS caregiving family dyads. *AIDS Care, 19*, 901–909.

Wight, R. G., LeBlanc, A. J., De Vries, B., & Detels, R. (2012). Stress and mental health among midlife and older gay-identified men. *American Journal of Public Health, 102*(3), 503–510.

Wight, R. G., LeBlanc, A. J., & Lee Badgett, M. V. (2013). Same-sex legal marriage and psychological well-being: Findings from the California health interview survey. *American Journal of Public Health, 103*(2), 339–346.

Chapter 11
Falling in Love in Later Life

Margaret Hellie Huyck

11.1 Introduction

Falling used to be fun. I remember tumbling in a snow drift or in a pile of hay, and gleefully getting myself up. As a teen we had trust exercises in which we stood in the middle of a circle of people, shut our eyes, and fell back—with the thrill of being caught and rescued from harm. Now, I fear falling more than anything else. I have taken several classes in learning how to prevent falls, how to fall safely if it seems inevitable, and how to regain my upward stance when I do fall.

Thus, the notion of "falling in love" evokes very mixed feelings in me. I recall when I wanted nothing more than to experience love and could easily imagine tumbling into the experiences I read about in books and pop magazines. I went through the period of learning how to trust falling in love, and how to recover when it did not work out. At this point I have a lot of learning and experience behind me, and I am much more cautious about even contemplating the complex emotions and relationships that may accompany passion and "love."

We are born to be social. At all ages, we long to be recognized as special by at least one other, evoking the tender care that can ensure survival in the early years—and perhaps in the later years as well. We need touch, and as we mature we desire the more intimate attention and caressing of passion and sensuality. These are crucial components of some forms of love. We are also born with a desire for autonomy, the need to feel competent and independent. Balancing these needs is a lifelong challenge.

Falling in love means granting a special kind of power to the beloved—to make us feel better and invulnerable, and to leave us feeling abandoned and empty if the relationship ends. We can only fall in love if we are confident we can survive its loss.

M. H. Huyck (✉)
Psychology, Illinois Institute of Technology, Chicago, IL, USA

Much more research has focused on love, sex, courtship, and marriage during early adulthood than in later life. Research is very sparse and this area may be considered as a research gap. One of the early, anecdotal studies of romantic relationships formed in later life was reported in 2001 by Edith Ankersmit Kemp and Jerrold Kemp (2001). They recruited 15 couples where at least one partner was over age 55 when the relationship started. They interviewed couples who were married, living together, or living separately but in a committed relationship. Each partner was interviewed separately, and then together. They found that the capacities to love deeply and to be as sexually active as health allows do not change. In fact, they found evidence that many of the individuals had difficult, sometimes horrendous childhoods and painful earlier marriages, but they were still able to form satisfying later unions. They were able to learn over adulthood how to manage and overcome earlier adversities. These new relationships gave individuals the chance to find personal strengths not previously developed. They also found that a common thread with all the couples who had a solid relationship—there was a foundation of mutual acceptance and respect for the other person as he or she is.

Kemp and Kemp (2001) drew on the work of developmental psychologists to compare early and late life unions. Erik Erikson observed that intimacy in young adulthood implies the fusion of individual identities in mutual intimacy; in later life the commitment is more to companionship between individuals who have developed their own identity and remain differentiated (Erikson, 1986).

The reality is that many of us now have many more years in which to experience love. We have a longer healthy lifespan, and a shorter period of serious disability and final decline. In addition to changes in our bio-medical experiences, many social changes lead to new options. When I entered the field of gerontology in 1961, an American woman on average experienced widowhood before the last child left home. Now we have the potential of a long period of marriage after the "empty nest"—and many individuals decide they do not wish to spend that time with the partner of their earlier years. Divorce rates rose overall in the 1970s, 1980s, and 1990s in the USA, and have declined somewhat in this century (Swanson, 2015). However, divorce rates have climbed for America's 50+ population (Stepler, 2017). Divorce is still most common among young adults (24/1000 married persons in 2015), but among the older group it has risen from 5 to 10/1000 married persons from 1990 to 2015 (Stepler, 2017). Birth rates have declined, which means fewer years preoccupied with child rearing and more options for career and personal development, especially among the better educated. Cohabitation has become more socially acceptable, and more common, at all ages.

Over the past half century, we have experienced substantial revisions in how we define and experience gender, though these changes have not been experienced equally in all segments or in all ways. In some ways, the gender stereotypes have remained remarkably consistent in the last 30 years. As researchers Haines, Deaux and Lofaro (2016) pointed out, the activities of women and men, and the way they are represented in society, have changed since the early 1980s and yet, very basic beliefs about gender persist. Among a young adult sample in 2014, they found substantial agreement between men and women in how they stereotyped each sex, though they were more likely to believe the stereotypes about their own sex. People were very likely to believe that men avoid "traditional" female roles. The most notable change was that women and men were believed to be more equally engaged in financial roles in 2014 than in 1983. Interestingly, recent research with adolescents indicate that there are "many ways to be a girl, but one way to be a boy" (Miller, 2018; Plan International USA, 2018).

In the USA the middle and upper classes are more likely than working class individuals to have challenged the status of women, with the expectations that women should have the opportunities and responsibilities more similar to those of men in previous decades; many of those women are now older, and they view romantic possibilities quite differently than when they were much younger. Working class women seem to have remained more accepting of traditional social gender roles. One analyst examined the recent voting records in the 2016 Presidential election, and noted that the women supporting the Republican candidate were poorly educated, working-class white women (Fearn, 2016). She speculated that they may rely more on their traditional roles as mother and homemaker for power, and are reluctant to embrace the kind of occupational competition championed by more advantaged women (Ibid.).

The consequences of the complex gender role shifts on love in later life are not yet clear. One psychiatrist whose practice includes many older men drew on his clinical observations to craft a novel *The Lonely Hearts Club* (Friedman, 2012) about men who gather frequently to work out and share coffee—but who are unable to share anything like real intimacy, with each other or with a woman. A journalist who recognized the kinds of men portrayed in the novel from her own experiences dating older men concluded that the men were unable to confront the changes in gender roles; they had never learned to express or share emotions (other than competition and anger), and are bewildered by what contemporary women want of them (Hodgkinson, 2012).

In this chapter, I will focus on adults who are in their sixties or older, which is a time when individuals are expected socially to move toward redefining their life with less emphasis on paid work and parenting—though many become heavily involved with grandchildren (Many remain in long-term marriages, some very happily and some not). In my own research with 130 couples we found a group of wives whom we dubbed "widows in waiting" because they were, in fact, looking forward to the time when they could move into the relative freedom of widowhood (Huyck & Gutmann, 1992). As indicated in Table 11.1, in the USA a majority of women and

Table 11.1 Marital status by age and sex, 2016 rate per 1000 NOT married and living with spouse

Age	Female	Male
65–74	45.1	27.2
75–84	60.8	29.9
85+	82.3	43.7

Source: US Census (2016)

a minority of men over 65 are not married and living with a spouse. These are, presumably, the candidates for "falling in love in later life."

The difficulties involved in looking for love in later life, and the ambivalence that ensues, have emerged in personal discussions with many of my acquaintances, older women who are relatively well-educated and socially involved:

- "I think men want 'a mouse with a house' or 'a nurse with a purse'—and most feminists don't want to be either."
- Linda: "I had 'the love of my life' at 68—but he turned out to be alcoholic, temperamental (he would march out of the house in the midst of an argument), etc. When he became very ill, I was summoned to the hospital; I called his two children (both local) and they said 'we're so glad he has you'. I told them to come get him. We did not reconcile, and I don't think I would risk anything like that again."
- Halina: "At my age (82) I no longer think of men as potential romantic partners. They are interesting in some way, or helpful, but I don't even think about romance."
- A professional black woman reflected on her own history: "I was married twice, and then I learned better. The first time I typed all my husband's papers so he could get through school. That didn't last very long. The second one was really short—I discovered he was violent, and I was right out of there. I'm still interested in a relationship, but I'm not good at the wife stuff—having dinner on the table, doing the laundry, and that. I am a good partner. My ideal at this point would be to have someone who has his own place, and we could get together and have a good time."
- In an episode of the British television drama *Father Brown*, the parish secretary (age 50s or 60s) is confronted with the sudden reappearance of her husband, a magician who disappeared from her life some 20 years ago. He has come back to woo her—but when he finally admits that he is dying of alcoholism and his previous lover has abandoned him, she sends him packing. Interestingly, some of the characters who are aware of the situation urge her to reconcile and care for him; others warn her against being taken advantage of, as she had been earlier.
- The journalist cited earlier (Hodgkinson, 2012) was very direct: "I have been looking for another life companion, someone exciting with whom to walk into the sunset for our remaining years. So far, this special man has eluded me. And I am far from alone in this. So many of my female friends of a certain age are searching for love, on the internet or elsewhere, and coming up with precisely zero…The men we meet are not what we are looking for … We ask ourselves and each other: what's the matter with them? Why do older men make such dreadful partners?…Older men are often totally incapable of opening up to new women…Older men can fall passionately in love when they're older, but it is less likely because there is less spontaneity and less emotion at this age…"

Similar ambivalence is evident in conversations with men.

- Wes (age 66): "I'm just getting through a divorce I didn't want, and I don't know how long it will take until I can trust anyone, or myself, to be close again."
- John (age 78): "I really don't like change."
- Saul (age 92): "I really like to have a warm body to cuddle with, but at my age I don't think I could go through all that again. I just wish I could go back and really appreciate my second marriage."

However, men also experience falling in love. Paul who fell in love with Arlene (read her account further down) at 66 says "falling in love in later life is more meaningful because you have a foreshortened sense of time, which you probably don't have when you are younger—you might even think this is your last chance, or you may have got to the point where you thought it would never happen/or never happen again, and then…wham!!"

11.2 Attraction and Dating

Falling in love begins with attraction. We sense, believe, or at least hope that this new person can enhance our life if we can be in a closer relationship. In the quotes above, some are fairly cynical about the possibilities. However, the fact is that the rise in online dating among older adults in the USA suggests that there are those who are more optimistic.

One study of online dating examined prioritized relationship goals for new romantic relationships within a sample of 5829 users of the U.S. eHarmony.com website between October 2002 and March 2012 (Menkin, Robles, Wiley, & Gonzaga, 2015). The sample was 20–95 years old, 50% male and 86% non-Hispanic White, 67% had an associate's or higher degree. Relationship goals were assessed by asking how important each of 30 characteristics was in finding a partner for a relationship. Factor analysis identified three main factors: Sexual Attraction, Interpersonal Communication, and Individual Companionate Characteristics. They examined the effects of gender and age for "young" users (under age 40), "middle-age" users (aged 40–50), "young-old" users (aged 60–74), and "old-old" users (aged 75 years and above). Overall, users valued companionship more than sexual attraction, with no consistent differences by age. As predicted, men valued sexual attraction more than did women at all ages, and women valued companionate characteristics more than did men at all ages. The clearest gender difference was evident in the over-80 age group, where men valued sexual attractiveness highly, and women valued it little, with no overlap in the male–female distribution.

Very similar findings were reported in a study of Internet personal ads of 600 heterosexual men and women aged 20–75+. Alterovitz and Mendelsohn (2009) find that irrespective of age, men are more likely to look for physical attractiveness while women are more likely to seek status.

A national portrait of dating relationships in older adulthood in the USA was constructed by Brown and Shinohara (2013) using data from the 2005–2006

National Social Life, Health, and Aging Project, with a nationally representative sample of 3005 individuals aged 57–85. Roughly 14% of singles were in a dating relationship. Dating was more common among men than women and declined with age. Compared to non-daters, daters were more likely to be college educated and had more assets, were in better health, and reported more social connectedness. Daters were more likely to be divorced than widowed.

Several studies have examined gender differences in the meanings of dating in later life. Men tend to be more interested than women in formalizing these relationships through marriage (Brown & Shinohara, 2013; Dickson, Hughes, & Walker, 2005). A classic study of dating in later life by Bulcroft and O'Connor (1986) reported that women emphasized the greater esteem and identity they gained among their peers, feeling that relationships with men provided elements not found in their female support systems. Men emphasized having an outlet for intimacy, self-disclosure, and often sex.

A qualitative analysis of interviews with 15 older white women, aged 62–79 years, living in a large city in the Western United States revealed some of the complexities of dating for an advantaged group of women (Dickson et al., 2005). The women expressed needs for independence and companionship, as well as gender role conflict. The most important theme was the need to maintain independence, often only realized fully in later life (with divorce or widowhood). They did not want to lose financial independence, and they feared taking on a caregiver role. Most of the women wanted to maintain an intimate relationship, but felt pressured by men to proceed to marriage. The women also discussed the changing etiquette of dating. They preferred to have the man initiate the date, and also pay for dinner (although they no longer assume that he will do so). However, they wanted to meet a new date in a public space, and preferred to pay for their own lunch.

11.3 Sexuality and Sensuality

Sensual pleasure begins in infancy, and the desire to be touched continues until death. "Bad touching" can lead us to repress this normal desire at any point along the life course. Normally, these general sensual desires develop to focus more specifically on genital feelings and are described as sexual pleasures. We recognize now that the desire for sexual pleasure is also maintained until very late in life, though we also know that every society regulates the expressions of sensual and sexual desire at every phase of life. The social norms governing sexual expression vary by culture, social class, historical time, and gender; when these norms change individuals are often confused about what feelings and behaviors are "normal," "permissible," "optimal," or even legal.

One example of the change in cultural norms is evident in the catalogs of products marketed to older adults in the USA. In several catalogs there is a section called Sexual Health, which displays, in vivid colors, various devices designed to provide stimulation of the clitoris, vagina, penis, and anus—all known to be primary sites for sexual pleasure. Readers are guided with taglines such as these: "the secret to amazing clitoral stimulation"; "Put the fun into foreplay." "Pure G-spot pleasure"; "Bends to your every desire," "Amazing prostate stimulation"; "Harder, fuller erections," "Tease and please the tip of your penis" (Feelgoodstore, 2019). Such explicit information was not available to the general markets until very recently.

A national poll on healthy aging in the USA (AARP/University of Michigan, 2018) included questions about respondents' perspectives on relationships and sex and their experiences related to sexual health. The 1000 respondents were aged 65–80. Nearly three in four (72%) said they were in a current romantic partnership (married, partnered, or in a relationship). Most of those with a romantic partner have been in the relationship 10 years or longer (92%); only 4% were in a relationship of less than 5 years. Most older men (84%) and many women (69%) agreed that sex is an important part of a romantic relationship. Men were more likely to report being sexually active than women (51% vs. 31%), as were both men and women reporting they were in very good, good, or good health compared to those with fair or poor health. Half of the men (50%) reported being extremely or very interested in sex as compared to 12% of the women. Younger respondents were more likely than older respondents to report being extremely or very interested in sex (34% aged 65–70, 28% aged 71–75, and 19% aged 76–80).

A similar survey on sexual attitudes and practices conducted by AARP sampled 1670 adults aged 45 and over in August of 2009 (AARP, 2010). This sample included 630 Hispanic respondents and was administered in both Spanish and English. The researchers compared results with patterns identified in surveys done in 1999 and 2004. They pointed out that "the sexual revolution continues in the older population … Opposition to sex among those who are not married is down by half over the past 10 years (from 41% in 1999 to 22% in 2009) and belief that there is too much emphasis on sex in our culture today is down since 2004." Similar to the findings in the 2017 survey, "men continue to think about sex more often than women, see it as more important to their quality of life, engage in sexual activities more often, are less satisfied if without a partner, and are twice as likely as women (21% vs. 11%) to admit to sexual activity outside their primary relationship."

Both sexual frequency and sexual satisfaction are higher among unmarried and dating individuals than among those who are married. Regardless of gender, respondents with a regular sexual partner have a more positive outlook on life, both positive and future, than do those who do not have a regular sex partner. This particular gender gap is larger for men than for women. Among men, about half (52%) say their current quality of life is high, as compared to 30% of those without partners. Among women, the gap in current quality of life is only five points—48% among those with partners and 43% among those without partners.

"Sexual activity" includes many different behaviors, in later life as in earlier life. The 2010 AARP study reported on the frequency by gender and age for six sexual activities: sexual intercourse, kissing or hugging, sexual touching or caressing, self-stimulation, oral sex, and anal sex (AARP, 2010). They did not ask about the use of "sex toys." More than one in five (22%) said they engage in self-stimulation at least once a week; the presence of a sexual partner does not matter.

Variations in the emphasis on these options was described by my acquaintance "Helen," one of my more candid respondents, describes the variety of reasons for engaging in sexual encounters, and the changing qualities of sexuality over the life course.

With my first husband, it was passionate attraction from the beginning. We "necked" for several years (as was common in that era), but finally succumbed and had Real Sex. I loved it, but we needed to do it twice for me to have an orgasm. We got better at it, but he never lasted as long as I wanted, and I usually wanted more. When that relationship ended and I began to consider other options, I went through an exploratory phase where I had several relationships which were not even as satisfying as my first one. By the end of that period I was almost non-orgasmic, and I sought out sex therapy to see if there was something seriously wrong with me. Then I became involved with a man who was my very serious fuck-friend for 25 years. I was totally responsive, and we were obsessed with each other. My next lover was recently widowed. He was older and impotent but lusted after oral sex—and we absolutely bonded with this erotic tie. I realized how little standard intercourse had to do with my sensual satisfaction. After he died, I met a widower who seemed to appreciate sensuality as much as I, and we got together. I now experience the full pleasures of sensual touch, sexual and otherwise; I feel totally loved and desired. I am thankful every day that he is in my bed and in my life. We don't know what comes next, but we are enjoying this time.

11.4 Relationship Status: Personal and Social

By the time we get to later life, we have already moved through many relationship statuses, both personal and social. We have acquired new relationships, negotiated complex new personal and social statuses (think about becoming a wife/daughter-in-law/sister-in-law) and then ex-wife, step-mother, widow. When we contemplate entering a new romantic relationship in later life, there are a number of crucial decisions to be made. Some decisions relate to the extent and ways we will interact with each partner's prior family (or families) and friends. Others relate to ways we define the new relationship, socially and legally: to live together or separately? To recognize the new relationship legally through marriage, with a personally fashioned commitment ceremony, or informally? What are the potential benefits and concerns associated with each of these options?

11.4.1 Partnered but Living Separately

Another option for later-life romances is for each to retain their own home, and agree to spend time together. This can be the most flexible, and seems to be attractive for those having a home they like, hate the prospect of moving or rearranging their own household to accommodate another person, have a pet (or more than one) that is unacceptable to the new partner, or who just need control over their own space and lives more than they desire companionship. This option is most attractive to those who can support themselves and are not trying to minimize costs by sharing space. The benefits include retaining the maximum sense of autonomy in later life. One of the downsides was identified by a friend who was in a caring, committed relationship with a man for several years; when he became ill and died, she was offered none of the social support provided to widows or cohabiting partners.

11.4.2 Cohabitation

Living together, without the legal sanctions of marriage, is an increasingly popular option at all ages. This social option has allowed many seniors to decide to enjoy the benefits of shared living, either before or instead of making other, more legal, commitments. There are several reasons why couples may choose to cohabit rather than marry:

- **Financial**: If a woman (or man) could lose a pension upon remarriage, it may be too costly (Bowden, 2012). The penalties are more common for those who remarry before age 60 after divorce; there are no problems if you are receiving benefits on your own work record or are widowed.
- **Medical**: If long-term care is needed but personal finances are not adequate to pay for the care needed, programs such as Medicaid may pay for such care. In calculating the ability to pay, resources from both spouses are considered in terms of a married couple. However, in the USA only the resources of the person needing care are considered in calculating eligibility for Medicaid support. Policies and practices regarding funding long-term care vary by country, and by state within the USA, and are changing—so the only guide is to remain informed. This will not be an issue for all older adults, but it is for many.
- **Assets:** Setting up a new household, as with cohabitation, means deciding who is going to give up a home. If one partner has a home that is comfortable for the new partnership, and the other does not, it may make sense to move in together and not maintain two separate households. However, this brings with it the need to anticipate what will happen when one partner dies. If the homeowner dies first, the survivor of an informal partnership may not qualify for a homestead exemption (it depends on the state). The heirs of the homeowner may wish to dispose of the property (including the contents and the real estate) and the survivor may be vulnerable to eviction if the home is not also titled in his or her name (Bowden, 2012). One solution for the cohabiting couple would be to title the house as a life estate so the survivor can live there until the latter dies, and then the owner's heirs inherit (Bowden, 2012). Another strategy is for both partners to sell their homes, and move to a new shared space. This, however, means dealing with all the complex issues of defining ownership and rights of transmission to heirs.
- **Cohabitation Agreements**: Each couple can draw up a list of agreements on how they will share their lives, which can meet their own needs rather than the laws of the state. Such an agreement should list all significant assets of both parties, whether there will be a joint bank account, who is going to pay for what,

how they are going to handle the purchase of significant household items, and how to determine who owns these items if they split up. If one partner owns real estate—including the home the cohabiting couple lives in—the agreement can include buy-out and right of first refusal provisions. There can be provisions covering personal liability issues and debts, as well as whether there will be "palimony" in the event of a split (Bowden, 2012).

11.4.3 Remarriage

Later-life remarriages are increasingly common, more so for divorced than widowed persons, and more common for men than for women. Marriage, a formal, legally, social-proclaimed status of special relationship, is associated for many with the kind of commitment they seek. Because it is a legal status, marriage confers both rights and obligations on each partner and on all organizations that deal with the couple (such as hospitals and Social Security). What the rights and obligations are depend on the country, state, locale, and historical period, but the fact that they exist is crucial. It means that anyone contemplating marriage should be fully informed about what the protections and obligations are at that time.

Many of the legal specifications concern financial and economic matters. As one headline advised, "Remarry in haste, and you'll repent in poverty" (Insley, 2007). Some critical financial issues to consider include: (Bravias Financial, 2017)

(a) Candidly **identify and discuss your financial situations**: What assets, debts, and obligations does each person have? What are your credit scores? Will you pool finances completely, partially, or not at all? Where will we live—your place, my place, or a new place we buy together? How will our marriage affect college financial aid for our children/grandchildren from previous marriages/relationships?

(b) **Update life insurance, medical directives, and beneficiary designations**, to make sure the documents reflect your current wishes.

(c) **Retirement planning**: Find out how benefits you or your partner are receiving or may be eligible to receive will be affected by remarriage (Frigon, n.d.). Some divorce settlements stipulate that retirement benefits be split with an ex-spouse; some pension benefits end with the death of the primary covered person. Check very carefully not only private pensions but public pensions. Many divorced or widowed seniors in the USA receive Social Security from their former spouses, and remarriage can affect these benefits. If you are divorced after at least 10 years of marriage, you can collect retirement benefits on your former spouse's Social Security record if you are at least 62 and if your former spouse is entitled to or receiving benefits. If you remarry, you generally cannot collect benefits on your former spouse's record unless your later marriage ends (whether by death, divorce, or annulment). However, if you are a widow, widower or surviving divorced spouse who remarries after age 60 you are entitled to benefits on your prior deceased spouse's Social Security earnings record. If you are receiving alimony from a divorce, the alimony will likely end once you remarry. Depending on the laws in each state and the divorce settlement specifications, alimony may end even if the divorced is only living with someone else.

(d) **Prenuptial agreement**: While these are not usual for first-time marriages, they are often more important for remarriages or late life marriages. These make most sense if you have assets you want to preserve for children from a previous marriage, you own a business you want to keep in the family, or you have endured a costly divorce. Consider including your adult children in the conversation.

(e) **Long-term care**: Formal need for institutional long-term care is common as we get much older. Family members, particularly spouses, typically provide most of the care needed for elders who remain at home. However, when cognitive or physical frailties worsen, institutional care may be the only responsible option. Some individuals and couples have long-term care insurance policies, but most do not. In the USA, options are for private coverage, or Medicaid when private resources are exhausted. In both cases, the assets of the couple are considered, rather than the assets of either spouse. In the case of Medicaid, there is a policy of "look back" to examine whether assets have been transferred within the past 5 years to another party that could have been used to pay for medical coverage. This applies to all couples, but may have a differential impact on recently married couples.

(f) **Estate Planning**: As implied by the cautions above, estate planning is a key issue when approaching later life remarriage. This is particularly important when both members of the new couple have pre-existing relationships with children, grandchildren, organizations, siblings and so on, that they wish to honor and/or support after their death. Conflicts over estate items (silver, jewelry, art) as well as financial assets are common when a remarried parent dies who has willed all his/her possessions to the surviving spouse. Lawyers knowledgeable about elder law, estates and trusts should be consulted to think through what each partner wants to happen after death, and to take the legal steps required to ensure this happens.

In spite of the complexities involved in later life remarriage, many couples do remarry. One path to remarriage is well described by our colleague Arlene Vetere, who shares her personal reflection on falling in love in later life.

The Ending

In 2005, my beloved husband, Graham, died after a year-long illness. I felt like I died with him. He was 71. I was 55. We had been together for 23 years. Our relationship had reached a stage of deep trust and contentment, despite a somewhat turbulent start. Although I had a wonderful family, and wonderful friends and colleagues, and a job I really enjoyed, the light went out of my life and I believed that my life as a woman, and as a sexual woman, was over. I think I survived by turning to my work. I worked seven days a week and seven evenings a week. I stopped watching television. It was dangerous to take time off—it only emphasized my grief and loneliness.

The Beginning

One year after Graham died, I decided I needed to do something. I had always wanted to ride a motor bike. I found a riding school that was owned by a woman and started taking lessons. It became an enjoyable social focus for me—taking riding lessons with an instructor and another trainee, stopping for refreshment half way through—and so much so, that I was reluctant to take my bike test and end my lessons. However, I passed my test, bought a Harley Davidson, and started riding around the country lanes on my own. And yes, this also emphasized my loneliness because previously, Graham and I had enjoyed cycling together. My young neighbor rescued me by suggesting I join a motor bike club so that I could go on their group "ride outs." This is what I did, and this is where I met Paul, 3 years after Graham's death. I was 58 and Paul was 66. Neither Paul, nor I, was looking for a couple relationship. I was looking for riding comrades and Paul was already part of such a group.

In writing this brief reflection on my experience of falling in love in later life, I consulted some of my older women colleagues who had had similar experiences. We are all living longer it seems and serial monogamy is the language of the new sociology! Some shared themes emerged from our conversations. The most prominent theme was the "roller coaster" ride of emotion—in my case I often felt that I preferred my grief state to that of waking up to emotion I never expected to feel again—alternating excitement and anxiety, doubt and certainty, and all underpinned by the questions: what is this? Do I need this? Do I want this?? Clearly we can experience the heady state of falling in love at any age, but when this occurs in later life, it is contextualized by many lived experiences, expectations, and discourses, both of ourselves and of what we think others expect of us—at our age!! For me, I had forgotten the rules of dating, even if I had known them when I was younger! As I had fallen in love with a man, for example, was it acceptable for me to ask him out? To pay for dinner? And so on. I was a feminist, but was he? This I had yet to find out....

I was sexually attracted to Paul—was he to me? How could I know this was not going to remain a platonic and enjoyable friendship? Worries about my body emerged—I was now quite wrinkly, and may I say, bits had dropped off!! This felt very different to my earlier experiences of sexual exploration and getting to know another's body. But again, another difference emerged, life experience had helped me speak about sensitive matters and to confront them—and to my relief, Paul had similar concerns about his body. So being in the same boat together helped us take risks.

Another theme that was highlighted in my discussions with my women colleagues was that of inheritance. Clearly this is important in the stepfamily literature, but it takes on a sharper focus if our children are adults with their own families. Falling in love and marrying in later life can raise anxiety in both family systems about the distribution of property and assets in the event of the death of one. So writing another will that both looked after each other, but did not dilute the inheritance of children and grandchildren was important in settling any concerns about outsiders coming into a family at a late stage. As it happens, Paul did not have children—so almost overnight, it seemed to him, he became a stepfather to my sons, and even more poignantly, he became a step-grandfather. Learning new roles in new relationships is always a challenge, but when we do not have mental representations of those roles, we find ourselves, yet again, in the position of the pioneer.

For many younger people who cohabit and marry, one of their tasks is to build a life together—they may have children, find accommodation and make it a home, look after older relatives, pursue paid employment, build new community friendships as a young family, and so on. When we fall in love in later life, we have done many of these things. Paul and I both had a home, full of possessions and memories of our previous separately lived lives. When we decided to live together, we had to decide whether we sell both homes and buy a new one together, or sell one and live in the other. Our compromise was to keep my bungalow, but both make an equal financial contribution to a modern extension of the premises that made the house Paul's too. But for me, the hardest part was to let go of half my possessions to make room for half of Paul's. We can say possessions are possessions—it is relationships that matter—but for me, my possessions were imbued with memories of my children growing up and of my life with Graham.

Where Are We Now?

So, to bring this brief reflection up to date, Paul and I married after 3 years. We are very contented with life together. My family have fully accepted him, and he, them. He is retired from paid employment, and I continue to earn a living. We have to navigate every day these different expectations of how we spend our time. Our past experience (of our mistakes!) in intimate relationships has taught us both the signal importance of being clear, direct and straight forward about our feelings and wishes, to listen carefully to each other even when upset ourselves, and to always acknowledge and heal hurt feelings and misunderstandings. We both find it easier to be calm in difficult moments. This is our secure base and on which we continue to develop our trust in each other and in our relationship.

This reflection has been from my perspective, and that of my colleagues, as older women living in the UK, who have fallen in love with men. Clearly the perspectives of others is not reflected in this account."

11.5 Finding Love in Later Life

For those who would like to experience a special love in later life, the literature offers some suggestions.

The book *Autumn Romance: Stories and Portraits of Love after 50*, shares the stories of 29 couples who welcomed love into their lives (Denker, 2010.). The study of 15 couples who partnered in later life offers a set of suggestions (Kemp & Kemp, 2012, pp. 349–350):

(a) First, it is never too late to be in love.
(b) There needs to be a certain amount of negotiation and change in an older couple's union, but it is essential to have a deep internal acceptance of your partner as he or she is.
(c) In every good, older relationship, there is a balance between togetherness and separateness, and this balance varies with each couple.
(d) Sexual satisfaction is possible throughout life. Age is no barrier.

(e) Your loving partnership is more important than any small issues that bother you. Do not hold grudges.
(f) A sense of humor can make problems seem much smaller, and it helps keep a spark alive in an older relationship.
(g) Accept that your partner has had previous loves. It is good to be able to share freely your past lives with each other without undue jealousy.
(h) Your children and grandchildren may or may not accept your new partner. Keep in mind that the relationship with your mate needs to be primary.
(i) Early in your relationship, discuss financial arrangements, particularly how expenses will be shared. In time, consider to whom each will leave his or her assets, the advisability of Power of Attorney for Health Care, long-term care insurance, and alternatives for various types of retirement living.
(j) When forming a relationship in later life, one of you is likely to eventually become a caretaker. Feelings of resentment are normal. You need not blame yourself as long as your actions are kind and responsible.
(k) As you and your partner come closer to the end of life, know you might experience the pain of a loss. Be aware that the present joys are worth the pain.

This review illustrates some of the significant changes that are occurring in the ways we experience romantic and companionate love in later life. Many individuals continue to seek and value this special relationship. More desire the relationship than achieve it, but many more now realize the pleasures of later life intimacy than in earlier decades (Bowden, 2012). There are some persistent differences in what men and women seek in such relationships, presumably anchored in differential patterns of socialization and life experiences.

Most of the research so far has explored patterns associated with middle-class Americans; we do not really know how the desires and experiences may differ for working class and minority older Americans. However, the desire to be recognized by another person as special and cherished applies to all humans. This desire persists throughout life, and we must understand and support social structures that honor and support the ways those desires are fulfilled.

References

AARP (2010). *Sex, romance and relationships: AARP survey of midlife and older adults*. Publication D19234. Retrieved May 20, 2018 from https://doi.org/10.26419/res00063.001.
AARP/University of Michigan (2018). *National poll on healthy aging: Let's talk about sex*. Retrieved May 20, 2018 from healthyagingpoll.org.
Alterovitz, S. S. R., & Mendelsohn, G. (2009). Partner preferences across the life span: Online dating by older adults. *Psychology and Aging, 24*(2), 513–517.
Bowden, M. (2012, August 17). *Bankrate retirement*. Retrieved from Marriage vs. living together after 60 https://www.bankrate.com/retirement/marriage-vs-living-together-after-60.
Bravias Financial. (2017, August 28). *5 Critical Financial issues to consider in remarriages*. Retrieved from https://braviasfinancial.com/news/5-critical-financial-issues-to-consider-in-remarriage.

Brown, S. L., & Shinohara, S. (2013). Dating relationships in older adulthood: A national portrait. *Journal of Marriage and Family, 75*(5), 1194–1202.

Bulcroft, K. & O'Connor, M. (1986). The importance of dating relationships on quality of life for older persons. *Family Relations, 35*(2), 397–401.

Denker, C. (2010). Autumn romance: Stories and portraits of love after 50. Philadelphia, PA: A-Shirley Publishing.

Dickson, F., Hughes, P., & Walker, K. (2005). An exploratory investigation into dating among later-life women. *Western Journal of Communication, 69*(1), 67–82.

Erikson, E. (1986). *Vital involvement in old age*. New York: W.W. Norton.

Fearn, H. (2016, November 10). *These are the real reasons women voted for Donald Trump—and they're terrifying*. Independent. Retrieved from www.independent.co.uk/voices/donald-trump-president.

Friedman, D. (2012). *The lonely hearts Club*. Chicago: Peter Owen.

Frigon, B. J. (n.d.). *BJF Law*. Retrieved from Finding love in later life: The financial and legal implications https://www.bjflaw.com/finding-love-in-later-life-the-financial-and-legal-implications.

FeelGood Store Catalogue (2019). www.feelgoodstore.com

Hodgkinson, L. (2012, May 29). *DailyMail.com*.Why DO older men find it so hard to fall in love again? Retrieved from www.dailymail.co.uk/femail/article-2151924/Why-Do-older-men-find-it-so-hard-to-fall-in-love-again?

Huyck, M. H., & Gutmann, D. L. (1992). Thirtysomething years of marriage: Understanding husbands and wives in enduring relationships. *Family Perspective, 26*(2), 249–265.

Haines, E., Deaux, K. & Lofaro, N. (2016). The times they are a changing...or are they not? A comparison of gender stereotypes 1983-2014. *Psychology of Women Quarterly, 40*(3), 353-363.

Insley, N. M. (2007, March 4). *Remarry in haste and you'll repent in poverty*. The Guardian. Retrieved from https://www.theguardian.com/money/2007/mar/04/lifeandhealth.

Kemp, E. A., & Kemp, J. (2001). *Older couples: New couplings—finding and keeping love in later life*. Bloomington: Unlimited Publishing.

Menkinm, J., Robles, T., Wiley, J., & Gonzaga, G. (2015). Online dating across the life span: Users' relationship goals. *Psychology and Aging, 30*(4), 987–993.

Miller, C. C. (2018, September 14). *Many ways to be a girl, but one way to be a boy: The new gender rules*. The New York Times. Retrieved from www.nytimes.com/2018/09/14/upshot/gender-stereotypes

Plan International USA (2018, September 18). *The state of gender equality for U.S. adolescents*. Retrieved from http://www.planinternationalusa.org.

Stepler, R. (2017, March 9). *Led by baby boomers, divorce rates climb for America's 50+ population*. Retrieved from http://www.pewresearch.org/author/rstepler.

Swanson, A. (2015, June 23). *144 years of marriage and divorce in the United States, in one chart*. Retrieved from https://www.washingtonpost.com/news/wonk/wp/2015/06/144.

US Census (2016). Table A1. Marital status by age and sex. In *America's families and living arrangements*. Retrieved from https://www.census.gov/data/tables/2016/demo/families/cps-2016.html

Chapter 12
Polygamous Marriages: An Arab-Islamic Perspective

Alean Al-Krenawi

12.1 Introduction

Polygamy takes various forms and is practiced in several regions of the world. Polygyny is the union of one man to multiple wives; polyandry is the marriage of one woman to multiple men; and polygynandry the union of multiple husbands to multiple wives (Al-Krenawi, 2001; Elbedour, Onwuegbuzie, Caridine, & Abu-Saad, 2002). The practice of polygyny, the union of one man to a number of women, remains an ongoing issue in many countries, irrespective of legislation allowing or prohibiting the practice. The reasons for this are multifaceted, deriving from a complex mesh of social, cultural, economic, and political factors (Bao, 2008; Ozkan, Altindag, Oto, & Sentunali, 2006).

The prevalence of polygyny is particularly high in the Middle East. Specific local factors underpinning the practice include the tenets of the Islamic faith, which permit men (in certain circumstances) to take up to four wives; cultural practices and perceptions concerning valid or valued configurations of the family entity; and agricultural and population needs (Al-Krenawi, 1998; Al-Krenawi & Graham, 1999a; Elbedour et al., 2002; Shepard, 2012; Slonim-Nevo & Al Krenawi, 2006). Perhaps due to the diversity of factors contributing to the practice, opinions regarding the phenomenon vary widely across different demographic groups in the Middle East, even among those who do practice polygyny (Al-Krenawi, Graham, & Ben-Shimol-Jacobsen, 2006).

The practice of polygynous marriage in the Middle East typically occurs among the older generations, often informed by a desire to preserve and maintain traditional ways of life. Polygyny has a rich history spanning both the pre-Islamic and Islamic eras. However, a decline in the practice has been noted in the recent past, in

---

A. Al-Krenawi (✉)
Ben-Gurion University of the Negev, Beersheba, Israel
e-mail: alean@bgu.ac.il

© Springer Nature Switzerland AG 2020
A. Abela et al. (eds.), *Couple Relationships in a Global Context*,
European Family Therapy Association Series,
https://doi.org/10.1007/978-3-030-37712-0_12

part due to the spread of Western values and modernity (the two are not necessarily coterminous) across Middle Eastern societies. That said, entrenched pockets of polygynous practices still persist, resistant to both social and state-enforced trends and entreaties. Modernization has reduced, to a significant degree, the advantages that may be derived from the practice of polygyny—with regard to the perceived benefit of producing large families for agricultural or other economic gain, for instance. Nevertheless, the traditional power and prestige associated with polygynous marriage appear to trump the economic losses in many Middle Eastern societies (Kressel, 1996)—a construct also observed in other contexts, such as among second-generation Thai citizens of Chinese extraction (Bao, 2008).

It is fair to assume that the men involved benefit in diverse ways from a polygynous family construct. However, insufficient research has been carried out by researchers and mental health practitioners regarding the association between polygynous relationships and the mental health of women spouses in these relationships (Al-Krenawi, 1999). This is particularly true when recognizing that polygamous women typically report higher rates of emotional distress, psychological disorders, stress and familial conflict than those in monogamous relationships (Al-Krenawi, 1998; Elbedour et al., 2002). This knowledge gap is also evident with regard to considering the different experiences of polygyny by spouses in these relationships; that is, differences between the first and subsequent wife; the impact on the wife's/mother's mental health; and of the experience of polygyny more generally and multiple issues within such marriages. This chapter will address aspects of this knowledge gap, offering a greater understanding of this potentially vulnerable demographic group through an overview of available literature.

12.2 The Social, Mental–Emotional, and Well-Being Basis for Polygynous Marriage

Many studies view polygyny as a way for men to maximize the number of their offspring: a means of extending the family lineage and legacy by means of a human reproductive strategy (Al-Krenawi, 1998, 2001). In the Middle Eastern and African contexts, most certainly, large families are a source of social and cultural capital, more so if the family line is populated with male issue (Daoud, Shoham-Vardi, Urqula, & O'Campo, 2013). Social pressure is the most common reason for men to marry more than once; this is mainly associated with the expectation for a man to produce multiple sons, as a means of perpetuating his lineage and (often) as an ostensible display of social standing. Infertility, specifically the failure to bear male offspring, and mental or physical illness are all circumstances that are commonly associated with the husband choosing to marry a second wife (Al-Krenawi, Slonim-Nivo, & Yuval-Shani, 2008).

In some cultural or social contexts, fertility issues or the failure to bear sons (at times framed as one and the same issue) are deemed to be the fault of the wife. In other contexts, these "failings" are attributed to sorcery, black magic, or other forms of unquantifiable intervention. In such circumstances, men may resort to taking a second wife as a solution. The first wife will remain a part of the household, and in some cases assumes the status of a "senior" or first wife (see Shoneyin, 2010, for a rich exploration of polygyny in an African context). It is also known for men to take a second (and third) wife after the demise of the first wife's reproductive capacity—again linked to social pressures and the assertion of status and virility.

Several cultural settings also encourage the phenomenon of exchange marriage, in which two men marry the sister of the other; when one marries a second wife, the other man does likewise in order to maintain honor in his family. This practice can also serve as a catalyst for polygynous marriage (Al-Krenawi et al., 2008). Here, the first marriage is usually matched and arranged by the parents with considerations of class, land, and power relations within the family. Second and other subsequent marriages, however, are usually free choice and informed by reasons of intimacy and attraction.

While the academic literature on the various issues is still growing, there are many representations of polygyny in fiction and other forms of cultural output explicating these factors. For example, polygyny may also be explained by sexual and moral rather than economic reasons, as some men attempt to resist illegitimate and immoral sexual temptation by marrying another wife (Al-Krenawi et al., 2008; Bao, 2008).

So far, the logic of polygyny has been presented primarily from the perspective of the man. Indeed, it is correct to note that the impulse is largely directed by men and this, undoubtedly, contributes to polygyny being framed as a patriarchal and oppressive practice (Sweet-McFarling, 2014). In some circumstances, nonetheless, divorced and widowed women may also consent to becoming the second or third wife of an already married man. The social positioning of an unmarried woman in a society defined by masculine values contributes to this, as does the presumption (tested or not) that single men would not consider them for marriage. In such circumstances, women may feel a loss of status and economic well-being, thus triggering them to accept a polygynous marriage (Al-Krenawi & Graham, 1998).

Across the Middle East, it is also (relatively) common for a widow to marry the brother of her deceased husband. The reasons for this are several. It may be to ensure that family property or assets inherited by the widow remain in the possession of the deceased's family (Al-Krenawi et al., 2008; Hund't, 1976). It may also be related to broader social practices in the specific community, such as a brother "inheriting" responsibility for his deceased brother's spouse.

A significant factor in women's well-being in relation to polygyny is that some societies have high mortality rates, or a wide differential between male and female mortality rates. Examples include societies defined by conflict and war, or societies with an unfortunate juxtaposition of weak workplace health and safety regulations and industrial accidents. In such circumstances, the equilibrium between men and women is often lost, leading to an increased ratio of women to men (Al-Krenawi et al., 2008). Thus, the number of single women who want (or need, depending on societal dictates) to marry is higher than the number of single men who wish and desire marriage. It has in fact been argued that Islam permits polygyny as a result of social necessity; it is predicated upon the need to protect the rights of widowed women and other women through marriage and not upon temporary, lustful pleasure (Al-Sherbiny, 2005).

12.3 The Social Influence of Religion on Middle Eastern Polygynous Marriage

Polygyny is illegal in many countries. However, this restriction does not necessarily reflect the prevalence of the phenomenon. Israel, a Middle Eastern country that subscribes to (broadly) Western and modern values is one example. Even though polygyny is illegal, the practice nevertheless manifests amongst the country's minority Arab-Bedouin population. The legal restrictions are often circumvented by way of men not registering the marriage with the appropriate state authorities, that is, marrying in secret. This state of affairs is rendered more complex by the fact that Israel does not have a mechanism for civil marriage, and marriages are contracted under the relevant religious authority. Consequently, it is de facto impossible to completely outlaw polygyny in Israel, given that it is recognized under Islamic law.

In many other Muslim communities, an increased prevalence of polygyny has been stimulated by the emergence of Islam as a powerful element in society and a means for religious justification. Polygyny did exist before the advent of Islam; yet, the faith and its tenets legitimized the practice, albeit under specific conditions. A man is permitted to marry up to four wives under the Islamic conceptualization of polygyny. However, the marriages must be maintained fairly and justly (Quran, Sura 4, ch. 3). Strict conditions under the Islamic law have to be met in order to ensure that the marriages are true to the spirit and practice of the Islamic faith. The man must treat his spouses equally, regardless of their differences (perceived or actual) in terms of age, attractiveness (beauty), character, social status, or other virtues.

The man is obliged to demonstrate that he has the means to take responsibility for the multiple spouses and their offspring. This equal treatment and care of the spouses by the man is obligatory. It should be noted, nonetheless, that some Islamic scholars have argued that this condition is inherently impossible to satisfy, anchoring this to a broader critique regarding the interpretation of the relevant verses of the Quran and subsequent *Hadiths* (interpretational guidance derived from the practices of the Prophet Mohammed). The Quran makes it quite clear that if men doubt their ability to behave equally and justly with their wives, they should content themselves with only one wife (Quran, Sura 4, ch. 3). In this sense, the role of Islam with regard to polygyny can be interpreted as seeking to protect a range of natural and human rights of women—the right to marriage, to form a family, and to have and raise children.

12.4 Characteristics of the Family Structure in Polygynous Marriages

Polygynous wives may live together in the same household, or reside in separate households with their own children (Al-Krenawi et al., 2008). "Senior" wives, the first wives, are commonly perceived as possessing a higher status than the "junior" wives. They usually have more control over the other wives and they typically have more privilege and influence, financially and socially, with the husband (Al-Krenawi et al., 2008; Broude, 1994). Husbands in high-functioning polygynous families, underpinned by the practice of Islam, often reason that their symbolic respect for the senior wife is to adhere to God's order (Al-Krenawi et al., 2008).

Sometimes, however, the husband may surprise the first wife by not telling her before the fact of his decision to marry another wife (Al-Krenawi & Graham, 1999a, 1999b), creating the potential for dysfunction in the family unit. In the Bedouin Arab population of Israel, for instance, the senior wife in low-functioning polygynous families may have less influence than the junior wife (Al-Krenawi et al., 2008). As the junior wives are usually chosen by the man due to attraction, rather than familial arrangement, he may offer her more in terms of economic resources, social support, and attention (Al-Krenawi & Graham, 1999a). It has also been noted that senior wives often manifest specific demographic characteristics which may diminish their standing in the family unit. These include older age, higher number of children, lower education, and absence of professional or other status outside the home (Al-Sherbiny, 2005). Rather scant research attention has been given to the consequences of these factors; specifically, the emotional and psychological needs of the senior wife, or her feelings with respect to the change in domestic circumstances.

Ultimately, daily interactions between the men, wives, and children determine the level of family functioning. So much so that this has been shown to be a leading determinant of both positive and negative effects on the mental health of the family members (Al-Krenawi & Graham, 2001, 2004, 2006a, 2006b; Al-Krenawi et al., 2006; Al-Krenawi, Graham, & Izzeldin, 2001).

12.5 The Psychosocial Manifestations of Polygynous Marriage in Middle Eastern Society

The level of conflict, competition, and cooperation among the wives in polygynous setups varies depending on the women's personal feelings and ideals with regard to their married life. Even though it can provide certain benefits for the household as a whole, polygyny is more commonly a source of jealousy and anguish for the women, with conflicts arising from tensions regarding the perceived status of the wives with regards to each other and to their husband, and from clashing personalities. Women often experience constant stress within the home environment, typically emerging from feelings of disappointment and betrayal triggered by the lack of attention they receive from the spouse. The very circumstances that result in polygyny often have a clear impact on broader psychological health and functioning. Frequently, husbands remarry because they are no longer satisfied with their sexual relationships, or because the senior wife has not (or cannot) satisfy a primary social "imperative" (the production of a son or sons, for instance). Thus, the supposed "senior" wife feels devalued, especially in the wake of a new, often unequal distribution of household and emotional resources. Families in which family functioning is low, and where feelings of anger and jealousy are not acknowledged and negotiated, become vulnerable due to the higher likelihood of intergenerational suffering—including emotional turmoil, stress, and disengagement (Al-Krenawi et al., 2008).

It has been empirically documented that more mental health and social problems are manifested within polygynous marriages, compared to monogamous marriages. In a systematic review of relevant literature, consisting of 22 cross-sectional study samples in which 1913 polygamous women and 3326 monogamous women were represented, Shepard (2012) identified that somatization, depression, anxiety, hostility, paranoid ideation, psychoticism, psychiatric disorder, general symptom severity (GSI), low self-esteem, reduced life and marital satisfaction and problematic family functioning were all significantly found to be more prevalent among the polygamous women than among the monogamous women.

The phenomenon of "First Wife Syndrome," emerging from the specific circumstances created by the practice of polygyny, should be more broadly acknowledged and researched by policymakers and mental health providers. Studies have demonstrated that senior wives experience more anxiety, paranoid ideation, and psychoticism, compared to second and third wives, as well as more feelings of loneliness and lower marital and family satisfaction (Al-Krenawi, 2013). This finding reinforces other studies done across the Middle East. Chaleby (1985) found a disproportionate number of women in polygamous marriages (mostly senior wives) among psychiatric outpatient and inpatient populations in Kuwait. A more recent Turkish study found that the participants from polygamous families, especially senior wives, reported more psychological distress (Ozkan et al., 2006). A study conducted in the United Arab Emirates with first wives—and the children of first wives—identified a range of psychological problems emerging from polygyny, many linked to the unexpected manifestation of the phenomenon (Al-Shamsi & Fulcher, 2005). Al-Sherbiny (2005) concludes that "[t]his new native category of psychiatric disorders, which has no Western equivalent, is justified by the almost constant pattern of reaction of Arabic [sic] women to polygamy." (p. 18).

However, it is important to avoid an ab initio presumption of dysfunction within the polygynous context. Certain conditions may allow for higher family functioning to take place within the setting of a polygynous marriage. These include: accepting polygyny as fate, or the will of God; perception of equal distribution of economic resources and attention by the husband; avoidance of minor conflicts; respectful attitudes between the wives; and open communication between all the siblings and between the children and the other wives (Al-Krenawi et al., 2008). Similarly, a comprehensive content analysis of the existing scholarship on consensual non-monogamies (including polygyny) notes that the topic remains largely under-researched, with much of the research attention directed to its social interpretation, and much less to familial concerns or training and counseling (Brewster et al., 2017).

Indeed, over the years, different researchers have started exploring various modes of addressing this unexamined phenomenon (Al-Krenawi, 1998; Al-Krenawi & Graham, 1999a, 1999b; Moosa, Benjamin, & Jeenah, 2006). Al-Krenawi (1998) has proposed and reported on a creative multiphase model of therapy for a polygamous family context which is based on cultural values, sensitivity to co-wives and subfamilies dynamics and distress, and husband–wives interactions. Respectfully acknowledging and addressing the various attitudinal influences, as well as the causes and symptoms of the behavioral, psychological, and physical problems encountered by the different family members, while finding the most potentially successful leverage for change, were key components which led to a successful outcome.

Vignette

A multiphase therapy intervention was carried out with a Bedouin-Arab family from the Negev, Israel, which consisted of a husband, multiple wives, and their children. The husband was 55 years old, healthy, wealthy and had no formal education. He lived with his youngest wife and did not afford much attention to his other wives or their children. The latter wives were illiterate and their ages ranged from 18 to 50 years. Each lived in her own house with her own children and received financial support and occasional visits from the husband. The children's ages ranged from 5 months to 30 years; some were still at school, others had dropped out, and many had graduated from high school. At the onset of therapy, the wives were complaining of somatization, nervousness, undifferentiated illnesses and emotional distress and some were concerned about their children's health or misbehavior. The intervention consisted of several phases: the first was the case conference; the second, individual meetings with the senior wives; the third, group therapy; the fourth individual meetings with the youngest wife and subsequent invitation to group meetings with the other wives; fifth a meeting with the husband; and sixth ongoing group sessions with all the wives. Prior to meeting, the wives required reassurance that everything discussed would remain confidential and that the husband would not be aware of the meetings. During phase two and three, although it emerged that there was competition, hostility, and jealousy among the senior wives and inter-wife communication was scarce, common issues were also revealed including how their husband neglected them emotionally and instrumentally and spent most of his time with the youngest wife, how they perceived him as rude and difficult, and how the children born to different wives were mutually hostile. Given this scenario, the intervention was planned (1) to establish good relationships among the co-wives; (2) to build a coalition among all the co-wives through the use of group therapy; (3) to use the children's problems as leverage to get the husband involved in the therapy without diminishing his self-esteem or causing trouble for the wives. As a result of an individual interview with the husband where he promised to take a greater interest in all his children's well-being and by using the youngest wife (who was the husband's favorite but who had realized during the therapy that she might suffer a similar fate to the other wives should he remarry), as a mediator between him and the other wives and their children, the relationship between the co-wives improved and the wives' and children's medical, psychological, emotional, and/or social problems decreased. Over time, the children functioned better within and outside the family and they began to refer to each other as brothers and sisters, while the wives became mutually supportive and there was reduced between-family hostility. This led to an amelioration in the husband's relationships with all his children and wives, and the younger wife still felt she was in a privileged position given that she was willing and able to intervene to maintain the positive outcomes. After about 3 months of therapy initiation, once there was consensus that the problems were being resolved, the wives group therapy was terminated (For more information see Al-Krenawi, 1998).

12.6 Perceptions of the Current and Future Direction of Polygynous Marriage

Public opinion, in the Middle East and beyond, is sharply divided on the practice of polygyny. Polygynous marriage is perceived by some to be a challenging situation: it deprives women and children of their rights, tears husbands between homes, imposes heavy financial burdens on the husband and elicits emotional turmoil among all involved (Al-Krenawi, 2010; Moosa et al., 2006; Tomori, Francisco, Kennedy, & Kajula-Maonga, 2013; Uggla, Gurmu, & Gibson, 2018). This point of view is particularly apprehensive of the economic, psychological, and educational strain that the practice imposes on children in polygynous households, given the complex and sometimes inchoate structure of the familial unit and the many children in the single household (Elbedour et al., 2002).

It is also believed that fairness and equal distribution of love is not feasible under the circumstances of polygyny. A study of family drawings conducted with Bedouin children from polygynous families demonstrated that the children were able to present complex and multifaceted representations of their families in drawings, including hierarchical structures and familial alliances (Lev-Weisel & Al_Krenawi, 2000). Significantly, however, representations were influenced by the placement of the child's mother in the family unit: children of "senior" wives tended to reflect this status in their drawings, while the children of "junior" wives ignored this. Additionally, the children of the senior wife all (albeit in a small sample) omitted the representation of a father character in their drawings, suggesting a manifested distancing due to the other, newer wives and families.

There is no clear line of thought concerning a societal response to polygyny. It has been argued that education and time will provide a medium- to long-term solution. Others think that aspirations to change are doomed to ineffectuality within the patriarchal society. Traditionalists argue that polygyny is an option all men should have, in order to provide for a large and fruitful family, with male offspring as the primary motivation for honor and prestige (Al-Krenawi, 1998, 2001). A significant number of the young and educated also believe that polygyny is justified (Al-Krenawi & Graham, 2004, 2006a, 2006b). Conditions of time, place, society, resources, and facilities differ regarding this issue and influence accordingly. In an interesting ethnographic study of online polygamous communities, Sweet-McFarling (2014) argues, quite spiritedly, that broader perceptions of polygynous relationships are inflected by the essentializing presumption that the phenomenon is dominated by the "older man-(much) younger women" paradigm. Descriptions of the manifestations of polygyny in the Middle East do, it must be acknowledged, bear out this "essentialization" to some extent. But, at the same time, researchers have a responsibility to problematize received wisdom, and to identify the underlying rationale that informs a specific social phenomenon. This can only emerge from a closer engagement with the "why" of the phenomenon—a stance not overly represented in the existing literature.

Sweet-McFarling (2014) further notes that within the context of her research environment—the USA—some change can be identified in the cultural perception of polygyny. Polygyny was traditionally considered as the preserve of the Mormon faith (a belief system that has incurred significant disdain—and occasionally overt discrimination—in the USA). But nuanced, sometimes empathetic, representations in popular television programs and documentaries (like HBO's "Big Love," the National Geographic Channel's "Taboo," and TLC's "My Five Wives") are encouraging a subtle shift in perspective and engagement. It may well be that this will prompt increased research activity, on the basis of engaging with observable social phenomenon and thus achieving an understanding of a fuller range of its possible implications for society at large.

12.7 Implications for Practice and Future Directions

This overview of contexts, experiences, and influencing factors around polygyny suggests that a revised approach to polygyny will be useful in the sphere of therapy and public policy. Practitioners and policymakers need to be aware of the potential psychological, familial, and economic effects of polygyny on women and the family unit. Further research is required to compare the experiences of women in polygynous marriages based on their order (first, second, and third, etc.), such as a deeper exploration of the First Wife Syndrome. Senior wives have been noted as being particularly vulnerable to psychological distress in association to marital status (Al-Krenawi, 2001, 2010; Al-Krenawi, Graham, & Gharaibeh, 2011; Al-Krenawi & Slonim-Nevo, 2008; Shepard, 2012). Likewise, Daoud et al.'s (2013) study, while identifying a higher risk of poor mental health for women in polygynous relationships, also notes that social support structures—both in the immediate context of the polygynous family and in the broader context of a community or society that acknowledges the existence of the phenomenon—have an influential role to play.

Regression analysis has also revealed that family functioning was the primary indicator of inventoried symptoms for psychological distress of wives within polygamous marriages (Al-Krenawi & Slonim-Nevo, 2008). Thus, future research needs to focus on developing, implementing, and evaluating family intervention program for polygamous families as they function in different communities in the world. Notably, the same regression analysis also revealed that economic status may be a mediating variable by which to ease psychological distress in polygynous women. Future studies must, therefore, not only look toward the structure of the family, but also investigate the mediating variables that play a major role in the intricacies of family dynamics (Al-Krenawi & Slonim-Nevo, 2005a, 2005b; Elbedour et al., 2002; Shepard, 2012). Possible sites for best allocating services when there is dysfunction and/or related health problems may be through the work of community health clinics and traditional healers (Al-Krenawi & Graham, 1999a, 1999b). Al-Krenawi and Graham (2006b) found that while 4% of sampled patients were referred to mental health practitioners, 84% visited their community health clinic instead.

Similar arguments apply in considering the experience of polygyny from the perspective of the children of polygynous relationships. Al-Sharfi, Pfeffer and Miller's (2016) systematic review of papers on this topic indicates that the children of polygynous relationships are more susceptible to experiencing issues of low esteem, underachievement, and poor mental health than children from monogamous relationships. They do concede, however, that the impact of polygyny on children may well be mediated by broader social cues, including education and economic circumstances. Similarly, an unpublished paper by Adel Jeda'an suggests that the issue of mental health within the polygynous context should take into account a child's sense of "self-concept," as informed by the child's experience of the family unit as secure or insecure. A deeper appreciation of these factors, informed by research, will guide policy development and guide practice in the counseling, psychotherapeutic and educational settings.

12.8 Conclusion

As Middle Eastern societies take steps toward Western visions of modernization, remnants of their cultural identity maintain a stronghold on the people. The future of polygyny in the Middle East is ambiguous; however, policymakers and practitioners must investigate the effects of its current practice. This approach should strive to strike a balance between "normalizing" polygyny and delegitimizing it ab initio. As Bao (2008) notes, the former approach conceals power relation dynamics and prevents exploration of the phenomenon (and its dysfunctionalities) in a broader social context. With the latter, as we have seen above in the case of Israel, blanket delegitimization—no matter how well intentioned—leaves policymakers and professionals ill-equipped to negotiate the challenges that polygyny does present. Recognizing and targeting mediating variables on the family function will play a vital role in preventing and treating the mental health issues facing polygynous families, especially among the children and women involved. Notably, immediate attention is needed to address the plight of some women, given that based on current literature it can confidently be stated that there is greater prevalence of psychological distress among polygynous women than their monogamous counterparts.

References

Al-Krenawi, A. (1998). Family therapy with a multiparental/multispousal family. *Family Process, 37*(1), 65–81.
Al-Krenawi, A. (1999). Women of polygamous marriages in primary health care centers. *Contemporary Family Therapy, 21*(3), 417–430.
Al-Krenawi, A. (2001). Women from polygamous and monogamous marriages in an outpatient psychiatric clinic. *Transcultural Psychiatry, 38*(2), 187–199.
Al-Krenawi, A. (2010). A study of psychological symptoms, family function, marital and life satisfactions of polygamous and monogamous women: The Palestinian case. *International Journal of Social Psychiatry, 58*(1), 79–86. https://doi.org/10.1177/0020764010387063
Al-Krenawi, A. (2013). Mental health and polygamy: The Syrian case. *World Journal of Psychiatry, 3*(1), 1. https://doi.org/10.5498/wjp.v3.i1.1
Al-Krenawi, A., & Graham, J. R. (1999a). The story of Bedouin-Arab women in a polygamous marriage. *Women's Studies International Forum, 22*(5), 497–509.
Al-Krenawi, A., & Graham, J. R. (1999b). Gender and biomedical/traditional mental health utilization among the Bedouin-Arabs of the Negev. *Culture, Medicine and Psychiatry, 23*(2), 219–243.
Al-Krenawi, A., & Graham, J. R. (2001). Polygynous family structure and its interaction with gender: Effects on children's academic achievements and implications for culturally diverse social work practice in schools. *School Social Work Journal, 25*(3), 1–16.
Al-Krenawi, A., & Graham, J. R. (2004). Somatization among Bedouin-Arab women: Differentiated by marital status. *Journal of Divorce and Remarriage, 42*(1/2), 131–144.
Al-Krenawi, A., & Graham, J. R. (2006a). A comparative study of family functioning, health, and mental health awareness and utilization among female Bedouin-Arabs from recognized and unrecognized villages in the Negev. *Health Care for Women International, 27*(2), 182–196.
Al-Krenawi, A., & Graham, J. R. (2006b). A comparison of family functioning, life and marital satisfaction, and mental health of women in polygamous and monogamous marriages. *International Journal of Social Psychiatry, 52*(1), 5–17.
Al-Krenawi, A., Graham, J. R., & Ben-Shimol-Jacobsen, S. (2006). Attitudes toward and reasons for polygamy differentiated by gender and age among Bedouin-Arabs of the Negev. *International Journal of Mental Health, 35*(1), 46–61.
Al-Krenawi, A., Graham, J. R., & Gharaibeh, F. A. (2011). A comparison study of psychological, family function, marital and life satisfactions of polygamous and monogamous women in Jordan. *Community Mental Health Journal, 47*(5), 594–602.
Al-Krenawi, A., Graham, J. R., & Izzeldin, A. (2001). The psychosocial impact of polygamous marriages on Palestinian women. *Women and Health, 34*(1), 1–16.
Al-Krenawi, A., & Slonim-Nevo, V. (2005a). A comparative study of polygamous and monogamous marriages as they affect Bedouin-Arab women. In R. Lev-Wiesel, J. Cwikel, & N. Barak

(Eds.), *Guard your soul mental health among women in Israel* (pp. 149–167). Beer-Sheva: Ben-Gurion University of the Negev, in cooperation with Myers-JDC-Brookdale Institute. Retrieved April 1, 2019, from http://in.bgu.ac.il/en/humsos/womcen/Documents/%D7%A9% D7%9E%D7%A8%D7%99%20%D7%A0%D7%A4%D7%A9%D7%9A-%20%D7%90%D7 %A0%D7%92%D7%9C%D7%99%D7%AA.pdf.

Al-Krenawi, A., & Slonim-Nevo, V. (2005b). Psychosocial functioning of children from monogamous and polygamous families: Implications for practice. In M. Ungar (Ed.), *Handbook for working with children and youth* (pp. 279–293). Thousand Oaks, CA: Sage.

Al-Krenawi, A., & Slonim-Nevo, V. (2008). The psychosocial profile of Bedouin Arab women living in polygamous and monogamous marriages. *Families in Society, 89*(1), 139–149.

Al-Krenawi, A., Slonim-Nivo, V., & Yuval-Shani, B. (2008). Polygynous marriage in the Middle East: Stories of success and failures. *Ethnology, 47*(3), 195–208. Retrieved July 7, 2018, from https://ethnology.pitt.edu/ojs/index.php/Ethnology/article/viewFile/6031/6211.

Al-Shamsi, M. S. A., & Fulcher, L. C. (2005). The impact of polygamy on United Arab Emirates' first wives and their children. *International Journal of Child & Family Welfare, 8*(1), 46–55.

Al-Sherbiny, L. A. M. (2005). The case of the first wife in polygamy: Description of an Arab culture-specific condition. *Arabpsynet Journal, 8*(2), 18–27.

Al-Krenawi, A., & Graham, J. R. (1998). Divorce among Muslim Arab women in Israel. Journal of Divorce & Remarriage, 29(3–4), 103–119.

Al-Sharfi, M., Pfeffer, K., & Miller, K. A. (2016). The effects of polygamy on children and adolescents: A systematic review. Journal of family Studies, 22(3), 272–286.

Bao, J. (2008). Denaturalizing polygyny in Bangkok, Thailand. *Ethnology, 47*, 145–161.

Brewster, M. E., Soderstrom, B., Esposito, J., Breslow, A., Sawyer, J., Geiger, E., … Sandil, R. (2017). A content analysis of scholarship on consensual monogamies: Methodological roadmaps, current themes, and directions for future research. *Couple and Family Psychology: Research and Practice, 6*(1), 32.

Broude, G. J. (1994). *Marriage, family, and relationships. A cross-sectional encyclopedia*. Denver, CO: ABC-CLIO.

Chaleby, K. (1985). Women of polygamous marriages in an inpatient psychiatric service in Kuwait. *The Journal of Nervous and Mental Disease, 173*(1), 56–58. https://doi. org/10.1097/00005053-198501000-00009

Daoud, N., Shoham-Vardi, I., Urqula, M. L., & O'Campo, P. (2013). Polygamy and poor mental health among Arab Bedouin women. Do socioeconomic position and social support matter? *Ethnicity & Health, 19*(4), 385–405.

Elbedour, S., Onwuegbuzie, A. J., Caridine, C., & Abu-Saad, H. (2002). The effect of polygamous marital structure on behavioral, emotional, and academic adjustment in children: A comprehensive review of the literature. *Clinical Child and Family Psychology Review, 5*(4), 255–271.

Hund't, G. (1976). Conflict types between Bedouin women. In M. Sde-Boker (Ed.), *Notes on the Bedouin* (Vol. 7, pp. 19–29). Beer-Sheva: Ben-Gurion University of the Negev.

Kressel, G. M. (1996). *Ascendancy through aggression: The anatomy of a blood feud among urbanized Bedouins. (Mediterranean Language and Culture Monograph Series 12)*. Wiesbaden: Harrassowitz.

Lev-Weisel, R., & Al_Krenawi, A. (2000). Perceptions of family among Bedouin-Arab children of polygamous families, as reflected in their family drawings. *American Journal of Art Therapy, 38*(4), 98.

Moosa, M. Y. H., Benjamin, R., & Jeenah, F. Y. (2006). A review of multispousal relationships: Psychosocial effects and therapy. *South African Journal of Psychiatry, 12*(2), 12–14.

Ozkan, M., Altindag, A., Oto, R., & Sentunali, E. (2006). Mental health aspects of Turkish women from polygamous versus monogamous families. *International Journal of Social Psychiatry, 52*(3), 214–220. https://doi.org/10.1177/0020764006067207

Shepard, L. D. (2012). The impact of polygamy on women's mental health: A systematic review. *Epidemiology and Psychiatric Sciences, 22*(01), 47–62. https://doi.org/10.1017/ s2045796012000121

Shoneyin, L. (2010). *The secret lives of Baba Segi's wives*. New York: William Morrow and Company.

Sweet-McFarling, K. (2014). *Polygamy on the web: An online community for an unconventional practice*. (Unpublished master's dissertation). Colorado State University.

Slonim-nevo, Vered & Al-Krenawi, Alean. (2006). Success and failure among polygamous families: The experience of wives, husbands, and children. Family process, 45(3), 311–330.

Tomori, C., Francisco, L. V., Kennedy, C. E., & Kajula-Maonga, L. (2013). The changing cultural and economic dynamics of polygyny and concurrent sexual partnerships in Iringa, Tanzania. *Global Public Health, 8*(7), 857–870. https://doi.org/10.1080/17441692.2013.815249

Uggla, C., Gurmu, E., & Gibson, M. A. (2018). Are wives and daughters disadvantaged in polygynous households? A case study of the Arsi Oromo of Ethiopia. *Evolution and Human Behavior, 39*(2), 160–165.

Chapter 13
The Couple Relationship When One of the Partners Has an Acquired Physical Disability

Elaine Schembri Lia

13.1 Introduction

John and Lilian have been together for the past forty years. They have had typical instances of ups and downs in their relationship but no matter what, they persevered and with time they have successfully managed to bring up three children, who are all now in their thirties and settled in their lives.

Lilian and John are the proud grandparents of four grandchildren. They had been enjoying their first year of retirement together after some intensive years of work in their bakery when John had a stroke, which left his body half-paralysed. This impairment severely impacted the lifestyle which John and Lilian were used to, since because of John's mobility difficulties the couple now had limited access to their community. John had also become clinically depressed following the impairment and despite aspiring not to be a burden for Lilian, his level of dependence on her seemed to increase from day to day, both physically and psychologically. Lilian feels exhausted by the situation; however, she feels it is her duty to support John in all his needs. She strongly rejects their children's pleas to admit John into a retirement home, as she believes that as long as she can manage, John's place is at home with her.

The couple has applied for community services. A psychiatric team operating from the community follows John. An occupational therapist and a physiotherapist who visit him at home on a weekly basis also monitor him. In addition, the parties receive home support services that cater for some of their housekeeping needs. When the aide is at home Lilian can go shopping and see to the chores which require her to be away from John for a period of time; this also serves as a source of respite for her. Moreover following John's impairment the couple has also accessed a state-funded financial support scheme and a disability pension, which help with some of their financial struggles. Regrettably, while John and Lilian's income is now limited, expenses have drastically increased for them, given that they also had to do some house alterations to make their house more accessible for John. The couple claim that even though the services they receive cannot restore John's health and typical functioning, at least they sustain them in the challenges arising from the situation they found themselves in.

E. Schembri Lia (✉)
Department of Family Studies, Faculty for Social Wellbeing, University of Malta, Siggiewi, SGW, Malta

© Springer Nature Switzerland AG 2020
A. Abela et al. (eds.), *Couple Relationships in a Global Context*,
European Family Therapy Association Series,
https://doi.org/10.1007/978-3-030-37712-0_13

The above scenario is just one example of the way in which couples can be faced with an acquired physical disability over their life course. With the ever increasing life expectancy and the improvement in technology and medical procedures, individuals who would have previously died due to life-threatening health conditions or impairments are now able to live for years with some limitation or other, undeniably impacting on their couple relationships and family lives both positively and negatively. Indeed, even though today's couples and families are able to enjoy the presence of loved ones in their lives for longer years, and might fear less than their ancestors the possibility of an early death, current generations also face the ever increasing probability that they might have to live through some impairment or other in their relationships. As research informs us, this stage is not approached in the same way by all couples, and the challenges which different dyads face, along with the ways in which together they work through them, is dependent upon a number of factors, some of which actually lie outside the couple constellation itself.

This chapter will review how heterosexual couples work through an acquired physical disability, which is obtained in later life. Different scenarios which might lead to these situations, along with the processes involved in managing their impact on the couple and their relationship will be highlighted. Issues pertaining to psychotherapeutic work, which can sustain couples faced with such challenges in the long term, will also be addressed.

Despite possible similarities in the actual physical impairments of members pertaining to homosexual and heterosexual couples, there may also be differences in the challenges which same-sex and heterosexual couples face in the course of their relationship following a disability. This is especially so in view of enduring stigma which might add further challenge to members of homosexual dyads who might therefore need different means of intervention and support as a result.

13.2 What Leads to an Acquired Physical Disability?

Even though when we think about acquired physical disabilities we often think about elderly couples impacted by some form of health condition in later life, as in the case of John and Lilian, there are different contexts which might lead couples to have to deal with such struggles. For example, acquired physical impairments may be the result of stroke, cancer, cardiac disease, neurological conditions, genetic or hereditary disorders, brain injury, chronic illnesses, war, accident and physical trauma. Not all of these conditions necessarily impact individuals and couples later on in life; indeed, there are couples who are still in their early adult years who have to cope with newfound physical impairments following accidents or ill-health.

There are different kinds of acquired physical impairments and no one situation or impairment might necessarily impact the individuals concerned in the same way. For example, there are conditions which might lead to complete or partial paralysis or loss of the limbs. Others may lead to complete or partial loss of sensation and language, including visual and hearing impairments. Still others might lead to problems with fine or gross motor skills or difficulties with balance, as well as others which might disturb the functioning of various physiological systems, such as digestive, urological and sexual. Most acquired physical disabilities include a multitude of these physical manifestations.

Often, acquired physical impairments are visible and chronic. However, this is not always the case, as in the situation of some neurological conditions or autoimmune diseases, such as fibromyalgia, arthritis or pain-inducing conditions. Physical impairments might occur in the presence or absence of other disabilities, such as intellectual impairments.

As the social model of disability informs us (Barnes & Mercer, 2005), impairments become a disability when the individuals impacted are not sustained by a society which is accessible and which enables those affected to thrive and participate equally in the community. This also applies to those who sustain an acquired physical impairment.

13.3 What Are the Implications of an Acquired Physical Disability on the Individual Parties and Couples?

Acquired physical disabilities do not only lead to physiological impairments, but most acquired physical impairments also impact the affected individuals in different areas of functioning, including the emotional, psychological and interpersonal functioning. Indeed, acquired physical disabilities have been known to impact adjustment, happiness and quality of life (Stiell, Naaman, & Lee, 2007). These consequences obviously then also affect one's psychosocial functioning.

In this regard, acquired physical disabilities and the impact which these have on the individuals affected need to be considered not only in the societal context in which they occur but must also take into account the relationships in which they develop (Schembri Lia & Abela, 2016). Time and again, research carried out with couples has shown that not only are the challenges faced by partners affected by a physical impairment multiple and distinct, but the parties also influence the perceptions and processes which occur over time in dynamic and circular ways (Eriksson, Tham, & Fugl-Meyer, 2005; Schembri Lia & Abela, 2019).

Indeed, research suggests that the impact of a physical limitation on people with impairments and their spouses typically varies. This variance often depends on the type of diagnosis given, the functional implications of the impairment, the pre-morbid health status of the individuals impacted and the coping strategies they have available (Rodrigue & Hoffmann, 1994). Such differences need to be considered when working with couples impacted by an acquired physical impairment. Whereas some couples might have the stability, health, resources and strategies necessary to cope with the limitations imposed on them by an impairment, others may struggle to face the challenges put upon them by their physical limitations. Even more, adequately dealing with an acquired physical disability at a particular point of the couple life cycle stage might not necessarily mean that the same couple will adequately deal with the same impairment later on in life. For example, even though at present Lilian and John are overall coping well with the limitations put upon them by John's disability, they might eventually come to a stage when they struggle to deal with the same impairments should Lilian also develop some impairment herself. This is especially the case if their social context or support system changes over time.

Thus, adjustment post-disability is very often not a linear, one-time process (Blank & Finlayson, 2007; Bowen, MacLehose, & Beaumont, 2011). Research suggests that when faced with an acquired physical impairment couples go through a number of stages. For example, the individual partners are said to first have to accept the diagnosis of a disability. This is often a critical stage to the ensuing couple life (Chance, 2002; Esmail, Huang, Lee, & Maruska, 2010). Early on, Devivo and Fine (1985) had found that in the case of spinal cord injury the highest chance of separation and divorce post-disability occurs in the early adjustment phases, typically occurring in the first three years after the disability.

Yet adjustment after impairment, particularly in the face of unpredictable and degenerative conditions like multiple sclerosis, might require individuals to go through the same stages on multiple occasions as the disability progresses and new impairments develop (Blank & Finlayson, 2007; Bowen et al., 2011; Esmail, Munro, & Gibson, 2007). Such multiple occurrences, as well as the uncertainty typical in these situations, adds further to the stress and dynamics of the individuals concerned, hindering their adjustment and the stability of the couple unit over time. For example, in an epidemiological study with people diagnosed with multiple sclerosis, the number of individuals who reported being divorced or separated increased with the level of severity of disease and impairment, from 6 to 18% in men and from 8 to 13% in women (Hammond, McLeod, Macaskill, & English, 1996). For men with multiple sclerosis, it seems that the worst outcomes result when they are forced to depend on their partners for physical care such as transfers and dressings; in these instances it seems that the physically impaired men feel incompetent as sexual partners and as a consequence they develop poor self-worth, doubt their masculinity and consequently withdraw or become inactive in the relationship, potentially leading to its breakup (Esmail et al., 2010).

Couples who find it difficult to accept the losses which follow an acquired physical impairment may attempt to deny the existing problems. They may try to maintain the status quo established prior to the disability or may set unrealistic standards for themselves post-disability (Esmail et al., 2007). Such defences can have devastating implications for the couple's life together, and might lead to depressive or violent reactions as well as emotional breakdowns and problems with intimacy for the individuals over time (Aloni & Katz, 2003).

On the other hand, couples who actively pursue adjustment after having acquired a physical impairment have to come to terms with the implications of this disability for themselves as individuals and as a couple (Beauregard & Noreau, 2010). These implications may include the obvious physical impairments as well as other complications arising from the physical limitations, which might include the need for long hospitalisation and rehabilitation, repeated hospital admissions and check-ups, as well as invasive physical and nursing care procedures.

After acquiring the disability, partners might—as individuals and as a couple—have to deal with other adjustments which might challenge their coping. Though linked to the impairment, and often co-occurring with it, these adjustments might not necessarily be as obvious to clinicians. For example, the individuals impacted might have to relocate to a house which is more accessible. Partners might also have to change jobs or adjust their lifestyles and routines to meet the needs arising from the disability. There may be added financial struggles as a result of reduced income. Degenerative disorders like multiple sclerosis may also add further tensions and worries about an uncertain future as the partners struggle to understand what to expect or how the condition will evolve over time. Moreover couples might also have to let go of previous plans or dreams to make space for new visions and aspirations.

I remember the case of a young married couple where the male spouse, previously the main family breadwinner, had sustained a severe spinal cord injury at work. Following his disability, this individual could no longer go to work, leading his wife, who had now also become his main carer, to seek an out-of-home lesser-paid job. This led the couple to experience severe financial difficulties and to have to let go of previously cherished pastimes. To add to the stress, the couple also eventually had to move house since they used to live on the fifth floor with only staircase access to the outside world, leaving the man in question stranded on most of his days. In relocating, the couple had to accept to live in a home which was much smaller than the one they had before. They also had to sell some of their assets to afford an in-house care assistant for the spouse. In working through such moves and changes, the couple also had to take care of the needs of their five-year old daughter, who back then had just transitioned into primary school. They no longer envisioned having another child, as they were aware that this would just add more stress to their family; they decided upon this even though a big family had been their dream since the early days of their courtship. Needless to say, the situation placed all the family on a tough roller coaster of psychological, emotional and situational upheaval.

Indeed, research suggests that following a disability, it is typical for couples to have to cope with vulnerable emotional states such as loss, fear, shame, guilt, melancholy, uncertainty, helplessness and anger. Literature (e.g. Buchanan & Elias, 2000; Chan, 2000a; Feigin, 1998) shows us that very often, acquired physical impairments challenge the self-identification, sense of coherence, personal values, self-worth, quality of life and well-being of the disabled persons and their loved ones. These reactions might occur at different times for the disabled and the non-disabled partners. For example, in their research with couples who faced spinal cord injury Angel and Buus (2011) found that the non-disabled partners' crisis often began when the disabled partners' situation stabilised and became more accepted, prolonging the duration of instability for the couples and the distress experienced as a result of such over time. Studies show that the partners of persons with acquired physical impairments typically experience levels of psychological distress which are at the same level or even higher than those of the disabled parties (Baider et al.,

Gotay, & Hannum et al., as cited in Stiell et al., 2007). In this regard, these processes and variances often further contest the existing couple dynamics, adding to the stress and turmoil experienced by the partners over time and complicating their adjustment process.

Adding to this, many times acquired physical impairments also impact the couples' expression of their sexual intimacy. For example, physical conditions such as diabetes, multiple sclerosis, traumatic brain injuries or paralysis might impact the disabled parties' sexual functioning in terms of desire, arousal and orgasm, directly impacting the couples' sexual lives and expression. Sometimes, rather than the condition in itself, the medication necessary to deal with the physiological limitations or the consequent psychological problems might affect the sexual aspect. Conversely, severe physical impairments which might necessitate physical care from the partners, as in the case of stroke, paralysis or degenerative neurological conditions, might also challenge the couple's sexual expression. It is difficult to be a sexual partner and a carer at the same time but it is also difficult to feel sexually appealing to someone who has been taking care of your most intimate needs, possibly challenging your own self-worth and esteem as a male or female. There is ample research supporting the manifestation of these challenges post-disability (Aloni & Katz, 2003; Beck, Robinson, & Carlson, 2009; Bélanger, 2009; Bowen et al., 2011; Dickson, O'Brien, Ward, Allan, & O'Carroll, 2010; Esmail et al., 2007; Perrone, Gordon, & Tschopp, 2006; Quinn, Murray, & Malone, 2014; Schembri Lia & Abela, 2019).

Adding to this, tertiary sexual dysfunctions such as psychosocial and cultural belief systems that interfere with sexual satisfaction as well as misperceptions about sexuality and sexual performance in the case of physical impairments, may also lead to challenges to body image, identity and self-concept that hinder the sexual relationship. For example, in talking about this issue in relation to individuals affected by traumatic brain injury, Aloni and Katz (2003) wrote that 'diagnostic labels such as *organic brain damage* are often associated with social stigma and interpersonal rejection that can interfere significantly with attempts to initiate intimate relationships' (p. 8). In this regard post-disability couples may need to explore the meanings and understandings they have associated with their intimate and sexual experiences. They may also have to explore alternative ways in which they can sexually relate, possibly further adding to the frustrations and challenges caused by the acquired physical impairment and necessitating care and attention in this regard even in their rehabilitation processes. At the same time, couples may struggle to voice these challenges with the professional team supporting them and unless the latter highlights or talks about such, these difficulties may never be addressed.

Furthermore, the life adjustments mandated by an acquired physical impairment such as financial burdens, role changes and added responsibilities, may in themselves hinder the couples' cognitive availability to sexually relate by adding to the strains and concerns experienced by couples (DiGiulio, 2003). It is important to keep in mind that the experience of burden on care-giving partners has been found to increase with the amount of daily living support given, the disabled persons' psychological problems, the overall length of care-giving time and the caregiver's age (Post, Bloemen, & deWitte, 2005). This increased burden can lead to reduced well-being and quality of life on behalf of partners which limits their sexual availability, especially in the face of conflicts between what the disabled individuals expect of their caregivers and what the non-disabled partners are willing to provide.

Adding yet another layer to the challenges experienced by couples post-disability is adjustment to the roles, routines and lifestyles, which the partners used to share prior to the impairment. For example, couples who are also parents might have to rework the way in which they parent and the roles and responsibilities each assumes in this regard (Piercy & Piercy, 2002). Non-disabled partners may have to take on added chores in relation to parenting, such as driving duties or attendance to school or recreational activities, which prior to the disability used to be shared. Partners who struggle to cope emotionally with the disability, or whose community support is limited, may find it difficult to be fully present as parents in their children's lives. Yet again the children in question would also be going through their own adjustment processes following the disability, necessitating additional care and support from their parents and adding further challenges to the couple who are also parents.

13.4 How Does Systems Theory Support Us in Understanding and Working with These Couples?

Early systemic thinkers (Lederer & Jackson, 1968) argued that the couple relationship is not a function of individual partners but an interdependent system with a life of its own, co-created by the partners through their interactions over time. This systemic perspective implicates that the way each partner deals with the challenges following a disability not only impacts the coping of the other partner but also influences the type of interactional cycles occurring in the couple relationship. This was also explicated by Schembri Lia and Abela (2019). Indeed, research shows that disabled people's life satisfaction following an acquired physical impairment is significantly related to the spouses' life satisfaction (Achten, Visser-Meily, Post, & Schepers, 2012).

In this regard if we want to fully support partners to adjust through their challenges following a disability, it is essential to understand 'the way that reciprocal couple support operates in [disabling] situations; the mechanisms that enable couples to support each other effectively; and how they succeed in maintaining the quality of their relationship under these life circumstances' (Gilad, Lavee, & Innes-Kenig, 2009, p. 454). Stiell et al. (2007, p. 65) present the following scenario:

> Negative interactive cycles are the product of the interaction between the partners' way of coping with threat. For example, one partner may become anxious, with an accelerated need for information and soothing just as the other becomes withdrawn and unavailable. The withdrawal of one intensifies the anxiety of the other, which further primes the withdrawal of the first. The resulting cycle of defensive emotion and behaviour add to the

distress already present due to the [disabling] chronic illness, and robs couples of their most powerful antidote: comfort and connection from each other.

From this perspective, the adjustment of couples post-disability is no longer seen in terms of the stand-alone process of adjustment and coping of each individual partner, but as one which is undeniably impacted by the adjustment and coping of the other party in interdependent and circular ways, as presented by Schembri Lia and Abela (2019).

In talking about the development of couple support schema post-impairment, Gilad et al. (2009) stated that couples who manage to thrive following a disability share interchangeable interactions in a cyclical process based on trust:

> Providing support represents the individual's reaction to the other's need for support. The recipient tends to request support on the basis of previous support experiences, and in turn provides support to the assisting spouse, and so on. All supportive transactions rely on the sense of availability, and shape it in turn... Support providing and receiving behaviours are further shaped by individuals' beliefs, that is, their support schemata. These inner beliefs, constructed in the personality development process, are reinforced by the totality of recent transactions in couple relations (p. 454).

Such systemic understanding is in line with the social model of disability presented by Barnes and Mercer (2005) which postulates that when faced with a disability, individuals need to have the internal structures and mechanisms necessary to adjust to their challenging realities as well as a reliable and supportive social context which helps them and enables them to move on. In considering adjustment from a systemic perspective, the social context in question extends beyond the individuals' community, social accessibility, the perceptions available around the disability and the prevalent societal discourse. It also focuses on the dynamics and interactional processes occurring in the most intimate relationships of the individuals, that is, those present between the partners.

13.5 Gender Differences in the Context of Disability and the Couple Relationship

Research suggests that there seems to be a difference in the risk of separation and divorce following an acquired physical impairment depending on whether the disabled person is male or female. In their study with couples who had been impacted by serious medical illness, Glantz et al. (2009) found that when the affected party was the woman, partner abandonment through separation or divorce was more likely. They proposed that remaining in a relationship with a seriously ill partner reflects a commitment on behalf of the non-disabled spouse towards the relationship, which is more likely to prevail in women. Interestingly such a finding did not coincide with earlier research presented by Chappell and Kuehne (1998) who had found that husbands who acted as caregivers tended to express less negative sentiment towards their spouses than women care providers did. In their research

Chappell and Kuehne had hypothesised that men perceived caregiving to be a choice whereas women perceived caregiving as an obligation, thereby experiencing it as more burdensome.

Literature also suggests that there is a difference in the way in which male and female disabled individuals relate to their non-disabled partners. For example Esmail et al. (2007, 2010) as well as Schembri Lia and Abela (2019) found that disabled women tend to assume a self-sacrificing position towards their non-disabled partners, to suffer in silence and to attempt to minimise the impact of the disability on their partner, on their newly assumed roles and on the couple relationship itself, including the sexual relationship. By taking such a position, women also minimise any adverse impact on the couple dynamics occurring after the disability is acquired. Such research stands in stark contrast to the findings of McCabe (2002) who had found that men with acquired physical impairments tended to experience less sexual interest following the occurrence of the physical dysfunction further negatively impacting their relational experience.

Such gender considerations therefore need to be taken into account when making sense of the processes that couples go through following a disability and the positions which each of the partners assumes and why they do this. For example, Weinert and Long (1993) found that male caregivers tend to have fewer outside sources of support than female care providers; this leads men to experience bigger strains as a result of their caregiving roles than females do. Likewise, Kramer (2002) found that male care providers tend to have fewer confidantes than their wives, increasing their chances of isolation and caregiver burden. In these varying circumstances, unless the professionals working with couples post-disability take an interest in the contexts surrounding their experiences, they may potentially miss out on what guides the partners' understanding of the roles and dynamics which they may be assuming.

13.6 What Supports Partners to Adjust Post-Disability?

Relationship permanency after the occurrence of an impairing event has long been cited to be beneficial to the disabled individuals' quality of life and quality of care (McCabe, McDonald, Deeks, Vowels, & Cobain, 1996). Benefits cited in the literature include less antidepressant use, greater participation in clinical trials and a lower chance of hospitalisation, including at the point of death (Glantz et al., 2009). Indeed a healthy connection between the disabled and the non-disabled partner has been cited to be more important to the disabled person's life satisfaction than the physical aspect itself (Keefe et al., 2004; McNeff, 1997).

Perceiving the disability as 'the ultimate test' for the couple (Dickson et al., 2010, p. 1115), couples who find in each other and in the relationship a sense of accomplishment are strengthened rather than destroyed by the disability. Many individuals who acquire a physical disability have been cited in the literature to state that dealing with their impairment has triggered in them a process of personal growth and increased their feelings of pride and self-worth (Gordon & Perrone, 2004;

Schembri Lia & Abela, 2019). Dickson et al. (2010) reported that even though some non-disabled partners testified to the complete loss of their spousal identity post-disability in view of the newfound carers' roles they had to assume, others reported the emergence of a novel 'caregiver' identity, which made them feel proud in their ability to cope and assist their loved ones.

In this regard, partner availability and satisfactory partner support have been found to contribute to the quality of life and stability of the couple relationship over time by enhancing relationship satisfaction (Cutrona, Russell, & Gardner, 2005). Gilad and Lavee (2010) stated that partner availability and support enhances and strengthens trust and security in the relationship and it contributes to a sense of commitment to the growth of the relationship even in the face of adversity. Moreover, supportive attitudes and positive comments from the non-disabled partners also seem to enable success even in the sexual well-being of persons with disability (Li & Yau, 2006). It could be that such behaviours project a sense of acceptance to the disabled individuals, which in turn enables them to develop a positive identity and self-esteem, thereby increasing their chances of sexual satisfaction.

Specific characteristics in the disabled individuals and the non-disabled partners have also been associated to enhance dyadic coping (e.g. Beauregard & Noreau, 2010; Chan, 2000b; Radcliffe, Lowton, & Morgan, 2013). For example, being of a young age, enjoying financial security, having a good sense of optimism as well as having an internal locus of control are characteristics which research has repeatedly associated with better adjustment to physical impairments such as spinal cord injuries. Chan, Lee, and Lieh-Mak (2000) found that the more able to function independently the disabled individual is, the less likely it is for the couple to experience relationship problems. On the other hand, the openness of the non-disabled partners to be with disabled individuals as well as to establish a flexible balance between accepting the limitations presented by the disability and pushing for the disabled individuals' sense of autonomy and resilience, even in the light of social disapproval, have been found to positively influence adjustment and coping for couples post-disability (Schembri Lia & Abela, 2016, 2019).

Furthermore the quality of the relationship prior to the disability has been found to play a major role in the type of adjustment which occurs post-disability (Chan et al., 2000). For example, the partners' ability to self-sacrifice, empathise with each other, persevere in the face of adversity as well as being committed to relationship permanence were found to be key to positive outcomes (Schembri Lia & Abela, 2019). Perrone et al. (2006) also added communication as one of the factors contributing to the satisfaction of caregiver spouses. Indeed, couples who develop good communication strategies have been found to describe more positively their emotional, physical and sexual relationship post-disability (Esmail et al., 2007, 2010; Verschuren et al., 2013). This should come as no surprise given that the flexibility and negotiation of roles, identity and rules post-disability may only occur in the presence of a climate which encourages reflection and communication between the partners.

Guided by a strengths-focused and resilience-based approach to disability, like the one presented by Walsh (2011), we also know that the more able a couple is to maintain previously established rituals and routines such as family times and celebrations, even in the face of disability, the better able couples are to move forward following an impairment. Families who thrive are ones who are able to move away from making the impairment the centre of their family life and instead find ways in which they can support each other to adjust and to live their lives fully even in the face of physical challenges (Schembri Lia & Abela, 2016).

The availability of support from the social networks surrounding couples impacted by a disability has also been identified as a vital contextual factor and resource in the way in which a disability is lived and negotiated (Chan, 2000a; Radcliffe et al., 2013). For instance the adequate provision of information by the medical systems enables couples to know what to expect and to make sense of the disability. Likewise, even though it seems that not all couples make use of it to the same extent (Winslow & O'Brien, 1992), community support, such as the provision of home health aide, visiting nurses, occupational therapy and physical therapy have also been considered as important factors which mediate caregiver stress and reduce the burden experienced as a result of the disability (Revensen & Majerovitz, 1991). The presence of accepting social networks and the availability of friends may also enable couples to thrive post-disability. Urey, Viar, and Henggeler (1987) found that couples who experienced most distress following an impairment were the ones to least participate in social and recreational activities, whether individually or as a couple.

13.7 How Can Practitioners and Clinicians Support Couple Adjustment Post-Disability?

Francesca and Anthony have been together for the past seven years. They met in their late teens and immediately felt attracted to each other. Spending the first year of their relationship dating, they quickly became inseparable, and though young and still studying, they were eager to take matters seriously and actively pursued their relationship.

Some three years into their courtship Anthony and Francesca started to cohabit. All was going well and their relationship continued to flourish as each party was keen on assuming and sharing roles and responsibilities. The couple planned on having a family with many children, travelling and growing old together.

Two years down the line Francesca got pregnant. The couple was ecstatic by the new addition and they happily planned for their newborn's arrival. When the day came for Francesca to give birth, the couple hastily took off for hospital, planning for minimal medical intervention and visualising the joy they would experience upon their return home with their little one.

Regrettably a different story unfolded for Francesca and Anthony though. Following a long and traumatic birth process, Francesca experienced a severe neurological injury, which led to autonomic and motor dysfunction. Whereas the baby's health was optimal and she could be released after just a couple of days, Francesca had to be kept for treatment and rehabilitation in hospital for a number of weeks. Unlike what the couple had envisioned, Anthony had to take time off work to be able to see to the needs of their newborn along with supporting Francesca to deal with her injuries. He also had to seek their extended families' support to be able to see to all their needs. In spite of resorting to community support and intervention, it took a number of months for Francesca to be able to spend a whole day on her own with their growing baby. Despite gaining some neurological functions over time, she still could not move independently.

This unexpected change impacted the couple on multiple levels. Even though Francesca and Anthony remained committed to each other and to their relationship, seeking ways in which they could re-establish their lifestyles and routines, the situation also demanded of them a number of adjustments and decisions which were not always easy to handle.

Williams (1984) used the term 'narrative reconstruction' to describe the conceptual strategies which people employ following a biographical discontinuity, such as the occurrence of a chronic illness, to establish their sense of coherence, stability and order. According to Williams these strategies involve re-framing the life-changing event within the framework of one's life story, assigning meaning to the events that have disrupted that life story and altering the course of one's life to adjust to that event. Other strategies include linking up and interpreting different aspects of one's biography rather than focusing solely on the impairment. Williams claimed that such processes allow people to 'realign the present and past and self with society', thereby creating a redefined self (p. 197). It is this 'redefined self' that couples like Francesca and Anthony who are challenged by an acquired physical impairment need to work through in dealing with the consequences of their physical changes. And it is in this redefinition process that very often individuals who seek psychological or couple intervention need support in.

Literature consistently shows that when working with individuals who are dealing with a physical impairment, it is very important for the partners to also be involved in the rehabilitation process (Bowen et al., 2011; McCabe et al., 1996; Quinn et al., 2014). This involvement extends to psychotherapeutic interventions which should aim to highlight and explore the challenges presented by the impairment for both partners (Schembri Lia & Abela, 2019).

Taylor (2015) emphasised that professionals working in these circumstances should sensitively work with couples to initiate conversations which encourage them to voice their concerns as well as express and discuss their emotions with regard to the disability and its aftermath. On the same lines Rolland (1994) suggested that couples dealing with disability often benefit from a flexible approach to therapy which combines individual and conjoint sessions and which considers the different issues which the partners face following a disability. Such intervention should also extend to the exploration of intimacy and sexuality issues for the couples over time (Schembri Lia & Abela, 2019).

Mills and Turnbull (2004) pointed out that when working with disabled persons and their partners, couple therapists should aim to create safe and contained settings in which the couples can share their thoughts and feelings honestly and openly with respect, empathy and compassion. They also stated that such therapists should aim to identify, explore and eliminate dysfunctional communication patterns and cognitive distortions, particularly those that belong to the loss cycle, which the couples might have. In line with the findings of Schembri Lia and Abela (2019) and following Hoffman (as cited in Barker & Chang, 2013), therapists working with couples who have to deal with an acquired physical impairment should therefore enable partners to process the adjustment cycles arising from the disability and to explore the circular and reciprocal patterns of interaction occurring between the partners, in the hope of flexibly promoting accommodation based on the feedback being given and received.

Other research (Esmail et al., 2010; Hepworth, 2007) suggests that clinicians should adopt interventions which enable the parties to establish meaningful roles in their relationship. Emotionally Focused Couple Therapy has been cited as being particularly useful in such instances (Chawla & Kafescioglu, 2012).

Even more, Schembri Lia and Abela (2019) speculate about interventions that can be useful to practitioners and clinicians in their work with couples facing adjustments related to movement following an acquired impairment. These interventions may also be applied to other physical impairments and disabilities. For example, specific therapeutic techniques that may help as presented by Schembri Lia and Abela include externalisation and enactment. These may be particularly useful in supporting the partners to distance themselves from the impairment and to consider each as an individual partner who is distinct from the role that he or she assumes towards the disability. Moreover, as presented by Schembri Lia and Abela, the sharing of stories with clients by therapists, including therapeutic ones but also success stories about other couples and families, may also help partners to visualise a positive future and a way out of a possibly tragic perspective. Furthermore, Schembri Lia and Abela highlighted that scaffolding partners and supporting them to establish a new sense of meaning to their life stories in the face of their disability is also important. Finally, 'prescribing rituals and routines which shift the focus away from the disability, looking for exceptions, re-framing, asking circular and reflexive questions as well as solution-focused interventions' were also described by Schembri Lia and Abela (p. 17) as possible therapeutic interventions which may be useful in these therapeutic contexts.

Reflexivity by the therapists working in the context of disability is of utmost importance, especially when they face difficulties to understand the impact of specific kinds of impairments on the couples. Therapists need to reflect upon the interventions they use, the therapeutic goals they set, the positions they adopt during therapy as well as the working alliance they create (Stiell et al., 2007). They also need to strongly reflect upon their own understanding of disability and to monitor for any possible projections occurring during therapy as this can then enable them to intervene appropriately (Segal, 2003). Both supervision and the use of multidisciplinary practices are necessary in this regard.

13.8 Conclusion

Dealing with an acquired physical impairment is no easy feat for couples, irrespective of the stage in which it occurs in their life cycle. At the same time, specific characteristics and positions adopted by the individual partners or by the couples can enable dyads to adjust to their disabling realities and to find a new way of being together. Support networks may also be highly beneficial. Follow-up and lines and opportunities for intervention need to be offered at different points in time. Society at large also needs to be accepting and facilitating in the face of a possible disability. It should enable partners to be open to the possibility of a relationship with an impairment, especially when considering the progresses being done in the medical field enabling life longevity and rebound from life-threatening health conditions and serious ill-health. In this regard, psycho-education about issues pertaining to disability as well as services providing support in the face of acquired physical impairments should be available and easily accessible to the general public. Such strategies should hopefully limit the challenges and adjustment difficulties faced by couples impacted by an acquired physical impairment and lead the way for couples to redefine their stories and identities over time.

References

Achten, D., Visser-Meily, J., Post, M., & Schepers, V. (2012). Life satisfaction of couples 3 years after stroke. *Disability and Rehabilitation, 34*(17), 1468–1472. Retrieved from https://doi.org/10.3109/09638288.2011.645994

Aloni, R., & Katz, S. (2003). *Sexual difficulties after traumatic brain injury and ways to deal with it*. Joseph C. Thomas: US.

Angel, S., & Buus, N. (2011). The experience of being a partner to a spinal cord injured person: A phenomenological hermeneutic study. *International Journal of Qualitative Studies on Health and Well-Being, 6*(4), 1–11. Retrieved from https://doi.org/10.3402/qhw.v6i4.7199

Barker, P., & Chang, J. (2013). *Basic family therapy* (6th ed.). New Jersey: Wiley.

Barnes, C., & Mercer, G. (Eds.). (2005). *The social model of disability and the majority world*. Leeds: The Disability Press.

Beauregard, L., & Noreau, L. (2010). Spouses of persons with spinal cord injury: Impact and coping. *British Journal of Social Work, 40*, 1945–1959. Retrieved from https://doi.org/10.1093/bjsw/bcp140

Beck, A. M., Robinson, J. W., & Carlson, L. E. (2009). Sexual intimacy in heterosexual couples after prostrate cancer treatment: What we know and what we still need to learn. *Urologic Oncology: Seminars and Original Investigations, 27*, 137–143.

Bélanger, D. (2009). Traumatic brain injury and sexual rehabilitation. *Sexologies, 18*, 83–85. Retrieved from https://doi.org/10.1016/j.sexol.2009.01.008

Blank, C., & Finlayson, M. (2007). Exploring the impact of multiple sclerosis on couples: A pilot study. *Canadian Journal of Occupational Therapy, 74*(2), 134–142. Retrieved from https://doi.org/10.2182/cjot.06.0015

Bowen, C., MacLehose, A., & Beaumont, J. (2011). Advanced multiple sclerosis and the psychosocial impact on families. *Psychology and Health, 26*(1), 113–127. Retrieved from https://doi.org/10.1080/08870440903287934

Buchanan, K., & Elias, L. (2000). Personality and behaviour changes following spinal cord injury: Self perceptions-partner perceptions. *Axone, 21*(2), 36–39.

Chan, R. (2000a). How does spinal cord injury affect marital relationship? A story from both sides of the couple. *Disability Rehabilitation, 22*(17), 764–775. Retrieved from https://doi.org/10.1080/09638280050200269

Chan, R. (2000b). Stress and coping in spouses of persons with spinal cord injuries. *Clinical Rehabilitation, 14*(2), 137–144. Retrieved from https://doi.org/10.1191/026921500675826560

Chan, R., Lee, P., & Lieh-Mak, F. (2000). Coping with spinal cord injury: Personal and marital adjustment in the Hong Kong Chinese setting. *Spinal Cord, 38*, 687–696. Retrieved from https://doi.org/10.1038/sj.sc.3101085

Chance, R. (2002). To love and be loved: Sexuality and people with disabilities. *Journal of Psychology and Theology, 30*(3), 195–208.

Chappell, N., & Kuehne, V. (1998). Congruence among husband and wife caregivers. *Journal of Aging Studies, 12*(3), 239–255. Retrieved from https://doi.org/10.1016/S0890-4065(98)90002-0

Chawla, N., & Kafescioglu, N. (2012). Evidence-based couple therapy for chronic illnesses: Enriching the emotional quality of relationships with Emotionally Focused Therapy. *Journal of Family Psychotherapy, 23*(1), 42–53. Retrieved from https://doi.org/10.1080/08975353.2012.654080

Cutrona, C., Russell, D., & Gardner, A. (2005). The relationship enhancement model of social support. In T. A. Revenson, K. Kayser, & G. Bodenman (Eds.), *Couples coping with stress* (pp. 73–97). Washington, DC: American Psychological Association.

Dickson, A., O'Brien, G., Ward, R., Allan, D., & O'Carroll, R. (2010). The impact of assuming the primary caregiver role following traumatic spinal cord injury: An interpretative phenomenological analysis of the spouse's experience. *Psychology and Health, 25*(9), 1101–1120. Retrieved from https://doi.org/10.1080/08870440903038949

DiGiulio, G. (2003). Sexuality and people living with physical or developmental disabilities: A review of key issues. *The Canadian Journal of Human Sexuality, 12*(1), 53–68.

Devivo, M., & Fine, P. (1985). Spinal cord injury: Its short-term impact on marital status. Archives of Physical Medicine and Rehabilitation, 66(8), 501–504. Retrieved from https://www.researchgate.net/publication/19134494_Spinal_cord_injury_Its_short_term_impact_on_marital_status

Eriksson, G., Tham, K., & Fugl-Meyer, A. (2005). Couples' happiness and its relationship to functioning in everyday life after brain injury. *Scandinavian Journal of Occupational Therapy, 12*(1), 40–48.

Esmail, S., Huang, J., Lee, I., & Maruska, T. (2010). Couples' experiences when men are diagnosed with multiple sclerosis in the context of their sexual relationship. *Sexuality and Disability, 28*, 15–27. Retrieved from https://doi.org/10.1007/s11195-009-9144-x

Esmail, S., Munro, B., & Gibson, N. (2007). Couples' experience with multiple sclerosis in the context of their sexual relationship. *Sexuality and Disability, 25*, 163–177. Retrieved from https://doi.org/10.1007/s11195-007-9054-8

Feigin, R. (1998). The relationship between the sense of coherence and adjustment to disability studied in the context of marital interrelations. *Marriage and Family Review, 27*(1–2), 71–90. Retrieved from https://doi.org/10.1300/J002v27n01_06

Gilad, D., & Lavee, Y. (2010). Couple support schemata in couples with and without spinal cord injury. *Rehabilitation Counseling Bulletin, 53*(2), 106–116. Retrieved from https://doi.org/10.1177/0034355208328522

Gilad, D., Lavee, Y., & Innes-Kenig, O. (2009). The structure of dyadic support among couples with and without long-term disability. *Journal of Behavioural Medicine, 32*, 453–465. Retrieved from https://doi.org/10.1007/s10865-009-9216-5

Glantz, M., Chamberlain, M., Liu, Q., Hsieh, C., Edwards, K., Van Horn, A., & Recht, L. (2009). Gender disparity in the rate of partner abandonment in patients with serious medical illness. *Cancer, 115*(22), 237–242. Retrieved from https://doi.org/10.1002/cncr.24577

Gordon, P., & Perrone, K. (2004). When spouses become caregivers: Counseling implications for younger couples. *Journal of Rehabilitation, 70*(2), 27–32.

Hammond, S., McLeod, J., Macaskill, P., & English, D. (1996). Multiple sclerosis in Australia: Socioeconomic factors. *Journal of Neurology, Neurosurgery and Psychiatry, 61*, 311–313.

Hepworth, J. (2007). When illness moves in: Helping couples process the trauma of sickness. *Psychotherapy Networker 31*(3). Retrieved from https://www.questia.com/read/1P3-1258716161/when-illness-moves-in-helping-couples-process-the

Keefe, F., Affleck, G., France, C., Emery, C., Waters, S., Caldwell, D., ... Wilson, K. (2004). Gender differences in pain, coping, and mood in individuals having osteoarthritic knee pain: A within-day analysis. *Pain, 110*, 571–577. Retrieved from https://doi.org/10.1016/j.pain.2004.03.028

Kramer, B. J. (2002). Men caregivers: An overview. In B. J. Kramer & E. H. Thompson (Eds.), *Men as caregivers: Theory, research and service implications* (pp. 3–19). New York: Springer.

Lederer, W. J., & Jackson, D. D. (1968). *The mirages of marriage*. New York: W.W. Norton.

Li, C., & Yau, M. (2006). Sexual issues and concerns: Tales of Chinese women with spinal cord impairments. *Sexuality and Disability, 24*(1), 1–26. Retrieved from https://doi.org/10.1007/s11195-005-9000-6

McCabe, M. (2002). Relationship functioning and sexuality among people with multiple sclerosis. *Journal of Sexuality Research, 39*(4), 302–309. Retrieved from http://www.ncbi.nlm.nih.gov/pubmed/12545413

McCabe, M., McDonald, E., Deeks, A., Vowels, L., & Cobain, M. (1996). The impact of multiple sclerosis on sexuality and relationships. *Journal of Sexuality Research, 33*(3), 241–248. Retrieved from http://www.jstor.org/stable/3813584

McNeff, E. A. (1997). Issues for the partner of the person with a disability. In M. L. Sipski & C. J. Alexander (Eds.), *Sexual function in people with disability and chronic illness: A health professional's guide* (pp. 595–616). Gaithersburg: Aspen Publishers.

Mills, B., & Turnbull, G. (2004). Broken hearts and mending bodies: The impact of trauma on intimacy. *Sexual and Relationship Therapy, 19*(3), 265–289. Retrieved from https://doi.org/10.1080/14681990410001715418

Perrone, K., Gordon, P., & Tschopp, M. (2006). Caregiver marital satisfaction when a spouse has multiple sclerosis. *Journal of Applied Rehabilitation Counseling, 37*(2), 26–32.

Piercy, S., & Piercy, F. (2002). Couple dynamics and attributions when one partner has an acquired hearing loss: Implications for couple therapy. *Journal of Marital and Family Therapy, 28*(3), 315–326. Retrieved from https://doi.org/10.1111/j.1752-0606.2002.tb01189.x

Post, M., Bloemen, J., & deWitte, L. (2005). Burden of support for partners of persons with spinal cord injuries. *Spinal Cord, 43*(5), 311–319. Retrieved from https://doi.org/10.1038/sj.sc.3101704

Quinn, K., Murray, C., & Malone, C. (2014). The experience of couples when one partner has a stroke at a young age: An interpretative phenomenological analysis. *Disability and Rehabilitation: An International, Multidisciplinary Journal, 36*(20), 1670–1678. Retrieved from https://doi.org/10.3109/09638288.2013.866699

Radcliffe, E., Lowton, K., & Morgan, M. (2013). Co-construction of chronic illness narratives by older stroke survivors and their spouses. *Sociology of Health and Illness, 35*(7), 993–1007. Retrieved from https://doi.org/10.1111/1467-9566.12012

Revensen, T., & Majerovitz, S. (1991). The effects of chronic illness of the spouse: Social resources as stress buffers. *Arthritis Care and Research, 4*, 63–72. Retrieved from https://doi.org/10.1002/art.1790040203

Rodrigue, J., & Hoffmann, R. (1994). Caregivers of adults with cancer: Multidimensional correlates of psychological distress. *Journal of Clinical Psychology in Medical Settings, 1*, 231–244.

Rolland, J. S. (1994). In sickness and in health: The impact of illness on couples' relationships. *Journal of Marital Family Therapy, 20*(4), 327–347. Retrieved from https://doi.org/10.1111/j.1752-0606.1994.tb00125.x

Schembri Lia, E., & Abela, A. (2016). Not broken but strengthened: Stories of resilience by persons with acquired physical disability and their families. *Australian and New Zealand Journal of Family Therapy, 37*, 400–417. Retrieved from https://doi.org/10.1002/anzf.1156

Schembri Lia, E., & Abela, A. (2019). The couple relationship when the female partner has an acquired physical disability. *The History of the Family*. Retrieved from https://doi.org/10.1080/1081602X.2019.1663549

Segal, J. (2003). Your feelings or mine? Projective identification in a context of counselling families living with multiple sclerosis. *Psychodynamic Practice, 9*(2), 153–171. Retrieved from https://doi.org/10.1080/1353333031000104794

Stiell, K., Naaman, S., & Lee, A. (2007). Couples and chronic illness: An attachment perspective and emotionally focused therapy interventions. *Journal of Systemic Therapies, 26*(4), 59–74. Retrieved from https://doi.org/10.1521/jsyt.2007.26.4.59

Taylor, B. (2015). Does the caring role preclude sexuality and intimacy in coupled relationships? *Sexuality and Disability, 33*, 365–374. Retrieved from https://doi.org/10.1007/s11195-015-9394-8

Urey, J., Viar, V., & Henggeler, S. W. (1987). Prediction of marital adjustment among spinal cord injured persons. *Rehabilitation Nursing, 12*(1), 26–30. Retrieved from https://doi.org/10.1002/j.2048-7940.1987.tb00545.x

Verschuren, J., Zhdanova, M., Geertzen, J., Enzlin, P., Dijkstra, P., & Dekker, R. (2013). Let's talk about sex: Lower limb amputation, sexual functioning and sexual well-being: A qualitative study of the partner's perspective. *Journal of Clinical Nursing, 22*(23–24), 3557–3567. Retrieved from https://doi.org/10.1111/jocn.12433

Walsh, F. (2011). Resilience in families with serious health challenges. In M. Craft-Rosenberg (Ed.), *Sage encyclopaedia of families and health*. London: SAGE Publications.

Weinert, C., & Long, K. A. (1993). Support systems for the spouses of chronically ill persons in rural areas. *Family Community Health, 16*, 46–54.

Williams, G. (1984). The genesis of chronic illness: Narrative re-construction. *Sociology of Health and Illness, 6*(2), 175–200. Retrieved from http://onlinelibrary.wiley.com/doi/10.1111/1467-9566.ep10778250/pdf

Winslow, B., & O'Brien, R. (1992). Use of formal community resources by spouse caregivers of chronically ill adults. *Public Health Nursing, 9*(27), 128–132. Retrieved from https://doi.org/10.1111/j.1525-1446.1992.tb00087.x

Part IV
Global Trends in Couple Relationships

Chapter 14
Framing Couples in the Media: Coupledom, Well-Being and Comedy

Brenda Murphy

14.1 Introduction

Couples are everywhere—in 'real life' and in the media—and research informs us that being in a good couple relationship improves well-being and can even improve longevity. Alongside this, positive psychology reports that humour is an important variable in well-being. 'Couple identity' and 'well-being' are central themes in this chapter and I extend those themes into the world of screens. I challenge traditional definitions of 'couple' and heteronormative standpoints while I chart the various mediated identities of coupledom on screen and deconstruct those media portrayals of couples, within a comedy genre. I do this in order to unpack those representations of couples as they intersect around age, race, class, ethnicity, gender and ability/disability. The theoretical framing for this chapter is cultural studies (textual analysis and semiotics), gender studies, intersectionality and positive psychology.

This chapter is organised into three sections: in Sect. 14.2 I examine couples as an ideological construct; coupledom and its role for our well-being; and the positive power of humour. In Sect. 14.3 I introduce the reader to textual analysis and semiotics as I unpack and map coupledom in the selected sitcoms. And in Sect. 14.4 I comment on emergent themes such as the process of framing important issues, the subsequent normalising impact of that framing and the authentic casting of actors. Finally I spotlight moments where race and gender coalesce and traditional gender roles are challenged; and observe how the selected comedies resist traditional patriarchal media discourses which commodify and objectify.

B. Murphy (✉)
Department of Gender Studies, University of Malta, Msida, Malta
e-mail: brenda.murphy@um.edu.mt

14.2 Couples and Humour

The ideology surrounding couples is culturally bound and the notion that coupledom and significant relationships are 'good for us' and our well-being is emerging in contemporary literature.

14.2.1 Couples and Couple Identity: **The Ideology of Definitions**

Couples are everywhere—in 'real life' and in the media—but how we define 'couples' can open up or close down our understanding of the relationship (Box 14.1).

Conventional definitions of couples can be problematic as they are likely to narrow our thinking, rendering us blind to and exclusionary of other versions of coupledom. Dominant narratives and ideology surround and uphold the concept, meaning and subsequent research into and about couples. This can impact on the performances of coupledom, the acceptance, and the thinking about coupledom in any given space.

Budgeon (2008) discusses the placement of the couple relationship at the centre of the normative practice of sexuality and considers how it is underpinned by an *ideology of marriage and family*. She maintains that this ideology is based on the assumption that everyone desires a sexual partnership, that a sexual relationship is the only truly important personal relationship. She argues that those who are in one are significantly happier and more fulfilled than those who are not, and she observes

Box 14.1
dictionary definitions
couple:

1. Two people or things of the same sort considered together, e.g. 'a couple of girls were playing marbles'— also: a pair, duo, dyad etc.
2. Two people who are married or otherwise closely associated romantically or sexually also: husband and wife, twosome, partners, lovers, cohabitees etc.

Oxford Dictionary Online

The conventional family is the so-called 'nuclear' family where such a couple has two or three children. And the conventional home is the house which this family owns and where they live out their private life, away from the gaze of other people.

Open University Open Learn Online

that 'the ideological force of couple culture is such that its privileged status is rarely recognized or questioned' (2008, p. 302). Budgeon claims that while the couple relationship is a well-established norm, scholars seldom turn their gaze to those who are not in a couple relationship. Indeed, within the sociology of the family there is 'a tendency to privilege the heterosexual, co-resident, usually married, couple and their children as the unit of analysis thus rendering invisible the range of intimacies falling outside this form but which nonetheless are being practised in everyday life' (2008, p. 302).

While mapping couple identity and coupledom on screen, I challenge the conventional cultural framings that surround and produce coupledom in order to disturb constraints around concepts of coupledom that may be boxed in by and around notions of family and marriage. Ferreira Rodrigues (2014) notes that history has recorded various forms of relationships between humans, which has led to the emergence of new, metamorphosed intimate relationship formats. This democratisation has impacted on marriage relationships and resultant shifts in society, which have opened new possibilities for expanding consciousness and psychological development.

Indeed research *has* broadened when studying couple identity and well-being. For example, Abela, Calleja, Piscopo, and Vella, (2016) extended their study noting that the couple relationship is highlighted while taking into account dating participants, married persons, and cohabiting partners, and single persons, whether separated, divorced or simply single, were also included in the study (Abela et al., 2016). In an equally broadening set of thinking on the subject, Sullivan and Lawrence (2016) define couples as 'long-term committed intimate relationships such as marriage [as] an integral part of our lives and confer many benefits' (2016, p. 1), which I interpret as *such as marriage* but not limited to marriage.

14.2.2 *Coupledom and Well-Being*: **Coupledom Is Good for Us**

While Sullivan and Lawrence, (2016) broaden their definition of couples as long-term committed intimate relationships, in that spirit they go on to report that 'people in satisfying marriages report greater life happiness, live longer and are less vulnerable to mental and physical illness' (2016, p. 1). Skerrett and Fergus, (2015) also support coupledom as being 'good for us' and in *Couple Resilience* they define and explore resilience and we-ness. For them, we-ness is the stuff that does not necessarily get verbalised, but is demonstrative of a true partnership. They flag how important 'we-ness' is for keeping partners co-supportive when challenged by the brutal reality of aging, illness and traumatic loss.

Research in other disciplines also reports that to be in a good couple relationship is related to better psychological and physical health; impacts positively on well-being and can actually improve longevity. According to longevity researcher Susan

Pinker (2016), a significant indicator for a long life was *emphasis on close personal relationships*, i.e. having someone in your life who will call a doctor if you are ill, or sit with you if you are having a crisis—a 'significant other'. We are currently encountering more and more mainstream reporting that being in a relationship adds up to overall well-being—better physical and mental health (Robles, 2014) and better well-being (Abela et al., 2016; Abela, Frosh, & Dowling, 2005).

14.2.3 *Humour and Well-Being*: Humour Is Good for Us

Above, I argue that a good couple relationship, in whatever shape we wish to frame it ideologically, is profoundly 'good for us'. I broaden the picture to include humour (or comedy) as the second key variable in this story, as it too has been researched and shown to bring about well-being in life. For example Edwards (2013) has identified humour as one of 24 character strengths considered ubiquitously important for human flourishing.

Hatzipapas, Visser, and van Rensburg (2017) have been exploring laughter as an intervention to promote well-being and they provide a comprehensive and valuable review. They note that laughter is a familiar action for most individuals and thinkers, from the philosophers (Plato, Aristotle and Hobbes) to modern psychologists, who have written about and contemplated 'laughter'. However, they note that there is little academic literature and research on laughter and the therapeutic use of laughter to enhance psychological well-being in the human and social sciences.

For Hatzipapas et al. the ability to laugh helps us to develop an affinity towards positive emotions, and their expression, which in turn has a positive influence on our affect. They cite Fredrickson (2001) who claims that positive emotions contribute to personal well-being. This occurs by broadening thought-action or expanding the individual's attention and ideas. It also helps undo the effects of negative emotions and thus increases psychological resilience and personal resources. The generation of positive experiences can then contribute to and have a long-lasting effect on personal growth and development—and our overall well-being.

14.2.4 *Onscreen Humour and Laughter*

Research into onscreen humour and its impact on our well-being is scant. Hatzipapas et al. cite Cousins (2017) as one of the first authors who wrote about laughter as a therapeutic intervention based on his own experiences in overcoming a serious chronic disease. They describe how he subjected himself to continuous viewings of his favourite comedy shows. He advocated that 10 min of laughing gave him 2 h of drug-free pain relief. In addition, Berk et al. (1989) examined the effects of laughter on neuroendocrine hormones that are involved in classical stress responses. The researchers concluded that joyful laughter modifies or reduces some of the neuroendocrine hormone levels associated with stress. Similar results were found in an experiment where participants were exposed to a humorous video of their choice, compared to participants in the control group that viewed a tourism video. Hatzipapas et al. cite research findings that show that when exposed to humour, cortisol levels and self-reported stress levels decrease (2017: 203).

As a prescription, laughter can do no harm. It has no side effects, and if taken '3 times a day' in units of 30 min, (most sitcom's are 20–30 min in length) then audiences will further enhance their well-being by limiting their screen time to 1 h and 30 min, instead of the global average which is 2 h and 56 min[1] or American average which is 3 h 58 min daily watching TV in 2017.[2]

14.2.5 Comedy and Coupledom Are Good for Us ... Couples and Humour on Screen

Coupledom, in whatever form it takes, is a prevailing state of being for many of us, in our daily lives and lived experience. And just as we are coupled with significant others in the real world, that reality is reflected in the mediatised world of screen too. Within and across all the possible genres of media entertainment *comedy* remains one of the most robust in terms of annual programming produced for both large and small screen. Comedy programmes are the second most popular genre in the USA at 18%, after drama (33%)[3]; in Europe comedy is second most popular at 13.84%, after drama (53.18%).[4]

In this section I marry (pardon the pun) *humour* and *coupledom*. Couples are persistently and consistently portrayed in mainstream media, i.e. film and TV, across all genres—horror, family drama, music vids, children's programmes and comedy. They feature as central images to sell (in advertising), to entertain (dramas, etc.), to inform (news and documentaries, etc.). A word search on IMDb (the Internet Movie Database) for the word 'couple or couples' in title returned 849 titles [couple 782/couples 67], marriage as a keyword returned 7544 titles, love returned 12,632 titles, and divorce returned 2794 titles. On screen, the imaginings and portrayal of 'love' (regardless of context) appeared to dominate, followed by 'marriage', 'divorce', and then 'couple'—all terms imply coupledom in the first instance (Box 14.2).

---

[1] Eurodata's 'One Television Year in the World' report found that global individual viewing time for TV stood at 2 h and 56 min per day in 2017 http://www.mediametrie.com/eurodatatv/communiques.php

[2] https://www.statista.com/statistics/186833/average-television-use-per-person-in-the-us-since-2002/

[3] Genre breakdown of the top 250 TV programs in the USA in 2017 https://www.statista.com/statistics/201565/most-popular-genres-in-us-primetime-tv/

[4] Most popular television show genres in Europe 2016 https://www.statista.com/statistics/563611/most-popular-tv-show-genres-in-europe/

Box 14.2 Questions for reflection
Ask yourself…

1. *How does the media portray couples?*
2. *Does it 'support' the imagined concept of couples,*
    or does it denigrate and dismiss the status and role?
3. *What kind of couples are depicted in the media and*
    how does the media frame 'coupledom'?
4. *Does it portray the myth of the perfect couple,*
    —does it idealise romance and reinforce stereotypes etc.
    or does it portray dysfunctional, divorced, unhappy couples?
5. *What roles are the couples portrayed in… strict gendered roles?*
6. *How is betrayal framed and featured?*

The media is an integral space in our lived experiences and it reflects and shapes beliefs and understandings, and upholds dominant ideologies (alongside *family, religion, the state,* and *education*) (Fiske 2010; Adorno 1991).

Relationships and coupledom are often portrayed in the media—the framing is sometimes positive and sometimes negative—with themes ranging from the stereotype of the perfect couple and images of idealised romance, to unhappy couples, embedded in storylines about betrayal, misery and discontent, and, depending on the genre, are sometimes framed around stories of femicide and homicide. In general, the media portrays couples in a wide range of *roles*—hyper-romantic, romantic, modern, traditional, dysfunctional, historical, supportive, tragic, funny, violent etc. Furthermore couples appear in a variety of media *formats* and *genres* such as music videos, advertising, news programmes, films, TV dramas, soaps and comedies—to name a few.

In the next section I explore the kind of couples depicted in the media texts selected, and examine how the media frames 'coupledom'. I will flag portrayals of the 'myth of the perfect couple' and moments when it reinforces stereotypes, idealises romance, and isolate moments when it portrays dysfunctional, divorced, unhappy couples. I will also highlight the roles couples are portrayed in with special attention to rigid and fluid gendered roles.

14.3 Framing Couples: Decoding Comedy

In this section, I examine positive portrayals of couples in the media, specifically in comedy as a media genre, holding humour as significant in maintaining well-being. Six contemporary, mainstream comedy programmes where 'coupledom' is central to the plot are identified as examples of a particular representation of culture. Many contemporary sitcoms would have satisfied the criteria of this research, for example Modern Family would have been an obvious choice as a successful programme; however I selected the comedy series based on the fact that they all contain a broad range of the intersectional variables mentioned above and was limited by the usual constraints of time and space. The programmes selected afford an opportunity to analyse mediated portrayals of couples and relationships on contemporary screens. The main body of analysis is focused around the core couple relationships and I plot the semiotic signifiers that signify well-being and coupledom.

14.3.1 *Informing the Story:* **Methods and Standpoints**

The theoretical framing for this chapter is cultural studies and I draw, theoretically and methodologically, on textual analysis and semiotics while retaining a gender studies lens. I look to intersectionality and positive psychology to contain the arguments and the methodological tools are qualitative textual analysis and feminist intersectionality.

The selected comedy programmes, where 'coupledom' is central to the plot are: *The Odd Couple* (about Felix and Oscar sharing a home), *The Middle* (about Frankie and Mike and their three children), *Speechless* (about Mia and Jimmy and their three children), *The Carmichael Show* (about Jerrod and Maxine, his parents, and his brother and ex-wife), *Boy meets Girl* (about Judy and Leo), and *Grace and Frankie* (about Grace and Frankie, their estranged husbands, Grace's two daughters, and Frankie's two sons).

In the process of decoding all the texts, I give additional attention to *Grace and Frankie* and engage in a closer analysis, locating numerous contemporary issues that impact on coupledom and how coupledom is performed. These six comedy series make reference to inter-generational and intra-generational relationships, race, and ethnic identities, class and gender relations, and ability/disability.

14.3.2 *Excavating Comedy: Locating Coupledom*

Textual analysis is the methodological key for unlocking and unpacking media *texts*. It is the umbrella term for several powerful analysis tools such as content analysis, discourse analysis, semiotic analysis, narrative analysis, rhetorical analysis and ideological analysis. These tools facilitate to deconstruct, unsettle and challenge meanings that are embedded in media programmes. I have adopted a semiotic approach in order to locate media generated meanings around 'coupledom'. Semiotics permits and supports an interrogation of the media texts and the sitcoms that portray coupledom as a central theme to the plot.

14.3.3 Something About Semiotics…

When carrying out semiotic analysis (SA) the requirement for generalisable data is not applicable. The core tenets of SA are that each text (i.e. a piece of media, advert, novel, photograph or anything that can be 'read') stands for itself, and the meaning it produces is specific to the research. The researcher occupies the role of specialist or expert reader (Johnson 1983, 1986; Johnson et al., 2004), and others (Hall, 1997; Hawkes, 2003; Williamson, 1988) argue that there is no 'wrong' reading or interpretation. The power of SA lies in its ability to locate ideology and *preferred meanings* that have been written into the texts by the producers; and to locate other meanings, brought to the text by the readers or audiences.

The texts are selected in the same spirit as we would 'sample' for a qualitative study—i.e. seeking respondents that 'fit' the narrative being explored. If I am researching young men's experiences as second-generation migrants, then I only need to speak to young men, who are second-generation migrants—no others. In this study, I have identified contemporary sitcoms that depict couples and coupledom across a broad range of contexts so as to include stories located and embedded in age, race, class, ethnicity, gender and disability. Those parameters have facilitated the selection of the programmes analysed.

The texts: contemporary comedies selected are detailed below, including the storyline background, i.e. *Sitcom Bio*, and the logic behind the selection, i.e. *Rationale for the selection*. I then provide a vignette analysis—*Locating codes for 'coupledom' and 'well-being'*—where I describe how the characters are framed as a couple and decode the themes of coupledom and well-being in that comedy.

The programmes: I open this textual analysis with *The Odd Couple*, and close with *Grace and Frankie* as both sitcoms breach 'conventional couple' dyads. The others in the sample set are closer to 'normalised' versions of coupledom.

14.3.3.1 The Odd Couple

Sitcom Bio: This series is a remake of the 1968 American comedy film and 1970 TV series which was written by Neil Simon, based on his play of the same name. The comedy features Oscar Madison, the slovenly apartment owner, and Felix Unger, the obsessively tidy friend, who comes to live with Oscar after his wife kicks him out. The two friends form a bond and share an apartment, but their ideas of housekeeping and lifestyles are very different.

Rationale for selection: The sitcom depicts a couple who are bonded by friendship and need, rather than romantic ties. The two men form an unusual 'family' structure in that they live together, perform the day-to-day maintenance duties that sustain family life (cooking, eating together, household chores, etc.), and they support each other in various practical and emotional ways. The intersectional variables mentioned above—age, race, class, ethnicity, gender (hetero & LGBTQI) and ability/disability—are middle age, American, professional, white, heterosexual, and same-sex relationship.

Locating codes for 'coupledom' and 'well-being': Two men, in a non-romantic relationship, are bonded by their situation and location. They share an apartment and their lives. In doing so they are situated in a shared lived experience, and within that space they are portrayed in traditional/stereotypical 'husband/wife' roles. Felix is the 'the traditional female'. He keeps the house clean, cooks like a professional chef, attends to the laundry and other chores, and is attentive to emotions—his own and those around him.

Oscar is 'the stereotypical male'. He has a visible job, success and money. He is messy, often inconsiderate towards Felix and his feelings, often unappreciative of the 'unpaid domestic labour' that Felix takes on, and is portrayed as sexually active and successful in dating, etc.

The sitcom successfully 'plays on' and parodies traditional gendered roles, while bringing humour, absurd scenarios and likable characters to the audience/viewer/reader. Well-being is marked throughout, as the two characters ultimately 'look out' for and care for each other.

14.3.3.2 The Middle

Sitcom Bio: An American sitcom about a lower middle class family living in Orson, Indiana. The programme features Mom and Dad (Frankie and Mike) and their three children (Axl, Sue and Brick). The comedy is about their day-to-day struggles with home life, work and raising children.

Rationale for selection: The sitcom depicts a heteronormative couple and traditional family structure. The intersectional variables are: middle age; American, working class, white, heteronormative, with one character who is gently flagged as having a disability.

Locating codes for 'coupledom' and 'well-being': Frankie, the mother, narrates the series so there is a female voice throughout the programme. In the early part of the series, Frankie is a used-car salesperson and later she trains as a dental assistant. Mike, her husband, manages a local quarry and likes sports. The kids are quite different from one another. The oldest son, Axl, fulfils the stereotype of traditional masculinity. He is a sporty, popular and lazy teenager. He does well in sports but is not academic, his room is untidy, he is a messy eater, drinks from the milk carton, has lots of girlfriends and is portrayed as sociable and outgoing. Sue, the middle child and only daughter, fulfils the stereotype of traditional femininity. She is an enthusiastic young teen but socially awkward. She is tidy, neat and always tries to be helpful, both around the house and in 'taking care of' and attending to family and friend's emotional needs. She studies, is attentive to all the social rules and aims to please. Brick is the youngest son. He is an intelligent and introverted compulsive reader with odd behavioural traits loosely hinted to derive from Asperger syndrome. The actor who plays Brick—Atticus Shaffer—has *type four osteogenesis imperfect*, which is a form of *brittle bone disease*. Brick is often overlooked by the rest of the family, is self-contained but socially awkward.

The series portrays the most traditional versions of coupledom and family life. Both couples work and struggle to make ends meet. Their priority is to give their kids a 'better life'. Traditional gender roles prevail—Frankie works full time but is also portrayed as responsible for food, laundry, cleaning house and kids. She also attends to everyone's emotional lives, in both the nuclear family and the extended family. Mike is the silent taciturn, emotionally blocked, non-communicative husband, whose word, when spoken, is the 'last word' in that it carries a lot of weight and ends arguments. He is portrayed as stoic and a stabilising influence in the family, although Frankie complains about his lack of affection at times. The gentle humour that surrounds the couple as they work together to meet the daily challenges of family life is familiar and easy to identify with meaning that the viewer does not struggle to identify with the scenarios as they are 'normal', recognisable and relevant, and resolved with humour.

14.3.3.3 Speechless

Sitcom Bio: An American television sitcom that explores both the serious and humourous challenges a family faces with a teenager who has a disability. The DiMeo family consists of Mom and Dad, and three children—a traditional family structure. Maya, the mother, is British; she fights hard for justice for her children, especially their eldest son, who has cerebral palsy. The father, Jimmy, brings a 'don't care what others think' attitude to the series and is also ready to do anything for his children. For both parents their first priority is to give their children every opportunity to be the best and the happiest they can be.

The children consist of two sons and a daughter. The eldest son, JJ, is mainstreamed in high school. He has cerebral palsy and is unable to speak. He communicates by using headgear with a laser pointer to indicate various words, letters, and numbers on a board attached to his wheelchair, while others read aloud what he 'says'. Ray, their scholarly middle child acts as the 'voice of reason' in the family, and Dylan is the practical, competitive, athletic daughter.

Rationale for selection: The sitcom depicts a heteronormative couple and traditional family structure—a 'normal' family. The intersectional variables are: middle age; American/British, middle class, white, heteronormative, with one of the central character having a disability.

Locating codes for 'coupledom' and 'well-being': The parents are constantly portrayed as a united team. They are seen to have the same goals, and a shared philosophy, which holds the children 'central' in everything they work for and do. They are often portrayed in the storyline as giving each other space to be themselves and pursue their own interests. Each is seen as supporting the other in their, sometimes 'off the wall' plans or schemes.

14.3.3.4 The Carmichael Show

Sitcom Bio: This American sitcom follows stand-up comedian Jerrod Carmichael as he navigates through life with his therapist in-training girlfriend and his heavily opinionated family. The series ran from 2015 to 2017. It stars Jerrod and follows a fictional version of his family in Charlotte, North Carolina.

Rationale for selection: The sitcom depicts a heteronormative couple. The intersectional variables are: young; American, middle-class, Afro-American, heterosexual characters.

Locating codes for 'coupledom' and 'well-being': The main characters are Jerrod and his girlfriend Maxine. They are living together and later marry. They are both depicted as having careers and disposal income and are equally successful in their lives. The other family members include Jerrod's father Joe, mother Cynthia, and brother Bobby and his ex-wife Nekeisha.

The series systematically makes statements on social and political issues such as gender equality, Trump vs. Obama, race and social justice. The well-being codes are embedded in the story line around these issues above, and the couple challenge each other and Carmichael's more conservative family on all of these issues.

The central couple are supportive of each other, affectionate, and use humour to make important social points to each other and to the rest of Carmichael's family. The other couples in the series—Carmichael's parents, and his brother and estranged wife, reflect other 'ways of being' a couple. The parents hold traditional roles—he works outside the home, she is a homemaker, religious and conservative. The other couple, Bobby and Nekeisha, are still friends and have a relationship and role in each other's lives, even though they are romantically separated. The codes for well-being are woven throughout, as the series uses humour to address topical social and political issues, while offering 'solutions' to some of the issues raised.

14.3.3.5 Boy Meets Girl

Sitcom Bio: This is a British (BBC Two) sitcom and it tells the story of the developing relationship between 26-year-old Leo and 40-year-old Judy. The script, by Elliott Kerrigan, was discovered through the Trans Comedy Award, a 2013 BBC talent search for scripts with positive portrayals of transgender characters. Judy, is played by Rebecca Root and both actress and character are transgender, making this the first BBC comedy to feature transgender issues prominently, and the first sitcom to star a transgender actor.

Rationale for selection: The sitcom depicts a transgender woman and a heterosexual man as a couple. The intersectional variables are: young, British, lower-middle-class or working class, white, age, transsexual and heterosexual characters.

Locating codes for 'coupledom' and 'well-being': This programme uses humour in order to spotlight and subsequently normalise alternative relationships. The reader is introduced to two characters that are human, likable, and easy to identify with. It challenges the 'norms' of coupledom—Judy is transgender, and Leo is younger than Judy. It is more common for storylines to feature 'May to September' relationships where the female is younger than the male, which is more familiar in 'real life'. The programme is funny, tender, positive and provocative. It explores what it means to be a man or woman, in a relationship, and how important it is to live a courageous life.

Coupledom is written into the text continuously—the deep desire for a significant 'other' is present at the beginning of the series as Judy seeks a relationship, but is systematically hurt by men's reactions to her. 'Attraction' and 'acceptance of each other' are the main messages as Judy and Leo meet and fall in love. Well-being is coded throughout as the message that 'to be in a couple' is *the* sought after state for both Judy and Leo, and on finding each other, they can deal with life and the world together. The series captures the excitement and inherent heartache of 'non-traditional' love in a northern British town.

14.3.3.6 Grace and Frankie

Grace and Frankie is the final programme analysed in this set of texts. I began this textual analysis with The Odd Couple and close with a similar 'odd couple' relationship. Like Felix and Oscar, Grace and Frankie come to live together when their marriages end. Unlike the Odd Couple, the series addresses a huge imbalance in the gendered portrayal of women, older women, and women in lead roles, which is a media issue and a gender issue. This series affords an excavation of a contemporary successful sitcom that addressed numerous issues that impact on coupledom and how coupledom is performed.

Sitcom Bio: This is an American comedy starring Jane Fonda and Lily Tomlin in the title roles Grace and Frankie. The two women's lives become joined when they find out that their husbands are not just work partners, but have also been romantically involved for the last 20 years and plan to marry. The women, with an already strained relationship, try to cope with the circumstances together, become friends.

Rationale for selection: This programme challenges many variables—it is about older couples, and particularly older women. It is well documented in media research that as women age they disappear from the screen in a way that older men do not (GMMP, 2010, 2015; Ross, Boyle, Carter, & Ging, 2018). The series is about traditional heterosexual relationships in coupledom and family life, the breakdown of marriage, same-sex relationships, love and acceptance, ageism, female sexuality, and female success.

Locating codes for 'coupledom' and 'well-being': The series follows Grace, a retired cosmetics entrepreneur, and Frankie, a hippie art teacher, whose husbands, Robert and Sol, are successful divorce lawyers in the same law firm in San Diego. They are stunned when their husbands inform them that they want divorces, and their lives are turned upside down when Robert and Sol announce that they are in love with each other and want to get married. The women, who have never particularly liked each other, are forced to live together and learn to unite and cope with difficulties.

The conventional relationship is challenged in this series as Grace and Frankie are not a 'conventional couple' or family, and they are not romantically or sexually involved or committed through marriage and shared children. But as the series progresses they become a couple in every other sense of the word. They live together, run the house and home together, look out for and look after each other, bicker over small things, argue over bigger things, and develop deep love ties that are portrayed when they put each other's needs before their own. While the versions of coupledom are not 'everyday typical', some of the scenarios are, and the emotions that are portrayed as a core element in the series are identifiable for the reader. For example, Grace's initial reaction to her husband Robert's announcement that he wants a divorce is fury. Frankie's reaction is sorrow 'I can't remember the last time I slept without you'. The men are depicted as struggling and pained by their leaving too. All responses are relatable to the viewer.

Grace and Frankie share indignation as well as panic, sorrow and anger. Grace complains that Robert and Sol get to live happily ever after *and* retain a moral high ground, as they have not 'run off' with a younger woman (which would generate negative gossip), instead they have 'come out' to themselves and the world (which is implied as a positive step in their personal growth). They also find that without important husbands, they become invisible—old friends do not call, and strangers do not always acknowledge them. This flags a real scenario in contemporary society, where is it documented that older people are not acknowledged, valued or considered to have power, especially older women.

The codes for well-being are rich in this programme. The sitcom genre and its implied and embedded humour, continue to act as a prevailing 'well-being producer'. And while the series *is* a sitcom but is serious about relationships and emotions as it features both the broken marriages *and* the lasting bonds of the husband wife dyad, *and* the lasting bonds of the newer friendship coupledom. The embedded well-being messages are around resilience and survival. The two women are portrayed as 'remaking the self', and retaining a positive outlook on life and the challenges it brings.

Sitcoms rarely feature older females and when they do they are usually not a named production. They are more likely to be a 'side kick' to the main storyline and main characters. For example, Betty White had a leading role in TV Land's 'Hot in Cleveland', but she is not the focus. She served as a 'witticism punching bag' for the other characters in the show, and older actors, especially female actors tend to be cast as grandparents or neighbours—who take on (grand) child-minding or require extra care themselves.

The storyline for *Grace and Frankie* systematically challenges traditional stereotypes that surround aging and older adults. Grace and Frankie are portrayed as sexually vibrant women—they join forces to launch a vibrator for older women and Frankie develops an organic gynaecological lubrication made from yams. They date, are physically active and outgoing, attend parties, etc.

Well-being research shows that stereotypes can affect health and 'researchers have identified numerous theories of how stereotypes of aging impact older adults, primarily internalization/stereotype embodiment, stereotype threat, downward social comparison/resilience, and (more recently) stereotype boost and upward social comparison/role models' (Dionigi, 2015). Media research also shows that older women find it difficult to retain a place in the media—within journalism, in acting roles, and in onscreen jobs, meaning that older women are almost entirely missing from media content production and portrayal (GMMP, 2010; GMMP, 2015; Ross et al., 2018[5]). Grace and Frankie reposition 'aging women'. The sitcom challenges negative stereotypes that can impinge on well-being and the text offers reimagined roles and lived experiences for all readers to engage with.

14.4 Concluding Scenes: *Fin*

By making us laugh, all comedies, by their very nature, have well-being written into the very fabric of their existence as their humour generates positive feelings and outcomes. The very act of laughing has been shown to affect health in an overall positive way as well as contributing to social well-being. I argue that by framing serious, sometimes painful subjects within a humorous discourse, it may help reframe our responses to that negative moment or scenario.

In this section I comment on emergent themes and spotlight moments where race and gender coalesce and traditional gender roles are challenged; I observe how the selected comedies resist traditional patriarchal media discourses which often commodify and objectify women, while raising some questions to ponder at another time. Finally, I comment on the treatment of couple relationships in the broader media space.

14.4.1 Normalising Effects; Authentic Framing

Unpacking complex relationship and social issues seem to be present in each of the sitcoms analysed and this act of portrayal must have a normalising effect on ability/disability, race politics and gender politics. For example, while analysing the texts I was struck by the authenticity of the casting of actors. For example in *The Middle*, the actor who plays Brick—Atticus Shaffer—has Type Four Osteogenesis Imperfecta which is a form of *brittle bone disease*—but his role is *not* about his disability. — In the storyline Brick displays motor and phonic tics including echolalia (repeating words just spoken by someone else), palilalia (repeating one's own previously spoken words), and lexilalia (repeating words after reading them),

---

[5] Ross et al., (2018)—broadly in line with the global data, our findings also show that there is an inverse relationship between sex, age and visibility so that as a woman's age increases, her visibility in the news decreases: a mere 20% of all sources/subjects who were perceived as being over the age of 50 years were women. This is in line with the European data which shows that women comprise only 19% of everyone in the 50–64 year age group.

and there are allusions to autism spectrum disorder (ASD) although none of these are 'named' in the script. Indeed the family mostly ignore his 'odd' behaviour and by doing so, normalise it. In *Speechless*, Micah Fowler, the actor cast to play JJ, has cerebral palsy and is an advocate for CP as a result of his role in Speechless; and in *Boy meets Girl* the actor who plays Judy—Rebecca Root—is transgender. And in *The Carmichael Show*, as race and gender coalesce, traditional gender roles are challenged and positive readings around race and gender emerge. The series depicts strong women who are portrayed as decision makers and women with agency.

14.4.2 Media Sins: Commodification and Objectification

Feminist media researchers have challenged mainstream media for decades, and media producers have been accused of various 'crimes against humanity' but especially against women. This occurs most blatantly in advertising and in music videos but subtly in all other genres too. Women portrayed on screen are persistently commodified and objectified. They are subjected to the tyranny of the beauty myth (Wolf 1990; Kilbourne, 1999, 2002) the male gaze (Mulvey, 1975) and the subsequent male framing of sexuality (McNair, 2002), and the media holds a largely patriarchal lens in order to frame society's stereotype of femininity.

When embarking on this research I anticipated spotlighting examples that would highlight moments of commodification and objectification. In particular, objectification of women and women's bodies, which would feed into and highlight moments of commodification of 'love and romance'. However, in the six sitcoms analysed there was only subtle evidence of such commodification and objectification, and it was often named and addressed in the script at some point in the series, unlike most other media genres. Some of the texts actively resisted this lens, and contained overt resistance to patriarchal discourses and other subtle discursive practices. Indeed this observation would suggest that sitcoms, as a genre, not only promote and support personal and social well-being by serving up humour and laughter to the reader, the sample above are also the least guilty of documented 'media sins' as outlined above, and therefore may be instrumental in promoting social and personal well-being in a 'positive portrayal' that may warrant further research.

14.4.3 Media Portrayal and Representation of the Couple Relationship

The media has the potential and role to serve as a source of information in the portrayal couples and families. However literature on this topic is scant and when it does exist, it is quite narrow in scope. For example, in 1996 Bachen & Illouz focused on *young peoples imagined vision of romance* and how those understandings move from one moulded by the media and associating romance with luxury and leisure consumption, to one characterised by a tension between what media have promised them and their growing understanding of the complexities of love. Tanner, Haddock, Schindler Zimmerman, and Lund, (2003) examined *images of couples and families in Disney (animated) movies*. In their work they identified four emergent themes: (a) where family relationships were a strong priority, (b) where families are diverse, but the diversity is often simplified, (c) where fathers were elevated, while mothers were marginalised, and (d) where couple relationships were created by 'love at first sight' were easily maintained and were often characterised by gender-based power differentials. In 2005 Leon and Angst examined portrayals of *stepfamilies in film* and looked at media images around remarriage. They found that stepfamilies were typically depicted in a negative or mixed way. In addition, stepparent–child relations, remarried couple relationships, and issues related to former partners were frequently portrayed.

While the media occupies a significant space in our daily lives and in our lived experiences, and while it has the capacity to reflect and shape understandings of coupledom, it is under researched in and around *how* it portrays couple relationships.

14.4.4 Final Cut or Finale

Distinct from issues around portrayal and representation of coupledom it is also useful to also ask how media, and its presence and usage, impacts on couples. From an ethnographic anthropological standpoint we might want to ask how we, as social actors, 'use' the media. What is the role the media plays in couples' lives? Is the 'act of watching TV' used as shared time together or is it used to distract from day to day or even more serious issues? Does the 'act of watching TV' become incorporated into other routines like eating or working? Do particular genres aid or damage the couple relationship?

Finding or making time to communicate is key to maintaining couple relationships. Is the act of watching TV and screen a distraction from our couple relationships? Watching TV takes up a significant portion of our adult waking day (see above) and if we are dedicating so much time to the screen this must surely be distracting us from, and robbing us of, time to spend or invest in the maintenance of our significant and meaningful relationships.

Literature specifically examining the role the media is playing in the lived experiences of couples, is scarce. Researchers are more likely to examine specific topics such as sexual media and its impact on couples, or to broadly explore the role media technologies, including communication technologies, are playing in couples' lives. For example Bridges and Morokoff (2011) assessed how sexual media use by one or both members of a romantic dyad relates to relationship and sexual satisfaction. And in 2011 Coyne et al. examined the communication technologies that individuals in serious, committed, heterosexual, romantic relationships were using to communicate with one another. They looked at the frequency of use, and the association between the use of these technologies and couple's positive and negative communication.

The most useful work in understanding the role the media is playing in couples lives is by Hertlein (2012) who examined how digital technology, i.e. media in its broadest understanding, is affecting couple relationships and family life. She was interested in this unprecedented age of technology and notes that few articles in family journals address online behaviour, intimacy patterns and influences on the ways couples and families communicate through technology. In her work she describes the process of how technologies are affecting couple and family life. However, Hertlein is looking at the widest application of screens and screen interaction (mobile phones, internet etc.) as opposed to the use of watching TV, movies and films—as media texts.

Media texts, like the ones deconstructed in this chapter, are programmes that entertain and inform and they persist to play a part of our lives. They have the potential to be uplifting and to portray positive examples of coupledom that enrich us. There are, of course, negative examples of couple relationships, but they are more likely to be located in other genres such as dramas, soap operas or movies. Comedy writers craft humour into programmes which have the scope to entertain us, uphold coupledom in its broadest construct, and while doing so, serve up a large slice of well-being.

References

Abela, A., Calleja, N., Piscopo, S., & Vella, S. (2016). *Report sustaining relationships: Couples and singles in a changing society*. Malta: The President's Foundation for the Wellbeing of Society.

Abela, A., Frosh, S., & Dowling, E. (2005). Uncovering beliefs embedded in the culture and its implications for practice: The case of Maltese married couples. *Journal of Family Therapy, 27*(1), 3–23.

Adorno, T. (1991). 'Culture industry reconsidered' in The Culture Industry: Selected Essays on Mass Culture. London: Routledge.

Bachen, C. M., & Illouz, E. (1996). Imagining romance: Young people's cultural models of romance and love. *Critical Studies in Mass Communication, 13*(4), 279–308.

Berk, L. S., Tan, S. A., Fry, W. F., Napier, B. J., Lee, J. W., Hubbard, R. W., … Eby, W. C. (1989). Neuroendocrine and stress hormone changes during mirthful laughter. *American Journal of the Medical Sciences, 298*(6), 390–396.

Bridges, A. J., & Morokoff, P. J. (2011). Sexual media use and relational satisfaction in heterosexual couples. *Personal Relationships, 18*, 562–585.

Budgeon, S. (2008). Couple culture and the production of singleness. *Sexualities, 11*(3), 301–325.

Coyne, S. M., Stockdale, L., Busby, D., Iverson, B., & Grant, D. M. (2011). "I luv u:)!": A descriptive study of the media use of individuals in romantic relationships. *Family Relations 60*, 150–162.

Dionigi, R. A. (2015). Stereotypes of aging: Their effects on the health of older adults. *Journal of Geriatrics, 2015*, 9.

Edwards, K. R. (2013). The role of humor as a character strength in positive psychology (Electronic Thesis and Dissertation Repository, 1681).

Fiske, J. (2010). Understanding Popular Culture. London & New York: Routledge.
Fredrickson, B. L. (2001). The role of positive emotions in positive psychology: The broaden-and-build theory of positive emotions. *American Psychologist, 56*(3), 218–226.
Ferreira Rodrigues, T. (2014). Meaning in couples relationships. *Psychology in Russia: State of the Art, 7*(3), 126–135.
GMMP. (2010). http://cdn.agilitycms.com/who-makes-the-news/Imported/reports_2010/global/gmmp_global_report_en.pdf.
GMMP. (2015). http://cdn.agilitycms.com/who-makes-the-news/Imported/reports_2015/global/gmmp_global_report_en.pdf.
Hall, S. (1997). *Representation: Cultural representations and signifying practices. Culture, media and identities series.* London: Open University, Sage.
Hatzipapas, I., Visser, M. J., & van Rensburg, E. J. (2017). Laughter therapy as an intervention to promote psychological well-being of volunteer community care workers working with HIV-affected families. *SAHARA-J: Journal of Social Aspects of HIV/AIDS, 14*(1), 202–212.
Hawkes, T. (2003). *Structuralism and semiotics.* London & New York: Routledge.
Hertlein, K. M. (2012). Digital dwelling: Technology in couple and family relationships. *Family Relations, 61*, 374–387.
Johnson, R. (1983). What is cultural studies anyway? Stencilled occasional paper, September 1983, *general series: SP No 74,* Birmingham: Centre for Contemporary Cultural Studies. Retrieved July 2018, from https://www.birmingham.ac.uk/Documents/college-artslaw/history/cccs/stencilled-occasional-papers/56to87/SOP74.pdf
Johnson, R. (1986). What is cultural studies anyway? *Social Text, 16*, 38–80.
Johnson, R., Chambers, D., Raghuram, P., & Tincknell, E. (2004). *The practice of cultural studies.* London: Sage.
Kilbourne, J. (2002). *Killing us softly 3, advertising's images of women.* Northampton MA: Media Education Foundation.
Kilbourne, J. (1999). *Can't buy me love, how advertising changes the way we think and feel.* New York: Touchstone.
Leon, K., & Angst, E. (2005). Portrayals of stepfamilies in film: Using media images in remarriage education in family relations. *Interdisciplinary Journal of Applied Family Science, 54*(1), 1–168.
McNair, B. (2002). *Striptease culture: Sex, media and the democratisation of desire.* London: Routledge.
Mulvey, L. (1975). Visual pleasure and narrative cinema. *Screen, 16*(3), 6–18.
Open University Open Learn. Retrieved July 2018., from http://www.open.edu/openlearn/body-mind/psychology/the-gap-lovers-must-fill-what-exactly-conventional-relationship
Oxford Dictionary. Retrieved July 2018., from https://en.oxforddictionaries.com/definition/couple
Pinker, S. (2016). *The secret to living longer may be your social life.* Ted2017. Retrieved July 2018, from https://www.ted.com/talks/susan_pinker_the_secret_to_living_longer_may_be_your_social_life/transcript?language=en
Ross, K., Boyle, K., Carter, C., & Ging, D. (2018). Women, men and news. *Journalism Studies, 19*(6), 824–845.
Robles, T. F. (2014). Marital quality and health implications for marriage in the 21st century. *Current Directions in Psychological Science, 23*(6), 427–432.
Sullivan, K. T., & Lawrence, E. (Eds.). (2016). *The Oxford handbook of relationship science and couple interventions.* Oxford: Oxford Uni Press.
Skerrett, K., & Fergus, K. (Eds.). (2015). *Couple resilience: Emerging perspectives.* New York: Springer.
Tanner, L. R., Haddock, A., Schindler Zimmerman, T., & Lund, L. K. (2003). Images of couples and families in Disney feature-length animated films. *American Journal of Family Therapy, 31*(5), 355–373.
Williamson, J. (1988). *Decoding advertising.* New York & London: Marion Boyars.
Wolf, N. (1990). The Beauty Myth: How Images of Beauty Are Used Against Women. London: Chatto & Windus.

Chapter 15
Keeping Couples Together when Apart, and Driving Them Apart when Together: Exploring the Impact of Smartphones on Relationships in the UK

Mark McCormack and M. F. Ogilvie

15.1 Introduction

Research on gender and sexuality has recognized the impact of technological change in how sexual acts, identities, and cultures are organized in society (e.g., Döring, 2009). The internet and computer-based technology have revolutionized the ways in which romantic relationships are initiated and maintained (Coyne, Stockdale, Busby, Iverson, & Grant, 2011). One focus of this research has been on smartphones and the effects this pervasive technology has on couples' social and romantic lives (Hertlein & Ancheta, 2014). However, this research frequently adopts a quantitative approach that seeks to understand potential negative effects of smartphone use during dating, and to examine the influence of smartphone use on a range of psychological variables on long-term happiness and well-being. There is less focus on the impact of smartphones on the romantic and sexual activities of people in long-term relationships, particularly in respect to an experiential or phenomenological understanding of people's lives. Indeed, much of the research has focused on the social dynamics facilitated by these behaviors rather than understanding how people feel about smartphones and technology in their lives.

This study examined how individuals perceive the impact of smartphones and related technology on romance, intimacy, and sex for people in long-term relationships. Using in-depth, qualitative interviews with 30 people from a diverse range of backgrounds across England, and adopting an inductive analysis, this research shows that while smartphones are central to contemporary romantic relationships, they are also a cause of stress and tension. These tensions can be subtle and complex,

---

M. McCormack (✉)
Department of Social Sciences, University of Roehamptom, London, UK

M. F. Ogilvie
Department of Sociology, Durham University, Durham, UK

but have the potential to negatively impact relationships if they are not dealt with. While participants had strategies to deal with some of these issues, there was also dissatisfaction with the use of smartphones in their lives.

15.2 Technology, Smartphones, Sex, and Relationships

The emergence of the internet and computer-mediated communication has resulted in significant change in how people form and maintain social, sexual, and romantic relationships (Drouin, Vogel, Surbey, & Stills, 2013; Turkle, 2011). As part of this, the internet has created opportunities for online sexual gratification and the development of distinct online social and sexual identities (Mowlabocus, 2010; Waskul, 2003). These online spaces have also enabled individuals to explore sexuality and make connections with like-minded individuals who share their sexual tastes (Döring, 2009), including by constructing sexual communities through blogs and social networking sites (Wignall, 2017). Sites like Facebook and Twitter are used to transmit sexual content, facilitating online sexual subcultures (Drouin & Landgraff, 2012; Wignall, 2017).

The internet has also changed the means used to develop, maintain, and enhance relationships (Coyne et al., 2011; Sprecher, 2009). Social networking sites have been utilized by couples as a way of demonstrating commitment to each other by displaying positive posts about their partner, uploading photos of activities they do with their partner, or using social media to publicly define that their relationship is "official" (Rappleyea, Taylor, & Fang, 2014). Many couples also use the internet for relationship education (Hertlein & Ancheta, 2014), as a way to manage conflict and reduce anxiety (Bergdal et al., 2012).

Advances in technology and the accessibility of sexually explicit media have also made it easier for couples to enhance the sexual components of their relationship. This includes watching pornography together, engaging in sexual acts via live-camera, using sex toys that have a mobile app as a remote control, and sexting (texts containing sexual content) (Bergdal et al., 2012). Drouin et al. (2013) found that 78% of their sample of people in committed relationships had sent "words only" sexts to their partner, while 49% had sent picture or videos to their partner, and 12% had engaged in live video sex with their partner. It has also had a positive influence on long-distance relationships, as well as with couples who live apart in the same town (known as Living Apart Together relationships) (Levin, 2004).

Some of the earlier research on sexuality and technology focused on computers as the medium through which to access the internet. However, smartphones have become the most popular and accessible way to engage with social media applications and stay connected to friends and partners. Location-based social network apps available on smartphones, such as Tinder and Grindr, labelled "hook-up apps," also enable people to arrange to meet either socially or sexually in the real world (Gudelunas, 2012; Macapagal, Coventry, Puckett, Phillips, & Mustanski, 2016).

Smartphone users describe their relationship with this technology as fun but compulsive (Jung, 2013). Existing research suggests that smartphones negatively affect romantic relationships, interrupting meaningful communication between partners (Duran, Kelly, & Rotaru, 2011), leading to lower relationship satisfaction and increased conflict, and endangering individual well-being (McDaniel & Coyne, 2016). Partners of smartphone users report jealousy and other negative emotions as a result of smartphone use (Krasnova, Abramova, Notter, & Baumann, 2016; Roberts & David, 2016). Su (2016) argues that increased connectedness leads to increased vulnerability because people find silence and being alone difficult to acclimatize to, in the context of constant communication provided by smartphones. Social media sites can also lead to a lack of trust in a relationship through adding new friends, unwanted posts, and the ease of private messaging (Hertlein & Ancheta, 2014).

However, the issue of smartphones and their influence on relationships is complex with a greater frequency of phone calls between partners being associated with positive outcomes, including fewer doubts about partners' commitment to the relationship and increased confidence in the relationship (Jin & Peña, 2010). Indeed, smartphones can be useful tools for establishing and maintaining diverse forms of sexual relationships (Bergdal et al., 2012). One reason for this apparent dissonance may be a focus on testing the effects of smartphone use through survey methods and hypothesis testing, rather than a more inductive and qualitative approach to the issue.

15.3 Changing Sexual Norms

The rise of internet technology and its impact on sexual lives has occurred simultaneously with changing norms of sex and sexuality. One key trend of the past 60 years has been the increasing acceptance of nonmarital sex (Cherlin, 2004). While 29% of Americans stated that nonmarital sex was acceptable in the 1950s, this had increased to 58% by 2012, and people report having more sexual partners over this period (Twenge, Sherman, & Wells, 2015). These changes were spurred by modern methods of contraception, particularly the Pill, which greatly reduced the possibility of pregnancy from sex. In this context, sex moved from the reproductive arena of marriage toward a recreational and pleasurable activity between consenting adults (Twenge, 2014). Attitudes toward same-sex sexuality have also liberalized (Twenge et al., 2015), as a radical shift in lesbian, gay, and bisexual people's experiences has seen society become more inclusive of diverse sexualities (Anderson & McCormack, 2016; Weeks, 2007).

This liberalization of sexual attitudes has required new ways to understand contemporary sexual practices. One way is through thinking of sex as a leisure activity. This involves moving away from understanding sex through a moral lens and a medicalized framework of risk and harm to viewing sex as "part of a complex social structure in which pleasure and risk are balanced" (Wignall & McCormack, 2017: 802). Understanding sex as leisure is particularly helpful when considering the prevalence of casual sex and "hooking up" in many youth cultures, the visibility of sexually explicit entertainment and media, and the accessibility of pornography (Mulholland, 2013). The leisure sex model, rooted in the liberalization of attitudes toward nonmarital sex, discusses diverse forms of sexual desire and identity that have recently become highly visible, including greater acceptance of sexual minorities and various sexual communities and kink activities (McCormack & Wignall, 2017; Wignall & McCormack, 2017).

This framing of sex as leisure enables consideration of risks and benefits, rather than a focus on social harm. It also recognizes how sex is considered for some as a serious, skillful activity (Newmahr, 2010). Framing sex as a leisure activity also places responsibility on the individual involved to project sexual competency, responsibility, and knowledge. Thus, even when some sexual activity is framed as a casual leisure activity, the broader leisure framework still recognizes how sex has become widely understood and experienced as important to individual well-being.

Recognizing the complexity of the genesis of shifting sexual attitudes, the trend of sexual liberalization also has its limits. Greater acceptance of sexual behaviors outside of marriage is limited to premarital sex and same-sex sexual activities, excluding extramarital sexual behaviors, which are still deemed to be "wrong" (Twenge, 2014). The liberalization of sexual attitudes is circumscribed by a set of values based around consent and safety, with behaviors outside these norms still quite stigmatized (Newmahr, 2010).

15.4 Situating Leisure Sex and Technological Change in Sociological Theorizing

The liberalization in attitudes toward many consensual sex acts is the result of structural changes in society (Giddens, 1992). Research surrounding these cultural changes has highlighted an increase in people focusing on their own needs and desires, rather than the beliefs and values of broader social groups (Fukuyama, 1999). There has also been an increase in secularism and a sharp decline in adolescents' religious affiliation between the 1970s and 2010s (Chaves, 1994; Twenge, 2014). While precise terminology is debated, this has often been referred to as individualization, and amounts to a significant reordering of how society is structured in the West.

This rise of individualization also resulted in people taking more decisions in their lives as they distance themselves from the power of institutions (Beck, Giddens, & Lash, 1994). In this context, Lash and Wynne (1992: 3) contend that individuals must "reflexively construct their own biographies," and meaning in people's lives is created through their actions rather than the institutions they inhabit. People's social worlds become infused with reflexive human knowledge due to social changes such as increased geographic mobility, the influence of mass media, and greater access to a range of materials.

Indeed, this form of society has been one in which risk has become a major social concern (Beck, 1992; Giddens, 1991). Contrasting with threats of previous eras that tended to be beyond the control of individuals, risk is defined as "a systematic way of dealing with hazards and insecurities induced and introduced by modernization itself" (Beck, 1992: 21). This is particularly true of sexuality, where moral panics related to children and sex focus on technology, sexualization, and threats to "childhood innocence" (Best & Bogle, 2014; Fahs, Dudy, & Stage, 2014). In this context, the risks of sex and sexuality are targeted at the expense of notions of pleasure (Fine & McClelland, 2006).

This focus on the risks of sex can be closely connected to the transformation of intimacy occurring within a late-modern capitalist society. That is, while the liberalization of attitudes to a number of sexual behaviors can be seen to have had a positive effect for a number of people, this focus on the individual means that broader social forces that structure sex in society receive less focus than they otherwise might—including how political institutions or moral discourses can influence how sexual activities and identities are socially perceived. As a result, individuals are blamed for their behaviors rather than the social institutions that influence them—whether it be cheating (Anderson, 2012), selling sex (Weitzer, 2009), or other stigmatized sexual behaviors such as kink and polyamory (Rubin, 1984). In this context, it is important to understand how individuals perceive smartphones and related technology to have impacted upon their sexual and romantic lives.

This connects with a key debate in the literature about whether the growth of internet technology enhances relationships. Turkle's (2011) exploration of the role of technology in people's relationships rejects this position, arguing that technology facilitates a greater number of connections but harms the growth of serious and meaningful relationships. She contends that "The ties we form through the Internet are not, in the end, the ties that bind" (Turkle, 2011: 280). Indeed, a trend in the literature is that while internet technology has enabled social and sexual *connections* (Gudelunas, 2012; Macapagal et al., 2016), it has hindered the development and *maintenance* of meaningful relationships (Hertlein & Ancheta, 2014; McDaniel & Coyne, 2016; Turkle, 2011). Even so, the ways in which internet technologies impact romantic relationships lack research that employs rich interview data, and this study seeks to address this issue in greater detail.

15.5 A Note on Methods

This study draws on 30 in-depth interviews with individuals from England who were in a heterosexual relationship to examine the influence of smartphones and related technology in their lives. Participants were aged 18–55, and the initial recruitment process required them to have been in a relationship for at least 1 year. Heterosexual couples in long distance relationships were excluded from participation due to their reliance on technology and smartphones for all methods of communication with their partners. There was a diverse range of participants in terms of class, ethnicity, age, and educational background. An equal number of men and women were interviewed.

The other requirement for participation in the study was that individuals must have engaged with at least two forms of social media, which we used as a broad category to guard against people who actively distanced themselves from using contemporary technology. Our focus in interviews was on use of smartphones and other related technology, which includes tablets, laptops, and personal computers in the home. As such, while we generally refer to smartphones in this chapter, we occasionally reference other technologies as guided by the data.

Interviews were undertaken by a team of researchers (see McCormack, 2015), and while participants were recruited through convenience sampling, effort was made to recruit people of different ages, from different parts of the country and in relationships for different lengths of time. An inductive approach to analysis was used that identified themes. Further coding and thematic analysis occurred alongside deeper engagement with the literature, combining existing frameworks on technology in relationships with our own themes specific to smartphone use in relationships to develop a theory grounded in the data and prominent literature (Urquhart, 2013). Ethical approval was gained from the authors' university, and this included ensuring that participants gave informed consent. While funding was provided by Durex, the authors maintained academic independence in all aspects of the research process.

15.6 Results

15.6.1 The Benefits of Smartphones in Relationships

Interview data demonstrated that technology and smartphones were central to the organization of romantic relationships for most participants (Byrne & Findlay, 2004; Sprecher, 2009). All but one participant owned a smartphone and those who did regularly communicated with their partner on it at some point in their relationship. Participants spoke about the value of smartphones during the early stages of relationships, particularly for keeping in contact between romantic dates (see also Bergdal et al., 2012). Rather than being used solely for organizing dates, participants discussed how smartphones were an integral component of communication in the early stages of dating, and vital in establishing romantic relationships. This was particularly true of participants aged under 35, with one woman in her thirties saying:

> I'd say that at the start, it played a big part in our relationship because we would text each other and that's actually how we stayed in touch. We met and had sex obviously, but we kept in touch by text and emails and that built the foundation of our relationship.

Some participants spoke of messaging each other hundreds of times a day in the early stages of the relationship, with one participant saying he sent "literally thousands and thousands of messages."

This use of smartphones to communicate in a relationship persisted after the early stages for many participants (Pettigrew, 2009). For example, a female participant aged 33, said:

> We can always get in touch with each other. He calls me on his break at midnight just to tell me goodnight. We are apart the majority of the day, so we stay in contact through texts, or liking each other's photos on Instagram, or sending each other cute articles from Buzzfeed. Little reminders like that really help.

A 24 year old male participant's perspective was that the primary value of smartphone communication was for this regular contact: "It's literally there for contact when we're away from each other." Similarly, a 22 year old man said, "I just text her during the day to check in with her, so she knows I'm thinking of her."

A small number of participants who either did not have a smartphone or had one that was old (including not having internet browsing or free texting services), spoke about feeling they were "missing out" on this technology. For example, a 23 year old man said, "I used to have snapchat but my phone is too slow for it. I think my social and sex life would flourish a bit more if I got a new phone and was more into it."

In addition to these forms of relationship maintenance, participants also spoke about the use of smartphones for mundane activities, including organizing leisure activities and planning housework and other duties during the day (Pettigrew, 2009). For example, a male participant aged 28, said, "If I'm bored at work, I'll text and ask what the plans are for that night. It's nice to touch base, and also helps me get through the day." All participants with smartphones did this, with some arguing that these communications decreased the likelihood of arguments by averting potential issues before they occurred. For example, a female participant aged 38, who had been in a relationship for 7 years, said: "It's the texts during the day, where we can plan and stuff that means we don't forget things, and stops arguments from happening."

Participants also discussed the value of smartphones and technology in fostering conversation when together (c.f. Turkle, 2011). One female participant, aged 23, said:

> I don't know what older people used to speak about, they didn't know what was going on in other peoples' lives. There is only so much you can talk to about with somebody you see every day—these [social networking] sites give us talking points.

Similarly, another female participant, aged 32, asked, "What did people used to talk about before they could use their phones to show people YouTube videos and stuff like that?" He added, "You couldn't use phone calls to speak to people and find out where they were when you're meeting up with them."

The other key theme related to the benefits of smartphones was for the benefits they had in enhancing participants' sexual lives (Drouin et al., 2013). Twenty participants discussed sending flirtatious or sexual messages to each other, while 12 had sent pictures of a sexual nature to each other. One female participant, aged 27, said: "We've taken sexy pics of me, but not of sex. They were sexual, scintillating but not slutty." Another female participant, aged 55, said of her smartphone:

> When I discovered it could record little videos, I did silly little strip-teasey routines for a laugh. It was fun, yeah, I really enjoyed it... When I first met my partner, I also filmed myself masturbating, and I hoped he could pick up some tips, but I didn't want to do it in front of him, so I filmed it. I remember it was quite exciting and was worth doing.

While this narrative came from the oldest participant, the younger participants appeared to be more open in general to using their smartphones in this sexual capacity (Gordon-Messer et al., 2013), highlighting a possible generational difference.

One man, aged 25, spoke of the value of smartphones in filming sex. He said, "It gives you different perspectives of sex and enables you to see what you're doing in a different way. We can also text and sext when she's away which is great, too." A 25 year old female participant said, "If I buy new bathing suit or bikini, I'll send him a picture of me in it or if I'm going to his in the evening, I'll send him a hint of what I'm wearing." Interestingly, no participants spoke about worries regarding ending a relationship and the pictures being retained and shared maliciously by the ex-partner, colloquially known as "revenge porn."

Some participants did not send explicit pictures because of worries over other people seeing them if their phone is lost or on display at work (Baym, 2010). Participants who did sext also spoke of deleting sexual photos to reduce any risk of others seeing them. One female participant in her thirties said, "I'm a teacher and I sometimes leave my phone lying around. It's really important that there are no sexual photos on my phone, in class or the staffroom." A young male participant said, "It's that standard issue of your grandma is looking at a photo and you're terrified of what she'll see if she swipes left. I delete them because of that."

However, other participants who had not sent sexual pictures were open to the idea, particularly if they were single in the future. One women aged 32 said:

> My friend does it all the time, she's just got loads of cocks on her phone. I can have his dick in real life though, so no need for pictures. If I was single then I would probably do it more, it would be exciting, the anticipation of it I guess.

Eight of the participants had also recorded videos of themselves engaging in sexual activity with their partner, either together or using Skype or other messaging services with camera facilities. This often occurred on laptops or tablets rather than smartphones, and was praised as a way to keep in contact and maintain sexual relations when apart. As a female participant aged 26 said, "I'm not that into sex and technology, but when my boyfriend was in America, we did it a few times because it was the best option." As other research has shown (Dir, Coskunpinar & Cyders, 2014), there was no evidence of negative effects from sexting or the filming of sex. Thus, participants recognized the benefits that smartphones and technology had in their romantic relationships, both emotionally and sexually.

15.6.2 The Costs of Smartphones on Relationships

While participants overwhelmingly valued smartphones and technology in their lives, the majority also recognized that their pervasive usage came at a cost to their relationship (Krasnova et al., 2016; Turkle, 2011). For four participants, it served to question the fidelity of partners, and undermine trust. One female participant, aged 24, said:

> It's just an open door. There are so many ways you can get away with things. It's been said before—the delete button is so easy to use. You can hide anything. Somebody could be cheating on you for months and you wouldn't know about it because they can delete everything.

Similarly, another female participant, aged 55, said:

> When you go on Facebook and you can see if people are active or whatever—you see the green light. If I go on at funny hours and I see his online I do wonder what he's up to, who's he talking to, and what's he saying? At half 8 in the fucking morning.'

Another female participant, aged 38, commented:

> When the first iPhone was purchased by him I used to call it the third person in our marriage and I hated her with a passion, she used to sit between us, and I really disliked her… it has become a third arm for a lot of people.

While these views have resonance with research that sees trust undermined through the use of social networking sites, they were articulated by just four participants—three of whom stated that smartphones had been used as a way of facilitating cheating by partners in the past. Interestingly, all four participants were female, and it may be that there is a gendered component to these concerns around infidelity (Rappleyea et al., 2014).

These four participants also discussed tracking their partners' activities through monitoring their use of social networking sites, apps, and their texts. The female participant concerned about smartphones as an "open door" with delete functions being "so easy to use," said:

> It can be awful. Reading messages that should never have been read, from both sides. Just technology in general. You can write letters to people with it, emails, texts, documented forever. Sometimes you forget to delete it until it's too late. It causes tension through lack of trust.

The great majority of participants valued technology in their lives, yet they still expressed frustration at the tensions it caused in their relationships—something McDaniel and Coyne (2016) call "technoference." One key theme was how smartphones led to social distance between partners when at home together, often through multitasking when interacting with their partner (see Krishnan et al., 2014). One female participant said, "It hinders [communication] because sometimes I'll be on Facebook and he'll be on a sporting app while we are both in bed; then we realize that we are literally sitting in bed together, but living in different worlds."

Another participant, female and aged 29, raised smartphone apps as a particular distraction in her relationship:

> He is obsessed with Candy Crush and often plays it on his phone and iPad. He'll do that in the pub when we're with friends, which drives me insane. And he'll do it when we're watching a film, so he's not concentrating and then he'll ask what is going on in the film which is ridiculous…it really annoys me because it's very uncivilized.

Similarly, another male participant in his twenties, said:

> When I first got my smartphone I got this one app, and it was really addictive. She asked me to delete it because a month of my life was ruined by this game. I had to do it every night before bed so it would be ready for in the morning. I'd do it every night. …Sometimes when we were cuddling I would play on the game behind her head. Sometimes I would play on the apps rather than cuddle my partner.

Others, particularly those 30 or older, discussed work intruding into their relationships because of smartphones. One said, "I have clients texting me at 5 in the morning cancelling their sessions. I think it would be better if I had a shut off period where I wasn't allowed to use my phone after certain times." A male participant, aged 42, said, "[My partner] can't disconnect from work. She'll be checking emails first thing in the morning and last thing at night."

A related issue was the way in which smartphone usage changed over the duration of a relationship, being used as an indicator about the quality of the relationship more generally (Jin & Peña, 2010). For example, a female participant aged 55, said:

> It's nice when you hear the text coming in, and you think, aww, that means he's thinking about me. It's a sort of signal, you know, you're in someone's thoughts, if they're texting you. But again, I've found in the past year or two I've dropped off—like it used to be that I would always text him back immediately, but now I don't as much, but he hasn't seemed to notice. I want him to notice, but he doesn't. He hasn't said anything.

A small group of participants found that the level of communication on smartphones diminished as the relationship progressed in this manner, and were troubled by what it meant as a "sign," rather than discussing the issue openly with their partners, supporting the idea of discussing smartphone usage in the initial stages of a relationship.

Participants also felt that smartphones impacted sexual activity, with 12 of the 30 having delayed sex because of smartphone use. One participant said she had delayed sex when "in the middle of my Candy Crush game," while another said that he did so, "As a form of 'I can't be arsed.'" He added, "So maybe we would have both gone to bed at the same time and so to not take things any further I might make myself look busy on my phone." A female participant in her thirties used a similar technique, saying: "Sometimes I know from his body language he wants to have sex. He gets a funny look. I just don't look at him, go on my phone, and say I'm busy."

Participants spoke of smartphones impacting sex in other ways as well. One woman in her thirties said, "I may want sex and he might not be aware of that, because he's distracted on his phone." Others spoke about hurrying sex in order to respond to a text message or notification. While half of participants spoke of smartphones impacting on sex in this way, this tended to be temporary infractions rather than more permanent disruptions to sex. As one participant said, "I'll make him wait until I'm done with my updates, but I'll still have sex with him."

15.6.3 Strategies to Deal with Smartphones in Relationships

While frustration existed as a result of smartphone use for the majority of participants, most had developed strategies for dealing with these issues (see Miller-Ott, Kelly, & Duran, 2012). The key strategy that people used was to organize times when smartphones were banned from use in the house. A number of rules were developed by participants, including not having smartphones easily accessible at dinner, out with friends, during sex, or before sleeping. One participant, male and aged 27, said:

> My girlfriend used to check her phone lot in bed, and my hobby is reading. So where I've tried to ban her using the smart phone in bed, she said to me that in that case you shouldn't be reading so much in the bedroom. So there's that dynamic now. We're only trying to use the bedroom now for sleeping and sex and do things like reading in other places.

A female participant aged 29, who had been in a relationship for 5 years, spoke about how these rules were negotiated:

> If I try and insist on the "phones down" rule, he sees that as me telling him what to do. He doesn't like that and rebels against it. The only time it stands in our house is when we have candle-lit dinners. Then, phones are away and not picked up... More generally, it really, really annoys me and we fight about it all the time.

Interestingly, highlighting how technology use is interpreted subjectively by individuals (Nodin, Carballo Dieguez, & Leal, 2013), this participant added, "I think I manage my phone use really well. But my friends get mad with me for not responding to anything. I like to focus on the here and now with the person I'm with, but they get annoyed that I don't respond to texts."

Others spoke about deleting particular apps because they recognized it was impacting too much on their free time. One participant said, "I just knew I was spending too long on this game, so I deleted it. It was bad for the relationship and for my work." Another participant, male and aged 42, said, "I used to have my work email linked up to my phone. But I would check it all the time. Now, if I check it on my phone, I have to go through my browser. It's really made me check it less and that's been great."

However, while participants highlighted a number of strategies they had developed to manage tensions about smartphones in their relationship (Miller-Ott et al., 2012), these were not always effective. One male participant, aged 25, said, "Smartphones are just this huge distraction from each other. We still find ourselves sat on our phones rather than engaging with each other." Similarly, another participant highlighted the persistence of the issue:

> She always gets in trouble because we'll just be sat there chatting and all of a sudden she'll be on Facebook. And I'll say, "Hi, I'm here." I've actually messaged her whilst she's on Facebook to say I'm still here. Then, she'll get embarrassed and put her phone down.

A female participant, aged 33, commented, "It infuriates me and we fight about it, but it keeps on happening. It's fine at dinner, but he'll use his phone everywhere else." Thus, while strategies were developed, these tended to be successful only in particular contexts and settings with issues persisting in other venues. That being said, the majority of participants felt that smartphones had an overall benefit to their lives and that the costs were manageable as long as issues were addressed.

15.7 A Qualitative Perspective on Technology and Relationships

Despite being an area of substantial interest and in a topic area—gender, sexuality, romance and the family—where qualitative research often thrives, questions regarding the influence of internet technology on romantic relationships has not had sufficient qualitative exploration. Addressing this gap, this study examined how individuals perceive the impact of smartphones and related technology on romance, intimacy, and sex for individuals aged 18–55 in long-term heterosexual relationships. All participants documented smartphones and technology as having a significant impact on the ways in which they negotiate romantic relationships, from the early stages of dating to their everyday practices in long-term relationships. Recognizing a range of benefits of this technology, the key positive for most participants was that smartphones served to keep them in close contact with partners when apart (c.f. Turkle, 2011). However, the primary concern, particularly with smartphones, was that this technology could drive couples apart when they were together—supporting the notion that smartphones can result in "technoference" (McDaniel & Coyne, 2016) that can disrupt relationships. Many participants recognized this quandary, and sought to develop strategies to resolve some of the issues that smartphones caused.

The need for strategies and explicit rules to counter tensions in relationships brought about through smartphones is perhaps unsurprising. Oulasvirta, Rattenbury, Ma, and Raita (2012) show that smartphone use becomes habitual, and that this increases the likelihood of frequent checking of smartphones. As such, explicitly developing strategies to counter such habituated behavior is likely a necessary step to try and relieve some of these tensions. This use of strategies to negotiate smartphone use to avoid tensions is compatible with the trend of individualization, where people frame life experiences within narratives of risk and control (Twenge, 2014).

One dominant theme in the literature regards the risk of smartphone addiction (Ahn & Jung, 2016). Smartphone addiction refers to a lack of control in moderating technology use, to the extent that it has damaging consequences for the user. Some argue this is akin to gambling and compulsive shopping (Choliz, 2010), while others focus more on associated risks, such as use while driving (Salehan & Negahban, 2013). Perhaps because this study adopted an inductive analytic approach, smartphone addiction was not discussed as an issue. Rather, issues with smartphones were discussed in a more mundane way, still recognizing serious issues, and sometimes speaking with regret at the impact they have had, but focusing more on the impact on the relationship rather than classifying such behaviors as signs of excessive dependence.

It is possible that smartphones will impact differently upon couples who are non-monogamous as well as in same-sex relationships (Anderson, 2012). The jealousy described by some participants in this study might be less important for relationships where partners are permitted to engage in sex with other people. However, initial research finds similar patterns in some areas (Macapagal et al., 2016). This is likely attributable to the fact that many of the tensions of smartphone use are not about the *sexual* or *gendered* components of coupled relationships, but about how communication in relationships is affected (both positively and negatively) by technology.

15.8 Conclusion

This research provides important insights regarding the role smartphones and broader communications technology play in couples' lives in the twenty-first century (Turkle, 2011; Twenge, 2014). Participants in this study used smartphones for diverse reasons with a range of benefits: These included increased communication while apart and the offer of emotional support throughout the day and while geographically separated. Participants spoke about the importance of short communications during the day that reminded partners or themselves they were loved. Yet alongside these benefits, tensions related to smartphone use remained. While people were developing strategies to deal with these issues, these only worked in particular contexts and not for all individuals. Thus, while smartphones drew couples together when apart, they also isolated couples when together. Further research exploring this quandary would be a useful endeavor, including study into how such issues may best be resolved and how these experiences may change over the course of a relationship.

References

Ahn, J., & Jung, Y. (2016). The common sense of dependence on smartphone: A comparison between digital natives and digital immigrants. *New Media & Society, 18*(7), 1236–1256.

Anderson, E. (2012). *The monogamy gap: Men, love and the reality of cheating*. New York, NY: Oxford University Press.

Anderson, E., & McCormack, M. (2016). *The changing dynamics of bisexual Men's lives*. New York, NY: Springer.

Baym, N. K. (2010). *Personal connections in the digital age*. Cambridge, UK: Polity.

Beck, U. (1992). *Risk society: Towards a new modernity*. London, UK: Sage.

Beck, U., Giddens, A., & Lash, S. (Eds.). (1994). *Reflexive modernization: Tradition and aesthetics in the modern social order*. Cambridge, UK: Polity Press.

Bergdal, A. R., Kraft, J. M., Andes, K., Carter, M., Hatfield-Timajchy, K., & Hock-Long, L. (2012). Love and hooking up in the new millennium: Communication technology and relationships among urban African American and Puerto Rican young adults. *Journal of Sex Research, 49*(6), 570–582.

Best, J., & Bogle, K. A. (2014). *Kids gone wild: From rainbow parties to sexting, understanding the hype over teen sex*. New York, NY: New York University Press.

Byrne, R., & Findlay, B. (2004). Preference for SMS versus telephone calls in initiating romantic relationships. *Australian Journal of Emerging Technologies and Society, 2*(1), 48–61.

Chaves, M. (1994). Secularization as declining religious authority. *Social Forces, 72*(3), 749–774.

Cherlin, A. J. (2004). The deinstitutionalization of American marriage. *Journal of Marriage and Family, 74*, 102–127.

Choliz, M. (2010). Mobile phone addiction: A point of issue. *Addiction, 105*, 373–374.

Coyne, S. M., Stockdale, L., Busby, D., Iverson, B., & Grant, M. D. (2011). "I luv u :)!": A descriptive study of the media use of individuals in romantic relationships. *Family Relations, 60*, 150–162.

Dir, A. L., Coskunpinar, A., & Cyders, M. A. (2014). A meta-analytic review of the relationship between adolescent risky sexual behavior and impulsivity across gender, age, and race. *Clinical Psychology Review, 34*(7), 551–562.

Döring, N. (2009). The Internet's impact on sexuality: A critical review of 15 years of research. *Computers in Human Behavior, 25*(5), 1089–1101.

Drouin, M., & Landgraff, C. (2012). Texting, sexting, and attachment in college students' romantic relationships. *Computers in Human Behavior, 28*(2), 444–449.

Drouin, M., Vogel, K. N., Surbey, A., & Stills, J. R. (2013). Let's talk about sexting, baby: Computer-mediated sexual behaviors among young adults. *Computers in Human Behavior, 29*(5), A25–A30.

Duran, R. L., Kelly, L., & Rotaru, T. (2011). Mobile phones in romantic relationships and the dialectic of autonomy versus connection. *Communication Quarterly, 59*(1), 19–36.

Fahs, B., Dudy, M. L., & Stage, S. (2014). *The moral panics of sexuality*. Basingstoke, England: Palgrave.

Fine, M., & McClelland, S. (2006). Sexuality education and desire: Still missing after all these years. *Harvard Educational Review, 76*(3), 297–338.

Fukuyama, F. (1999). *The great disruption: Human nature and the reconstitution of social order*. New York, NY: The Free Press.

Giddens, A. (1991). *Modernity and self-identity*. Stanford, CA: Stanford University Press.

Giddens, A. (1992). *The transformation of intimacy: Sexuality, love and eroticism in modern societies*. London, UK: Polity.

Gudelunas, D. (2012). There's an app for that: The uses and gratifications of online social networks for gay men. *Sexuality & Culture, 16*(4), 347–365.

Hertlein, K. M., & Ancheta, K. (2014). Advantages and disadvantages of technology in relationships: Findings from an open-ended survey. *The Qualitative Report, 19*(22), 1–11.

Jin, B., & Peña, J. F. (2010). Mobile communication in romantic relationships: Mobile phone use, relational uncertainty, love, commitment, and attachment styles. *Communication Reports, 23*(1), 39–51.

Jung, Y. (2013). What a smartphone is to me: Understanding user values in using smartphones. *Information Systems Journal, 24*(4), 299–321.

Krasnova, H., Abramova, O., Notter, I., & Baumann, A. (2016). Why phubbing is toxic for your relationship: Understanding the role of smartphone jealousy among "generation Y" users. Paper presented at *Twenty-Forth European Conference on Information Systems*, Istanbul, Turkey.

Lash, S., & Wynne, B. (1992). Introduction to Ulrich Beck's risk society. In U. Beck (Ed.), *The risk society: Towards a new modernity*. London, UK: Sage.

Levin, I. (2004). Living apart together: A new family form. *Current Sociology, 52*(2), 223–240.

Macapagal, K., Coventry, R., Puckett, J. A., Phillips, I. I. G., & Mustanski, B. (2016). Geosocial networking app use among men who have sex with men in serious romantic relationships. *Archives of Sexual Behavior, 45*(6), 1513–1524.

McCormack, M. (2015). *The role of smartphones and technology in sexual and romantic lives*. Durham, NC: Durham University.

McCormack, M., & Wignall, L. (2017). Enjoyment, exploration and education: The consumption of pornography among young men with non-exclusive sexual orientations. *Sociology, 51*(5), 975–991.

McDaniel, B. T., & Coyne, S. M. (2016). "Technoference": The interference of technology in couple relationships and implications for women's personal and relational well-being. *Psychology of Popular Media Culture, 5*(1), 85–98.

Miller-Ott, A. E., Kelly, L., & Duran, R. L. (2012). The effects of cell phone usage rules on satisfaction in romantic relationships. *Communication Quarterly, 60*(1), 17–34.

Mowlabocus, S. (2010). *Gaydar culture: Gay men, technology and embodiment in the digital age*. London, UK: Ashgate.

Mulholland, M. (2013). *Young people and pornography*. Basingstoke, England: Palgrave.

Newmahr, S. (2010). Rethinking kink: Sadomasochism as serious leisure. *Qualitative Sociology, 33*(3), 313–331.

Nodin, N., Carballo Dieguez, A., & Leal, I. M. P. (2013). Sexual use of the internet: Perceived impact on MSM's views of self and others. *New Media & Society, 16*(5), 719–736.

Oulasvirta, A., Rattenbury, T., Ma, L., & Raita, E. (2012). Habits make smartphone use more pervasive. *Personal and Ubiquitous Computing, 16*(1), 105–114.

Pettigrew, J. (2009). Text messaging and connectedness within close interpersonal relationships. *Marriage and Family Review, 45*, 697–716.

Rappleyea, D. L., Taylor, A. C., & Fang, X. (2014). Gender differences and communication technology use among emerging adults in initiation of dating relationships. *Marriage and Family Review, 50*(3), 269–284.

Roberts, J. A., & David, M. E. (2016). My life has become a major distraction from my cell phone: Partner phubbing and relationship satisfaction among romantic partners. *Computers in Human Behavior, 4*(1), 134–141.

Rubin, G. (1984). Thinking sex: Notes for a radical theory of the politics of sexuality. In C. S. Vance (Ed.), *Pleasure and danger* (pp. 267–319). Boston, MA: Routledge and Kegan Paul.

Salehan, M., & Negahban, A. (2013). Social networking on smartphones: When mobile phones become addictive. *Computers in Human Behavior, 29*, 2632–2639.

Sprecher, S. (2009). Relationship initiation and formation on the internet. *Marriage & Family Review, 45*(6–8), 761–781.

Su, H. (2016). Constant connection as the media condition of love: Where bonds become bondage. *Media, Culture & Society, 38*(2), 232–247.

Turkle, S. (2011). *Alone together: Why we expect more from technology and less from each other*. New York, NY: Basic Books.

Twenge, J. M. (2014). *Generation me: Why Today's young Americans are more confident, assertive, entitled – And more miserable than ever before*. London, UK: Atria.

Twenge, J. M., Sherman, R. A., & Wells, B. E. (2015). Changes in American adults' sexual behaviour and attitudes, 1972-2012. *Archives of Sexual Behavior, 44*(8), 2273–2285.

Urquhart, C. (2013) Grounded Theory for Qualitative Research. London: Sage.

Waskul, D. (2003). *Self-games and body-play*. New York, NY: Peter Lang.

Weeks, J. (2007). *The world we have won*. London, UK: Routledge.

Weitzer, R. (2009). Sociology of sex work. *Annual Review of Sociology, 35*, 213–234.

Wignall, L. (2017). The sexual use of a social networking site: The case of pup twitter. *Sociological Research Online, 22*(3), 21–37.

Wignall, L., & McCormack, M. (2017). An exploratory study of a new kink activity: "Pup play". *Archives of Sexual Behavior, 46*(3), 801–811.

Chapter 16
Online Dating: Modern Options of Searching for a Partner and Its Implications for Psychotherapy

Christiane Eichenberg, Jessica Huss, and Cornelia Küsel

16.1 Introduction

Establishing sexual and romantic contacts as well as relationships via the internet or mobile communications has become a normal way of getting to know each other. In the USA, around 30% of those aged between 18 and 29 use dating websites or dating apps (Statista, 2018a). Today, every third couple gets to know each other online (Hogan, Li, & Dutton, 2011). The average number of subscribers worldwide for the online dating app Tinder alone in the second quarter of 2018 is 3,769,000 (Statista, 2018b). A positive attitude toward online dating is moderated by the extent of affinity with the internet and the time spent online, but not by general attitudes toward romantic relationships (Anderson, 2005).

Generally, the internet works via a large number of free offers, although in the area of "online dating" there is a strong willingness to spend money: forecasts predict that online dating platforms will generate revenues of 3.11 billion Euros by 2022 (Statista, 2018c). Hence, it can certainly be stated that romantic love is mixed with economic rationality (Dröge & Voirol, 2011). According to a survey conducted in 2016 (Statista, 2017), 17% of women and 14% of men surveyed would pay between 11 and 25 euros per month for an online partner portal or app if all requested features are available. Many online dating websites offer so-called "premium

---

C. Eichenberg (✉)
Institute of Psychosomatics, Medical Faculty, Sigmund Freud University, Vienna, Austria
e-mail: c.eichenberg@sfu.ac.at

J. Huss
University of Kassel, Kassel, Germany

C. Küsel
Computer Science Department, Bundeswehr University, Munich, Germany
e-mail: cornelia.kuesel@unibw.de

© Springer Nature Switzerland AG 2020
A. Abela et al. (eds.), *Couple Relationships in a Global Context*,
European Family Therapy Association Series,
https://doi.org/10.1007/978-3-030-37712-0_16

memberships" for a monthly fee that offer a broad spectrum of features, while basic memberships are usually very limited in their functionality.

In the psychological online dating research over the past 20 years, various major research topics can be identified, including the types and motives of online dating, the course of online dating and the formation of relationships, as well as advantages and disadvantages of this form of relationship search including corresponding negative trends. The implications of these findings for psychotherapeutic practice and research desiderata will be described.

16.2 Types and Motives of Online Dating

When taking a closer look at online dating services, it is essential to differentiate between diverse types of portals (see also Eichenberg, Huss, & Küsel, 2017): (1) single exchanges, which focus on casual flirting contacts; (2) partner exchanges, which are mostly similar to traditional contact advertisements and where suitable partners are suggested by the provider using algorithms; (3) erotic dating/casual dating portals for nonbinding sex contacts; (4) niche providers, i.e., specialized platforms with the objective of connecting people with specific preferences and needs; and (5) the most current offer of "social dating" (e.g., Tinder), which is usually operated via smartphone and involves the special feature that GPS services display contacts in the user's immediate proximity (location-based real-time dating; Handel & Shklovski, 2012).

Besides regional and national dating apps, there are also worldwide ones. The market for dating apps is large and in some cases not entirely manageable. Hence, there are also websites that regularly select and rate the "best dating apps" and present them in a review (partly sponsored). Many dating apps are commercial and linked to other social networking companies. Very well-known geosocial networking apps, that is, apps that take location into account, are presented below (without a claim to completeness):

- Tinder (https://tinder.com): A geo social networking app whose "swipe" feature allows you to quickly decide whether you like or dislike the proposed profile photo, name, and age. If both sides give a like (swiping to the right), a "match" is created. If the information does not meet the user's expectations, they can swipe to the left to reject the suggestion.
- Bumble (https://bumble.com): This dating app works similarly to Tinder, although if two profiles match the woman must initiate the first contact. Additionally, there is the option to meet new people by using Bumble BFF (Best Friends Forever) or make business contacts with Bumble Bizz. Bumble Boost involves a fee-based premium function that makes it possible to see who likes you, while "matches" can be extended by 24 h.
- PlentyOfFish (https://www.pof.com): One of the oldest and largest dating apps. First, a test must be taken so that the app can suggest people based on the user's given information about preferences and characteristics. PlentyOfFish is free of charge.

- App Hater (https://www.haterdater.com): An alternative to the previous dating apps in which partner suggestions are not based on common preferences but rather dislikes. Further features are similar to other apps, such as Tinder or Bumble. Furthermore, there are "hated things" categories that contain additional funny GIFs and the percentage of users who also do not like the topic, with the main aim of increasing the fun factor.
- Grindr (https://www.grindr.com): The largest geosocial networking app for gay, bi, trans, and queer people, alongside Scruff (https://www.scruff.com) and Jack'd (https://jackdapp.com). However, other dating apps also allow you to specify the preferred gender of a potential date.

The usage of online dating websites is independent of one's income and education. Men between 30 and 50 years of age and young adults between 18 and 22 use online exchanges extensively (Valkenburg & Peter, 2007). In terms of their social integration, users hardly differ from nonusers: they meet friends equally often in their free time and participate just as strongly in the associative life of groups (Brym & Lenton, 2001). Gender differences regarding interaction behavior prove that contact initiations are much more frequent among men than women (Skopek, 2010). However, women are more likedy to ignore a request compared with men (Brym & Lenton, 2001; Fiore, 2004). Generally, there is no correlation between the use of and specific behavioral patterns during online dating and various personality traits (Blackhart, Fitzpatrick, & Williamson, 2014).

The motivations are heterogeneous and have been classified into intrapsychic (leisure time, security/intimacy, self-assurance, control) and interpsychic (communication, flirtation, sex) needs, which may vary depending on gender (Aretz, 2016). A survey of male Grindr users ($N = 92$) showed that 38% of the men use the app to find new sexual partners and 18.5% use it to pass the time when they are bored. They also claimed to use several dating apps simultaneously (Goedel & Duncan, 2015). A survey conducted among $N = 409$ heterosexual students revealed that 39% had already used geosocial networking apps and 60% regularly use them. The main reasons for the usage were for fun and to meet other people (Griffin, Canevello, & McAnulty, 2018). Only a few (4%) said that they used apps to make loose sexual contacts, although the majority (72% of men and 22% of women) were open to meeting sexual partners via apps (ibid.).

There are also online dating sites for singles who want children, such as the German Website https://www.match-patch.de/partnersuche/ or https://www.loveandkids.dk in Denmark. Despite the gender-specific trends, it is also becoming clear that both women and men are moving beyond gender role stereotyped expectation patterns on the internet (Döring, 2000b). In a survey about the motivations of single persons, it was reported that 20% of men also think about starting a family when looking for a partner online. In the case of partner choice, women have a stronger preference for income rather than physical attributes (Hitsch, Hortacsu, & Ariely, 2010).

Interracial dating is also investigated, whereby the findings indicate that, for instance, white heterosexual people are predominantly attracted by other white users' online profiles, including the preferred characteristics matching the expected stereotype (Alhabash, Hales, Baek, & Oh, 2014).

16.3 A Theoretical Framework to Understand Relationships on the Internet

Various theories can be applied regarding the possible effects of the internet on the initiation of relationships. Theories of computer-mediated communication (CvK) are very pertinent (see Döring, 2003 for a review). Likewise, the psychological theories highlighted below offer a helpful conceptual framework (Eichenberg, Huss, & Küsel, 2017; Whitty, 2008).

16.3.1 Disinhibition Effect

The so-called "online disinhibition effect" (Suler, 2004) describes a tendency for users to feel freer on the internet and give in to their impulses more easily than in face-to-face situations due to a weaker social control. Two aspects of this effect are described: due to the lack of physical presence and the associated possibility of behaving anonymously, people on the internet reveal more secrets, private details, or intimate feelings such as fears or shame, i.e., they are emotionally more honest ("benign disinhibition"). This means that the encounter is experienced as if one is meeting an old friend even during the first face-to-face meeting (Huels, 2011). However, the disinhibition effect also promotes harsher antisocial behavior ("toxic disinhibition", see Cyber Crime Abuse, Sect. 16.6 below).

16.3.2 Hyperpersonal Theory

According to the hyperpersonal theory, problems connected to the absence of social references and the presence on the internet can be easily overcome. Walther, Slovacek, and Tidwell (2001) claim that the advantage of CvK is that people can strategically deal with their self-presentation ("time for reflection"), which in the negative case favors the creation of a false or exaggerated self-image. In the more favorable and much more frequent case (Döring, 2003; Heller & Dresing, 2001), it can also support a more honest and authentic self-representation.

16.3.3 Object Relation Theories

Equivalent to the concept of "transitional space" (Winnicott, 2002), the internet can be described as an extension of the individual's intrapsychic world (Braun, 2009). It is a space that neither exists in fantasy nor emerges in its given physical reality. It is rather characterized as a space in which playful-experimental encounters of subjective imagination and the real world imply a potential of development and change. Thus, the internet is a space in which forces that change reality can be discovered, developed, and tested on real things that can be perceived in terms of their still-unknown possibilities. Accordingly, online relationships can be understood and depicted as a liberating experience through the possibility of experimenting with the self-representation. This type of experimenting can be likened to the concept of "trial dealing" put forward by Freud (1945).

16.3.4 Attachment Theory

The different attachment types which are based on the attachment theory (Bowlby, 1940; Slade, 1998) are also relevant for romantic relationships in adulthood (see Hazan & Shaver, 1987) and it can be assumed that these are also applicable to the chosen forms of relationship initiation and development on the internet.

The central uniqueness of intimate relationships established via modern media lies in an accelerated self-disclosure compared with face-to-face situations ("disinhibition effect"). This can result in intensive intimacy in online relationships. Another approach which can be applied to online dating is the relational approach, e.g., the adaption of theories concerning digital partner choice based on Pierre Bourdieu's relational sociology (Schmitz, 2017).

16.4 The Online Dating Itinerary

In the literature, the course of online dating is explained in various ways through ideal-typical steps (for instance, Döring, 2000a, 2010; Aretz, Gansen-Ammann, Mierke, & Musiol, 2017). During the partner search in online contact exchanges, the focus person and the target person gain a first impression of each other before they chat via private networks. Hence, the profile creation is strategically important. Impression management or self-presentation is a classic concept of social psychology that can also be applied to online dating, describing the controlled impression of oneself in other people (Chester & Bretherton, 2007). Klohnen and Mendelsohn (1998) showed that by presenting one's own ideal self (instead of the real self), the perceptions of the potential partner are close to one's own ideal self-conception. On the other hand, interested recipients not only examine the online profile regarding the explicit profile information and whether it is trustworthy, but they also evaluate implicit details about the presented person, such as correct expression and spelling (including in private messages) to draw conclusions about the profile owner (Derlega, Winstead, Wong, & Greenspan, 1987). Therefore, the way in which personality is presented and interpreted in the context of online dating is a very complex and strategic process.

The study by Bruch and Newmann (2018) ascertained that people are more likely to look for people who are more attractive than themselves during online dating. In addition, women and men use different communication strategies depending on the perceived attractiveness, i.e., the more attractive the other person is perceived, the longer the messages/emails will be. These results seem to complement those of impression management in online dating. The search for a more attractive partner is also related to the advantages of online dating, whereby the seekers are more likely to approach "ideals," i.e., more attractive people than themselves. The offense of a potential rejection is less drastic than in "face-to-face" situations, since users simply do not receive an answer or match online in the worst case (see for instance Tinder).

Therefore, one can understand why the users invest more time in the communication with attractive partners. Online dating gives the impression of being able to make new contacts all of the time. Why not try "the best," especially when the costs (low risk of rejection) are so low? Moreover, it would be a great self-affirmation for oneself to find a partner who is more attractive and still wants to start a relationship. More important questions would then arise in terms of the progress and stability of the relationship. In online dating, getting to know each other from "inside out" takes place. When the first photo passes the test, "physical appearance" is not that important compared with the conversation. Nevertheless, physical appearance may once again play a role during the first face-to-face meeting. This all depends on the quality of the relationship that would have been built online.

The further development of the relationship originally initiated via the internet follows a typical sequence. The media change implies that the communication is extended to "rich" media to deliver a more nuanced impression of the potential partner. Characteristically, the first step is to transfer the conversation to private mail or messenger. The contact frequency during this phase is usually very high (e.g., regular message exchange until the early hours of the morning). In comparison with the initial phase of a traditional (offline) love relationship—which is characterized by occasionally going out together—internet love affairs/contacts typically include a more continuous and intense engagement during the initial phase (see also Eichenberg, Huss, & Küsel, 2017). A first critical media interchange is the transition from text-based internet and smartphone communication to telephone calls. Exchanging telephone numbers is a sign of trust. Nervousness and timidity can be felt on the phone. These nonverbal cues are not so apparent on the internet due to the lack of visual and audio interaction. It can be presumed that users often consider the use of the telephone as problematic because the imagined voice during writing is replaced by a real voice. Hence, the first telephone call may be accompanied with a feeling of distance or disappointment for some, while others feel immediately excited by the voice and the intimacy of the exchange and experience the relationship as more familiar.

The first date is the most critical phase in the development of the relationship, because it is crucial in the ultimate decision concerning whether the relationship will be maintained or ended under the motto "Real life gave me too much information." Since an online relationship needs to cope with many critical stages including the change of media, it is deemed sensible not to wait too long for the partner's "reality check." This is because the projections could become so powerful that the individual's expectation of a perfect partner can hardly compete with a real person. Partners tend to rate themselves more positively when the time between online contact and the first date is shorter (Ramirez & Zhang, 2007).

Case study
M. (32) states in her first session that she fell in love with an older man on the internet. They have been chatting until late at night via WhatsApp for 3 months and have been in contact virtually all day. She reports that P. is her "dream man" and that she has never experienced such intensive intimacy and solidarity. He felt the same way about her and now they have got engaged. Although she has such a strong desire, she would be very frightened to get to know P. in real life. She is sure that she would not love him less "face-to-face," although she is afraid that the dream would burst if he were to see her. She would be devastated. All of her hopes were attached to the relationship and at the same time—to please him—she had sent him old photos in which she was significantly slimmer. She says that she could hardly stand the inner tension between the desire for him and the fear of rejection.

M. was taught the special features of relationships initiated on the internet during psychoeducation, which gave her some relief. In the course of therapy, biographical references to her anxious avoidance attachment style when forming relationships were analyzed. In the end, she met P., and she realized that her idea of P. was mainly characterized by projections and idealizations that bore little relation to the real person. She lost interest in the contact and decided to look for a partner in her personal environment.

16.5 The Further Development of a Relationship Initiated Online

The research focuses on how the online initiation of relationships affects their further development, as well as what differences exist in the course of relationships initiated online and offline.

Two hypotheses have been investigated in many studies (see also Eichenberg, Huss, & Küsel, 2017): on the one hand, the "rich-get-richer" hypothesis that extroverted users and those who have many social contacts also experience positive consequences from internet use (see Kraut et al., 2002); and on the other hand, the opposite "social compensation" hypothesis, that is, that introverted users with few social contacts use the internet to compensate for these real deficits (see also Bargh & McKenna, 2004). Numerous studies (e.g., Abbas & Mesch, 2016; Lee, 2009; Valkenburg & Peter, 2007) could prove the rich-get-richer hypothesis in their research work. However, other studies (Poley & Luo, 2012; Stinson & Jeske, 2016) have indicated that the rich-get-richer and social compensation hypotheses are rather less significant concerning online dating, but that social influence—for instance, by peers—has a stronger impact on engaging in online dating.

Utz (2000) proved that online contacts can become stable bonds or friendships. Döring's (2000a) analysis of 109 online experience reports of cyber lovers who documented their relationships showed that most of the relationships initiated on the internet developed well. Wolf, Spinath, and Fuchs (2005) proved by means of a survey study that the use of online partner exchanges can also lead to a serious partnership (30% of men and 33% of women who use an online partner exchange). Another survey by Baker (2004) compared $N = 800$ couples who met online with a control group of the same size. The results show that online couples more commonly married shortly after their first contact. These couples described their marriage as "happy," "harmonious," and they looked optimistically to the future. Current studies show that a partnership initiated via social networks is not exposed to a higher risk of divorce or separation and is considered just as happy as relationships initiated offline (Hall, 2014).

Noor, Djaba, and Enomoto (2016) used literature reviews to ascertain the effects of social networks and dating websites on marriages and divorces in the USA. One question was whether social media has a positive or negative impact on the quality of life during the initiation of new or existing partnerships. The findings show that in countries such as the USA, where many have used social networks (for instance, Facebook, Bumble, and PlentyofFish) the divorce rate increased in the following year. This suggests that social websites increase the possibility of meeting new contacts, although they can also cause jealousy, cheating, or even separations. These findings only apply to the USA and the media-independent fluctuations in marriage and divorce statistics must also be considered.

Modern media not only makes it possible to find a partner but it also simplifies the options for modern forms of living together and supports pluralization in terms of founding a family (Eichenberg, Huss, & Küsel, 2017; Eichenberg & Küsel, 2019).

16.6 Advantages and Risks of Online Dating

Online dating offers specific advantages in contrast to the traditional "real-life" getting to know each other, including geographically and temporally independent partner search, more control of self-representation and people with the same interests being more easily found with the help of concrete selection criteria. Additionally, online dating facilitates and favors the primary initiation of numerous relationships. Online dating also increases self-disclosure due to the lack of physical contact (Eichenberg, 2010). The direct and immediate possibility of deciding whether a suggested partner meets one's own criteria is also an advantage of online dating. Sexual preferences can be lived out or tested without shyness, which can help to reduce uncertainties and build self-confidence (Döring, 2009). Physical advantages include no unwanted pregnancies, no sexually transmitted diseases, and no risk of direct sexual assault.

However, online dating is also associated with disadvantages such as personal security, distrust of the truth of self-representation, and privacy (Griffin et al., 2018). Not only unrealistic expectations due to the potential idealization of the encounter as an "optimal partner" but also the pressure to correspond to a certain image to gain attention are among the potential risks of online dating. For example, a study on the body image of Tinder users showed that they ($N = 102$) have a lower satisfaction with their own body and more often tend to objectify their own body and that of others (Strubel & Petrie, 2017). Online dating also increases the cognitive orientation to assess the partner based on verbal information, which becomes more important and is analyzed more closely due to the lack of multiple sensory channels (Geser & Bühler, 2006). Nonbinding contacts imply the risk that initiated contacts are broken off faster or even completely without giving reasons (see "ghosting" below). Online dating can also support escapist tendencies, vis-à-vis problems that occur in the current partnership which are not dealt with constructively. Instead, a dream or fictitious reality (with the online affair) is built up.

16.7 Negative Trends in the Context of Online Dating

In addition to the risk of being deliberately deceived by the other party due to the special features of internet settings (Lo, Hsieh, & Chiu, 2013), sexual risks are cited as potential dangers (Couch, Liamputtong, & Pitts, 2012), which also exist in offline contacts. Constellations are also mainly organized via the internet. This includes "barebacking" or "riding without a saddle," whereby people search the internet for contacts who will provide unprotected sexual intercourse. For instance, some people look for HIV-infected partners with the aim of deliberately infecting oneself with the virus (see Eichenberg, 2009).

Dangers for specific groups are identified such as cyber-bullying in online dating among young people (Alvarez, 2012; Zweig, Dank, Yahner, & Lachmann, 2013). In this context, the individual protective behavior—especially of women—has also been examined (Cali, Coleman, & Campbell, 2013). The following examples describe various negative trends that may occur in connection with online dating.

Sexting: The sending of private erotic photos was intensively discussed in public, especially regarding dangers such as the violation of individual rights and the unwanted distribution of photos (Martyniuk, Dekker, & Matthiesen, 2013). Sexting can also occur intentionally in the context of online dating, since it is also practiced in the course of getting to know each other to create intimacy. Of course, this is associated with the danger—as with any disclosure of very intimate information—that this intimacy may be abused after separations. The prevalence rates of sexting strongly vary due to the different research methods (Englander & McCoy, 2018), whereby no generalizable statements are possible.

Love scamming: Love scamming (or romance scamming) refers to deception involving payments by pretending to be in love. Persons' feelings are used to get money by using fake profiles, for instance, for a trip to get to know each other. If the victim then pays the money, there is no meeting and it is likely to be postponed again and additional money will be demanded. Only if the victim stops paying money because the suspicion of fraud arises does the contact end and the online profile of the so-called "scammer" disappears (Wahr, 2013; Whitty, 2016).

Case study

R. (52) has been divorced from her husband for several years and the children have already moved out. She has been using Facebook to chat with her friends for a year. She also enjoys surfing on other people's profiles. Around 4 months ago, she was contacted on Facebook by a stranger, a very handsome man, 10 years younger than her and a successful businessman. He complimented her and was very interested in her. He came online in the morning to say "good morning" and when she came home from work there were already lovely messages waiting in her inbox. The man soon confessed his love to her and even though R. did not understand why this man was attracted to her, she enjoyed his attention and fell increasingly in love with him. She wanted to meet him, although the dates never took place due to sudden events in the man's life: his mother became ill, he needed money for her operation, he lost his passport and could not take the plane. R. always helped him out with increasing sums of money. She loved this man and wanted to support him. She happened to see a report on TV about the so-called "love scammer" and she discovered that this man was exhibiting similar behavior patterns that she had witnessed when she was still with her husband.

R. collapsed. She could no longer sleep, cried a lot and was no longer able to work. She criticized herself for falling for this deception and sought psychotherapeutic help. Her traumatic relationship experience with the scammer was treated within trauma therapy.

Ghosting: This describes the sudden disappearance of a person and the end of a relationship by cutting all contact (Freedman, Powell, Le, & Williams, 2018), whereby the ghosted person wonders what might have gone wrong. Collins and Gillath (2012) ascertained that avoidance/withdrawing from contact is the least appropriate method to end a relationship and it is related to attachment avoidance. Ghosting is facilitated by apps and online platforms due to physical distance and is chosen due to boredom, negativity, a need for security, and above all a perceived better alternative (Le Febvre, 2017). Ghosting can occur at any time during online dating, from after a few minutes to a longer period (ibid.).

Internet infidelity: If people living in a partnership secretly use dating apps, this can become a problem in the partnership (Schneider, Weiss, & Samenow, 2012). It is possible to communicate online with another (alternative) partner, which can result in relationship problems, separation or divorce (McDaniel, Drouin, & Cravens, 2017; Vossler, 2016). A study of $N = 338$ married couples/individuals showed that behaviors associated with "internet infidelity" were significantly related to lower relationship satisfaction, higher relationship ambivalence, and lower connectivity (ibid). Hertlein and Blumer (2014) listed seven potential threats that could lead to internet infidelity: anonymity, accessibility, affordability, approximation, acceptability, ambiguity, and accommodation (Vossler, 2016). A review by Vossler

(2016) showed that internet infidelity and associated behavior have a negative impact on couples and families (ibid.). Loss of confidence and in some cases even traumatic effects are described (Cavaglion & Rashty, 2010; Mao & Raguram, 2009).

Online jealousy: Another consequence of sexual interaction on the internet is the problem of "digital jealousy." Thus, information that people can read about their partners in social networks can provoke jealousy (Muise et al., 2009 cited by Aretz, Becher, Casalino, & Bonorden, 2010). However, studies indicate that digital jealousy is not a medium-specific phenomenon, but rather it strongly depends on a person's disposition to jealousy as well as the trust in one's own relationship and relationship commitment. The strong correlation between dispositional and digital jealousy implies that persons with a high tendency toward jealousy also perceive content on the internet as more threatening than persons whose dispositional jealousy is rather low (Aretz et al., 2010). Nowadays, it is a challenge in each partnership to determine as a couple which behaviors are referred to as "cheating" in the context of social media usage.

Cyberstalking: A relative new form of crime in the private sphere is the phenomenon of stalking, which means the obsessive stalking of people paired with harassment and threat, which begins with a narcissistic fantasy of attachment (Hoffmann, 2006). Cyberstalking mainly occurs with ex-partners (Dreßing, Bailer, Anders, Wagner, & Gallas, 2014). The spectrum in which this development manifests itself ranges from invasions of privacy to direct and hidden threats and it finds new forms of expression on the internet. Social networks in particular—from which an enormous amount of private information (such as habits and preferences) emerges—can open up opportunities for perpetrators. In contrast to offline stalking, cyberstalking refers to stalking activities that are carried out using communication devices such as mobile phones or the internet. The peculiarity of these media devices for the stalkers is that they help to disguise their identity and allow them to act largely undetected. Examples of cyberstalking include sending threatening emails, buying and selling articles on the internet under the victim's name, creating homepages under the victim's name, faking a foreign identity on the internet to gain the victim's trust and thus gain personal data and posting internet advertisements in the victim's name or with contact details (Al Mutawa, Bryce, Franqueira, & Marrington, 2016; Bocij & McFarlane, 2002; Lyndon, Bonds-Raacke, & Cratty, 2011). Fox and Tokunaga (2015) highlighted that "Facebook stalking" has nothing in common with criminal stalking but it becomes a problem, especially for the person performing the stalking. This means that after the breakup of partnerships the ex-partner's profile continues to be visited to receive information from his/her life and thus to remain "connected," which ultimately makes the separation process more difficult.

Cybercrime abuse/toxic disinhibition: Toxic disinhibition describes aggressive, offensive, rough, antisocial, and offensive behavior (so-called flaming behaviors) on the internet. Three factors favor this approach, namely anonymity, invisibility, and overall the lack of eye contact (Lapidot-Lefler & Barak, 2012). This behavior can also occur in online dating by suddenly offending, unintentionally sexualizing, or criticizing the appearance in an inappropriate form. Cyber aggression victimization can also happen to intimate partners, whereby aggressive online and offline behaviors can be linked (Marganski & Melander, 2018).

16.8 Conclusion

Online dating is a relatively new area of study, in which investigating the effects on the long-term relationship stability of online-established partnerships is a research gap. In the case of negative trends, further studies are needed to focus on personality traits that are related—for example—to ghosting and whether people with insecure attachment behavior could even initiate a promising partnership through online dating. It should be clarified whether insecure attachment behavior is exacerbated due to the special features of computer-mediated communication. On the one hand, insecure attachment behavior can reinforce fears of relationships due to the more anonymous and less binding communication on the internet. On the other hand, those mentioned aspects can also help people with an insecure attachment behavior to approach potentially intimate partners in a context experienced as individually safe. It would also be helpful to ascertain which people with which motives benefit from online contact and relationship initiation.

More diverse research methods are increasingly being used in online psychological research. To our knowledge, the approach of using *PageRank scores* like in the study by Bruch and Newmann (2018) has not yet been used to analyze online data. Thus, it was ascertained that people look online for a partner who is perceived as more attractive than oneself. However, the ideas of partnerships also depend on culture. Therefore, it has to be examined whether this is also the case in other countries or with people living in rural areas, as well as whether there may be differences between different age groups.

Regarding therapy, the problems associated with modern media use are increasingly becoming a topic of discussion. Therefore, it is also important that psychosocial professionals are familiar with the trends in digital media. At the same time, they should also be informed about the constructive potential of the internet as a place for seeking a relationship.

Internet-associated problems (see Eichenberg & Kühne, 2014) are not genuinely new disturbances, since the use of media does not cause problems in itself, but rather acts as a catalyst. Nevertheless, they have their own peculiarities and dynamics. For example, the perpetrators can act more subtly and above all more anonymously during cyberstalking. The supposed anonymity on the internet can support their criminal actions in the sense that the direct reactions of the victim are not visible to the perpetrators and they can act undetected. This example shows that treatment strategies such as trauma therapy must consider the special dynamics of the internet setting.

Internet addiction in general (Montag & Reuter, 2017; Weinstein & Lejoyeux, 2010) has already been well researched and manuals for its treatment are available (e.g., Wölfling, Jo, Bengesser, Beutel, & Müller, 2012), including research on cybersex addiction in particular (Weinstein, Zolek, Babkin, Cohen, & Lejoyeux, 2015; Wéry & Billieux, 2017). It is now widely agreed that internet addiction is a substance-free addiction, that is, a behavioral addiction (see American Psychiatric Association, 2013 (DSM 5); see also Kuss, Griffiths, & Pontes, 2017). Thus, internet addiction should be treated like substance-related addictions with the exception that normal use is intended after a phase of abstinence. It therefore needs to be examined whether the use of online dating portals and apps can be addictive and how the phenomenon of an "online dating burnout" can be understood as well as psychotherapeutically treated.

Today, we experience patients in psychotherapeutic practice for whom receiving as many messages or "likes" as possible seems to be more important than initiating contacts with whom they subsequently meet in real life. Likewise, the consumer character can be predominant for some: many dates that often remain unique occurred alongside a long-term feeling of loneliness. If patients suffer from this, a more functional approach regarding online partner search should be developed when applying a behavioral therapeutic perspective. From a psychodynamic perspective, a biographical understanding of the dysfunctional partner search on the internet is necessary for the patient. Overall, a connection between internet addiction in general and insecure attachment styles has already been demonstrated (Eichenberg, Schott, Decker, & Sindelar, 2017).

Last but not least, the internet not only offers the option of initiating online partnerships, but it also provides help with partnership problems, for instance, via online counseling and therapy. Psychosocial workers should also be informed about these possibilities as well as corresponding evaluation studies. The US program *OurRelationship* is an online intervention (plus short telephone contacts) that lasts for 8 h based on evaluated couple therapy concepts. In a randomized study with $N = 600$ persons (300 couples), it was shown that the partnership satisfaction significantly improved through the intervention. Other areas (domains of individual functioning) also benefited from the online program, whereby symptoms of depression and anxiety could be reduced, while work performance and life satisfaction were increased (Doss et al., 2016).

References

Abbas, R., & Mesch, G. (2016). Do rich teens get richer? Facebook use and the link between offline and online social capital among Palestinian youth in Israel. *Information, Communication & Society, 21*, 63–79. https://doi.org/10.1080/1369118X.2016.1261168

Al Mutawa, N., Bryce, J., Franqueira, V. N. L., & Marrington, A. (2016). Forensic investigation of cyberstalking cases using Behavioural Evidence Analyses. *Digital Investigation, 16*(Suppl), S96–S103. https://doi.org/10.1016/j.diin.2016.01.012

Alhabash, S., Hales, K., Baek, J., & Oh, H. J. (2014). Effects of race, visual anonymity, and social category salience on online dating outcomes. *Computers in Human Behavior, 35*, 22–32.

Alvarez, A. R. G. (2012). "IH8U": Confronting cyberbullying and exploring the use of *Cybertools* in teen dating relationships. *Journal of Clinical Psychology, 68*, 1205–1215. https://doi.org/10.1002/jclp.21920

American Psychiatric Association. (2013). *Diagnostic and statistical manual of mental disorders (DSM-5)*. Arlington, TX: American Psychiatric Publishing.

Anderson, T. (2005). Relationships among Internet attitudes, Internet use, romantic beliefs, and perceptions of online romantic relationships. *Cyberpsychology & Behavior, 8*(6), 521–531.

Aretz, W. (2016). Match me if you can: Eine explorative Studie zur Beschreibung der Nutzung von Tinder. *Journal of Business and Media Psychology*. Retrieved from http://journal-bmp.de/2015/12/match-me-if-you-can-eine-explorative-studie-zur-beschreibung-der-nutzung-von-tinder/.

Aretz, W., Becher, L., Casalino, A., & Bonorden, C. (2010). Digitale Eifersucht: Die Kehrseite soziale Netzwerke. Eine empirische Untersuchung. *Journal of Business and Media Psychology, 1*, 17–24.

Aretz, W., Gansen-Ammann, D.-N., Mierke, K., & Musiol, A. (2017). Date me if you can: Ein systematischer Überblick über den aktuellen Forschungsstand von Online-Dating. *Zeitschrift für Sexualforschung, 30*, 7–34. https://doi.org/10.1055/s-0043-101465

Baker, A. J. (2004). *Double click: Romance and commitment among online couples*. Cresskill, NJ: Hampton Press Book.

Bargh, J. A., & McKenna, K. Y. A. (2004). The Internet and social life. *Annual Review of Psychology, 55*, 573–590. https://doi.org/10.1146/annurev.psych.55.090902.141922

Blackhart, G. C., Fitzpatrick, J., & Williamson, J. (2014). Dispositional factors predicting use of online dating sites and behaviors related to online dating. *Computers in Human Behavior, 33*, 113–118.

Bocij, P., & McFarlane, L. (2002). Online harassment: Towards a definition of cyberstalking. *Prison Service Journal, 139*, 31–38.

Bowlby, J. (1940). The influence of early environment in the development of neurosis and neurotic character. *International Journal of Psycho-Analysis, XXI*, 1–25.

Braun, C. (2009, June). Gruppenheimat im Cyberspace? *Digitale Medien, Suchtgefährdung, Online-Therapie*. Berliner Institut für Gruppenanalyse BIG (Lecture).

Bruch, E. E., & Newmann, M. E. J. (2018). Aspirational pursuit of mates in online dating markets. *Science Advances, 4*, eaap9815. https://doi.org/10.1126/sciadv.aap9815

Brym, R. J., & Lenton, R. L. (2001). *Love online: A report on digital dating in Canada*. Report. Retrieved from http://projects.chass.utoronto.ca/brym/loveonline.pdf.

Cali, B. E., Coleman, J. M., & Campbell, C. (2013). Stranger danger? Women's self-protection intent and the continuing stigma of online dating. *Cyberpsychology, Behavior, and Social Networking, 16*, 853–857. https://doi.org/10.1089/cyber.2012.0512

Cavaglion, G., & Rashty, E. (2010). Narratives of suffering among Italian female partners of cybersex and cyber-porn dependents. *Sexual Addiction & Compulsivity: The Journal of Treatment & Prevention, 17*, 270–287.

Chester, A., & Bretherton, D. (2007). Impression management and identity online. In A. Joinson, K. McKenna, T. Postems, & U.-D. Reips (Eds.), *The Oxford handbook of internet psychology* (pp. 223–236). Oxford, UK: Oxford University Press.

Collins, T. J., & Gillath, O. (2012). Attachment, breakup strategies, and associated outcomes: The effects of security enhancement on the selection of breakup strategies. *Journal of Research in Personality, 46*, 210–222. https://doi.org/10.1016/j.jrp.2012.01.008

Couch, D., Liamputtong, P., & Pitts, M. (2012). What are the real and perceived risks and dangers of online dating? Perspectives from online daters. *Health, Risk & Society, 14*, 697–714. https://doi.org/10.1080/13698575.2012.720904

Derlega, V., Winstead, B., Wong, P., & Greenspan, M. (1987). Self-disclosure and relationship development: An attributional analysis. In M. E. Roloff & G. R. Miller (Eds.), *Interpersonal processes: New directions in communication research* (pp. 172–187). Thousand Oaks, CA: Sage.

Döring, N. (2000a). Romantische Beziehungen im Netz. In K. Thimm (Ed.), *Soziales im Netz. Sprache, Beziehungen und Kommunikationskulturen im Netz* (pp. 39–70). Opladen: Westdeutscher.

Döring, N. (2000b). Feminist views of Cybersex: Victimization, liberation, and empowerment. *Cyberpsychology & Behavior, 3*, 863–884. https://doi.org/10.1089/10949310050191845

Döring, N. (2003). *Sozialpsychologie des Internet. Die Bedeutung des Internet für Kommunikationsprozesse, Identitäten, soziale Beziehungen und Gruppen im Internet* (2nd ed.). Göttingen: Hogrefe.

Döring, N. (2009). The internet's impact on sexuality: A critical review of 15 years of research. *Computers in Human Behavior, 25*, 1089–1101. https://doi.org/10.1016/j.chb.2009.04.003

Döring, N. (2010). Wie wir Liebes- und Sexualpartner im Internet finden: Der aktuelle Forschungsstand. *Psychosozial, 4*, 33–49.

Doss, B. D., Cicila, L. N., Georgia, E. J., Roddy, M. K., Nowlan, K. M., Benson, L. A., et al. (2016). A randomized controlled trial of the web-based OurRelationship program: Effects on relationship and individual functioning. *Journal of Consulting and Clinical Psychology, 84*, 285–296. https://doi.org/10.1037/ccp000006

Dreßing, H., Bailer, J., Anders, A., Wagner, H., & Gallas, C. (2014). Cyberstalking in a large sample of social network users: prevalence, characteristics, and impact upon victims. *Cyberpsychology, Behavior, and Social Networking, 17*, 61–67. https://doi.org/10.1089/cyber.2012.0231

Dröge, K., & Voirol, O. (2011). Online-dating. Zwischen romantischer Liebe und ökonomischer Rationalität. *Zeitschrift für Familienforschung, 23*(3), 337–357.

Eichenberg, C. (2009). Internetnutzung und Sexualität aus gesundheitspsychologischer Perspektive. In B. U. Stetina & I. Kryspin-Exner (Eds.), *Gesundheit und Neue Medien. Psychologische Aspekte der Interaktion mit Informations- und Kommunikationstechnologien* (pp. 85–111). Wien: Springer.

Eichenberg, C. (2010). Zusammen – getrennt: Paarbeziehungen im Internet aus medienpsychologischer und psychodynamischer Perspektive. In H. G. Soeffner (Ed.), *Unsichere Zeiten. Herausforderungen gesellschaftlicher Transformationen. Verhandlungen des 34. Kongresses der Deutschen Gesellschaft für Soziologie in Jena 2008 (CD-ROM)*. Wiesbaden: VS Verlag.

Eichenberg, C., Huss, J., & Küsel, C. (2017). From online dating to online divorce: An overview of family relationships shaped through digital media. *Contemporary Family Therapy, 39*, 249–260. https://doi.org/10.1007/s10591-017-9434-x

Eichenberg, C., & Kühne. (2014). *Einführung Onlineberatung und –therapie*. München: Reinhardt UTB.

Eichenberg, C., & Küsel, C. (2019). Kinderwunsch und Internet. *Psychotherapeut, 64*(2), 134–142.

Eichenberg, C., Schott, M., Decker, O., & Sindelar, B. (2017). Attachment style and internet addiction: An online survey. *Journal of Medical Internet Research, 19*, e170. https://doi.org/10.2196/jmir.6694

Englander, E., & McCoy, M. (2018). Sexting – Prevalence, age, sex, and outcomes. *JAMA Pediatrics, 172*, 317–318. https://doi.org/10.1001/jamapediatrics.2017.5682

Fiore, A. T. (2004). *Romantic regressions: An analysis of behavior in online dating systems*. (S.M. thesis, Massachusetts Institute of Technology).

Fox, J., & Tokunaga, R. S. (2015). Romantic partner monitoring after breakups: Attachment, dependence, distress, and post-dissolution online surveillance via social networking sites. *Cyberpsychology, Behavior, and Social Networking, 18*, 491–498. https://doi.org/10.1089/cyber.2015.0123

Freedman, G., Powell, D. N., Le, B., & Williams, K. D. (2018). Ghosting and destiny. Implicit theories of relationships predict beliefs about ghosting. *Journal of Social and Personal Relationships*. https://doi.org/10.1177/0265407517748791

Freud, S. (1945). *Formulierungen über zwei Prinzipien des psychischen Geschehens. Gesammelte Werke (VIII)*. London, UK: Imago.

Geser, H., & Bühler, E. (2006). *Partnerwahl online*. Retrieved from http://socio.ch/intcom/t_hgeser15.htm.
Goedel, W. C., & Duncan, D. T. (2015). Geosocial-networking app usage patterns of gay, bisexual, and other men who have sex with men: Survey among users of Grindr, a mobile dating app. *JMIR Public Health and Surveillance, 1*, e4. https://doi.org/10.2196/publichealth.4353
Griffin, M., Canevello, A., & McAnulty, R. D. (2018). Motives and concerns associated with Geosocial Networking App usage: An exploratory study among heterosexual college students in den United States. *Cyberpsychology, Behavior, and Social Networking, 21*, 268–275. https://doi.org/10.1089/cyber.2017.0309
Hall, J. A. (2014). First comes social networking, then comes marriage? Characteristics of Americans married 2005 – 2012 who met through social networking sites. *Cyberpsychology, Behavior, and Social Networking, 17*, 322–326. https://doi.org/10.1089/cyber.2013.0408
Handel, M. J., & Shklovski, I. (2012). Disclosure, ambiguity and risk reduction in real-time dating sites. In *GROUP '12 Proceedings of the 17th ACM International Conference on Supporting Group Work* (pp. 175–178). https://doi.org/10.1145/2389176.2389203.
Hazan, C., & Shaver, P. (1987). Romantic love conceptualized as an attachment process. *Journal of Personality and Social Psychology, 52*, 511–524.
Heller, J., & Dresing, T. (2001). Chat - Kommunikationsmedium mit Entwicklungspotential. In R. Bader, W. Schindler, & B. Eckmann (Eds.), *Bildung in virtuellen Welten - Praxis und Theorieaußerschulischer Bildung mit Internet und Computer* (pp. 83–90). Frankfurt, Germany: Gemeinschaftswerk der Evangelischen Publizistik.
Hertlein, K. M., & Blumer, L. C. (2014). *The couple and family technology framework: Intimate relationships in a digital age*. New York, NY: Routledge.
Hitsch, G. J., Hortacsu, A., & Ariely, D. (2010). What makes you click? – Mate preferences in online-dating. *Quantitative Marketing and Economics, 8*(4), 393–427.
Hoffmann, J. (2006). *Stalking*. Heidelberg, Germany: Springer.
Hogan, B. J., Li, N., & Dutton, W. H. (2011). *A global shift in the social relationships of networked individuals: meeting and dating online comes of age*. Oxford, UK: Oxford Internet Institute/University of Oxford.
Huels, D. J. (2011). Beginning romantic relationships online: A phenomenological examination of Internet couples. *Dissertation Abstracts International: Section B: The Sciences and Engineering, 72*(5-B), 3135.
Klohnen, E. C., & Mendelsohn, G. A. (1998). Partner selection for personality characteristics: A couple-centered approach. *Personality & Social Psychology Bulletin, 24*(3), 268.
Kraut, R., Kiesler, S., Boneva, B., Cummings, J., Helgeson, V., & Crawford, A. (2002). Internet paradox revisited. *Journal of Social Issues, 58*, 49–74.
Kuss, D. J., Griffiths, M. D., & Pontes, H. M. (2017). Chaos and confusion in DSM-5 diagnosis of Internet gaming disorders: Issues, concerns, and recommendations for clarity in the field. *Journal of Behavioral Addictions, 6*, 103–109. https://doi.org/10.1556/2006.5.2016.062
Lapidot-Lefler, N., & Barak, A. (2012). Effects of anonymity, invisibility, and lack of eye-contact on online toxic disinhibition. *Computers in Human Behavior, 28*, 434–443. https://doi.org/10.1016/j.chb.2011.10.014
Le Febvre, L. E. (2017). Phantom lovers. Ghosting as a relationship dissolution strategy in the technological age. In N. M. Punyanunt-Carter & J. S. Wrench (Eds.), *The impact of social media in modern romantic relationships* (pp. 219–236). Lexington: Lanham, MD.
Lee, S. J. (2009). Online communication and adolescent social ties: Who benefits more from Internet use? *Journal of Computer-Mediated Communication, 14*, 509–531. https://doi.org/10.1111/j.1083-6101.2009.01451.x
Lo, S.-H., Hsieh, A.-Y., & Chiu, Y.-P. (2013). Contradictory deceptive behavior in online-dating. *Computers in Human Behavior, 29*, 1755–1762. https://doi.org/10.1016/j.chb.2013.02.010
Lyndon, A., Bonds-Raacke, J., & Cratty, A. D. (2011). College students' Facebook stalking of ex-partners. *Cyberpsychology, Behavior, and Social Networking, 14*(12), 711–716.
Mao, A., & Raguram, A. (2009). Online infidelity: The new challenge to marriages. *Indian Journal of Psychiatry, 51*(4), 302–304.

Marganski, A., & Melander, L. (2018). Intimate partner violence victimization in the cyber and real world: Examining the extent of cyber aggression experiences and its association With in-person dating violence. *Journal of Interpersonal Violence, 33*, 1071–1095. https://doi.org/10.1177/0886260515614283

Martyniuk, U., Dekker, A., & Matthiesen, S. (2013). Sexuelle Interaktionen von Jugendlichen im Internet. *Medien & Kommunikationswissenschaft, 61*, 327–344. https://doi.org/10.5771/1615-634x-2013-3-27

McDaniel, B. T., Drouin, M., & Cravens, J. (2017). Do you have anything to hide? Infidelity-related behaviors on social media sites and marital satisfaction. *Computers in Human Behavior, 66*, 88–95. https://doi.org/10.1016/j.chb.2016.09.031

Montag, C., & Reuter, M. (2017). *Internet addiction. Neuroscientific approaches and therapeutical implications including smartphone addiction.* Cham, Switzerland: Springer.

Noor, S. A., Djaba, T., & Enomoto, C. E. (2016). The role of social networking websites: Do they connect people through marriage or are they responsible for divorce? *Journal of International Social Issues, 4*(1), 40–49.

Poley, M. E., & Luo, S. (2012). Social compensation or rich-get-richer? The role of social competence in college students' use of the Internet to find a partner. *Computers in Human Behavior, 28*, 414–419. https://doi.org/10.1016/j.chb.2011.10.012

Ramirez, A., Jr., & Zhang, S. (2007). When online meets offline: The effect of modality switching on relational communication. *Communication Monographs, 74*, 287–310. https://doi.org/10.1080/03637750701543493

Schmitz, A. (2017). *The structure of digital partner choice. A Bourdieusian perspective.* Cham, Switzerland: Springer.

Schneider, J. P., Weiss, R., & Samenow, C. (2012). Is it really cheating? Understanding the emotional reactions and clinical treatment of spouses and partners affected by cybersex infidelity. *Sexual Addiction & Compulsivity: The Journal of Treatment & Prevention, 19*, 123–139.

Skopek, J. (2010). *Partnerwahl im Internet - Eine quantitative Analyse von Strukturen und Prozessen der Online-Partnersuche* (Dissertation University Bamberg).

Slade, A. (1998). Attachment theory and research: Implications for the theory and practice of Individual psychotherapy with adults. In J. Cassidy & P. Shaver (Eds.), *The handbook of theory and research*. New York, NY: Guilford Press.

Statista. (2017). *Wenn ein Partnerportal bzw. eine Dating-App alle Leistungen erfüllen würde, die Ihnen wichtig sind, was wären Sie dann bereit im Monat für eine Mitgliedschaft zu bezahlen?* Retrieved from https://de.statista.com/statistik/daten/studie/666188/umfrage/umfrage-zu-der-zahlungsbereitschaft-fuer-partnerportale-und-dating-apps-in-deutschland-nach-geschlecht/.

Statista. (2018a). *Share of internet users in the United States who have used online dating sites or apps as of April 2017, by age group.* Retrieved from https://www.statista.com/statistics/706499/us-adults-online-dating-site-app-by-age/.

Statista. (2018b). *Durchschnittliche Anzahl an Abonnenten von Tinder weltweit vom 1. Quartal 2015 bis zum 2. Quartal 2018 (in 1.000).* Retrieved from https://de.statista.com/statistik/daten/studie/806485/umfrage/abonnenten-von-tinder-weltweit/.

Statista. (2018c). *Prognose zum Umsatz im Markt für Online-Partnervermittlungen weltweit für das Jahr 2022.* Retrieved from https://de.statista.com/themen/885/online-dating/.

Stinson, S., & Jeske, D. (2016). Exploring online dating preferences in line with the "social compensation" and "rich-get-richer hypothesis". *International Journal of Cyber Behavior, Psychology and Learning, 6*, 75–87. https://doi.org/10.4018/IJCBPL.2016100106

Strubel, J., & Petrie, T. A. (2017). Love me Tinder: Body image and psychosocial functioning among men and women. *Body Image, 21*, 34–38. https://doi.org/10.1016/j.bodyim.2017.02.006

Suler, J. (2004). The online disinhibition effect. *Cyberpsychology and Behavior, 7*(3), 321–326.

Utz, S. (2000). Social information processing in MUDs: The development of friendships in virtual worlds. *Journal of Online Behavior, 1*(1). Retrieved from http://www.behavior.net/JOB/v1n1/utz.html

Valkenburg, P. M., & Peter, J. (2007). Who visits online dating sites? Exploring some characteristics of online daters. *Cyberpsychology and Behavior, 10*, 849–852. https://doi.org/10.1089/cpb.2007.9941

Vossler, A. (2016). Internet infidelity 10 years on: A critical review of the literature. *The Family Journal: Counseling and Therapy for Couples and Families, 24*, 359–366. https://doi.org/10.1177/1066480716663191

Wahr, D. (2013). *Liebe auf Anzahlung. Vorschussbetrug und Internet-Scam*. Books on Demand.

Walther, J. B., Slovacek, C. L., & Tidwell, L. C. (2001). Is a picture worth a thousand words? Photographic images in long-term and short-term computer-mediated communication. *Communication Research, 28*, 105–134. https://doi.org/10.1177/009365001028001004

Weinstein, A., & Lejoyeux, M. (2010). Internet addiction or excessive Internet use. *The American Journal of Drug and Alcohol Abuse, 36*(5), 277–283.

Weinstein, A. M., Zolek, R., Babkin, A., Cohen, K., & Lejoyeux, M. (2015). Factors predicting cybersex use and difficulties in forming intimate relationships among male and female users of cybersex. *Frontiers in Psychiatry, 6*. https://doi.org/10.3389/fpsyt.2015.00054. Retrieved from http://journal.frontiersin.org/article/10.3389/fpsyt.2015.00054/full

Wéry, A., & Billieux, J. (2017). Problematic cybersex: Conceptualization, assessment, and treatment. *Addictive Behaviors, 64*, 238–246. https://doi.org/10.1016/j.addbeh.2015.11.007

Whitty, M. T. (2008). Revealing the 'real' me, searching for the 'actual' you: Presentations of self on an internet dating site. *Computers in Human Behavior, 24*, 1707–1723. https://doi.org/10.1111/j.1752-0606.2008.00088.x

Whitty, M. T. (2016). Do you love me? Psychological characteristics of romance scam victims. *Cyberpsychology, Behavior, and Social Networking, ahead of print*. https://doi.org/10.1089/cyber.2016.0729

Winnicott, D. W. (2002). *Vom Spiel zur Kreativität*. Stuttgart, Germany: Klett-Cotta.

Wolf, H., Spinath, F. M., & Fuchs, C. (2005). Kontaktsuche im Internet: Erfolgsfaktoren und die Rolle der Persönlichkeit. In K.-H. Renner, A. Schütz, & F. Machilek (Eds.), *Internet und Persönlichkeit* (pp. 205–219). Göttingen, Germany: Hogrefe.

Wölfling, K., Jo, C., Bengesser, I., Beutel, M., & Müller, K. (2012). *Computerspiel- und Internetsucht. Ein kognitiv-behaviorales Behandlungsmanual*. Stuttgart, Germany: Kohlhammer.

Zweig, J. M., Dank, M., Yahner, J., & Lachmann, P. (2013). The rate of cyber dating abuse among teens and how it relates to other forms of teen dating violence. *Journal of Youth and Adolescence, 42*(7), 1063–1077. https://doi.org/10.1007/s10964-013-9922-8

Chapter 17
Fidelity, Infidelity, and Non-monogamy

Tina Timm and Adrian Blow

17.1 Introduction

Intimate relationships have the power to be the greatest source of safety, comfort, and security between two people, but consequently, also have the power to be the greatest source of pain if those needs are not met or if trust is broken. Research on adult attachment has explored how one's attachment style, established in infancy, continues to affect how adults partner and their ability to be emotionally and physically connected. Referred to as an "internal working model," men and women come into adulthood with an unconscious template of what they can expect in a relationship. Someone whose emotional and physical needs were met early in life by responsive caregivers typically go forward into the world expecting this will continue, and when they partner, they trust that if they are vulnerable or need their partner, then he or she will provide that comfort.

Unfortunately, the opposite is also true. Individuals who learned that caregivers do not always provide comfort and safety when needed will move into adulthood being too delf-protective or ambivalent to tolerate closeness. This makes sense if an individual's internal template says, "Don't bother trusting others, they will just hurt you." Consequently, they will have trouble feeling safe even with the most responsive partner. Finding someone who is not emotionally responsive is perhaps easier because at least it fits with what one has come to expect. In a review of the literature on adult attachment and sexuality, Stefanou and McCabe (2012) found that higher

---

T. Timm (✉)
School of Social Work, Michigan State University, East Lansing, MI, USA
e-mail: timmt@msu.edu

A. Blow
Department of Human Development and Family Studies, Michigan State University, East Lansing, MI, USA
e-mail: blowa@msu.edu

levels of anxious and avoidant attachment were related to less satisfying sexual relationships, higher levels of sexual dysfunction, and different sexual intercourse frequencies and motivations for sex. Any one of these variables may have implications for why people have affairs.

Humans are wired to be relational (Johnson, 2004). At the most primitive level, people seek connection. Even when the protective part of them firmly believes that people are not to be trusted and that relationships are not needed, there is another part of them that still craves this closeness. This push and pull of human relationships takes many different forms, but ultimately is at the core of fidelity and infidelity.

What is fidelity? What is infidelity? Many people view this answer in a simplistic way—fidelity is being sexually faithful to your partner, infidelity is not. However, as any relationship clinician can tell you, it is not that simple. The definition and meaning of these words is individual to each person and each relationship. Fidelity is actually defined as "faithfulness to a *person, cause, or belief*, demonstrated by continuing loyalty and support" (Oxford Dictionary, 2019). This broad definition very quickly challenges one of the commonly assumed beliefs about fidelity, most notably, the assumption of monogamy. A person can be *faithful* to a partner, but that does not necessarily mean being *sexually exclusive*. Non-monogamy is not infidelity if each person is faithful to the relational agreement. They are still being loyal to their partner.

In some countries, men having multiple wives is common, and while there are many potential problems with polygamy, many live satisfying lives in these relationships, and these are not considered betrayals. Individuals may also live in polyamorous relationships or open relationships, and infidelity is not an issue. These relationships involve engaging in sexual relationships outside of the primary relationship, but with the *consent* of all individuals involved. The term consent is key here. The bottom line is that infidelity is relationally defined and the standards for fidelity may vary across relationships. By this we mean that each relationship and by extension, each individual in each relationship, has beliefs that determine whether infidelity is the issue or not. As clinicians, we must move away from narrow, perhaps value laden, definitions of fidelity and assumptions to help clients to explore this complex relational landscape.

One definition of infidelity provided by Blow and Hartnett (2005) suggests that "Infidelity is a sexual and/or emotional act engaged in by one person within a committed relationship, where such an act occurs outside of the primary relationship and constitutes a breach of trust and/or violation of agreed-upon norms (overt and covert) by one or both individuals in that relationship in relation to romantic/emotional or sexual exclusivity" (pp. 191–192). This definition suggests that infidelity can be sexual, emotional, or both and that an act could be considered infidelity when the agreed upon rules of a relationship are breached. Some of these rules are established by cultural norms and others are established by explicit conversations and agreements. Sexual acts can range from sexual intercourse to passionate kissing. Even more benign types of touch, such as hugging or sitting too closely can be considered a betrayal by some. Emotional involvement brings in another complicated variable. In this age of technology, the authors have worked with couples in which friending someone of the opposite sex on social media was considered to be infidelity. On the extremes of the definition, some infidelity beliefs can lead to a stifled relationship and controlling behaviors that are indicative of other problems in the relationship.

From this standpoint, establishing and communicating about boundaries is crucial in relationships. Often these boundaries are unspoken until there is a breach. For example, I (AB) worked with a couple who had never had an explicit conversation about pornography use. One day, the wife walked into the bedroom and her husband was viewing pornography. They presented in therapy because she had a large emotional reaction to this discovery. Therapy consisted of them having numerous conversations about the role of pornography in their relationship. It absolutely felt like a betrayal for her that he was engaging in this behavior. Other couples are open to pornography use, although there may be unspoken rules about what kind. For example, AB was supervising a case in which the spouse was fine with her partner watching pornography, but felt betrayed when she discovered her partner watching same sex male porn. This constituted a betrayal to her even though they had not explicitly discussed this type of pornography.

17.2 Desire, Infidelity, and Non-monogamy

The literature suggests many reasons for infidelity or non-monogamy. One of the complicated factors is that of desire both at the individual and relational level. Clinicians have long struggled with this as a concept and it was not until the 1970s that Helen Singer Kaplan even identified it as a distinct phase of the sexual response cycle (Kaplan, 1979). What became apparent in therapy was that some individuals were coming to seek help, not because of problems with the physical arousal or the ability to orgasm, but rather because someone did not desire to even try to get to those phases. Kaplan hypothesized that people needed to want to have sex before actually engaging in sexual activity and the concept of "inhibited sexual desire" (ISD) was added as a distinct sexual problem.

This then led to another complicated issue, as to what is considered a normal level of sexual desire. Can someone have too little? Can someone have too much? Is having no desire a problem? Is thinking about and wanting sex all the time a problem? For many years having no desire, or being asexual, was pathologized. There is a move toward more acceptance of asexuality as a viable option, and that does not mean anything is wrong with the person. Some even encourage it to be seen as a perfectly acceptable way to live, whether by choice, for example, Catholic Priests, or just psychologically not caring to ever be sexual (though careful assessment should be done in these cases to rule out sexual anxiety or phobia). There are many asexual people who are living perfectly happy lives, many in long-term satisfying relationships, sometimes with other people who also have low to no desire or just an acceptance of the partner as a non-sexual person.

However, the relationships that come to therapy are usually ones where there is relational discord as a result of the low desire, often referred to as a "desire discrepancy." This term is also used when both partners have what seems to be "normal" levels of desire. As a therapist we often get the question, "Am I normal?" or more commonly asked by the higher desire partner, "Can you fix my partner?" The high desire person thinks there is something wrong with the lower desire person and vice versa. Their fights often devolve into various forms of pathologizing language—one is "frigid," while the other is a "sex addict." The truth is that there is not necessarily anything "wrong" with either of them, they are just different. However, these differences can lead to infidelity and/or perhaps the negotiation of a non-monogamous relationship.

Historically, the sexual response cycle was primarily a linear model. First, you wanted to have sex (desire), then as a result of that, and subsequent physical engagement with a partner, the body would respond in positive ways (arousal). If arousal was sufficient and stimulation maintained, orgasm might result. Again, relying on clinical observation, an interesting phenomenon revealed itself—that for women in particular, the desire and arousal phases of the model were very much intertwined and in some cases reversed (Basson, 2005). They might not have any desire to have sex, but if they got aroused first, the desire would follow. Mitchell, Wellings, and Graham's research (Mitchell, Wellings, & Graham, 2014) has continued to explore how desire and arousal are blurred, hereby supporting the merging of female sexual arousal disorder and hyposexual desire disorder into one diagnostic category. Sharing this research can be a psychoeducational intervention to help couples lead more satisfying sexual lives. If couples wait around, or psychologically require the low desire partner to feel desire before engaging in sexual activity, they may be waiting a very long time. However, if they are willing to reverse that, and make a behavioral choice to be sexual, desire can potentially be awakened.

Lack of communication around sexual issues, including desire discrepancies, is a common reason for infidelity or a move to non-monogamy. David Schnarch (1991) would argue that a lack of differentiation is what prohibits couples from negotiating this issue. It is therefore "easier" to just have an affair, than to tell your partner you are unhappy or to work through the discomfort of negotiating a different sexual relationship. Or, perhaps one has communicated about one's unhappiness, but this has not resulted in any change in behavior, and instead of continuing to fight, an individual may choose to have an affair. Others who are more differentiated and can hold on to themselves will continue to advocate for their needs. In the face of no response, they may ask for a consensual non-monogamous relationship. The following case illustrates this scenario.

Randy and Lori had been married for over 30 years. Sexual activity had been steadily decreasing for years and despite Lori bringing up the topic many times, she felt unheard and unloved at Randy's lack of willingness to make any effort to improve their sex life. It was only when he discovered that Lori was having an affair with a co-worker that he fully realized how seriously unhappy she was. They came in to therapy in crisis, both not sure where to go from this point. Randy's lack of desire was clearly systemic. There were a combination of factors at play; (1) He had been in a high stress job for many years and had turned to eating and alcohol to soothe this, (2) The unhealthy eating, and subsequent weight gain, led to high blood pressure that needed to be controlled with medication, (3) The medication affected his ability to get erections and when that started, he was too embarrassed to talk to Lori and just withdrew, never initiating and finding excuses to not have sex when she asked.

Over time, this combination of factors took his sexual desire to basically zero. During therapy it became clear that there was a deep love and affection for each other and both of them wanted to stay married. However, the difference in sexual desire continued to be a problem and Lori also revealed that the weight gain had made her repulsed by his body. He was willing to work on losing weight, but Lori was skeptical as he had said this many times before. Essentially they had three options: (1) Leave things as they currently were, (2) Work on restoring a sexual relationship, or (3) Open up the relationship and negotiate a consensual non-monogamous agreement. Lori was clear that she could not do #1. Despite her love for Randy, she did not want to live a life as a nonsexual person. Lori was willing to do #2 at some point, but not willing to wait to see if in fact he would follow through with the weight loss and neither were sure he could/would regain his erectile functioning. She was interested in talking about #3, but hesitant because she did not want the relationship to end. On Randy's part, he would be comfortable with #1, but Lori had eliminated this as a viable option. He was open to #2, but skeptical that his desire would ever match hers and empathic that she had brought this up for many years and he had not done anything to address it. He was more interested in physical affection than overt sexual activities. Regarding #3, the thought was anxiety-provoking but he felt that with enough safeguards in place, and assurance that she wanted to stay married, he would consider it.

Over the course of 6 weeks, a consensual non-monogamous relationship was discussed and a relational contract established. This painful relational crucible was hard, but necessary to push their marriage to the point of complete honesty and truthfulness about what they needed. Both of them agreed that it was better than the hurt and betrayal that resulted from the discovery of the secret affair.

In cases like this, it is essential for the clinician to examine their own biases and beliefs around monogamy while keeping a careful eye to the power dynamics in the relationship (Timm, 2018). Monogamy has been, and continues to be the socially constructed norm of what a relationship "should" be. Many could argue that we live in a monogamist society that actively discriminates against individuals and couples who choose non-monogamy. The concept of client self-determination is essential to clinical work related to this issue.

However, that does not mean that consensual non-monogamy should be embraced in all situations. All relationships have power dynamics, both emotional and contextual. While everyone theoretically has a right to say no to their partner who proposes a consensual non-monogamous relationship, in reality that may not be the case, for instance, where the person who does not want the non-monogamous relationship is not emotionally strong enough or is financially dependent in such a way that they do not feel like they actually have a choice. The more powerful person in the relationship can exploit this for their gain to the detriment of his/her partner. One of the recommendations for determining this is to meet individually with each partner to assess for violence, abuse, or other types of control (financial, social, emotional) and determine if they are truly able to consent. If there are situations where the clinician does not feel the partner legitimately has the ability to say no, this must be skillfully taken back to the couple therapy. As a clinician, the most important word to embrace is that it is *consensual* non-monogamy. It is not ethical practice to support a therapeutic intervention where consent is not forthcoming from both partners. It requires strong therapeutic alliances with both partners and sustained communication to address these issues and sort out what would constitute legitimate consent.

In the case of Randy and Lori, issues of power and consent were thoroughly explored. Both of them were financially viable independently and reported being able (and willing) to leave the relationship if they felt their values or emotional well-being were being compromised. What made this couple a good candidate for consensual non-monogamy is their deep love for each other, unwavering desire to stay married, excellent communication skills, and willingness to develop a plan that made each of them feel safe emotionally. Once the agreement was reached, I reiterated that either of them could ask for a renegotiation of the contract if something was not working well. They could do this on their own, or come back to see me. When we ended our initial work, we set up an appointment for a 3 month follow-up to see how it was going. At that session, I (TT) met both together and individually. This strategy continues to give ample opportunity for the partner who did not initially ask for the non-monogamous relationship to share how it is going without the influence of having their partner in the room. It is essential that consent be an ongoing process rather than just something that is given at the beginning. In this case, things continued to go well at the 3 month follow-up and I have not heard from them again.

There are theoretical differences in thinking about desire and also a prevailing relational myth. The prolific work of John Gottman has established what he calls the Sound Marital House (Gottman, 1999). This model includes a number of things, including, knowing each other's world, fondness, turning toward each other, maintaining a positive perspective, managing conflict, making dreams come true, and creating a shared meaning. Likewise, Susan Johnson's work on Emotionally Focused Couples therapy (EFT) is attachment based, with the goal of helping the couples to become a secure base for each other (Johnson, 2004). These two models are widely respected, but clinically sometimes an emotionally safe relationship is also one that is devoid of passion. The best friend model of relationships can at times end up being highly non-sexual. Esther Perel's (2007, 2017) work addresses this issue directly. Perhaps relationships need a little mystery to foster desire. Maybe knowing everything about your partner is a version of enmeshment that actually decreases desire. As a sex therapist, I (TT) often get referrals from local couples' therapists who have done excellent work at getting a couple's relationship to a healthy place. They can communicate more effectively, they like spending time together again, and have learned how to be there for each other emotionally. The therapist thought that once these elements were in place, that a healthy sexual relationship would be the natural outcome, and for some couples it is. However, for others, they will present saying, "We get along really well, but it is like we're roommates." The desire and passion did not actually flow out of an improved relationship.

In part this may be that in order to maintain a safe relationship, partners do not reveal themselves. Intimacy is hard. When you love deeply, there is a lot to lose if you are rejected. Some affairs are a direct result of the inability of couples to be vulnerable around what they really want sexually. People are afraid to reveal fantasies for fear that their partner will think they are weird, or a pervert. If a person takes these desires and acts them out with an affair partner, it is less risky. In this day and age, it is easy to screen for openness to a wide range of behaviors online. If you like bondage, it is easy to find someone on the internet who likes that too. If you try it once with that person and it does not work out, you never have to see them again. There is very little to risk emotionally. Contrast this to asking your partner to "tie you up" if you have never done that before. There are a wide range of reactions you could get, some of which could be positive, but the risk of it being negative makes people not even ask. It can also explain why some men experience situational erectile dysfunction—they can achieve and maintain erections with a prostitute for example, but not with their primary partner. With less intimacy they do not have to be emotionally vulnerable.

One of the many things that make the treatment of affairs so difficult is how varied the reasons or motivations are for having the affair. While there are many different ways to organize types of affairs, Williams (2017) proposes five categories of affairs; impulse, proximity, avoidant, addiction, and stage of life affairs. *Impulse affairs* are typically brief, unplanned encounters, sometimes referred to as "opportunistic" affairs. The focus is largely on sex, not a relationship and it is not uncommon for it to involve alcohol. One-night stands are a classic example of this type of affair. *Proximity affairs* are ones that happen as a result of spending a lot of time with someone who you may have common interests. The mutual fondness can become a slippery slope, leading to a loosening of boundaries and almost "accidental" development of attraction. This type can easily happen with colleagues and close friends. *Avoidant affairs* are the classic type where the person is unhappy in the primary relationship and instead of facing it head on, they avoid it by turning to another person. Avoidance fosters an emotional void that clearly makes someone more susceptible to anyone else in his/her environment who shows interest. Some people consequently "explore" other relationships to potentially find what is missing. This can include sexual identity affairs among couples that have ongoing conflict that has not been resolved. *Addiction affairs*, sometimes called sexual compulsivity, serial philandering, or out of control sexual behaviors, are typically people who feel inadequate in some way and use sex to feel better. The term addiction is controversial, but this term refers to people who appear to lack control of their sexual behaviors in relation to fidelity. People in this category often have narcissistic tendencies and rationalize their sexual needs. The behaviors and relationships vary widely and can have substantial, relational, financial, and sometimes legal consequences. The last category is *stage of life affairs*. These are affairs that happen during or because of being in a transitional stage of life. They can flow from an existential crisis, for example being disillusioned with life and wanting to feel more fulfilled. These individuals may finally have resources to experience a life they could not have had before. They may long for a high school sweetheart or an old flame because they are feeling the effects of aging.

17.3 Sexual Communication

One of the most common complaints of couples seeking help is "We can't communicate." First, it is helpful to educate a couple about one of the most basic tenets of communication, the first one is, that you cannot, not communicate (Watzlawick, Beavin, & Jackson, 1967). For example, that silence they are frustrated with is not actually a lack of communication; it is communicating a lot. If your partner says, "Hey, let's make out" and the other person ignores them, that is communication. It is not clear communication, because the silence can mean a lot of different things, but they are clearly communicating "I do not want to kiss you." Most of the time, couples are "communicating" just fine, it is just they do not like what is being communicated. There is a big difference. Another important communication principle that couples often fail to understand it that the listener throws out the content of what is said and focuses almost exclusively on the tone and the non-verbals. For example, if your partner says, "Yes, I'll have sex" but with a look of disgust, what is communicated is a direct contradiction to the words and the partner knows that in fact they do not want to. So a lot is being communicated, what is missing is an open, honest discussion about sexuality. We need to help clients to talk about needs, fears, hopes, insecurities, dreams, longing, desire, passion, fantasy, and so on. As part of all clinical work with couples, we need to help facilitate these conversations, but it is even more imperative when grappling with issues of infidelity. The topics that cannot be talked about at best miss opportunities for more sexual fulfillment and at worst push the topic underground where the only "safe" place where it can be revealed is with a different partner where there is less chance of judgment or rejection.

17.4 Assessment

Thorough assessment is key in relational therapy, but even more so when the presenting problem is related to infidelity and/or consensual non-monogamy. There are many different factors that will affect the course of treatment, and secrets are particularly pernicious when it comes to positive relationship outcomes (see Atkins, Eldridge, Baucom, & Christensen, 2005). These factors can be at the individual, relational, and societal levels. In conducting an assessment, some can be done at the relational level, but information gleaned in individual interviews is also essential and this is what we recommend.

17.4.1 Individual Interviewing

Interviewing individuals within the context of couples therapy can be a landmine for therapists, so much so that some therapists simply refuse to do it. The most obvious reason for this is related to secrets. What do you do if the client shares information in the session that they are not able or willing to disclose in the couples therapy? Going into all the ways to conduct individual assessments in couples work is beyond the scope of this chapter. The most important recommendation for clinicians is to have clear rules about how information gained in the individual sessions will be handled and that these rules are clearly communicated to couples. For some clinicians this is a strict, "No secrets rule" meaning that couples are told to not say anything in the individual sessions that they would not feel comfortable talking about in the couples therapy. While this is by far the easiest, and recommended for beginning therapists, it has the potential to push information underground that is essential to treatment. The problem of course is that the air tight, "no secret rule" actually negates the usefulness of an individual session. If everything discussed in the individual session can be said to the partner, then what would the added value be? A more nuanced rule is one that explains the therapeutic dilemma and gives more latitude for sharing honestly. The therapist then has the responsibility to thoroughly process what information is essential to treatment and then find ways to encourage or support the person to move toward the increased intimacy it would require to share with their partner. In some cases, couple therapy would not be advised if there was a secret such as an ongoing affair, and in these cases, it is better to proceed with both parties individually until the affair has ended.

The most basic assessment must determine the degree to which both parties are committed to working on the relationship. This is important in that couple therapy is set up to fail when one person has a foot out of the relationship. In some cases the commitment has already been clearly established, essentially that is the reason the couple sought therapy—they want to stay together but found that healing on their own has been difficult. Other couples, especially closer to the time of infidelity discovery, are deeply ambivalent about whether or not the relationship can be saved. This ambivalence can be with either party, or with both. Obviously for the person who is hurt he/she wonders if the whole story has been revealed and they are grappling with the reasons why it happened, wondering if they will ever be able to trust again, and assessing their own ability to commit to someone who did this to them. Therapists often think it is only the hurt party who makes this decision and this is not the case. Depending on the reasons for the affair, the person who committed the infidelity may be assessing whether or not they want to stay, especially if the work to save the relationship seems daunting or there were significant relational problems prior to the affair. Sometimes the individual has fallen in love with the affair partner. This typically makes it harder to discontinue the affair and in fact sometimes the affair does not end. If there are able to end it, there can be a period of grieving that has to be done in isolation as very few partners could be expected to comfort them regarding their loss. And lastly, some people do end up leaving their primary partner for the affair partner as they truly do see themselves as being happier with that person. If one or both partners are really far out of the relationship, this needs to be brought to light sooner rather than later. Some people need the safety of the therapy to disclose this level of honesty. There is sometimes an underlying motive to engage a therapist, not to actually work on the relationship, but to get the partner involved in therapy so they will have an individual therapist to support them post-disclosure to leave. It is more useful to know this early and as a result, the goals of therapy will be different—perhaps helping with a separation, mediation, or effective co-parenting. Most times, the ambivalence is because they want to see if therapy will work before committing themselves back to the relationship. As the therapist, we want them to commit to the relationship for the therapy to be most effective. So we are stuck in a catch 22. One way out of this is to get the couple to commit to putting both feet in for 8–10 sessions to give therapy a chance, but not locking them in to making a forever decision.

Particularly in the crisis phase, there is additional information that is important to ask about. Some of this is basic self-care information. Are they eating? Are they sleeping? To what degree are they experiencing classic post-traumatic stress responses such as flashbacks, intrusive thoughts, nightmares, hypervigilance, and inability to concentrate (Glass, 2004; Glass & Wright, 1997)? There are usually a wide range of reactions and emotions including depression (Gorman & Blow, 2008). Some of these may need immediate behavioral interventions. How much alcohol or other substances are they using to cope with the overwhelming feelings? What are their support systems? Who knows about what has happened? These types of assessment questions are important to ask at the outset of treatment and continue evaluating along the way.

17.4.2 Infidelity Specific Assessment

Second, it is important to assess the nature of the infidelity. At a most basic level, we want to know "What we are up against?" Some types of affairs are easier to recover from. The type of variables that may influence that are questions like, Was there only one affair or have there been multiple betrayals? Typically multiple affairs are worse. Who was it with? Strangers tend to be much easier to handle than someone who the hurt party knew closely. How long did it last? One-night affairs typically have less meaning than ongoing relationships that lasted years. How did discovery happen? A partner who willingly discloses it builds more honesty than when the partner discovers it. The questions will always linger, "If I had not found out, would it still be going on? Is the partner really sorry for the affair, or are they just sorry they got caught?" It goes without saying that discovering the partner actually engaging in the affair directly will have long-lasting effects, including flashbacks of what they saw. Most importantly, the clinician also needs to know, "Has it ended?" and if so, "When and how?" If it has not, "What is the plan?" It has been interesting over the years to see the hurt partner sometimes not feel empowered to set boundaries around the affair partner, essentially changing a situation of infidelity into a form of consensual non-monogamy (albeit with complex relational variables at play). Essentially by not saying, "You can't see this person anymore," they condone the relationship. However, this can be affected by both gender and power. Perhaps the women is not financially viable on her own and so she compromises on her own personal values in order to stay in the relationship.

17.4.3 Relationship History

One of the most important things you want to know about the relationship history is whether or not there have been affairs by either party in the past, or other types of betrayals of trust that could constitute an attachment injury (Johnson, Makinen, & Millikin, 2001). If there are previous issues that have compromised safety, these may also have to be addressed or else they may impede progress in therapy. In addition to the current relationship, it is helpful to know about the individual's relationship history. Have they been unfaithful to others in the past? Have they had other partners who have been unfaithful?

As standard practice it is essential to know basic information such as how long they have been together? How did they meet? If married, how long did they date before they got engaged? How long was the engagement? A description of the wedding? When in the course of their relationship did they become sexual? What has that been like over time? The answers to these questions give you an idea of the quality of their relationship both in terms of the content and the process of how they answer them.

17.4.4 Current Relationship

A good assessment will also reveal the relational dance or patterns in their relationship. The beginning stages of EFT (Johnson, 2004) provide an essential roadmap as to how to proceed in identifying relationship patterns. For example, if the relationship interactional style is a classic pursue–withdraw dynamic, this tendency will be amplified in the wake of an affair.

Particularly in the post-discovery phase, the therapist must assess for violence, both toward the partner and the person they had the affair with. There may be fantasies of hurting the affair partner and the imminent desire and danger of that need to be directly assessed. It is not uncommon for hurt partners to do a variety of stalking behaviors, both virtually on the internet, and physically, such as driving by their house or place of employment. In the crisis phase, it is typical to have increased conflict and volatile interactions. If there is a history of violence, this could put partners at increased risk. It is key to ask not just about hitting, but any physical contact or violent behavior that has happened during fights. This includes, but is not limited to, throwing things, holding someone against their will, pushing, grabbing roughly and forced sexual interactions, among others. There is also a wide range of behaviors used to control others that do not involve physicality, such as verbal abuse, financial control, and isolation.

17.4.5 Family of Origin

It is also helpful to get a brief family history. This can glean helpful information regarding what they may have learned about gender, power, sexuality, conflict, communication, religious upbringing, and any other pertinent issue(s). This information can be asked in the presence of the partner as they are usually a helpful source of additional information both verbally and non-verbally. If there is a history of infidelity in the family of origin this may bring up specific issues that may need to be addressed.

17.4.6 Societal Influences

Sexuality is socially constructed. Each culture defines what is "normal" and "not normal." For example, sexuality in the USA is still heavily influenced by religious belief systems that only sanction heterosexual relationships, forbid sex before marriage, see infidelity as a sin, and advocate for monogamy within the relationship. Formative messages around sexuality can be fear based to control sexual thoughts and behaviors. Consequently, there is a lot of shame around feelings that differ from these teachings. Even individuals who do not grow up within any specific religion are still steeped in messages promoting heterosexism and monogamy. Having an affair is definitely frowned upon despite the statistics that show how prevalent it is. The person who just had an affair is often portrayed in a negative light. Polyamory (belief and practice of having more than one loving relationships at a time) is rarely talked about, thereby marginalizing individuals and relationships who embrace that as a way of being. Therapists should be challenged to assess their own constructions of sexuality and be willing to embrace the complexity of relational structures that can bring fulfillment to individuals and relationships.

17.5 Non-monogamous Relationships

Consensual non-monogamous relationships, often referred to as "open relationships" take many different forms. Estimating their prevalence is difficult, as it is in measuring the frequency of infidelity (Blow & Hartnett, 2005). As discussed earlier, non-monogamy is not infidelity if it is agreed upon by both partners. However, infidelity can and does happen in non-monogamous relationships, most notably when the boundaries of the agreement are broken. The assumption that an open relationship means "anything goes" is false. The assumption that if a relationship is open, someone does not have a right to be hurt or insecure is false. From an attachment theory perspective, an individual still needs to feel secure in their relationship/s, and this security comes from a clearly negotiated agreement on the rules of the relationship and from partner/s who build trust by adhering to these rules.

Couples dealing with infidelity show up in treatment for a variety of different reasons. Some know they are unhappy sexually and need help figuring out what to do about it. They may have never considered being non-monogamous, but it may be a viable option. Some know they want to open their relationship, but need help discussing what that would look like. Some couples have had non-monogamous relationships where betrayal has occurred, and some couples are happily non-monogamous and they just need help with general relational problems but within the safety of a therapeutic space where they know they would not be judged for not being monogamous.

It is an advanced relationship skill to be able to negotiate the boundaries of a non-monogamous relationship. Attempts to guess or assume what is meant by the other person to be non-monogamous are highly problematic. Discussions and agreements need to be made. Some couples make verbal agreements, others write a more formal contract of what the expectations are, including how and when the contract can be altered. Therapists need to encourage couples to talk about issues including, but not limited to:

- What is the goal/desire of the non-monogamy (e.g., to maintain sexuality if the primary partner is unable/unwilling, to increase eroticism, a desire to be polyamorous)?
- Who will be with other people (e.g., both partners together, just one of them, both of them can be with other people individually)?
- Who will the other partners be (e.g., sex workers, single people, other couples)?
- How will they be selected (e.g., apps, internet, in person, jointly selected, or by one partner)?
- Parameters of sexual activities with other people (e.g., oral sex, intercourse with or without protection).
- How much time can be spent away from the primary relationship (e.g., afternoons, overnights, weekends, vacations)?
- How much money is allotted to other relationships/activities (e.g., per month, per year)?

The following case illustrates a couple where a husband asked to include another person in their sexual relationship and his wife was open to it. It also shows the importance of ongoing communication and negotiation when issues arose that they could not resolve on their own.

Jill and Garrett, a heterosexual couple in their 30s have been consensually non-monogamous for 2 years. The current arrangement came about when Garrett disclosed an ongoing fantasy he had of having sex with two women at the same time.

Jill (the primary partner) was open to the idea, but needed to feel safe with the implementation of the fantasy. Much of the plan was discussed and negotiated prior to coming to therapy and they had been successful in its application. As a couple, they initially agreed to the following rules: (1) Both of them would be involved in the selection process of the third party. Jill had the "first right of refusal," meaning that even if Garrett liked the person but she did not, that person would not be selected. (2) Sexual activity with the third party would only take place with Jill present. (3) Sexual activity between Garrett and the third party could include oral sex, but not vaginal or anal intercourse. (4) Jill did not want to engage in sexual activities one-on-one with the third party. This covered many of the important boundaries that should be discussed prior to embarking on any non-monogamous relationship. They added more rules to this list after beginning to include the third party. For example, Jill felt more comfortable if sex did not happen in their master bedroom as she wanted that to be reserved for only their relationship. Other parts of the house were fine, or it could be at a hotel. They decided that ongoing communication would only be between Jill and the third party for purposes of setting up days and times.

However, a number of issues came up over time that started to cause relational difficulties and they decided to come to therapy for help. The most troubling one for Jill was the decrease in frequency of sex between just the two of them. While she was fine with including another person at times, she felt that this was becoming the only way Garrett wanted to be sexual. The second was related, in that he constantly was looking for new partners and wanting her to do the same. She was happy with having one partner at a time, but he wanted more options given the difficulty in having one person available as frequently as he would like. When they came to therapy, I met with each one of them individually before we met together. In particular, I wanted to assess whether or not this arrangement was completely consensual, or were there elements of coercion involved. This is a very important part of the process and it is imperative to address issues of gender, power, and patriarchy. As it turns out, Jill was starting to feel "pressure" to do more. Along with this, she felt unappreciated that she had agreed to do this, and now it was affecting the activities that she enjoyed most. Garrett was relatively confused about why Jill was unhappy. He denied that it had affected their sex life and in fact felt like it had only enhanced their time together. He also felt it was just logical and practical that they have more than one partner at a time. The couple therapy helped Jill to have more of a voice around what she needed to feel heard and safe with the ongoing non-monogamy. As a result of the therapy, they agreed to only include someone else no more than one time a month in their relationship. They also agreed that they would be sexual together alone at least twice a week. Jill agreed that having more than one person was fine, but she did not want to be responsible for constantly looking for new people. Garrett agreed that he would not ask her to look for new people as long as they had two or three partners willing to engage with them. It was also crucial for Garrett to be more reassuring toward Jill and communicate more frequently his desire for her and satisfaction with her as his life partner. After this last agreement was reached we concluded therapy.

17.5.1 LGBTQ Couples

While there are data that show that some LGBTQ individuals may be more accepting of non-monogamy than their heterosexual counterparts (see Blow & Hartnett, 2005), we believe that the relational processes of healing from infidelity and negotiating consensual non-monogamy are the same. We strongly advocate for the same principles with these couples as discussed earlier, especially related to power and consent. Infidelity is determined by each relationship and is an ongoing negotiation between parties. The same is true for ongoing consent to non-monogamy.

17.6 Conclusion

Clinical work with infidelity and consensual non-monogamy is complicated. It is fraught with intense emotions and laced with underlying assumptions about what sexuality should be. However, helping couples negotiate a significant relational crisis like this has the potential to not just restore stability in their relationship, but actually achieve more fulfilled intimacy both physically and emotionally. Working with these couples takes skill and openness on the part of the therapist. Even when treatment is done well, some couples will choose to not stay together. The key is sustained engagement around the difficult conversations while fostering secure attachment. We encourage therapists to increase their comfort in working with both affair recovery and non-monogamy (Timm, 2018; Timm & Blow, 2018).

References

Atkins, D. C., Eldridge, K. A., Baucom, D. H., & Christensen, A. (2005). Infidelity and behavioral couple therapy: Optimism in the face of betrayal. *Journal of Consulting and Clinical Psychology, 73*, 144–150.

Basson, R. (2005). Women's sexual function: Revised and expanded definitions. *Canadian Medical Association Journal, 172*(10), 1327–1333. https://doi.org/10.1503/cmaj.1020174

Blow, A. J., & Hartnett, K. (2005). Infidelity in committed relationships I: A methodological review. *Journal of Marital and Family Therapy, 31*(2), 183–216.

Fidelity (Def. 1). *Oxford Online.* Retrieved October 1, 2019, from https://www.lexico.com/en/definition/fidelity.

Glass, S. P. (2004). *Not "just friends": Rebuilding trust and recovering your sanity after infidelity.* New York, NY: Atria Books.

Glass, S. P., & Wright, T. L. (1997). Reconstructing marriages after the trauma of infidelity. In W. K. Halford & H. J. Markman (Eds.), *Clinical handbook of marriage and couples interventions* (pp. 471–507). New York, NY: Wiley.

Gorman, L., & Blow, A. (2008). Concurrent depression and infidelity. *Journal of Couple & Relationship Therapy, 7*(1), 39–58. https://doi.org/10.1080/15332690802129705

Gottman, J. (1999). *The marriage clinic.* New York, NY: W. W. Norton.

Johnson, S. M., Makinen, J. A., & Millikin, J. W. (2001). Attachment injuries in couple relationships: A new perspective on impasses in couples therapy. *Journal of Marital and Family Therapy, 27*, 145–156.

Johnson, S. M. (2004). *The practice of emotionally focused couple therapy: Creating connection.* New York, NY: Brunner-Routledge.

Kaplan, H. S. (1979). *Disorders of sexual desire.* New York, NY: Simon and Schuster.

Mitchell, K. R., Wellings, K. A., & Graham, C. (2014). How do men and women define sexual desire and sexual arousal? *Journal of Sex and Marital Therapy, 40*(1), 17–32. https://doi.org/10.1080/0092623X.2012.697536

Perel, E. (2007). *Mating in captivity: Unlocking erotic intelligence.* New York, NY: Harper.

Perel, E. (2017). *The state of affairs: Rethinking infidelity.* New York, NY: Harper.

Schnarch, D. M. (1991). *Constructing the sexual crucible: An integration of sexual and marital therapy.* New York, NY: Norton.

Stefanou, C., & McCabe, M. P. (2012). Adult attachment and sexual functioning: A review of past research. *Journal of Sex Medicine, 9*(10), 2499–2507.

Timm, T. M. (2018). Brief therapy with non-monogamous couples: Challenging the status quo. In D. Flemons & S. Green (Eds.), *Quickies: The handbook of brief sex therapy* (2nd ed.). New York, NY: W.W. Norton.

Timm, T. M., & Blow, A. J. (2018). Healing the relational wounds from infidelity. In D. Flemons & S. Green (Eds.), *Quickies: The handbook of brief sex therapy* (2nd ed.). New York, NY: W.W. Norton.

Watzlawick, P., Beavin, J. H., & Jackson, D. D. (1967). *Pragmatics of human communication: A study of interactional patterns, pathologies, and paradoxes.* New York, NY: Norton.

Williams, D. C. (2017). *What's done in the dark: Affair-proofing and recovery from infidelity -- Self help guide for couples.* Amazon Digital Services: BookLogix.

Chapter 18
Understanding Long-Term Couple Relationships

Carrie Cole and Donald Cole

18.1 Introduction

A young couple walks into my office for their first appointment. He jumps in quickly when I ask them the reason for their coming. "She's driving me crazy! Last week I was driving down the freeway. All of a sudden she starts yelling at me, 'Why are you slowing down to look at those cars? We don't need a new car! You just waste all our money!' This happens all the time and I'm sick of it!"

As I listened to more of their story, it was clear to me that they really loved each other and wanted to stay together forever but they were interacting in a way which we now know will lead to relationship breakdown and separation.

18.1.1 The Need for Relationship Science

In the early 1970s a young psychology professor became interested in the very question of this chapter. How can we understand long-term relationships? Why do some couples progress from year to year with a sense of connection and satisfaction and others decline and end? Dr. John Gottman began seeking the answers to this question while he was an assistant professor at Indiana University. He and his colleague and friend Dr. Robert Levenson teamed up as research partners to seek a scientific way to learn about couples and discover what we can actually predict.

C. Cole (✉)
Research Department, The Gottman Institute, Seattle, WA, USA
e-mail: carrie@gottman.com

D. Cole
The Gottman Institute, Seattle, WA, USA
e-mail: don@gottman.com

Before that time (and even today), most of the "theories" of long-term relationships were really little more than the hypotheses of well-meaning psychologists or therapists who based their guesses on some psychological system or on the anecdotal evidence gleaned from the couples they tried to help in therapy. George Bach, in his book *The Intimate Enemy*, provides a great example of this process. Dr. Bach hypothesized that couples became distressed in relationships because they were harboring deep resentments that needed to be expressed. He devised a therapy based on this idea which guided couples into taking turns expressing their resentments and frustrations. He even went so far as to have the couples punctuate their anger by striking the partner with a foam rubber bat, called a Bataka (Bach, 1965). Therapy might go something like this: "I hate that you are such a slob around the house, *Whack!*" "Well, I hate that you are so cold in bed and never want to have sex, *Whack!*"

This approach, as wrongheaded as it might seem today, fit well with the theory Dr. Bach was using. The problem was (and often still is) that there were no data on which to base such an approach. Now we know, according to Carol Tavris (1989), that over 3000 studies on anger show that this type of venting actually increases anger and hostility rather than lowering them. There is no magic catharsis of anger through this kind of venting. In fact, Gottman, along with Levenson and many other colleagues, discovered that the happy, stable couples take the opposite approach to conflict. When something was bothering them, they would find a gentle way to bring up the subject (Gottman & Levenson, 1983).

18.1.2 Overview of the Scientific Research

Dr. John Gottman and his associates studied couples for over 45 years, using a variety of methods. They observed videos of couples' interactions and analyzed them second by second using the SPAFF coding system (Gottman, McCoy, Coan, & Collier, 1996). They analyzed the stories of couples' relationships using the Buehlman coding system (Buehlman, Gottman, & Katz, 1992). Physiological measurements were used to understand what was going on "under the skin" for couples (Gottman & Levenson, 1984). In addition to the laboratory, couples were observed in an apartment setting to understand what they were like when they were just "hanging out together." Some couples participated in a 20-year-long study to see how things changed or stayed the same over time (Driver & Gottman, 2004).

Thanks to this careful research, it is now possible to begin to understand relationships with scientific precision and mathematical accuracy. Through the careful study of couples and their interactions we now know the differences between couples whose relationships improve over time and those who decline and separate. Using these methods, John Gottman was able to predict which couples would maintain their relationships over time, and which couples would separate, with over a 90% accuracy rate (Gottman & Levenson, 2002).

18.2 A Scientific Theory of Relationships: The Sound Relationship House

Gottman's work has led to a formulation of a systematic way of understanding relationships. In addition, it provided the clinician with a way of understanding the strengths and weaknesses in relationships. The theoretical framework is known as The Sound Relationship House Theory.

The levels depicted in the diagram below represent traits that are found in relationships that are successful over time. Starting from the bottom, "Building Love Maps" is the process of couples learning about their partner's world and showing interest in them.

The second level, "Sharing Fondness and Admiration" describes the expression of positive feelings between the couple.

The third level of the house "Turning Toward vs. Turning Away" is an analysis of patterns of interaction observed in couples. Interactions begin with a "bid" for attention such as a comment "I really like this song." Turning toward occurs when the partner responds to the bid. They might say "So do I," or "What is this called?"

These first three levels, taken together constitute the Friendship System of the relationship. See Fig. 18.1.

The fourth level of the Sound Relationship House theory is known as "The Positive Perspective." This describes the overall emotional quality of the relationship. When couples have a positive friendship and manage conflict effectively, they tend to have overriding positive thoughts and feelings about their partner which provides an emotional buffer helping them repair miscommunications and negative moments.

The fifth level of the house is called "Manage Conflict." All couples have conflicts, but the successful couples manage them in ways that are mostly positive. They accept and discuss their differences. They are gentle with one another when they deal with problems and repair miscommunications. They stay calm when dealing with conflict and take breaks to "cool off" when necessary, avoiding escalation, criticism, defensiveness, contempt, and stonewalling. Conflict management is by itself the second system of the relationship (Fig. 18.1).

The sixth level of the theory is "Making Life Dreams Come True." Successful partners are interested in each other's deep needs and dreams and seek to honor

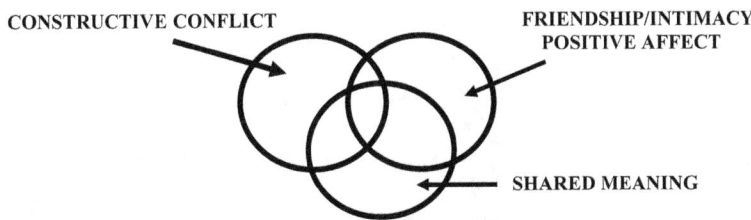

Fig. 18.1 Three systems of the SRH

them as much as possible. These relationships also develop share dreams over time and they work together to bring those dreams to fruition.

The seventh level is known as "Creating Shared Meaning." Successful couples find meaningful goals to pursue together. They find ways to go through the years together in a way that feels important and meaningful. The third major system of the relationship is known simply as shared meaning and it contains both levels 6 and 7 (Fig. 18.1).

The levels of the house are held together by two essential concepts, trust and commitment (Fig.18.2). Trust develops in a relationship when one experiences the partner as "being there" for them especially when there are difficulties. Commitment represents the state of knowing that the current relationship represents the life each person desires and they make no comparisons to possible alternatives.

As mentioned above, there are three systems within a relationship: Friendship System, Conflict Management System, and Shared Meaning System. The Friendship system includes building love maps, sharing fondness and admiration and turning toward levels. The second system is Constructive Conflict and the third system is Shared Meaning which includes make life dreams come true and create shared meaning levels. As figure two illustrates, these systems may overlap at times. For example a couple might have an ongoing conflict about the way they want to celebrate holidays, a shared meaning issues.

Fig. 18.2 The sound relationship house

18.2.1 The Theory in Practice: The Friendship System

The love mapping begins immediately in relationships. People are usually curious about each other and ask questions. They want to know about each other's work, families, likes, and dislikes. They look for commonalities and enjoy the differences. They have long conversations that sometimes last into the wee hours of the morning.

Not all relationships begin this way. According to Gottman's research, some couples show little interest in their partner from the very beginning. Even though the relationship might progress to commitment and even marriage these couples feel that they have never really known one another. Somehow, they skipped this important step (Buehlman et al., 1992).

The love mapping process continues throughout the life span of the successful couples. People change, they grow and develop over time. For example, a younger person might not think about becoming a parent, but later they find themselves considering that step. The successful couples stay up to date with these kinds of changes in each other's lives. They learn about the stresses their partner is having at work or how they feel about their aging parents. However, many couples fail to keep up with these changes. Even though the relationship began with good love mapping, the process faded over time. These couples find that their conversations have declined in depth and frequency and they feel further away from each other. If this process continues unabated, a decline in relationship satisfaction will follow.

A second component of the friendship system in Gottman's theory has to do with the couples' tendency to express or withhold expressions of fondness, affection, and respect. Successful couples offer expressions of gratitude and admiration to each other on a regular basis. They respect each other. They are verbally and nonverbally affectionate with each other. They are specific in their praise. For example, saying something like "I really appreciate your doing the dishes for me tonight." They also speak positively about their partners to others. For many couples this sharing fondness and admiration process is no longer happening. These couples have fallen into a habit of mind where they are more likely to notice and point out negatives. They focus on perceived flaws in their partner's personality or behavior. This is a pattern that easily leads to escalating arguments or avoidance of one another.

The third component of the friendship system is called Turning Toward. At the University of Washington, John Gottman added a new component to his research. An apartment was built on campus and couples spent 24 h just hanging out together in that apartment. Their interactions were observed, physiological measurements were recorded, and blood and urine samples were gathered for analysis. He noticed that people were making "bids" for attention to their partner. Partners responded in one of three ways: (1) they turned toward their partner by responding to them; (2) they turned away by ignoring or tuning out the bid; or (3) they turned against by snapping at or belittling their partner. Imagine a scenario where one partner looks out the window and says, "Cool boat." A turning toward partner would respond by putting their book down, join their partner at the window for a momentary interaction "Oh, yeah," or the partner might enthusiastically say "Wow! That is a cool boat, do you ever want to do something like that?" A turning away response would be silence as though the partner had never spoken. A turning against response would sound something like "Can't you see I'm busy? Don't bother me with a stupid boat!" At a 5-year follow-up, couples who had turned toward each other's bids an average of 86% of the time were still happily married but those who had only turned toward each other's bids 33% of the time were divorced or very unhappy in their relationship (Driver & Gottman, 2004).

The fourth level of the Sound Relationship House is known as the Positive Perspective. Robert Weiss coined the terms "Positive Sentiment Override" and "Negative Sentiment Override" to describe the emotional attitude people had about their relationships (Weiss, 1980). When couples are turning toward one another, sharing fondness and admiration and building love maps, they have a tendency to remain in a positive perspective about the relationship. On the other hand, when the friendship system is not being attended to, negativity creeps in and overrides the positive perspective. Couples like this have a chip on their shoulder and are sensitive to any perceived slight from their partner. Imagine two couples experiencing the same event. The husband is at home expecting his wife to arrive at 6 p.m. At 6:15 he begins to anxiously call her cell phone and she does not answer. If they are in a positive perspective, he thinks to himself, "I hope she's okay. Maybe she forgot to charge her phone." When she gets home he asks, "What happened? I've been trying to call." She says, "I'm sorry. My phone was at the bottom of my purse and I couldn't reach it." He says, "That's okay, but please be more careful. You know I get worried." However, imagine a second couple in negative sentiment override. He starts thinking "I wonder where she is, or who she's talking to? She's deliberately avoiding my call!" He is much less likely to accept her apology about the phone being at the bottom of her purse and the relationship becomes even more negative. This scenario serves to illustrate that this is a transitional level between friendship and conflict.

18.2.2 The Theory in Practice: Conflict Management System

Conflict management is the next level of the Sound Relationship House theory. The term "management" is central here. Gottman and Levenson conducted longitudinal study of couples and discovered that 69% of their conflicts were perpetual over time and had no solution (Gottman & Levenson, 2002). These conflicts are based on differences in personality or basic feelings and needs and will likely persist over the years. One partner might be adventurous and love travel while the other is much more comfortable in familiar surroundings and would rather stay close to home. This kind of difference will likely never change, but couples can successfully maintain dialog about the issue and accept these differences. Other couples however fail to sustain the dialog and find themselves in gridlocked conflict instead. The couple mentioned at the beginning of this chapter is an example of this gridlocked pattern. She believed he was careless about money, was materialistic, and would eventually bankrupt the family. He believed that she was uptight, never wanting to have any fun in life, and was worrying about every little thing. Their arguments about money became increasingly negative and threatened to destroy the relationship altogether.

This couple's experience illustrates an important concept in Sound Relationship House theory. The emotional perspective of the relationship can be pushed toward the negative even if the friendship system is functioning well. That was the case with this gridlocked couple. They were fairly successful at sharing fondness and turning toward bids, but their gridlock conflict had become so destructive that they were seeing the relationship as mostly negative and were considering a divorce. Shifting the conversation from gridlock back to dialog was the central therapeutic task for this couple.

This couple, like so many others, was engaging in negative exchanges that escalated as they tried to solve this problem. Early in their research, Gottman and Levenson identified four patterns that were highly predictive of relationship breakup. They labeled these "The Four Horsemen of the Apocalypse." They are: criticism, defensiveness, contempt, and stonewalling. The presence of these during conflict conversations predicted divorce or relationship breakup with over 90% accuracy (Gottman & Levenson, 1992).

- Criticism: Placing the blame for a problem inside the partner. It often takes the form of harsh complaining such as "Why do you always spend too much?" or "You never want to have any fun!"
- Defensiveness: Refusing to take responsibility for the problem. The defensive partner tends to attack back, "You waste as much money as I do!" or to whine about feeling unfairly criticized "I work hard, why can't I have nice things?"
- Contempt: Belittling the partner with an attitude of superiority. Contempt goes beyond criticism. It has a tone of superiority and talking down to the partner. "I learned the value of money when I was five. You'll never learn, will you?"
- Stonewalling: Shutting down all verbal and nonverbal communication during conflict. The stonewalling partner ends communication. They often break eye contact, look away, and refuse to respond to direct questions.

Successful couples avoid these negative patterns most of the time. If they do find themselves talking to one another with this level of negativity they repair the relationship. We will talk more about repair below.

18.2.2.1 The Six Skills for Effective Conflict Management

Couples who have positive friendship and emotional connection were more likely to engage in effective conflict management. Positive feelings of closeness and intimacy are essential beginning steps toward dealing with differences and problems in the relationship. John Gottman also observed that couples who were successful over the years practiced six conflict management skills that helped keep them out of gridlock and away from the four horsemen. These six skills are: softened startup, effective repair, physiological self-soothing, accepting influence, honoring each other's dreams, and compromise.

Skill Number 1: Softened Startup

The way couples began their conflict conversations proved to be very important. When the conflict began with a harsh startup which included attacking and blaming statements the conversations remained negative 96% of the time. In Gottman's laboratory it was discovered that long-term successful couples maintained positive affect during conflict conversations 80% of the time (five positive to one negative exchange). The unsuccessful couples demonstrated slightly more negative than positive affect during their conversations: .8:1 positive to negative (Gottman & Levenson, 2002). So when couples began their conflict conversations harshly, they were much more likely to remain negative and failed to achieve that 5:1 positive to negative ratio.

A softened startup has three parts. It begins with how the speaker feels. This requires an emotion such as "I'm worried." The speaker then describes the situation neutrally. They focus on what they see, hear, or the message that they get. They then ask for what they want or need. A simple example would be "I'm worried about the time. I need us to hurry." This avoids the harsh, critical startup, "Why do you always make us late!" We have had a lot of personal experience with this one!

Skill Number 2: Repair and De-escalation

The second skill successful couples use is repair and de-escalation. Instead of using the escalating four horsemen language as described above, they use positive ways of expressing themselves. They talk about their feelings and needs instead of how the partner is flawed or at fault. They take responsibility for their part of miscommunication rather than making excuses and they know how to stop and recover when things get too heated. All couples fail at the de-escalation task at times and that is when they seek to repair the relationship. Repair, it turns out, is a defining difference between couples who maintain a satisfying relationship over time and those who do not. All couples disagree and miscommunicate. All couples have perpetual differences that cause stress and negative emotions. The couples who are able to maintain a positive perspective are more likely to repair effectively (Gottman, Murry, Swanson, Tyson, & Swanson, 2002).

Repairing the relationship happens in two settings. Successful couples often stop themselves or their partner if something was spoken with harshness and negativity and make an immediate repair attempt. They would say things like "Sorry, that came out wrong. Let me try again." They also have the ability to process arguments or regrettable incidents that had occurred in the past. They listen to each other's perspective about the event and offer heartfelt apologies.

Skill Number 3: Physiological Self-Soothing

A key element in the long-term success of couples is physiological calmness which is the third skill. During laboratory conversations they exhibited lower heart rates, lower galvanic skin responses, lower respiration, and lower pulse transit time.

Flooding occurs when a person's heart rate is elevated above 100 bpm due to escalating negative emotions. When one or both members of a couple find themselves in a flooded state during conflict, they lose a sense of empathy and perspective, they are more likely to engage in the four horsemen, and they lose their sense of humor. When some people flood, they shut down in a stonewalling manner and stop engaging with their partner while others become more critical and contemptuous. If they do try to engage in conversation with their partner in this state, they will likely repeat themselves and fail to listen effectively. Successful couples avoid flooding situations most of the time and if they do become flooded, they take effective time-outs to self-soothe.

Skill Number 4: Accepting Influence

Couples in successful long-term relationships demonstrate the skill of accepting influence from one another. They sincerely say things like "That makes sense" even if they have a different point of view. They take in their partner's perspective as equally valid as their own. Unsuccessful couples had more difficulty with this skill. They were more likely to say, "No" or "You're wrong." In heterosexual relationships this skill of accepting influence proved to be most important for the men to exhibit. Typically, women accepted influence at a high rate, but men less so.

One might believe that this concept of accepting influence is based on a Western ideal of egalitarian relationships, though it proved to be an important factor even among couples whose relationships were based on a more male-dominant model. In those situations, the patriarch still had the choice to accept his wife's point of view or not on matters delegated to her role. Those patriarchal cultures demonstrate a power imbalance but in the successful marriages the wife's power was affirmed even if it was limited (Gottman, Driver, Yoshimoto, & Rushe, 2002).

Skill Number 5: Honoring Life Dreams

A defining characteristic of successful couples is understanding and seeking to fulfill their partner's life dreams. Dreams are often longings or promises that we make to ourselves, often going back to childhood. Gridlocks occur when couples are either unable or unwilling to honor each other's deepest dreams. Often these dreams are shaped by powerful experiences from childhood or past experiences. Sometimes people remember those experiences as very positive and they dream of having them repeated with their partner, for instance, the person whose family always sat down to dinner together at 6:00 pm in the evening and shared their day. For that person, dinnertime was a very positive experience that they want repeated in their current relationship. They might have entered the commitment with an unspoken idea that they would create a family dinner ritual just like the one they had as a child. Alternatively, a person's prior experiences might be remembered very negatively. This was the case with the couple who were fighting about automobiles at the beginning of the chapter. They both grew up in impoverished families, but she dreamed of having a good job and saving money for the safety of herself and her children.

Safety was the deep meaning of money and savings for her. On the other hand, he dreamed of having enough money to have all the nice things for himself and his children that he was denied in his past. Having money to him meant having a sense of equality and power. They found it impossible to honor each other's dreams because each felt like they had to give up their own and gridlock was the consequence. Successful long-term couples dialog about these important topics and they find ways to understand and honor their partners' dreams without having to give up their own. Then they are able to make effective compromises that allow for both dreams to be honored.

Skill Number 6: Compromise

Compromise begins with understanding one another and desiring that their needs and dreams can be honored. Couples approach the conflict from a win-win mentality which starts by honoring the deep needs and dreams of the partner. They find areas of flexibility that they can share and live with a lot of give and take. Let us take one more look at our first couple. During therapy they were able to understand what money and spending meant to each other. He got it, that she was not trying to take things away from him but that she was trying to feel safe. She got it too, that he was not trying to spend every penny they made, but he just needed to feel good about his lifestyle. Now they can compromise. They established a budget and savings plan that they both could live with. They started a pattern of talking about spending ahead of time. With the conflict managed better, the underlying love began to blossom again.

18.3 The Theory in Practice: Shared Meaning

Now we look beyond the issues of friendship and conflict management and take a look at the "Why do I want this?" question of a committed relationship. Over and over again couples say, "I want us to grow old together." Long-term successful couples find ways to go through time together that makes sense, that feels right for both. They laugh at private jokes in the bathroom and the bedroom. They build in celebrations of life with friends and family. All the work of conflict management is a means to an end, the goal of sharing a loving long-term life with someone who makes it all worth living.

18.4 The Theory in Practice: Trust and Commitment

Trust and commitment are the walls that hold everything together. They grow and develop as couples move beyond the hormonally driven period of "falling in love" and begin to seek the answer to important questions about the relationship.

First, "Will my partner be there for me?" Not just will my partner be sexually faithful to me, although that is extremely important, but also on a more global scale, in terms of prioritizing my side over others and giving importance to my needs. We need to know that our partner is there in the good and bad and that that they can repair things with us when they do not go perfectly well. Trust grows when we answer "Yes!"

Commitment is a little different. Commitment is based on a question we ask about both ourselves and our partner. Sometimes we take a look at the path we have chosen and the companion we have chosen to walk that path with us. Do we cherish this person and the life that we share? Do they cherish us, forsaking all others? For all its ups and downs, do we know that this is the place, the path for us? On the other hand, do we wonder if life would be better somewhere else, with someone else? Is our partner just marking time with us until someone better comes along? Do we compare what we have with a real or imagined alternative? The couples who last have answered these questions for themselves. They know this is the partner they want (Gottman & Silver, 2012).

18.5 Moving from Theory to Practice

We have spent the first half of this chapter laying out the basics of relationship science and the theory that has developed from it about what a lasting relationship is like. There is a lot of interesting science there but this science is not just about psychological observations, physiological measurements, and mathematical analysis; it is about real people who desire a meaningful, satisfying life with a partner. Some have wondered if these ideas, this theory, really applies to people outside of the USA where most of the original science was done. As with any theory, more work needs to be done. We are constantly learning more and more about couples, their interactions and their happiness. It is a joy to be able to apply that science to the task of helping couples find the satisfaction, stability, and meaning that they seek.

As Clinical Director and Research Director for the Gottman Institute we have had the privilege and opportunity to talk to couples from all over the world. Therapists trained in the Gottman method have seen couples in China, Singapore, India, Australia, Israel, Miramar, and Turkey to name a few. We have worked with Native American families in Oklahoma. We have trained therapists from all parts of the world in the Gottman method and everywhere we hear the same message. The principles discovered by Gottman and his associates make intuitive sense to the couples and the therapist who seek to help them.

Gottman's theory relies on an understanding of emotion derived from Paul Ekman whose pan-cultural work brought an understanding of how people from all over the world, from every culture, share a common emotional experience of the world. Ekman was able to describe basic human emotional responses and define the universal facial expressions which accompany them. He also examined the "display rules" which cultural influence imposes on the public expression of emotion

(Ekman & Friesen, 1975). Attachment theory has taught us that people have a basic need to bond with others in loving association and connection (Johnson, 2004). We have discovered the importance of expressions of caring and of gentleness when there are difficult conversations. Studies of gay and lesbian couples have shown that their relationships follow these same patterns. This has helped to bring about the beginning of an understanding of relationships that is truly global. There is more to learn. We know little about polyamorous relationships, for example, but therapists are called upon to try to help so the need for ongoing science is very real.

18.6 What About Sex?

No conversation about relationships is complete without talking about the sexual side of life. Emily Nagoski helps us understand that people have a dual control system when it comes to sexual arousal. Both the accelerator and the brake are at work, speeding up sexual desire or slowing it down (Nagoski, 2015).

Carol and Steve are an average couple in many ways. They are reasonably happy with each other, but when it comes to their sex life, they are in trouble. Steve complained for years that they were not having sex as often as he would like and Carol felt pressured. Sexual encounters, when they did happen, were different as well. They no longer spent time in bed talking, laughing, and cuddling. Their kisses had become simple "pecks" before going to work or at bedtime. When sex did happen, Steve always initiated and sometimes felt like he was having to beg her. He hated being turned down, so often he did not ask.

It was obvious to me as their therapist that their bids for attention and turning toward process was not working. His complaining and pressuring were pushing on Carol's brake, not her accelerator. The touching, laughing, cuddle time had been an accelerator for them, but they were no longer spending that time. The same was true for kissing which had all but disappeared. Carol's reluctance to initiate sexual contact was a definite break for Steve. It made him feel unwanted and distant. As a result, he disengaged more and complained more, both things pushing on Carol's brake.

Successful, long-term couples function well as sexual partners even as they advance through the various stages of life (Gottman & Gottman, 2007). They build love maps of each other's erotic world through asking questions and talking. These couples learn what accelerates their partner and they make those bids. They make it a point to turn toward each other's bids, both sexual and non-sexual. They also understand what pushes the brakes for their partner. They are able to avoid pushing their partner's brakes, but they also understand that sometimes their partner just is not ready sexually and they honor those needs.

Steve and Carol had a lot of talking to do. They had spent years unconsciously creating the very relationship they did not want. Before they could begin to rebuild their sexual connection, they had to repair the relationship from years of failed bids and turnings away. It took time to process the pain of detachment, to hear each other's perspective and find the path to repair but they were able to do that. They then began a journey of learning about their partner's needs, fears, and wishes when it came to sex. Steve was amazed to learn that Carol not only wanted sex but wanted it with him. Carol was surprised to learn that Steve wanted more than intercourse. He really wanted closeness and affection just like she did. They both had to overcome their tendency to avoid discussing sexual issues. This is a common problem for many couples. As they began to recover, the sense of love and closeness that comes from physical touch returned and they find themselves happier in all areas of the relationship.

18.7   What About Stress?

It is hard to talk about modern life without the word "stress" coming up. It seems like being stressed out is the norm for most people. Relationships can suffer from that stress, but they can also be a source of soothing. One of the ways couples can soothe each other is through a stress-reducing conversation. In Gottman workshops, couples are encouraged to develop a daily conversation designed to create an alliance between them as they face their life stresses. The couples spend 30 min at the end of the workday re-connecting. They talk about the events of the day especially the stressful ones. They take turns listening. They empathize with their partner and ask questions. They avoid problem-solving. They also avoid taking the side of the person who is the source of their partner's stress. They only talk about events and problems that are outside of the couple relationship. As a result, they experience their partner as a friend, an ally who really understands them. Guy Bodenmann spent a year in John Gottman's lab. He took this idea of the stress-reducing conversation back to Switzerland and expanded it into a couple's program called *Couples' Coping Enhancement Training* (Bodenmann & Shantinath, 2004). Bodenmann found that couples who are able to shield their relationship from the damaging effects of life stress, improved relationship quality.

Stacy and Chris both work in high-stress, high-tech jobs. By the time they reunited in the evening they had very little emotional energy left for each other. They did not argue. Instead they found themselves avoiding each other most of the time. Neither wanted to discuss work at home because these conversations typically went awry. Chris was convinced that Stacy never really listened but rather wanted to give quick and easy answers to the problems. Stacy was frustrated as well. It seemed that any complaint made about a co-worker led to Chris pointing out how Stacy was making the situation worse. Fortunately, they learned about the rules of engagement around the stress-reducing conversation that helped them reconnect with each other. They learned to take turns as speaker and listener instead of trying to compete for the floor. They also learned to just listen, ask questions, and give empathy and support rather than attempting to solve their partner's problems. They both described a new sense of lightness between them. This became so important to them that they made it a part of their daily routine. They built a ritual of sitting together on the back porch with a glass of wine and discussed their day. They now look forward to their reunions at the end of the day.

18.8 What About the Fights?

Some couples fight, and they fight hard. When they get upset, they bring out the four horsemen and attack each other. These fights can do real damage to the relationship and cause injury. But even couples who do not fight very often can injure each other. In these cases, the quick apology is not good enough. If one apologizes too soon, the apology might fail because the injured party does not believe that their partner understands what they are apologizing for. They do not understand what got triggered and why it cut so deep. We offer a five-step process to repair these kinds of injuries called *The Aftermath of a Fight or Regrettable Incident*. Couples need to know that their feelings and their perspective have been heard at the deepest level by their partner. They need to understand their partner's experience as well. They need to know that their partner is willing and able to take responsibility for their part of the argument. Then they are able to repair the damage.

David and Sarah were a young couple and they struggled with a multitude of arguments. It seemed that every conversation ended in a fight where one or both partners got flooded. It was difficult for them to grasp that there could be two subjective realities. They usually ended up in fights about whose perspective was the right one. The four horsemen were the rule, not the exception. It seemed like their relationship had no hope. It was hard for them to master the *Aftermath of a Fight* and their many attempts often led to new and more negative fights. They actually destroyed multiple copies of the guide sheet to the *Aftermath of a Fight* along the way.

However, they stuck with the program and after many months they began to understand that their partner was not automatically wrong just because they saw things differently. They began to understand each other's trigger points and how those were getting stirred up. Eventually they were able to listen to each other's triggers in a new way. They realized that there were some injuries from their past that made them more vulnerable in this relationship. The identification of those painful parts of their history helped them not vilify each other and instead be a source of empathy around those past events as they saw how something they might have innocently done reopened old wounds. From that point on they could each see how they contributed to the escalation of the fight and work to make it better in the future.

Learning from the moments when we are at our worst is something we see again and again in the couples whose relationships are both lasting and satisfying. They are able to lower their defensiveness and take in their partner's point of view, knowing that there are two sides to every story (Wile, 1988).

18.9 Conclusion

In this chapter we have introduced the research of John Gottman and his associates into the realities of relationships. We have glanced at the lives of successful couples and struggling couples alike and gained a sense of how they differ, glimpsing into the lives of a few real couples to see how these insights helped them change and grow. Therapists around the world have benefited as they have applied this theory and the methods which have grown from it to the lives of couples in many cultures. The research goes on and the work continues.

References

Bach, G. (1965). *The intimate enemy: How to figntfair in love and marriage.* New York, NY: Basic Books.
Bodenmann, G., & Shantinath, S. O. (2004). The couples coping enhancement training (CCET): A new approach to prevention of marital distress based upon stress and coping. *Family Relations, 53*(5), 477–484.
Buehlman, K., Gottman, J., & Katz, L. (1992). How a couple views their past predicts their future: Predicting divorce from an oral History Interview. *Journal of Family Psychology, 5*, 295–318.
Driver, J. L., & Gottman, J. M. (2004). Turning toward versus turning away: A coding system of daily interaction. In P. Kerig & D. H. Baucom (Eds.), *Couple observational coding systems* (pp. 209–225). Hillsdale, NJ: Erlbaum.
Ekman, P., & Friesen, W. (1975). *Unmasking the face.* Los Altos, CA: Malor Books.
Gottman, J. M., Driver, J., Yoshimoto, D., & Rushe, R. (2002). Approaches to the study of power in violent and nonviolent marriages, and in gay male and lesbian cohabiting relationships. In P. Noller & J. A. Feeney (Eds.), *Understanding marriage: Developments in the study of couple interaction* (pp. 323–347). Cambridge, UK: Cambridge University Press.
Gottman, J. M., & Gottman, J. S. (2007). *And baby makes three.* New York, NY: Crown.
Gottman, J. M., & Levenson, R. (1984). Why marriages fail: Affective and physiological patterns in marital interaction. In J. Masters (Ed.), *Boundary areas in social and developmental psychology* (pp. 110–136). New York, NY: Academic Press.
Gottman, J. M., & Levenson, R. W. (1983). Marital interaction: Physiological linkage and affective change. *Journal of Personality and Social Psychology, 45*(3), 587–597.
Gottman, J. M., & Levenson, R. W. (1992). Marital processes predictive of later dissolution: Behavior, physiology and health. *Journal of Personality and Social Psychology, 41*, 83–96.
Gottman, J. M., & Levenson, R. W. (2002). A two-factor model for predicting when a couple will divorce: Exploratory analyses using 14-year longitudinal data. *Family Process, 41*, 83–96.
Gottman, J. M., McCoy, K., Coan, J., & Collier, H. (1996). The Specific Affect Coding System (SPAFF). In J. M. Gottman (Ed.), *What predicts divorce: The measures.* Hillside, NJ: Erlbaum.
Gottman, J. M., Murry, J. M., Swanson, C., Tyson, R., & Swanson, K. (2002). *The mathematics of marriage: Dynamic nonlinear models.* Cambridge, MA: MIT Press.
Gottman, J. M., & Silver, N. (2012). *What makes love last?* New York, NY: Simon & Schuster.
Johnson, S. M. (2004). *The Practice of emotionally focused couple therapy* (2nd ed.). New York, NY: Brunner/Routledge.
Nagoski, E. (2015). *Come as you are.* New York, NY: Simon & Schuster.
Tavris, C. (1989). *Anger: The misunderstood emotion.* New York, NY: Touchstone Books/Simon & Schuster.
Weiss, R. L. (1980). Strategic behavioral relationship therapy: Toward a model for assessment and intervention. In J. P. Vincent (Ed.), *Advances in family intervention, assessment and theory* (Vol. 1, pp. 229–271). Greenwich, CT: JAI Press.
Wile, D. B. (1988). *After the fight.* New York, NY: Guilford Press.

Chapter 19
Why and How Couples Leave Relationships: A Twenty-First Century Landscape

Jim Sheehan

19.1 Introduction

This chapter examines the phenomenon of couple separation as it presents itself to couple therapists and consultants towards the end of the second decade of the twenty-first century. Against a background where increasing numbers of adults experience themselves as members of a global society and as workers in a global economy, two distinct but linked perspectives will be adopted in pursuit of a deep understanding of the phenomenon. The first perspective is grounded by the effort to understand why couples separate. This *why* of separation will focus on the reasons individuals give to themselves, to each other, and to others for their parting from intimate partners. The second perspective concerns the *how* of couple separation. At this level the exploration will be interested in the relational processes that accompany different kinds of couple separation and how these processes appear to provide opportunities at the same time as exacting costs of different kinds in the lives of separating adults, their children, and those close to them.

The chapter will develop its exploration of the theme in three parts. The first part considers a variety of factors impacting the broader social context in which contemporary couples live a shared existence. Taken together, these contextual factors can be thought of as the still evolving 'conditions of life' in which couples succeed or fail in the maintenance and development of a shared life. The second part of the chapter draws upon a series of three vignettes of separating couples. With each vignette the 'why' and 'how' of separation will be addressed with the assistance of a range of sociological and psychological theory. The vignettes are confined to employed, heterosexual couples who are parents and do not reflect the separation challenges of same-sex couples, couples without children, couples where one member suffers

---

J. Sheehan (✉)
Department of Family Therapy, Vid Specialised University, Oslo, Norway

from significant physical or psychological illness or couples whose persistently low income levels constantly threaten the continuity of their relationships. While these latter groups are part of the broad picture of couple separation they remain, by comparison with income-earning, parental heterosexual couples, a smaller part of the total picture. The chapter will conclude with some brief reflections on questions raised by the images of couple separation presented in the vignettes when set against the background of the contextual factors described in the first part of the chapter.

The chapter is written from the perspective of a couple therapist and consultant whose professional experience over the last 40 years has been gained in both public service and private consultancy in a western European capital. As such, it contains all the biases one might expect from a practitioner situated in a relatively stable political context and in a cultural milieu marked by Western individualist assumptions. Notwithstanding the problematic contexts in which separation decisions are made, within the couple vignettes portrayed in the second part of the chapter a relatively high degree of voluntariness is assumed to underpin decisions by couple members to depart from, or remain in, intimate relationships. It is acknowledged that, at a global level, neither political stability nor voluntariness in couple leave-taking can be assumed. While outside of the direct professional experience of this writer, the chapter acknowledges the plight of those couples and their families trapped in contexts of war and political terror who are either forcefully separated from each other or who make enforced 'decisions' to leave each other for the greater good of saving the lives of some or all of their children.

19.2 Factors Shaping the Character of Twenty-First Century Couple Life

While there are a host of factors which shape the emerging character of contemporary couple life, just six of the most important factors are considered here. While some of these contextual factors emerge from developments in contemporary communications technologies, others can be seen as ongoing responses to the requirements of a developing global capitalism. In describing them it is not suggested that any of these factors, either alone or in combination, can be ascribed causal status in relation to couple separation. When taken together, however, the factors are like a set of fast-flowing rivers in which the contemporary couple must paddle their own, often fragile, canoes.

19.2.1 The Mobile Telephone, the Internet and Social Media

The ubiquitous presence and use of mobile telephones by many couple and family members place them at the heart of a very contemporary paradox. This paradox consists in the fact that while couple and family members are regularly drawn physically together at several points in the day, their attachment to their mobile phones and other modern communications apparatuses positions them simultaneously in a variety of other worlds far removed from couple and family. This paradox of physical proximity to one another being accompanied by different kinds of psychological retreat from each other is captured well by the Polish sociologist, Bauman (2003, p. 64), who describes how homes 'have turned from shared playgrounds of love and friendship into the sites of territorial skirmishes, and from building sites of togetherness into the assemblies of fortified bunkers'.

This tendency for homes to develop into sites of separated togetherness had been noted a decade earlier by Schluter and Lee (1993, p. 37) who observed how 'we have stepped into our houses and closed the door, and then stepped into our separate rooms and closed the door'. With the assistance of different kinds of technological devices, the home, they propose, has been transformed into 'a multipurpose leisure centre where household members can live, as it were, separately side by side' (ibid.). Notwithstanding the extraordinary opportunities created by the mobile telephone and the computer such technologies have that strange capacity to make present to us that which is far away at the same time as distancing us from that which is near.

The mobile telephone has become the key symbol of a virtual proximity made possible by our advancing communications technologies. However, the arrival of virtual proximity, Bauman (2003, p. 62) suggests, 'renders human communications more frequent and more shallow, more intense and more brief'. For Bauman, virtual proximity brings about the separation of communication from relationship. Our contemporary communications technologies allow us to communicate with the outside world through the making of a multiplicity of connections. However, no amount of 'connections' ever materialise into 'relationships' which require much more effort and 'engagement' by individuals. Relationships, we are reminded, require us to be more 'engaged' with another person and such engagement takes more time and more effort than simply being 'connected' to them (Bauman, 2003, p. 63).

In the years since Bauman's comments there has been a considerable amount of empirical research which offers a more nuanced, though not always consistent, picture of those variables of couple and family functioning that appear most related to family members' use of contemporary information and communications technologies. In a review of existing literature in this domain Carvalho, Francisco, and Relvas (2015) found that four variables seemed most related to such technologies. These were: family communication; family cohesion; family roles, rules and intergenerational conflict; and family boundaries.

Several studies (Devitt & Roker, 2009; Hertlein, 2012; Lanigan, 2009) have shown how the use of modern information and communications technologies have facilitated the daily management of family activities in real time and contribute to the maintenance of couple and family relationships, while others (Lanigan, 2009; Stern & Messer, 2009) have shown how the technologies actively foster the development of new patterns of family communication that are realised at low cost. Transnational families, mentioned later in this chapter, are one group of families where such low-cost modern technologies facilitate both the maintenance and re-creation of family bonds notwithstanding geographical distance (Bagicalupe & Lambe, 2011). Use of the technologies has also been shown to assist with the realisation of effective co-parenting relationships and decision-making after separation and divorce (Ganong, Coleman, Feistman, Jamison, & Markham, 2012). Such positive findings are counterbalanced, to some degree, by other studies (Nie, 2001; Watt & White,

1999) that highlight the negative influence the technologies can have on the quality of family relationships and communication. One example of the latter is the way that disconnection between verbal and nonverbal signals can lead to either misunderstanding between couple and family members or to those same individuals becoming isolated from each other within the same family dwelling (Cardoso, Espanha, & Lapa, 2008; Huisman, Catapano, & Edwards, 2012).

With respect to family cohesion a somewhat contradictory picture emerges. While some studies (Chesley & Fox, 2012; Plowman, McPake, & Stephen, 2010) suggest the use of the technologies tends to increase the time families spend together as well as enhancing communication and intimacy among family members, other studies (for example, Williams & Merten, 2011) highlight how large amount of technological equipment and high frequency of use seems to be related to a reduction of both family time and intimacy between family members. With respect to couple life, Coyne et al. (2012) suggest that the use of certain technologies (specifically, the playing of video games) appears to facilitate the occurrence of couple conflict. Many studies (for example, Bagicalupe and Camara, 2011; Lanigan, 2009; Mesch, 2006) note how the development of technological abilities in children and adolescents creates a digital gap, and with it a hierarchy reversal, between themselves and their parents thus facilitating the emergence of intergenerational conflict. In contrast, there seems to be a relative lack of research focus on the impact on couple relationships of a parallel digital gap opening up between couple members themselves.

Where family boundaries are concerned Carvalho et al. (2015) note that a variety of studies (Lanigan, 2009; Mesch, 2006; Stafford & Hillyer, 2012) point to the potential of the technologies to alter the permeability of these boundaries due to changes in the flow of information. Domestic use of the technologies carries the potential to bring about a blurring of necessary boundaries between the family environment and the external world. Such potential weakening of family boundaries may increase the exposure of households to vulnerabilities (Hertlein, 2012; Lanigan, 2009) and inadvertently draw families into situations where there is a lack of privacy or where the safety of their members is compromised (Davies & Gentile, 2012; Williams & Merten, 2011). Notwithstanding the emergence of some contradictory findings in the abovementioned studies, one matter seems increasingly clear. The use of modern information and communications technologies has an influential role in all stages of relationship from relationship initiation and relationship development right through to the post-separation behaviours of divorcing pairs (Eichenberg, Huss, & Kusel, 2017; Sheehan, 2018).

What might such reflections mean for the life of the contemporary couple? These reflections certainly have relevance for those couples whose members have become immersed in communications technologies that privilege the making of multiple connections that are necessarily brief and focussed in character. Sheehan (2018) asks whether the ongoing immersion in the technologies in question, while fostering communications skills that are relevant for many daily life tasks, might have an inhibiting role in the development of relationship skills which allow couple members communicate with each other about more complex and deeper aspects of each other's experience.

19.2.2 The 'Saturated' Character of Postmodern Couple and Family Life

The north American social psychologist Gergen (1991a, 1991b) chose the term 'saturated' to describe the emerging character of postmodern family and couple life as it presented itself to observers in the final decades of the twentieth century. The postmodern family, he suggested, is a place where its members 'feel their lives scattering in intensifying busyness' (1991a, p. 28). By the final decade of the last century we were witnessing family and couple members who had become embedded in a multiplicity of relationships at different times throughout the day which bring them into contact with a host of different cultures, attitudes and ideas. With the aid of all contemporary communications and other technologies such as the computer, the mobile telephone, cars, trains and planes individuals have the means to engage in a large number of different activities in locations far removed from each other. And, at the level of our social relations, Gergen suggests that 'we ingest myriads bits of others' being—values, attitudes, opinions, life-styles, personalities—synthesising and incorporating them into our own definition of self' (p. 28). However, as the postmodern individual looks inwards they are likely to observe 'a maelstrom of partial beings in conflict' (p. 28). It is this experience of the world and of self that Gergen refers to as 'social saturation'. Notwithstanding efforts to coordinate overloaded schedules, couple and family members inevitably end up in varying degrees of conflict with each other and with a sense of fragmentation and chaos marking their lives as each of their members is pulled outwards towards an ever-expanding range of activities and relationships in which they are embedded away from couple and family life.

Typically, the postmodern individual in couple therapy wonders where they will find the energy to rebuild the relationship from which they have withdrawn in favour of one hundred other activities, relationships and obligations outside of couple life. The difficulty of finding a balance between work and family is exacerbated by exceeding demands on the workplace in the twenty-first century (Burnett, Swan, & Cooper, 2014) which some career driven couples buy into to move on. On the other end of the spectrum, workers with a low level of education find themselves exploited by having to take on precarious jobs and work irregular hours to earn a living (Abela & Renoux, 2014).

19.2.3 Sex and the Cyberworld in Contemporary Couple Life

The internet has increased the availability of different kinds of sexual opportunities to any individual who has both the opportunity and technological skills to gain access. Some couple therapists in the western world (Goldberg, Petersen, Rosen and Sara, 2008) report significant increases in couples seeking therapy because one or both of their members are shunning 'real-world' sex opportunities within their couple in favour of 'webcam' or other online sexual experiences with an unknown other or others. In the mid-1970s Shorter (1975) noted that one key factor facilitating the emergence of the 'postmodern' couple and family was the gradual replacing of property, first with sentiment and later with sex, as the bond uniting a man and a woman. More recently it has been suggested (Sheehan, 2018) that with a combination of the greater availability of extra-dyadic, internet-facilitated, sexual opportunities for individuals and a weakened norm relating to couple sexual fidelity, we may now be witnessing a beginning of the dislodgement of sex as the bond uniting the couple and, with such dislodgement, a new kind of destabilisation of couple life.

19.2.4 Global Workers in a Global Economy

The time when young workers, equipped with whatever skills and qualifications they had acquired, could expect to find permanent employment or ongoing income-earning opportunities close to their families of origin or even in the country where they grew up has long disappeared. The capacity of young workers to earn a livelihood has become growingly dependent on their mobility within a global economy. The consequences of this development are that, in contrast to their parents' generation, a great many more of their peers will form couple relationships with partners from countries and cultures other than their own and will go on to create transnational marriages and, in time, to experience transnational divorces. As can be seen from one of the vignettes below the transnational divorce provides many challenges for its participants regarding resolution of such issues as the residence and contact arrangements for partners and children following divorce.

19.2.5 A Changing Set of Power Relations Between Men and Women in Domestic and Social Domains

Over the last 300 years most parts of the industrialised world have seen a gradual release of women from the confines of child-bearing and child-rearing roles within family structures dominated by patriarchal values. Whether we see the many changes in the position of women as driven solely by the unrelenting spread of global capitalism or by a mixture of economic and cultural factors, the concrete reality for many contemporary couples is that they reside in societies which, officially at least, adopt social policies that foster gender equality in the domestic, workplace and other social and cultural domains. However, transitions along this pathway towards gender equality happen at different speeds in different locations and, depending upon other contextual factors in a couple's life, can provide significant challenges to couple stability.

19.2.6 *Income Level and the Fate of Couple Relationship*

One strand in separation and divorce research in recent decades has been the effort to specify predictors of divorce within different domains. Within demographic and economic domains Amato (2010) lists 'being poor' and 'experiencing unemployment' among a group of major risk factors for separation and divorce (p. 651). Many couples in different parts of the globe, whether through low levels of education (another risk factor for divorce) or depressed local economies, live on inadequate incomes for different periods of time. For them 'being poor' becomes a condition of life, a constant background against which they must attempt to provide for the basic necessities of life (ongoing shelter, food, clothing) for themselves and their children. Clinicians are not surprised to find that such economic risk factors for separation and divorce are often combined in couples' lives with specific interpersonal risk factors such as domestic violence (Lawrence & Bradbury, 2001), infidelity (Hall & Fincham, 2006) and frequent conflict (DeMaris, 2000).

In summary, then, the twenty-first century couple must manage their relationship against the background of a number of challenges, each of which may be perceived as opportunities from another angle. Couple members are constantly drawn away from the centre of their relationship by the constant use of communications technologies that favour connection-making rather than relationship-building and by 'saturated' lives that always require their presence elsewhere. Their easy access to extra-dyadic sexual opportunities in the cyberworld and beyond carries the potential to reposition the place of sexuality within their own couple bond. As workers in a global economy they must be ready to privilege residential mobility over stability in the interests of continuing employment and livelihood and must be ready to negotiate an ever-changing set of power relations between women and men within their couple. In addition to these challenges a group of couples, varying in size from one state to another, must take on the task of managing their relationship in the context of poverty and inadequate income over longer or shorter periods of time.

19.3 Events and Processes Within Contemporary Couple Separation

What does contemporary couple separation look like? There are a host of different kinds of couple separation, each brought into being by unique couples making unique decisions in unique circumstances. The theme will be explored here through three vignettes of separating couples. The vignettes are fictional constructs and do not reflect the actual circumstances of any couple known to the writer, directly or indirectly. The vignettes, however, remain faithful to relational processes observed by the writer in many different separating couples since the turn of the century.

19.3.1 The Disappearance of Feelings: Paul and Hilda

Paul and Hilda met when they were both 23 years and pursuing the same postgraduate program in Business and Finance at an élite London-based university. Paul was the second of four children of Irish parents living in Dublin while Hilda was the eldest of four sisters raised in Berlin by German parents. The couple had fallen 'head-over-heels' in love with each other shortly after their arrival in London and started to live with each other on a full-time basis 6 months into the relationship. Over the next 6 years they both, with the aid of fellowships, completed their postgraduate and doctoral studies in London before engaging in postdoctoral studies which brought them a range of shared travel opportunities to exotic places.

By the time they were 30 years they had both commenced very well-paid employments in Dublin with different finance institutions and by the time they were 35 years they were the parents of 2-year old twin boys and the owners of a home that was rapidly appreciating in value. They both worked very hard and both achieved a number of promotions within their employing institutions within a surprisingly short space of time. They managed the care of the boys with the assistance of a child-minder who came to their home from 7 am, when they both left for work, to 7 pm, when they both arrived home from work, 5 days per week.

When their boys were 3 years old, the couple commenced couple therapy at Hilda's request following a 6-month period in which they had been having frequent arguments about relatively minor matters and little or no sex. She described for Paul and their therapist how her 'feelings' for Paul seemed to have 'disappeared' and that this seemed to have happened almost unnoticeably, even to herself, over the previous year. She felt she still 'loved' Paul but was no longer 'in love' with him. She had also become disenchanted with Ireland and no longer felt excited by living 'on a small island cut off from mainland Europe.' Following a number of exploratory sessions over a 3-month period she felt she could no longer stay in her marriage to Paul as she could not envisage a future with Paul in the absence of 'strong feelings' for him. Paul was devastated initially and wanted Hilda to take some time to see if they, together, could re-find the feelings they had shared for each other for so long. Following a number of further sessions in which there were no changes in Hilda's feelings, Paul felt that it was time to 'surrender' and commented to the therapist that 'I just can't fight this. I don't think her feelings are going to return'.

The couple moved quickly into mediation where they managed to reach a full agreement within four sessions about the care of the children and financial matters despite Hilda's expressed intention to take up her employer's offer of a promotion which involved taking responsibility for the company's European division from its London base. Their agreement, which formed the basis of their subsequent divorce, saw the children move to London with Hilda with Paul taking care of the boys in her London accommodation every second weekend as well as having the boys back in Dublin for six scheduled 5-day periods during the year. Within 9 months of the completion of mediation Hilda and Paul were both in the early stages of new relationships in London and Dublin and had redefined their relationship as 'co-parents who share friends'.

In the above vignette we can see that the transitions in the relationship from its inception, through its major changes, to its final cessation all occurred within the framework of a discourse of romantic love. In this particular couple's positioning within this discourse their 'feelings' had been spoken about as something independent from themselves and as something over which they had, ultimately, little or no control. Hilda's feelings had 'disappeared', as she described, 'almost unnoticeably' to herself. Paul, for his part, while devastated initially, was equally in the grip of this discourse which did not allow him to be critical of his partner for something over which she did not have control or of himself for failing to assist his partner in refinding these 'feelings' for him. As he said to their therapist; 'I just can't fight this'. Øfsti (2008), in her study of Norwegian therapists' discourses of love, intimacy and sexuality, noted the objectifying function accorded by some of her participants to the phenomenon of 'being in love' and she suggests that within the culture of her study's participants the phenomenon of *being in love* is so taken for granted that it almost acquires 'the ontological status of a natural phenomenon' (p. 104).

If the *why* of the above couple's separation can be explained in terms of Hilda's repositioning within a discourse of romantic love, it was their joint positioning within the same discourse that enabled the *how* of their separation to be realised within a relatively amicable, conflict-free, mediation process. It is also clear that their own experiences of success at work, friendship networks that stretched between London, Dublin and Berlin, supportive extended family networks, flexible employment patterns and sufficient money for regular travel between London and Dublin all contributed towards making the transition as manageable as possible for themselves and their boys.

If the first vignette portrays a type of separation which, notwithstanding the transitional crisis it signifies for the individuals involved, is marked by very low levels of couple conflict, high levels of cooperation within a continuing shared parenthood, and low levels of personal cost associated with the transition, the second vignette reflects the opposite end of the post-separation couple conflict spectrum. In this vignette we see how the separation crisis can develop into a process that extends over several years, is marked by very high levels of interpersonal conflict, low levels of trust in the parenting relationship, and has the potential to exact extraordinarily high levels of personal cost in the lives of parents, children and others close to them.

19.3.2 Domestic Violence and the Transnational Couple: Naomi and Emmanuel

Naomi, a 32-year old teacher from Ireland, met Emmanuel, a 34-year old French-Canadian, on a summer yoga retreat week in the south of Italy. She was the only child of Irish parents who were both art teachers. She had grown up in a household where her father drank heavily and intermittently abused her mother physically. She was the mother of two boys aged 4 and 2 years she had with a previous partner from whom she was separated from before the birth of her youngest son. Emmanuel was the only son of his Canadian father and Parisienne mother who had a prolonged high-conflict separation during his adolescence due to his father's numerous infidelities. While academically bright, Emmanuel had failed to achieve in school and had spent 12 years unsuccessfully trying to occupy positions made available to him in different companies and businesses owned by his father in the Toronto area where he had grown up. He had also developed a pattern of binge drinking in his early adulthood which played a significant role in his employment failures. When he met Naomi he had recently emerged from an 8-week residential addiction treatment program in Toronto and his participation in the yoga retreat was part of a self-care plan agreed with his after-care counsellor.

The couple made such a strong connection, emotionally and sexually, on the yoga week that Emmanuel decided to extend his European stay in order to spend more time with Naomi in Ireland. Within a 6-month period they were residing together in Ireland with Naomi's children and within 18 months Naomi had given birth to their own daughter, Lucy. When Lucy was 2 years the couple decided to move to live in Paris for a couple of years with the twin objectives of Emmanuel being able to get better-paid employment than he had been able to realise in Ireland and of enabling the development of a bond between Lucy and Emmanuel's mother who had been residing alone in Paris for several years. After 18 months in Paris Emmanuel returned to a pattern of binge drinking and began to be emotionally abusive to Naomi. Despite Emmanuel having regained his sobriety, Naomi insisted that the family return to Ireland where she was able to resume her teaching job. Emmanuel once again lost his sobriety and began to be physically abusive to Naomi in the middle of one of his binge drinking episodes. Naomi immediately made an application in the Irish courts for an order excluding Emmanuel from the home. Following his court-ordered exclusion from the home and having nowhere else in Ireland to live and no local supports Emmanuel returned to Paris to stay with his mother.

Over the next 2 years Emmanuel, with the financial assistance of both his mother and father, was in and out of the Irish courts struggling over his desire to achieve what he considered an appropriate level of contact with their daughter, Lucy. He felt that Naomi was trying to cut him out of his daughter's life as she appeared to have cut her sons' father out of their life. On the other hand, Naomi insisted that her reluctance to agree a contact regime for Lucy was related to lack of assurances about Emmanuel's continuing sobriety and his ability to provide safe care and safe return for Lucy. Following a number of court hearings, professional evaluations and appeals in the family courts, final orders for contact were made which allowed Emmanuel to have Lucy in his care in Ireland for one weekend every month and for four 4-day periods per year in France on condition that his mother would always be present to supervise this contact in both countries. Emmanuel remained angry about the supervised element of the contact orders and refused to have any direct communication with Naomi about the pragmatics of each contact period. This communication was managed for him by his mother who had maintained a positive relationship with Naomi. Despite the distance, hostility and lack of trust in the parental relationship the contact periods went without incident for 6 months and

Lucy returned home to her mother after each period with positive reports of her experiences with her father who clearly spoilt her a lot while in his care. However, in the middle of the second Paris-based contact period Naomi received a call from Emmanuel's mother indicating concern at Emmanuel's failure to meet her at the exit of a theme park where she had earlier left him and Lucy to spend the day together. Efforts to reach him on his mobile proved fruitless and within 24 h the French police had established that he had taken a flight from Paris to Toronto with Lucy. It was 3 weeks before Interpol and the Canadian police finally found Emmanuel and Lucy staying at a small rural motel 300 km outside Toronto.

When Lucy was seen by local child protection social workers in the area where she was located, they found an 8 year old girl who was both distressed and brainwashed. She told the social workers that she had been beaten repeatedly by her mother in Ireland and that her mother would not believe her when she told her she was being bullied at school. Emmanuel told the professionals he had taken Lucy away for her own protection and, with the financial assistance of his father, he engaged a very experienced legal team in efforts to have Lucy remain with him in Canada. Naomi, having initiated legal proceedings under the Hague Convention to have Lucy returned to Ireland, was re-introduced to her daughter after a gap of almost 4 weeks. To her utter dismay Lucy kicked and screamed and refused to stay with her in the hotel room she had obtained with the help of local lawyers. Due to a variety of legal delays it was 6 months before the Canadian court hearing the Hague Convention proceedings ruled that Lucy's country of 'habitual residence' was Ireland and that she should be returned there in the care of her mother and that Ireland was the appropriate jurisdiction for the hearing of all further disputes between the parents about her care. Lucy continued to protest as she boarded the plane back to Ireland in the company of her mother and an assisting professional.

When we consider the *why* of the couple separation portrayed in the above vignette, it is clear that a mixture of domestic abuse and addiction were the immediate precursors to, and reasons for, the ending of the relationship. While these experiences of abuse are particularly traumatic for victims and their witnessing children, the developing relational processes that unfold as part of the *how* of separation can be even more traumatic. In such high-conflict post-separation dramas, individuals in transnational couple separations may have to engage in legal proceedings in more than one jurisdiction, leave their employments for periods of time to contest child abduction and related proceedings, leave their other children for long periods of time in the care of relatives or friends, and incur significant financial debt due to loss of earnings, legal fees and unanticipated child-minding costs. Indeed, high-conflict relational processes after separation can traumatise and injure their participants in many different ways both in the short and long term. While the conflict is raging the participants often remain in elevated states of emotional arousal as they try to anticipate or counter the next move of their adversary ex-partner.

Conflict at this level over the emotional goods that are embodied in parent–child relationships is like a hypnotic glue which often transfixes the obsessional gaze of conflict participants on each other to the detriment of being able to see and appreciate a broader picture, including the picture of their child's needs for a relationship with each of them. Insecure attachment styles (Bowlby, 1969, 1973) play their part in trapping participants in cycles of fear of each other that lead to behaviours that often, paradoxically, bring about the very thing they fear most, that is, the temporary or more permanent loss of their child from their life. Other costs for adults in high conflict disputes over child residence and contact may include losing a foothold on career pathways, disengagement from friendship networks as well as disconnection from health-promoting leisure activities (Sheehan, 2018). By comparison with the couple in the first vignette who were able to form new romantic bonds within a year of residential separation, high conflict ex-partners, for the most part, tend to have little energy or emotional availability to engage with the possibility of developing new intimate bonds.

When we consider the costs for children like Lucy of being at the centre of prolonged conflict between her parents about her care, such children regularly suffer the emotional burden of the conflict in a way that restricts their normal social development due to having to comply with court orders aimed at the maintenance of their relationship with both parents. Such children work hard to maintain their relationship with both parents and must participate in two familial worlds that remain sharply divided and disengaged from each other. While there is a certain amount of evidence suggesting that child abduction, when it occurs, does inflict harm on children (Agopian, 1984; Hegar & Grief, 1991), sometimes long-term harm (Grief, 2000, 2009), it is also clear that this is not always the case. Where the abducting parent is a victim of domestic violence the abduction of the child by the victim parent to a safe context may be the first significant step towards the improvement of the child's circumstances.

However, in the case of children like Lucy in the above vignette the experience of abduction by a non-resident parent allied to their verbal interference with the child's experience of a prior positive bond with their resident parent (brainwashing) can prove to be a psychological violation with both short- and long-term consequences for the child's trust in the world around them. Such abducted children regularly lose out academically as they are often displaced from their normal school settings for prolonged periods of time and, like some of their parents, become disengaged from their friendship networks and associated recreational and sporting pursuits. When restored to the care of their traumatised resident parents they often require extensive therapeutic assistance.

19.4 Transnational Divorce Processes

A feature of the second vignette is that the separating couple at its centre is a transnational couple. Earlier in this chapter we noted how the increasing mobility of young and not so young workers within a global economy was likely to lead to an ever-increasing number of transnational couple relationships and marriages. While not enough is known about the long-term outcome of different kinds of transnational relationships/marriages and divorces by comparison with couples whose members share the same state-of-origin, Sportel's (2016) study of a sample of 26 divorced individuals who had been part of Dutch-Egyptian or Dutch-Moroccan marriages throws some light on the 'why' and 'how' of a small group of transnational divorces. While some of the study's participants saw themselves as victims of *Bezness* (a kind of false love in which one party emotionally manipulates another into contracting a legal marriage for the purposes of gaining a visa or progressing their legal entry process into their partner's country) it was clear that many of the participants seemed to be able to work out post-separation arrangements regarding the residence and care of partners and children in a relatively amicable way. However, the study found that when conflict did arise about these matters it often became very intense and involved child abduction and other high conflict strategies. Another particularly abusive means of bringing about a separation in transnational relationships noted by Sportel is when a male takes his female partner and children back to her country of origin for a holiday and, without warning, returns to his own country alone at the same time as destroying the residence papers and passports of his partner and children.

Despite the continuing efforts of non-governmental organisations to combat this practice, such partner 'dumping' can make it next to impossible in some instances for women to legally contest their interest in marital property or to secure financial support for the care of their children which, through manipulation, becomes fully their responsibility. By comparison with the Irish/French-Canadian couple at the centre of the second vignette whose states shared the same language and were both signatories to the Hague Convention, the Sportel study shows how the transnational separation and divorce process is regularly circumscribed by the complex interactions between marital status, migration law and family legislation in the countries of origin of both couple members.

If the above two lengthy vignettes reflect two ends of a separation-related conflict continuum, the third vignette reflect another typical kind of couple separation with its own unique pathway to conflict resolution and associated costs.

19.4.1 Infidelity and Its Wounds: Hannah and Roger

Hannah and Roger were both 39 years and the married parents of a 14-year old girl and boys of nine and 7 years when Roger's infidelity came to light through Hannah's discovery of sexual text messages on his phone. Hannah was a nurse in the family's local hospital in the northeast of the UK while Roger was employed as a stores manager in their local supermarket. While Hannah was on night shifts in the hospital Roger began watching pornography on his own personal computer as well as going on dating sites before commencing a pattern of chatting to other women online. Eventually he began to date some of these women and had a number of sexual liaisons before making a stronger connection with one particular woman. When Hannah confronted him about the text messages she discovered he told her the truth about what he had been doing. Notwithstanding his apology and assurance that he would stop the activities, Hannah insisted that he leave the home while she had an opportunity to consider her position. She was traumatised by the discovery and Roger's subsequent revelations and quickly came to a decision that she wanted their separation to be permanent.

In the moment of her crisis Hannah leaned on her 14-year old daughter for emotional support. Her daughter, on learning of her father's behaviour, refused to have anything to do with him despite Roger's efforts to contact her after he left the house. When he tried to meet her outside her school she ran away from him and refused to go to school for a period until she was reassured through third parties that he would not approach her school again. After 4 weeks of separation her younger brothers began to spend two 3-h periods per week with their father. This pattern of outings lasted for a month before both boys refused to go with their father. At different times they told assisting mental health professionals that they felt either sick or bored while with their father or that they found their father to be 'mean' in ways they were unable to specify. Court applications by Roger for contact periods with his two sons followed this refusal and notwithstanding professional evaluations and subsequent court orders for continuing contact for the boys with Roger the children became more resistant to such contact. Within 20 months of the infidelity discovery and subsequent residential separation and following six court appearances over the same period neither Hannah nor any of the three children were having any communication with Roger either directly, by telephone or online. Roger began to feel hopeless and helpless around the loss of relationship with all his family members and, on the advice of his therapist, let go of any further efforts to seek the court's assistance in overcoming what he saw as Hannah's alienation of the children from him. His hope that the children would eventually come back to him when they were older was not realised.

For many years couple therapists have noted that infidelity is one of the most common reasons that couples seek assistance (Whisman, Dixon, & Johnson, 1997). Yet the extent to which couple separation decisions are directly attributable to infidelity disclosure/discovery remains unclear. It also remains unclear whether the ease of availability of sexual opportunities online or the use of the internet in finding affair partners has increased the prevalence of infidelity in populations having internet access. One thing seems clear to clinicians, however, and that is that infidelity disclosure or discovery in relationships where fidelity is either the stated or assumed norm regularly has a traumatic impact on either one or both couple members and puts the continuity of the relationship at risk (Hall & Fincham, 2006; Weeks, Gambescia, & Jenkins, 2003).

In the vignette described above the traumatic wounds experienced following affair discovery was the trigger for the redrawing of emotional boundaries between a mother and her teenage daughter which, in turn, became the platform for the alienation of younger children from a 'wounding' father. Given that not all affair discovery leads to relationship termination and not all relationship cessation following affair discovery/disclosure leads to the complete eclipse of children's relationship with an unfaithful parent, it is important to consider why some wounded parents seem able to bear their traumatic wound without allowing their personal sense of betrayal jeopardise the ongoing relationship of their children with the other parent.

Attachment theory (Bowlby, 1969, 1973) may go some way towards providing a possible answer to this puzzle. It may be that those wounded parents who have more secure-autonomous adult attachment styles (Howe, 2011) have access to more relationship resources in the form of trusted friends and family members to help them absorb traumatic news than those wounded partners with more problematic adult attachment styles where traumatic news appears to drive them into an abyss of fear, rage and a sense of chaotic abandonment without nearby adult supports to help process what has happened. As the vignette suggests the short and long-term costs for both children and adults resulting from the trauma of infidelity discovery in certain circumstances can be immense.

19.5 Concluding Reflections on the Vignettes in the Context of Postmodern Couple Life

What kinds of questions and reflections might the foregoing images of separating couples propose about the character of both contemporary couple formation and dissolution? Just three reflections will be made here. The first concerns the question of 'feelings' as the basis for couple formation and dissolution; the second concerns the persistence of a certain range of adult behaviours as a continuing basis for relationship endings; and the third concerns the contribution that negotiations about gender equity within couple relationships can make to either couple separation or stability.

While the status of 'feelings' as a determinant in couple formation as well as in couple decision-making about termination was more explicitly present within the first vignette there were indications that it was probably a significant factor in couple formation within all vignettes. While many contemporary couples enter therapy with one member struggling with the question of staying or leaving because of the disappearance of 'feelings', the power of the discourse of romantic love within such dialogues about separation is regularly contextualised by other discourses relating to shared parental responsibility, shared lifestyle and, perhaps, shared financial debt. Different cultures and subcultures will vary in the extent to which the power of discourses about romantic feelings hold unrivalled sway. We need to know more about those couples who remain together even when one of the partners has experienced the disappearance of 'feelings' that are deeply important to them. Does the partner in this position continue to quietly pursue what Øfsti (2008, p. 95) calls 'emotional peak experiences' outside their relationships or do they find alternative bases through which they gain satisfaction in their couple life? Or do these couples find other resolutions? Difficult research!

Effects of a different kind are at the heart of two particular studies focused on predictors of divorce. Building upon the earlier work of Gottman (1993) on divorce prediction, the first of these (Gottman & Levenson, 2000) was a long-term, prospective, longitudinal study which found that a different set of variables predicted early divorcing (in the first 7 years) than later divorcing (the period running up to the time when the first child is 14 years old). Negative affect during conflict predicted early divorcing but it did not predict later divorcing. By contrast, the lack of positive affect within events-of-the-day and conflict discussions predicted later divorcing but did not predict early divorcing. The second study (Lavner & Bradbury, 2012) was aimed at identifying risk factors early in marriage that distinguish initially satisfied couples who eventually divorce from those who remain married. This study, which looked at relationship outcomes for couples with high levels of satisfaction in the first 4 years of marriage, found that divorcing couples displayed more negative communication, emotion and social support as newlyweds compared with couples who did not divorce.

While couple consultants see some pairs whose dilemmas are focussed on the presence or absence of 'feelings' or on whether their respective expectations of the relationship are sufficiently complementary to allow them contemplate an ongoing shared future, I suspect that most couple consultations occur in the context of problematic behaviour in one partner threatening the continuity of the couple bond. Domestic violence, infidelity of different kinds, along with addiction-related behaviours remain, I suspect, the stuff of most couple consultations/therapies that lead towards a separation decision. And, regularly, such decisions are made by individuals who are not as well-resourced personally, psychologically, socially or financially as the couple members in the first vignette who found a way to create a new life and forge new attachments in a relatively short period of time. Many couple separations are traumatic events for one or both partners where separation often compounds the unhealed wounds from earlier lives and gives rise to mental health challenges that were not present during the time of the relationship.

Finally, the question of gender equity is now more consciously present in the dialogues about heterosexual couple separation than it was even at the end of the last century. A strengthening discourse about women's rights and entitlement to equality in different spheres is as much a reality in many societies as is the lack of equity within the lived relationships between men and women in different institutions within those same societies. The couple as an institution feels the tensions created by this gap between aspiration and lived reality as much and more than any other social institution. Often the couple consultant is witness to women's decision-making about separation whose meaning is intimately bound up with an assertion about entitlements to equity in contexts where the requirements for such equity are either ignored or denied.

References

Abela, A., & Renoux, M. C. (2014). Families living on the margin in affluent societies. In A. Abela & J. Walker (Eds.), *Contemporary issues in family studies: Global Perspectives on partnerships, parenting and support in a changing world* (pp. 302–316). Chichester, UK: Wiley-Blackwell.

Agopian, M. W. (1984). The impact on children of abduction by parents. *Child Welfare, 63*(6), 511–519.

Amato, P. R. (2010). Research on divorce: Continuing trends and new developments. *Journal of Marriage and Family, 72,* 650–666.

Bagicalupe, G., & Camara, M. (2011). Adolescentes digitales: El rol transformador de las redes y las interacciones virtuales. In R. Pereira (Ed.), *Entre impotencia, resiliencia y poder: Adolescentes en el Siglo XXI* (pp. 227–241). Madrid, Spain: Morata.

Bagicalupe, G., & Lambe, S. (2011). Virtualizing intimacy: Information communication technologies and transnational families in therapy. *Family Process, 50,* 12–26.

Bauman, Z. (2003). *Liquid love.* Cambridge, UK: Polity Press.

Bowlby, J. (1969). *Attachment and loss* (Vol. 1: Attachment). London, UK: Hogarth Press.

Bowlby, J. (1973). *Attachment and loss* (Vol. 2: Separation: Anger and anxiety). London, UK: Hogarth Press.

Burnett, S. B., Swan, J., & Cooper, C. (2014). Working families: Who cares? In A. Abela & J. Walker (Eds.), *Contemporary issues In family studies: Global Perspectrives on partnerships, parenting and support in a changing world* (pp. 215–226). Chichester, England: Wiley-Blackwell.

Cardoso, G., Espanha, R., & Lapa, T. (2008). Dinamica familiar e interaccao em torno dos media: Autonomia dos jovens, autoridade e control paternal sobre os media em Portugal. *Revista Cominicacao e Sociedade, 13,* 31–53.

Carvalho, J., Francisco, R., & Relvas, A. P. (2015). Family functioning and information and communication technologies: How do they relate? A literature review. *Computers in Human Behaviour, 45,* 99–108.

Chesley, N., & Fox, B. (2012). E-mail's use and perceived effect on family relationship quality: Variations by gender and race/ethnicity. *Sociological Focus, 45,* 63–84.

Coyne, S. M., Busby, D., Bushman, B. J., Gentile, D. A., Ridge, R., & Stockdale, L. (2012). Gaming in the game of love: Effects of video games on conflict in couples. *Family Relations, 61,* 388–396.

Davies, J. J., & Gentile, D. A. (2012). Responses to children's media use in families with and without siblings: A family development perspective. *Family Relations, 61,* 410–425.

DeMaris, A. (2000). Till discord do us part: The role of physical and verbal conflict in union disruption. *Journal of Marriage and the Family, 62,* 683–692.

Devitt, K., & Roker, D. (2009). The role of mobile phones in family communication. *Children and Society, 23,* 189–202.

Eichenberg, C., Huss, J., & Kusel, C. (2017). From online dating to online divorce: An overview of couple and family relationships shaped through digital media. *Contemporary Family Therapy, 39,* 249–260.

Ganong, L. H., Coleman, M., Feistman, R., Jamison, T., & Markham, M. (2012). Communication technology and postdivorce coparenting. *Family Relations, 61,* 397–409.

Gergen, K. J. (1991a). The saturated family. *The Family Therapy Networker, 15*(5), 27–35.

Gergen, K. J. (1991b). *The saturated self.* New York, NY: Basic Books.

Gottman, J. M. (1993). *What predicts divorce?* (p. 1600). New York, NY: Psychology Press.

Gottman, J. M., & Levenson, R. W. (2000). The timing of divorce: Predicting when a couple will divorce over a 14-year period. *Journal of Marriage and Family, 62*(3), 737–745.

Grief, G. L. (2000). A parental report on the long-term consequences for children of abduction by the other parent. *Child Psychiatry and Human Development, 31,* 59–66.

Grief, G. L. (2009). The long-term aftermath of child abduction: Two case-studies and the implications for family therapy. *The American Journal of Family Therapy, 37,* 273–275.

Goldberg, P. D., Peterson, B. D., Rosen, K. H., Sara, M. L. (2008) Cybersex: The impact of a contemporary problem on the practices of marriage and family therapists. *Journal of Marital and Family Therapy 34*(4), 469–480

Hall, J. H., & Fincham, F. D. (2006). Relationship dissolution after infidelity. In M. Fine & J. Harvey (Eds.), *Handbook of divorce and relationship dissolution* (pp. 153–168). Hillsdale, NJ: Erlbaum.

Hegar, R. L., & Grief, G. L. (1991). Abduction of children by parents: A survey of the problem. *Social Work, 36,* 421–427.

Hertlein, K. M. (2012). Digital dwelling: Technology in couple and family relationships. *Family Relations, 61,* 374–387.

Howe, D. (2011). *Attachment across the Lifecourse: A brief introduction*. London, UK: Palgrave.
Huisman, S., Catapano, S., & Edwards, A. (2012). The impact of technology on families. *International Journal of Education and Psychology in the Community, 2*, 44–62.
Lanigan, J. D. (2009). A sociotechnological model for family research and intervention: How information and communication technologies affect family life. *Marriage and Family Review, 45*, 587–609.
Lavner, J. A., & Bradbury, T. N. (2012). Why do even satisfied newlyweds eventually go on to divorce? *Journal of Family Psychology, 26*(1), 1–10.
Lawrence, E., & Bradbury, T. N. (2001). Physical aggression and marital dysfunction: A longitudinal analysis. *Journal of Family Psychology, 15*, 135–154.
Mesch, G. (2006). Family relations and the internet: Exploring a family boundaries approach. *Journal of Family Communication, 6*, 119–138.
Nie, N. H. (2001). Sociability, interpersonal relations, and the internet: Reconciling conflicting findings. *American Behavioral Scientist, 45*, 420–435.
Øfsti, A. K. S. (2008). *Some call it love: Exploring Norwegian couple therapists' discourses of love, intimacy and sexuality* (Doctorate of Systemic Psychotherapy, University of East London at the Tavistock Clinic).
Plowman, L., McPake, J., & Stephen, C. (2010). The technologisation of childhood? Young children and technology in the home. *Children and Society, 24*, 63–74.
Schluter, M., & Lee, D. (1993). *The R factor*. London, UK: Hodder and Stoughton.
Sheehan, J. (2018). *Family conflict after separation and divorce: Mental health professional interventions in changing societies*. London, UK: Palgrave.
Shorter, E. (1975). *The making of the modern family*. New York, NY: Basic Books.
Sportel, I. (2016). *Divorce in transnational families: Marriage, migration and family law*. London, UK: Palgrave Macmillan.
Stafford, L., & Hillyer, J. D. (2012). Information and communication technologies in personal relationships. *Review of Communication, 12*, 290–312.
Stern, M. J., & Messer, C. (2009). How family members stay in touch: A quantitative investigation of core family networks. *Marriage and Family Review, 45*, 654–676.
Watt, D., & White, J. M. (1999). Computers and the family life: A family development perspective. *Journal of Comparative Family Studies, 30*, 1–15.
Weeks, G. R., Gambescia, N., & Jenkins, R. E. (2003). *Treating infidelity: Therapeutic dilemmas and effective strategies*. New York, NY: Norton.
Whisman, M. A., Dixon, A. E., & Johnson, B. (1997). Therapists' perspectives of couple problems and treatment issues in couple therapy. *Journal of Family Psychology, 11*, 361–366.
Williams, A. M., & Merten, M. J. (2011). iFamily: Internet and social media technology in the family context. *Family and Consumer Sciences Research Journal, 40*, 150–170.

Chapter 20
Between the Couple and Living Alone

Lynn Jamieson

20.1 Introduction

It may seem paradoxical to include a chapter on living alone in a volume on 'couple relationships' but the pervasive trend towards living alone at all stages of the adult life course makes academic dialogue about the relationship between 'the couple' and living alone increasingly urgent. It is over simplistic to assume a state of emergency in couple relationships signalled by the increase in the proportion of adults living alone at all ages (Jamieson & Simpson, 2013; Wasoff & Jamieson, 2005). This increase is, however, clearly related to changing patterns of entering and leaving couple relationships as shown in the documentation of demographic trends further elucidated by qualitative research. Living alone as a young adult is relatively common across the rich world, but particularly in northern and western Europe and parts of North America where it is normative to leave the parental home early in young adulthood (Jamieson & Simpson, 2013; Klinenberg, 2012; Sobotka & Toulemon, 2008). However, it is also becoming increasingly common in Asia (Yeung & Cheung, 2015; Ho, 2015; Raymo, 2015; Yip & Forrest, 2014). Levin and Trost (1999) suggested that once it became socially accepted normal practice for a heterosexual couple to live together without being married, a trend that occurred first in the Nordic countries, then LATs, living-apart-together, that is, being self-defined as a couple but choosing not to live together, also became more imaginable (Levin, 2004). There has been much research and debate.

For instance, European studies in France (Beaujouan, Regnier-Loilier, & Villeneuve-Gokalp, 2009), Spain (Castro-Martín, Domínguez-Folgueras, & Martín-García, 2008); Germany (Ermisch & Seidler, 2008) and the UK (Coulter & Hu, 2017; Duncan & Phillips, 2010, 2008; Haskey & Lewis, 2006) have established

L. Jamieson (✉)
Centre for Research on Families and Relationships, University of Edinburgh, Edinburgh, UK
e-mail: Lynn.Jamieson@ed.ac.uk

that choosing a long-term or permanent arrangement of being a couple without living together remains relatively unusual, except perhaps in later life. Nevertheless, the trends of living alone and of formation and dissolution of couple relationships are not independent and their mutual influences need to be unpacked.

In general, as the age of first marriage has risen, and the likelihood of living together prior to marriage has increased, so also has the number of young adults who have some experience of living alone prior to living with a partner. Analysis of longitudinal household survey data indicates that living alone all of adult life is far more unusual than spending part of the adult lifespan prior to age 75 living alone (Wasoff & Jamieson, 2005). In southern Europe, it is not very remarkable for young people to live with their parents until they marry, hence continuing to combine the transitions of establishing a new household, entering co-resident partnership and changing legal status to married (Aassve et al., 2006). This pattern is utterly exceptional in northern Europe where these transitions are now typically separated in time and by interceding transitions (Lesthaeghe, 2010). Leaving the parental home almost always occurs well before marriage. For example, in the UK living away from the parental home rather than marriage is the required proof of independence and adulthood, although the practical possibilities of leaving home vary with economic circumstances, family support and local housing markets (Heath & Calvert, 2013; Stone, Berrington, & Falkingham, 2011). For young people who have left home, returning is typically seen as undesirable, except as a temporary stop gap measure. Marriage is typically separated from the transition to a co-resident partnership since the overwhelming majority of those who marry have already established co-residence. In other words, marriage is no longer regarded as a necessary step to establishing a long-term committed partnership, although it is still experienced as publically demonstrating commitment and establishing stronger security for children by legalising the arrangement. However, differences are diminishing between Southern and Northern Europe as cohabitation and living alone both become more common among young adults (Lesthaeghe, 2010).

Living alone in the twenties to the forties age group is the corollary of disrupted partnerships as well as delayed partnership. When heterosexual parenting couples separate, most typically children and their mother become a lone parent family and men often become a one-person household. This and men's slightly lower rates of partnering, typically explain the excess of men living alone over women at working ages. These trends, however, do not signal a demise in the desire for or idealisation of being partnered, at least not yet (Jamieson & Simpson, 2013). Depending on a person's cultural and biographical circumstances, living alone is typically experienced as either a normal stage of development, a part of becoming an independent adult, or as a necessary but undesired phase of life resulting from one of three conditions, failure to find a partner, the breakdown of a couple relationship or constraints preventing living with a partner although this is desired. Relatively rarely do young adults make an active choice to live alone as a way of avoiding couple relationships or wish to remain living alone despite becoming committed to a long-term couple relationships (Coulter & Hu, 2017). It remains likely, however, that as living alone becomes increasingly normalised then the weight placed on having a co-resident partner may wane. Also, any experience of living alone may modify subsequent partnership, including expectations of the relationship, the pace and complexity of making any move to co-residence, and the desired balance between sustaining a sense of autonomy versus investment in an identity as a couple.

Dialogue about the relationship between living alone and couple relationships is relevant to debates about the future of relationships and has the potential to enhance more immediately grounded understandings of the experiences of people living alone and in couples here and now. This chapter is structured around three such topic areas. The first concerns the circumstances and orientations to co-resident coupledom of the population who live alone, including those who define themselves as in a couple relationship. While cultural assumptions may suggest that a person who lives alone is likely to be single or perhaps divorced or widowed, without a romantic, sexual or legal partner, this is not, of course, necessarily the case. Those living alone yet in couple relationships are more varied and numerous than the minority proportion who choose to be LATs. They may be in the phase that most co-resident couples have had gone through of becoming and being a couple before living together. Those not in couples may be desperately seeking, biding their time, or, more rarely, indifferent or hostile to becoming a couple. In order to understand the changing trajectory of couple relationships and living alone, it is important to remain mindful of the variety of stages in and ways of being a couple, informed by an understanding of whether and how those who live alone see themselves and their future in terms of being a couple. The second concerns how the experience of living alone is changing the experience of becoming a co-resident couple. The proportion of people with experience of living alone has grown in many countries across all ages of adult life. As more people live alone prior to living with a partner, the process of transition to a co-residential coupledom changes, as the meaning and practical valence of moving in together is modified. It is obviously a very different sort of transition than the once traditional move from living as a grown-up child in the parental home to forming a new home as a married couple helped by their wedding gifts. People who have lived alone prior to becoming a couple bring different types of material and experiential baggage than those leaving the parental home. Knowing how people who live alone think and feel about that transition from their own home alone to a home as a couple adds to understanding the adjustments required in couple relationships as well as of the experience of living alone.

The third is more directly linked to the idealisation of couple relationships and concerns the continued misrepresentations in popular discourse perpetuating harmful assumptions and stereotypes that play coupledom off against singlehood and/or living alone. Living alone is a domestic-residence arrangement, a one-person household, dwelling and conducting domestic life alone but people living alone are often caricatured by assumptions about their relationships that blur solo-living and partnership status. Two gendered stereotypes of working-age people who live alone haunt popular culture—the swinging single, usually male, avoiding any responsibility or commitment to others and the desperately seeking sad-and-lonely, usually female. These stereotypes set out a contrast between living alone and normal men and women, gesturing towards conventional gendered script about creating families and living happily ever after. They suggest that normal men are saved from being irresponsible, and normal women are saved from being sad and lonely, by living in co-resident heterosexual committed couples. Such stereotypes diminish the lives of people living alone. They may not amount to explicit misogyny and homophobia but are a close cousin and remain a supporting act.

This chapter draws on the international research literature and a UK study initiated by the author, *Solo Living,* funded by the Economic and Social Research Council, and conducted in Scotland (Jamieson & Simpson, 2013). This involved telephone interviews with 140 men and women aged 25–44 who were identified as living alone in the Scottish Household Survey, (SHS) and face-to-face interviews with a much smaller subsample. The study was designed to compare the men's and women's experiences of living alone in cities versus more rural areas. Hence, although more men live alone than women in this age group, and there are many more people living alone in cities than in small towns and rural areas, our sampling strategy sought equal numbers of men and women, urban and rural residents. The transcriptions of the telephone interviews and follow-up in-depth interviews were read and reread, coded and analysed thematically.

20.2 Orientations to Couple Relationships Among Young Adults Living Alone

In a growing number of parts of the world, some young people come to see living alone as a normal part of their development as an independent adult. As the previously cited literature shows, establishing a home alone as a young adult typically carries no determined stance against living with a partner in the future. The *Solo Living Study* found that a substantial proportion of young adults living alone are in some type of romantic and/or sexual relationship and some are already anticipating living with their current partner. Of course, the possibility of living alone also requires access to suitable housing and the economic means to maintain a household, conditions that vary across socio-economic backgrounds and have become more difficult for many young people since the economic crisis of 2008. In the UK, students now typically need financial support from their parents to be able to afford to live away from home at the point of going to university or college. However, many students continue to move away from home to live in student accommodation, share rented properties with friends or in some cases to live alone, or transition to living alone at the end of their studies, particularly if they then secure employment. For example, Jake, age 28, represents the relatively privileged among young people who transition from shared arrangements to private renting alone or 'getting on the property ladder' by buying a home alone. He talks about living alone as a necessity for early-career geographically mobile young professionals.

> It used to be I think the case in my parents' generation that people lived with their parents until they got married and then they lived with their husband or wife. I don't think that's the

case anymore. I think people are much more independent and more nomadic and move around a lot more, as I have done. So when you move around a lot, living alone is I suppose an inevitable consequence of that.

Jake had successfully used his degree and professional qualification to gain a foothold in a graduate career that helped him acquire a mortgage of a two-bedroom city-flat in Scotland. He also knew he could rely on his middle-class parents for financial assistance. He assumes a future in which he will be co-resident with a partner. His way of talking about living alone in the meantime has no sense of regret or embarrassment. He was using internet dating as a way of meeting people, and, at the time of interview, had been developing a relationship for 2 months with a young woman whom he described as *'a potential rather than a serious partner'* because, in his words, it was too early to know yet whether it was going to become 'serious'.

Owner occupation and privately rented housing are unaffordable for many young people in precarious or lower income employment, but this does not extinguish the aspiration to live independently of parents. Among our interviewees, Alice's housing trajectory represents this less privileged group of young people living alone. She was living alone in a rural area, aged 36 when we first interviewed her and was renting a housing association apartment organised by her local council after waiting 9 years to get such a tenancy.

> I didn't live with my parents through choice, it was through necessity ... because I couldn't afford to rent privately, and obviously to get an association house or a council house you have to wait on a list ... It took me years to get a house [...] I had my bags packed and all [laughs]. As soon as I was offered it I took it.

Alice was not in a relationship at the time of interview but when asked about internet dating said 'that is my New year's resolution'. There were relatively few possibilities of meeting potential partners locally but she was looking forward to a local pub opening and anticipated that it would have a darts team, as playing darts was how she met previous boyfriends. However, she also stressed a relaxed approach 'If it happens it happens, if it doesn't, it doesn't'. Unlike Jake, however, she also expressed considerable wariness about co-residence.

While Jake and Alice see living alone as perfectly normal ways of being independent adults that require no apology, there were also interviewees who seemed to partially accept the negative views of living alone that permeate the stereotypes discussed in the final section of this chapter. They acknowledged a position of deficit, a second-best, I-have-no-other-choice situation, because of their lack of a partner. This was a view more frequently articulated in rural areas, perhaps because of the more intense social pressures: *Well, I'd prefer to live with the man of my dreams, but since he's not here, I live alone* (Sue, age 34); *I'd rather be living with a lassie [Scots for a young woman] but I've not had much luck getting a girlfriend at the moment.* (Benjamin, age 33).

In the *Solo Living Study* the majority of the young adults living alone were or had been in couple relationships and some had previous experience of a living together as a couple. Those who had fallen out of co-resident or long-standing relationships spoke of missing intimate contact and the comfort of companionship but also of needing recovery time and being careful not to rush into new partnerships. Even when circumstances meant that living alone began with an ambience of regret at the loss of a relationship, a sense of peace and pleasure sometimes grew with time living alone rather than the episodes of loneliness. The pleasure of living alone then added to wariness about actively seeking a new co-resident partnership. On the other hand, some aspects of living alone could remain difficult; eating alone and cooking-for-one remained a challenge for many. The experience was rather different for those who were parents at the time of separation and remained in contact with their children. This typically meant also remaining in touch with their ex-partner. Some communication and collaboration with their children's co-resident parent was necessary in order to manage routines of hosting children for holidays or weekends. These parents typically made their home into a second home for their children and organised domestic routines around their coming and going. Responsibilities for children, in turn, made some parents wary about entering into new partnerships because of the potential implications for the time and space they could give their children in their lives. The failure of previous 'serious' relationships, and particularly relationships with children, has an impact on the experience of living alone as well as modifying openness to and timing of re-partnering.

Those who had never lived with a partner and were not in a couple relationship at the time of interview typically assumed having a co-resident partner at some time in the future. Some felt this would just happen naturally, *I would just hope to eventually, I suppose, meet somebody to want to settle down with* (Jessica, age 31) and some were more actively seeking a partner Those who were in couple relationships were often considering co-residence or, like Jake, thinking it was still too early to know if this was 'the one' with whom they wished to make such a commitment. The exceptions were typically not interested in having children either stating that they had never been interested or, for some gay men, had never considered it feasible or, for some heterosexual women, that they had already left it too late. Alice, for example, said: *Never wanted children, never will. Can't wait 'til I'm too old to have them by accident*. She was adamant that she would prefer an LAT relationship to cohabiting: *I would like someone in my life but they have their house, I have my house*. She immediately followed this up with the comment: *I'd be nobody's slave* and later elaborated on her assessment of the likely gender inequalities were she to cohabit with a boyfriend. She was not the only women in the study to conclude that co-residence would carry a risk of becoming her partner's domestic servant and this seemed to be particularly unattractive to women who felt that it was now too late to have children. Alice also had little faith in the long-term harmony of couple relationships citing as her evidence: *all my friends are divorced; living with my mum and dad I can hear their arguments*. Alice is relatively unusual in her consistent stance against co-resident coupledom, but her reference to couple dissolution among friends is a device that women seeking a partner sometimes also drew on to stress the value of not rushing into relationships, the normality of periods living alone and absurdity of a discourse equating the absence of a partner with deficiency in a person.

20.3 How Living Alone Changes Becoming a Couple

When a couple shift from separate residences to living together, the different resources they bring include income, material stuff, social connections, skills and tacit knowledge. All of these are typically modified by living alone. When a couple considering co-residence each have their own household, the issue inevitably arises of who makes the move to whom or whether both leave their current home to establish a new joint household. There may be inequalities in the size or value of homes and the desirability of their location that come into play and for working men and women living in different cities, proximity to employment is also unavoidably an issue. These were the issues, for example, on the mind of Alexandra when she started a new relationship at age 41. At the time of interview, she had not yet explicitly discussed such issues but was already considering them:

> Although we're both seeing it as a long-term relationship, it's still, you know, early days to kind of like discuss those kind of things and well not discuss them but think about them but actually act on them because there's, it has, I can't think what the, knock on effect with kind of like my work, his work, where we live, who's house and I think I said you know, I've lived on my own for 20 years. I'm quite selfish now and also, his house is tiny. And I've got a bigger house. So it's kind of practical issues about where and…Yeah lots of things that really you know, in the next year will be discussed and sorted but it's kind of scary thinking about them at the moment.

For a couple coming together who have both been living alone, each will have developed predispositions honed through their experiences of establishing their own household and being in sole charge of their own domestic affairs. While it cannot be presumed that years of living alone will result in enhanced skill in looking after a property, managing domestic affairs and developing definite tastes in how a home looks, these are all possibilities. While not everybody who lives alone creates a home in which décor, furniture and contents project their identity and preferences, somebody who has taken pride in such a home may find it difficult to accommodate different tastes or accept indifference to its aesthetic. Living alone also involves control over scheduling time and use of space whether by maintaining conventional routines or choosing to do things differently. Adjusting to living with another person may prompt the recalibrating of schedules and accommodating to different uses of space. It should not be assumed that living alone reduces skills in negotiating shared space with others, since it is possible to live alone and yet maintain a highly hospitable and welcoming space that often serves as a home-from-home for others. However, research indicates that people who live alone often gain pleasure in their self-reliance, some develop predispositions to solitude and many worry about whether they have become 'selfish' in ways that will make it more difficult to live with others. For some women, the self-reliance of living alone heightens wariness about entering into a relationship which feels like providing service and taking orders.

Most interviewees wished for a relationship that approximates equality accepting that this will involve some degree of 'give and take'. Prior experiences can be deliberately set aside but this often requires sustained effort and negotiation. For example, for a dual-earner heterosexual couple who share a strong desire to strive for equality of domestic effort and discuss avoidance of falling into practices that reproduce conventional gender roles, it can be difficult to overcome having been brought up in households where their parents adhered to gendered scripts and they previously learned gendered skills resulting in the woman being the better cook and more sensitised to standards of cleanliness as the subsequent example of Megan demonstrates. Not 'falling into gender' (Miller, 2011) requires on going vigilance and dialogue, including a deliberate effort at skill sharing, prioritising mutual learning. Renegotiating a relationship of equals in the face of predispositions arising from experiences of exclusive control of time and space may similarly require effort combined with an understanding of the challenges involved.

Although Megan was living alone at first interview, by the second interview she had actually moved in with her partner. This interview is quoted at length because it illustrates the multiple ways in which the experience of living alone impacts on the challenges of living together. Megan had also changed employers to a less stressful workplace that enabled her to use her professional skills within conventional working hours, rather than having to take work home with her in the evening. This was informed by a medical condition that was generally under control but sometimes meant she experienced episodes of chronic fatigue. The job change involved a cut in salary. When asked if this was a concern she replied: *It's not a concern because I've moved in with Alan* acknowledging the greater economic security of sharing financial responsibilities and cost savings of living as a couple in comparison to living alone. She went on to explain that when they started to consider living together as a couple, they quickly reached the view that Megan should move in with Alan and keep ownership of her own flat which she could rent out. Alan's flat was bigger and this arrangement gave them lower costs and the psychological security of knowing that they had not done anything irrevocable because they both still had their own homes and could return to their previous living arrangements if living together was not a success.

Megan talked about their attempts to be fair to both parties as they worked through various aspects of the challenge of moving into somebody else's house including dealing with the volume of clothes, kitchen utensils, books and other personal items that came from two households and the sensitivity necessary on both sides to each other's needs.

> if you ever move in with a guy and you have to sort out his clothes make sure he's not there … He very bravely attempted to try and bring his things into a smaller area. … I am very much of the opinion that if you don't need it, you haven't used it for at least a year, charity it and that's what I did. Alan's more [for keeping things] [laughs] … he did make a very good attempt and then between the two of us we did the rest. The most complicated bit actually is places like the kitchen … trying to decide whose bowls to keep, whose, you know…

Megan recognised that there was much more to the business of making room for her things in Alan's house than equalising physical space for personal items. It was also about creating a situation in which she felt at home without destroying Alan's sense of being at home. This required both of them to have a sense of control over space and of their identity being expressed within the space.

> I had to bring things to make this my space because when I moved in we didn't do any decoration, the house is in its colouring as Alan chose it and so therefore I very much had to make my mark on it without taking over at the same time. Very, very delicate balance to do that and to make sure that he wasn't seriously affected by that or sort of feeling that I was taking over his space completely and so one of the things I have done is put up photographs of my family in the living room.

She went on to describe items that they had both agreed could be put up in other rooms and the fact that her books were 'on display' in the sitting room:

> So every room just about has something like that of mine in it, which grounds me. One of the things that touched me most about moving in here was I had a lot of books and I thought Oh! Gosh! Where am I going to put all these books and I did sort of [cut] them back a bit and got rid of a few to charity but it's books [laughs] you know, I can't get rid of them no matter how and if I do I just buy more so it was kind of we had to find space and Alan set aside spaces for my books and so all my books are in the living room out on display which really means a lot to me because he knows how much I enjoy reading.

However, before getting to this stage there was much discussion. This included the sensitive topics of financial commitments and responsibilities. It also included explicit discussion of their divisions of housework. Megan declared that:

> we discussed everything. It was quite thorough. Money was definite. I wanted to see the breakdown of all the bills, not that I didn't trust him but I needed to know myself what the difference [in terms of costs] would be and also what he had in terms of, you know, things like insurance. I'm moving in with things. I want to make sure they are going to be covered.

Once they were living together, they found that they could make some further adjustments that reduce their costs and environmental impact

> We did have two cars when I moved in, we've gone down to one so that was definitely a, you know, a conscious thought process, several reasons, environmental and money and space.

Another area of discussion and negotiation prior to moving in was over sociability, ensuring that friendships were not neglected as a result of living together, that patterns of hosting and being hospitable to others at home could still be managed without conflict and that leisure activities that were important to them prior to co-residence could be maintained.

> One of the things that is very important to me is to have good communication with friends. I think that's something that I've noticed with other friends that if they move in with their partners or get into more serious relationship it dies off and I was determined not to let it happen. … my social life hasn't stopped at all when I moved in here.

Maintaining her separate social life and prior interests were an aspect of sustaining a sense of autonomy and personal identity alongside her increased investment in being and acting as a couple (Askham, 1983; Gabb & Fink, 2015; Van Hooff, 2013). Another aspect of these difficult balancing acts touched on in Megan's account involves one of the pleasures interviewees sometimes claimed for living alone—the freedom to come and go without any requirement to be accountable to somebody else, versus the communication about coming and going that is required for the practical coordination of connected lives that are practicing mutual care for and about each other. Megan acknowledged an obligation that she and Alan communicate about elements of their social life that they continued to conduct separately:

> As I said earlier Alan has a very, very busy career and works very long hours so therefore he would not expect me to sit at home if he had to work, if he's got a function on in the evening he will tell me in advance so I can maybe arrange something else. And one of the other things I do which is very important to me is exercise and I have set exercise times that he knows about, where I am going to be, these nights I am going to be at this place doing this…

At the same time, this must not mean micro-surveillance of each other and some freedom to not consult had to remain. The experience of living alone meant being used to private down time at home without having to consult anyone else about what form this took. For Megan, it was important to be able to spend time at home without any sense of pressure to talk, make polite conversation or report the details of how she was choosing to relax.

> I don't feel like I have to be in the same room as him, there's no need to go and make conversation, I can watch what I like on TV, you know, these kind of things I think are what make it home as well, it's a place to relax and then I feel that he really has worked hard adjusting to make me feel like that and vice-versa. … he has a play station and we manage to work round when he plays his play station and when I have my old movies on so I can do the ironing, and I say to him if 'I'm going to iron I'm sorry but I want the TV on my programmes.

However, as is discussed further in the next section, the sharing of housework did not work out as they had discussed. Despite both being in the same profession and Megan having further to commute to work, Alan was ultimately judged to have less time, less skill and less interest in doing the housework. He was in a higher-paid, higher-status, long-hours-culture job, the type of job that Megan had left. Megan's adjustment in her work commitment at the time of moving in with Alan effectively enabled the justification that his employment commitments trumped his obligations to perform domestic work. Over several decades, the research literature on dual earning couples has observed this pattern of women downsizing their employment commitment around the time of co-residence more often than men, subsequently doing significantly more domestic work than men (e.g., Mansfield & Collard, 1988; Van Hooff, 2013). Philosophical acceptance of 'falling into gender' was perhaps facilitated by Megan's sense of her own need to withdraw from a high stress career because of a medical condition that made her vulnerable to episodes of disabling ill health. The research literature on co-resident couples shows that mothers who have prioritised the well-being of children over their own careers are often similarly philosophical about such adjustments.

20.4 Idealising Coupledom and the Gendered Stigmatising of Living Alone

In European and Euro-American societies, co-residential couple relationships remain the normative family form and living arrangement for adult life. Co-residential coupledom is routinely idealised as offering the most satisfactory living arrangement and support system for well-being across adulthood, as well as being lauded by moral commentators as the foundation of family life and the most appropriate arrangement for bringing up children. Legal acknowledgement of same-sex couple relationships has extended the category but it remains fiercely debated whether this has modified the emphasis on and valorisation of couple relationships in ways that enable a more general diversity in ways of doing and being in relationship that provide love and care (Butler, 2002; Richardson, 2004; Roseneil, Crowhurst, Santos, & Stoilova, 2017). The emphasis on the primacy of the couple designates other arrangements as second best and the tendency to proselytise on behalf of coupledom amplifies a stigmatising discourse suggesting a deficit or inadequacy in the lives and the personages of those outside the co-residential couple arrangement.

For example, Annabel (age 30, urban) was made to feel uncomfortable by the many ways in which her friends communicated dissatisfaction with the fact that she had no partner, lived alone and is childless. These included her friends' repeated efforts at matchmaking, their eager suggestions that any man she might be seeing should move in with her, and prounouncements such as *"Oh, you don't know what you are missing!"* by a married friend who had recently had a baby.

That something more censorial, controlling and insidious is in operation than the valorisation of loving couple relationships is indicated not only by its bruising impact on the person being constructed as-if in deficit but also by the fact that such a discourse is not equally directed at men and women. Feminists have long argued that women play a part in policing and maintaining patriarchal systems. Annabel's women friends are helping to sustain a view that it is particularly important that women should be partnered and have children, a view which is consistent with a conventional patriarchal gender regime that is intolerant of independent women outside the protection and supervision of a man. Support for such a regime is not the motivation. If this claim was put to her friends, they would likely repudiate support for such an 'old fashioned' view of couple dynamic, rather emphasising that they take it for granted that couple relationships should be between equals. However, given that many couples aspiring to be equals 'fall back into gender' (Miller, 2011) perhaps they would also have to admit to slippage between this ideal of equality and their own couple relationship. Nevertheless, it is their failure to see success in and celebrate Annabel's independence that lends tacit support to gender inequalities and stereotypes. While men may also be cajoled for not having a partner, as another professional young women interviewee noted: *'If you are a woman who lived on her own and are happy to live on your own then there's something wrong with you. And that's an assumption made by both sexes. But if it's a man* [living alone], *then that's fine.'* (Lauren, age 37).

The differential stereotyping of men and women living alone reflects the legacy or continuity of patriarchal control over women and the double standard in sexual conduct reflected also in discourses around 'spinster' and 'bachelor' (DePaulo, 2015; Lahad, 2017; Reynolds, Wetherell, & Taylor, 2007; Simpson, 2006, 2016; Trimberger, 2006). Men living alone are more likely to be stereotyped as 'foot loose and fancy free' assumed to be 'having a good time' whereas women living alone are more likely to be stereotype as 'sad and lonely'. However, it seems that growing numbers of women have the opportunity to defy these stereotypes, even if it is relatively rare to be as clear about this as Sophie:

> I have a very male attitude towards relationships. Yes. So I don't mind having relationships but they—I really only want to have them on my terms and my terms are not about buying joint properties and certainly are not about moving. My life, my career is up here, my career is very important to me. (Sophie, age 38)

In the 1970s, feminists argued that the staging of romance and falling in love enabled individual women to enter couple relationship blinded to or sometimes despite knowing that they were participating in an arrangement that reproduced gender inequalities. One element of this analysis was pithily captured in the adage 'it begins by sinking into his arms and ends with your arms in his sink'. Women now have much greater capacity to resist this specific scenario but can also be complicit in its continuity. As noted in the previous section, the constituency of women living alone who are actively resisting living with a partner often recognise that 'hands in the sink' remains a plausible prediction of the trajectory of a co-residential partnership. Alice quoted above went into detail about what she thought would happen if she were living with a local boyfriend: '*It'd* [It would] *be like, where's me* [my] *tea?* [laughter] *Where's my shirt?*' When the interviewer asked about the possibility of a 'new man', she said, '*There's no such thing.*' In contrast, Megan had not anticipated any such inequality when she decided to make the move to a co-residential couple relationship. However, she then accepted 'falling back into gender' as part of the give and take of becoming a co-resident couple, acknowledging her partner's longer working hours which excused his lack of housework underpinned the higher earnings that were an aspect of her own financial security. However, she went on to describe how she now considers herself as naïve to have ever thought that she could have had a 50/50 division of labour with any man of her generation given gender differences in learned predispositions and standards around cleanliness, tidiness and the house 'looking nice':

> maybe it's just a generational thing, I do not know, but in my opinion boys are not brought up the same as girls, they are not expected, especially boys of my age, they are not expected to do the same amount round the house and home as a girl would be.

It remains much more difficult for a woman than a man to live alone in many cultures, which invidiously stigmatise women who are living independently of parental control and outside of a partnership with a man. It would be extremely dangerous and near impossible for a young woman to live alone without parental support in parts of Asia, the Arab world and Islamic Africa where women's chastity is a matter of family honour, parents continue to exercise significant control over partnering, and remaining unpartnered and childlessness amounts to 'social death'. In Euro-American cultures, gender differences in the stigmatisation of living alone are softer but yet they still endure, making it difficult for women to claim contentment with living alone (Klinenberg, 2012, p 68; Jamieson & Simpson, 2013; Simpson, 2006, 2016). Ironically, the persistence of stereotypes also makes it more difficult for women to be very open about a desire to be partnered, for fear of being viewed through the stereotype as deficient and desperate (Macvarish, 2006). A sense of being outside the mainstream and socially excluded has been sufficiently strong to inspire blogs, social media networking and campaigning organisations (DePaulo, 2006, 2015; Klinenberg, 2012; Lahad, 2017; Trimberger, 2006).

Some women living alone, particularly professional urban women, were protected from stigmatising discourses and pressure to find a partner by friendship networks in which women living alone predominated. For example, Lauren described the normalcy of solo-living among her friends whom she characterised as educated women in the early 30s to mid 40s age-group:

> You get to like sort of late 30s and it's not uncommon for people to be living on their own either because it's the first time they've done it… due to separation of or a marriage breakdown or because that's just what they've always done since they've left home.

At the same time, though, she remained aware of gendered stereotypes about solo-living women that circulate in the wider culture. The sparser population of rural areas and lower levels of living alone mean that rural solo-living women are less likely to have a protective network of other solo-living friends and more likely to be very visible as a woman who is living alone. Nevertheless, some rural women maintained a fierce independence and determination to conduct couple relationships without bowing to conventional gender roles.

20.5 Conclusion

In the countries where the trend of living alone in the years of adulthood before midlife is advanced, those living alone typically see this as a phase that will end with co-resident coupledom. Nevertheless, Levin and Trost (1999) were correct in suggesting that the idea of being a couple and yet living apart is increasingly imaginable, albeit only a very small minority of those in early adulthood to midlife express a preference for long-term 'living apart together'. Those who do typically also reject having children or feel they are already 'too old' or their circumstances make having children too difficult. For some women, the self-reliance of living alone heightens wariness about relationships with men which risk feeling like providing service and taking orders. Enjoyment of living alone makes continuing to live alone imaginable as a possible alternative future to being in a couple. As more working-age men than women live alone, particularly in the 30–59 age group, (European Social Survey) the experience it affords is not equally distributed.

Hesitation and delay in taking up co-residence is a likely outcome when two people living alone become a couple. Desire for delay is modified by routes into living alone. Those who have entered from a failed co-residential relationship often cite the need to recover or to protect time for the children of their relationships. However, living alone in itself causes delay in co-residence by adding new layers to the aspects of everyday life which require renegotiation in the process of making a new life together. Demographers note that delay in co-residential partnering is linked to delayed parenting and unintended infertility. On the other hand, the time taken may enhance the quality of the relationship.

When a couple come to live together, awareness of the pleasures of living alone can heighten efforts to attain fairness and awareness of the need to equalise belonging, ownership and autonomy in command of space and time within their home and their relationship. If women experience living alone prior to living with a male partner, awareness of the balancing acts between self-identity and identity as a couple may help to enhance the gender equality of heterosexual relationships or at least heighten awareness of 'falling into gender'. For some women, fear of falling into conventional gendered divisions of labour makes co-residence with any man a risky future; they do not wish to extend their domestic work to looking after another adult nor to reduce other commitments such as their focus on their career. Once having children is off the agenda, women's tolerance of 'falling back into gender' may be reduced and their wariness of co-residence enhanced. As yet, a shared culture of how to manage transitions from living alone to living with others is not well developed.

Conventional understandings of gender also inform the negative stereotypes of living alone that are the flip side of the over-idealisation of couple relationships as the true source of living happily ever after. There is no tradition of congratulating or celebrating the anniversaries of those who live alone and contentment in living alone is treated as particularly deviant among women. Consistent with the legacy of a tradition of patriarchal hostility to independent women outside the control by men, women are more likely to receive belittling remarks about 'missing out' by living alone while men are more likely to get compliments on their freedom or domesticity. Many who live alone in young adulthood want to become a couple but only some women and men take on a self-description that expresses a sense of lack. Since women alone are portrayed more negatively they have more reason to actively resist the stereotype and can end up self-censoring themselves to never acknowledge feeling lonely or any desire for a partner. Current stereotypes are likely to intensify the pain for those who long to find a partner and silence honest dialogue about the ups and downs of living alone. Cultural acknowlegdment of the achievements of those who live alone while remaining open and hospitable to others is overdue, along with recognition that this balancing act is relevant to couple relationships seeking to combine autonomy and mutual support, intimacy and equality.

Acknowledgments I note gratitude to my colleagues and research participants and acknowledge the sad loss of Roona Simpson. She lived alone and died peacefully at home supported by friends and family.

References

Aassve, A., Iacovou, M., & Mencarini, L. (2006). Youth poverty and transition to adulthood in Europe. *Demographic Research, 15*(2), 21–50.

Askham, J. (1983). *Identity and stability in marriage*. Cambridge, MA: Cambridge University Press.

Beaujouan, E., Regnier-Loilier, A., & Villeneueve-Gokalp, C. (2009). Neither single, nor in a couple. *Demographic Research, 21*, 75–108.

Butler, J. (2002). Is kinship already always heterosexual? *Differences: A Journal of Feminist Cultural Studies, 13*, 14–44.

Castro-Martín, T., Domínguez-Folgueras, M., & Martín-García, T. (2008). Not truly partnerless. *Demographic Research, 18*, 436–468.

Coulter, R., & Hu, Y. (2017). Living apart together and cohabitation intentions in Great Britain. *Journal of Family Issues, 38*(12), 1701–1729.

DePaulo, B. (2015). *How we live now*. New York, NY: Simon and Schuster.

Duncan, S., & Phillips, M. (2010). People who live apart together LATs – How different are they? *The Sociological Review, 58*, 112–134.

Duncan, S., & Phillips, M. (2008). New families? Tradition and change in modern relationships. In A. Park, J. Curtice, K. Thomson, M. Phillips, M. Johnson, & E. Clery (Eds.), *British Social Attitudes: the 24th Report*. Sage, London.

Ermisch, J., & Seidler, T. (2008). Living apart together. In J. Ermisch & M. Brynin (Eds.), *Changing relationships*. London, UK: Routledge.

Gabb, J., & Fink, J. (2015). *Couple relationships in the 21st century*. London, UK: Palgrave Macmillan.

Haskey, J., & Lewis, J. (2006). Living apart together in Britain. *International Journal of Law in Context, 2*, 37–48.

Heath, S., & Calvert, E. (2013). Gifts, loans and intergenerational support for young adults. *Sociology, 47*, 1120.

Ho, J. H. (2015). The problem group? Psychological wellbeing of unmarried people living alone in the Republic of Korea. *Demographic Research, 32*, 1299–1328.

Jamieson, L., & Simpson, R. (2013). *Living alone*. London, UK: Palgrave.

Klinenberg, E. (2012). *Going solo*. London, UK: The Penguin Press.

Lahad, K. (2017). *A table for one*. Manchester, UK: Manchester University Press.

Lesthaeghe, R. (2010). The unfolding story of the second demographic transition. *Population and Development Review, 36*(2), 211–251.

Levin, I. (2004). Living apart together. *Current Sociology, 52*, 223–240.

Levin, I., & Trost, J. (1999). Living apart together. *Community, Work and Family, 2*, 270–294.

Macvarish, J. (2006). What is 'the Problem' of Singleness? *Sociological Research Online 11*.

Mansfield, P., & Collard, J. (1988). *The beginning of the rest of your life?* London, UK: Macmillan.

Miller, T. (2011). Falling back into Gender? Men's Narratives and Practices around First-time Fatherhood. *Sociology, 45*, 1094–1109.

Raymo, J. M. (2015). Living alone in Japan: Relationships with happiness and health. *Demographic Research, 32*, 1267–1298.

Reynolds, J., Wetherell, M., & Taylor, S. (2007). Choice and chance: Negotiating agency in the narrative of singleness. The *Sociological Review, 55*, 331–251.

Richardson, D. (2004). Locating sexualities: From here to normality. *Sexualities, 7*(4), 391–411. https://doi.org/10.1177/1363460704047059

Roseneil, S., Crowhurst, I., Santos, A. C., & Stoilova, M. (Eds.). (2017). *Reproducing citizens*. London, UK: Routledge.

Simpson, R. (2006). The intimate relationships of contemporary spinsters. *Sociological Research Online, 11*(3), 125.

Simpson, R. (2016) Singleness and self-identity: The significance of partnership status in the narratives of never-married women. *Journal of Social and Personal Relationships, 33*(3), 385–400.

Sobotka, T., & Toulemon, L. (2008). Changing family and partnership behaviour. *Demographic Research, 19*(6), 85–138.

Stone, J., Berrington, A., & Falkingham, J. (2011). The changing determinants of UK young Adults' living arrangements. *Demographic Research, 25*(20), 629–666.

Trimberger, K. (2006). *The new single woman*. Boston, MA: Beacon Press.

Van Hooff, J. (2013). *Modern couples?* Farnham, UK: Ashgate.

Wasoff, F., & Jamieson, L. (2005). Solo living, individual and family boundaries. In L. McKie & S. Cunningham-Burley (Eds.), *Families and society: Boundaries and relationships*. Cambridge, UK: Polity Press.

Yeung, W.-J. J., & Cheung, A. K.-L. (2015). Living alone: One-person households in Asia. *Demographic Research, 32*, 1099–1112.

Yip, N. M., & Forrest, R. (2014). Choice or constraint? Exploring solo–living for young households in Hong Kong, *Urban research group–city U on cities working paper series*, WP1, 1–14, City University of Hong Kong, http://www.cityu.edu.hk/cityuoncities/upload/file/original/705520140620144948.pdf (accessed 12/12/2018)

Part V
Supporting Couple Relationships

Chapter 21
Systemic Therapy and Narratives of Attachment

Arlene Vetere

21.1 Introduction

This chapter will outline an attachment narrative approach to working with couples in systemic psychotherapy. Rudi Dallos and I have been working for over 20 years to integrate modern attachment theory, narrative theory and trauma theory into systemic theory and practice with individuals, couples, families and with supervision of therapeutic practice (Dallos & Vetere, 2009, 2014, 2017). Such integration leads to powerful intergenerational explanations of distress and resilience in family members' relationships. Crucially, integrative formulation makes clearer to all participants in the therapy how to understand and resolve loss and hurt and how to heal and repair relationships within a collaborative framework. It is with such integrative formulations that we, as practitioners, can hold ourselves ethically accountable for our thinking and practice to all those involved in the therapeutic work (Vetere, 2006).

In writing this chapter it is important to both acknowledge those therapists and researchers and their colleagues who have influenced our work and/or who are engaged in similar integrative projects, for example, Guy Diamond, Diamond, and Levy (2014) and Robert Marvin, Cooper, Hoffman, and Powell (2002) in the USA; Susan Johnson (2004) in Canada; Carmel Flaskas (2002) in Australia and John Byng-Hall (1995) and Pocock (1997) in the UK. There are, of course, some similarities in our approach to integration, but here I shall identify a few differences, for example, (a) we work inter-generationally across the family life cycle with all close relationships, including those of close work colleagues in teams; (b) we specifically theorise narrative as skill development and the emotional and social conditions under which coherent relational narratives can emerge; (c) we are strongly influenced by and indebted to the research of Patricia Crittenden and the development of

---

A. Vetere (✉)
VID Specialized University, Oslo, Norway

her dynamic maturational model of attachment (Crittenden, 2006); (d) specifically, we are influenced by the discursive analytic work done with the Adult Attachment Interview (Crittenden & Landini, 2011); and (e) we have developed the application of our therapeutic work with attachment narratives across a range of clinical settings, including eating disorders (Dallos & Draper, 2015), alcohol use (Vetere, 2014), family violence (Sammut Scerri, Vetere, Abela, & Cooper, 2017), supervision and consultation work with professional teams (Vetere, 2017). In this chapter though, I shall focus on therapeutic work with couples.

I am a clinical psychologist and systemic therapist who has been working therapeutically with couples for 35 years. And in that time they have taught me much, for which I am grateful. I have learned to look for the attachment significance when couples stumble in their attempts to connect. In striving for intimacy, yet reeling with hurt and disappointment when they cannot connect, knowing they want connection, yet not knowing what it looks like, or feels like, or what to do, I have learned to respect their wish for connection in how I will persist and make a commitment to them. I undertake longer term systemic work as needed, as time is necessary for some couples to develop their reflective functioning (Vetere & Sheehan, in press). When adult intimate encounters trigger unresolved procedural memories of exposure to unprotected and uncomforted danger in childhood, I have learned to help them be curious about what the danger is, what it represents, and why it remains so dangerous.

Reflection and observation is the way to process and reintegrate experience, and for some couples this can take years. My undertaking is to stay with them on this journey. I have been exposed to their hurt, pain, rage and disappointment, in its many forms and manifestations. And I have lived with their moments of deep connection, renewed intimacy and emerging joy in the possibilities of trusting again. And, as I myself have aged, I find I need supervision more often as my response to this exposure is to become overly empathic. Thus looking after myself as a therapist has now emerged as a more significant emotional focus—for me, and in my teaching and training.

21.2 Attachment Strategies as Attempted Solutions: Styles of Protective and Defensive Processes

Attachment theory is a developmental theory of the social regulation of emotion in families (Bowlby, 1973, 1988). Through subsequent research it has evolved into a theory of arousal regulation with a focus on interactive regulation and non-conscious relational responding (Schore & Schore, 2008). Our early experiences of being cared for by our key attachment figures can shape how we learn both to understand and to manage our emotional experiences and physiological arousal when we are upset, distressed, afraid and in need of comfort and reassurance. Our responses to the non-availability of our attachment figures or to unpredictable care, that is, never knowing if we shall be left in the corner to cry or scooped up and cuddled and comforted, as one man described it to me in the therapy, can lead to a form of compulsive self-reliance in the former, or to a chronic preoccupation with our own arousal in the latter. With the former we learn that our feelings are not a good guide to action and they have not achieved what we want, that is, being listened to when we are upset with comfort, compassion and reassurance. With the latter we may be exposed to unpredictable care in an emotional context where our attachment figures themselves cannot manage their own arousal in difficult moments and are less able to help us make meaning of what is happening, to name emotional states, and to learn to manage them.

For some children who live with fear in their households, where their caregivers may be frightened and/or frightening, it may never be safe to think about what is happening for fear of being physiologically flooded and overwhelmed with panic. In this context a more extreme strategy of self-protection might emerge, such as dissociation, numbing and splitting (Van der Kolk, 2015). Both the above strategies of self-protection, i.e. a dismissing withdrawal, or a hyper-activated arousal state, make the development of intimacy in adult couple relationships harder to achieve. Both these extremes of care-giving have taught us that interpersonal trust is difficult to achieve. Indeed we may not have experienced a felt sense of personal safety in early relationships, yet yearn and struggle as adults to achieve felt security. However, research would suggest that most people achieve a balance of self-protective strategies, that is, being able to exclude feeling and deactivate arousal when needed and to become preoccupied and aroused at times of danger and threat, but importantly, these strategies are enacted in less extreme ways.

Attachment theory does not pathologise dependency in our relationships, nor does it pathologise our strategies of self-protection when we perceive danger and threat. These strategies are considered to be adaptive to the relational context and political, economic and social circumstances in which we live. As these strategies are learned, and sometimes over-learned, they are subject to revision and change. Children can develop different attachment strategies with different caregivers and as they grow and develop and new relationships are made, with friends, teachers, relatives, and subsequently dating relationships, colleagues, and so on, throughout the life cycle, opportunities emerge to experiment and experience new ways of relating.

Couple therapy is based on the notion that our self-protective strategies can be revised and changed (Crittenden, 2006). Central to this process is the development of interpersonal trust and the deconstruction of threat and danger with the creation of relational safety and felt security. Initially and possibly very slowly, this may be with the therapist or other professional practitioner who refers the couple to the therapy. The referrer can sometimes be the stable third or bridge into the more challenging process of therapy, where partners may fear confronting their difficult experiences and ward off vulnerable feelings. The task in therapy is to help those partners who rely on the deactivation of emotion in difficult moments to 'warm up' and take emotional risks to explore such warded off feelings, such as fear, sadness, shame, hurt and humiliation. This is sometimes expressed as self-blame and fear of being unacceptable to others. Similarly, those partners who are chronically and unhelpfully physiologically aroused need help to calm themselves down, to learn to comfort and self soothe, so that they can think about what is happening and thus avoid the tendency to blame others reactively. The task in therapy is to help partners integrate their relational experiences, that is, to connect thought with feeling, so that they might learn to be curious about what is happening. Neurologists and trauma theorists would suggest that the only known brain pathway to reorganise the perceptual systems of the brain is through reflection and thus, integration (Levine, 2015; Siegel, 2012; Van der Kolk, 2015).

Systemic therapists have long recognised behavioural patterns of 'approach–withdraw' or pursuer–distancer in couple relationships in difficult moments, for example, when one or both fear abandonment or rejection, feel themselves to be a disappointment or experience the other as disappointing. In such instances, their stress arousal system is activated and they risk falling back into well-established patterns of self-protection and defensiveness. Damasio (1994) termed these patterns 'dispositional representations', where well-rehearsed behavioural patterns become neural templates that predict future responses to similar situations.

The key to understanding this is the perception of danger. The attachment system is activated when we perceive danger, for example, a threat to our self-esteem, or a threat to the integrity of our relationships, such as fear of abandonment or rejection. Susan Johnson in her work with Emotion Focused Therapy further explored and theorised the attachment significance at the heart of such painful and unresolved repeating patterns of interaction in couple relationships (Johnson, 2004). It is the unresolved hurt and loss in these difficult relational moments that continue to haunt us and then act as triggers for further unhelpful emotional and physiological arousal in future difficult interactions. John Gottman's (2011) research strongly suggests that all couples deal with the tasks of being in a relationship and that patterns of criticism, defensiveness, stonewalling and contempt can be observed. However in relationships felt by the couple to be emotionally safe, contempt is much less likely to be seen, and criticism, stonewalling and defensiveness are much less extreme.

Attachment theory considers autonomy and dependence to be different sides of the same attachment experience—we know our own minds and make better informed and more thoughtful decisions when there is a least one other person we can turn to for support and understanding. Van der Kolk writes that social support—the perception that others are accessible and responsive to us—is one of the best defences against the development of trauma responses when we feel frightened and endangered (Van der Kolk, 2015). Safety and protection are at the heart of attachment theory. Our attachment system is activated when we perceive relational threat and danger from our partner. Our initial response might be a form of protest anger when we reach out with strident demands to be paid attention to, to be listened to, to feel heard and understood.

Speaking from my own personal experience, such a request is unlikely to achieve the desired response, and if we are not heeded, we could flip into the anger of despair when we rubbish and reject the very response we want and need. Feeling ourselves to be unheard, unseen and thus unknown by a loved one can be enraging. Bowlby termed these two forms of protest anger as the anger of hope and the anger of despair (Bowlby, 1973). Bowlby also observed that these expressions of protest anger concealed the experience of vulnerability in such a difficult interactional moment, when we fear we are loved less, fear we are not wanted, fear we are a disappointment to our partner, hurt and sadness because they have disappointed us and possible feelings of shame that we are not deserving of their attention, comfort and care.

The therapeutic task is to make it safe enough in the therapy to identify and acknowledge these unexpressed and unprocessed vulnerabilities, to help the partners explore and name their experiences, to both feel understood and heard in their own right before we throw light on the relational pattern and invite them to be curious and empathic of the other's experience. We work slowly and patiently in such moments, supporting each partner to remain calm. Such empathy is needed for healing and the development of trust—acknowledgement, compassion and comfort and sometimes apology and forgiveness (Vetere, 2017). The role of a self-regulated therapist is crucial in these moments of potential healing. As Diana Fosha (2000) observed, the roots of relational resilience are to be found in the sense of being understood by and existing in the heart and mind of a loving, attuned and self-possessed other. For some partners, their relationship with their couple therapist may afford their first experience of embodied, felt security.

John and Mary are a couple, recently retired from busy and influential paid employment. They have been together since their college days, and have travelled the world for work while raising their family. Since retirement they have struggled with the challenge of living together full-time. Such full-on full-time living emphasises their different approach and style in their expectations, intentions and lived experiences with each other. There can be no hiding in work or travel or family.

When the therapy began, I was not convinced that John could or would want to utilise the experience to deepen his intimate connection with Mary. I found him to be emotionally well-defended. But I could not have been more wrong. As a man who values facts over opinions, and the value of practical work and support, he has made clear his wish for a close connection with Mary, his love for her, and his desire to please her. Although his efforts might appear somewhat clumsy (as they have not yet become polished with practice) he persists in trying to do things well for her.

Mary does not see these efforts. She continues to complain that he gets it wrong—not just for her, but for their children as well. When Mary learned to trust me more she felt she could say what she was thinking—"he is lying!". "What he says and does in this therapy room is a lie! He does not do this at home!". And herein lies Mary's hurt, the disappointment and the preoccupation with the pain—the deep attachment significance of the erosion of trust over many years of marriage. As a child, Mary was neither seen nor heard—but she learned that crumbs of comfort could be hers if she cared for others, thus subjugating her own needs. During the long years of their marriage she experienced John's focus on practical matters as evidence that he did not see her or hear her. Her efforts to be seen and heard were a constant source of disappointment and frustration to her, so that latterly when John tried to make his wish for connection with her visible, she herself could neither see it nor believe it.

Enabling their reconnection needed a mutual trust in me, our relationship together and the therapy process. Supervision of the therapy and of me, with Mary and John's consent and knowledge, formed a systemic therapeutic triangle. This triangle provided the containment needed for the longer term persistence, patience, compassion and commitment that helped them heal their mutual years of hurt and disappointment. Slowly they began to believe that contentment could be theirs as they lived a more yielding life together. We worked therapeutically for 3 years. Now, Mary and John will meet with me once every 3 or 4 months for a review. We all hold hope for their future together.

21.3 Attachments as Representations

Our attachment experiences with our key attachment figures are thought to be representational and layered, that is, how we hold people and experiences in mind in our various memory systems. Nonverbal memory is both procedural and sensory. Procedural memory is memory for actions, that is, how and what we do with our attachment figures—how we give and receive affection, how we run our arguments, how we look after each other, and so on. Sensory memory is memory for sensation and emotion—our embodied experiences of the touch, smell, taste and the look of a loved one, the feeling of safety and warmth, the feeling of anxiety when we are left, for example. Verbal memory is semantic, episodic and integrative. Semantic memory organises our thoughts, values, attitudes, intentions and so on in relation to our attachment experiences with people we love. Episodic memory is sometimes called narrative or autobiographical memory. This is memory for storied experience and how we use memory for action, feeling and thought to describe and explain experience—ours, theirs and shared experiences. Episodic memory can recruit all these memory resources to describe attachment experiences, and yet still remain reactive. Integrative memory is our ability to integrate and narrate experience from a meta-position, with curiosity and a wish to understand what is happening in the moment. This is what is called a coherent narrative (Bruner, 1990).

Reflective and coherent narrating can only happen if we remain sufficiently calm. In the context of couple therapy when we recount or re-experience a difficult interactional moment and our arousal and self-protective strategies are activated we risk our fight-flight system taking over! Therapists need to support partners in staying sufficiently calm so they can recruit all their memory resources in the service of self and other understanding, with the capacity for reflection still intact. Our reflective abilities are located in our prefrontal cortex. When we perceive danger, the perceptual message gets to our fight-flight system faster than to our prefrontal cortex, for obvious evolutionary survival reasons, but in therapy, if we are to heal our hurts and unresolved losses, we need assistance to remain self-aware.

In my own experience, the capacity to remain calm enough and to listen to what someone you love wants you to hear when they themselves are unhelpfully aroused and possibly angry, is a very sophisticated life skill that takes time and patience to develop. It is thus no accident that the adult attachment researchers advise us to give over more time to healing in couple relationships, than we do to assessment, formulation and intervention (Mikulincer, Shaver, & Pereg, 2003). Thus as we get to know the couple and their relationship concerns, we listen to how they talk about themselves, about each other and what happens between them. In the early stages of therapy, when recounting disappointing and distressing experiences, we listen to their strategic fallback position, that is, to whether there is a reliance on semantics and the dismissing of emotion, or a preoccupation with affect and arousal and a limited capacity to think and/or reflect on the experiences. This provides us as therapists with crucial information on how partners have constructed a sense of safety, what might be contributing to emotional distancing, and where we first meet them in their comfort zone.

Thus we can construe our attachment representations as layered. As noted above, Damasio coined the phrase 'dispositional representations' to replace Bowlby's ideas of an internal working model (IWM). The internal working model was thought to be made up of our expectations and beliefs about relationships based on our repeated encounters with our attachment figures. Thus, depending on the responses we elicited and the mutuality of the attachment process, our ideas and beliefs about ourselves as loveable, and worthy and deserving of the care and attention of others were formed and subject to change in future relationships. Dispositional representations are thought to be neurological patterns of activity that result from repeated interactions with our attachment figures, including our thoughts, and that predispose us to action when we encounter similar attachment situations in the future. Dispositional representations are thought to be reworked each time we think of our attachment figures and the disposition to act connects us to our environment, particularly our relational context, in a particular way, along with our ideas about the expected outcome. Distortions in perception can either exaggerate or minimise the probability of safety and danger in our encounters, and when working to help stop violent behaviour within the family, for example, we need to pay attention to whether too much information is brought forward, so everything is dangerous, or not enough information is brought forward, so danger is minimised.

21.4 Intergenerational Attachments: Corrective and Replicative Scripts

Family culture can be considered as a dynamic interaction of beliefs, behaviour, intentions and practices over time, handed on from one generation to the next as guidance, teaching and learning and also as a system of mutual influence between the respective generations. John Byng-Hall (1995) was probably the first UK-based family therapist to integrate attachment theory into his practice. He was interested in patterns of care, affection and care-giving across the generations—how they develop, and how they change. He suggested that family members make comparisons across the generations in terms of similarities and differences between how their own parents were with each other as a couple, and with them as children, and how this is repeated or changed in the next generation, and so on.

Byng-Hall's idea that we make comparisons across the generations is important because it allows us to construe our parents' intentions and our own intentions in a positive frame, that is, that they/we have tried to repeat what was good about care-taking and care-giving experience, or correct what was felt to be unhelpful about these experiences. This opens up discussions around whether our attempts to repeat or change behaviours and patterns have been successful or not, and possibly how they might be altered, strengthened, and elaborated.

In our work with a couple, we might invite a comparative process of reflection designed to illuminate intentions to do things differently, or intentions to preserve and protect ways of relating with intimate partners. For example, prompt questions could start with: 'What are your thoughts about how similar or different your relationships with each other and with your children are to that of your parents' (and grandparents') relationships?' 'What have you tried to make similar or different to either/any of the relationships?' 'What do you value versus feel critical about in either of your parents' relationships?' 'Does what you have tried to repeat or change, work?' 'How would you know?' 'Is there anything that you want to alter, strengthen, develop or abandon about what you have been trying to repeat or to change?' 'What do you hope your children will learn from you for the future of their relationships… And the future of their children?'

The use of future-oriented questions in these discussions is helpful because it makes it possible for partners and parents to speak with hope and from a position of aspiration for the future of their children and (potential) grandchildren, and so on. Thus may we then bring the conversation back into the here-and-now and reflect on what they want to happen next in their attachment relationships. When working with past trauma in couple relationships, we sometimes find that the attempt to correct, and not to repeat abusive patterns of interaction, can lead a partner to be overly rigid in their attempts and to struggle to seek and receive feedback on their efforts. It seems it does not always occur to us to tell our partners that we are trying not to repeat our parents' patterns that we were exposed to in childhood and neither does it always occur to us to seek feedback on whether our attempts are working in the ways we hope for. Thus we can see that our intentions are to make things better, and even though these attempts are conscious, they are often still reactive, and not sufficiently reflective. Yet again, the therapeutic task is to help acknowledge these good intentions, even when they appear not to succeed, and to support the couple in reviewing and renewing their efforts for an empathic connection based in a new shared understanding.

21.5 Creating the Secure Base in Therapy

Interpersonal trust is the emotional weave of our relationships and unresolved losses and hurts create a gulf in a couple relationship. Trust is built on our perception and experience of our partner as accessible and responsive to us, for most of the time

(Gottman, 2011). And, if we experience a misattunement, it is thus possible to acknowledge this, to speak about it, and to repair it. We need understanding, patience, commitment and curiosity to help make things feel right. However, many couples who come into therapy have experienced many breaches of trust and do not feel emotionally safe or secure enough to speak about their vulnerability and their hurt. They may blame themselves or they may blame their partner—feelings of shame and humiliation can often be concealed within the sadness and fear that accompanies a loss of trust, for now, and for the future.

A husband and wife came into therapy, at the wife's instigation, because he had announced he wanted a divorce. She wanted to try to make the relationship work in a more satisfying way for both of them, and she was clear that she loved her husband and wanted to be with him. He continued to say that he wanted to part, and I agreed to be a consultant to their couple process. They had two school aged children, and both agreed that whether they parted or remained together, they needed to prioritise the well-being of their children. As I got to know them, and they began to trust in the process of our meetings, it emerged that the husband wanted a divorce because he could no longer bear the idea or the feeling that he was, and had been, a deep disappointment to his wife. This filled him with shame and he deadened his feelings by overworking.

She, of course, had no idea he felt this way in his relationship with her. She could not understand why he did not respond to her requests for connection. He in his turn did not understand that his limited and somewhat ambiguous responses to her attempts to reach him emotionally both confused and frightened her. This confusion was intolerable to her as it resonated with childhood experience of ambiguous and unclear parental communication. In these moments her fear motivated her to increase her efforts to reach her husband, to get some connection, to seek reassurance, and as her attempts became more strident and more seeking of certainty, he, in turn, retreated further, and became unobtainable. She would then collapse into her own withdrawal, reinforcing for him his felt experience of fundamentally letting her down and being a disappointment to her.

Again, in the therapy, it emerged that his own father had been violent to him, shamed him as never amounting to much as a boy/man, and his mother, who was also frightened of her husband, could do little to protect, encourage and reassure him. As the therapy progressed, and the husband understood his wife's confusion and fear, and her attempts to seek reassurance through a strident search for certainty, he was able to feel his compassion and empathy for her flow again. She similarly, when she understood how frightened and shamed he had been as a child, realised that her pursuit of him in these difficult moments meant he could no longer 'see' her in her own right, rather that he reacted as the shamed and spurned child he had been. He suggested that they should be able to take emotional risks with each other and invited her to join him. Graciously, and clearly, she told him she could not take these risks to make herself more vulnerable while he was still unsure about divorcing her.

He decided he no longer wanted a divorce and asked his wife if she would have him. She would, and she did.

Thus we can see how the therapist begins the process of rebuilding trust, initially through creating a secure connection with each partner, and through esteem shown for their relationship, whether they continue to stay together, or whether they decide to part. The therapist supports each partner in exploring their perceptions and experiences in a difficult moment, and helps to clarify and throw light on warded off feelings. The task is to help integrate experience: thought, feeling, action and intention, and facilitate reflection and thus choice. Careful exploration and acknowledgement of experience helps to calm and settle partners before they are invited to stand in the emotional shoes of the other, and explore the other's experience. The therapist works slowly, helping partners to process their experiences.

21.6 Comfort and Reassurance

In conclusion, let us turn to the importance of comfort and comforting at the heart of safety and protection in attachment theory. Comfort in our close relationships is complex. It can be understood as both a noun and a verb. Exploration of our experiences of seeking comfort, of giving comfort, and of receiving comfort can be both poignant and affirming. For some couples we meet, one or both may have experienced comfort from the very person who abused them, thus pairing care and danger into a complicated, ambiguous and hard-to- navigate territory of experience. Bowlby believed that even when we have not experienced safety and comfort in our close relationships as children, and have no embodied memory of felt security to draw on as a template for care and care-giving, we still yearn and strive for it—even though we do not know what it looks like, feels like, does like, and have no stories to tell of comfort.

Thus opening up the conversational space around comfort and comforting, helping people learn to soothe and calm themselves when they feel sad and threatened, is often a process for middle therapy as trust grows in the process of the work. We may ask about childhood experience. For example, we may ask what happened, as a child, if you hurt yourself, or if you were unwell. If this question is asked too soon, it may be perceived as dangerous and threatening. Someone who deactivates emotion may reply blandly, even hypothetically, and briefly, that someone took care of them. Such deactivation is often made visible when the person struggles to find an example of comfort and comforting to illuminate their response. Similarly someone who struggles to manage their arousal when triggered by such an enquiry might erupt with an emotional response, but struggle to formulate or think through an event. Gentle enquiry, whilst supporting and validating their experiences, both in the past and the present, could continue to explore their learning, using the notion of corrective and replicative scripts, and intergenerational learning in families around care and comfort. We might ask how their parents comforted them, or how they comforted each other, or about what they know of their parents' experiences of being comforted by grandparents. Asking about experience through the generations can give some thoughtful distance when asking about poignant experience and help people stay reflective in the moment. We can ask what they are trying to do the same, and what they are trying to do differently. We can ask how they know if it is working, and whether they want to expand, elaborate, strengthen or change their efforts and practices. We can ask future questions, such as, what do they hope their children will learn from them about the importance of comforting, and for the future of their children's children, and so on.

21.7 Conclusion

Healing and repair in our close relationships, and establishing a felt sense of security can often take time. We are supporting couples in learning new ways of relating and laying down new neural patterns as dispositional representations of attachment experiences. This requires risk-taking. This requires patience and commitment from all involved in the therapy. And the foundation of growth and resilience is found in interpersonal trust.

References

Bowlby, J. (1973). *Attachment and loss: Separation, anxiety and anger.* New York, NY: Basic Books.
Bowlby, J. (1988). *A secure base.* New York, NY: Basic Books.
Bruner, J. (1990). *Acts of meaning.* Cambridge, MA: Harvard University Press.
Byng-Hall, J. (1995). *Rewriting family scripts: Improvisation and systems change.* New York, NY: Guilford Press.
Crittenden, P. (2006). A dynamic-maturational model of attachment. *Australian and New Zealand Journal of Family Therapy, 27*, 105–115.
Crittenden, P., & Landini, A (2011). Assessing Adult Attachment: A dunamic-maturational approach to discourse analysis. New York: Norton.
Dallos, R., & Draper, R. (2015). *An introduction to family therapy.* Chichester, England: Wiley.
Dallos, R., & Vetere, A. (2009). *Systemic therapy and attachment narratives: Applications across a range of clinical settings.* London, UK: Routledge.
Dallos, R., & Vetere, A. (2014). Systemic therapy and attachment narratives: Attachment narrative therapy. *Clinical Child Psychology and Psychiatry, 19*, 494–502. https://doi.org/10.1177/1359104514550556
Dallos, R., & Vetere, A. (2017). Systemic practice and narratives of attachment. *Human Systems, 28*, 55–71.
Damasio, A. (1994). *Descartes' error: Emotion, reason and the human brain.* New York, NY: Penguin.
Diamond, G., Diamond, G., & Levy, S. (2014). *Attachment based family therapy for depressed adolescents.* Washington, DC: APA Books.
Flaskas, C. (2002). *Family therapy beyond postmodernism.* Hove, England: Brunner Routledge.
Fosha, D. (2000). *The transforming power of affect: A model for accelerated change.* New York, NY: Basic Books.
Gottman, J. (2011). *The science of trust.* New York, NY: Norton.
Johnson, S. (2004). *The practice of emotionally focused marital therapy.* New York, NY: Brunner/Mazel.
Levine, P. (2015). *Trauma and memory. Brain and body in a search for the living past.* Berkeley, CA: North Atlantic Books.

Marvin, R., Cooper, G., Hoffman, K., & Powell, B. (2002). The circle of security project: Attachment based intervention with caregiver-preschool child dyads. *Attachment and Human Development, 4*, 107–124.

Mikulincer, M., Shaver, P., & Pereg, D. (2003). Attachment theory and affect regulation: The dynamics, development, and cognitive consequences of attachment-related strategies. *Motivation and Emotion, 27*(2), 77–102.

Pocock, D. (1997). Feeling understood in family therapy. *Journal of Family Therapy, 19*, 283–302.

Sammut Scerri, C., Vetere, A., Abela, A., & Cooper, J. (2017). *Intervening after violence: Therapy for couples and families*. New York, NY: Springer.

Schore, J., & Schore, A. (2008). Modern attachment theory: The central role of affect regulation in development and treatment. *Clinical Social Work Journal, 36*, 9–20.

Siegel, D. (2012). *The developing mind, second edition: How relationships and the brain interact to shape who we are*. New York, NY: Guilford Press. ISBN 978-1-4625-0390-2.

Van der Kolk, B. (2015). *The body keeps the score*. New York, NY: Penguin.

Vetere, A. (2006). The role of formulation in psychotherapy practice. *Journal of Family Therapy, 28*, 388–391.

Vetere, A. (2014). Alcohol misuse, attachment dilemmas, and triangles of interaction: A systemic approach to practice. In R. Gill (Ed.), *Addictions from an attachment perspective: Do broken bonds and early trauma lead to addictive behaviours?* London, UK: Karnac.

Vetere, A. (2017). An attachment narrative approach to systemic supervision practice. In A. Vetere & J. Sheehan (Eds.), *Supervision of family therapy and systemic practice*. New York, NY: Springer.

Vetere, A., & Sheehan, J. (eds) (in press) Long term systemic psychotherapy. London: Palgrave Macmillan.

Chapter 22
Supporting Parents as Partners: The Couple Context of Parenting, a Personal and Academic Journey

Carolyn Pape Cowan and Philip A. Cowan

22.1 The Journey

22.1.1 The Personal Story

This chapter presents an expanded version of a talk that we gave at the International Commission on Couple and Family Relations, early in February of 2018. It was no coincidence that we were in Malta. We were excited to be there because the couples group intervention that we developed in California in the 1970s and then revised and expanded in collaboration with our colleagues Marsha Kline Pruett and Kyle Pruett was beginning an intervention trial attended by Maltese couples who were parents of very young children. In California and Canada, the intervention is called Supporting Father Involvement. In England and Malta, the same intervention is called Parents as Partners. As we reflected back to the origins of our intervention approach, we realized that the path from the 1970s to the present represented a convergence of events in our own lives as a couple and emerging ideas in the fields of Psychology, Sociology, and Family Studies. We hope that it will be helpful to the international cadre of Conference participants to understand our intervention if we also present the personal and academic background that led us to follow what has become a more than 40-year pathway.

Like many projects that hope to address social problems, the adventure began with events in our own lives. We became a couple in Toronto, Canada, where we married in 1958 at the age of 21 (Phil) and 19 (Carolyn). Both of us had worked with children as teenagers and wanted children of our own. Our first, Joanna, was born in 1961 and Carolyn took a leave from teaching elementary school. Two years

---

C. P. Cowan (✉) · P. A. Cowan
University of California, Berkeley, Berkeley, CA, USA
e-mail: ccowan@berkeley.edu; pacowan@berkeley.edu

© Springer Nature Switzerland AG 2020
A. Abela et al. (eds.), *Couple Relationships in a Global Context*,
European Family Therapy Association Series,
https://doi.org/10.1007/978-3-030-37712-0_22

later, in early September we moved to California with our second baby (Dena) about to be born so that Phil could take a position in the Department of Psychology at the University of California, Berkeley. And 2 years later in 1965, Jonathan joined our family.

In a state famous for earthquakes, we experienced three psychological tremblors over the next few years. First, with the countless joys of raising three delightful children came the unexpected challenges, sleeplessness, and sometimes disorientation of going through the uncharted territory of early parenthood. Second, having moved 3000 miles from our families and friends, and engaging in the first stages of a very exciting but stressful job, we did not anticipate the difficulties involved in such a major transition, especially early on without family and friends as guides and supports. And third, not to be minimized, we were starting a family and careers in the 1960s, a time of changing roles and expectations, along with increased family disruptions not only in America, but in most industrialized countries of the world.

The parenting part of our lives was going well, but we began to lose the initial closeness of our relationship as a couple that we relied on to cope with the external stresses. We did not realize then how much the feelings that we were experiencing but not talking about were experienced by many couples, who like ourselves, had uprooted from rural settings, small towns, or big cities to begin their adult lives. Furthermore, while we rarely talked about this directly with couples we were getting to know, it began to look as if many of them were going through similar rocky transitions. It was the fact that "nobody talked about it" that led us to the notion that groups in which both partners felt safe to share their experiences with other couples might alleviate some of the distress of attempting to deal with unspoken concerns on our own.

We looked around for help, but found little. Many parenting classes were available, but that was not what we needed. Berkeley was a haven for individual therapists, but that was not what we needed either, at least not at first. A prominent local therapist and her husband had become close friends of ours, so we felt we could not consult her on a professional level, although they later became very helpful when we confided in them about our strained relationship.

At the time (the 1960s and early 1970s), Phil was an academic, and Carolyn was on leave from teaching. We began to look to the published literature to help us understand what was happening to us and whether there was anything that we and other couples could do to avoid, or at least reduce, what seemed like the inevitable challenge of partners becoming parents. We eventually found four relatively new ideas that were emerging out of the social ferment of the culture and the growing tendency in the social sciences to regard families as interconnected systems rather than collections of individuals in defined roles (mother, father, child).

22.1.2 *The Intellectual Journey*

Research on the transition to parenthood Sociologists and psychiatrists had begun to study what happens to couples when they become parents. Countering the usual expectation that the transition to parenthood was a joyful time, the literature suggested a rather dark picture. A study that interviewed partners after they had become parents made news by stating that the transition to parenthood was a "crisis" for most couples (Lemasters, 1957). Psychiatrists, relying on testimony from patients wrote articles with titles such as: "Pregnancy as a precipitant of mental illness in men" (Freeman, 1951). This information, while daunting and dramatic, was in a strange sense somewhat comforting. Rather than a failure on our part to negotiate this transition competently, the strain associated with becoming a family might be normative. Why did no one seem to know this?

While the early research on the transition to parenthood looked back nostalgically on the positives of life before baby, over the next decades more than 50 studies followed parents from mid-pregnancy for periods ranging from a few months to 5 years postpartum. All but a handful of these studies reported the same outcomes (Twenge, Campbell, & Foster, 2003): Although not all new parents experience some form of distress, the large majority (around 75–80%) show consistent declines in various measures of marital or couple relationship satisfaction. Of course, this is bad news for young couples. What makes it a public health problem is that declining marital satisfaction in such a large proportion of parents, especially when it involves ongoing unresolved conflict, increases the risk of negative effects on children's cognitive, social, and emotional development (Cummings & Schatz, 2012).

The ideology of prevention Was there any way that this marital slide could be prevented? This question arising from our personal struggles was reinforced by a very strong movement in American psychology and psychiatry during the 1960s, stimulated by the social optimism of the culture in which oppressive institutions could be, and should be, changed. The metaphor frequently cited by prevention practitioners of the 1960s still holds: Instead of fishing drowning bodies out of the river, we should go upstream to see what is pushing them in. The message could be framed as: "Instead of waiting until psychological problems become serious and dangerous, let's think of ways to intervene early when small changes could have long-lasting consequences." Over the years, this ideology formed the basis of the science and practice of prevention with studies of interventions in public health, schools, and families (Coie et al., 1993).

The family as a system In the first half of the twentieth century, our home discipline of psychology was focused primarily on the study and treatment of individuals. After all, "psyche" refers to the mind, soul, or spirit of one individual at a time. But in the 1950s a powerful idea emerged, at first in the study and treatment of families in which one member was diagnosed with severe mental illness (Singer & Wynne, 1965; Watzlawick, Bavelas, & Jackson, 1967). Observations of families in laboratory and treatment settings revealed that although one individual (child, mother, father) received the diagnosis and was the identified patient, the disorder was maintained (and perhaps caused) by distorted communications among family members in couple, parent–child, or sibling relationships. Very quickly, the general principles of family systems theory were generalized far beyond families with mental illness: The defining characteristic of a system is that "the whole is greater than the sum of the parts." An individual's behavior is a product of interactions among all family members, not simply a function of the individual's personality. Just as resistance to change is located in the system of relationships, so is the possibility that change in one relationship will reverberate throughout the system. And, for many family theorists (Minuchin, 1974; Satir, 1972), the relationship between the parents is key to understanding family dynamics, because "the couple is the architect of the system."

Our question was: what specific aspects of the family system ought to be targeted in an intervention? Before we designed the content of our couples group curriculum, we developed a model based on the literature that has guided our thinking over the years. The model focused on five major family domains that function in interconnected ways as risk or protective factors for the development of the individuals and relationships in the family.

1. The transmission of positive and negative patterns across the generations
2. The hopes, expectations, anxieties, and mental health status of each parent
3. Couple communication challenges and healthy problem-solving strategies
4. Parent–child relationships and the effects of different parenting styles
5. Life stresses and social supports outside the nuclear family

Research available in the 1970s and continuing to the present day suggests that without any intervention, negative patterns in our families of origin tend to be repeated in the next-generation through parents' discrepant expectations or mental health problems, which lead to unresolved overt conflict or silent withdrawn tendencies in the couple, which, in turn, lead to harsh, permissive, or neglectful parenting (Caspi & Elder, 1988). This negative cycle can be exacerbated by stressful conditions outside the immediate family (neighborhood, work-related, financial) that are not buffered by external supports from friends, services, or institutions (Conger, Conger, Elder, & Lorenz, 1992).

Parenting and the importance of fathers From the perspective of 2018, it may be difficult to realize that family system ideas represented a Copernican revolution, although as we shall see, in many areas of family service, the systemic view has not been put into practice. The clearest example in our experience lies in the realm of parenting interventions. Classes to teach effective parenting skills have been on offer in the USA since before the twentieth century up to the present. From the perspective of family systems theory though, almost all of these classes have a major flaw stemming in part from the fact that almost 90% of the participants are women.

Until the 1980s fathers were generally unseen in studies of child development, except when researchers investigated the impact of father's absence (at war or incarcerated) or as a consequence of parental divorce (Wallerstein & Kelly, 1980). Studies of father–child relationships began to emerge slowly at first (Lamb, 1977; Parke & Beitel, 1986) and then in a torrent, increasing in frequency over the decades (for reviews, see Lamb, 2010; Tamis-LeMonda & Cabrera, 2013). Taken as a whole, the studies demonstrate conclusively that whatever the marital status of the parents, positive father involvement makes a major contribution to the children's development and the well-being of the mother and the father.

Beginning in the 1980s and 1990s, social and political commentators were becoming alarmed at the increases in divorce and children born to single mothers (Blankenhorn, 1995; Popenoe, 1993). From the studies reporting increased risks of poverty and child behavior problems associated with fatherlessness, these commentators concluded that (1) fathers are absolutely necessary for children to develop well, (2) too many fathers are unmotivated to assume a "responsible role," and (3) from a policy perspective, everything should be done to discourage divorce, get single mothers married, and persuade fathers to become involved parents.

While acknowledging the increase in risk associated with father absence, we believe that these policy claims are misguided because most children in single parent families grow into adulthood indistinguishable from their two-parent counterparts (Silverstein & Auerbach, 1999). Still, a second positively involved parent in addition to the mother represents an often-untapped resource who can make added and sometimes unique contributions to the developing child. We are still puzzled by the fact that so many parenting classes, while "welcoming fathers," do not reach out to recruit them or make their potential contributions an equal focus of the curriculum.

The couple relationship context of parenting As we continued to recapture our own relationship, we were struck by a contradiction in all that we had read. The transition to parenthood was described as a crisis for the couple. The disruption of the couple relationship through high unresolved conflict or divorce was considered problematic for children. But as we have described, fathers were relatively absent from the research and from parenting interventions, and the couple relationship was addressed in interventions only when it had deteriorated, sometimes past the point of no return. Family theorists had described the couple as architects of the family—shapers of the environment that had the potential to protect the child from internal and external stormy weather—but there were no services for average couples experiencing the normative bumpy road to parenthood.

Sometime after our initial attempts in the 1970s to design a preventive intervention that included both partners, family research began to provide reinforcement for our intuitions. Studies in the 1980s through the present day make several points clear. First, there is a strong correlation between the level of unresolved conflict between parents and the child's level of acting out, aggressive behavior or social withdrawal and symptoms of depression. Second, even very young children are highly aware of the tenor of their parents' relationship; especially if the parents fight and children blame themselves for their arguments, the children are at risk for both academic and emotional problems. Third, and perhaps even more important, non-intervention studies suggest that couple relationship distress spills over into the parent–child relationship. When mothers and fathers are at odds and either volatile and aggressive or sullen and withdrawn, each parent is more likely to be harsh and punitive, remote or disengaged, or unable to set appropriate limits (Cui, Durtschi, Donnellan, Lorenz, & Conger, 2010; Erel & Burman, 1995).

In Sect. 22.2, we describe how the findings in our intervention studies corroborate the results of these correlational studies. While the majority of services available to young families—when there are services at all—focus on the mother's or baby's health or parenting skills, the couple relationship that provides a context to each parent–child relationship has largely been ignored. We initially made this observation in considering the dynamics of two-parent families. But over the decades, we have found that the same general statement holds for parents who are married, cohabiting, separated, or divorced.

Silos: The isolated components of the family service field We want to highlight an additional point that may have become apparent in our description of the different strands of research and theory that influenced our thinking about what couples need when they are forming their families. In the course of our journey, as we and our colleagues mounted couples group interventions in the USA, Canada, and the U.K. for middle-class, working-class, and low-income families, we learned that policy decisions about funding family-related programs and the evaluation of these programs are made by a bewildering and sometimes bewildered array of politicians and program administrators who operate independently in a series of fragmented, isolated departments or, metaphorically, silos.

At the federal level, the USA has a plethora of administrative units tasked with providing family support. One example: within the Administration for Children and Families (ACF), there are separate departments to deal with programs for Developmental Disabilities, Child Care, Child support enforcement, Child Abuse and Neglect, Native Americans, and the Office of Family Assistance (OFA). Within OFA are separate programs supporting "healthy marriage" and "responsible fatherhood," which have not coordinated their activities until very recently. Administrative responsibility for policy and programs is often spread among different organizations (e.g., https://www.fatherhood.gov/content/federal-programs-and-resources) that inform potential applicants about ten departments that administer funds to support fatherhood programs.

Similarly siloed arrangements occur at state and local government levels in terms of service delivery systems available for family members. Parenting classes, popular for more than a century, are often offered through University extension or community education institutions and attended primarily by mothers. Therapies for children with behavior problems typically involve a parent, but here too, fathers have not been included. In recent decades, based on concerns about "father absence," programs to encourage fathers' active involvement in the lives of their children became popular, typically delivered to groups of men by male staff, with scant or no attention to the relationship between the parents and no assessment of their effectiveness. Couple relationship enhancement or couple relationship education programs, beginning in the mid-twentieth century, bring both partners together, but rarely focus on parenting issues or children unless they come up as a source of disagreements between the parents.

The family policy paradox, as we will show, involves the fact that all of the agencies and departments we have mentioned, and many more that we have not, focus attention on improving the lives of family members, especially children. Yet, despite having the same goal, they rarely collaborate or talk to each other to learn about successful strategies, modify strategies that do not work, or coordinate activities and decisions. As we will describe, our Supporting Father Involvement/Parents as Partners couples group intervention makes a case for bringing down the siloed walls in order to develop a more collaborative, systemic approach to formulating policies and programs to help parents, children, and families function in more effective, satisfying ways.

22.2 The Destination: An Evidence-Based Integrative Couples Group for Parents

While there have been slight modifications in our intervention approach over the years, the general structure and process of these couples group interventions have remained constant, despite the fact that the name of the various intervention programs changed depending on the target population. Our central idea was to include both parents in the intervention and to focus on strengthening the relationship between them in order to create an environment that supports the development of their children. We wanted to work with families as early in their development as possible—expectant and new parents making the transition to parenthood (Becoming a Family, C. Cowan & Cowan, 2000), parents whose first children are about to start their academic careers as they make the transition to primary school (Schoolchildren and their Families, Cowan, Cowan, Ablow, Johnson, & Measelle, 2005), and parents whose relationships are especially vulnerable based on their low incomes or their own or their children's mental health challenges (Parents as Partners and Supporting Father Involvement, Casey et al., 2017; Cowan, Cowan, Pruett, Pruett, & Wong, 2009).

Each group includes five or six couples, and a male–female co-leader pair trained to work with couples and parent–child relationships. In the low-income communities, we have also included a Case Manager to help refer the parents to other services as needed (housing, legal, health) and to facilitate their consistent attendance at the groups. The groups typically meet weekly for 16 weeks to talk about and share their challenges of being partners and parents, although our first trial with expectant parents extended for 24 weeks from mid-pregnancy to 3 months postpartum.

We had the radical idea that parents do not so much need to be told what to do or not to do but will benefit from having a safe setting in which we can encourage them to examine their values and goals and think about the relationships they experienced in their families of origin that undoubtedly influence their goals, so that they can become more conscious about where they are heading and why. The groups foster more deliberate sharing of these ideas than partners typically do, which encourages an atmosphere in which they can discover what works for each of them—by listening to each other, getting ideas from other couples and the facilitators, and taking time to try some slight shifts in their day-to-day lives to move them a little closer to the kind of partners and parents they are hoping to be.

From the beginning, the content of the program was determined by the list of five known risks and buffers to adults' and children's development: each family member's adjustment and distress, the quality of the couple relationship and each of the parent–child relationships, the relationship patterns from each parent's family of origin, and the stressors and supports that each family is contending with. The program is delivered in both open-ended and structured conversations, exercises, role-plays, materials such as videotapes of couples or parents and children, and occasional "homework" to try between meetings.

22.2.1 The Transition to Parenthood: Becoming a Family (BAF, C. P. Cowan & Cowan, 2000)

We have written extensively about the issues couples face in becoming parents for the first time. Identities and roles change. Parenting infants who communicate but cannot talk is often a baffling enterprise. Relations with the parents' families of origin often require rethinking and renegotiation. Outside stresses from work, friends, and other events often increase as parents juggle the internal demands of family-making. And, as we have experienced and observed, all of these changes have consequences for the couple.

This BAF study of partners becoming first-time parents was funded by the US National Institute of Mental Health (NIMH) as a preventive venture for community couples making the transition to first-time parenthood. The couples groups spanned 24 weeks, encompassing the last 3 months of pregnancy and the first 3 months of parenthood. Each of the 2-h meetings begins with an open-ended check-in during which the couples are welcome to bring both successes and dilemmas arising from last week's meeting or from any of the events occurring in their lives and relationships. The check-in is followed by structured exercises, role-plays, discussions, and mini-presentations by the Group Leaders.

A few examples:

The self Before their first babies were born and again later, we asked men and women in our Becoming a Family project to draw a circle we call "the Pie" to represent their sense of themselves in the major aspects of their lives. They divide the circle into sections they name based on how large each aspect of life *feels*, not the amount of time spent in each role—husband/wife/partner/worker/son/daughter/electrician/artist/leisure, and so on. Compared with men who did not have babies, who showed a significant increase in the size of the "partner/lover" aspect of self over the next several years, new fathers were squeezing "partner/lover" into a smaller space once the babies were born to accommodate the significant increase in the "father/mother" or "parent" piece of the Pie. The expectant mothers did the same, and after the babies were born, the couples realized that this squeeze often led to strain in their relationship as a couple. One major issue was where their time for intimacy had gone and another at the top of their lists was what had happened to the "who does what?" of their lives, which reflected a more traditional division of labor at home that they had predicted. This challenge to their expectations of becoming more equal partners than their parents had been surprised them. Not only did they discover in the group discussions that many new parents were experiencing this strain, but with both partners in the room, we could encourage them to think about what small shifts in "who does what?" might lead to a bit more time for intimacy, less conflict and strain as partners, and more satisfaction.

Parenting Another issue that often surprised the new parents was their different inclinations about how to respond when their baby was upset. Unlike new gadgets, new babies come without a "user's manual" so parents often turned to different sources for advice. There were at least two problems with this strategy: one expert's advice about picking up a crying infant and another's suggestion that they let him cry it out were often in conflict—as the two parents' ideas often were—and either way of handling a distressed baby might not fit these particular mothers, fathers, or babies.

Family of origin Similar dilemmas came up about how to handle the grandparents' reactions to the new grandchild, which included who would come to meet the baby first and the tendency of the grandparents to feel criticized if the new parents adopted a different way of handling the baby than they had done when their children (the new parents) were young. We also know now, but did not when we were forming our own family, that patterns in our original families tend to get repeated without some thought or intervention. The groups allowed space for both partners to consider which relationship patterns had served them well as they were growing up and which they hoped to modify to create more nurturing and satisfying relationships in their new family.

Outside the family Contemporary partners are faced with managing a delicate balance between work and family demands while trying to maintain a relationship as partners and with friends. Many men tell us that they want to be more involved with their children than their fathers were with them; a majority of modern women aspire to manage work or a career while being caring parents. How to manage all that when bosses and babies vie for their time and energy can feel daunting and sometimes overwhelming.

The couple relationship Regardless of the specific topic of each group meeting, the couple relationship becomes the focus of our intervention in a number of ways. First, we leave some time for couples to talk with each other before engaging in a group discussion. Second, couples exchange information with other couples about how they are coping with very similar issues. Third, when partners disagree—about an issue in their relationship or a parenting strategy (a frequent occurrence)—we help them focus not on "the right answer" but on how they could work together productively to take account of or resolve their differences.

Fourth, as we extended the interventions to varied groups of parents, we realized that we needed a more explicit focus on couple communication. For example, group leaders described three styles of communication—attack, withdraw, and confide (Wile, 2008). Partners from two different couples were asked to role-play a discussion in the style of attacking and withdrawing; then, with the group's help, they were invited to discuss how these tense interactions could be turned into conversations in which both partners could begin to confide the vulnerable feelings the issue brought up for them. An extension of this exercise is to ask the group while the participants were attacking or withdrawing—"what do you think your children saw and heard?"—sometimes asking an adult to pretend to be the child overhearing this argument—to heighten their awareness of the potential negative impact of parents' unresolved conflict on their children. These role-plays often brought the point home dramatically.

The results The study was conducted in the form of a randomized clinical trial, with couples randomly assigned to participate in the groups or to simply be interviewed about their lives over time. We found promising benefits of meeting with clinically experienced co-leaders and other couples expecting a baby: Compared to parents who were not offered the intervention in the random trial, parents who participated in the couples groups were able to stave off the common slide in marital satisfaction over time that we and others found in new parents in most countries who do not have the possibility of intervention (Twenge et al., 2003). The intervention parents maintained their relationship quality over 6 years between pregnancy and their first child's transition to school (Schulz, Cowan, & Cowan, 2006). Notably, a comparable group of couples who did not have a baby during these years who were recruited into the program from the same Obstetrics/Gynecology clinics and private practices also maintained their relationship satisfaction over the 6 years, suggesting that without intervention, new parents are vulnerable to declining satisfaction as a couple over the early years of parenthood.

22.2.1.1 Schoolchildren and Their Families (SAF, Cowan et al., 2005)

This study for parents of a first child about to make the transition to elementary school was funded by the US National Institute of Mental Health. The participants were couples who responded to recruitment efforts at pre-school setting in 28 different cities and towns in the wider San Francisco Bay Area and to notices in local media.

Results Compared to parents offered *a brief consultation* with staff once a year between pre-kindergarten and second grade, those offered *the 16-week couples group* showed benefits for the parents, their relationships as couples and with their children, and the children's adjustment. We also tested a slightly different emphasis in two sets of couples groups, one focusing a little more on couples' issues in the open-ended part of each meeting, the other focusing a little more on parent–child issues, while the rest of the content was identical in the two sets of groups.

Parents in both sets of groups showed less harsh, authoritarian parenting styles after the groups ended (as we observed them), but the couples in the groups with the added focus on couples' issues also showed reductions in conflict and volatility as a couple while working on a challenging problem (as observed). This study's variation supported the notion that focusing on challenging couple issues has the potential to affect both parenting *and* couple relationship quality. Children showed benefits in both versions but those whose parents had the groups emphasizing couples' issues showed reduced aggression and increases in achievement scores 5 years later. Ten years later, when all the children had made the transition to high school in grade 9 at age 14–15, children of parents in both the couple-focused and parenting-focused groups were less hyperactive and aggressive than children in the control group, and parents from the couple-focused groups were still more satisfied with their relationships than parents in the control group with no intervention (Cowan, Cowan, & Barry, 2011).

22.2.1.2 Supporting Father Involvement (SFI, Cowan et al., 2009)

This 10-year study was funded by the California Office of Child Abuse Prevention to offer ways to strengthen fathers' involvement in their children's lives in five counties with a preponderance of poor families. In this venture, we were joined by colleagues Marsha Kline Pruett and Kyle Pruett, who collaborated with us to modify the 16-week program to make it even more accessible for low-income families and to provide ongoing guidance to project staff. The first trial involved 286 Mexican American, African American, and European American families, in which the groups and assessment interviews were offered in English or Spanish. We also made some of the exercises a little more hands-on and active and offered less written material, something we have continued to do with the UK intervention with much success.

Because the father involvement movement at that time (2002) typically brought men together in groups with male leaders, we designed our evaluation to test the effects of fathers-only groups or couples groups meeting for 16 weeks, or a one-time group of couples meeting for 3 h, where we focused on the importance of fathers in their children's lives (a low-dose control group). The same male–female leader pairs worked with families in all of these study conditions. These different conditions were offered randomly as parents in four counties expressed interest in the program. We then followed all of the parents for the next 18 months to see whether any of the intervention models was more effective—in getting fathers involved with their children and the mothers of their children, in any changes in their parenting styles, or in their children's behaviors as reported by the parents.

Results of the first trial The parents offered the *one-time 3-h meeting* did not change or got worse, and their children's behavior problems increased over 18 months. In families offered the *16-week fathers-only groups*, the fathers became more involved in their children's care, the children's behavior problems remained stable, but the parents' satisfaction with their couple relationships declined. In families offered the *16-week couples group*, the fathers became more involved with the children, the mothers' and fathers' parenting stress declined, the children's behavior problems remained stable—and the parents' satisfaction as couples remained stable.

Results of the second and third trials These results were comparable to a second trial with another 276 families, who showed similar positive benefits of a couples group, with the added finding of increased income after the groups ended (Cowan, Cowan, Pruett, Pruett, & Gillette, 2014). A third trial with 239 couples included similar community families from the same five counties (Pruett, Cowan, Cowan, Gillette & Pruett, 2019), but this set of groups also included families referred by the staff of the Child Welfare Service (CWS), who had come to their attention because of earlier domestic violence or child abuse or neglect. Each couples group included parents referred from the community *and* by CWS staff. This time, we randomly offered a 16-week group to start immediately or in 6 months.

Several months after the groups ended, CWS-referred and community parents from the immediate groups showed significant declines in couple distress—couple conflict, conflict about their children, and violent problem-solving—and reductions in harsh parenting. This trial supported the idea that mixing couples with more and less distress made a difference to a majority of the couples' lives, even those in serious difficulty—and that their children benefited from the parents' reduced stress and conflict. One year after the intervention ended, the reductions in distress as a couple and harsh parenting continued, which led to reductions in the children's aggression and symptoms of depression.

A vignette of one couple, based on before and after videotapes

Before the group intervention. A couple is asked by a project staff member to choose an issue about parenting that they disagree about and discuss it for 10 min to try to make some headway on resolving the disagreement. The experimenter leaves the room. The issue this couple chose was getting their 8-year-old daughter to bed. The father sits facing front, arms folded in front of his chest. Sitting beside him, the mother keeps turning to him when she speaks. She starts with several suggestions, including to give the daughter more choices. When he gives in immediately, she says "we're supposed to be *discussing* this." The conversation becomes heated with her suggesting and him objecting. Finally, she says loudly, "how many times have you actually tried to put her to bed?" Still not looking at her, he gets quieter, tries to defend himself, and then withdraws.

After the group intervention ends. Eighteen months later the couple came in to the program site again. The topic they choose is the same—getting a child to bed, but this time their conversation focuses on the older son rather than the daughter. This time, they sit facing each other. The mother starts with suggestions. Instead of rejecting them, the father contributes an example and adds an additional suggestion. She responds with still another idea. He says in a friendly voice "I don't think that's a good idea." In response she advances yet another plan. He says "we can try that" and suggests some additional details. He suggests that they both get involved in carrying out the plan. She agrees. He re-states the plan to make sure that he understands it.

Of course, this is only one example but it does reflect the overall data showing that (1) couple conflict declines and (2) this decline is associated with an increase in collaborative parenting, and in each of their individual approaches to the child.

22.2.1.3 Participants' Evaluations of the Groups

Beyond the parents' scores on the assessment materials we examined to look at potential changes in interventions participants, we were interested in the parents' own evaluations of their work in the couples groups. Comments from fathers and mothers in all of the interventions described above were mostly positive and amazingly similar. A wide range of parents have told us that, unlike other programs they have participated in, our groups are helpful because they do not lead them to feel stigmatized because they are economically poor or struggling with conflict—and because both parents are taking part together. Perhaps the single most frequent comment has been that the biggest take-home message they come away with is "we are not the only ones struggling." Groups have great power to *show* the members—rather than simply telling them—how widespread couples' concerns are. The group's emphasis on the importance of strengthening their relationships as partners and parents to overcome the conflicts and challenges that get in the way of their being able to react in caring ways gives them new ways to understand their struggles and new ideas to try to make their day-to-day lives and relationships feel more satisfying. Because we have both parents in the room, we can focus on challenges in their key relationships in ways that reading materials or parenting classes or groups for mothers or fathers alone cannot hope to match.

22.3 Conceptual Significance of Our Intervention Approach

When interventions are systematically evaluated, they not only provide evidence concerning whether the interventions are effective, but also shed light on our theories about how families function, or fail to function. We believe that the results we have presented document the benefits of using clinically skilled co-leaders to work with both parents—both as a preventive intervention for middle-class and working-class families and as a helpful intervention for families in poverty and those with serious mental health challenges. Furthermore, we believe that our findings, and findings from studies of other couples group interventions, have something to teach us about the couple relationship context of parenting.

Looking back over the last 40 years of intervention creation and evaluation, we believe that our work has added support to a fundamental assumption of family systems theory. In contrast with thousands of parenting programs that are attended by mothers, we have shown that groups for both parents that include a focus on the couple relationship provide value-added impact on family relationships and child outcomes (Panter-Brick et al., 2015). Parenting is a team effort, and both members of the team need to be involved and collaborative, even when the intimate couple relationship has come to an end.

In the Schoolchildren and their Families intervention we found that a focus on the couple relationship in the open-ended check-in portions of each meeting provided benefits for the couple relationship as well as the parent–child relationship, and that these benefits were passed on to the children. In the Supporting Father Involvement study, we found that couples groups provided stronger positive effects than groups for fathers only. And, consistent with family systems theories, in all of our studies, we demonstrated that there is a series of dynamic spillover effects in which improvements in couple relationship quality are followed by improvements in parent–child relationship quality, which, in turn, are followed by benefits for the child in terms of higher academic achievement and lower levels of aggressive, hyperactive, shy withdrawn behaviors, and depressive symptoms.

Also consistent with family systems theory, our couples group curriculum goes beyond a singular focus on communication skills to address risk and protective factors associated with individual well-being, three-generational continuities and discontinuities, parenting principles, and coping with life stresses and enlisting supports outside the nuclear family.

The findings of our studies lead us to a critical conclusion concerning how family services are organized in most of the Western countries with which we have had some experience. Contrary to the family systemic approach, the funding mechanisms and service delivery organizations hoping to strengthen families have been isolated in silos in which fathers, mothers, and children are viewed separately, or at best in pairs. Just as families are most profitably viewed as dynamic interacting systems, so should the organizations that minister to families avoid the isolation and lack of communication that unfortunately constitutes the norm.

The research results reported here indicate that our intervention has been successful as measured by statistical findings that determine whether participation produces positive changes in parents and their offspring. Another important criterion of success is whether others outside the original investigator group attempt to adopt and evaluate the intervention approach. At this writing, with active involvement of the Cowans and the Pruetts as trainers and consultants, the Supporting Father Involvement program, sometimes with a different name, is now operating in the USA, Canada (Kline Pruett, Gillette, & Pruett, 2016), the UK (Casey et al., 2017), and Malta, with plans to begin soon in Israel.

22.4 Ending on a Personal Note

We began this journey with an attempt to deal with the unanticipated strain associated with becoming parents of young children. Among other things, the disruptions we felt as a couple led to four decades of working together—first to cope with our own issues, and then to design a couples group intervention that is proving helpful for many other families. We are excited about the ever-expanding dissemination of this approach to working with parents in different communities and countries. All of the clinical trials have brought us into relationships with a vital, hard-working cadre of professionals in different countries who are enthusiastic about the promise of these ways of helping men and women become the kind of parents and partners they hoped to be.

And what of the family we created with a marriage in 1958 and three children born in the early 1960s? Our two daughters and our son are now parents and partners themselves who made their own transitions to parenthood some time ago and are actively nurturing our seven grandchildren, six of whom have already embarked on their college careers. We have learned a great deal in this rich and gratifying journey bringing our personal and professional lives together.

References

Blankenhorn, D. (1995). *Fatherless America : Confronting our most urgent social problem*. New York, NY: Basic Books.
Casey, P., Cowan, P. A., Cowan, C. P., Draper, L., Mwamba, N., & Hewison, D. (2017). Parents as partners: A U.K. trial of a U.S. couples-based parenting intervention for at-risk low-income families. *Family Process, 56*(3), 589–606.
Caspi, A., & Elder, G. H. J. (1988). Emergent family patterns: The intergenerational construction of problem behaviour and relationships. In R. A. Hinde & J. Stevenson-Hinde (Eds.), *Relationships within families: Mutual influences* (pp. 218–240). Oxford, UK: Clarendon Press.
Coie, J. D., Watt, N. F., West, S. G., Hawkins, J. D., Asarnow, J. R., Markman, H. J., ... Long, B. (1993). The science of prevention - A conceptual-framework and some directions for a national research-program. *American Psychologist, 48*(10), 1013–1022. https://doi.org/10.1037/0003-066x.48.10.1013
Conger, R. D., Conger, K. J., Elder, G. H., & Lorenz, F. O. (1992). A family process model of economic hardship and adjustment of early adolescent boys. *Child Development, 63*(3), 526–541.
Cowan, C. P., & Cowan, P. A. (2000). *When partners become parents: The big life change for couples*. Mahwah NJ: Lawrence Erlbaum.
Cowan, C. P., Cowan, P. A., & Barry, J. (2011). *Journal of Family Psychology, 25*, 240–250.
Cowan, P., Cowan, C. P., Pruett, M. K., Pruett, K., & Gillette, P. (2014). Evaluating a couples group to enhance father involvement in low-income families using a benchmark comparison. *Family Relations, 63*(3), 356–370. https://doi.org/10.1111/fare.12072
Cowan, P., Cowan, C. P., Pruett, M. K., Pruett, K., & Wong, J. J. (2009). Promoting fathers' engagement with children: Preventive interventions for low-income families. *Journal of Marriage and Family, 71*(3), 663–679.
Cowan, P. A., Cowan, C. P., Ablow, J. C., Johnson, V. K., & Measelle, J. R. (2005). *The family context of parenting in children's adaptation to elementary school*. Monographs in parenting series. Mahwah, NJ: Lawrence Erlbaum Associates, xvii, 414p.
Cui, M., Durtschi, J. A., Donnellan, M. B., Lorenz, F. O., & Conger, R. D. (2010). Intergenerational transmission of relationship aggression: A prospective longitudinal study. *Journal of Family Psychology, 24*(6), 688–697.
Cummings, E., & Schatz, J. N. (2012). Family conflict, emotional security, and child development: Translating research findings into a prevention program for community families. *Clinical Child and Family Psychology Review, 15*, 14–27. https://doi.org/10.1007/s10567-012-0112-0
Erel, O., & Burman, B. (1995). Interrelatedness of marital relations and parent-child relations: A meta-analytic review. *Psychological Bulletin, 118*(1), 108–132.

Freeman, T. (1951). Pregnancy as a precipitant of mental illness in men. *British Journal of Medical Psychology, 24*, 49–54.

Kline Pruett, M., Gillette, P., & Pruett, K. D. (2016). Supporting father involvement to promote co-parent, parent and child outcomes in a Canadian context. *Psychology and Psychological Research Interational Journal, 1*(1), 000111.

Lamb, M. E. (1977). Father-infant and mother-infant interaction in the first year of life. *Child Development, 48*(1), 167–181.

Lamb, M. E. (2010). *The role of the father in child development* (5th ed.). Hoboken, NJ: Wiley.

Lemasters, E. E. (1957). Parenthood as crisis. *Marriage and Family Living, 19*(4), 352–355. https://doi.org/10.2307/347802

Minuchin, S. (1974). *Families and family therapy*. Cambridge, MA: Harvard University Press.

Panter-Brick, C., Burgess, A., Eggerman, M., McAllister, F., Pruett, K., & Leckman, J. (2015). Practitioner review: Engaging fathers - Recommendations for a game change in parenting interventions on a systematic review of the global evidence. *Journal of Child Psychology and Psychiatry, 22*(11), 1187–1212.

Parke, R. D., & Beitel, A. (1986). Hospital-based intervention for fathers. In M. E. Lamb (Ed.), *The father's role: Applied perspectives*. New York, NY: Wiley.

Popenoe, D. (1993). American family decline, 1960-1990. *Journal of Marriage and the Family, 55*, 527–541.

Pruett, M. K., Cowan, P. A., Cowan, C. P., Gillette, P. & Pruett, K. D. (2019). Supporting father involvement: An intervention with community and child welfare-referred couples. *Family Relations, 68(1)*, 51–67

Satir, V. (1972). *Peoplemaking*. Palo Alto, CA: Science and behavior books.

Schulz, M. S., Cowan, C. P., & Cowan, P. A. (2006). Promoting healthy beginnings: A randomized controlled trial of a preventive intervention to preserve marital quality during the transition to parenthood. *Journal of Consulting and Clinical Psychology, 74*(1), 20–31.

Silverstein, L. B., & Auerbach, C. F. (1999). Deconstructing the essential father. *American Psychologist, 54*(6), 397–407.

Singer, M. T., & Wynne, L. C. (1965). Thought disorder & family relations of schizophrenics: IV. Results & implications. *Archives of General Psychiatry, 12*(2), 201–212.

Tamis-LeMonda, C. S., & Cabrera, N. J. (2013). *Handbook of father involvement: Multidisciplinary perspectives* (2nd ed.). New York, NY: Routledge, Taylor & Francis Group.

Twenge, J. M., Campbell, W. K., & Foster, C. A. (2003). Parenthood and marital satisfaction: A meta-analytic review. *Journal of Marriage and Family, 65*(3), 574–583. https://doi.org/10.1111/j.1741-3737.2003.00574.x

Wallerstein, J. S., & Kelly, J. B. (1980). *Surviving the breakup: How children and parents cope with divorce*. New York, NY: Basic Books.

Watzlawick, P., Bavelas, J. B., & Jackson, D. D. (1967). *Pragmatics of human communication : A study of interactional patterns, pathologies, and paradoxes*. New York, NY: Norton.

Wile, D. B. (2008). *How conflict can improve your relationship* (revised ed.). Oakland, CA: Collaborative Couple Therapy Books.

Chapter 23
Supporting Links Between Living Apart Together (LAT) Couples Through Online Couple Therapy

Pierre Cachia

23.1 Introduction

We live in an age in which ease of travel and greatly improved communication technology allows relationships to emerge, develop and be nurtured across continents. The advent of Living Apart Together (LAT) couples and the possibility of offering partners in such relationships, therapeutic support while they are living away from one another, reflect the impact these advances are having on our personal, romantic, familial and therapeutic relationships.

This chapter examines the application of webcam-mediated couple psychotherapy and, discusses, the challenges and opportunities the online medium affords couple therapists seeking to support couples 'living apart together'. Over the past 2 years, I have been responsible, together with my colleagues at Tavistock Relationships in London, for the setting up a of an innovative psychoanalytically-informed service offering online couple psychotherapy and individual relationship counselling. Here I draw on the experience gained in setting up this service, supervising the team of experienced clinicians, and my own online practice with couples, reflecting about how online couple therapy provides a potentially irreplaceable means of supporting LAT couples. Composite case studies will illustrate some of the experiences and the learning this has afforded me.

P. Cachia (✉)
Tavistock Relationships, London, UK
e-mail: pcachia@tavistockrelationships.org

23.2 The Therapeutic Model

Tavistock Relationships was founded in 1948 as the Family Discussion Bureau and has today grown to become the primary organisation in couple psychotherapy in London and is a centre of excellence in couple psychotherapy, training and research. The main face-to-face service has grown to deliver thousands of sessions annually (Annual Review, 2017), with the online service representing a small, but growing development that benefits immensely from the experience accumulated over years of clinical practice here. The theoretical framework employed in this practice draws broadly from objects relations approaches, predominately those with a Kleinian inspiration, coupled with the intrapersonal influence offered by Jungian thought.

A detailed account of the work of Tavistock Relationships is available in Ruszczynski's (1993) *Psychotherapy with Couples* and a more updated elaboration of the approach being available in Morgan's *A Couple State of Mind: Psychoanalysis of couples and the Tavistock Relationships Model* (Morgan, 2019). Moreover, Lanman, Grier, and Evans (2003) inform us that

> Psychoanalytic couple psychotherapists are concerned with aspects of couples' functioning that the couple initially may be unaware of. This form of therapy aims to facilitate change in the relationship between the partners. It focuses not simply on partners as individuals and not only on the conscious and rational level, but also on the interaction between partners that operates unconsciously, which, if not engaged with, can interfere powerfully with the possibility of lasting change. The approach considers a couple's relationship in terms of how the functioning of the two individuals can be perceived as fitting together to form one predominant joint mode of relating (p. 255).

They point out a number of key aspects of the approach, namely, the importance of couple psychological fit and flow of the shared, patterned processes inherent to couple dynamics, whether these be conscious to the couple or less so. These are considered to be of vital importance in understanding and supporting change when working towards a more fulfilling relationship.

The Psychoanalytic Couple and Family Institute of New England (2013) defined this approach in a very similar manner. Couple psychoanalytic psychotherapy is seen to involve an integration of psychodynamic and family systems theory alongside developments in neurobiological understanding of attachment, unconscious emotional communication and affect regulation. This wide theoretical matrix allows an appreciation of each partner's early relational histories and how these might translate into creative or problematic self-reinforcing patterns of relating within the couple.

The face-to-face application of this methodology is well established and is increasingly supported by research findings. A large naturalistic study of clinical outcomes at Tavistock Relationships has shown that couple psychotherapy led to significant reduction in both personal and relational distress (Hewison, Casey & Mwamba, 2016).

23.3 Cautiously Venturing into Cyberspace

Delivery of psychoanalytic psychotherapy to clients via online media, particularly when it comes to couple work, is in its infancy and faces a number of real challenges. Hilty et al.'s (2013) review of telemental health interventions suggests that these are often effective. However, studies looking specifically at psychotherapeutic interventions with couples were not included in their sample. This absence reflects a continuing lack of research in the field. My preferred position is one of cautious exploration and resonates with that of Scharff (2013) when she states that 'The field of teletherapy is so new that standards of practice and learning resources are still being developed. None of us has enough experience as yet to be definitive but we all feel the need to open the topic for discussion' (p. xix).

The medium itself presents a number of challenges in its therapeutic application. Firstly, there is the instantaneous nature of cyberspace with the resultant expectation that therapists, when working online, are immediately available and efficiently responsive before and during therapy. Most clients' experience of online services has been shaped by the likes of eBay and Amazon where speed and immediacy are key. The painstaking attention to detail typical of the psychotherapeutic process, whichever orientation one subscribes to, stands in stark contrast with the 'culture' dominating cyberspace.

Additionally, the online medium drastically modifies the therapeutic frame so that it can no longer be defined by the four walls of the therapist's consulting room, or the temporal arrangements in which therapy takes place. Indeed, these features come to give way to the framing offered by the two-dimensionality of the therapist's screen and other peculiarities of the technology we employ as well as the manner this is managed by all parties involved. Furthermore, the therapist might find that clients are located in a very different time zone so that the therapist's first session might coincide with the ending of the clients' day. While in session, the couple will often move in and out of screen shot, modify the composition and tone of the visuals available to their therapist in particular ways, and provide entry into chosen areas of their home or workplace. These elements represent valuable communication to the therapist which the couple composes with conscious intent or less so. Many of these elements are novel and often surprising to therapists who are venturing into online work for the first time. Neumann (2013) tells us that the impact of proving therapy through the internet has a profound and pervasive effect on the therapeutic process itself:

> Using the internet as a vehicle for treatment affects the way that conscious and unconscious material is received, experienced, and processed by both patient and analyst. It impacts the types of transference/countertransference, the types of defences used, and the nature of the unconscious material such as dreams and associations that emerge. It effects the analyst's capacity to foster a therapeutic alliance and the nature of the enactment that are likely to occur. (p. 179)

Sceptics argue that these changes are so profound as to render the viability of online therapy questionable. My own experience and, I believe, of the clients I have worked with directly or through supervisory process, does not support such assertions. It is of course essential that one remains fully cognizant that the work is not a pseudo face-to-face therapy and the reality of the technology is kept firmly in mind. Sherer-Mohatt and Scharff (2013) reflecting on online therapy with individuals, suggest that the computer needs to be thought of as a 'metaphor for state of mind' (p. 27) and the therapist therefore 'interacts in the language of technology, works in the displacement, and gradually interprets the conscious parallel between aspects of the computer and parts of his mind' (p. 36). While this might sound somewhat techno-centric, it is no more so than the therapist consideration of how a client might make use of their chair or how they might open or close the consulting room's door. In many ways doors, chairs, clocks on consulting room walls and mobile phones are bits of technology we have grown accustomed to relating as inhibiting and even mediating meaning within the therapeutic process. High-definition cameras, microphones and broadband bandwidths are new additions that in online therapy are not only present but the vehicles of connection.

Notwithstanding the cautious reserve displayed by many with the psychotherapeutic professions some couples find the medium meets their needs well. The reasons couples seek online support are diverse. The medium offers the convenience of not having to commute to the therapist's consulting room, reducing the time and expense involved. While there are privacy risks involved with any form of online transaction, couples often appreciate the increased confidentiality afforded by a medium that allow them to seek help while avoiding questions about their whereabouts from family and friends. However, there are some couples for whom online couple therapy is the only viable option.

About half of all inquiries for online couple therapy at Tavistock Relationships throughout 2017/2018 involved couples with one partner either living permanently outside the UK or frequently travelling away from home due to work commitments. These couples have at times attempted face-to-face therapy but were unable to sustain the required commitment. Other couples do not have access to qualified specialists in couple and relationship counselling within a commutable distance, while others are faced with mobility restrictions and find the online medium well worth considering.

23.4 Living Apart Together

Couples who identify themselves as part of a couple but reside in two different households are often referred to as 'living apart together' or by its acronym, LAT, the term being first used by a Dutch journalist in 1978 (Haskey, 2005). Amato and Hayes (2013) suggest that the growth of such relational arrangements reflects the growth of individualism in the Western world. While I do not doubt that sociological changes have energised the emergence of the LAT lifestyle, I want to suggest that, this must have been greatly facilitated by advances in technology leading to increasingly accessible and effective means of communication and travel.

They identify two types of LAT couples which, as I will discuss later on, has some relevance to the manner in which LAT couples seek help. First, Transitory

LAT couples are often relatively short term but may seek and attain increased commitment and stability when they can be described as Stable LAT couples, the second typology.

Notably, Amato and Hayes use the term 'Alone Together Marriages' to describe one of four types of marriage based on levels of happiness and interaction. These couples are characterised by high levels of happiness and low levels of interaction. While parallels between LAT couples and this type of marital coupling is worth considering it is important not to confuse the two. LAT couples can certainly be distressed and while they do live apart their level of interaction can be extremely intense with continuous communication, often mediated digitally via Facebook messenger, Skype, WhatsApp or any other of the myriad social media accessible to them.

Duncan, Phillips, Roseneil, Carter, and Stoilova (2013) briefing on research carried out in the UK in 2011 and 2012 indicate that nearly 9% of the population are in a relationship but not living with their partner. This figure excludes all married couples in similar living arrangements so that the number of couples in such arrangements is certainly significantly higher. In this discussion, the term LAT is being used in this wider sense and includes married couples living separately.

Duncan et al.'s research found that the LAT couple state is often an explicit choice with about 30% believing that the relationship had not matured sufficiently to progress to cohabitation and another 30% indicating a distinct preference to preserving separate households and prioritising other responsibilities (including parenting). Twenty percent of respondents indicated that financial pressures meant shared residence was not viable while only 10% of LAT couples reported that the arrangement was a result of developments in their studies or career. Significantly, the ethnicity of LAT couples in the UK is, more or less, in line with that of the general population. About a quarter of LAT couples have children, which is less than in the general population and they also tend to be younger partners with 43% being under the age of 24.

It is also interesting to note, particularly when considering the provision of online therapy, that LAT couples often live in proximity even if they do not share residence with only 16% living 50 miles away from one another, and about half of these having partners residing outside the UK. Needless to say, this chapter considers the application of online couple therapy specifically to this latter group for whom access to conventional face-to-face therapy is more or less impossible. While there are no figures available for the number of married couples in such arrangements, it is safe to assume that in large metropolitan areas like London, the total number increases significantly if taking into account the married population.

The picture in other countries is similar in that, for example, 26% of LAT couples in study of German LAT couples chose this arrangement as the relationship had not yet matured sufficiently (Reuschke, 2010). The transition to cohabitation is seen as a possible desirable outcome. Indeed, in Italy and Spain, LAT couples are nearly exclusively transitional in nature reflecting, at least in part, difficulties faced in attaining financial autonomy (Billari, Rosina, Ranaldi, & Romano, 2008; Castro-Martín, Domínguez-Folgueras, & Martín-García, 2008).

Mortelmans, Pasteels, Régnier-Loilier, Vignoli, and Mazzuco (2015) compared incidence of LAT couples across ten European countries and found that this is somewhat variable. Belgium, France and Norway having similar numbers of persons in LAT relationships as the UK while other countries report deflated numbers. Bulgaria, Lithuania report only about 5% and Estonia and Georgia less than 2%.

23.5 LAT Couples Seeking Online Relationship Support

The trajectory of LAT couples approaching online couple psychotherapy services is probably as varied as in the general population. However, I have come across a number of presentations, which I wish to highlight as they each present us with different clinical challenges and opportunities. First of all there are those LAT couples transitioning to a non-LAT arrangement and, at the other end of the spectrum, there are couples struggling to settle into an LAT arrangement. Finally, there are LAT couples who use distance so as to make proximity tolerable as they seem limited in their capacity to manage the intensity of the couple experience. I will illustrate these presentations clinically and then discuss their challenges and opportunities.

23.5.1 Couples Transitioning from LAT to a Shared Living Arrangement

Mary and Patrick are a long-term LAT couple in their early sixties who are actively contemplating in transitioning to a shared residence as they move towards semi-retirement. They approached therapy after their previously relatively harmonious shared lives was rocked by a massive disagreement as how to manage aspects of their wealth. Patrick's eldest daughter from his first marriage had recently divorced and was experiencing financial difficulties. He decided to gift her a significant amount of money to support her relocation but this triggered a major crisis in the couple that spilled around them and ended up involving Mary's children as well. This happened against the backdrop of the couple's planned move towards living more permanently in one home.

The couple lived most of their lives apart. Early on they both were based in London and shared a home but often travelled and spent days and, at times weeks not seeing one another. Over the past 10 years or so, Mary has been working for a large multinational and has been permanently based in Copenhagen. He lives in a small but comfortable apartment which generally resembled a bachelor's pad in its utilitarian functionality while her home was larger and rather more richly decorated. He travels regularly, mostly around the UK, spending many nights away sleeping in hotels. The couple meets as often as they can to spend a few days together, mostly in Mary's residence or away on well-planned group holidays.

On exploring their shared history, it became clear that the LAT lifestyle had served them both well and had been a feature of their past relationships as well. It felt like a natural choice required to accommodate their ambitions and driven personalities and their marked need for autonomy. Their shared desire for retirement (or semi-retirement) related to a growing sense that they had achieved their career goals and a sense of entitlement to a less stressful and demanding lifestyle. Their success meant they could finally enjoy what they had dreamt of separately.

Getting hold of a shared vision was clearly considerably challenged by different wants leading them to face real difficulties in coming up with a shared trajectory towards their goal. Patrick envisaged a more sanitary life with less travel and a slow-paced existence ideally living in a home with lovely sea views. He dreamed of the pleasure of living without a travel planner and targets to reach. He envisaged Mary to be there accompanying him, rather silently, soaking in a much desire peace. However, Mary experienced his idyllic vision as equivalent to incarceration. The very thought of joining him on this 'not doing too much' caused her to feel suffocated as her retirement was to be filled with activities, the ticking off of a long and exciting bucket list she had compiled and now desired to see fulfilled

They attempted having a few sessions with a London-based couple therapist but the experience was disrupted by their frequent travel. When I first met them online, they were highly agitated and there was talk of giving up on being a couple. I feared that if we could not establish a solid weekly routine, difficult issues would be unpacked and then shelved again, in a manner parallel to what they seemed to be describing happening time and time again between them. I resisted attempts to meet them fortnightly and after much deliberation (over a number of sessions) the couple settled into a solid weekly routine that helped them manage their worries. Much thought was devoted to finding a day and time we could all commit to, so that whether they were in their individual homes, away from home or in the same residence, we could meet weekly.

Initially sessions centred on the transfer of monies to Patrick's daughter. The conflict seemed to have been experienced as a major breach of trust and a sense that the injury could not be recovered from. Patrick was desperate to make up, with his only complaint being that his anxieties in relation to his daughter's welfare was being dismissed by his wife. The emphasis on this one central complaint eventually started to give way to a tentative voicing of other concerns indicating that the couple had compiled lists of perceived offences that had been left unspoken.

Helping the couple see how anxious they were with discussing the ordinary, everyday irritations inherent to a shared life helped them experiment with greater frankness. For the first few months the couple's communication was mostly limited to our sessions and when I shared my observation of how inhibited much of their communication seemed to be they reacted with scepticism. Over time they came to appreciate their own anxieties and gained some sensitivity to one other's vulnerability as we developed links between their manner and the relational and familial histories they had been through. Their ability to speak their mind with greater honesty improved and contact outside our sessions became more frequent. One could say that therapy helped them develop a great empathic capacity towards self and other thereby being less apprehensive of exchanges between them.

Online couple psychotherapy with LAT couples transitioning to share conviviality offers unique opportunities. Central to the shared household is the increased time spent together and the need of a more consistently shared vision of what togetherness will involve. The discipline of weekly online therapy provides the perfect opportunity for the couple to engage in and experiment with a sustained process of interaction which the therapist witnesses in vivo and is then able to comment about. Couples often share unconscious phantasies that over time crystallise into shared unconscious beliefs about one another. Over time it became clear that Patrick and Mary shared a deeply held unconscious belief that there was a real danger of mutual colonisation if they did not venture away on opposed paths from time to time. One could think of their sustained choice of the LAT lifestyle as, at least in part, a creative adaptation to these anxieties which the LAT lifestyle allowed them to avoid much exploration of. The relatively steady progress in therapy indicated that these anxieties were not annihilatory in nature and of a type present in most couple relationships.

One can consider this couple's falling in love and subsequent adoption of the LAT lifestyle as related to an 'unconscious choice' of partner (Pincus, 1960; Morgan 1995) which allowed for the accommodation of their anxieties as well as their ambitions. It is important that this is not understood to mean that an LAT lifestyle is necessarily a more defensive choice than living in a shared household, or indicative of greater psychological vulnerability. Cleavely (1993) eloquently points out that the fact a relationship serves defensive needs is not in itself counter-developmental, in that 'the marriage relationship offers a unique opportunity for dealing with the unresolved conflicts of earlier relationships. The marital relationship offers scope for each partner to be parent and child of the other' (p. 57). This type of LAT couple can be considered to have achieved a creative couple relationship (Morgan, 2005) but now face a transition requiring them to again examine aspects of self and relationship that had hitherto not needed such attention.

The containment offered by regular contact with the couple therapist is in my view the key to success with the regularity of weekly intervals probably being ideal as they allow close enough contact to allow the unpacking of the narratives the couples bring as the associated transference. Regularity results in the couple not being able to deploy the avoidance, defensive or contextual, available to them as a result of their LAT lifestyle—the forum offered by the therapeutic space means that there is ample opportunity to discuss matters that could be easily avoided otherwise. It is essential, in my view, for the couple therapist not to collide with avoidant strategies and support the couple progress in thinking about what they normally avoid looking at, whether this be good or bad experiences. The process of educating couples about the importance of bringing their communications to the therapy session and in particular to avoid communicating with the therapist in a manner that excludes the partner is crucial. I often find it essential to underline the fact that my email communication is addressed to the couple and that it would be undermining of therapy for the therapist to be burdened with secrets or to be used as a go-between.

Online webcam-mediated therapy with its unique capacity to link up three persons in three different locations offers the flexibility required by LAT couples with the added advantage that as they progress in their therapy and become more capable of sustaining greater togetherness, they can be seen together perhaps even sitting alongside one another on a sofa. The therapist actually becomes witness to their increased comfort with psychological and physical space and the manner in which they manage these changes in proximity regulation.

23.5.2 Couples in the Process of Establishing an LAT Lifestyle

The establishing of an LAT lifestyle may happen early in the couple's relationship history or at a later stage, at times as a way of managing personal or contextual factors impinging on the couple. Sometimes these two realities combine and, in this case, led Silvia and Raymond, a professional couple in their late thirties, to be drawn towards an LAT lifestyle in order to facilitate being a couple.

Silvia and Raymond had met 2 years previously and very soon came to feel very much committed to one another. They shared common interests and values, including a degree of reverence for the idea of marriage, coupled with a sense of caution about relationships, as well as an open-minded and adventurous disposition. Regrettably, their eagerness was not shared by Silvia's family who refused to have any contact with Raymond on the basis of his race and religious affiliation.

When an opportunity surfaced for Raymond to work in Asia they both felt this provided a chance to diffuse the familial tensions that risked undermining their happiness, together with a great opportunity for career progression and financial stability. They agreed that this prospect was worth considering and that they would seek to remain a couple even if the geographical distance created some apprehension. They were excited that they would soon be financially independent of familial support. They made all preparations for the move being supportive of one another and dreaming of being re-united to settle together in some future place of their choosing. Eventually Raymond settled in his new apartment and a routine developed with regular planned meetings and frequent contact on the phone and Skype.

They were both surprised as they started to experience difficult feelings expressed through increased irritation towards one another when they communicated via social media or in person. When they did manage to meet, their togetherness was joyful and re-affirming of their love for one another but surprisingly Raymond found himself becoming increasingly irritable and angry with Silvia leaving her feeling very much rejected and dismissed at the very moment she longed for a good parting. The stance adopted by Silvia's family and the fact that Raymond now lived away from his family left them both feeling isolated and with no one to celebrate their relationship with. Indeed, many of their friends assumed that their relationship was soon to come to its natural conclusion and end. Unsure as how to manage their deepening sense of crisis they sought online couple therapy. They did not feel distance was the issue here.

In the initial conversation with their online therapist it soon became clear that this couple were facing a real challenge in adjusting to becoming a couple, while facing the added pressures of working through their differences, expectations and disappointments over a distance. The couple came across as warm and very much interested in one another and neither of them had any significant mental health difficulties.

The process of establishing a couple involves managing the individual partners' loyalties to their respective family systems. In adopting the LAT lifestyle, the couple had only slightly postponed the need to engage in this process. Their therapist felt that this was unlikely to prove particularly problematic as the couple seemed to have the internal resources and the willingness to address this developmental need. What was clearly very challenging was the fact that the limited contact they were having did not afford them the opportunity to process and more fully support one another. Texts and video conference calls felt a bit too distant to allow the discussion of subtle, largely unaware feelings and when they did meet up, they were eager to enjoy one another and not contaminate their time with talk about familial tensions.

In reality, Silvia was 'left' to visit her family alone and therefore unable to present herself as a couple since her partner was hundreds of miles away. While she understood the reason for him not being with her, she could not avoid the uncomfortable feelings stirred up in her when she attended social functions alone. On his part, Raymond also harboured some discomfort about the fact that Silvia visited her family without him. In psychoanalytic terms, they each risked projecting the anger and upset stirred up by external 'irritants' towards one another.

It also became apparent that they both felt alienated and bereft of significant others and now feeling stuck with the choices they had made—both of the LAT arrangement and of one another. In choosing Raymond, Silvia had driven a wedge between her and her family while choosing to move abroad meant Raymond missed those he held dear and at times found himself blaming Silvia for his choice. The therapist was required to position herself as a 'thinking or reflective partner' empathic to their life choices but also willing to engage in thinking about the feelings this stirred up. Significantly, Raymond spoke of how spending a weekend together felt reminiscent of his experience of returning home from boarding school. His experience had not, in itself, been a negative one but he recalled missing his family and particularly the family dog with whom he lost complete contact between visits.

The therapist was intrigued by the couple's description of the couple's experience of parting and coming together. The suggestion that Raymond became irritable because it stirred up long forgotten upset seemed to resonate and free up the couple's thinking. Sylvia was then also able to see how her retreat away from her partner on sensing his irritability only reinforced his own sense of something being amiss. Couple therapy provided a new type of space where such feelings could be explored rather than suppressed. Central to analytic couple psychotherapy is the notion of projection and projective identification (Klein, 1946, 1952; Rosenfield, 1971) where unbearable feeling states are pushed into the other as means of communicating inner experience along with managing it. The process is akin to that described by Scheinkman and Fishbane (2004) in their seminal paper entitled 'The

Vulnerability Cycle: Working with Impasses in Couple Therapy' which describes in systemic terms, how vulnerability is defended against by the application of defensive strategies which in turn trigger the other party's sense of vulnerability and leads to adoption of a defensive stance. Breaking the cycle is key to unlocking creativity in the couple and prevention, what Morgan (1995) has termed projective gridlock. In psychoanalytic approaches, the appreciation of the defence is discerned through the careful monitoring of the couple's exchanges, together with the transference feelings evoked in their therapist.

This development in the couple then heralded another change. Feeling closer and better supported in their partnership, they could contemplate making their choices known to family and resolve to manage the fallout together. They considered having a baby although they both understood that for the time being they were comfortable with living apart and chose to postpone this for a while.

To my mind, this type of couple is again presenting with a need to adjust and develop a shared way of being that is respectful of their individual sensitivities and the trajectory they are embarking on. For couples who are still in the process of establishing themselves, they are not supported by past shared experiences of triumph over adversity. The hope is that online couple therapy will support these couple solve that which is upsetting them and end the therapy with a sense that they have successfully and jointly managed difficulty. For more established couples struggling with a newly established LAT lifestyle, therapy offers an opportunity to examine their choices in a safe and non-judgemental manner, examine whether these choices are respectful of one another' needs, and work towards creative solutions. Whether couples choose to sustain the LAT lifestyle or adopt a more conventional arrangement is not a major concern for the couple therapist whose only real focus is to support the couple to come to a place where the couple can more fully meet their shared desires and aspirations, whatever shape these may come to take.

23.5.3 LAT Couples Troubled by Togetherness

The prototypal secure individual is able to offer their partner a secure base (Bowlby, 1988) and their shared experiences then allow the emergence of a security enhancing a 'third'—their relationship (Clulow, 2001). If proximity to another person instigates fear, the relationship inevitably risks becoming problematic but if this can be managed and does not overwhelm the ego, then partners may be able to use the relationship to address their anxieties. Colman (1993) discussed this in terms of containment—a process in which the couple is able to communicate and think about difficult experiences, often stirred up simply as a result of one another's continued presence, in a manner that dispels the very fears that instigated difficult moments in the first place.

Couple therapy is in many ways aimed at supporting couples in making these valuable links to their own experience, of self and other, in a way that renders experiences manageable. In Bionian (1962) terms, the couple offers one another reverie and if this cannot be managed, the couple therapist is called upon to fulfil this function temporarily.

Defensive avoidance of closeness happens, from time to time, in every relationship whether it be romantic, social or professional. When the experience triggers off unbearable pain and a real fear of annihilation and instigates somatic agitation or detachment, the couple loses its capacity to fulfil the crucial function of providing containment and security. Couples presenting to therapy in this manner are some of the most troubled and difficult to help.

Anita and Sergio sought help with their relationship because they would no longer bear the cyclic ups and downs that characterised their relationship since its very start 2 years previously. They had met at a University in the North of the country in the final year of their studies after which they moved in together, to seek employment and to saviour the vibrancy of the capital. These first few months allowed them to enjoy a period of intensely passionate engagement. They partied, enjoyed their new surrounding and when things were less thrilling they partied harder. Disagreements were never easy and they engaged in them in an equally passionate manner. It seemed, however, that these disagreements intensified and became more frequent as both voiced concerns about the other's behaviours in relation to third parties. Envy became unbearable and repeatedly led to recriminations being exchanged with increasing intensity. Eventually Sergio decided that he had had enough and after having threatened to leave for months he moved out and went back to his native Italy. Anita experienced his actions as further proof that he was a betrayer, a person intent on letting her down—how else could he have planned to move back to Italy without her knowing?

The dramatic parting was rather predictably not to be the end of this couple's shared life. Within a few weeks they had re-established contact and they both felt that things were better. Indeed, distance now seemed to support their liking of one another. Anita was no longer plagued by anxieties and anger about his contact with ex-girlfriends. He felt less hemmed in by her monitoring and reactivity. They could talk about how irrational they had been at times and the distance between them seemed to allow for greater fondness and tenderness to be found and shared. Sergio even recognised that he was often provocative of Anita's insecurities when he felt irritated by her. When Sergio did manage to get back to London things were generally good. However, over time the previous sense of dread, a sense that something was not quite right started to disturb their coming together. Eventually Anita made up her mind of wanting to end the relationship and he was devastated. He promised to change, be calmer and less controlling. They agreed to seek help and eventually identified an online couple therapy provider.

Significantly very little of the above narrative was revealed in the initial assessment process. They joined their online therapist from two locations and spoke of how they experienced one another's envy and provocations as destructive. They were clearly upset but not too agitated. They started regular online therapy with the understanding that they would honour their commitment to the therapy sessions both when apart and on the occasions when they were in the same location. Soon after the process started their shared anxiety around commitment emerged with intensity around payment for sessions (they refused to pay for any session in advance) and wanted to make clear that that they were only committing to the upcoming session and not necessarily the one after that. The therapist, faced with such claustrophobic fears and a pervasive sense of dread, struggled to provide a place that felt safe enough for therapy to proceed.

With this particular couple, online couple therapy served to make explicit their shared sense of dread, to recognise the impossibility of their situation including the fact that they could not come to place trust in their therapist when aroused by one another's presence. Guiding them towards seeking individual therapy emerged as the only viable option. Recommending that a couple, in recognition of their personal difficulties and the limitations of what we are able to offer them, focus their energies away from couple therapy is painful and may feel like failure. However, in my view it remains a very valuable outcome. Recognising the limitations of our treatment methodology and the therapist's capacity to help a couple manage affect is important in dispelling omnipotence on the part of therapist and clients.

This third type of couple seem to have adopted the LAT lifestyle not because they value its benefits but as a defence from proximity which while desired, powerfully triggers off intense anxiety and defensive retaliation against the perceived source of threat. The oscillating periods of calm and fury presents risks that the online medium amplifies as the therapist is likely to feel much more powerless being physically distant from the couple. In many ways this third presentation is a more intense version of couple adjusting to the LAT lifestyle but whose personality characteristics renders the cycles of proximity and distancing rather unbearable for one or both.

Paradoxically, the online medium offers a unique opportunity here. Our experience with couples that tend to become overly agitated and somewhat dysregulated in joint online sessions, seem to be able to manage the intensity of the couple therapy process when they join the session from different spaces so that the session takes place as a three-way conference call. It seems that the boundary offered by not being in each other's physical presence facilitates exchanges and thinking. Perhaps for this third 'type' of LAT couples the three-way conference call format can be prescribed with gradual exposure of shared two-way conference calls. Here again online therapy affords the couple therapist a novel method of intervention that merits further exploration and careful application.

23.6 The Management of Risk in Online Couple Psychotherapy

When couples present, whether online or in person, with significant levels of dysregulation and a history of violence, online couple work is likely to be unwise and possibly unethical. If violence has happened in the past, however slight, incidents need to be examined very carefully and the safety of all involved carefully considered. Use of controlling strategies by one or both of the partners, even when not manifest in physical violence, should alert the couple therapist to increased levels of risk. Couple therapy depends on the exchange of feelings, beliefs and personal perspectives and if these cannot be tolerated then individual therapy might be a safer and preferred option. The identification of coercive control behaviours is counter-indicative of online couple therapy.

When therapy is progressing well, the therapist needs to keep an eye on the possibility that developments triggers off new fears and associated defensive (or perhaps offensive) strategies presenting increased risk to the partners themselves and in particularly any children they might have. The issue of management of risk when working remotely with couples who have children is beyond the scope of this chapter but suffice to say that remote working does not exonerate the provider from ethical responsibilities with regards to safeguarding.

23.7 The Effect of Technology on the Therapeutic Process

Online couple therapy is surprisingly intense and personal. The couple open up the psychic and physical space they live in for the scrutiny, however benign, of their therapist. They are also able to configure their surroundings and therapy arrangements at will. Some of the couples I see online opt to join their couple sessions from different, brightly lit rooms in the same house, at times expressing a view that the space in front of one laptop is too small for them to share while other couples sit on a sofa, holding hands in close proximity and with more subdued lighting. The meaning of such gestures for these couples and the associated communicative elements within them are subject to the therapist's interpretation and reflection. The transference reactions of the therapist, as with face-to-face work help inform practice but with online work, the therapist needs to be open to be surprised by the creativity of the couple's presentation and to value it. Interestingly, such presentations are often subject to the couple's reflections as well, because through webcam technology, they are offered the opportunity to look into the 'mirror' presented by their own image visible on their screen. Memorably, one of my client couples told me that their relative size on the screen, distorted as it was by the wide-angle of the camera, reflected the relative space they occupy in their relationship. He loomed large and was the force behind activity in their relationships, the female partner, slightly further from the camera, looked diminutive as was indeed her energy for their relationship.

Technology modifies the therapist's presence. In many ways the couple have more control being able to dictate much of the setting but the therapist's power is not necessarily diminished. Firstly, words are being spoken into the clients' living spaces, with the therapist working with an LAT couple choosing for example, to reflect about the diverse manner the partners furnish their living spaces. Secondly, the online medium amplifies elements in the communication process. We are all familiar with how unflattering the webcam camera can be as the short focal length amplifies facial features, typically the nose, because it is closer to the lens. Equally, gestures may be amplified and come to surprise the viewer. Gesturing to a couple that the therapist wishes to speak or that they need to tone down their exchanges may result in the appearance of the therapist's hand moving rapidly towards the clients face and filling the screen! For some clients this can be rather startling. Equally, if the therapist's camera is capturing their faces and little else, clients will get a very detailed view of every eye movement, every reaction to surprise, humour or disgust.

The camera and technology we use in online work offer us a window through which we are allowed to examine a couple's relationship. Paradoxically, my experience suggests that, while the online therapy process is necessarily intrusive (perhaps even more so than other therapies tends to be), it offers more anxious couples enough distance to tentatively engage in therapy. This is in line with research suggesting that a positive experience with online therapeutic intervention allows more vulnerable clients to more easily engage with face-to-face intervention (Jones et al., 2014). The perception that online work is less threatening perhaps, or the setting less alien, facilitates the client's initial tentative engagement with this slowly changing as the therapist becomes less of an image and more of an active presence.

23.8 Final Thoughts

Online couple psychotherapy offers living apart together couples an opportunity to access professional help in an effort to develop their relational capacities. Its remote execution exercises the couple's use of communication technology in a manner that supports the quality of the connection between them while living apart. Online therapy is mediated via increasingly stable, secure and bandwidth efficient technologies we now have access to but it is the therapist's modelling of a way of thinking and relating towards the couple, their environment and the technology itself that remains at the core of the therapeutic process. The experience allows couples Living Apart Together to internalise a method of thoughtful reflection and communication that is designed to outlive their encounter with online couple therapy.

References

Amato, R. P., & Hayes, N. L. (2013). 'Alone together' marriages and 'Living apart together' relationships. In A. Abela & J. Walker (Eds.), *Contemporary issues in family studies: Global perspectives on partnerships, parenting and support in a changing world* (pp. 31–45). New York, NY: Wiley.

Billari, F. C., Rosina, A., Ranaldi, R., & Romano, M. C. (2008). Young adults living apart and together (LAT) with parents: a three-level analysis of the Italian case. *Regional Studies, 42*(5), 625–639.

Bion, W. R. (1962). *Learning from experience*. New York, NY: Basic Books.

Bowlby, J. (1988). *A secure base: Parent-child attachment and healthy human development*. London, UK: Routledge.

Castro-Martín, T., Domínguez-Folgueras, M., & Martín-García, T. (2008). Not truly partnerless: Nonresidential partnerships and retreat from marriage in Spain. *Demographic Research, 18*, 443–468.

Cleavely, E. (1993). Relationships. In Ruszczynski & Stanley (Eds.), *Psychotherapy with couples: Theory and practice at the Tavistock Institute of Marital Studies* (pp. 55–69). London, UK: Karnac.

Clulow, C. (2001). *Adult attachment and couple psychotherapy*. London, UK: Routledge.

Colman, W. (1993). Marriage as a psychological container. In S. Ruszczynski (Ed.), *Psychotherapy with couples: Theory and practice at the Tavistock Institute of Marital Studies* (pp. 70–96). London, UK: Karnac.

Duncan, S, Phillips, M, Roseneil, S, Carter, J., & Stoilova, M. (2013). *Living apart together: Uncoupling intimacy and co-residence*. Retrieved from http://natcen.ac.uk/media/28546/living-apart-together.pdf.

Haskey, J. (2005). Living arrangements in contemporary Britain: Having a partner who usually lives elsewhere and living apart together (LAT). *Population Trends, 122*, 35–45.

Hilty, D. M., Ferrer, D. C., Parish, M. B., Johnston, B., Callahan, E. J., & Yellowlees, P. M. (2013). The effectiveness of telemental health: A 2013 review. *Telemedicine and e-Health, 19*(6), 444–454.

Hewison, D., Casey, P. and Mwamba, N. (2016). 'The effectiveness of couple therapy: Clinical outcomes in a naturalistic United Kingdom setting', *Psychotherapy, 53*(4), pp.377–387.

Klein, M. (1946). Notes on some schizoid mechanisms. *International Journal of Psychoanalysis, 27*, 99–110.

Klein, M. (1952). Notes on some schizoid mechanisms. In J. Riviere & M. Klein (Eds.), *Developments in psycho-analysis*. London, UK: Hogarth Press.

Lanman, M., Grier, F., & Evans, C. (2003). Objectivity in psychoanalytic assessment of couple relationships. *British Journal of Psychiatry, 182*, 255–260.

Jones, M., Kass, E. A., Trockel, M., Glass, A. I., Wilfley, D. E., & Taylor, C. B. (2014). A population-wide screening and tailored intervention platform for eating disorders on college campuses: The Healthy Body Image Program. *Journal of American College Health, 62*(5), 351–356.

Morgan, M. (1995). The projective gridlock: A form of projective identification in couple relationships. In J. Fisher (Ed.), *Intrusiveness and intimacy in the couple* (pp. 12–33). London, UK: Karnac.

Morgan, M. (2005). On being able to be couple: The importance of a "creative couple" in psychic life. In F. Grier (Ed.), *Oedipus and the couple* (pp. 9–30). London, UK: Karnac.

Morgan, M. (2019). *A couple state of mind: Psychoanalysis of couples and the Tavistock relationships model*. London, UK: Routledge.

Mortelmans, D., Pasteels, I., Régnier-Loilier, A., Vignoli, D., & Mazzuco, S. (2015). Analysis of determinants and prevalence of LAT. *Families and Societies, 25*. Retrieved from http://www.familiesandsocieties.eu/wp-content/uploads/2015/01/WP25MortelmansEtAl.pdf

Neumann, D. A. (2013). The frame for psychoanalysis in cyberspace. In J. S. Scharff (Ed.), *Psychoanalysis online: Mental health, teletherapy and training* (pp. 171–181). London, UK: Karnac.

Pincus, L. (Ed.) (1960). Marriage. Studies in emotional conflict and growth. London: Methuen.

Reuschke, D. (2010). Living apart together over long distances—time–space patterns and consequences of a late modern-living arrangement. *Erdkunde, 64*(3), 215–226.

Rosenfield, H. (1971). Contribution to the psychopathology of psychotic states: The importance of projective identification in the ego structure and the object relations of the psychotic patient. In E. B. Spillius (Ed.), *Melanie Klein today* (vol. 1, pp. 64, 117–137). London, UK: The New Library of Psychoanalysis.

Ruszczynski, S. (Ed.) (1993). Psychotherapy with Couples: Theory and Practice at the Tavistock Institute of Marital Studies. London: Karnac.

Sherer-Mohatt, K., & Scharff, J. S. (2013). The computer as a metaphor for a state of mind. In J. S. Scharff (Ed.), *Psychoanalysis online: Mental health, teletherapy and training* (pp. 27–47). London, UK: Karnac.

Scharff, J. S. (2013). *Psychoanalysis online: Mental health, teletherapy and training (library of technology and mental health)*. London, UK: Karnac.

Scheinkman, M., & Fishbane, M. D. (2004). The vulnerability cycle: Working with impasses in couple therapy. *Family Process, 43*(3), 279–299.

Tavistock relationships annual review 2017. Retrieved from https://tavistockrelationships.ac.uk/images/uploads/images/Tavistock_Relationships_Annual_Review_2017_web_version.pdf

Chapter 24
No Couple Is an Island: Communities of Support in Couple Relationships

Kevin Schembri

24.1 Introduction: No Couple Is an Island

To different extents, all couples—whether in a long- or short-term loving relationship, married or not, with or without children, and irrespective of their age, sexual orientation or religious beliefs—need external support to grow together and cope with the challenges of life. A major provider of support in couple relationships is the community. Depending on the contexts and needs of specific couples, different types of communities offer distinctive kinds, levels and patterns of support. Some communities of support are formal. These may be official, well-structured or attached to an institution or entity. They may also feature professional, committed or experienced members. Other communities are informal or unofficial, such as family members, friends, neighbours and colleagues. Such communities may simply comprise people with the same objectives, values and experiences. These two types of communities of support also exist in the virtual world, in the form of online groups, fora, or social networks. Some couples even experience society at large as a global community of support.

This chapter offers an overview of the need for communities of support, and their role and dynamics in couple relationships. It presents the strengths and positive impact of such communities, but also draws attention to their possible limitations which, at times, bring about more harm than good.

K. Schembri (✉)
Faculty of Theology (Humanities A Building), University of Malta, Msida MSD 2080, Malta
e-mail: kevin.m.schembri@um.edu.mt

© Springer Nature Switzerland AG 2020
A. Abela et al. (eds.), *Couple Relationships in a Global Context*,
European Family Therapy Association Series,
https://doi.org/10.1007/978-3-030-37712-0_24

24.2 Need for Support

Most couples feel strong and invincible at the outset of their journey together. Yet, new and challenging situations require them to learn how to keep their relationship alive and flourishing. Some of these challenges are external to the life of the couple and may be directly linked to rapid social, cultural and demographic developments. It can be said that over the last decades, perhaps also at great cost for those who pioneered the way, various cultural changes have led couples to experience greater freedom of choice, an equitable distribution of duties and responsibilities, and more emphasis on authenticity rather than on social conformity. Nonetheless, many of today's couples feel overwhelmed by an engulfing 'liquid' culture and new social order that are highly marked by indifference and disconnection. This atmosphere often generate uncertainty, arbitrariness and fear of commitment (Bauman, 2000; Zimbardo & Coulombe, 2016). Couples, particularly in Western societies, may need social support as they struggle with a fast and stressful pace of life, with challenges posed by work-life imbalance and financial hardship, with pressures to consume ever more goods and services, and with an extensive use of social media and constant online connection. Other testing external factors comprise political and economic instability, evolving norms, laws and religious beliefs that are gradually changing the format and meaning of relationships, on-going trans-border commuting, and the endless plague of poverty, wars, persecution and forced migration. The demise of various traditional social structures actually denies couples the external support they received in the past. It is precisely for these reasons that communities of support can play a vital role in the life of today's couples. Indeed, they may well become imperative.

Besides, couples may also need support to address internal issues and overcome difficult trials in life, particularly at transition points in their relationship. After all, relational and coping skills are not a given, and every couple will sail stormy waters. The various stages in the life of a couple very often overlap and merge. Often, transition from one stage to the next is rarely distinct or clear cut, with one phase morphing into another. Writers who have given some attention to life cycle issues do not agree on the number of these stages. Generally, the developmental stages in the life of a couple are grouped in three phases: formation, expansion and contraction (Carter & McGoldrick, 1980; Gerson, 1995; Nichols & Everett, 1986; Nichols & Pace-Nichols, 1993). According to Framo (1994), each of these stages is 'a shock to the system because roles have to be reassigned, values reoriented, status positions shifted, loss and mourning dealt with, and needs met through new channels' (p. 90).

In the phase of formation, couples may need external support to learn how to grow in their relationship and include their partner as they realign their relationships with relatives and friends. For those blending two families or entering a relationship following divorce, formation may entail welcoming and adjusting to children and relatives from previous relationships. The support which communities offer at this stage may consist of material, financial or practical assistance. It may even take the shape of educational advice or mentoring towards acquiring relational skills, coping with social expectations, and managing a relationship in conjunction with other personal, familial and social duties. At the outset of their journey together, young or new couples may easily feel alone, discouraged, or simply overwhelmed by the many obstacles that lie ahead of them. In trying to establish social or professional status and financial stability for themselves, they may isolate themselves from their families and peers or, worse, become alienated from each other. Hence, the presence of a caring community at this initial stage can make all the difference in their life.

Several communities continue to offer backing and accompaniment when couples progress through into the stage of expansion. This phase is usually marked by major forward-looking steps undertaken by the couple, such as getting married, welcoming children, developing a project or business, or even moving to another state or country. For couples who form a family, social support may be needed as they take on parenting roles and make space to accept children into their lives. Parenting adds new dimensions to the couple relationship. Research shows that couples are often shocked by the impact of this new reality and marital satisfaction steadily declines over the childbearing periods (Framo, 1994; Hiedemann, Suhomlinova, & O'Rand, 1998). The extended family may play an important part at this point, as couples also attempt to realign relationships with their relatives, particularly their parents, to include them into the dynamic of parenting and grand parenting. As children become adolescents and then young adults, couples face the need to increase flexibility of boundaries and allow an increased number of entries and exits into their family dynamic. At this point in life, couples may also need external support to cope with midlife relational issues, together with the ageing process of their own parents and grandparents. It is not unusual that they start facing deep existential questions concerning the meaning of life and commitment, the limitations of human activity and relationships, and the presence of suffering in life.

This phase is followed by that of contraction where couples start to face the process of letting go or closure with regard to certain projects developed over the years. Couples who formed or blended a family see their children grow into young adults and leave home. They may struggle to cope with the empty nest syndrome resulting from the departure of the youngest child. At this stage, couples often attend to both their individual and couple needs for the first time in many years. They may desire assistance to renegotiate their own connection as a couple, rediscover meaning in spending time together, and adjust their relationship with their grown-up children, in-laws, and possibly, grandchildren (Bates Harkins, 1978; Gorchoff, John, & Helson, 2008). The phase of contraction entails the final stretch of life, marked by the retirement of the couple. This stage could be the longest, and for some, the most difficult, since living longer allows more time for differences to develop within the relationship. At this point, children and projects play less active roles in the daily lives of couples. Presence and accompaniment may be needed by the couple to accept this shift in generational roles and maintain their own functioning and interests in the face of physiological decline. The support of a community might also be needed when having to deal with the ageing or death of the parents and grandparents, not to mention those of any siblings, relatives, peers and even of their own partners.

24.3 Types of Support

The support offered to couples by different communities can take different forms. It can be practical or material, as in the case of intergenerational initiatives within extended families, neighbourhoods or other communities. For instance, parents with busy schedules amalgamate resources with their own elderly parents or other retired couples; in doing so, the latter find company and assistance in young children and adolescents, whilst parents find responsible carers for their children at no or minimal financial cost. Practical support may also take the form of a positive network of friends or neighbours, where couples agree to help each other by upholding and promoting similar rules and values. This dynamic helps couples to rely upon each other and becomes a source of empowerment, protection and support for all. Support may also consist of material or financial assistance to young or newly established couples or to couples struggling with diverse problems.

Support provision can also be of a moral or psychological nature. In such cases, communities become confidants and sources of care for couples. They turn into safe spaces where couples can let off steam and share their stories without fear of judgement or rejection. At certain moments in life, particularly when faced with major decisions, couples may need to bounce off their ideas and evaluate their concerns with other persons they both trust. Certain communities offer mentoring and counselling for those who need them. Researchers distinguish between two forms of moral support at this level. Instrumental moral support attempts to deal directly with an issue and is characterised by the supporting community making specific suggestions, giving helpful advice, or providing access to helpful information. Alternatively, emotional support is aimed at the management of emotions and entails being present, reassuring others and providing genuine encouragement (Cohen, Gottlieb, & Underwood, 2000; Pasch, Harris, Sullivan, & Bradbury, 2004).

Paul and Claire have been actively engaged in marriage preparation courses for more than twenty years. Looking back on these two decades, they now realise that the most valuable support they have offered to young or newly established couples was their availability: 'Many times we find ourselves listening to these couples about their concerns or difficulties. They say they have nobody to talk to or that they cannot trust others. Some individuals tell us that they cannot even talk to their partner about certain issues simply because their partner does not listen or attempt to understand'. Paul and Claire's comments and experience give value to the thought that intergenerational sharing can be highly beneficial and effective. This, too, became evident in a study on peer support between veteran and freshly diagnosed patients. The survey indicated that interaction between beginners and experienced persons reduces feelings of isolation, conveys social support, and communicates realistic hope about the future through role modelling (Chambers et al., 2013).

The moral support of a community may be highly important for a couple when coping with stress and anxiety related to work–life imbalance. Research shows that this matter is becoming an increasing source of conflict within couple relationships (NCFR, 2017; Symoens & Bracke, 2015). Support becomes even more vital when the couple goes through tough experiences, namely illness, infertility, financial instability, betrayal, and loss of a loved one. Along with others, these circumstances can carry with them a range of negative psychological effects, including feelings of depression, anxiety, isolation, anger, shame, inadequacy and helplessness. They may also result in addictions, violence or self-harm. A community which is present, accessible and supportive during such times of test and distress proves to be a pillar of strength and a safe haven. It helps foster feelings of security, belonging and friendship. Such a community generates a 'go-to place' which can be a lifeline for many couples. It propels them to persist at seeking new and creative ways of sustaining their future. Just knowing that one is not alone can be a game-changer during such overwhelming situations.

A third form of support provision is spiritual. Research demonstrates that couples with high regard for religion or spirituality appear to have more satisfying relationships. Faith seems to strengthen their commitment towards each other and enables them to deal with the more challenging times in their relationship (McAdams, 2010; NCFR, 2016; Perry, 2014; Sabey, Rauer, & Jensen, 2014). For this reason, certain communities provide couples with authentic spaces where they can find spiritual belonging, pray together, and grow in faith, hope, and serenity. Said communities help couples reach beyond their inadequacies and view the possibility of living life with a greater sense of purpose. They do this by providing them with pointers towards the transcendental.

Spiritual support may also be offered through acts of intercession, that is, when members of a community bless couples by wishing them well or praying for their needs. A few months ago, the son of a couple who is actively involved in a local community of faith had to undergo an emergency operation abroad. The couple received a lot of practical and financial support from the other members of the community; yet they maintain that they were mostly touched and encouraged by the numerous assurances of intercession they received throughout the entire rough and emotional episode which protracted over time. Finally, communities offer spiritual support through authentic lived witness. In doing so, they become reliable and authentic reference points for couples. They empower them to live out a value system of their own choice, even if it means going against the flow.

24.4 Benefits and Limitations

Persons affect each other in complex and reciprocal ways (Mikulincer, Florian, Cowan, & Cowan, 2002). Considerable research signals that supportive behaviour between partners fosters emotional healing and security, better health outcomes, positive resilience and higher life satisfaction (Carr, Freedman, Cornman, & Schwarz, 2014; Gabb, Klett-Davies, Fink, & Thomae, 2013; Nimtz, 2011; Reis, Clark, & Holmes, 2004). This is also true for the support of a community. Researchers associate social support with better mental and physical health of individuals and consider it a key element of relationship maintenance and marital well-being

(Bradbury & Karney, 2004; Cohen et al., 2000; Devoldre, Davis, Verhofstadt, & Buysse, 2010).

The presence of a helpful community plays a vital role in how couples adjust to stressful experiences. Communities of support have the capacity to create an atmosphere that allows couples to develop fresh insights and to realise that they are not the only ones aspiring to certain goals or facing a specific hardship. For instance, with regard to couples struggling with infertility, various studies show that social interactions and external support are linked to lower levels of depression, anxiety and stress. One survey conducted with couples undergoing IVF treatment demonstrated that those who participate in a support group derive psychological benefit on completion of the group sessions, with women reporting less stress and men greater optimism (McNaughton-Cassill, Bostwick, Arthur, Robinson, & Neal, 2002). Another study about the influence of one's perception of social support on his or her partner's way of adjusting to infertility stress revealed that low support from family or friends increases anxiety in women and their partners (Martins, Peterson, Almeida, Mesquita-Guimarães, & Costa, 2014).

Authentic communities of support are also beneficial because they offer a space where the couple may grow together. This is central in the journey of a couple, because, at times, an individual progresses and integrates issues in life quicker than his or her partner, leaving the other behind. Conversely, there are instances when the support of a community may be needed purely on a personal level. This brings to mind Angele's story. The most challenging episode in her marital relationship, she recounts, was the birth of her first child. She was alone, feeling overwhelmed with the challenges of this new dynamic. Her husband, however, did not experience or share any of her sentiments, emotions and turmoil. During this difficult time, Angele sought professional help and also the support of a group of friends. This assistance proved priceless and actively helped her towards healing, growing stronger and remaining in the relationship. She is happily married to this very day.

Couples who experience the support of a community may find it easier for themselves to open up to the needs of other couples and be ready to offer support if and when the need arises. When Emmanuela's husband was in hospital for a long period, facing a life-threatening illness, she felt emotionally shattered. She felt helpless with the practicalities of everyday life since she relied entirely on her husband; suffice to say that she did not have a driving licence. Yet, she managed to cope with the situation thanks to the support of family members and friends, who often offered to drive her to hospital and to entertain her children whilst she was at work or visiting her husband. This experience of support touched her and her husband in such a profound way. As a way of giving-back, they were inspired to set up and coordinate a community that supports young and new couples. In short, it can be said that the benefits of the 'first' community begot the 'second' community.

On the contrary, when certain dynamics within communities are taken for granted or not tackled properly, they may bring about more harm than good. Communities may end up draining couples, drowning their identities, and robbing them of the little time they have available for themselves. They may also become spaces of escapism. It is not unusual that couples become involved in a group or network of peers simply to avoid being alone at home. In such cases, communities alienate couples from the fundamental value that no one and nothing can replace the role of one's partner. There are also communities, including members of the extended family and in-laws, who are overprotective or render couples extremely passive, since the latter no longer feel the need to be creative or try to respond to the challenges they face. Respondents in a qualitative study about the expectations and lived experiences of couples in Malta highlighted the negative effects that relationships with in-laws sometimes have on the couple relationship, particularly where one partner may still be enmeshed with his or her parents' system (NCFR, 2017).

Communities may also harm couples if they lack proper coordination or responsible handling of delicate issues. At times, friendly bonds, good intentions and informal support may not be enough. When addressing sensitive matters, communities must strive to offer professional mentoring, keep clear boundaries regarding sharing and confidentiality, and make appropriate referrals when necessary. Couples may also experience failure, cynicism and confusion when they come across communities that fail to distinguish between positive and negative forms of support provision. Negative support provision would include criticising or blaming couples, expressing negative affect at them, and minimising or maximising their problem (Cohen et al., 2000).

It is also possible that couples get attached to a community of support but experience a sense of disappointment when they find out that the other members are too busy to attend to them. Couples may also be let down and scandalised by the presence of cliques, struggles of power, or attitudes of arrogance, exclusion and moralism. A lack of authenticity shown by those most held in high esteem, may be extra painful. Vincent attends a rehabilitation community with his wife. He recounts that every session starts with the words: 'Thank God I am not God'. He believes that this principle is the foundation of the success of the group because 'one of the main problems seems to be when one or more persons take over the management of the support system and dominate proceedings by imposing their beliefs onto others'. In his recent treatise on the theme of love in the family, Pope Francis raises this issue. He refers to the accompaniment provided by Catholic communities to millions of couples and families around the world and acknowledges that this support has not always been perfect. The leader of the Catholic Church observes that at times, those engaged in this sterling service thought that they could provide sufficient support to couples and giving meaning to marital life simply by stressing doctrinal and moral issues. He admits that sometimes, a community wrongly attempts to 'replace' rather than 'make room' for the consciences of individuals, who are capable of carrying out their own reflection or discernment in complex situations and very often respond as best they can to the challenges of life notwithstanding their limitations (Francis, 2016).

In fact, there are couples who wish and feel the need to open up to others but are afraid because of a negative experience in a past community. Certain blockages are not easy to undo and such feelings get worse when communities of support are imposed on couples or when partners do not agree about the need or format of such communities.

24.5 Two Further Questions

Considering this overview of communities of support and couple relationships, a twofold question arises: what prompts a community to offer support to couples within or beyond its fold, and which factors move a couple to open up to this dynamic?

Provision of effective social support is not a straightforward issue. Many researchers consider the factors that contribute to social support as an important research objective (Lakey & Cohen, 2000; Lindorff, 2005; Rafaeli & Gleason, 2009). Some identify the set of personal characteristics possessed by support providers as one such factor (Pierce, Lakey, Sarason, Sarason, & Joseph, 1997; Verhofstadt, Buysse, Devoldre, & De Corte, 2007). Others consider empathy as a major characteristic that is likely to move an individual or a community to offer support. Devoldre et al. (2010) speak of empathy as a multidimensional phenomenon that encompasses both cognitive and affective elements. In the case of a community of support, the cognitive dimension of empathy is expressed when the community attempts to understand the internal experience of a couple by taking their perspective. The affective dimension is demonstrated when the community experiences the same or similar emotions to those of a couple; for instance, the community has feelings of distress, discomfort, or concern when witnessing a couple going through negative experiences. Research signals that the experience of empathy is linked to the following reactions: being more helpful to those in need, offering supportive responses to peers, and engaging in greater self-disclosure (Batson, 1991; Devoldre et al., 2010; Reis & Collins, 2000; Trobst, Collins, & Embree, 1994).

On the other hand, experience shows that there is no single answer with regard to what moves a couple to open up to a community of support. While it is true that no couple is an island, it is also true that couples are like different islands. A study amongst African American spouses specified that couples who preferred to seek external help, often resorted to the support of religious/spiritual figures or communities and family members. The participants expressed mistrust in professionals, due to perceiving them as being more familiar with research and statistics than with real-life experience and the sacred nature of marriage (Vaterlaus, Skogrand, & Chaney, 2015). In another survey, most participants indicated that they would seek support through couple counselling before individual counselling. Nonetheless, women appeared to be more likely to seek any form of counselling in comparison to men, and, unlike fathers, mothers prefer couple counselling over individual counselling (Gabb et al., 2013). A comparative analysis of profiles of couples attending community-based couple counselling and others partaking in relationship education services demonstrated that couples in the first group were more likely to be married and/or to have children, expressed serious relationship issues, scored higher on depression and aggression, had difficulty in managing their income, and were less educated than those of the second group (Schofield et al., 2015).

Some of these findings echo a recent research conducted in Malta. The quantitative survey showed that those seeking relationship support were less than 15%, being mostly middle-aged, having a higher level of education and having dependent teenage children. Gender, locality of residence and income adequacy were not associated with help-seeking behaviour. The findings also indicated that members of the clergy were still the most sought-after providers of relationship support on the island, followed closely by family therapists or marriage counsellors, and to a lesser extent relatives or friends. Those who did not seek help with their relationship attributed this to the fact that they felt they did not need to. Other reported reasons included being uninformed, showing distrust about available services, and feeling ashamed, shy or afraid (NCFR, 2016). Then there are couples who do not manage to approach or sustain a healthy relationship with a community simply because they find its setting overwhelming or due to the complexity and strain of their own situation (McNaughton-Cassill et al., 2002).

The answer to the question about what moves a couple to open up to a community of support also depends on the personalities, characters and aptitudes of the couple itself, as evident in the following experiences encountered by the author during family work. Michael's family portrays four different interactions between couples and communities. His parents were active members of a local religious community for more than forty years. He observes how this community helped his parents' marital relationship to mature and flourish in a beautiful way. On his part, he has also been involved, together with his wife, in another community for more than twenty years and they cannot see themselves otherwise. His two younger sisters are married with children, but their relation to structured communities is different. One of the sisters and her husband are somewhat attached to a community on an on-and-off basis and mostly find support within an informal group of friends. The other couple is solely focused on their family; they practically have very few friends and no social time beyond the parameters of the house.

On her part, Jacqueline is not too much of a people person. She admits that at this stage in life, she feels that her place is within the family, preparing healthy food, listening to the husband after a long day at work, welcoming the kids when they return from school, and so on. Nonetheless, every year, she attends, along with her husband and children, a weekend live-in and some outdoor picnics with the same group of families. This community of families is coordinated by a family worker who enjoys the trust of all the couples. Jacqueline and her husband find great support in these encounters because they offer spaces of leisure and rest for the whole family and bring them in contact with other couples who share similar values, struggles and experiences. At the same time, the rhythm of this type of community is just enough for them. It offers a relaxed support system, which neither requires a lot of commitment, nor engulfs their family schedule. Jacqueline and her husband believe that they must be the builders of their own family; however, knowing that they have friends to fall on to if need be, infuses them with a high sense of serenity.

Amanda had a serious alcohol problem that was tearing the family apart. José, her partner, was struggling to cope with the situation. Their three children were still very young, and pressures were piling up. He was also losing his faith, hope and optimism. Several years into the marriage, just as he had decided to leave the relationship, Amanda found support in a self-help group and managed to stop drinking. On his part, José joined a support group for partners of persons struggling with alcohol problems. He recounts: 'Eventually, acceptance of the past and trust set in. Our lives started to converge again and become focused. We then joined a prayer group together and our relationship became stronger and our family became a family again'. When their youngest son came out as gay, José and Amanda joined a network of parents who share a similar experience. Enriched by these positive experiences of social support, today they coordinate a structured community which aims to sustain financially unstable couples.

24.6 Conclusion

This chapter has shown that there are no determinate answers to the question as to why a couple opens up to a community of support. This move often depends on the background, personalities and aptitudes of the couple itself. It has also demonstrated that there exist limitations and dynamics within certain communities of support, that, when taken for granted or not tackled properly, may bring about more harm than good. Nonetheless, we have also seen that when couples share their vulnerability in a safe space like that offered by a community of support, they can receive the encouragement, inspiration and nourishment with which to grow and reach their full potential, both individually and as a couple. Authentic communities of support become for these couples like vehicles that transport them from their initial hesitations to the continued searching for meaning in life and for stability irrespective of the hardships. They provide them with a pathway upon which they may cultivate their own identity and become transformed into flourishing citizens who are appreciative of the journey travelled and sensitive to the needs of others who are travelling a similar path. For such couples, the moments of celebration and joy are consequently even more meaningful since their journey in pain and darkness is deeply and sincerely shared and lived in community. They know all too well, that no couple is an island!

References

Bates Harkins, E. (1978). Effects of empty nest transition on self-report of psychological and physical well-being. *Journal of Marriage and the Family, 40*(3), 549–557.
Batson, C. D. (1991). *The altruism question: Toward a social-psychological answer.* Hillsdale, NJ: Erlbaum.
Bauman, Z. (2000). *Liquid modernity.* Cambridge, MA: Polity Press.
Bradbury, T. N., & Karney, B. R. (2004). Understanding and altering the longitudinal course of marriage. *Journal of Marriage and the Family, 66*, 862–881.
Carr, D., Freedman, V. A., Cornman, J. C., & Schwarz, N. (2014). Happy marriage, happy life? Marital quality and subjective well-being in later life. *Journal of Marriage and Family, 76*(5), 930–948.
Carter, E. A., & McGoldrick, M. (1980). *The family life cycle: A frame work for family therapy.* New York, NY: Gardner.

Chambers, S., Schover, L., Halford, K., Ferguson, M., Gardiner, R., Occhipinti, S., & Dunn, J. (2013). ProsCan for couples: A feasibility study for evaluating peer support within a controlled research design. *Psycho-Oncology, 22*(2), 475–479.

Cohen, S., Gottlieb, B. H., & Underwood, L. G. (2000). Social relationships and health. In S. Cohen, B. H. Gottlieb, & L. G. Underwood (Eds.), *Social support measurement and intervention: A guide for health and social scientists* (pp. 3–28). New York, NY: Oxford University Press.

Devoldre, I., Davis, M. H., Verhofstadt, L. L., & Buysse, A. (2010). Empathy and social support provision in couples: Social support and the need to study the underlying processes. *The Journal of Psychology, 144*(3), 259–284.

Framo, J. (1994). The family life cycle: Impressions. *Contemporary Family Therapy, 162*, 87–116.

Francis. (2016). *Post-synodal Apostolic Letter Amoris Laetitia on love in the family*. Vatican City, Rome: Libreria Editrice Vaticana.

Gabb, J., Klett-Davies, M., Fink, J., & Thomae, M. (2013). *Enduring love? Couple relationships in the 21st century. Survey findings: An interim report*. Berkshire, UK: Open University.

Gerson, R. (1995). The family life cycle: Phases, stages, and crisis. In R. Mikesell, D. Lusterman, & S. McDaniel (Eds.), *Integrating family therapy: Handbook of family psychology and systems theory* (pp. 91–111). Washington, DC: American Psychological Association.

Gorchoff, S., John, O. P., & Helson, R. (2008). Contextualizing change in marital satisfaction during middle age: An 18-year longitudinal study. *Psychological Science, 19*(11), 1194–1200.

Hiedemann, B., Suhomlinova, O., & O'Rand, A. (1998). Economic independence, economic status, and empty nest in midlife marital disruption. *Journal of Marriage and the Family, 60*, 219–231.

Lakey, B., & Cohen, S. (2000). Social support theory and measurement. In S. Cohen, L. G. Underwood, & B. H. Gottlieb (Eds.), *Social support measurement and intervention: A guide for health and social scientists* (pp. 29–52). London, UK: Oxford University Press.

Lindorff, M. (2005). Determinants of received social support: Who gives what to managers? *Journal of Social and Personal Relationships, 22*, 323–337.

Martins, M. V., Peterson, B. D., Almeida, V., Mesquita-Guimarães, J., & Costa, M. E. (2014). Dyadic dynamics of perceived social support in couples facing infertility. *Human Reproduction, 29*(1), 83–89.

McAdams, K. K. (2010). *Understanding religiosity: A preliminary evaluation of a process model linking religiosity to relationship outcomes*. (Doctoral dissertation, Michigan State University, Michigan).

McNaughton-Cassill, M., Bostwick, J. M., Arthur, N. J., Robinson, R. D., & Neal, G. S. (2002). Efficacy of brief couples support groups developed to manage the stress of in vitro fertilization treatment. *Mayo Clinic Proceedings, 77*(10), 1060–1066.

Mikulincer, M., Florian, V., Cowan, P. A., & Cowan, C. P. (2002). Attachment security in couple relationships: A systemic model and its implications for family dynamics. *Family Process, 41*(3), 405–434.

National Centre for Family Research. (2016). *Sustaining relationships: Couples and singles in a changing society*. Malta: The President's Foundation for the Wellbeing of Society.

National Centre for Family Research. (2017). *Sustaining relationships: The expectations and lived experiences of couples in Malta*. Malta: The President's Foundation for the Wellbeing of Society.

Nichols, W. C., & Everett, C. A. (1986). *Systemic family therapy. An integrative approach*. New York, NY: Guilford Press.

Nichols, W. C., & Pace-Nichols, M. A. (1993). Developmental perspectives and family therapy: The marital life cycle. *Contemporary Family Therapy, 15*, 299–315.

Nimtz, M. A. (2011). *Satisfaction and contributing factors in satisfying long-term marriage: A phenomenological study*. (Doctoral dissertation, Liberty University, Virginia).

Pasch, L. A., Harris, K. W., Sullivan, K. T., & Bradbury, T. N. (2004). The social support interaction coding system. In P. Kerig & D. Baucom (Eds.), *Couple observational coding systems* (pp. 319–334). New York, NY: Guilford.

Perry, S. L. (2014). A match made in heaven? Religion-based marriage decisions, marital quality, and the moderating effects of spouse's religious commitment. *Social Indicators Research, 123*(1), 203–255.

Pierce, G. R., Lakey, B., Sarason, I. G., Sarason, B. R., & Joseph, H. (1997). Personality and social support processes: A conceptual overview. In G. R. Pierce, B. Lakey, I. G. Sarason, & B. R. Sarason (Eds.), *Sourcebook of social support and personality* (pp. 3–18). New York, NY: Plenum.

Rafaeli, E., & Gleason, M. E. J. (2009). Skilled support within intimate relationships. *Journal of Family Theory and Review, 1*, 20–37.

Reis, H. T., Clark, M. S., & Holmes, J. G. (2004). Perceived partner responsiveness as an organizing construct in the study of intimacy and closeness. In D. J. Mashek & A. Aron (Eds.), *Handbook of closeness and intimacy* (pp. 201–225). New York, NY: Psychology Press.

Reis, H. T., & Collins, N. (2000). Measuring relationship properties and interactions relevant to social support. In S. Cohen, L. G. Underwood, & B. H. Gottlieb (Eds.), *Social support measurement and intervention: A guide for health and social scientists* (pp. 136–194). New York, NY: Oxford University Press.

Sabey, A. K., Rauer, A. J., & Jensen, J. F. (2014). Compassionate love as a mechanism linking sacred qualities of marriage to older couples' marital satisfaction. *Journal of Family Psychology, 28*(5), 594.

Schofield, M. J., Mumford, N., Jurkovic, I., Jurkovic, D., Chan, S. P., & Bickerdike, A. (2015). Understanding profiles of couples attending community-based couple counseling and relationship education services. *Journal of Couple & Relationship Therapy, 14*(1), 64–90.

Symoens, S., & Bracke, P. (2015). Work-family conflict and mental health in newlywed and recently cohabiting couples: A couple perspective. *Health Sociology Review, 24*(1), 48–63.

Trobst, K. K., Collins, R. L., & Embree, J. M. (1994). The role of emotion in social support provision: Gender, empathy, and expressions of distress. *Journal of Social and Personal Relationships, 11*(1), 45–62.

Vaterlaus, J. M., Skogrand, L., & Chaney, C. (2015). Help-seeking for marital problems: Perceptions of individuals in strong African American marriages. *Contemporary Family Therapy, 37*(1), 22–32.

Verhofstadt, L. L., Buysse, A., Devoldre, I., & De Corte, K. (2007). The influence of personal characteristics and relationship properties on social support in marriage. *Psychologica Belgica, 43*, 195–217.

Zimbardo, P., & Coulombe, N. D. (2016). *Man (dis)connected. How the digital age is changing young men forever*. London, UK: Penguin Random House.

Chapter 25
Policy Perspectives on Couple Relationships

Sue Vella, Angela Abela, and Suzanne Piscopo

25.1 Introduction

This chapter is based on a thematic review of the works in this volume, with a view to identifying common principles that underpin couple relationships today while also incorporating broad policy reflections. Policy is here taken to refer to the guiding principles and purposive interventions by the state to achieve desired objectives. Policy instruments generally comprise regulation, benefits, programmes and services, education and awareness raising.

Taking a state-centred approach to couple well-being is by no means intended to undervalue civil society and the myriad ways in which couples derive support from their communities. Indeed, in a 'mixed economy of welfare' (Powell, 2007), communities play as great, if not greater, a role in contributing to couple well-being than the state and market. That said, the chapter draws on the old feminist adage that 'the personal is political': many apparently personal problems have their roots in social structures and hence may be ameliorated, at least in part, by appropriate legislation and policy intervention.

With the signing of the Universal Declaration of Human Rights (UDHR) in 1948, all men and women of 'full age' were to have equal rights to marry and to

---

S. Vella (✉)
Department of Social Policy and Social Work, Faculty for Social Wellbeing,
University of Malta, Msida, Malta
e-mail: sue.vella@um.edu.mt

A. Abela
Department of Family Studies, Faculty for Social Wellbeing, University of Malta,
Msida, Malta

S. Piscopo
Department of Health, Physical Education and Consumer Studies, Faculty of Education,
University of Malta, Msida, Malta

found a family, as long as both spouses freely and fully consented. Society and the State were to protect the family, while everyone was to have the right to legal protection against arbitrary interference with their privacy, family and home (UN, 1948). These rights also featured in the 1950 European Convention for the Protection of Human Rights and Fundamental Freedoms and have since been embedded also in the Charter of Fundamental Rights of the European Union (EU, 2012).

Attitudes to state action in respect of 'private life' differ across time and place. Writing of the broader and better established field of family policy (within which policies for couples generally feature), Hantrais (2004) points out that not all governments explicitly target 'the family' as a focus for policy, nor would many admit to seeking to influence family composition or behaviour. However, a number of social and demographic trends with a marked impact on society have buttressed the legitimacy of state action for families, particularly a decline in fertility levels; population ageing; decreasing rates of marriage and increasing rates of divorce and their impact upon children; rising levels of female employment and an evolving breadwinner model; and poverty, especially among lone parents. Furthermore, the quality of the parental relationship as well as improved work–life balance have increasingly been seen as central to the well-being of couples and their children.

In exploring similarities and differences between the chapters in this volume, we recognise that culture is pervasive, and imbues social life with different values and meaning. Cultural sensitivity is increasingly required of both policy makers and practitioners in a progressively more fluid and intercultural world. While it is our firm intention in this chapter to be respectful of cultural differences, ambitious exercises like these bring home the importance of deepening one's understanding and respect for difference, steeped as we are in Western research and the situated values that define our personal and professional lives.

The sections that follow deal in turn with each of five principles that emerged from the thematic review and, given the wide coverage of this volume, also include necessarily broad-brush policy reflections. These five themes include equal status, consent, capability, commitment and care. Authors' names not followed by a year of publication refer to chapters in this volume.

25.2 Equal Status

The characteristics and behaviours expected of women and men are shaped by social context, and these differences are too often accompanied by power differentials in respect of decision-making, command over resources, responsibility for unpaid work, and influence in the public sphere. Traditional gender roles also shape patterns of relating. Many chapters in this volume touch upon equality legislation while others make reference to prevailing cultural beliefs around gender.

In respect of equality before the law, a number of authors describe the progressive strengthening of equality legislation over the twentieth century. Øfsti speaks of state feminism in Scandinavia, where equality is now embedded in political structures and processes as well as in social norms. Maestre illustrates how equality between married partners was established in France by the mid-twentieth century, followed by legal protections for unmarried couples by 1999 and marriage for same-sex couples by 2013. Piscopo et al. describe the relatively rapid promulgation of legislation in Malta, including divorce in 2011, civil unions for same-sex couples in 2014, cohabitation law in 2017 and marriage for same-sex couples also in 2017.

In some jurisdictions, equality of legal rights remains intricately bound to religion; this often means that women remain subject to men in both the private and public spheres. In Israel, as al Krenawi notes, marriage can only be contracted through a religious authority. Fayad (n.d.) and Weiss (2019) point out how the monopoly of the rabbinic courts over marriage and divorce in Israel upholds patriarchal norms and effectively deprives women of autonomy and redress. Kashyap illustrates how women in ancient India had greater freedoms and were largely considered equal to their husbands. However, this changed under the patriarchal and caste-based rules introduced by Hinduism as women's independence was exchanged for the guardianship of their fathers, then of their husbands and eventually their sons. Perhaps inequality before the law is at its starkest in the case of polygyny, where men—but not women—are entitled to marry more than one spouse, with all that this may entail in terms of the division of resources, power and attention. As discussed by al Krenawi, although Islam requires a husband to treat all wives equally, in effect polygyny often has deleterious consequences on the mental health of the wives concerned.

While most chapters refer to evolving social expectations of gender equality, if one takes a global perspective it becomes clear that the law—as a critical policy instrument in this area—has been slow to catch up. A recent report by the World Bank (2019) has found that only six countries across the world, all in Europe, ensure full legal parity between women and men. This report is based on eight indicators: freedom of movement; starting a job; getting paid; getting married; having children; running a business; property and inheritance; and getting a pension. On average, the global score is 75, meaning that women only enjoy three quarters of the legal rights of men with respect to the eight indicators mentioned above. That said, the score has gone up from 70 ten years ago, and has risen due to the promulgation of gender equality legislation in 131 countries. The scores vary widely across the world, with average regional scores as indicated below. The countries closest to gender parity are in the OECD high-income group, followed by Europe and Central Asia. Over this period, the greatest regional change has occurred in South Asia, and the smallest in the Middle East and North Africa (MENA) region. Most of the top improving countries were from Sub-Saharan Africa (Fig. 25.1).

Most reforms appear to have had an economic impetus and occurred in respect of labour rights, particularly non-discrimination in employment; protection from sexual harassment; and, in some countries where it existed, removing the need for permission to take up work. However, getting married and having children were the second and third areas most likely to have seen reforms over the 10-year period under study. Most of these reforms included greater recognition of domestic violence as a crime (considered further below) and granting women the same rights to

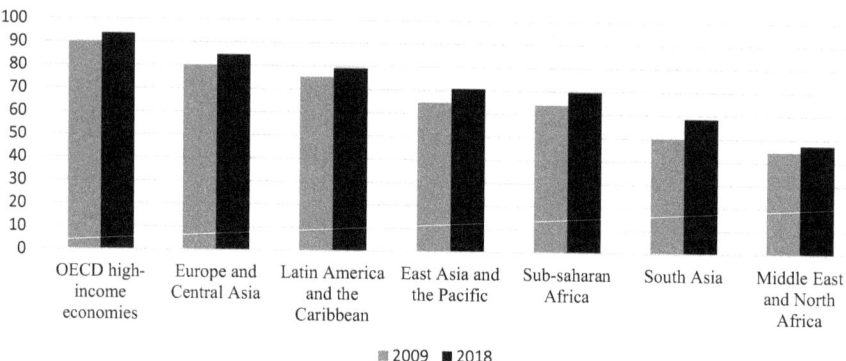

Fig. 25.1 Global gender equality average scores based on eight indicators. (Source: World Bank, 2019)

divorce and remarry as men. Least reform occurred in an area that is critical to women's autonomy—that of managing assets—where very much still needs to be done to ensure that women enjoy similar rights to men regarding the ownership, administration and inheritance of property.

Legal differences often mirror widely held cultural beliefs as to whether gender is socially constructed or whether women and men are different but complementary. That gender is socially constructed, with all this implies for the effectiveness of law and policy, appears to be broadly accepted across much of the Western world yet less so in the east and south. For instance, as Kashyap recounts from her female students, while the notion of gender equality is gaining ground in India (at least among those with higher education), this equality is seen in terms of complementarity rather than sameness. Similarly, Rashad et al. speak of the tension between women's rising aspirations to autonomy and choice, and men's reluctance to cede the rights that they traditionally derive from their breadwinner status. Despite a degree of difference across countries in the MENA region, the recent Masculinities Survey cited by the authors indicates that patriarchal views on the distinct roles of women and men persist; most respondents believe that gender equality is not part of their traditions and culture, though the majority of men and (more so) women declare that more needs to be done to promote equality.

Thus, in addition to greater legislative effort in many countries, the active mainstreaming of gender equality across all levels of education would seem critical to ensure further progress on this issue. As UNESCO (2015) underscores in a recent guide on this topic, teachers should be trained and supported to foster gender equality, both in and through the formal curriculum as well as through informal socialisation processes in the classroom and school more broadly.

The issue of equality also arises in respect of same-sex couples who, as Frost notes, do not enjoy legal recognition in the vast majority of countries, and indeed face discrimination and even persecution in some. Wang and Xia describe how in

China, where same-sex marriage is not legal, same-sex couples often feel they have to enter into fake marriages with third parties to hide their relationship, or simply have ceremonies to inform their family and friends of their union.

In its first report on LGBT rights, the United Nations (2011) note how governments have too often overlooked the violence and discrimination arising from gender identity and sexual orientation. The UN calls for the abolition of the death penalty in cases of consensual sex; for laws that criminalise homosexuality to be repealed; and for anti-discrimination laws to be widely enacted. The World Economic Forum (2018) notes a clear East–West divide in the rights afforded to same-sex couples, with those in the West enjoying far greater legal protection while in 73 countries, mostly in the Middle East, Africa and Asia, homosexuality remains illegal and is punishable by imprisonment or even, in a few jurisdictions, by death. For further reference, ILGA is the world federation of LGBTIQ associations and provides an annual world map of regulations affecting same-sex couples (ILGA, 2019).

The Council of Europe contends that legal recognition is a matter of equality before the law and is necessary to confer same-sex couples with protections enjoyed by opposite-sex ones, such as parenting rights and obligations, inheritance rights and survivors' pensions. The Council of Europe cites jurisprudence from the European Court of Human Rights which, they note, can only be read as 'placing a positive obligation on states parties to the ECHR to provide legal recognition to same-sex couples as a way to protect their right to family life' and urges its member states to do more to eliminate discrimination based on sexual orientation in the area of family rights (Council of Europe, 2017).

While registered partnerships have become increasingly accepted in many Western jurisdictions, controversy persists as to whether such legal recognition should extend to marriage itself. Even though international law does not oblige states to allow same-sex partners to marry, a number of jurisdictions have chosen to do so. The Netherlands was the first to allow same-sex marriage in 2000, and has since been followed by 27 other countries as of May 2019 as indicated in the map below by the Pew Research Centre (Fig. 25.2).

As with gender equality more broadly, legal recognition of the rights of same-sex couples is necessary but not sufficient. The UN (2011) point out that legal provisions need to be accompanied by awareness-raising campaigns with a view to reducing homophobia, both at school level and beyond. Furthermore, law enforcement officials should be provided with sensitisation and training programmes to ensure that they deal appropriately with incidents of discrimination and violence in respect of LGBT persons. In the personal services field too, growing importance has been given to the training of therapists and counsellors in affirmative intervention with LGBT clients of various ages (Hinrichs & Donaldson, 2017; Whitman, Horn, & Boyd, 2007).

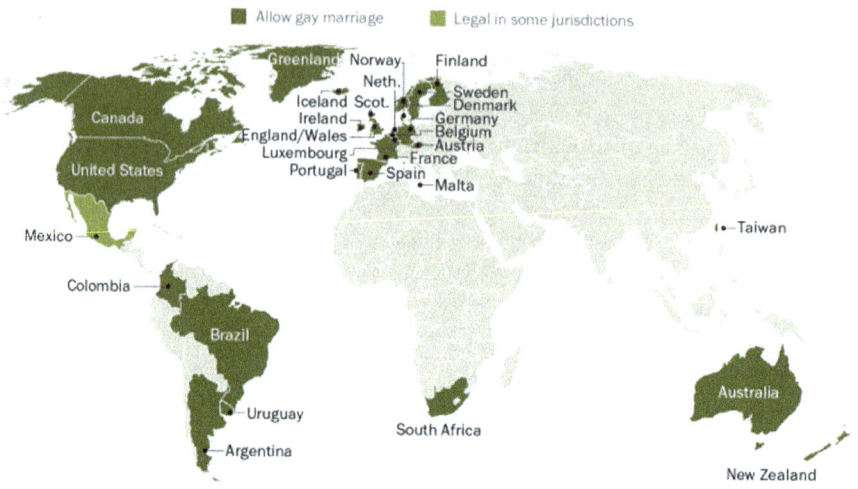

Fig. 25.2 Legal recognition of gay marriage across the globe, May 2019. (Source: Pew Research Centre (2019). Reproduced with permission)

25.3 Consent

A second theme that arises in various chapters is that of consent, both as a fundamental principle but also as an enduring and disputed issue in some cultural contexts.

Mate selection is one area in which consent is valued differently across time and space. In India, as noted above, freely chosen relationships gave way to arranged marriages as Hinduism sought to prevent inter-caste relationships. Despite social change and increasing female emancipation, arranged marriages are still widespread in India and are felt by parents to be a responsibility towards their child, rather than an imposition, and as important as providing a good education. Kashyap points out that young Indians increasingly aspire to exercise choice over who and when they marry and indeed, whether they marry at all. They are rarely forced to marry someone they would rather not. Yet, at least half her respondents would rather their parents choose a marriage partner for them. Speaking of China, Wang and Xia point out that while arranged marriage has been prohibited since 1950, the value of filial piety means that parents still have some influence upon young people's relationship decisions. Thus, although individual consent has been strengthened in both India and China, value is still placed upon parental guidance and support, and consideration is given to broader family prospects in one's selection of a mate.

'Free and full consent' has been upheld as a universal human right since 1948, yet marriage is not always freely undertaken. While in arranged marriages one or both partners are free to refuse, in forced marriages, at least one partner is not. Forced marriage occurs in many countries. For instance, the Forced Marriage Unit of the UK's Foreign and Commonwealth Office offers support in such cases to between 1200 to 1400 British nationals (or dual nationals) each year, having dealt with over 90 countries in 2017 alone (FMU, 2018). Many forced marriages involve minors who have not reached the age of consent, generally set at 18 in international agreements. Child marriage is still prevalent in some parts of the world and is considered a human rights violation with grave physical, psychological and socio-economic consequences, and is far more likely to affect girls than boys. Although most marriage laws set the legal age before which marriage cannot be contracted, loopholes do exist, for instance where parental consent may be granted, or where customary or religious laws supersede civil ones. Arthur et al. (2017) note that of the 191 countries they surveyed, 23 still do not have a minimum marriage age; in 30, girls under 18 can be married if customary/religious laws permit it; and in 99, they can be married below 18 if their parents permit it.

UNICEF (2018) notes that legislative developments have effectively prevented 25 million child marriages over the past decade, bringing the proportion of child brides down from one in four to one in five brides worldwide. Particular progress has been made in India, as government has invested more in young girls and their education and issued strong public messages that child marriage is illegal and harmful, and that it causes school drop-out, health complications and poverty risk (UNICEF, 2018). However, more than 150 million young girls are still likely to get married by 2030, many in sub-Saharan Africa, and UNICEF urges 'dramatic' efforts to address this issue.

The issue of consent would also seem to arise in polygynous marriages, which are permitted in Muslim-majority countries though with notable exceptions like Tunisia and Turkey where it has been banned for decades. Polygyny is also practiced (if illegally) in other religious traditions like Mormonism in some parts of the USA. As Jaafer-Mohammad and Lehmann (2011) note, polygamy existed before Islam; while Islam sought to regulate it, it did not make it either obligatory or universal. These authors note that while marriage in the Islamic tradition is based on both partners' consent, cultural practices shape and sometimes even contradict Islam. In effect, whether or not the first wife's consent is required for the husband to take a second or subsequent wife differs across jurisdictions, and some afford the first wife a greater say. For instance, in 2013 the Constitutional Court in South Africa ruled that living with dignity presupposes autonomy and control over one's life, and that respecting the dignity of their wife requires a husband to seek her consent before undertaking a subsequent marriage (Mudarikwa, n.d.).

The principle of consent also arises in the case of non-monogamy, often referred to as polyamory—the practice of romantic and/or sexual relationships with more than one person at the same time, where all parties are aware of and consent to the arrangement. In discussing non-monogamy, Timm and Blow contend that fidelity means being faithful to one's relational agreement rather than the more common interpretation of sexual exclusivity—one can still be faithful to one's partner if both consent to a non-monogamous relationship and communicate about the boundaries acceptable to each partner.

While at an interpersonal level it is hard to take issue with the liberty of consenting adults, at the level of services and legislation, polyamory is more complex. At a service level, Timm and Blow point out that power dynamics in a relationship may mean that a less powerful partner feels constrained to accept non-monogamy to avoid losing their partner entirely. In such cases, non-monogamy cannot truly be called consensual and therapists are to be vigilant for issues of safety and power when called upon to support a non-monogamous relationship. In respect of legislation, marriage laws usually require couples to commit to sexual exclusivity and there would not appear to be any examples of legislation which protects the rights of sexual partners, even of long-standing, outside the marital union. Avimar (2008) found that the polyamorous respondents in his study were not interested in pressing for plural marriage, because for them marriage entailed 'submission to government and bureaucracy, normalization and stagnation' (p. 275). For different reasons, Porter (2015) would agree that polyamory should not enjoy legal recognition. He acknowledges that states do not have as compelling a reason to ban polyamory as they do polygyny, where the human rights of women and children often need protection. Porter argues that while marriage is under-theorised, his review of arguments and evidence leads him to suggest that normative monogamy has played a crucial role in social and economic progress, protecting children and encouraging the investment of time and money in productive pursuits such as education, innovation and business rather than in multiple mate-seeking. The question remains as to whether and how the rights and responsibilities of all parties in polyamorous relationships can and should be protected, particularly in respect of the care and custody of children, but also property, maintenance and inheritance, during and after the relationship.

25.4 Relational Capability

A third theme to run through this volume is that of relational capability. Some of the main capabilities that arise in these chapters include reflexivity, communication, boundary negotiation and conflict resolution.

Reflexivity was underscored by many authors as an important relational capacity, increasingly so in the light of social change around gender roles, intercultural partnerships and relational permanence in even the most traditional societies. As Øfsti and Maestre point out, love relationships capable of satisfying both partners have increasingly become an end in themselves and not only a means to, say, economic security or having children. The ability to reflect upon oneself and one's relationship, and to be emotionally literate, now seems essential to strengthening contemporary relationships. Vetere speaks of how therapists often need to conduct systemic work over the longer term to help couples develop their reflective capacity and to integrate their experience. Singh illustrates through her vignettes how reflecting upon the influence of one's socio-political context on one's expectations of self and other as partners has become increasingly important to successful relationships.

Communication recurs repeatedly as a source of relationship satisfaction across countries. For instance, Wang and Xia note how couples who communicate positively have higher levels of relationship satisfaction, even if communication among Chinese partners may be less direct and involve less self-disclosure than among Western ones. As Frost notes, communication is important to relational quality not only among heterosexual but also same-sex couples. It is particularly important during difficult life situations; Schembri Lia illustrates that in the case of an incurred disability, good communication makes for better emotional, physical and sexual adjustment between the disabled partner and the caregiver. The need to communicate with clarity and sensitivity also endures into later life when, as Huyck discusses, people falling in love at an older age need skill to negotiate the financial and emotional complexities this may entail. The importance of communication is also made apparent by the rise in intercultural relationships where, as Singh shows, a couple's shared language may not allow one or both partners to express themselves as fully as they would wish, in turn lessening the quality of connection.

The ways in which communication is increasingly facilitated by technology, especially but not only among couples living apart, is also highlighted in this volume and described as a mixed blessing. Wang and Xia note how some couples, forced to live apart to make a living, maintain their relationship over digital media. McCormack and Ogilvie discuss the ways in which smartphones enable couples to keep in touch, to establish their relationship in its early days, and to enhance their sexual lives. Cachia illustrates the novel potential of technology in enabling therapeutic interventions among such couples. While acknowledging the discrepancy between the 'speed and immediacy' of cyberculture and the attention to detail required in therapy, Cachia discusses how online therapy can be used to provide the therapist with unique insight into the couples' context and to provide containment and support to couples living apart.

However, numerous authors also speak of the downside of smartphone use, including its potential to undermine trust and fidelity and to distract partners from communicating with each other when they are actually together. Sheehan queries whether technology-mediated communication—while facilitating daily life—might inhibit the deepening of relationship skills. Eichenberg, Huss and Küsel note how online communication may give rise to disinhibited self-disclosure as well as selective self-presentation. As these authors point out, internet-mediated communication comes with both risks and benefits, and more needs to be learned about its usefulness for, and its effects upon, different personality types.

Managing boundaries is another important capacity to emerge across different contexts. Both Jamieson and Huyck speak of the negotiation needed when moving in with a partner after a period of living independently, in respect for instance of the division of household chores, finances and relationships with extended families. Couples in more traditional societies may also require skill in balancing autonomy with respect for tradition in relation to parents and in-laws. Wang and Xia speak of how Chinese parents value family continuity and therefore negotiate with their adult children even about grandchildren. Kashyap illustrates the balance that many young Indians seek in both wanting and respecting their parents' guidance on the selection of a partner, while wishing to exercise a degree of choice in this regard. Schembri discusses the importance of community support to couple relationships, whether in practical, emotional or spiritual ways. He notes, however, that there are times when communities may prove intrusive, overbearing or lacking in empathy, and here, the ability of the couple to affirm its boundaries is important. Singh highlights the skill required by intercultural couples to negotiate major life decisions, such as where to live and the degree of closeness each partner wishes with their family of origin. Establishing boundaries around the practice of non-exclusive relationships, or ensuring equality among wives in polygynous marriage, must also require considerable negotiation skill to avoid power imbalance and ensure the well-being of all parties.

Conflict resolution is the last capacity to be highlighted here. As Cole and Cole point out, the ability to manage conflict is central to sound relationships. It requires partners to avoid negative exchanges and to keep talking, becoming proficient in a variety of skills that help lead to a constructive dealing with difference. The ability to resolve conflict is made more necessary by the fact that, as both Maestre and Øfsti note, the importance given to personal success for both women and men in various spheres of life may result in a collision of partners' interests. Conflict may also arise when partners subscribe to different 'love discourses'. Many contributors to this volume speak of emergent tensions between, for example, notions of love as virtue versus love as romance in Scandinavia (Øfsti); arranged marriage and romance in India (Kashyap); and between traditional gender roles and increasing choice and control for women in Arab countries (Rashad et al.). Singh speaks of the added challenges faced by intercultural couples over the meaning of their different backgrounds and how these impact their lives together in respect, for instance, of parenting.

The relational capabilities mentioned above can be fostered through relationship education, which imparts crucial principles and skills that increase the likelihood of healthy, stable and satisfying relationships, and which help prevent and resolve future problems (Wadsworth & Markman, 2012). In their meta-analysis of relationship education for individuals, Simpson, Leonhardt, and Hawkins (2018) find such education to have encouraging medium-term benefits, but call for rigorous evaluations of longer term impact. For couples too, relationship education has positive outcomes, though the earlier that couples participate in such education, the greater the benefits seem to be (Markman & Halford, 2005).

Relationship education is found to be particularly useful among adolescents, who go through rapid developmental change, and are likely to idealise romantic relationships without having the skills to ensure such relationships are healthy (McElwaina, McGillb, & Savasuk-Luxton, 2017). However, compulsory relationship education at school—particularly where this incorporates sexual education—has not been without controversy, with parents from various backgrounds uniting to insist that their children should have the chance to opt out of these classes and receive such instruction at home. This is particularly true in multicultural societies, manifested recently, for instance, in parents' protests in the UK (Savage, 2019), Los Angeles (Lindahl & Bharath, 2019) and Ontario (Canadian Press, 2016).

Following their review of relationship education research between 2003 and 2013, Markman and Rhoades (2012) make a number of suggestions to ensure that such education responds to social and demographic changes. They suggest that particular effort be invested in increasing the appeal of relationship education in general (both among couples with, and without, problems) and especially in engaging male participants. The authors make a case for the consideration of financial incentives to participate in relationship education, which they believe to be 'an excellent investment for a community' (p. 193).

In addition to the more traditional relational skills, couples can also receive support to develop their skills in managing finances and in parenting. Economic strain often has adverse effects on relationship quality, as worries about money create tension and spill over into negative behaviours and couple conflict (Pajarita, Orthner, Jones, & Mancini, 2006). This is true of both married and cohabiting couples (Hardie & Lucas, 2010). Academic interest in financial stress and relationship quality appears to have risen since the 2008 crisis. Policies to address financial stress among couples may be direct or indirect. Direct support would include adequate income maintenance through employment schemes and social security benefits. Indirect support—a discussion beyond the possibility of this chapter—must be intergenerational (addressing the needs of both parents and children), and multidimensional (through policy areas like education, employment, gender equality, housing, progressive taxation, affordable health and care, and addiction services).

However, financial stress does not only arise from inadequate income, but also from disagreement over how money should be managed, and training in financial skills has proven useful in this respect. Zimmerman and Roberts (2012) found that participation in a financial management course, and the subsequent implementation of practices learned, was linked to improved relationship quality. Financial issues frequently arise in therapy, leading Dakin and Wampler (2008) to suggest that it is important for therapists to be aware of income issues and what these mean in the context of clients' lives and prospects. Couples often find it hard to discuss money matters; Archuleta (2013) remarks that it is often easier for them to discuss sexual issues than financial ones. She encourages therapists to help couples clarify their financial expectations and their respective goals and values around money. Britt, Grable, Goff, and White (2008) go one step further, suggesting specialist 'financial therapy' to which relationship counsellors might refer couples who need it.

Turning to parenting, caring for children contributes to well-being in many ways (Nomaguchi & Milkie, 2017) yet the demands of parenthood are stressful. As Deater-Deckard and Panneton (2017) note, parenting stress is the norm not the exception. These authors discuss the many factors related to parenting stress and its impact on children's development, underscoring the need to mitigate this stress to avoid it becoming chronic and resulting in what they call maladaptive trajectories for the couple and children alike.

Again, policies to address parenting stress can be indirect or direct. Poverty alleviation plays a prominent role, as do family-friendly employment measures, and affordable and accessible mental health services. More directly, parent education programmes have received increasing attention as a valuable resource in enhancing parental competencies, improving family relationships and strengthening children's development. For instance, the Council of Europe launched Recommendation 19 in 2006 to encourage positive parenting, through family policies and services that help parents, especially vulnerable ones, to fulfil their tasks, as well as policies to enable work–life balance. The Council recommends an approach based on support, empowerment and partnership with parents, respectful of diversity and recognising fathers' important role (Rodrigo, 2010).

As the Cowans discuss in their chapter in this volume, involving the father in relationship education is of great benefit to the couple as partners and also as parents. Combining couple relationship education with co-parenting support was also found to have a significantly positive impact in a randomised controlled trial by Petch, Halford, Creedy, and Gamble (2012) who found that this combination was more likely than mother-focused programmes to reduce negative communication and parenting stress among women. In addition, combining couple relationship and co-parenting education was found to bring about an increase in relationship satisfaction among women and men deemed to be at high risk of maladjustment to parenthood. Their findings lead the authors to advocate for early intervention, recruiting parents during their transition to parenthood when they are likely to be more motivated to invest in their relationship.

25.5 Commitment

The fourth theme in this section is that of commitment. Cole and Cole describe commitment, along with trust, as 'the walls that hold everything together'; as a positive answer to whether we cherish a partner and forsake all others.

Marriage, as the formalisation of commitment, still enjoys widespread popularity, even if rates are falling and more rapidly in some regions than others. This volume suggests evidence of lower marriage rates, and later marriages, in countries as disparate as France, North Africa and China. However, this need not mean that marriage is less valued, and the lower and later rates of marriage may be attributable in part to the longer duration of education among both men and women. Also, not all couples have the right to formalise their commitment. As Frost notes, same-sex couples still face continued stigma in the vast majority of countries (and are indeed still criminalised in some) and very few countries provide their relationship with legal recognition. In some regions, religion still plays a strong role in dictating who may marry. For instance, inter-caste marriages are exceedingly rare in India and only constitute around five per cent of all marriages (BBC, 2019), while in Israel persons can only marry within their religious denomination (Davidson, 2019).

The OECD (2018) provides the crude marriage rate (CMR)—or marriages per 1000 of the population—for 44 countries for 1970, 1995 and 2016, illustrating a clear drop in most countries. Eurostat too notes that the CMR has halved in Europe between 1964 and 2014 (Eurostat, 2017). Partnership status data are summarised in the table below.

As seen in Table 25.1 below, rates of cohabitation as an alternative (or possible precursor) to marriage are on the rise, particularly among younger couples. Younger cohorts across the 44 countries surveyed by the OECD were more likely to cohabit than the general population; cohabitation rates also correlate with higher educational attainment. However, marked differences remain across regions, being quite high in Central and Southern America, the USA, New Zealand and some European countries, but low in Asia and the Middle East (Social Trends Institute, 2017). Furthermore, the evidence on who is most likely to cohabit is very mixed. For instance, in their review of the 2006–2013 National Family Growth Survey, Sassler, Michelmore, and Qian (2018) find that women from 'more advantaged' backgrounds were less likely to cohabit, and where they do, cohabitation occurs at a later point in the relationship than among those from less advantaged backgrounds. Also, cohabitees from advantaged backgrounds were more likely to eventually transition into marriage.

The recognition of cohabitation has been a controversial issue in many jurisdictions, particularly in respect of the higher dissolution rates of cohabiting relationships—at least, in the medium to longer term—and the well-being of children of such relationships. The Economist (2016) distinguishes three broad approaches to cohabitation. In one group of countries, cohabiting couples are treated like married ones if they have been together for a given period of time; this group includes countries like Sweden and Australia. Another grouping of countries only recognises marriage and treats cohabitees as single people, such as the UK, Italy and much of America. A third group offers formal alternatives to marriage, such as cohabitation agreements in the Netherlands or the *Pacte Civil de Solidarité* (PACS) in France. Europe has seen the introduction of civil union legislation, or partnership registration, in 22 of the 28 EU member states, though the entitlements that these confer vary quite widely, particularly around property and maintenance rights (European Union, 2019). In most countries, the legal and financial rights and obligations of cohabiting couples remain less than those of married couples. This sometimes gives rise to significant problems if the relationship ends through separation or bereavement—especially where women have given up work to become home makers (Sanchéz Gassen & Perelli-Harris, 2015).

Whether married or cohabiting, the choice to leave a relationship has come to seem increasingly possible. As Sheehan and others note, difficulties in maintaining

Table 25.1 Partnership status, OECD and EU 2011

Countries	Average: all over age 20			Average: aged 20–34		
	Not living with a partner	Married or registered partnership	Cohabiting	Not living with a partner	Married or registered partnership	Cohabiting
OECD	40.19	49.84	9.97	59.24	23.45	16.89
EU	40.73	50.93	8.35	60.49	24.86	14.42

Source: OECD (2018)

long-term relationships today emerge due to multiple factors such as changing gender expectations and different love discourses; intercultural differences; the pressures arising from stigma and discrimination; economic realities such as poverty and unemployment; the increasing reluctance to put up with domestic violence, infidelity and addictions; disparities in sexual desire and relationship skill deficits.

Longevity is no longer seen to be the main marker of relationship quality and, as Maestre notes, separation and divorce provoke less fear and are today more easily resorted to. This is true not only in the West; for instance, as Rashad et al. note, divorce rates are also increasing in the Arab region, particularly among younger cohorts and after shorter marriage durations. Looking globally, all states except for the Philippines and Vatican City have divorce laws. Lir Wang and Schofer (2018) examine the divorce rates in 84 countries between 1970 and 2008, and find these rates to be highest in the North and West of Europe, North America and Oceania, and the former Communist countries. Rates are lowest in Southern Europe and Latin America, while the rates in Asia and the MENA region vary considerably. Their data lead them to concur with other research in pointing out the positive correlation between divorce rates and national income, female employment and mass education, and the negative correlation between divorce rates and Catholicism and Islam. The authors contend that traditional understandings of marriage and family have been altered worldwide, as 'cultural principles of freedom, consent and gender equality, which are recognised and codified in world society, diffuse into national contexts' (p. 694) through the ratification of treaties and national ties with supranational organisations. Mass entertainment media, too, have contributed to reshaping ideas about family life. In one widely cited study, Chong and La Ferrara (2009) for instance, analyse divorce data from the censuses of 1970, 1980 and 1991 in Brazil and find a significant correlation between the rise in separations and divorces and access to the broadcasting of soap operas.

If in many countries divorce rates have risen, in others they have declined. The OECD (2018), for instance, captures divorce rates from 1970 to 2016 in 44 countries, of which 19 saw divorce rates fall from 1995 to 2016. This drop was particularly marked in Estonia, Belgium, the USA, the UK, New Zealand and Australia. Many urge caution against interpreting this decline as an indicator of greater couple stability. Referring to the USA and UK data, Luscombe (2018) acknowledges that millennials appear to be divorcing less than older cohorts, yet points out that the average age of marriage has risen, as have levels of cohabitation, and many young people lack the financial security they believe necessary to get married. This leads her to suggest that marriage has become 'self-selective' from among a shrinking group of relatively privileged people.

Countries do not only differ in terms of divorce rates but also in terms of the nature of divorce legislation. Divorce is easier to acquire in some jurisdictions than others, and is often a long and costly process especially in the context of a contentious separation. There has been a shift in many countries from fault-based divorce where one party needs to prove suitable grounds, to a no-fault based divorce which may be consensual or, in some jurisdictions, even unilateral. Writing of the USA, where no-fault divorces spread in the 1970s, Leeson and Pierson (2015) attribute this shift to many factors including partners' circumvention of fault-based legislation (through 'concocting' evidence and exploiting legal loopholes) and to socio-economic changes, such as women's growing economic independence and the decoupling of marriage and parenting. They cite Friedman (1984) in explaining how this shift reflects a move away from a moral view of the institution of marriage, to a contractual view more concerned with economic issues such as property, inheritance and alimony.

Policy choices over how liberal divorce laws should be vary widely across cultures and countries. Even if no-fault divorce may ease the process by making it less demeaning and less necessary to demonise one's partner, and possibly making it a shorter and less costly process, divorce can certainly cause pain and disruption. Apart from the emotional distress, if one spouse is in a weaker financial position, their standard of living may decline; non-custodial parents may disengage; and contact may be lost if one parent moves away to live and work elsewhere. There has been considerable research on the negative effects of divorce on children, and it is often observed that in most cases the effects of conflict start long before the divorce. Nevertheless, the debate endures on the extent to which protective factors (such as post-divorce parenting quality, father engagement and financial stability) can offset much of divorce's negative impact on child outcomes (Härkönen, 2013).

Stricter regulation of marriage is unlikely to bring about a drop in divorce rates, but various policy instruments exist to help prevent marital dissolution and mitigate the effects of divorce. These include marital counselling and therapy; legal aid; employment and income maintenance programmes for custodial parents after divorce; and co-parenting education. Amato (2010) highlights the promise of divorce education classes for parents, and of mediation services, or 'non-adversarial dispute resolution procedures', but notes that rigorous evaluation of both is still needed.

25.6 Due Care

The fifth and last theme to be considered is that of due care for the safety and well-being of loved ones. Vetere illustrates how our earliest experiences of care are fundamental to our ability to understand and manage our emotions, and to develop trusting and caring attachments with others. Although care, as both emotion and behaviour, has traditionally been associated with women, Cowan and Cowan describe how the idea of 'family as system' has developed over time to become a truism today. They speak of their work to include both mother and father in their parenting groups, because strengthening the parental relationship, and including the father in parenting, has proven the best way to support children's development.

The chapters in this volume are replete with different manifestations of care in our contemporary age. The need for respect for the equal worth, autonomy and aspirations of both partners, irrespective of gender or sexual orientation, runs through numerous chapters. This is given practical significance in shared decision-making; the sharing of household work and parenting; mutual support; and the honouring of relational commitments. Caring behaviours, such as spending attentive time together, communicating constructively, and the willingness to work on the relationship are repeatedly linked to relationship satisfaction across couple types.

The chapters and their vignettes also highlight situations devoid of, or lacking in, care. At the extreme end are honour killings, referred to by both Kashyap and Rashad et al. These are estimated to amount to 5000 persons across the globe each year, though advocacy groups consider this to be a gross underestimate (HVBA, n.d.) Intimate partner violence is also highlighted by a number of authors. Rashad et al. report research evidence that over a third of male respondents from Egypt, Palestine and Morocco believe that there are times when 'a woman deserves to be beaten', and over two-thirds believe that a woman should tolerate violence 'to keep the family together'. Domestic violence is singled out by Sheehan as still being one of three recurring reasons for separation-related consultations. Yang and Xia report that women seeking a divorce in China are most likely to be those who have experienced all types of violence.

The prevalence of domestic violence is also highlighted by the World Health Organisation (WHO, 2013), who note that three in ten of all women across the world have experienced physical and/or sexual violence by their intimate partner. While prevalence is greater in lower-income countries (rising to around 37% of ever-partnered women in Africa, the Eastern Mediterranean and South-East Asia) it is far from negligible in higher income countries, standing at 30% in the Americas and 25% in Europe. If domestic violence were a medical condition, its prevalence would surely constitute an epidemic.

The UN has made the elimination of violence against women and girls one of its Sustainable Development Goals for 2030. Yet, the World Bank reports that 24% of all countries still lack domestic violence legislation, and only in a third of all countries does such protection extend to unmarried partners (Tavares & Wodon, 2018). Moreover, not all countries incorporate the four facets of domestic violence—physical, sexual, economic and psychological—in their laws. For instance, over a third of all countries provide no legal protection against sexual violence, and over a half do not protect against economic violence.

As Tavares and Wodon (2018) point out, domestic violence legislation alone is not sufficient to address this problem. Indeed, the UN reports that even where such legislation exists, less than one in ten women seek police assistance, and less than one in four seek any help at all (UN, 2015). While the law is a necessary foundation, it must be accompanied by sufficient resources for enforcement and the support of survivors, as well as specialised training for the judiciary and law enforcement officials. Pressure and guidance from supranational organisations are also important. At European level, for instance, the 2011 Council of Europe Istanbul Convention was the first legally binding, multilateral agreement aiming to curb violence against women and it sets out a number of state obligations in the areas of prevention, awareness raising, education, protection and support, investigation and prosecution, among others (Council of Europe, n.d.).

Another contemporary manifestation of a failure to care is the abuse of internet technology. Eichenberg et al. discuss the potential of internet technology for forming new relationships but also its downsides, such as ghosting; the misuse of private erotic photos; and cyber-aggression towards one's partner. These authors, as does Maestre, also mention the ways in which infidelity may be facilitated by the internet. Less dramatic but also insidious is how smartphone use often diminishes the quality of partners' presence to each other when they are together, as Sheehan, Piscopo et al. and McCormack and Ogilvie all note.

Both legislative and educational efforts need to be stepped up around online abuse, or 'cyber violence'. In 2017, Amnesty International published new research on the extent, and impact, of online abuse against women, with almost a quarter of all females in the survey countries reporting that they have experienced such abuse at least once (Amnesty International, 2017). In 2018, the Human Rights Council of the UN General Assembly passed a resolution entitled *The promotion, protection and enjoyment of human rights on the Internet* (UN, 2018), affirming that those rights that people have offline should also be protected online and condemning, among others, all sexual and gender-based violence. One of the most harmful forms of cyber abuse, revenge pornography, can have devastating mental health effects (Kamal & Newman, 2016) and has resulted in cases of suicide across the globe. However, legislation that criminalises revenge porn has been too slow to develop, and in 2018 could only be found in the Philippines, Israel, Japan, the UK, Germany, France, Malta, Canada and the majority of American states (Centre for Internet and Society, 2018) and most recently, in Italy (ANSA, 2019). In view of this, education about online dating, and how people may optimise its benefits and manage its risks, appears to be an increasingly necessary part of relationship education. Some service providers are already providing concrete guidelines on this topic (for instance, Norton, 2019).

Lastly, the practice of due care after separation and divorce would, though difficult, seem to be another requirement of numerous contemporary couples. As Sheehan notes, there are as many types of couple separation as there are unique couples in unique circumstances. While some separations are amicable, others are protracted and acrimonious, with negative repercussions on the well-being of partners and their children. Financial stability, supportive friends and family, and a shared 'love discourse' (Sheehan, Øfsti) can ease a difficult separation process. Not all separating couples have these resources, as in situations of poverty or unemployment, domestic violence or addictive behaviour. Sheehan highlights how trauma is caused not only by the event that triggered the separation, but by high levels of conflict that can endure well after the separation itself. A commitment to care for each other must be incredibly difficult in many separation processes but would for this reason seem to be more necessary than ever, and to merit all possible support.

25.7 Concluding Note

This chapter has focused on five principles that run throughout the chapters in this volume which are both fundamental to couple relationships and which provide a basis for couple-related policy measures. The five principles are equality, consent, capability, commitment and care. A necessarily broad and supranational review of relevant data and policy measures highlights the important role of legislation in upholding these principles and laying the foundation for egalitarian, fulfilling and stable relationships. As noted, though, legislation is necessary yet not sufficient and must be complemented by an array of services and programmes for it to be effective. The proper implementation and enforcement of legislation requires sufficient, sensitised and well-trained resources. A major challenge continues to be posed by contexts where civil and religious rights are conflated; though religion continues to provide inspiration and solace to millions, this confluence does not always allow for legal protection of non-religious persons or indeed of aggrieved parties within a given faith tradition.

Legislation must also be accompanied by awareness raising, about a zero tolerance of violence of any sort but also about the values of care and respect, diversity and inclusion. Preventing and alleviating poverty is essential to address the relational and parenting strain generated by inadequate income. Relationship and parenting education can provide the skills required for both partners and their children to flourish. Counselling and therapy too are indispensable, not only for couples in distress, but also for those seeking to grow together and deepen their relationship.

Although legislation is the prerogative of the state, and benefits and services are generally financed and/or provided at national or local levels, the impetus for change very often originates outside statutory structures. While global differences persist on so many dimensions of couple relationships, supranational organisations have played a critical role in driving a shared vision and vocabulary of human and civil rights, and in shaping the aspirations of an increasingly connected world. The same can also be said of so many NGOs working worldwide to raise awareness and push for reforms that improve the well-being of women, men and children, while many also provide invaluable services to couples at various stages of their relationship. This chapter ends on a note of gratitude to these organisations, and to the global academic community, for shedding light on the experiences of couples worldwide and for holding out hope for a better future for all.

References

Amato, P. (2010). Research on divorce: Continuing trends and new developments. *Journal of Marriage and Family, 72*(3), 650–666.

Amnesty International. (2017). *Amnesty reveals alarming impact of online abuse against women.* Retrieved 30 May 2019 from https://www.amnesty.org/en/latest/news/2017/11/amnesty-reveals-alarming-impact-of-online-abuse-against-women/.

ANSA. (2019, April 2). *Revenge porn amendment ok'd by House*. Retrieved 1 June 2019 from http://www.ansa.it/english/news/general_news/2019/04/02/revenge-porn-amendment-okd-by-house_d9a61786-f7b6-4cca-9a57-55f0e343ff33.html.

Archuleta, K. (2013). Couples, money, and expectations: Negotiating financial management roles to increase relationship satisfaction. *Marriage & Family Review, 49*(5), 391–411.

Arthur, M., Earle, A., Raub, A., Vincent, I., Atabay, E., Latz, I., … Heymann, J. (2017). Child marriage laws around the world: minimum marriage age, legal exceptions and gender disparities. *Journal of Women, Politics & Policy, 39*(1), 51–74.

Avimar, H. (2008). Make love, now war. Perceptions of the marriage equality struggle among polyamorous activists. *Journal of Bisexuality 7*(3–4), 261–286.

BBC. (2019, April 14). *The couples on the run for love in India*. Retrieved 14 June 2019 from https://www.bbc.com/news/world-asia-india-47823588.

Britt, S., Grable, J., Goff, B., & White, M. (2008). The influence of perceived spending behaviours on relationship satisfaction. *Journal of Financial Counseling and Planning, 19*(1), 31–43.

Centre for Internet and Society. (2018). *Revenge porn laws across the world*. Retrieved 1 June 2019 from https://cis-india.org/internet-governance/blog/revenge-porn-laws-across-the-world.

Chong, A., & La Ferrara, E. (2009). Television and divorce. Evidence from Brazilian *novelas*. *Journal of the European Economic Association, 7*(2–3), 458–468.

Council of Europe. (2017). *Access to registered same-sex partnerships: it's a question of equality*. Retrieved 1 June 2019 from https://www.coe.int/en/web/commissioner/-/access-to-registered-same-sex-partnerships-it-s-a-question-of-equality.

Council of Europe. (n.d.) *Council of Europe Convention on preventing and combating violence against women and domestic violence*. Retrieved 4 June 2019 from https://www.coe.int/fr/web/conventions/full-list/-/conventions/rms/090000168008482e.

Dakin, J., & Wampler, R. (2008). Money doesn't buy happiness but it helps. *The American Journal of Family Therapy, 36*(4), 300–311.

Davidson, C. (Panellist). (2019, January 12). *Marriage in Israel*. BBC World Service, Heart and Soul podcast. Retrieved from https://player.fm/series/heart-and-soul-1301462/marriage-in-israel.

Deater-Deckard, K., & Panneton, R. (2017). Unearthing the developmental and intergenerational dynamics of stress in parent and child functioning. In K. Deater-Deckard & R. Panneton (Eds.), *Parental stress and early child development* (pp. 1–14). Switzerland: Springer.

European Union. (2012). *Charter of fundamental rights of the European Union, 2012/C326/02*. Retrieved 1 May 2019 from https://eur-lex.europa.eu/legal-content/EN/TXT/PDF/?uri=CELEX:12012P/TXT&from=EN.

European Union. (2019). *Civil unions and registered partnerships*. Retrieved 9 June 2019 from https://europa.eu/youreurope/citizens/family/couple/registered-partners/index_en.htm.

Eurostat. (2017). *People in the EU - statistics on household and family structures*. Retrieved 1 June 2019 from https://ec.europa.eu/eurostat/statistics-explained/index.php/People_in_the_EU_-_statistics_on_household_and_family_structures#Marriage.

Fayad, F. (n.d.) *Equality, religion and gender in Israel*. Retrieved 30 April 2019 from https://jwa.org/encyclopedia/article/equality-religion-and-gender-in-israel.

FMU. (2018). *Forced marriage unit statistics 2017*. London, UK: Home Office. Retrieved 6 June 2019 from https://assets.publishing.service.gov.uk/government/uploads/system/uploads/attachment_data/file/730155/2017_FMU_statistics_FINAL.pdf

Friedman, L. M. (1984). Rights of passage: Divorce law in historical perspective. *Oregon Law Review, 63*, 649–669.

Hantrais, L. (2004). *Family policy matters*. Bristol, UK: Policy Press.

Hardie, J., & Lucas, A. (2010). Economic factors and relationship quality among young couples: Comparing cohabitation and marriage. *Journal of Marriage and Family, 72*(5), 1141–1154.

Härkönen, J. (2013). *Divorce: Trends, patterns, causes, consequences*. Social Policy and Family Dynamics in Europe Working Paper 2013/3. Retrieved 11 June 2019 from http://www.su.se/polopoly_fs/1.133184.1366922030!/menu/standard/file/WP_2013_3.pdf.

Hinrichs, K., & Donaldson, W. (2017). Recommendations for use of affirmative psychotherapy with LGBT older adults. *Journal of Clinical Psychology, 73*(8), 945–953.

HVBA (n.d.) *Honour based violence awareness network – statistics and data*. Retrieved 20 June 2019 from http://hbv-awareness.com/statistics-data/.

ILGA. (2019). *Maps - Sexual orientation laws*. Retrieved 2 June 2019 from https://ilga.org/downloads/ILGA_Sexual_Orientation_Laws_Map_2019.pdf.

Jaafer-Mohammad, I., & Lehmann, C. (2011). Women's rights in Islam regarding marriage and divorce. *Journal of Law and Practice, 4*(1). Retrieved from http://open.mitchellhamline.edu/lawandpractice/vol4/iss1/3

Kamal, M., & Newman, W. J. (2016). Revenge pornography: Mental health implications and related legislation. *Journal of American Academy of Psychiatry Law, 44*(3), 359–367.

Leeson, P., & Pierson, J. (2015). Economic origins of the no-fault divorce revolution. *European Journal of Law and Economics, 43*(3), 419–439.

Lindahl, C., & Bharath, D. (2019, 17 May). *LA County's Chinese among those protesting state sex education curriculum*. Pasadena Star News. Retrieved 4 June 2019 from https://www.presstelegram.com/2019/05/17/la-countys-chinese-among-those-protesting-state-sex-education-curriculum/.

Lir Wang, C., & Schofer, E. (2018). Coming out of the penumbras: World culture and cross-national variation in divorce rates. *Social Forces, 97*(2), 675–704.

Luscombe, B. (2018, 26 November). The divorce rate is dropping. That may not actually be good news. *Time*. Retrieved 10 June 2019 from https://time.com/5434949/divorce-rate-children-marriage-benefits/.

Markman, H., & Halford, W. K. (2005). International perspectives on relationship education. *Family Process, 44*(2), 139–146.

Markman, H., & Rhoades, G. (2012). Relationship education research: Current status and future directions. *Journal of Marital and Family Therapy, 38*(1), 169–200.

McElwaina, A., McGillb, J., & Savasuk-Luxton, R. (2017). Youth relationship education: A meta-analysis. *Children and Youth Services Review, 82*, 499–507.

Mudarikwa, M. (n.d.). *Mayelane vs Ngwenyama on the importance of consent and its application to all polygynous marriages in South Africa*. Retrieved 29 April 2019 from http://resources.lrc.org.za/mayelane-v-ngwenyama-on-the-importance-of-consent-and-its-application-to-all-polygynous-marriages-in-south-africa/.

Nomaguchi, K., & Milkie, M. (2017). Sociological perspectives on parenting stress: How social structure and culture shape parental strain and the well-being of parents and children. In K. Deater-Deckard & R. Panneton (Eds.), *Parental stress and early child development* (pp. 47–73). Switzerland: Springer.

Norton. (2019) *The ultimate guide to online dating*. Retrieved 5 June 2019 from https://us.norton.com/internetsecurity-privacy-ultimate-guide-online-dating.html.

OECD. (2018). *SF3.1: Marriage and divorce rates*. Retrieved 30 May 2019 from https://www.oecd.org/els/family/SF_3_1_Marriage_and_divorce_rates.pdf.

Pajarita, C., Orthner, D., Jones, A., & Mancini, D. (2006). Poverty and couple relationships. *Marriage and Family Review, 39*(1), 27–52.

Petch, J., Halford, W., Creedy, D., & Gamble, J. (2012). A randomised controlled trial of a couple relationship and coparenting programme (Couple CARE for Parents) for high- and low-risk new parents. *Journal of Consulting and Clinical Psychology, 80*(4), 662–673.

Pew Research Centre. (2019). *A global snapshot of same sex marriage*. Retrieved 7 June 2019 from https://www.pewresearch.org/fact-tank/2019/05/17/global-snapshot-sex-marriage/.

Porter, J. (2015). L'amour for four: polygyny, polyamory and the state's compelling economic interest in normative monogamy. *Emory Law Journal, 64*(6), 2093–2139.

Powell, M. (Ed.). (2007). *Understanding the mixed economy of welfare*. Bristol, UK: Policy Press.

Canadian Press. (2016, 4 May). Ontario's Sex-Ed curriculum: Protests appear to be growing. Retrieved 4 June 2019 from https://www.huffingtonpost.ca/2015/05/05/opposition-appears-to-be-_n_7210744.html?utm_hp_ref=ca-ontario-sex-ed-protests.

Rodrigo, M. (2010). Promoting positive parenting in Europe: New challenges for the European Society for Developmental Psychology. *European Journal of Developmental Psychology, 7*(3), 281–294.

Sanchéz Gassen, N., & Perelli-Harris, B. (2015). The increase in cohabitation and the role of union status in family policies: A comparison of 12 European countries. *Journal of European Social Policy, 25*(4), 431–449.

Sassler, S., Michelmore, K., & Qian, Z. (2018). Transitions from sexual relationships into cohabitation and beyond. *Demography, 55*, 511–534.

Savage, R. (2019, 25 February). *Compulsory sex and LGBT+ education sparks religious backlash in the UK*. London, UK: Thomson Reuters. Retrieved 05.06.19 from https://www.reuters.com/article/us-britain-lgbt-education/compulsory-sex-and-lgbt-education-sparks-religious-backlash-in-uk-idUSKCN1QE24Z.

Simpson, D., Leonhardt, N., & Hawkins, A. (2018). Learning about love: A meta-analytic study of individually-oriented Relationship Education Programs for adolescents and emerging adults. *Journal of Youth and Adolescence, 47*(3), 477–489.

Social Trends Institute. (2017). *World family map 2017. Mapping family change and child wellbeing outcomes*. Retrieved 10 June 2019 from https://worldfamilymap.ifstudies.org/2017/files/WFM-2017-FullReport.pdf.

Tavares, P., & Wodon, Q. (2018). *Global and regional trends in women's legal protection against domestic violence and sexual harassment*. Retrieved 20 May 2019 from http://pubdocs.worldbank.org/en/679221517425064052/EndingViolenceAgainstWomenandGirls-GBVLaws-Feb2018.pdf.

UNESCO. (2015). *A guide for gender equality in teacher education policy and practices*. Retrieved 7 June 2019 from https://unesdoc.unesco.org/ark:/48223/pf0000231646.

UNICEF. (2018). *25 million child marriages prevented in last decade*. Retrieved 6 June 2019 from https://www.unicef.org/press-releases/25-million-child-marriages-prevented-last-decade-due-accelerated-progress-according.

United Nations. (1948). *Universal declaration of human rights*. Retrieved 5 May 2019 from https://www.un.org/en/ga/search/view_doc.asp?symbol=A/RES/217(III).

United Nations. (2011). *Discriminatory laws and practices and acts of violence against individuals based on their sexual orientation and gender identity*. United Nations Human Rights Council Nineteenth Session (A/HRC/19/41). Retrieved 10 June 2019 from https://www2.ohchr.org/english/bodies/hrcouncil/docs/19session/A.HRC.19.41_English.pdf.

United Nations. (2015). 'Violence against women'. *The World's Women 2015*. Retrieved 10 June 2019 from https://unstats.un.org/unsd/gender/chapter6/chapter6.html.

United Nations. (2018). *The promotion, protection and enjoyment of human rights on the Internet*. Retrieved 1 June 2019 from https://digitallibrary.un.org/record/1639840/files/A_HRC_RES_38_7-EN.pdf.

Wadsworth, M., & Markman, H. (2012). Where's the action? Understanding what works and why in relationship education. *Behavior Therapy, 43*, 99–112.

Weiss, S. (Panellist). (2019, January 12). *Marriage in Israel*. BBC World Service, Heart and Soul podcast. Retrieved from https://player.fm/series/heart-and-soul-1301462/marriage-in-israel.

Whitman, J., Horn, S., & Boyd, C. (2007). Activism in the schools: Providing LGBTQ affirmative training to school counsellors. *Journal of Gay and Lesbian Psychotherapy, 11*(3–4), 143–154.

WHO. (2013). *Global and regional estimates of violence against women: prevalence and health effects of intimate partner violence and non-partner sexual violence*. Retrieved 15 May 2019 from https://www.who.int/reproductivehealth/publications/violence/9789241564625/en/.

World Bank Group. (2019). *Women, business and the law 2019: A decade of reform*. Washington, DC: World Bank. Retrieved 1 June 2019 from https://openknowledge.worldbank.org/handle/10986/31327. License: CC BY 3.0 IGO.

World Economic Forum. (2018). *This is the state of LGBTI rights around the world in 2018*. Retrieved 2 June 2019 from https://www.weforum.org/agenda/2018/06/lgbti-rights-around-the-world-in-2018/.

Zimmerman, K., & Roberts, C. (2012). The influence of a financial management course on couples' relationship quality. *Journal of Financial Counseling and Planning, 23*(2), 46–54.

Index

A
Acquired physical impairments
　care-giving partners, 212
　challenges, 211
　complete or partial loss, 208
　couple life cycle stage, 210
　degenerative disorders, 211
　emotional states, 211
　gender, 214–215
　implications, 210
　multiple occurrences, 210
　physical care, 210, 212
　physical limitation, 209
　pre-morbid health status, 209
　rehabilitation processes, 212
　sexual dysfunctions, 212
　sexual intimacy, 212
　societal context, 209
　stress, 211
　visible and chronic, 209
Addiction affairs, 285
Adjustment post disability, 210
Administration for Children and Families (ACF), 364
Adult attachment, 279
Affair recovery, 293
Affection and emotional support, 139
Analysis of longitudinal household survey data, 330
Arab region couple relationships
　conscious choice framework, 100–103
　dominant forms, 87–93
　gender roles, 86
　marriage dynamics (*see* Gender equity attitudes)
　marriage satisfaction, 99
　opposing forces, 85, 86
　Urfi marriage, 86
Arab-Bedouin population, 196, 197
Arranged marriages, 110
　contemporary times (*see* Contemporary Indian society)
　traditional Indian society, 73–75
Attachment narratives, 348
Attachment representations
　dispositional representations, 353
　self-protective strategies, 352
Attachment theory, 265, 325
　autonomy and dependence, 350
　behavioural patterns, 350
　comfort and reassurance, 348, 349
　couple relationships, 350
　couple therapy, 349
　erosion of trust, 351
　interactional moment, 351
　perception of danger, 350
　self-regulated therapist, 351
　social regulation of emotion, 348
　strategies of self-protection, 349
Authentic communities, 396, 400
Autism spectrum disorder (ASD), 241
Avoidant affairs, 285

B
Bad touching, 182
Barebacking, 269
Becoming a couple
　domestic affairs, 335
　environmental impact, 337

Becoming a couple (*cont.*)
  inequalities, 335
  medical condition, 336
  micro-surveillance, 338
  mutual learning, 336
  philosophical acceptance, 338
  prior experiences, 335
  psychological security, 336
  scheduling time, 335
Best dating apps, 262
Best Friends Forever (BFF), 262
Birth rates, 178
Brittle bone disease, 235, 240
Buehlman coding system, 296

C
Catholic communities, 397
Catholic culture, 125
Child marriage, 409
Chinese couple relationships
  challenges
    gender inequality, 116, 117
    IPV, 117, 118, 120
    parenting and extended family, 116
  intracultural heterosexual, 107
  love/intimacy and sexuality, 108
  marriage and same-sex, 111–113
  mate selection, 109–111
  satisfaction
    communication, 114, 115
    parenting and extended family, 115, 116
    power and decision-making, 114
  traditional Chinese culture, 119
Cohabitation, 178
  agreements, 185
  asset, 185
  pension upon remarriage, 185
Comfort and reassurance, 356
Commitment
  CMR, 414
  controversial issue, 415
  divorce, 416
  emotional distress, 417
  longevity, 416
  long-term relationships, 416
  marriage, 414
  partnership status, 415
  protective factors, 417
  self-selective, 416
  supranational organisations, 416
Communities of support
  benefits and limitations, 395–397
  need
    accompaniment, 393

    advice/mentoring, 392
    contraction phase, 393
    internal issues, 392
    life cycle issues, 392
    marital satisfaction, 393
    midlife relational issues, 393
    parenting, 393
    social structures, 392
  types
    circumstances, 395
    emotional, 394
    instrumental, 394
    moral/psychological, 394
    religion or spirituality, 395
    work–life imbalance, 394
Community friendships, 189
Community services, 207
Compulsory relationship, 412
Computer-mediated communication (CvK), 264
Conflict management system
  accepting influence, 303
  conversations, 301
  differences, 300
  gridlocked pattern, 300, 301
  honouring life dreams, 303, 304
  intimacy, 301
  negative patterns, 301
  physiological self-soothing, 302
  relationship breakup, 301
  repair and de-escalation, 302
  softened start-up, 302
  therapeutic task, 301
Conflict relational processes, 321
Conflict resolution
  couple relationship education, 414
  financial stress, 413
  love discourses, 412
  parenting stress, 413
  relational capabilities, 412
  relationship education, 412
  social and demographic changes, 413
  social security benefits, 413
  traditional relational skills, 413
Confluent love, 50
Conjugal partnership, 82
Conscious choice framework
  delayed marriage, 100
  Egypt marriage market study, 102
  financial well-being, 101
  IMAGES MENA, 100
  mate selection preference, 103
  reconciliation, 100
  renegotiation, 101
  spinsterhood crisis, 101

Consensual non-monogamous, 283, 284
   affairs, 285
   intimacy, 285
   relational myth, 284
   sex therapist, 284
Contemporary couple separation
   disappearance of feelings, 318–319
   domestic violence, 319–322
Contemporary couples, 311
Contemporary Indian society
   arranged/love/self-chosen marriages, 77–78
   expectations, 79
   kinship bonds, 80
   marital roles, 76
   matrimonial service, 80
   parental attitudes, 80
   perceptions, 79
   procedure, 80
   romantic love, 81
   students' expectations, 78
   students' perception of marriage, 76–77
Contemporary partners, 367
Co-resident coupledom, 341
Co-residential coupledom
   gender inequalities, 339, 340
   legal acknowledgement, 339
   patriarchal systems, 339
   social media networking, 341
   solo-living, 341
   stereotypes, 340
   stigmatising discourse, 339
Counselling and therapy, 420
Couple counselling, 398
Couple diversity
   cultural sensitivity, 10
   globalization, 8
   immigrant women, 8
   intercultural, 8
   LAT, 7
   migration flows, 8
   qualitative research, 8
   reflexivity, 9
   same-sex, 7
   systemic psychotherapy, 9
Coupledom, 227, 243
   comedy programmes, 231
   IMDb, 231
   relationships, 232
Coupledom and well-being, 229
Couplehood and parenthood, 68
Couple identity, 227
Couple-level minority stress
   dyadic data, 168
   dyadic nature, 166
   identity, 166
   marriage, 168
   RDP/CUs, 168
   resilience resources, 169–171
   sexual minority, 165
   unequal legal status, 168
   unequal recognition, 168, 169
Couple life
   digital gap, 314
   divorcing pairs, 314
   fostering communications skills, 314
   global economy, 316
   income level, 317
   mobile telephones, 312, 313
   postmodern family, 315
   sexual opportunities, 315
   social and cultural domains, 316
   technologies, 313, 314
Couple relationships, 15, 152
   acquired physical impairment, 213
   arbitrary interference, 404
   arranged marriage (see Arranged marriages)
   attachment theory, 14
   belief systems, 4
   child outcomes, 371
   communities, 391
   context of parenting, 363–364, 371
   cultural context, 4, 5
   desire for children, 26–27
   education programs, 364
   emotions, 5
   fragility, 29–30
   gender equality, 6
   gender roles, 23
   globalization, 4
   good quality, 22–25
   impact, 27–28
   influence, 4
   interchangeable interactions, 214
   interdependent system, 213
   life circumstances, 213
   policy makers, 4
   policy, 403
   sexual activity, 21
   significance, 3
   social model, 214
   social networks, 391
   state-centred approach, 403
   therapeutic perspective, 4
   types, 21
Couple Resilience, 229
Couple satisfaction
   marital quality, 28
   marriages, 28

Couple separation, 311, 312
Couple therapy, 11, 56, 284, 287
　counsel, 63
　division, 64
　need, 63–64
Couples
　conventional definitions, 228
　cultural framings, 229
　family laws, 57
　humour (*see* Humour)
　normative practice, 228
Couples group interventions, 365
　conceptual significance, 371–372
　contemporary partners, 367
　couple relationship, 367
　family origin, 367
　radical idea, 365
　relationship patterns, 366
　transition to parenthood, 366
Couples post disability, 213
Courtly love in conflict
　couple therapist, 45
　discursive approach, 44
　psychological phenomena, 44
　pure relationship, 46–48
　romantic discourse, 48–49
　semi-reckless approach, 45
　status and property, 44
　virtuous love, 44, 45
Crude marriage rate (CMR), 414
Cultural sensitivity, 404
Current relationship, 289
Cybercrime abuse/toxic disinhibition, 271
Cyber-bullying, 269
Cyberstalking, 271, 272
Cyber violence, 419

D

Decoding comedy
　middle, 235, 236
　odd couple, 234
　semiotic analysis (SA), 234
　speechless, 236
　　boy meet girl, 237, 238
　　Carmichael show, 237
　　Grace and Frankie, 238–240
　textual analysis, 233
Digital jealousy, 271
Disability
　acquired physical impairments (*see*
　　Acquired physical impairments)
　heterosexual couples, 208
　life expectancy, 208
　psychotherapeutic work, 208

Disability pension, 207
Disappearance of feelings
　couple therapy, 318
　financial matters, 318
　intimacy and sexuality, 319
　type of separation, 319
Dispositional representations, 350, 357
　attachment figures, 353
　IWM, 353
　neurological patterns, 353
Divorce, 178
Domestic violence, 418
　abducting parent, 322
　abuse and addiction, 321
　communication, 320
　conflict participants, 321
　contact regime, 320
　high-conflict separation, 320
　legal proceedings, 321
　psychological violation, 322
　social development, 322
Dowry Prohibition Act, 74
Dual-earner couples, 23
Dual-earner heterosexual couple, 336
Dyadic minority stress processes, 166, 167
Dynamic maturational model, 348

E

Egypt marriage market, 102
Emotional peak experiences, 325
Emotionally Focused Couples Therapy (EFT),
　219, 284
Episodic memory, 352
Essentialization, 201
Estate planning, 187
Europe countries couple relationships
　conceiving and rearing children, 127
　European Social Survey, 126
　household, 127
　LAT, 126
　marriage rate, 126
　pluralism, 127
　satisfaction level, 126
Extra-marital relationship, 65–67

F

Face-to-face application, 376
Falling in love, 177
Family history, 290
Family origin, 367
Family policy paradox, 364
Family system
　couples group curriculum, 362

Index

risk/protective factors, 362
stressful conditions, 362
Family systems theory, 372
Fathers
  child relationships, 362
  responsible role, 363
  risk, 363
  social and political commentators, 363
Fertility rates, 28
Fidelity, 280
Financial therapy, 413
First wife syndrome, 198, 201
Framing couples
  commodification and objectification, 241
  decoding comedy (*see* Decoding comedy)
  media portrayal, 241
  normalising effect, 240, 241
Framing sex, 248
Free and full consent, 408
French
  couple formation and dissolution, 60–61
French couple
  age at time of marriage, 58
  consensual union, 58
  division of responsibilities, 61–62
  homosexual or heterosexual, 57
  moving in together, 59
  previous experience, 59, 60

G
Gandharva Vivah
  arranged marriages, 72
  classical literature, 72
  orthodox Hinduism, 72
  parental control, marriage, 72
  patriarchy, 72
  Rig Vedic times, 72
  self-chosen marriages, 72
Gender, 10
  couple therapists, 13
  family therapists, 12
  intimate partner violence, 11
  marital satisfaction, 11
  paradigm shift, 11
  pay gap, 10, 11
  power imbalance, 12
  social activities, 12
  traditional cultures, 12
Gender equity attitudes
  convergence and divergence, 96–98
  deviations, 95
  domestic violence, 97, 99
  frustrations, 96
  husband–wife comparisons, 96
  IMAGES MENA, 95
  power dynamics, 94
  statistics, 93, 94
  traditional household/childcare activities, 96
Gender Global Gap report, 12
Gender roles, 85, 99, 179
General symptom severity (GSI), 198
Ghosting, 270
Globalisation, 76

H
Heterosexual couples, 208
Heterosexual relationships, 249, 342
Hindu ideology, 72
Homophilia, 41
Homosexuality, 67, 159
Homosexuals seeking therapy, 67
Honour killings, 75
Household income adequacy, 135
Humour
  and laughter, 230, 231
  and well-being, 230
Hyperpersonal theory, 264

I
Ideological force, 229
Ideology of marriage and family, 228
Ideology of prevention, 361
IMAGES MENA, 99, 100
Impression management or self-presentation, 265
Indian traditional values, 82
individual's behavior, 361
Individual therapists, 360
Individualism and collectivism, 5
Individualistic romantic values, 82
Infidelity
  attachment theory, 325
  couple therapists, 324
  definition, 280
  disclosure/discovery, 324
  emotional support, 324
  loss of relationship, 324
  sexual intercourse, 280
  traumatic wounds, 324
Infidelity/non-monogamy
  desire discrepancy, 282
  ISD, 281
  psychoeducational intervention, 282
  sex addict, 282
  sexual response cycle, 281

Infidelity specific assessment, 288
Inheritance, 188
Inhibited sexual desire (ISD), 281
Initial assessment process, 386
Insecure attachment styles, 322
Integrative formulation, 347
Integrative memory, 352
Intercultural couple relationships, 8
Intercultural couples
   home, 150–151
   love, 151–154
   nonverbal and representational methods, 155
   spiritual ecogram, 154–155
   systemic techniques, 155
   systemic theoretical frameworks (*see* Systemic theoretical frameworks)
Interest technology
   qualitative research, 255–256
Intergenerational attachments
   comparative process, 354
   couple relationships, 354
   dynamic interaction, 353
Internal working model (IWM), 279, 353
International Commission on Couple and Family Relations, 359
International men and gender equality survey (IMAGES), 97, 98
Internet dating, 333
Internet infidelity, 270
Internet Movie Database (IMDb), 231
Internet technology, 419
   components, 246
   sexual norms, 247, 248
   social network apps, 246
Interpersonal trust
   couple relationship, 354
   feelings of shame and humiliation, 355
   perceptions and experiences, 356
Interracial dating, 263
Interracial relationships, 146
Intervention approach, 359
Interviewing individuals
   couple therapy, 287
   no secret rule, 287
   post-traumatic stress, 288
   therapy, 288
Intimacy, 5
Intimate partner violence (IPV), 116, 117, 120
Intimate relationships, 52, 69, 189, 279
Islamic conceptualization, 196

K
Kanyadan, 74
Khap/katta panchayats, 75

L
LAT couples
   online couple psycotherapy (*see* Online couple psycotherapy)
Later life
   attraction, 181, 182
   dating, 181
   falling in love, 181, 187, 188
   love, 180, 189–190
   marital status, 179
   relationship status (*see* Relationship status)
   sensuality, 182
   sexuality, 183, 184
   socialization, 190
Legislation, 420
Lesbian bed death, 161
LGBTQ Couples, 293
Lifetime partner, 82
Living alone
   become couple, 335–338
   breakdown, 330
   co-resident coupledom, 331
   couple relationships, 329
   coupledom, 339–341
   disrupted partnerships, 330
   family support and local housing markets, 330
   harmful assumptions, 331
   long-term couple relationships, 330
   parental home, 330
   solo-living, 331
   undesired phase of life, 330
   young adult, 329, 332–334
Living Alone Together (LAT), 126
Living Apart Together (LAT) couples, 375
   arrangement, 379
   conventional face-to-face therapy, 379
   ethnicity, 379
   happiness, 379
   interaction, 379
   online therapy, 379
   relationships, 246
   sociological changes, 378
   types, 378
Long-lasting love, 19
Long-term relationships, 48, 245, 272
   attachment theory, 306

Index
431

fights, 308
need, 295, 296
psychological observations, 305
scientific research, 296
sex, 306–307
shared meaning, 304
SRH (*see* Sound relationship house)
stress, 307
trust and commitment, 304, 305
Love, 177
Love discourse, 419
Love marriages, 75, 76
Love relationships, 5
Love scamming, 269, 270

M

Malta couple relationships
  legislative developments, 128
  marriage dissolution, 128
  marriage rates, 128
  marriage separation, 128
  Mediterranean, 125
  PFWS (*see* The President's Foundation for the Wellbeing of Society (PFWS))
  remarriage, 129
  same-sex civil unions, 129
  traditionalism and materialism, 127
  wedding tourism industry, 128
Marital counselling and therapy, 417
Marital coupling, 379
Marital satisfaction, 23, 198
Marriage counselling, 71, 76
Marriage couple relationships
  low marriage rate/late marriage, 112, 113
  registration and wedding, 111, 112
Marriage satisfaction, 99
Marriage unions dominance
  demographic macro-level dimensions, 91
  dissolution, 87, 90
  divorce incidence rate, 89
  divorce rate, 89
  duration, 89
  groupings, 87, 88
  institutions, 90
  population, 91
  spinsterhood, 87
Married life, 68
Mate selection
  biased social context, 110
  individual and contextual factors, 109
  intercultural couples, 110, 111
  parental preferences, 110
  personal traits and characteristics, 109
  same sex-couples, 110, 111

Media texts, 243
Middle East and North Africa (MENA), 405
Minority stress, 171
Modernization, 194
Monogamous relationships, 202
Monogamy, 283
Multiculturalism, 145
Multi-phase therapy intervention
  conference, 199
  group therapy, 199
  husband's relationships, 200
  individual meetings, 199

N

Napoleonic code, 56
Narrative reconstruction, 218
National Institute of Mental Health (NIMH), 366
Negative interactive cycles, 213
Neoliberalism, 76
New forms, couple relationships
  Messyar and *Muta'a*, 92
  nonconventional marital unions, 91
  Urfi marriages, 92
Nonbinding contacts, 269
Non-cohabitating couples, 61
Non-disabled partners, 213, 215
Non-monogamous relationship
  infidelity, 291
  issues, 292
  open relationship, 291
  selection process, 292
  sexual activity, 292
  skill, 291
  therapists, 291
  verbal agreements, 291
Non-monogamy, 409
Nonverbal memory, 352
Normalizing polygyny, 202
Nostalgic disorientation, 150

O

Office of Family Assistance (OFA), 364
Older couples, 29
Online couple psychotherapy, 389
  defensive avoidance, 386
  establishing of an LAT lifestyle, 380–383
  personality characteristics, 387
  prototypal secure, 385
  risk management, 387
  shared living arrangement, 380–383
  therapeutic process, 388–389
  treatment methodology, 387

Online dating, 261, 419
  advantages, 268
  gender differences, 263
  impression management, 266
  internet-associated problems, 272
  interpsychic, 263
  intrapsychic, 263
  love relationship, 266
  negative trends, 269
  nervousness and timidity, 266
  networking apps, 262, 263
  partner search, 265
  partnership problems, 273
  physical appearance, 266
  psychodynamic perspective, 273
  reality check, 266
  risks, 269
  types, 262
Online disinhibition effect, 264
Online therapy, 389
Open relationships, 291
Optimal partner, 268
Organic brain damage, 212
Oxford dictionary online, 228

P
PACS, 57
PageRank scores, 272
Parental communication, 355
Parental influence, 111
Parent–child relationships, 363, 366
Parenthood, 136
Parenting, 367, 371
  siloed arrangements, 364
Parenting interventions
  importance of father, 362–363
Parenting stress, 413
Patriarchal values, 316
Personal relationship, 32
PFWS, influencing factors
  macro level
    marital dissolution, 134
    technology, 134
    The mass media, 133, 134
  meso level
    formative experiences, 137
    household income adequacy, 135
    parenthood, 136
    relationship with in-laws, 136
    shared couple experiences, 136
    work–family balance, 135
  micro level
    affection and sexual intimacy, 139
    communication, 137
    conflict resolution, 138
    decision-making, 137, 138
    faith, 138
    humor, 138
    loyalty and fidelity, 137
Physical proximity, 313
Physiotherapist, 207
Planning and management skills, 23
Pluralism, 127
Policy reflections, 404
  commitment (*see* Commitment)
  consent, 408
    full and free, 408
    inter-caste relationships, 408
    issue, 409
    liberty, 410
    principle, 409
  due care, 417–419
  equal status, 404
    cultural beliefs, 406
    equality legislation, 404
    gender equality, 405, 406
    labour rights, 405
    legal recognition, 407, 408
    legal rights, 405
    LGBT rights, 407
    same-sex couples, 407
Polyamorous relationships, 410
Polyamory, 290
Polyandry, 193
Polygamy, 193, 280
Polygynandry, 193
Polygynous marriage
  academic literature, 195
  challenging situation, 200
  cultural settings, 195
  economic losses, 194
  essentialization, 201
  family property or assets, 195
  family structure, 197
  fertility issues, 194
  history, 193
  knowledge gap, 194
  mental health, 202, 203
  Middle East, 193
  modernization, 194
  Mormon faith, 201
  perspective, 195
  policymakers, 201
  psychological distress, 201, 203
  psychosocial manifestations, 197–199

Index

public opinion, 200
regression analysis, 202
self concept, 202
social influence, 196
social phenomenon, 201
social pressure, 194
societal response, 201
Positive attitude, 261
Post disability
   benefits, 215
   caregiver stress, 217
   characteristics, 216
   communication strategies, 216
   couple therapists, 218
   hospitalisation, 215
   intimacy and sexuality issues, 218
   narrative reconstruction, 218
   quality, 216
   rehabilitation process, 218
   relationship satisfaction, 216
   resilience-based approach, 216
   social networks, 217
   strategies, 218
   techniques, 219
   therapeutic interventions, 219
   treatment and rehabilitation, 217
   vital contextual factor, 217
Post-marriage, 171
Postmodern couple life
   consultations/therapies, 326
   divorce prediction, 325
   emotional peak experiences, 325
   feelings, 325
   gender equity, 326
   levels of satisfaction, 326
   problematic behaviour, 326
   risk factors, 326
   romantic love, 325
   social institution, 326
Post-separation couple, 319
Power
   socio-cultural context, 10
Power dynamics, 71
Premium memberships, 261
Prenuptial agreement, 187
Private life, 404
Procedural memory, 352
Proximity affairs, 285
Psychiatric disorders, 198
Psychiatrists, 361
Psychoanalytic Couple and Family Institute of New England, 376

Psychoanalytic couple psychotherapists, 376
Psychoanalytic psychotherapy
   cyberspace, 377–378
Psychoeducation, 267
Psychological language, 51, 52
Psychotherapeutic practice, 273
Pure relationship, 49
   heterosexual discourse, 51
   individualization and secularization, 51
   reflexivity, 50
   sexual and emotional equality, 50

R

Rationale for the selection, 234
Reality, 178
Reassurance, 355
Registered domestic partners or civil unions (RDP/CUs), 168
Relational capability
   communication, 411
   conflict resolution, 412–414
   managing boundaries, 411, 412
   reflexivity, 410
Relational qualities, 22
Relational therapy, 286
Relationship education, 139, 140
Relationship history, 289
Relationship status, 55
   cohabitation, 185–186
   remarriage, 186–189
   sense of autonomy, 185
Religious community, 399
Remarriage
   estate planning, 187
   financial situations, 186
   long-term care, 187
   medical directives, 186
   prenuptial agreement, 187
   retirement, 186
Request for consultation, 67
Romantic ideal, 71
Romantic love, 19, 81
Romantic relationships, 255

S

Same- and mixed-sex relationships
   differences, 160
      gender, 161
      stigmatised status, 161
   similarities, 160

Same-sex couple relationships, 113
Same-sex couples
    clinical and counselling interventions, 171
    couple-level minority stress (*see* Couple-level minority stress)
    devaluing discourse, 162
    heteronormative standards, 161
    interpersonal level, 162
    legal recognition, 167
    minority stress, 164
    negative impact, 162
    sexual minority, 162
    social and policy climates, 162
    social value, 163–164
    stigmatised status, 165
    structural level, 161
Same-sex marriage, 41, 129
Same-sex marriage campaign, 163
Same-sex relationships, 256
Same-sex sexuality, 247
Scandinavian
    coupledom, 52
    love, 52
    qualities and peculiarities, 42
    sociopolitical structure, 43
    successful life, 42
Scottish Household Survey (SHS), 332
Self-arranged/love-cum-arranged marriages, 78
Self-chosen marriages, 77
Semantic polarities, 154
Sensory memory, 352
Sensual satisfaction, 184
Service delivery systems, 364
Sexting, 252, 269
Sexual activity, 183
Sexual and romantic contacts, 261
Sexual communication, 286
Sexual desire, 283
Sexual relationships, 280
    benefits of smartphones, 250–252
    complexity, 248
    cost of smartphones, 252–254
    liberalization, 247
    risks and benefits, 248
    strategies to deal, 254–255
Sexuality, 290
Shared couple experiences, 136
Singledom
    divorce, 20
    life satisfaction, 20
Smartphones, 13, 245, 257
    addiction, 256
    communication between partners, 246
    duration, 254
    issues, 247
    level of communication, 254
Social dating, 262
Social harm, 248
Social networking sites, 246, 253
Social pressure, 194
Social problems, 359
Social support, 395, 400
    affective dimension, 398
    personal characteristics, 398
Socio-cultural expectations, 82
Sociologists, 360
Sociopolitical contexts, 151, 154
    gendered discourses, 149
    intercultural couples, 149
    psychotherapists, 149
Solo living, 332, 333
Sound relationship house
    building love maps, 297
    conflict management (*see* Conflict management system)
    creating shared meaning, 298
    friendship systems, 299–300
    levels, 298
    manage conflict, 297
    positive perspective, 297
    sharing fondness and admiration, 297
    systems, 297, 298
SPAFF coding system, 296
Spinsterhood, 10
Spousal relationships, 71, 76
Stage of life affairs, 285
State feminism, 43
Stress arousal system, 350
Successful couples, 308
Systemic psychotherapy, 347
Systemic theoretical frameworks
    clinical vignettes, 148
    cultural content, 148
    cultural issues, 147
    family life cycle, 146
    individualism–collectivism continuum, 148
    monocultural couples, 147
    positioning theory, 146
    racism, 147
    self-reflexivity, 147
    social GRRAACCEESS, 147
    sociopolitical context, 147
Systemic therapeutic triangle, 352
Systemic therapy
    attachment theory, 348–352
    collaborative framework, 347
    prefrontal cortex, 352
    reflective functioning, 348

Index

T

Tavistock relationships
   creative or problematic self-reinforcing patterns, 376
   face-to-face service, 376
   theoretical framework, 376
Technoference, 253
Technology
   commercialization of love, 14
   commodification, 14
   digital dating, 13
   financial stress, 14
   relationship quality, 13
   self-esteem, 13
Teletherapy, 377
The friendship system
   couples' tendency, 299
   love mapping process, 299
   partners response, 299
   positive perspective, 300
   transitional level, 300
   turning toward, 299
The President's Foundation for the Wellbeing of Society (PFWS)
   Computer-Assisted Telephone Interview, 130
   ecosystem analysis, 132–139
   implications, 139, 140
   Life and relationship satisfaction, 130, 131
   Maltese couples, 130
   quantitative study, 130
Therapeutic work, 348
Traditional Indian society
   act of violence, 75
   arranged marriages, 73, 74
   conjugal relationships, 74
   family structure, 73
   financial position and status, 75
   gender-based traditional values, 74
   honour killings, 75
   kinship group, 73
   marriage, 73
   payment of dowry, 74
Traditionalists, 201
Transitional space, 264
Transnational divorce processes
   conflict strategies, 323
   infidelity, 323–325
   marital status, 323
   non-governmental organisations, 323
   relationships/marriages, 322
Trial dealing, 265
Turning toward partner, 299

U

Universal Declaration of Human Rights (UDHR), 403
Urfi marriage, 86, 92, 93

V

Verbal memory, 352
Virtual proximity, 313
Voter referenda, 163

W

Webcam-mediated couple psychotherapy, 375
Work–family balance, 135
Working class women, 179

Y

Young adult
   communication and collaboration, 334
   co-resident partner, 334
   economic crisis, 332
   gender inequalities, 334
   potential implications, 334
   regret/embarrassment, 333
   romantic/sexual relationship, 332
   solo living, 333

CPSIA information can be obtained
at www.ICGtesting.com
Printed in the USA
LVHW010141110520
655319LV00003B/53